television and

radio

GIRAUD CHESTER
Exec. Vice-President
Goodson-Todman Productions

GARNET R. GARRISON
Univ. of Michigan, Ann Arbor

EDGAR E. WILLIS
Univ. of Michigan, Ann Arbor

Prentice-Hall, Inc., Englewood Cliffs, N.J. 07632

Library of Congress Cataloging in Publication Data

CHESTER, GIRAUD, (date).
   Television and radio.

   Bibliography: p. 519
   Includes index.
   1. Broadcasting—United States.   I. Garrison, Garnet R., (date) joint author.   II. Willis, Edgar E., joint
author.   III. Title.
PN1990.6.U5C5   1978   384.54'0973   77-26906
ISBN   0-13-902981-8

Television and Radio, 5th Ed.
Chester, Garrison and Willis

Printed in the United States of America
10   9   8   7   6   5   4

PRENTICE-HALL INTERNATIONAL, INC., *London*
PRENTICE-HALL OF AUSTRALIA PTY. LIMITED, *Sydney*
PRENTICE-HALL OF CANADA, LTD., *Toronto*
PRENTICE-HALL OF INDIA PRIVATE LIMITED, *New Delhi*
PRENTICE-HALL OF JAPAN, INC., *Tokyo*
PRENTICE-HALL OF SOUTHEAST ASIA PTE. LTD., *Singapore*

contents

PHOTOGRAPHS

FIGURES

TABLES

preface

When the first edition of this book was published in 1950, about 100 television stations were broadcasting programs several hours a day and about 5 million black and white television sets had been installed in American homes. As this fifth edition is written the number of television stations has risen to more than 960 and the number of television sets exceeds 120 million. Now virtually all American homes are equipped with at least one television set; 45 percent of these households have more than one set and 77 percent of them are equipped to receive programs in color. In the average home, people watch television more than six hours a day. From morning through the late evening hours, television commands the "strongest sustained attention" of most American families. In competition with television, radio has continued to maintain a place as a major mass communications medium, but since television's advent radio's hold on the American public has lessened markedly, especially in the evening hours, and its programming has undergone vital changes.

In preparing this new edition the latest developments in television and radio are fully recorded, but the basic intention of the previous editions has been maintained: to provide a comprehensive, up-to-date textbook for introductory courses in broadcasting. (Teachers and students should consult regularly such industry-publications as *Variety* and *Broadcasting* to remain abreast of further developments). Broadcasting courses are offered in several hundred colleges and universities. Faced with the problem of training students in the broadcasting skills and supplying them with a body of knowledge about the field, many teachers find it difficult to organize and present effective courses without the aid of a comprehensive textbook and adequate practice materials. It has been a matter of real gratification to us that the first four editions of this text won such wide acceptance from college teachers and students throughout the country. It is our belief that this fifth edition, prepared on the basis of our experience in teaching college courses, in educational broadcasting, and in commercial broadcasting, contains all the basic materials essential to a first course in broadcasting.

For courses concerned primarily with the social aspects of broadcasting, Part I, supplemented by such chapters from Part II as time will allow, may suffice. For courses concentrated on training in fundamental broadcasting skills, Part II, which introduces the student to television and radio studio practices and techniques, may be used alone or together with chapters chosen from Part I. Thus the text may cover two semesters of study in the order preferred by the individual instructor. Or the book may be utilized in one semester by concurrent assignments in Parts I and II; for example, in the same week, students may be asked to read Chapters 7 and 24. In our own teaching we have preferred to link content and skills in this manner. The chapter topics and the sequence of chapters in Part I remain as they were in the previous edition. The order of chapters in Part II has been rearranged to bring about a more logical progression of topics and the chapter on "Television Drama" has been eliminated. Some of the material in that chapter now appears in the chapter on "Directing."

Knowing how difficult it often is to obtain good exercise material for classroom use, we have provided ample broadcast copy for the various skills discussed in Part II, so that the text may be used as a working handbook. Some of the best scripts included in the earlier editions have been retained, but these have been supplemented with the most recent examples of broadcast copy. We have obtained clearance for the use of these selections in the classroom, *but we are obliged to caution all readers that these scripts are fully protected by copyright and common law and may not be broadcast without permission in writing from the individual authors or copyright holders, as the case may be.*

In most instances we have chosen to deal with television and radio concurrently because we believe that study of the nature and influence of the two communications media can most profitably proceed in this way. In the presentation of programming and production skills, we have tended to relate the two media by comparison and contrast, but there is separate treatment of matters that pertain to one medium but not to the other. We have also provided separate practice material for production exercises in television and in radio. Where institutions lack the equipment necessary for direct instruction in television, this text should at least help to orient students to the field of television and to prepare them for what they must later learn in the television studio. We believe that those instructors who want to combine instruction in television and radio will find in this book a reasonably adequate treatment of both.

Although in conception and execution this volume has been a joint project throughout, the reader may be interested in knowing the primary responsibilities of the three authors. The original writing of Part I, except for chapter 10, plus chapters 19 and 26 was by Chester. All the other chapters were originally written by Garrison except for chapter 10, which was written by Willis, who also did most of the rewriting that was required to bring this new edition up to date. One coauthor is an executive in the broadcasting industry; another was the director of broadcasting at a state university and is now a professor of broadcasting in that university; the third is a professor in the same university engaged in the teaching of television and radio courses. In this book, however, each of us speaks in his own right; the views we express are not to be ascribed to the company or institution with which we are affiliated.

A great many people have assisted us in preparing this revision. We express our appreciation to the numerous individuals, stations, networks, advertising agencies, publishers, and manufacturers who have permitted us to reproduce their materials, charts, and photographs. Specific acknowledgment is included in the book wherever the material appears. We express our special thanks to Fred Remley for his advice on technical matters, to John Rich for his assistance in obtaining scripts, and to Kathryn Notestine for her careful typing and preparation of the final copy.

We are also greatly indebted to the many good people from whom we have learned much of what we propose to teach. A complete accounting of this debt cannot be made here, and a long list of names of our intellectual creditors would be pointless. We must resort, therefore, to a blanket acknowledgment of our outstanding obligations to all our friends in education and in the television and radio industry who have given to us so generously of their knowledge and experience.

G. C.

G. R. G.

E. E. W.

part one

television
and
radio
in
society

social aspects
of broadcasting

It has been said that of all the peoples in the world, Americans, with their millions of television and radio sets, apparently stand most in fear of a moment of silence. It has also been said that the development of television and radio is the most significant technical advance in human communications since the invention of movable type. Surely no student of the twentieth century can fail to observe how television and radio have succeeded in permeating everyday life in America, changing social habits and creating new ones, upsetting staid political practices, affecting tastes in all forms of entertainment, building unprecedented demand for products and services never before so widely distributed, and providing the individual at home with an eye and ear to the world outside.

The full social impact of television and radio has not yet been fully gauged or charted, but all available evidence indicates that they represent a major force in American society.

So useful have these media of communication become that our whole society has become geared to them, and our daily lives are shaped by the messages they bear; yet, when broadcasting began some sixty years ago, hardly more than a moment in the span of human history, it was little understood as a science and even less as an art. It was of no concern to the public and was devoid of any social influence whatever. The change that has come over our society in these years is nothing less than revolutionary. To the responsible citizen of today, it becomes significant to ask what is the full story of broadcasting's impact on our way of life, and what social problems derive from its influence upon us?

This chapter will try to answer these questions by presenting a general outline of the role of television and radio in America. In doing so, it seems wise to discuss the following points: 1. the nature of the broadcasting media; 2. the dimensions of television and radio; 3. what television and radio convey to the American people; and 4. their effects on us and our ways of doing things.

BROADCASTING DEFINED

For the sake of convenience in this discussion, we may define broadcasting as the transmission through space, by means of radio frequencies, of signals capable of being received either aurally or visually or both by the general public.

There are numerous types of broadcasting: standard or AM (amplitude modulation) broadcasting of sound; FM (frequency modulation) broadcasting, a higher-fidelity form of sound transmission; television, the transmission of pictures and sound; facsimile, the transmission of still pictures and writing, with or without sound, to be received on photographic paper; shortwave transmissions overseas, police radio, Army and Navy radio, microwave relays, and highly specialized forms of broadcasting such as radar. When we use the term "broadcasting" in this volume, we mean only AM and FM radio, and television. There are, of course, many uses of television on a closed-circuit nonbroadcast basis to which some references will be made.

TRANSMISSION OF BROADCASTING

One way to gauge the scope of American broadcasting is to note how much effort and money go into the operation of the broadcasting system. In the 1970s, there were in operation nine national radio networks, more than 4500 individual AM radio stations, and approximately 3820 FM radio stations. There were four national television networks and more than 985 individual television stations.

Most of these stations transmit programs from sunup to sunset, and many continue until midnight and later. To produce income the commercial stations sell programs and time to advertisers. In 1975, according to the Federal Communications Commission, the revenues of the broadcasting industry were reported as follows: television, approximately $4.1 billion, and radio, $1.725 billion, making a total of $5.825 billion. That year industry profits from television (before federal income taxes) were $780 million; the profits from radio were $90.7 million. In 1976, TV revenues were almost $5.2 billion and TV pre-tax income exceeded $1 billion.

RECEPTION OF BROADCASTING

Television

By the late 1970s, the number of homes equipped with at least one TV set grew to more than 71 million or 97 percent of all homes. The total number of TV sets in households throughout the country reached 120 million, an increase from one million sets in 1949 and from 44 million sets in 1959. More than half of American homes were equipped with color TV sets, or 57 million sets, and it is estimated that 86 percent of TV homes could receive UHF signals, 45 percent had more than one TV set, and 15 percent were linked to cable systems. It is also estimated that television set owners paid more than $1 billion each year for repairs to their sets and for electric power to operate them.

According to the A. C. Nielsen Co., these television sets are being viewed about six hours per day in each home! It is clear that, as Frank Stanton, long-time president of CBS said, "The strongest sustained attention of America is now, daily and nightly, bestowed on television as it is bestowed on nothing else."

Radio

Family ownership of radio sets in America has reached the point of approximately total saturation. More than 98 percent of American homes have at least one radio set, and the total number of sets, 413 million, now is almost double the number of people in the country. Of these sets, 299 million are in homes and 114 million are out of homes.

Home radio sets are turned on considerably less than television sets, but listening to automobile and portable sets adds substantially to the listening done in homes. In a week the cumulative audience for radio reaches the 95 percent level. Radio, with its unique ability to entertain and inform individuals while they are engaged in some other activity, has become the "companion" of the American individual, following him from room to room, to public places, and on the highway.

It has been said, with much truth, that listening to the radio and looking at television are the great common denominators of the American people. They dominate all leisure-time activity, with television viewing clearly assuming the role of America's favorite leisure-time pursuit.

TELEVISION AND RADIO AS SOCIAL FORCES

With an audience as broad in scope as the American community itself, television and radio have become singularly powerful media to do good or evil in society. Their program offerings usually reflect the desires and values of our society, while their persistent command of our attention tends also to make them important creators of our values, desires, and tensions.

It is on those occasions when television and radio have turned America into a single thinking and feeling unit that the social force of these media has been made most evident. The power of radio was first indicated as early as 1933, when Franklin D. Roosevelt delivered his first inaugural address to an audience of many millions, assuring them that "the only thing they had to fear was fear itself." Roosevelt's fireside chats to audiences of 62 million people suggested the amazing potential of the radio medium—one individual, in a moment of time, bringing to bear upon a nation at large the full force of his vocal effectiveness. In the election campaign of 1976, some 77 million people watched the first debate between President Gerald Ford and Jimmy Carter and more than 100 million people saw at least one of the four debates between the presidential and vice-presidential candidates.

The power of television to direct public attention to a single event was first demonstrated dramatically in March, 1951, when the telecast of the Kefauver Crime Committee hearings brought daytime business operations to a practical standstill as millions of people sat glued to television receivers at homes and in public places. This power to produce "peak" audiences is characteristic of television today. In 1969 it was estimated that 125 million Americans watched Astronaut Neil Armstrong as he took man's first step on the moon, and from 350 million to 500 million viewers in other parts of the world joined them in watching that great event. When Richard Nixon left the Presidency in 1974, it is estimated that 61 million people viewed his resignation speech. The drawing power of television extends to the full range of nighttime entertainment programming. Successful shows are viewed regularly by from 30 to 40 million people.

Television and radio coverage of real happenings of importance throughout the world have made the American people direct eye and ear witnesses to events they could otherwise know only at second hand—such events as the Vietnam war, Watergate hearings, presidential nominating conventions, meetings of the United Nations Security Council, congressional committee hearings, the launching of astronauts, and numerous others. In this way television and radio encompass the press, the public platform, the theater, the music hall, and the "real world" outside, and communicate them to an eager and attentive audience comfortably situated at home.

The significance of television and radio as forces in our society can be understood more fully by an examination of the several major areas of belief and action in which their effects can be observed. In the rest of this chapter we examine these effects with respect to such areas as economics, enlightenment, culture, sports, and the problem of violence. In a later chapter we discuss the effects of broadcasting on politics.

TELEVISION, RADIO AND ECONOMICS

The economic significance of television and radio extends far beyond the dollar volume of their business alone. Their full significance is measured by their importance as advertising media for the distribution and sale of all forms of consumer goods. Television has established itself as the most effective advertising and selling medium ever developed, while radio's ability to persuade listeners to buy certain goods is indicated by the fact that advertisers spend close to a billion dollars a year to use radio.

The advertising effectiveness of radio and television has been demonstrated many times. In the early days of radio, Pepsodent's sponsorship of *Amos 'n Andy* resulted in a 76 percent increase in its sales. In 1939 sales of the Gillette Company increased 350 percent after it paid $100,000 for the right to broadcast the World Series. Radio's effectiveness as an advertising vehicle continued into the age in which television became the dominant medium. In the 1970s, radio advertising raised the sales of Blue Nun wine by 1700 percent in four years and radio was a major factor in making Nature Valley Granola number one in its share of the natural food market. A mix of radio and TV advertising increased business for the Midas Muffler Company 30 percent in one year.

Though radio has shown its advertising muscle many times, even its accomplishments have been outshone by those of television. Some years ago when the Dow Chemical Company began using television to advertise Saran Wrap, its sales within a year rose from 20,000 to 600,000 cases a month. In the same period Hazel Bishop lipstick company in four years raised its gross annual business from $40,000 to $12 million by committing 90 percent of its advertising budget to television. Television advertising accomplished similar results for the Alberto-Culver Company. By raising its television advertising budget from $219,000 to $23 million a year it increased its sales by 1500 percent in five years.

Television's record of success as an advertising medium has continued in more recent times. Using celebrity spokesmen, two companies in highly competitive fields substantially increased their business. When O. J. Simpson began running through airports on behalf of the Hertz rent-a-car company, he accomplished a 36 percent increase in the number of consumers who rated Hertz best among car-rental agencies. The tough-spoken commericials of Karl Malden for American Express Traveler's Cheques increased that company's business 15 percent in one year.

The success of television as an advertising vehicle has led a great many corporations to invest a major share of their advertising dollars in the medium. In 1975 for the fifth consecutive year corporate advertisers made television their number one advertising medium. In 1977 it is estimated that expenditures for all television will approximate $7.4 billion.

A special two-year study of the impact of television on the people of Fort Wayne, Indiana, was financed by the National Broadcasting Company. The research project was undertaken to determine what people did before television, how they spent their time, how they reacted to brand names, ideas, and products—and what they did after television. The results of the study, entitled *Strangers into Customers,* were as follows:

1. After getting TV, people became more conscious of advertising. Television accounted for 7 out of 10 advertising impressions people absorbed. Television became a greater advertising source than newspapers, magazines, and radio combined were before the family acquired its set. (85 percent vs. 80 percent.)

2. TV made people aware of a brand name (average brand awareness increased 45 percent), taught them what a product is and does (average brand-product association went up 59 percent), increased their ability to recognize a trademark (average trademark recognition increased 68 percent), taught consumers to identify a slogan or copy-point, and made the housewife rate a brand more favorably (average brand rating went up 41 percent).

3. TV presold durable goods, yielded great public-relations benefits, and brought out the advertised brand as a make people would consider and buy. After TV, a washing machine manufacturer was thought of 44 percent more often as "making the best," and 38 percent more housewives would "consider buying" a brand-name refrigerator.

4. TV increased the number of customers. TV brands usually increased at the expense of their non-TV competitors (a brand-name evaporated milk won 51 percent more buyers, while a competitor lost 14 percent). More nonbuyers changed to product buyers among the housewives who had sets. TV also brought its ad-

vertisers a bigger share of the market. (In the whole of Fort Wayne, TV brands increased their share of purchases by 19 percent in the typical package-goods field, while non-TV brands fell off 11 percent.)

5. The more a product was advertised on TV, the more buyer increase it got. The most advertised brands increased 48 percent among set owners, while the brands with small TV schedules increased only 28 percent.

6. TV worked fast and continued working. Those who had owned their sets longest, averaging a year or more, showed the highest buying levels for TV brands.

7. The effects of TV advertising were reflected sharply at the retailer level. Four dealers out of 10 stocked new brands as a result of TV advertising. TV advertising topped all other media in causing the dealer to give a brand more shelf space and special displays. On "doing the best job of moving goods in your store," dealers favored TV over newspapers almost 3 to 1, over magazines almost 10 to 1.

No wonder television is referred to by advertisers as a selling machine.

TELEVISION, RADIO AND ENLIGHTENMENT

Television and radio also serve as major sources of information and enlightenment for the American public. News broadcasts have long been among the public's favorite types of radio programs. During World War II, radio's ability to broadcast news bulletins a few moments after the actual events gave it a decided advantage over newspapers, which had to contend with the delays of typesetting. Radio first supplanted the press as the main and most trusted source of news, and it has now been supplanted in turn by television as the major source of news information for most people. Both media are established sources for the first word of unexpected news developments.

The coverage of special events, including natural disasters such as floods and hurricanes, and events of public importance such as a presidential inauguration, the visit of a foreign political leader, debates at the United Nations, or a presidential nominating convention, offers the public an opportunity to be present at the unfolding of history. Programs such as *Meet the Press, Face the Nation* and *Issues and Answers* subject national leaders to questions from newspeople that ventilate controversy on public matters and probe deeply into issues of current importance. Other series that provide enlightenment on matters of national and international importance are *Washington Week in Review*, in which Washington correspondents discuss the week's major stories, and *60 Minutes*, which employs a magazine approach to explore subjects of a social, cultural, or political nature. Programs of agricultural and consumer information and market and weather reports have come to play a vital role in the commerce of the nation. American farmers, especially, have become dependent on farm broadcasts for essential planting and marketing information. Formal and informal education programs have been presented by networks as well as by local commercial and noncommercial stations, and many of these have been successful. Broadcasts prepared for reception in schoolrooms have converted television and radio into schools-of-the-air in many cities and states. In the primary grades especially, televison and radio have been markedly effective in beaming lesson material to the classroom, where teachers and pupils may benefit by the greater facilities and skill at the command of the studio instructor.

TELEVISION AND CULTURE

The ways in which people choose to entertain themselves or to be entertained, their levels of taste, the place they assign to creative works of art, are all matters of cultural significance. At one time radio was an important factor in cultural life, but now that it has been transformed into essentially a local medium with many voices appealing to fractionalized audiences it has lost some of its impact, although there are areas in which its influence is still strongly felt. In popularizing various types of recorded music, such as rock, country and western, and other contemporary music styles, radio has had an enormous effect on the youth culture of the country, often, it has been said, conveying thinly veiled social themes and messages in the lyrics of the endlessly repeated broadcast songs. Though it still has an effect on the musical tastes of the nation, its main cultural role has been taken over by television. The fact that watching television represents the favorite leisure-time activity of the American people makes it an object of cultural concern. What kinds of programs do people watch so eagerly? What levels of taste do these programs represent? What place is assigned to works of artistic quality? To what extent does television develop cultural patterns of its own? To what extent does it create its own materials of entertainment and art? Or does it serve simply as a showcase for art and entertainment created elsewhere? To what extent has the public absorption in television affected interests and activities in other leisure-time pursuits, such as reading, conversation, sports, movie attendance, music study, painting, arts and crafts, to name a few?

These questions deserve serious consideration if we are to understand fully the relationship between television and American culture. We do not have final answers to all the questions, but as broadcasting has achieved a permanent place in our society, certain points have become clear. We know, for example, that by and large the kinds of programs that people watch and listen to in greatest numbers are those that combine the broadest elements of audience appeal in comedy, variety, drama, personality shows, and programs involving audience participation. We know that unlike other fields of communication such as magazine and book publishing, which are able to publish all kinds of magazines and books ranging from those with very specialized appeals, and therefore limited readership, to those with broad appeal and mass readership, the television medium has tended, especially during the evening hours, to broadcast only those programs that are likely to attract the largest audiences. The reason is simple: a program with limited appeal set into an evening network program schedule makes it difficult to regain the audience for the following program because many people tend to stay with the station to which they are tuned rather than change stations at the end of each program. Nevertheless, programs of superior artistic taste have been produced at great cost by national television networks in the hope that the public will turn to what is worthwhile rather than adhering to habitual tuning patterns. The concept of the "Special" program is based upon the idea that a program of superior quality, of whatever length necessary to do justice to its program material, will overcome habit patterns and attract an audience of substantial size. Although this objective is not always realized, the concept of the "Special" is now firmly established. Many cultural specials are broadcast a second time, and specials of a popular nature have been successful in attracting enormous audiences. In recent years the practice of presenting not a single "Special" program, but a "Special" series of limited length has come into being. The best example of this development is the so-called "mini-series," which dramatizes a novel or other work through a period of a few days or weeks. An outstanding success in this category was the dramatization through a period of about a week of Alex Haley's novel *Roots*. It drew the largest audiences in television history.

By and large, both television and radio in the past depended on the legitimate theater, the music hall, and the night clubs to provide them with performers and program material. Within less than 10 years of its beginning, the television industry discovered that its program demands could no longer be satisfied by turning to other entertainment media; as a result the broadcast media undertook to find performers of their own in large-scale talent and writer development plans. Thus, the media established substantial resources of their own, and television is now an important source of new talent in the country. Television will always continue to serve as a showcase for the best entertainment created elsewhere, but because of its huge economic resources and its great program needs, television underwrites in part or in whole artistic ventures on the legitimate stage and in motion pictures. NBC and CBS have participated in underwriting several theatrical ventures on Broadway, and there has been network activity in the production of movies not only for TV presentation but also for regular exhibition.

That the public's concentration on television has affected the nature of its interest and the extent of its participation in other leisure-time activities can hardly be doubted. Elmo Roper reported in one of his public opinion surveys that 78 percent of Americans regularly seek ready-made forms of spare-time activity, and that chief among these are television and radio.

At first it was feared that popular fascination with television would cause people to stop reading books and newspapers, going to movies or the theater, conversing with others, or participating in sports. When movie attendance dropped markedly in 1949 and 1950, many motion picture executives rushed to the conclusion that television was the primary cause of the loss at the box office. In time it was learned that the box office for quality motion pictures remained as good as ever, but that many people preferred to watch television rather than pay admission to see a mediocre movie. Many motion picture houses that specialized in the exhibition of Grade B films went out of business (almost 6500 in the first three years of television), and the importance of Hollywood as a center for the production of pictures for theatrical exhibition seems permanently reduced. The drop in the production of feature films, however, has been offset by the rise in the production of films designed specifically for the TV screen.

The effect of television on reading has been a major concern among those who worry about the cultural climate of our country. Considering the large number of hours that go into television viewing, one might assume that the time devoted to reading would decrease. Surprisingly, this seems not to be the case. Librarians reported that the circulation of books actually increased in the TV era, and they found that the interests of some of their customers in certain subjects were stimulated by TV viewing. Those who gain great pleasure from reading books are not likely to forsake reading for television; those for whom reading is a marginal pleasure are probably wooed away. The greater concern has been the effect of television on the development of reading habits in children, because we know that children have been almost wholly captivated by television. Professor Paul Witty of Northwestern University, who had conducted regular surveys of television viewing in the Chicago area, saw no great effect on the reading of children, even though he had found that elementary school children average about 21 hours of viewing a week, while high school students average about 13 hours.

Newspapers and magazines have suffered from the growth of television not so much from a loss of readers as from a loss of advertising revenue. Such mass-circulation magazines as *Colliers, Life,* and *Look* became extinct because the dollars that paid for many of the advertisements that used to fatten their issues went to television.

Another question of genuine concern is whether television tends to make people passive observers rather than active participators in cultural pursuits. Only as we gain greater perspective with the passage of time will we be able to reckon the full effects of television in this regard. It may be noted, however, that, at the very least, many people who always have been observers have been given an opportunity through television to observe cultural undertakings of real quality that they otherwise would never have experienced.

We know that the themes and values of television programs do have some effect on many viewers, although no comprehensive analysis and evaluation of these effects has yet been made. We know, for example, that in the popularizing of a song, radio and televison tend to form our tastes for us. A popular song becomes a success by being dinned into our ears through constant repetition. Special studies have shown that the sales of records regularly follow the peak of performances of the song on the air. As a result of this intense repetition, even successful songs are short-lived. In broadcasting classical music, radio undoubtedly has stimulated greater interest in the buying of records for home listening. We know that on specific matters like modes of dress and speech, large segments of the public are quick to imitate what they see and hear on the air. The reading of certain books has also been stimulated by their dramatization on the air.

SOCIAL EFFECTS OF TELEVISION AND RADIO

The social effects of television and radio are many and varied. For one thing, television and radio influence our daily living and buying habits. Group viewing at home, some say, has strengthened the family unit. Listeners and viewers are perceptibly and imperceptibly affected by the programs they hear each day. While broadcast stations try to adjust their schedules to popular living habits, the public in turn often adjusts its habits to the broadcast schedule. Farmers with sets in their homes stay up later at night than farmers without them. Topflight network television programs cause people to make a practice of staying home on certain nights. Refashioning of the living room to accommodate the television set has been the experience of many people. And, needless to say, the advertising we are exposed to on the air influences our buying habits. On a television series sponsored by the manufacturers of Kraft products, the commercial on one program was devoted to a cake frosting recipe made with cream cheese. The next day's mail brought 79,000 requests for the recipe. In following weeks, better than half a million more requests were received. Nor is the effect of commercial exhortation limited to adults only, as many parents who have been bombarded with pleas from their children to buy certain products can testify. A study by NBC of children's influence on buying as a result of their watching television had the following results:

1. Children frequently pay as much attention to television commercials as to the program itself. This is particularly true for the animated cartoon type, jingles, and gift offers.
2. Children not only like to watch the commercials—they remember them well enough to repeat them, and to both recognize and request the advertised products.
3. Nine out of ten mothers have been asked by their children to buy a TV advertised product; 89 percent of these requests resulted in purchase. The highest request rate is among the five- to eight-year-olds.
4. Children influence brand switching. Three out of five mothers have bought another brand of a product in addition to their regular brand, to satisfy the children's requests.

Television and radio have also demonstrated an exceptional ability to induce mass social action along lines of generosity. This was proved repeatedly during World War II. An outstanding example of broadcasting's influence on mass behavior during the war were the marathon broadcasts of Kate Smith on her War Bond drives. On February 1, 1944, in a round-the-clock appeal on almost every program of the CBS network, Kate Smith begged, cajoled, and demanded that her listeners buy War Bonds. By the end of her all-day drive, she had brought in a total of $105,392,700 in War Bond purchases, marking the greatest single radio bond-selling exploit during the war, an outstanding feat from every point of view. In recent years educational stations have demonstrated television's power to extract money from the public by holding TV auctions that in some cases have raised hundreds of thousands of dollars for the support of a single station's activities. Charity telethons have motivated viewers to donate even larger amounts of money. The muscular dystrophy telethons of Jerry Lewis year after year raised many millions of dollars for that cause.

The coverage of news events by broadcasters, particularly on television, seems to have a profound effect on the way people feel about the issues involved. The Vietnam war was the first in American history to be brought into living rooms on a day-to-day basis by television. Some sociologists believe that this constant exposure to its violence was a prime factor in causing many people to begin questioning the validity of American participation in that conflict. Mike Wallace's interview on CBS with a former soldier who confessed that he had killed unarmed Vietnamese civilians was instrumental in arousing national revulsion at the My Lai massacre.

Broadcasting also has a peculiar power to induce panic in insecure and suggestible listeners. This was demonstrated early in the history of radio, at the nervous expense of the public, in three fateful dramatizations of H. G. Wells' fantasy, *The War of the Worlds.* On Halloween weekend of 1938, which happened to fall in the period of the unsettling Munich war crisis, Orson Welles produced an adaptation of the fantasy that had hordes of Martians invading New Jersey. The program, done in a seminews style, created a panic on the East Coast despite frequent announcements during and after the program that the story was fictional. The panic did not subside until the next morning. Several persons were reported to have died of heart attacks, and many people prayed in the streets or fled into the country to seek refuge; hardier individuals seized arms and prepared to fight for their lives. Adaptations of the same script broadcast in 1944 in Chile and in 1949 in Ecuador caused even greater panic despite the fact that audiences were warned ahead of time that the program was to be all in fun. In Ecuador when the people learned it was all a hoax, an enraged mob, hurling gasoline and flaming balls of paper, burned down the radio station, killed at least six persons, and injured 15 others. Army troops and tanks had to be called out before order could be restored. In 1969 Station WJR in Detroit broadcast the program again as a historical curio, never believing that people would still take it seriously. In this instance no panic was created, but a number of people called the station wanting to be reassured that the nation was not being invaded by Martian monsters.

Just as broadcasting can induce panic through scare broadcasts, so it can often quell panic stemming from other sources, although the episodes described above suggest its limitations. During earthquakes, floods, and wartime aerial bombings, firm and confident voices carried by radio and television have calmed, reassured, and directed populaces into controlled and reasoned behavior. Broadcasts sent out during the destructive rampages of hurricanes and tornadoes are credited with providing crucial information that helped save many lives. Broadcasting helped to calm the people's fears after the assassination of President Kennedy. During the Detroit race riot of 1967, radio and television stations refrained for many hours from broadcasting news of what was happening to avoid exacerbating the situation; when knowledge of the events could no longer be kept from the public, they treated them as calmly and objectively as possible. We have every reason to believe that broadcasters will continue to serve the public in this way in crises to come.

As television and radio have won the acceptance of the American people, they have tended to establish or support certain social values and to accentuate various social trends. Television and radio programs, in their di-

rect advertising messages and in the implicit suggestions and appeals of dramatic shows, tend to convey to the listener and the viewer the social values
played up in commercials and scripts. Together with the press and the
movies, television and radio in this way define "success" for us, and give us
many of our social values.

Television and radio also have accentuated the standardizing and simplifying of the English language, which continues a social trend first noted in
the last century. Mass communication media, including newspapers, magazines, digests, and comic books, as well as television and radio, emphasize
brief and simple communication to the exclusion of more complex styles of
expression and argument. It is now difficult to get an audience to follow a
line of argument for more than fifteen minutes, whereas in former years, it
was not unusual for a skillful speaker to hold an audience rapt for hours, as
he wound his way through a long argument. Since many issues of great social importance do not lend themselves to brief presentation without the
danger of oversimplification and distortion of basic issues and meanings,
some observers look askance upon this social influence of broadcasting.

Television and radio also have a great influence on society by confer-
ring status on issues, persons, organizations, and movements to which broadcast time is made available. A broadcast discussion of an issue makes that issue more important in the public mind, just as the television or radio
appearance of a relatively unimportant individual boosts that person's prestige in the eyes of the community. As Professors Lazarsfeld and Merton have
pointed out, "The mass media bestow prestige and enhance the authority of
individuals and groups by *legitimizing their status.*" Television and radio audiences seem to subscribe to the circular belief: "If you really matter, you
will be at the focus of mass attention and, if you *are* at the focus of mass attention, then surely you must really matter."

TELEVISION AND SPORTS

An area in which television has had one of its greatest impacts is that of
sports. It has worked in two ways, both to damage sports and to provide
them with promotional and financial support. Television has hurt sports by
drawing people to the TV screen and away from the stadiums and arenas in
which games are played. As the televising of major league baseball games developed from 1949 to 1953, attendance at those games decreased from 21
million a year to 14.5 million. The effect on minor league baseball was even
more drastic, as millions chose to watch major league baseball on television
instead of going to their home-town stadiums to see players who had not yet
reached the big time. Through the decades of the 1950s and 1960s minor
league attendance sank from 42 million a year to 10 million, and the number
of clubs shrank from 488 to 155. The sport of boxing was almost killed by
television. Through the 1950s there was an enormous proliferation of boxing
shows; to cite an example, television stations in Detroit in the 1950s were
broadcasting five boxing shows a week, either locally produced or originating nationally. These shows lured patrons away from the boxing arenas and
created such a demand for talent that boxers were thrust into the national

spotlight before they were ready. The loss of patronage at the box office and the deterioration in the quality of the bouts brought the sport to a condition of bare survival.

There is another side to the picture, however. The money television pours into sports for broadcasting rights is a major element in the budgets of many teams, and in many instances TV revenue makes the difference between the financial success or failure of a team. Pete Rozelle, Commissioner of the National Football League, said: "There are 26 football franchises now. Without television half of them would not exist and the rest would be struggling." The fact that the American Basketball Association failed to gain a national television contract greatly complicated its effort to survive. It was denied both national exposure and the additional revenue it needed to supplement its income from gate receipts. The same problem contributed to the early demise of the World Football League.

It is estimated that television organizations spend more than $200 million a year for the rights to broadcast sports. In 1976 the American Broadcasting Company paid $25 million for the television rights to the Olympic games played in Montreal, Canada. The National Broadcasting Company contracted to pay more than three times that amount to broadcast the 1980 Olympic games from Moscow. In 1976 broadcasters paid $81.5 million for the right to broadcast professional and college football games on television and radio and nearly $51 million to broadcast major league baseball games. Other millions were spent to broadcast other sports, among them basketball, golf, and hockey.

The broadcasts made possible by these expenditures regularly attracted millions of viewers. Events that created a high degree of national excitement drew some of the largest audiences in television. As interest in the competition between the National and American Football Leagues (now Conferences) grew, the Superbowl telecasts began attracting larger and larger audiences until the number of viewers passed the 75 million mark. The telecasting of World Series games in prime time drew audiences of over 70 million. The cost to advertisers for commercial messages was in keeping with the number of people they attracted. Advertisers on the Superbowl paid $250,000 a minute and on the World Series $140,000 a minute.

While accepting this money from television, sports promoters have also taken steps to preserve the revenue from the sale of tickets at the box office. The National Football League would not permit the televising of any games in the local area until the Congress passed a law prohibiting blackouts of games when they were sold out. If the game was not sold out, there was no local TV coverage and a fan had to go to the stadium or be content to hear a description of it on the radio. The NFL continued to abide by this restriction even after the law expired. The NCAA exercises rigid control over the schedule of college football telecasts games to help maintain ticket sales at the various college stadiums throughout the country. Boxing promoters finally denied regular television access to major boxing events entirely, permitting only closed-circuit television in theaters, which produced revenue at the box office. In some ways television has helped sell certain sports events to the public by publicizing them, among them tennis, bowling, golf, wrestling, and roller derbies.

In addition to producing revenue from advertisers and affecting attendance at the actual events, television has had some other discernible effects on sports. One of the most obvious is the scheduling of events to suit the demands of television rather than the convenience of the people attending them. Thus an NBA professional basketball game began in Los Angeles at 11:00 A.M. Sunday morning so that it could reach a 2:00 P.M. TV audience in the East. Even the dates of games have been changed to accommodate the TV schedule makers. Those attending televised football games have noticed the time-outs that are called not for any reason connected with the game but to permit the televising of commercials. People attending the 1967 Superbowl game saw two perfectly legal kickoffs open the second half. The kickoff was repeated because the first took place when the network was in the middle of a commercial.

THE PROBLEM OF VIOLENCE

An aspect of broadcasting that concerns a great many people is the amount of violence in television programs. At frequent intervals various organizations make counts of the aggressive acts that punctuate video fare; these surveys all have a similar result: they demonstrate that television does involve a great deal of violence. In the summer of 1968, for example, when the nation was grieving over the violent death of Senator Robert Kennedy, a survey showed that television networks in prime time during one week portrayed 84 killings. In addition, 372 other acts of aggression or threats of violence were dramatized on the TV screen.

Many responsible leaders are concerned about the way this violence may affect viewers. There is particular concern about the effect on children. Some critics are convinced that television violence does great harm. Frederic Wertham, a noted psychiatrist, maintains that TV violence makes children callous, causes anxiety and tension, teaches the techniques of crime, and triggers juvenile delinquency. Senator S. I. Hayakawa, former President of San Francisco State College, noted that the young men and women who reached maturity in the 1960s were the first generation to have grown up in a television age. He speculated that their alienation, rioting, drug taking, and radical politics might be a result of their exposure to television.

There are some, on the other hand, who see violence on television as a positive good because it helps to dissipate aggressive impulses in a harmless way. P. M. Pickard, a British psychologist, believes that television violence helps children to escape from the terrors that arise from their own unresolved and frightening fantasies. Wilbur Schramm, an American media specialist, does not applaud TV violence, but he believes that most of the evils blamed on it arise from other causes, such as oppressive home life, bad environment, and disturbed personalities.

With experts in disagreement, it is not surprising that there are widespread demands for more scientific research on this question. At the request of Congress, the Surgeon General of the United States undertook studies to determine the effects of violence on television. Human beings are so complex, however, and the effects in question so difficult to measure, that research thus far has provided no definitive answers. The 1972 Surgeon-General's report, for example, could only provide the somewhat hesitant conclusion that the viewing of television violence can increase the subsequent aggressiveness of a young person. Professor Albert Bandura of Stanford University has conducted studies in which he showed preschool children pictures of adults kicking and punching large dolls. When he left the children alone in a room with similar dolls, he found they were more inclined to kick and punch them than were children who had not seen the pictures. Bandura concluded that children exposed to televised aggression learn aggressive patterns of behavior. Other scientists have questioned the significance of Bandura's findings, however, arguing that his experiments merely demonstrate that children are prone to imitate and that he failed to show that television developed inner hostility and aggression. Other studies have been similarly inconclusive.

In the 1970s the Rand Corporation initiated a number of studies designed to evaluate the effect of television on human behavior with special attention to the violence factor. In 1976 the results of two studies commissioned by ABC with grants totalling $1,000,000 were published. One study found that under certain conditions exposure to televised violence is capable of producing an increased inclination toward aggression in children. The second study found that exposure to aggressive content did not lead to heightened aggressive behavior, but it did tend to foster aggressive fantasies. The study did not find any causative relationship between television viewing and the criminal and violent actions of youthful offenders.

We do not yet know for certain what the effect of violence on viewers may be. In the absence of proof that TV violence is not damaging in effect, many people believe that we should play it safe and reduce the violence on television. In 1975, the television industry adopted a scheduling practice that sought to avoid telecasting programs containing violent themes and actions before 9:00 P.M. Though the institution of the "Family Hour," as the period before nine was called, came into question as the result of an adverse court decision, the step did represent an attempt by the broadcasting industry to deal in some way with the problem of violence.

There were also moves against violence from outside the broadcasting industry. In 1977, the American Medical Association announced that it had asked ten major corporations to review their policies about sponsoring excessively violent shows. This action was supported by J. Walter Thompson, the nation's largest advertising agency, which said that it was advising its clients to stop buying advertising spots in series that emphasized violence. The agency cited a survey showing that some viewers were boycotting products advertised on such shows. To help viewers identify violent series, the National Citizens Committee for Broadcasting undertook to rank series in terms of the violence they portrayed.

Questions for Discussion

1. In what ways can you justify the statement that "broadcasting can now be identified with American life itself"?

2. How do television and radio compare in influence with other social institutions such as schools, the family, and the church?

3. To what extent has your life been influenced by radio and television?

4. Has broadcasting tended to depress the artistic standards of our society?

5. What should be the ultimate mission of radio and television?

6. Is television making us a nation of spectators rather than participants? If so, is this a healthy development?

7. What should be the responsibility of television and radio to the American public?

8. "If you could use television once every six months, it would be a great amenity. But the world would have been a happier place if television had never been discovered. It contributes to the uneasiness of life today."—statement of the Archbishop of Canterbury after seeing television in the United States. Do you agree or disagree with this statement? Why?

9. Do you feel that radio-television coverage of the news is more objective than newspaper coverage?

the growth
of american radio

The growth of American radio is a dramatic chapter in the history of communications and the shaping of modern American life. The rise of broadcasting is the story of a struggle for control of inventions worth a king's ransom. It is a story of failure on the part of scientists and industrial leaders to recognize what we now accept as obvious: that radio's virtue is its usefulness as a public broadcast medium. It is a story of fumbling to find a sound means of financing a privately operated radio system; a story of governmental intervention in radio, at the request of both industry and the public, to replace chaos and piracy with order and stability; a story of great achievement by a mass communications medium that advanced from fledgling status to a dominant role in American life.

SCIENTIFIC ORIGINS AND DEVELOPMENT

Although the invention of radio was a natural consequence of scientific advances in the fields of electricity and magnetism, the path of radio's advance was uneven. The idea of broadcasting without wires of any sort, making use of unseen waves in space, did not come easily to the mind of man. Early inventors found it difficult to obtain financial support for their experiments. They ran into opposition from scientists and editors who could prove, on paper, the impossibility of effective radio broadcasting. The final scientific achievement of radio and television cannot be attributed to any single man or nation. It was made possible by the research of scientists in many nations: United States, Italy, Denmark, Canada, Great Britain, and others. The early period of scientific development is clouded with controversy. Rival scientists worked independently to produce similar solutions to the same technical problems. It would be risky indeed for the historian to try to unravel the morass of conflicting claims, which the patent courts could not clear up to the satisfaction of competing litigants.

In 1864, the British scientist James C. Maxwell laid down the theory of electromagnetism and predicted the existence of the electric waves that are now used in radio. Twenty years later, Thomas Edison worked out a system of communication between railway stations and moving trains without using

19

connecting wires. In 1887, Heinrich Hertz, a German, showed that rapid variations in electric current could be projected into space in the form of radio waves similar to light waves. Hertz thus founded the theory upon which modern radio is based.

By 1894, the investigations of Guglielmo Marconi, a twenty-year-old Italian, led him to conclude that Hertzian waves could be used for telegraphing without wires. The next year he secured a patent for wireless telegraphy in Great Britain. In 1901, Marconi's achievement was told to the American people in a front-page story in *The New York Times* headlined, "WIRELESS SPANS THE OCEAN." Marconi, working in Newfoundland, had picked up the Morse letter "s" transmitted by wireless telegraphy from England.

Marconi's discoveries stimulated the work of other scientists, and the next few years saw the refinement of wireless transmission. The main technical hurdle remaining in the way of wireless voice-broadcasting seemed to be the discovery of a means of high-frequency alternating transmission. Three prominent scientists worked independently on this problem. The result was the invention of the vacuum tube in 1904 by the Britisher John Ambrose Fleming, and its refinement by the Canadian Reginald Fessenden and the American Dr. Lee De Forest. The animosity that developed between Fessenden and De Forest makes it difficult to draw an accurate picture of the sequence of scientific events. Both men took out numerous patents on their inventions. De Forest, using his audion tube, projected speech by radio on December 31, 1906, five days after Fessenden accomplished the same thing with his heterodyne system. In 1908, De Forest broadcast recorded music from the top of the Eiffel Tower in Paris and was heard five hundred miles away.

THE STRUGGLE FOR CONTROL

Marconi was among the first to realize that the future of radio as a point-to-point broadcasting medium depended upon finding commercial applications for it and protecting patent rights. In 1897, the British Marconi Company was formed to acquire title to all of Marconi's patents. A subsidiary of the British company, known as American Marconi, was incorporated in the United States in 1899 and soon came to control almost all of America's commercial wireless communications, then limited to ship-to-shore transmissions and special point-to-point broadcasts. That such application of radio was to have commercial usefulness was made abundantly clear in 1910, when Congress passed a law requiring most passenger ships to have radio equipment and operators. This law amply justified itself when, two years later, the *Titanic,* on her maiden voyage, struck an iceberg and sank, but, owing to the prompt wireless call for aid, more than seven hundred passengers were saved. It is an interesting historical note that young David Sarnoff, later to be a major figure in the development of American broadcasting, was the wireless operator who received the distress calls from the sinking *Titanic*.

Although American Marconi dominated the field, a number of American-controlled companies undertook research in radio in order to cut in on the broadcasting business. They won several important radio patents and began to manufacture radio apparatus. Among these companies were General Electric, Westinghouse, and the Western Electric Company, the manufacturing subsidiary of the American Telephone and Telegraph Company. The further development of radio got snagged in a confused patent situation, however, which brought almost all manufacturing to a halt. Each manufacturer needed patents controlled by his competitors; each refused to license others or to exchange patents; therefore, if each company continued with its operations, it became vulnerable to patent-infringement suits.

This tangle was still unresolved when the government took over all wireless stations in World War I and asked all the companies to pool their inventions in the hope of devising practical radio-telephone transmitters needed by the Army and Navy. In return, the government assured the companies legal protection against patent suits.

When the war came to an end and wireless stations were returned to their owners, the confused patent situation once again prevented any extensive radio manufacturing. The situation was further complicated by a conflict of interests between the United States and Britain which, through the American Marconi Company, still controlled a substantial part of the wireless industry here. In early 1919, British Marconi undertook negotiations with General Electric for the exclusive rights to the Alexanderson alternator, a device considered of critical importance in long-distance radio transmission. The negotiations were virtually concluded when Rear Admiral W. H. G. Bullard, Director of Naval Communications for the U. S. Navy, appealed to General Electric not to sell the alternator to British Marconi because the British would then hold a practical monopoly on worldwide communications for an indefinite period.

Negotiations were dropped, and General Electric found itself without an outlet for the invention in which it had made a heavy investment. Under Admiral Bullard's guidance, General Electric evolved a plan by which a new company, controlled entirely by American capital and holding major radio patents, would be organized. The new company, formed in 1919, was the Radio Corporation of America. RCA bought all the patents and assets of American Marconi, entered into cross-licensing agreements with General Electric, Westinghouse, and Western Electric, and thus took a commanding position in the American radio field.

These agreements gave General Electric and Westinghouse the exclusive right to manufacture radio receiving sets and RCA the sole right to sell the sets. A.T.&T. was granted the exclusive right to make, lease, and sell broadcast transmitters, a monopoly of which the telephone company made much use in the next few years. In return these companies were assigned substantial stock holdings in RCA, which they did not dispose of for some time. During its first two years of existence, RCA was concerned with ship-to-shore communications, transoceanic point-to-point radio service, and sales of radio parts to amateurs for the construction of crystal receivers.

THE DAWN OF MODERN RADIO BROADCASTING

The early development of radio, therefore, centered around the perfection of point-to-point broadcasting as a substitute for transmission by cable or telephone lines. The main commercial criticism of radio was its lack of secrecy, making it unsuitable for private service, since unauthorized persons could overhear a broadcast conversation. How, then, it was asked, could this invention be turned into a money-making proposition? Efforts were directed toward developing radio as a confidential means of radio-telephony, with controls against eavesdroppers.

Finally, it was realized that radio's very lack of secrecy was its great commercial strength. Just who it was who first perceived this now obvious truth is not known, but the failure of many people associated with the rise of radio to recognize its best public applications demonstrates clearly how important it is for ideas of social utilization to keep abreast of discoveries in the scientific world. Of all the people connected with radio at this stage, Lee De Forest seems outstanding in his grasp of the possible use of radio as a *public* broadcast medium. He is reported to have said as early as 1909, "I look forward to the day when by the means of radio, opera may be brought into every home. Some day the news, and even advertising, will be sent out to the public on the wireless telephone."

In 1916, David Sarnoff, then an engineer with American Marconi and later the chief executive of RCA, also foresaw the public usefulness of the new communications medium. Sarnoff described a "plan of development" that would make radio a "household utility in the same sense as the piano or phonograph." Not only could radio be used to transmit and receive music, according to Sarnoff, but also to broadcast lectures, special public events, baseball scores, and various other subjects of popular interest.

De Forest's and Sarnoff's notion was not widely entertained, however, and by 1920 there were still only a few individuals who shared their grasp of radio's real future. At the University of Wisconsin, an experimental station (later called WHA) was operated by the University's Physics Department to broadcast weather and market reports. William E. Scripps, of the *Detroit News,* also appreciated the real virtues of broadcasting and started his experimental station, now WWJ, in the summer of 1920. In Pittsburgh, H. P. Davis, a Westinghouse vice-president, and Dr. Frank Conrad, a research engineer, opened the first commercially licensed radio station, KDKA, in November 1920, broadcasting the returns of the Harding-Cox presidential election as its first program.

THE FIRST FLUSH OF BROADCASTING

The new idea of radio as a public broadcast medium caught the imagination of the American people and spread like wildfire. From three stations in 1920, the number rose to over five hundred in 1923, and the sales of radio receivers rose from $2 million to $136 million in the same three-year period.

Many of these stations were owned and operated by concerns primarily interested in manufacturing and selling radio apparatus. These companies engaged in broadcasting for an obvious reason: unless there were stations to send out programs, the business of selling radio receivers would face collapse. The profit in radio had to be made on the sale of the radio set, while the broadcast program had to be supplied to the listener without charge. Westinghouse, RCA, and General Electric all opened up radio stations. Retail department stores then got interested in radio as a means of winning goodwill: Bamberger, Wanamaker, Gimbels, and the Shepard Stores set up stations. Newspapers, encouraged by the success of the *Detroit News* station, began broadcasting as a means of publicizing their papers. Colleges and universities plunged into broadcasting to provide experimental facilities for physics departments and to investigate the possibilities of educational radio. Numerous individuals afflicted with the radio fever rushed to open their own stations with whatever money they could scrape together. They used tiny five-watt transmitters which could be housed in small cabinets resembling ordinary receivers. Unofficial estimates of the number of these two-by-four stations ran as high as 1400 in 1924.

Still no way had been found to raise the money to pay for the operating expenses of the stations. Some people, like David Sarnoff, then general manager of RCA, believed that the manufacturers and distributors of radio receivers and parts should contribute to the cost of running broadcasting stations as a service to the buyers of sets and in order to stimulate sales. Others felt that radio stations should be operated by the government, or supported by endowment funds contributed by public-spirited citizens. Not yet born was the idea of selling radio time for advertising messages that is the foundation stone of modern commercial broadcasting.

In the first flush of broadcasting, however, the financial problem had not yet assumed urgent proportions. Radio required little by way of programming to attract an audience still thrilled by the very novelty of wireless communication. The main desire of many listeners was to be able to pick up on their battery-operated crystal headphone receivers the call letters of distant stations. Programs at first were really excuses for many stations to go on the air so that they might fulfill their true mission of announcing their call letters. Phonograph records were played and replayed to fill in the time between station identifications.

The broadcast quality of the primitive transmitting and receiving equipment of the early twenties was indeed poor, judged by present standards, but it was quite satisfactory to the audience of that day. One excited woman wrote to H. V. Kaltenborn, then beginning his career as a news commentator, "You came in last night just as clear as if you were talking over the telephone."

In these circumstances, broadcasters found themselves for the first two or three years under no great pressure to offer top-notch performers. Instead they relied on the phonograph and on the seemingly endless supply of free talent that came to the studio. Even the staff personnel of many stations could be had at virtually no cost. Good, bad, and indifferent musical artists were coaxed to the microphone with the promise of publicity. This was the period of the "great plague of mediocre sopranos badly transmitted and worse received."[1] After a time, however, performers became reluctant to give their services in exchange for publicity only, and a more sophisticated public began to demand higher-grade offerings. Entertainers, announcers, and engineers had cooled off from the early thrills and wanted to be paid for their work. Stations earned nothing, however. Where was the money to come from? One station was operating on an annual budget of $100,000 without tangible earnings of any kind. Westinghouse, having been amply repaid with publicity for its initial expenses, was seriously wondering whether there was a way out.

RADIO GOES COMMERCIAL

The solution eventually adopted came about through WEAF (now WNBC), the high-powered A.T.&T. station in New York City. The telephone company had set up WEAF to be operated as a "toll" station, available for hire to those wishing to reach the public by radio. The first sponsored program occurred on August 28, 1922, when WEAF broadcast a ten-minute talk delivered under the auspices of the Queensboro Corporation, a Long Island realty company.

The telephone company established a stringent broadcast policy that permitted only a conservative courtesy announcement to identify the sponsor. A.T.&T. ruled out the broadcast of direct advertising messages as being in poor taste for a communications medium that entered the privacy of the home with no forewarning as to the nature of the messages that would follow. Advertising was limited, therefore, to the simple statement of the sponsor's name, the intention being to maintain the dignity of radio and to prevent it from taking on the character of "huckstering."

The telephone company's attitude also reflected a fairly widespread belief, voiced by some newspapers that were apparently indulging in wishful thinking, that the radio medium was incapable of selling products through direct commercial announcements. The emphasis throughout this early period was on the use of radio by commercial companies solely to create public goodwill. This policy was emphatically approved by the then Secretary of Commerce, Herbert Hoover, who said in 1922, "It is inconceivable that we should allow so great a possibility for service, for news, for entertainment, for education, and for vital commercial purposes to be drowned in advertising chatter." The First Annual Radio Conference, held that year, recommended "that direct advertising in radio broadcast service be absolutely prohibited and that indirect advertising be limited to the announcements of the call letters of the station and of the name of the concern responsible for the matter broadcasted [sic]."

From 1922 to 1924, even limited goodwill commercial broadcasting was restricted almost entirely to WEAF. The telephone company claimed the sole right to sell radio time, and because of its control over patents, trans-

---

[1] Alfred N. Goldsmith and Austin C. Lescarboura, *This Thing Called Broadcasting* (New York, 1930), p. 146.

mission lines, and radio equipment it was able to enforce its will on other stations and to prevent them from carrying advertising. It was not until April 18, 1924, when A.T.&T. allowed independent stations to engage in sponsored broadcasting, that widespread advertising support for radio developed, and the system we know today began to take shape.

Advertising on the air soon increased markedly, and the distinction between direct and indirect commercial appeals began to wear thin. Advertisers and advertising agencies learned that radio campaigns were effective ways for marketing commercial products, and they turned over to radio stations a larger percentage of their advertising budgets. Whereas in 1922 WEAF's total advertising income for the whole year was about $5000, in 1930 the same station (which had been sold by the telephone company to RCA) was charging $750 for just one hour of evening radio time.[2] With this advertising money it became possible to hire high-priced entertainers to put on top-notch comedy, variety, and musical programs. Radio became "show business." Stars like Rudy Vallee expanded the dance-band formula by introducing radio "personalities" in 1929, the same year that *Amos 'n' Andy* began its long radio tenure. The continual improvement in the technical end of broadcasting persuaded renowned musical artists who had previously refused to risk their reputations on crude microphones and faulty amplifiers to break down and accept radio as a legitimate medium for their art. Opera singers like John McCormack and Lucrezia Bori led the musical flock to radio in 1926, and by the next year most of the big-name musical artists in the country appeared on program logs.

The better radio programs made possible by money obtained from radio advertising were undoubtedly welcomed by the listening audience, but opposition to the pressures which aimed to turn broadcasting into a carryall for various commercial appeals was still being voiced in responsible industrial and listener circles. The 1929 Code of the National Association of Broadcasters, for example, provided that after 6:00 P.M. commercial programs only of the "goodwill type" were to be broadcast, and between the hours of 7:00 and 11:00 P.M., no commercial announcements of any sort were to be aired!

Industry and public attitudes soon changed, however. If listening to a commercial message was going to make possible the broadcast of better entertainment programs, the public, with certain exceptions and within limitations, was willing to pay this price. The rules against direct advertising were at first relaxed, then gradually disappeared altogether.

Having established itself as the sole support of radio, advertising progressively took command of the entire broadcast operation. Programs began to stress more popular appeal in order to reach the type of audience desired by various advertisers. The standards for writing and presenting commercial messages on the air were guided almost entirely by considerations of effective selling. The earlier reservations placed upon the use of radio as an advertising medium because of the special way it gains access to our homes were no longer to be heard in broadcasting circles. The new trend was to reach its cli-

---

[2] *Ibid.,* pp. 279–281.

max 20 years later when, in 1943, one station broadcast 2215 commercial announcements in one week, or an average of 16.7 announcements every hour.[3]

FORMATION OF NATIONAL RADIO NETWORKS

If advertising was to become one foundation stone of American broadcasting, the national radio network was soon to become the other. The linking of two or more stations by land lines to carry the same program simultaneously was an essential aspect of the science, business, and art of radio. Single stations could not afford to produce elaborate shows to be transmitted to the audience in only one community; listeners in various parts of the country wanted to hear the best New York shows; advertisers with regionally or nationally marketed products wanted to launch their promotional campaigns simultaneously throughout the country. All of these desires combined to form the basis for the establishment of the national radio networks.

The A.T. & T. Network

Network broadcasting was inaugurated on January 4, 1923, when A.T.&T. broadcast a program simultaneously over WEAF and WNAC, a Boston station. Later that year, the telephone company set up a station in Washington, D.C., which it linked frequently with WEAF for network broadcasting, forming the nucleus of a network that expanded rapidly in the following years. By the fall of 1924, A.T.&T. was able to furnish a coast-to-coast network of 23 stations to carry a speech by President Coolidge.

The National Broadcasting Company

Meanwhile, RCA was making a start in network broadcasting. This was done despite the opposition of A.T.&T., which refused to furnish its telephone lines for use by competing networks and would not permit RCA to sell broadcast time to advertisers. RCA was compelled, therefore, to use inferior telegraph wires for "networking" and to make no charge for the use of radio time. Because of these obstacles, RCA's network did not grow as rapidly as A.T.&T.'s. In March 1925, when the telephone company network broadcast the presidential inauguration over a transcontinental network of 22 stations, the RCA network carried it over only four eastern stations.

This situation abruptly changed in 1926, when A.T.&T. decided to withdraw entirely from the radio broadcasting business, sold WEAF to RCA for $1 million, and transferred most of its radio properties to the so-called "Radio Group," made up of RCA, Westinghouse, and General Electric. These transactions cleared the way for the sale of radio time by the "Radio Group," and A.T.&T. agreed to make its telephone lines available to RCA.

---

[3] *Public Service Responsibility of Broadcast Licensees* (Washington, Federal Communications Commission, 1946), p. 44.

On September 9, 1926, RCA formed the National Broadcasting Company as a subsidiary corporation to take over its network broadcasting business and the station properties it had arranged to buy from A.T.&T. NBC began regular network operation in November of that year over a group of stations that came to be known as the NBC Red Network. In January 1927 it connected a second group of stations into what came to be known as the NBC Blue Network, thus controlling the only two networks in the country at that time. NBC continued to hold the predominant position in chain broadcasting for almost 20 years until, following a government order, it was forced to sell its second network in 1943.

The Columbia Broadcasting System

The network we now know as CBS came into being on January 27, 1927, under the name of United Independent Broadcasters, Inc. United's purpose was to contract time for a network of 16 radio stations, to sell time to advertisers, and to furnish programs for broadcasting. Before United actually got under way, the Columbia Phonograph Company became interested in the venture through the Columbia Phonograph Broadcasting System, which was organized in April 1927 to function as the sales agency of United. United contracted to pay each of its 16 stations $500 per week for 10 hours of radio time. It soon developed, however, that the sales agency could not sell enough time to sponsors to carry United under this arrangement, and the new network stood near the brink of collapse only a few months after its birth.

The Columbia Phonograph Company withdrew from the project, and all of the capital stock of the sales company was thereupon acquired by United, which took over the name of the Columbia Broadcasting System after dissolving the sales agency. William S. Paley and his family purchased a majority of CBS stock, the network began to thrive, and Paley assumed a role of leadership in broadcasting.

The Mutual Broadcasting System

The Mutual Broadcasting System, organized along radically different lines from NBC or CBS, did not come into being until 1934 when four stations, WGN, Chicago, WLW, Cincinnati, WXYZ, Detroit, and WOR, New York, agreed to work jointly to get advertising business for themselves. The network drummed up sales to advertisers and made arrangements with A.T.&T. for land-line connections among the four stations. With the coming of television and the decline of radio, particularly on the network level, MBS, which did not enter the television field, experienced difficult days. There was first a succession of owners and finally a bankruptcy proceeding, but even this crisis did not end the network's existence. It operated independently for a while and then became a subsidiary of the Minnesota Mining and Manufacturing Company. That company eventually sold it, and the network now operates as a subsidiary of the Mutual Broadcasting Corporation, servicing hundreds of affiliates throughout the country. It operates two radio networks, the Mutual Broadcasting System and the Mutual Black Network.

The American Broadcasting Company

The American Broadcasting Company came into being under its present name in 1945, after purchasing RCA's second network two years before. In 1953, ABC merged with United Paramount Theaters, Inc., to form a new corporation, American Broadcasting-Paramount Theaters, Inc., now known as American Broadcasting Companies, Inc. It operates four national radio networks, the American Contemporary Network, The American Information Network, The American Entertainment Network, and The American FM Network.

National Public Radio

After Congress established the Corporation for Public Broadcasting in 1967, the Corporation, in addition to its activities in television, established a radio network service for public and educational radio stations throughout the country. This noncommercial network is known as National Public Radio or NPR.

PUBLIC POLICY TOWARD RADIO

To make matters more difficult during broadcasting's first decade, the federal government was slow to make its position clear in its radio laws. Under international agreements, governments had assumed the responsibility to use certain radio frequencies and to provide protection for frequencies used by other countries. Radio's rapid growth quickly outdated the means by which these agreements were to be observed, however.

Early Radio Policy

Federal regulation of radio began with the Wireless Ship Act of 1910, which forbade any sizable passenger ship to leave the United States unless it was equipped with radio communication apparatus and a skilled radio operator. It was not until 1912, however, when the United States ratified the first international radio treaty, that the need for general regulation of radio became urgent. In order to carry out America's treaty obligations, Congress enacted the Radio Act of 1912. This statute forbade any person to operate a radio station without a license from the Secretary of Commerce.

Enforcement of the Radio Act of 1912 presented no serious problems until radio's value as a public broadcast medium was realized and there was a rush to get on the air. The Act of 1912 had not set aside any particular frequencies for privately operated broadcast stations, so the Secretary of Commerce selected two frequencies, 750 kilocycles and 833 kilocycles,[4] and li-

[4] The term "cycle" is now known as "hertz" in honor of the German scientist Heinrich Hertz, who contributed to the development of broadcasting. When writing of the history of broadcasting we shall continue to use the terms "kilocycles" and "megacycles," but when writing of the current scene we shall use the terms "kilohertz" and "megahertz."

censed all stations to operate on one or the other of these channels. The number of stations increased so rapidly, however, that the situation became extremely confused as radio signals overlapped and stations interfered with each other. On the recommendation of the National Radio Conference, which met annually from 1922 through 1925, Secretary of Commerce Hoover established a policy of assigning a specific frequency to each station.

The increase in the number of frequencies made available was still, however, not enough to take care of all the new stations that wanted to go on the air. The Secretary of Commerce tried to find room for all of them by limiting the power and hours of operation of some stations, so that several stations might use the same frequency. The number of stations multiplied so rapidly, however, that by 1925 there were almost 600 in the country and 175 applications on file for new stations. Every frequency in the standard broadcast band was by then already occupied by at least one station, and many by several. The new stations could be accommodated only by extending the standard broadcast band, at the expense of the other types of radio services, or by imposing still greater limitations upon time and power. The 1925 National Radio Conference opposed both of these methods and called upon Congress to remedy the situation through legislation.

Until Congress passed a new radio law, the Secretary of Commerce was powerless to deal with this trying situation. He could not simply refuse to issue any more broadcast licenses on the grounds that existing stations would be interfered with, because a court ruling denied him this authority. And, in April, 1926, an Illinois federal district court further tied his hands by holding that he had no power to impose any restrictions whatsoever as to frequency, power, or hours of station operations. A station's use of a frequency not assigned to it was ruled *not* a violation of the 1912 Radio Act, so there was nothing Hoover could do under then existing laws to prevent one station from jumping its frequency to that of its neighbor. This court decision was followed in July, 1926, by an opinion of the Attorney General that the Secretary had no power to issue regulations preventing interference between broadcast stations. Completely frustrated, Secretary of Commerce Hoover issued a public statement abandoning all his efforts to regulate radio and urging that the stations undertake, through gentlemen's agreements, to regulate themselves.

The Period of Chaos

Hoover's plea went unheeded. From July 1926 to February 1927, when Congress enacted new radio legislation, almost 200 new stations went on the air. "These new stations used any frequencies they desired, regardless of the interference thereby caused to others. Existing stations changed to other frequencies and increased their power and hours of operation at will. The result was confusion and chaos. With everybody on the air, nobody could be heard."[5] The situation became so intolerable that the President in his mes-

---

[5] *National Broadcasting Company* v. *United States,* 319 United States Reports at 212 (1943). This account is based largely on the historical review of public policy included in the majority opinion of the Supreme Court in this case.

sage of December 7, 1926, appealed to Congress to enact a comprehensive radio law. This time Congress took heed and legislation was enacted.

The Radio Act of 1927

The plight into which radio fell prior to 1927 could be attributed to a basic fact about radio as a means of communication—the radio spectrum simply was not large enough to accommodate every person who wanted to set up a broadcasting station. Regulation of radio by government was, therefore, as necessary to the development of radio "as traffic control was to the development of the automobile," according to the Supreme Court.[6] The Radio Act of 1927 proclaimed that the airwaves belong to the people of the United States and were to be used by individuals only with the authority of short-term licenses granted by the government when the "public interest, convenience, or necessity" would be served thereby. A temporary Federal Radio Commission was created to administer the law.

The new law automatically revoked the license of every radio station then operating, and allowed 60 days for applications for new licenses to be filed with the Federal Radio Commission. The Commission was given the authority to assign any power, frequency, or time limitations to the stations whose applications it approved. Meanwhile, temporary licenses were issued to most broadcasters so that they might continue in operation while the Commission worked out the jigsaw puzzle of fitting together all the broadcasters into the standard broadcast band, without interference between stations. The Commission required first of all that each station equip itself with frequency-control devices to prevent it from wobbling off its assigned frequency. After making extensive investigations, the Commission then issued regular licenses good for six months to all but about 150-odd stations for which it felt there was no room on the air.

In 1934, after reviewing seven years of temporary federal radio regulation, Congress was ready to write a permanent law embodying the "public interest, convenience, or necessity" approach, which had been tried and found successful. The Communications Act of 1934 created the Federal Communications Commission with substantially the same powers and responsibilities as the earlier Radio Commission, except that it was also given jurisdiction over wire communications. The development of radio broadcasting was turned over to competitive private enterprise, with limited government regulation. The 1934 statute, with certain amendments, remains on the books as the governing law of modern broadcasting.

Thus, anarchy of the airwaves became a thing of the past and order was established. Responsible broadcasters could feel confident that their assigned frequencies would be protected from radio pirates, and listeners were able to turn on their radio sets without being greeted by a melee of sounds from overlapping stations. Having bridged this critical period of its growth, radio was now prepared to step forward with its programming, to demonstrate the full artistic, communicative, and business capacities of the broadcast medium.

[6] *Ibid.,* at 213.

THE DEVELOPMENT OF RADIO PROGRAMMING

The period radio now entered saw the development and refinement of program types and the rise to stardom of entertainers who, in many cases, had won earlier recognition on the stage or in vaudeville. Jack Benny, Eddie Cantor, Fred Allen, Ed Wynn, Bing Crosby, Burns and Allen, Jimmy Durante, Edgar Bergen, Phil Baker, Bob Hope, and Fibber McGee and Molly won their places on the air in the thirties and set a pattern for comedy and variety that was maintained with little change over a score of years. The *Jack Benny Show* held forth Sunday evenings at 7:00 P.M. for more than 20 years without interruption.

In the programming of classical music, this period saw the start of Dr. Walter Damrosch's *Music Appreciation Hour*, which held a loyal audience of children and adults for a decade of Saturday mornings; the Sunday afternoon concerts of the New York Philharmonic Symphony Orchestra, and the Saturday afternoon broadcasts from the stage of the Metropolitan Opera House. Some years later the National Broadcasting Company formed its own symphony orchestra, under the leadership of Arturo Toscanini. The *Horn and Hardart Children's Amateur Hour, Uncle Don, Let's Pretend,* and other children's programs became regular features. These were the years, too, of the amateur-hour programs, which were made famous at first by Major Bowes and which brought to the air a copious supply of one-man bands.

Powerful personalities who won their followings through the effective use of the broadcast word also stand out in this period. They ranged from Franklin D. Roosevelt, whose fireside chats, delivered in a personal and intimate manner, captured the imagination and loyalty of most Americans, to men like the famous Dr. Brinkley, the patent-medicine man who advertised his goat-gland pills over the air to distraught men anxious to regain their lost youth. In between came firebrands like Louisiana's Huey Long and Father Charles E. Coughlin, the Detroit priest who became a storm center when he tried to build up a political movement through his radio broadcasts.

There were, too, the famous individual broadcasts that created momentary sensations. The broadcast reports of the trial and execution of Bruno Hauptmann, charged with kidnapping the Lindbergh baby, brought fame and fortune to Gabriel Heatter and Boake Carter. Actress Mae West won a permanent niche for herself in the annals of radio when, in reading a seemingly innocent script about Adam and Eve on an Edgar Bergen comedy show in 1937, she introduced an unexpectedly suggestive innuendo that, though it titillated some listeners, caused a flood of protests from offended listeners to swamp the network and the Federal Communications Commission.

In the broadcast of drama, radio at first found itself unable to surmount the limitations of a communications medium in which the audience could hear words, sound effects, and music, but could see nothing. Early dramatic broadcasts picked up Broadway stage plays by putting microphones over the actors' heads or in the footlights. These efforts to transplant stage plays to the air without any adaptation to the limitations of the radio medium resulted in programs little short of the grotesque. The effect on the listener was simply that of sitting in the theater blindfolded. Broadcasters soon realized that if radio drama was to win an audience, original material would have to be written and stage plays would have to be adapted especially for broadcast performance.

The first strictly dramatic radio program was *First Nighter,* launched in 1930. It was soon followed by the *Lux Radio Theater.* From this point it was only a step to the dramatization of mystery and adventure stories, such as *The Shadow, The Lone Ranger,* and *Bulldog Drummond.* The "stream-of-consciousness" technique to take the radio audience into the mind of a character, trick devices like echo chambers and filters to change vocal quality and perspective, and sound effects to intensify mood and to carry action, were made vital elements of radio dramatic techniques. In 1937 Archibald MacLeish wrote *The Fall of the City,* the first verse drama composed especially for radio. Writer-producers Norman Corwin, Arch Oboler, and Orson Welles won national fame for a succession of highly imaginative productions. Poet Stephen Vincent Benét contributed several original scripts that demonstrated the immense artistic possibilities of the radio medium.

These years also encompassed the period of "stunt broadcasting," when radio called the attention of the world to its great feats of wireless communication. Of especial fascination were the broadcasts from great heights and great depths or from widely separated points. Programs might be picked up from a glider in the air or from a bathysphere hundreds of feet under Bermuda waters. NBC broadcast two-way conversations between an aerial balloon flying high over the East Coast and an airplane off the Pacific Coast, between London and the balloon, and a four-way conversation between Chicago, New York, Washington, and the balloon. Like a child playing with a new toy, networks used their new shortwave equipment to broadcast a singer from New York accompanied by an orchestra in Buenos Aires or to pick up a piano concert from a dirigible in mid-Atlantic.

Such freakish broadcasts admittedly made small contribution to radio art, but they unquestionably prepared broadcasters for the more imposing tasks of covering important public events in different parts of the world. The hook-up of 19 widely separated broadcasting centers around the world in 1931 for a program dedicated to Marconi marked a great step forward in the science of broadcasting. Between 1933 and 1935 there were numerous broadcasts from Admiral Byrd's Antarctic Expedition. In 1934 a sensational on-the-spot description of the burning of the vessel *Morro Castle* off the New Jersey coast was brought to the public by radio. The dramatic farewell address of King Edward VIII who abdicated his throne for "the woman I love," and the impressive coronation of King George VI in 1937, were covered in the most elaborate overseas broadcast arrangements to that date.

The thirties also saw the rise of news broadcasting. Radio's capacities as a news medium were barely appreciated by the pioneer broadcasters of the twenties, who did little more than read over the air newspaper headlines and the front pages of late editions. Several newspapermen, like H. V. Kaltenborn of the *Brooklyn Eagle,* broadcast weekly news talks, but nothing like present-day news summaries was regularly scheduled in the twenties. In 1932 the Associated Press furnished presidential election bulletins to the networks, and the following year saw the new policy of interrupting broadcast programs with news flashes. But the advancement of radio as an effective news medium was temporarily brought to a halt by the pressure of powerful newspaper interests who feared the rivalry of broadcast news and therefore hoped to restrict radio's ability to compete with the press in the field of news dissemination.

There ensued, from 1933 to 1935, the "press-radio war," during which time radio news bulletins were limited by agreement to 30 words and by a time schedule that prohibited the airing of news while it was hot off the wires. The agreement finally broke down, and radio was free once again to broadcast news supplied by news agencies. Networks built up their own news staffs and sent correspondents to the important capitals and news centers of the world. Kaltenborn broadcast over CBS the actual sounds of battle in the Spanish Civil War, and NBC's Max Jordan broadcast an eyewitness account of Hitler's march into Austria and his reception in Vienna. During the Munich crisis in 1938, when for seemingly endless hours the nation turned to its radios to keep pace with the rapidly unfolding political events, the networks took leadership in supplying continual news bulletins and roundups of informed opinion in Europe. The voices of the chief actors in the international political scene, Hitler, Chamberlain, and Mussolini, were brought to American listeners with commentaries by network news analysts. Edward R. Murrow's dramatic broadcasts from London during the German air raids brought Americans a sense of actually being there as the bombs fell. Radio gave the mounting war crisis in 1939 sustained and comprehensive news coverage, establishing itself in the public mind as the primary source of news.

RADIO AND WORLD WAR II

From the outbreak of World War II through its conclusion, it was a well-organized, technically proficient, and confident radio system that brought to the American people the great speeches of Winston Churchill, news of the fall of France, the attack on the Soviet Union, and the flash reports of the Japanese attack on Pearl Harbor.

Even as the American military forces mobilized their strength, the radio industry made all its resources available to the federal government for war service. In contrast with World War I, however, when the government took over the operation of all wireless stations, World War II saw the basic radio organization left intact. The government merely enlisted the cooperation of the industry to publicize important morale and public-service announcements. Planned scheduling of war-information messages, bond-purchase appeals, and conservation campaigns were coupled with the systematic use of radio for instruction in civilian defense and responsibilities. All show business pitched in wholeheartedly, and the "win-the-war" theme permeated radio's offerings. The Office of War Information coordinated the government's wartime propaganda and information services. For the entertainment and information of soldiers and sailors overseas, the Army and Navy set up the Armed Forces Radio Service, with a network of stations in the Pacific and European war theaters. Entertainment programs at home were broadcast as usual, with the stars and formats of the thirties maintaining their popularity in the forties. Indeed, few new talents came to the fore; the war took its toll of the lives and energies of many young artists. Perhaps the most notable change in programming was the increase in news and one-man commentaries. The scheduling of news every hour became common; some use began to be made of recorders to transcribe actual events for airing at subsequent hours. Radio documentaries, casting the factual matter of the war into dramatic and semidramatic programs, were hailed as powerful new art forms.

In the field of special events, radio again scored its greatest triumphs, demonstrating anew its power to bring actual events into our homes and to make the world conflagration meaningful in terms of individual persons. From the broadcast of President Roosevelt's war message to Congress, to the eyewitness description of the signing of the surrender documents aboard the battleship *U.S.S. Missouri* in Tokyo Bay, there was a succession of outstanding programs. On D-Day in 1944, radio reporters were heard from invasion barges in the English Channel and on the Normandy beaches as the greatest military operation in history got under way. George Hicks' running narration from an amphibious ship under aerial attack provided a broadcast that few who heard it will ever forget.

The war was more than a great programming challenge to American radio, however. It also brought to the radio industry a period of unprecedented economic prosperity. The 900-odd stations then in existence enjoyed a lush advertising market protected from new competition by the government's refusal to license new stations for the duration. Although the shortage of consumers' goods created a sellers' market, many large manufacturing companies, mindful of the experience of World War I when some companies discontinued advertising and lost out in the public mind, continued their promotional work on a lavish scale. The wartime newsprint shortage, which cut down advertising space in newspapers, also served to drive more advertising money into radio. Institutional, or name, advertising was stimulated by the high wartime income taxes, which gave many corporations the alternative of spending large sums on advertising or turning the money over to the government in taxes.

The upshot of all this was that AM radio flourished. From 1938 to 1948, the advertising volume of the four networks more than doubled. From 1937 to 1944, broadcast profits of all networks and stations rose from $23 million to $90 million.

With income figures of such proportions, radio could not escape being viewed primarily as a money-making business rather than as a public-service enterprise. Entrepreneurs anxious to break into radio's magic circle could do so only by purchasing established stations. Radio property therefore acquired a high scarcity value and some stations changed hands at fantastic prices. Many realized from four to ten times the value of their assets. "In one instance the sales price was more than thirty times the original cost. In another, a station sold for 1534 times its net income."[7]

THE CHANGING FORTUNES OF AM RADIO

When World War II ended, 950 AM stations were on the air. When the lid was taken off new radio construction, the attractions of the industry's wartime profits brought on a horde of new broadcasters. Refined directional antennas that prevented station interference made it possible to license many new local stations operating on low power. The number of AM stations soon grew like Topsy. Five hundred new stations went on the air in 1946. Another 400 were authorized in 1947. By the end of 1948, 1900 AM stations were on the air producing an income of $145 million, compared to the $8,700,000 earned by the 50 television stations then in existence. By 1949, however, when the nation's economy suffered a temporary setback and the inroads from television first began to be felt by AM radio, total network radio billings slipped for the first time in radio history. One metropolitan AM station, purchased for $250,000 in 1944, was resold for only $150,000 in 1949. Another station dropped in sales value from a wartime $1,500,000 to $512,000 in 1949.

Thereafter, as television continued its rapid expansion, the future of AM radio became clouded with uncertainty. It was clear that network radio had suffered great damage from the competitive inroads of television, both in the reduction of audiences and in the loss of revenues. As the decade of the fifties advanced, the declines continued, and there were strong indications that national radio networks might soon vanish from the broadcasting scene unless the losses could be arrested.

Although the radio networks survived these years of change and expansion, network radio was no longer profitable, and the national radio networks continued their operations primarily to provide instantaneous national news and special events coverage. As far as audiences were concerned, the radio industry could not attract for a single program the number of people who viewed the most popular television programs, but the industry argued that, even under usual circumstances, the total number of people who listen to radio in a single week (in automobiles as well as in homes) equals or even exceeds the number who watch television.

The loss by radio to television of the "peak" evening audiences forced the radio industry into a period of intense self-study. From this study emerged new programming patterns: emphasis on news and music, developing popular disc jockeys, providing programs for audiences with special interests, and flexibility in attracting advertisers who could not afford television. With these approaches many AM stations found that they could operate very profitably even in competition with television. The number of sta-

[7] Charles Siepmann, *Radio's Second Chance* (Boston, 1946), p. 165.

tions continued to rise, and in some of the major metropolitan markets successful radio stations generated so much profit from advertising revenues that, in certain instances, they were sold for sums in excess of $10 million. Television forced AM radio to give up much of its glamour, but the future for many local AM stations still appears to be bright. Radio networks, on the other hand, must look forward to an existence that, at best, is likely to be marginal. In 1975, they lost $2.5 million.

FREQUENCY MODULATION (FM) RADIO

Although FM radio did not come to public attention until the end of the war, it had been known to the radio industry since its development during the previous 10 years by Major E. H. Armstrong of Columbia University. Using a much higher band of frequencies than AM radio (from 88 to 108 megacycles), FM has many advantages over standard radio. It is ordinarily free from static, fading, and interference noises. All stations within reception range come in with equal strength. Sound is transmitted with much greater fidelity than over AM radio. Because its coverage is usually limited to the line of sight from the top of the transmitter, FM is better suited for community and metropolitan centers than for rural areas. This limitation in coverage makes it possible for many FM stations, situated not very far apart geographically, to share the same frequency.

FM held high hopes to broadcast aspirants, critics, and educators because the construction and operating costs of an FM station were much less than those of an AM station. Schools and community organizations, as well as commercial entrepreneurs, might now consider entering the broadcasting business. Moreover, low-powered FM stations might hope to compete with high-powered stations on the basis of program quality only, since all signals in listening range would be heard equally well. In AM radio, low-powered stations were at a great disadvantage because many listeners made their dial choices primarily on the basis of signal strength, seeking the station they could hear with the least interference, regardless of program quality.

The Federal Communications Commission authorized commercial operation of FM radio in 1941, but the war held back further development until 1945, when the Commission shifted FM to its present frequency band and gave it the go-ahead. So high were hopes for FM that the chairman of the Commission predicted in 1946 that FM would replace AM radio in two or three years. By 1947, nearly 1,000 FM stations had been licensed, or more than the total number of AM stations before the war.

FM ran into a number of major stumbling blocks, however. First, it could not be heard on AM radio receivers without special converters, and AM programs could not be received on FM sets. This meant that FM's audience was limited to the number of people who invested in new, specialized radio sets. In 1947 the first inexpensive FM attachment for AM sets came on the market, and this problem was partially solved. Second, there was the problem of FM programming and advertising support. FM could not attract large audiences unless it offered distinctive programs; it could not get advertising to finance such programs unless it already had the audience. Some broadcasters skirted this dilemma by duplicating their AM programs over their FM outlets, but independent FM broadcasters without AM stations to lean on objected that such practices would hold back the development of FM, making it a stepchild of AM. Stations that had great investments in AM often looked on their FM licenses as a form of insurance and made little attempt to promote FM vigorously. Third, the absence of automatic tuning controls and the poor quality of cheap FM sets disappointed many listeners who did not find FM tone quality markedly superior to AM. Fourth, FM ran into heavy competition from the well-established AM field, now twice its prewar size, and from television, which hit the market almost simultaneously with FM radio.

In 1948, 300 new FM stations were constructed, but 125 applicants, in an unprecedented demonstration of pessimism in broadcasting, turned back their construction permits to the Federal Communications Commission. In 1949, the trend picked up steam, with licenses of even established stations being turned back. From 1949 through 1952, over 350 other FM station authorizations were returned to the Commission. Then slowly the picture brightened as new functions for FM were discovered. For one thing, AM licensees who were unable to obtain permission to broadcast on AM during evening hours recognized that an FM license provided an opportunity to continue broadcasting during the nighttime. For another, the high-fidelity capabilities of FM began to attract increasing attention, and FM stations specializing in the programming of good music became more and more common.

Although many FM stations continued to duplicate only the programs that were offered on AM outlets operated by the same owners, there was a steady increase in the number of FM stations that provided a program service not available on AM. The FCC moved to insure that the existence of FM stations would actually increase the diversity of programming available by requiring that in markets of 100,000 people or over a company operating both an AM and FM station would have to provide separate programming for the two stations at least 50 percent of the time. Later the FCC acted to make this restriction even more stringent. By 1979 FM stations in communities of 25,000 population or over may not duplicate the programming of a sister AM station more than 25 percent of the time.

The new interest in FM sparked a dramatic rise in the number of commercial FM stations as the total on the air rose over the 2700 mark. There was a corresponding rise in the number of FM receivers as most radios were made to receive both AM and FM signals.

In order to help FM stations commercially and to make for more efficient utilization of FM frequencies, the Federal Communications Commission has authorized FM stations to engage in such additional services as "functional music," which has many variations including, for example, restaurant, factory, and other background music; also "storecasting," background music in stores; and "transit radio," on passenger-carrying vehicles. These services are made possible through the multiplex system of broadcasting. This system involves the transmission on a broadcast frequency of a second program, which can be received only by individuals and organizations having the necessary multiplexing receiving equipment. Multiplexing has also made stereo broadcasting possible, for, using this system, the two signals needed to complete a stereo effect can be broadcast on the same frequency. The FCC authorized this type of broadcasting by FM in 1961, and a number of stations immediately began presenting stereo programs. Many others have since joined them in offering this type of service.

These developments have brought profitability to many commercial FM stations. In some cities, such as Washington, D.C., FM stations have sped past their AM competitors to become the most popular in the listening area. By 1975, AM and FM radio combined grossed $1.75 billion in annual revenues.

NONCOMMERCIAL FM RADIO

When the Federal Communications Commission authorized FM broadcasting, it set aside one portion of the band (88 to 92 megacycles) for use by noncommercial stations, also known as educational or public radio stations. Noncommercial FM broadcast service has continually expanded until now some 800 such stations are in operation. A number of academic institutions operate low-powered transmitters of 10 watts or less, which provide satisfactory coverage of college campuses and the small towns in which many are located. These can later be built into higher-powered stations if the necessary financial resources are made available and if spectrum allocations allow it.

SUMMARY

American radio grew from a fledgling enterprise to a great mass communications medium in less than 20 years. Radio's amazing growth involved a struggle for control of important patents and early failures to realize the true nature of the broadcast medium. The decision to finance broadcasting by the sale of time to advertisers, the formation of national networks, and the intervention of the federal government to establish order after radio had fallen into helpless chaos were each important landmarks in the advancement of radio. AM radio reached a pinnacle of financial success and service to the nation during World War II, but following the advent of television it has been obliged to accept a secondary position. FM radio made its entry on the broadcasting scene after the war, but despite its superior technical quality it had a slow development. With the recognition that FM could supplement the available broadcasting services by performing special functions, an expansion of facilities took place, and FM now plays a significant role on the American broadcasting scene.

Questions For Discussion

1. How did James Maxwell's contributions to the development of radio broadcasting differ from those of Guglielmo Marconi?

2. In what way did Ambrose Fleming, Reginald Fessenden, and Lee De Forest make similar contributions to the development of radio?

3. On what basis may stations WWJ, WHA, and KDKA be grouped?

4. Explain how many early radio station owners differed in their objectives from radio station owners of today.

5. Under what basic A.T.&T. philosophy did WEAF become a commercial station?

6. Of what significance was the decision in the 1920s to turn to advertising revenue as the financial support for radio?

7. How do you explain the change in public attitudes toward advertising on the air?

8. What events led to the Radio Act of 1927, and what changes in public policy were reflected in this law as compared to the Act of 1912?

9. What have been some of the leading programming changes in the last 20 years of radio?

10. List some of the pioneers and pioneer programs in the area of music, news, and drama programs

11. What significant role did A.T.&T. play in the development of network broadcasting, and how has it continued to play an important part in network activity?

12. How did the organization of the Mutual Broadcasting System differ from those of the other networks?

13. What were the main stumbling blocks to the development of FM?

14. Why do you think FM radio has now become so successful?

Television had its coming-out party at the New York World's Fair in 1939 and soon became the talk of the town. Television covered the opening of the fair and featured as its star attraction an address by President Roosevelt. Despite the significance of the event, only a few hundred receivers were able to tune in. The communications industry had not yet gone into production of TV receivers, and most of those in existence were homemade or special instruments developed for field testing.

Television actually has a longer history than its sudden presentation to the American people in 1939 suggests. Its origins can be traced back to 1884, when the German scientist Paul Nipkow invented the scanning disc that made television possible, and to 1923, when Dr. V. K. Zworykin patented the iconoscope, the television camera that preceded present-day cameras. Experimentation continued throughout the thirties, with RCA, CBS, and the DuMont laboratories working unceasingly on the refinement of television for commercial uses.

Shortly after the 1939 World's Fair, television's progress was interrupted by a series of governmental orders and then by World War II. In 1940 the Federal Communications Commission ordered a halt in the expansion of TV pending completion of an investigation to determine the best technical standards for TV transmission. In 1941, six months before America went to war, the Commission authorized full commercial television on the black-and-white, 525-line basis now in use, in contrast to the 441 lines previously used. The few TV stations then in existence began televising programs two to three hours a day, but there were only 4700 television sets in the entire New York area. When war came, the production of television sets stopped completely, and telecasting settled down to a skeleton schedule for the duration, with only six commercial television stations on the air.

Television ran into still another obstacle when controversies developed over which band it should be assigned in the broadcast spectrum and whether transmission should be in color as opposed to black-and-white. In March 1947 the Federal Communications Commission finally ruled out color television for the immediate future and authorized black-and-white television over 13 channels between 54 and 216 megacycles in the very-high-frequency (VHF) band. (Channel 1 was subsequently assigned by the Commission to fixed and mobile services instead of television.)

The effect of the Commission's action was swift. Within a year, the number of applications for TV stations jumped from less than 75 to more than 300. Almost a million television sets were sold in 1948, and several hundred advertisers were already buying time over television stations in 16 different cities. The American public had welcomed television with open arms.

THE PERIOD OF THE FREEZE

The rush to get into television was now so great that the 12 channels were no longer adequate. It became apparent during 1947 and 1948, as more and more television stations took the air, that serious signal interference was occurring in the service areas of some stations. Accordingly, in September 1948, with 36 stations on the air in 19 cities having approximately one-third the population of the United States, the Commission imposed a freeze on all new television assignments. The freeze applied to new applications only; 70 odd applicants who had received construction permits prior to September 1948 were permitted to proceed with the construction of their stations.

The freeze imposed upon television was not lifted by the Commission for almost four years, during which time the Commission investigated two important questions: 1. What frequency allocation plan would best provide a competitive and nationwide system of television free from signal interference; and 2. what policy should the Commission take regarding the development of color television?

Meanwhile, within the limitations of the freeze, television grew by leaps and bounds far beyond the expectation of its most ardent supporters. Although television sets cost as much as $750 to $1000 at first, the public investment in receivers was headlong. Those who could not afford their own sets visited neighbors or taverns that had sets. Programming at first was limited to evening hours, but as the public demand increased it was extended into the daytime. Many of the early programs were crude presentations—"simulcasts" of radio programs, and a seemingly endless succession of wrestling matches, roller-skating derbies, panel-quizzes, parlor games, dog acts, and acrobats. The first major television variety program was *The Milton Berle Show* on NBC, and it proved such a huge success that in 1948 and 1949 Tuesday night was known as "Berle Night" in New York City. The Berle show probably did more to stimulate television-set buying in the first years of television than any other single sales factor.

For television networks and stations, these first two or three years were extremely costly as well as exciting years. CBS and NBC plunged into television on a big scale. ABC found that it lacked the financial resources to undertake television network programming on a full scale and was forced to proceed cautiously in television while it sought new investment capital. The Mutual Broadcasting System did not attempt to develop a television network, but the Allen B. DuMont Laboratories, manufacturers of television sets without experience in radio broadcasting, went into the business of network programming and sales for several years along with CBS, NBC, and ABC. In 1955 DuMont ceased operating as a television network after numerous difficulties including inadequate station lineups and lack of top-quality programming. Television program production costs proved to be many times greater than had been known in radio, and because of the relatively small audience at first, as compared with the nationwide radio audience, the networks were unable to recover a good part of their program costs from advertisers. Some television stations lost as much as $1000 a day during this period. For the three years 1948–1950, the aggregate operating losses reported to the Federal Communications Commission by television networks and stations were $48 million. Of these losses, $27,500,000 were sustained by the four networks including their 14 owned and operated stations. Earnings from radio were poured into television, an ironic situation in which one communications medium financed the development of its competitor. Part of the loss in television was caused by the freeze, which prevented the networks from adding stations and increasing market coverage. For example, the city of Denver, Colorado, an important advertising market, had no television whatever during the four years of the freeze. In cities like Pittsburgh, only one station (owned by DuMont) was in operation, and the four networks had to share time over the single outlet. (However, this proved very fortunate for the station, which was able to profit greatly from its noncompetitive position. After the freeze DuMont sold the station to Westinghouse for $9,500,000.) The installation of coaxial cable and microwave radio relay facilities, necessary to link the stations into a network operation, was a costly and time-consuming operation. Not until September 1951 did A.T.&T. complete the network hookup to the West Coast. Stations not connected by the cable or radio relay were furnished film recordings ("kinescopes") of network shows for local showing. By 1951, many stations had passed the point of loss in television and were starting to show handsome profits from their operation. Public enthusiasm for the new medium continued unabated. Special-events coverage by television of baseball and football games, of the World Series, of the important meetings of the United Nations Security Council over the Korean War, the Kefauver Committee hearings, and the presidential conventions and campaigns of 1952 provided tremendous continuing promotion for television. By the time the freeze came to an end in July 1952, there were 108 stations on the air in 63 cities having two-thirds the population of the country. The number of television sets in the public's hands had risen from 1 million in 1948 to 17 million only four years later!

THE END OF THE FREEZE

On April 14, 1952, the Commission issued its final television allocation plan, known as the "Sixth Report and Order." This plan assigned to television, in addition to channels 2 through 13 in the VHF band, channels 14 through 83 in the ultrahigh frequency band (UHF) which ranged from 470 to 890 megacycles. Utilization of UHF frequencies in addition to VHF, according to the Commission, was the only way to make possible the establishment of more than 2,000 television stations on a nationwide and competitive basis. The Commission announced that it would resume accepting applications for new television assignments on July 1, 1952.

In the next six months, more than 900 applications were submitted and 175 new television stations were authorized. By May 1, 1954, a total of 377 stations had begun broadcasting and some 32,000,000 sets were receiving the programs. By 1976 more than 960 stations were in operation and some 120,000,000 sets were receiving programs. The sets were located in 71,000,000 different households or 97 percent of the households in the United States. The increase in stations made it possible for the networks to increase their station lineups and provide close to complete national coverage. The revenues earned by the television industry from the operation of networks and local stations went over $4 billion. The networks undertook television programming on a larger scale than ever previously envisaged, with top Broadway and motion picture talent appearing in major productions. Regular series costing the advertisers an average of $330,000 per hour episode and "specials" costing as much as $400,000 to $600,000 for a 60-minute program, plus another $165,000 for broadcast time, were considered effective advertising investments in the growing television medium. Television established itself, less than a decade after its start, as the outstanding mass communications medium of our time.

EDUCATIONAL NONCOMMERCIAL TV STATIONS

In the Commission's Sixth Report and Order, special provision was made for educational noncommercial television stations. Following the precedent set in its special allocation plan for FM radio stations, the Commission set aside 242 channel assignments for application by educational noncommercial television stations. The number of channels reserved for educational stations was increased several times until there are now 120 VHF and 533 UHF channels designated for educational use, a total of 653 reservations. As a result of these allocations, educational stations affiliated with universities and community educational groups have been established in more than 200 communities from coast to coast. A number of states have set up networks of educational stations. A few educational stations operate on commercial channels; stations in New York City and Iowa are examples of this type of service.

THE UHF PROBLEM

Although there was a great increase in the number of television stations with the end of the freeze, this expansion was accompanied by some very serious problems, notably that of new UHF stations. By May 1954, 132 communities had only VHF stations, 35 had both VHF and UHF stations, and 70 had only UHF stations. In the two years from 1952 to 1954, 29 UHF stations that went on the air were forced to cease operations and 89 others turned in their permits. By way of contrast, only four new VHF stations went off the air during the period, and 16 others surrendered their permits.

The numerous failures of new UHF stations became a matter of great concern not only to the investors who lost their money, but to the Federal Communications Commission and to Congress, which held hearings to determine whether the Commission's allocation plan should be changed. It was clear that the main reason for the difficulty experienced by many new UHF stations was the fact that all the television receivers in the hands of the public at the end of the freeze could receive VHF signals only and were unable to receive UHF stations without the owners spending various sums of money, often as much as $100, to convert them. The problem appeared even in those cities that began television broadcasting with a UHF channel. As soon as a VHF channel was introduced, the existing UHF channel, in most instances, began to experience difficulty. The problem was much more intense, of course, when a UHF station started operations in a community being served up to that time only by VHF. The new UHF station ran into overpowering competitive obstacles, related not only to the technical problem of reception, but also to the difficulty of obtaining a network affiliation and adequate local advertising support. For example, KCTY, a new UHF station in Kansas City, Missouri, faced competition from three established VHF stations. KCTY went on the air in June 1953, after investing approximately $750,000. The station expended more money in an attempt to win an audience, but the public was not willing to invest in converters to receive the station when it could obtain most of the top-rated programs from the existing VHF stations. Within six months after it went on the air, the station was offered for sale for $750,000, then $400,000, finally $300,000, but there were no takers. The owners finally disposed of the station for $1.

Congress and the Federal Communications Commission examined the UHF problem at length. The FCC, for example, established a UHF station in New York City to study the special problems that propagation of the ultrahigh frequency presents. The reception on UHF receivers installed in homes distributed throughout the New York area was studied to determine the quality of the signal. As far as the total problem of UHF was concerned, various proposals were suggested as possible solutions, including the following: 1. make television all UHF by transferring all present VHF assignments to the upper-band frequencies; 2. have all stations east of the Mississippi operate on UHF channels and all stations west of the Mississippi operate on VHF channels; 3. reallocate VHF and UHF assignments in cities where they are intermixed in order to make individual cities either all VHF or UHF, but not a combination of the two (this procedure, called deintermixture, was actually attempted by the FCC, but whenever it proposed to replace an existing VHF with a UHF channel, the opposition became so intense that it finally abandoned the policy); 4. require manufacturers to equip every TV set with an all-channel receiver to permit the reception of all existing VHF and UHF channels.

In 1962 the Congress put this fourth solution into effect by passing a law requiring that all TV sets sold in interstate commerce after April 30, 1964, be equipped to receive all TV channels. As older TV sets were replaced by sets made after 1964, the time gradually approached when all TV sets would be able to receive UHF as well as VHF stations. By 1976 more than 86 percent of TV homes could receive UHF signals.

Many new UHF stations have gone on the air since the passage of the all-channel law, and the capacity of these stations to secure an audience and earn an adequate financial return has been considerably enhanced. Still, the average UHF station does have many disadvantages in competing with its VHF counterpart. Everything else being equal, a UHF signal is inferior in range and quality to a VHF signal, and set owners must install a separate antenna to attain satisfactory UHF reception. UHF stations also were more difficult to tune than VHF stations, but the FCC moved to eliminate this last disadvantage by requiring that after July 1, 1974, all TV receivers with screens of nine inches or more have "comparable" tuning for both UHF and VHF reception. This meant that UHF stations could be "clicked" in just as VHF stations were.

COLOR TELEVISION

The development of color television first presented itself as an issue before the Federal Communications Commission as early as 1940, when it was decided that the quality and method of color transmission was not yet satisfactory. Again in 1945 and in 1947, the Commission reexamined the question of color television and decided that color picture transmission and reception was not yet technically satisfactory. The Commission nevertheless gave continued attention to the prospect of early approval of color television, and manufacturers in the television industry continued their research. CBS, which had developed a field sequential system of color television, proposed that the Commission approve its system. In October 1950, after extended hearings, the Commission officially approved the CBS system after finding that "of the systems then before it only this system produced an acceptable color picture." The CBS system used a mechanical device attached to the receiver and was "incompatible"—the pictures could be received only over new color receivers. Despite the Commission's ruling in favor of CBS, no television manufacturers except CBS-Columbia appeared willing to invest in the manufacture of color television sets using the CBS system. CBS itself was soon prevented from manufacturing color sets by a government order restricting the use of certain necessary materials that were in short supply during the Korean war. Finally, CBS itself appeared to lose interest in its own system, for which it had been unable to obtain industry support, while RCA continued experimentation on its electronic system with a view to perfecting it. The National Television System Committee (NTSC), an association of engineers and scientists including representatives of many companies engaged in the manufacture of television equipment, also commenced studies looking toward the development of a commercially practicable system of color television. In December 1953, after renewed consideration, the Commission issued a new set of rules for the NTSC electronic and compatible system of color television that is now in use. It turned out, however, that for a long period of time RCA was the only company that actively pushed the development of color television. Its broadcasting subsidiary, NBC, for example, immediately constructed new color facilities and put every major program on its network schedule into color at least once. Through the years it continued to increase its color programs. By 1967 virtually all network programs were being produced in color and most stations were broadcasting their own local programs in color in addition to providing outlets for the network color programs. The increase in color set ownership did not match the proliferation of color broadcasting, however. One obstacle was the fact that color sets on the average cost about twice as much as comparable black-and-white receivers. As viewers were constantly reminded by broadcasters that the program they were watching could be seen in color, however, their interest in acquiring color sets grew; increased sales in turn made it possible to reduce the price of sets. By 1976 more than half of U.S. households were equipped with color sets, with the prospect that within a few years almost all homes would have a color set. Unlike a simple increase in picture size, color adds an important dimension to television communication that enables it to transmit reality far more effectively than black-and-white television.

PAY TELEVISION

Another problem the Federal Communications Commission has had to resolve is what to do about proposals to utilize television frequencies for various systems of "pay-television," also known as "subscription-television" and "toll-television." The underlying theory of these proposals is that certain types of programs not telecast now by networks and stations could be made available to viewers if it were possible to charge the viewer directly for the program (i.e., use the "box-office" principle).

The method of pay television is to present a program (either on the air or through cables) together with a signal that scrambles the picture at the receiving end unless the viewer possesses a decoding device. Several systems have been used for this purpose. One used a coin machine that collected the money before each show was seen. The second employed a sealed tape on which viewer usage was recorded. A third utilized a standard IBM card bearing a printed circuit that acted as an "unscrambler" when a button on the device was pushed. At the same time the card was punched to record the fact that the show had been seen. A subscription-television system developed in California checked on program use through a signal sent by each receiving set to a central point. Other systems involved the use of a key device, telephone circuits, or a metering apparatus.

A number of experiments carried out to investigate the potentialities of pay-TV, both "on-the-air" and closed-circuit, failed to show that the public would support it on a regular basis. For a while interest lagged, but there was renewed activity as cable television systems spread throughout the country. People connected with these systems pay monthly fees to receive better-quality picture reception, and in many cases have many more program channels than their own receiving antennas make available. With cable television providing many different channel availabilities on the wires connecting the homes to the originating point, one or more of these channels may be authorized to transmit "pay-television" programs. Many industry observers now believe that "pay-television" will ultimately achieve its acceptance with specialized programming in that form (a fuller treatment of the development of cable television appears in Chapter 6). There has also been renewed interest in "on-the-air" pay-TV, as the FCC has approved a number of applications by UHF stations to broadcast programs on a pay-TV basis.

Another form of subscription television that does not use a broadcasting frequency is closed-circuit theater television, in which viewers pay to enter a theater to see a program projected on a large screen. Subscribers to this form of television have seen heavyweight championship boxing matches and other events. Pay-television, via cable, would presumably replace the use of theaters. Closed-circuit TV is also being used for a number of special purposes. Banks use it for drive-in services and to discourage robbers, stores use it to detect shoplifters, companies use it to introduce new lines to salespeople, medical schools use it to present demonstrations to physicians meeting in various locations throughout the country, and the courts use it to permit a prisoner restrained because of his unruliness to observe the trial. These are just a few of the uses being made of closed-circuit television, and new uses are being found every day.

SUMMARY

Many challenges still face the television industry. Television solved many problems in the past to rise in less than a decade to the place of dominance over all mass communication media in America. Television has become the foremost advertising medium in the country, the first choice of the people for leisure-time activity, the main source of popular entertainment, and the primary means by which most people maintain direct contact with governmental processes: a social, political, economic, cultural, and educational force of the first order; in short, the primary communications medium of the twentieth century.

Questions For Discussion

1. What was the first television show to become an outstanding success?
2. Why did the FCC impose a freeze on the construction of new television stations from 1948 to 1952?
3. Did the expansion of television facilities completely stop during the three-and-one-half year freeze on station application?
4. What two basic changes were inaugurated by the FCC at the conclusion of the freeze?
5. Why do you think television expanded so rapidly after the freeze was lifted?

6. In what way did the owners of UHF stations and FM stations have similar problems?

7. Do you think the problems that plagued UHF stations could have been prevented?

8. Describe three different methods that might be used for a pay-TV system.

9. Do you think it is proper for the Congress to pass legislation that would restrict or prohibit the development of pay-TV?

10. How has television changed in the period during which you have been watching it?

11. What is the future of television likely to be?

4

The key factor in public acceptance of television and radio is programming—the determination of what programs to put on the air and at what points in the program schedule. Only through successful programming that wins large audiences do television and radio become attractive to advertisers seeking mass circulation, and only through income obtained from these advertisers are commercial station program operations financed. The production, technical, and sales staffs of networks and stations work to little avail if they lack effective programming leadership.

THE PROGRAMMING FUNCTION

To understand television and radio programming, we must first have some insight into its scope and nature.

First, the programming function in both television and radio is of such vast proportions that it is difficult to convey its size accurately. As far as commercial operation is concerned, each of the more than 4,460 AM stations, 2,760 FM stations, and 710 TV stations plans a program schedule for every day of the week; most stations program 15 to 18 hours per day, and some more. The national television and radio networks program up to 15 hours a day and offer these programs to affiliated stations, which then need not produce programs for those hours. A single television network presents more than 6500 different programs in the course of a single season. Counting both network and local station offerings in both television and radio, literally tens of thousands of different programs are broadcast each day throughout the country.

Second, the programming function is continuous. Stations do not go on the air to broadcast only one or two programs at a time. Once they sign on in the morning, with few exceptions they program without interruption until sign-off. Television networks normally program in continuous blocks, with affiliated stations programming the intervening hours. It is the fact that programming is continuous that develops audience flow from one program to the next. Adult viewers and listeners tend to remain tuned to the same station unless they positively dislike the succeeding program or they know of a program more to their liking on another station. A very popular program on a station or network schedule provides an audience-in-being for the program that follows it. Similarly, a program with small appeal forces the following program to build its audience from scratch. This program-adjacency factor plays a great role in the preparation of program schedules. Programs are usually scheduled in blocks in order to build and hold audiences throughout the day and evening.

Third, the programming function is extremely competitive—it is, indeed, the most competitive aspect of television and radio. In the constant search to find and to develop "hit" programs, each network is in vigorous competition with other networks, and every station competes with other stations in the same market. Not only does the competition extend to programming effectively against the competitive programming of the other networks and stations, since they are seeking to attract the same audience, but also to the finding of new hit programs. Thus, a new hit on one network may have a devastating effect on the program broadcast at the same time by a rival network, as well as on adjacent programs. The big networks, always under pressure to win a majority of the available audience, usually try to meet program strength with program strength, which explains why two big hour variety shows or hour dramas may be scheduled at the same time over rival networks. Failure to compete in this fashion may cause the network to lose out competitively throughout the rest of the evening because of the effect of the failure on adjacent programs. Individual stations that can operate profitably if they attract only a minority of the audience often choose to schedule programs with specialized or local appeal against network hit shows, and this often proves very effective.

Fourth, the programming function, especially in television, is a very costly one in time, effort, money, and creative ability. Frank Stanton, former President of CBS, has stated that a typical CBS half-hour television dramatic program is the product of 1,374 man-hours, involving 154 people exclusive of the services of advertising, publicity, traffic, and sales personnel. For this half-hour seven members of the program staff spend 280 man-hours, 13 stagehands spend 195 man-hours, 10 cameramen operating three cameras spend 90 man-hours. The amount of money required to pay for this kind of effort is very large. A single one-hour episode of a prime-time series can cost $340,000 or more than $8,000,000 for a full season of 24 episodes. One episode of a half-hour program costs $170,000. In the 1976–77 season networks paid their program suppliers $500,000,000 for prime-time shows.

Fifth, the programming function, especially in networks, is extremely complex, because it is interrelated with almost all the other functions and operating processes of television—the availability of performing, writing, and production talent, production facilities, including studios, lighting and camera equipment, scenery, costumes, technical crews, network coaxial cables, and the advertising schedules and budgets of network clients, as well as the clearance of the same air time by affiliated stations in different time zones across the country.

Sixth, the programming function tends to seek stability in program schedules that will develop viewing and listening habits with the public, in order to be able to make long-term sales to advertisers, and to obtain relief from the relentless pressure of building new programs. The need to recover from damage caused by program failures induces most networks and stations to leave successful shows undisturbed until they weaken noticeably, although new shows that are obvious failures are sometimes terminated abruptly without even showing all of the episodes that have been produced.

Seventh, the programming function draws its creative ideas, materials, and talent from all possible sources: professional television and radio performers, and professional program packagers, talent bureaus, Broadway, Hollywood, night clubs, writers, singers, dancers, musicians, community theatrical groups, colleges, journalism, studio audiences, local-station talent, and auditions. The programming function must continually seek new program ideas and develop new program forms if television and radio are to maintain their holds on the public imagination.

Eighth, the programming function is highly speculative. There are no sure rules for predicting which program ideas will result in programs the public will like or which new performers will develop into star talent. If certainty of prediction were possible, there would be fewer failures in all ventures in entertainment—theater, movies, and sports—as well as television and radio! Programming deals with indefinable and intangible aspects of audience appeal.

The best programming executives possess an uncanny ability to evaluate the indefinable and intangible aspects of audience appeal, a thorough knowledge of program sources and show business in general, an acquaintance with program costs that will enable them to evaluate the risks involved in any program venture, and a high degree of boldness and courage.

RADIO PROGRAMMING

Let us turn now to an examination of radio programming—what its traditional patterns have been, what new forms have been developed, and how it is handled.

Until the advent of television, radio programming had become fairly well stabilized in content and pattern. The networks concentrated during evening hours on half-hour weekly program series in news, commentary, comedy-variety, situation comedy, mystery, audience participation, music, "personality," and dramatic shows. Programs like *Jack Benny, Lux Radio Theater,* and the *Bob Hope Show* occupied the same time period week after week for years on end. Most of the big network shows were actually produced by advertising agencies, with the network supplying only the studio facilities, engineers, and musicians. The networks themselves produced few commercial programs other than news shows. Although radio made enormous demands on writers for new material, top performers seemed to have an unending welcome in the American home (in contrast, as we shall see, to the experience of programming in television).

In the daytime hours, networks concentrated on audience participation shows and the soap operas—serial dramas with continuing characters and slow-moving action that were broadcast 15 minutes every day of the week.[1] NBC and CBS broadcast as many as 11 to 14 different soap operas each day, practically all of which were produced by agencies and independent program packagers. It was generally understood that the major advertising agencies controlled the production of programs on the networks.

Local radio stations affiliated with the networks rounded out their schedules with local audience participation shows, local newscasts, and programs of recorded and transcribed music. Only the larger local stations and the networks maintained staff orchestras for live music shows. Independent radio stations without network affiliations tended to rely more on "disc jockey" personalities who played records and talked informally for three or fours hours at a stretch. Local stations also programmed transcribed dramatic and musical programs supplied to them by program syndicators and by advertising agencies on behalf of commercial sponsors. Stations with more aggressive program departments tried to develop local talent to be used on their own shows, or sent newsmen out in the city with tape recorders to obtain on-the-scene interviews to be used on news programs.

Under the competitive inroads of television, network radio programming underwent substantial changes. The big-name performers moved over to television, and the major advertising support also abandoned radio for the new medium. Through the years the regular half-hour weekly shows gradually disappeared from network radio to be replaced by a flexible format of news, commentary, and feature talks designed for sale to small advertisers and available to listeners whenever they might tune in. A few longer programs are still broadcast, mainly the sound tracks of such television programs as *Meet the Press* and *Face the Nation,* and major sports and political events are covered, but network radio programming, on the whole, is devoted to short news and feature programs.

Local radio station programming is limited primarily to recorded music interspersed with news programs. Disc jockeys (DJ's) and local personalities provide program identification and develop listener loyalty to specialized program appeals. To most station managers and observers this combination provides radio with its best programming in competition with television. Stations may limit their music offerings to one type—"country and western," "classical," "middle-of-the-road (MOR)," "top forty," "soul," "rock," "jazz," and "underground." Several stations broadcast only news and news commentary, and some have an "all-talk" format that depends to a great extent on phone conversations with listeners. Some stations have an ethnic orientation, broadcasting programs primarily intended for blacks or for various foreign-language groups in the community. A few radio stations still provide a diversified bill of fare, providing recorded music of various types, news, feature programs, documentaries, phone conversations with lis-

---

[1] "A soap opera is a kind of sandwich, whose recipe is simple enough, although it took years to compound. Between thick slices of advertising, spread 12 minutes of dialogue, add predicament, villainy, and female suffering in equal measure, throw in a dash of nobility, sprinkle with tears, season with organ music, cover with a rich announcer sauce, and serve five times a week." James Thurber, "Onward and Upward with the Arts," *The New Yorker,* 24 (May 15, 1948), pp. 34ff.

teners, sports, farm news, and service programs, but most radio stations program "horizontally," whereas television stations program "vertically."

TELEVISION PROGRAMMING

When television programming started in 1948, it was hampered by the fact that only limited funds were available for programming purposes; even more seriously it suffered from a wide misunderstanding of the nature of the television medium. The fact that early network shows were "simulcasts" of radio programs (cameras placed in front of the radio performers) could be explained then by the lack of facilities for television's own use and by the lack of money for television program production. Far more difficult to justify, however, was the persistent if unthinking view that television programs were a simple extension of radio shows—in other words, hearing plus sight. This was, of course, true of a number of radio program forms, notably the audience participation, panel, and quiz shows, which retained their appeal in visually projecting the personalities of the contestants and celebrities. But it was certainly not true of comedy, variety, and drama, the main staples of network program fare. Nor could television handle music programming easily—not records, certainly, and even orchestral concerts presented television with problems that radio never had to face. Moreover, the half-hour program form, so firmly established in network radio, was transferred to television intact, and the evils that followed this transfer were numerous. Certain aesthetic forms like radio drama lent themselves to the half-hour form: the radio drama, utilizing the imagination to the fullest, was very successful in establishing characters, plot, and mood in a few moments, and then developing and resolving the story within 30 minutes. In live television drama, however, the half-hour form proved weak, with the writer rarely able to establish real characters or to develop his plot adequately. On the other hand, the full-hour live television drama for a brief period captured the attention of audiences, for it represented a quality of drama rarely achieved in the history of radio. Producers and directors such as Fred Coe, Martin Manulis, Albert McCleery, Herbert Brodkin, Alex Segal, Franklin Schaffner, John Frankenheimer, and George Shaeffer and writers such as Paddy Chayefsky, Tad Mosel, Reginald Rose, Gore Vidal, and Rod Serling acquired outstanding reputations for their part in presenting topflight original dramas on television. Then, as video tape came into existence and film techniques were improved, the pendulum began to swing the other way until finally live presentations of drama went into total eclipse.

THE "SPECIAL" CONCEPT

The regularity of the radio program schedule was also transferred to television, although the time and effort required to produce a television show was at least five to ten times as great as that required for radio. Moreover, in contrast to radio, the television audience tends to lose interest in performers, especially comedians, who appear on the air very frequently. As a result, many programs that had been broadcast successfully on radio for many years often failed after a season or two in television. Performers complained of the lack of time to prepare for a weekly television show. Even programs that were produced specifically for television ran for shorter periods of time than their radio counterparts. There have been a few long-lived series on television, and certain comedians retained their appeal for many years, but program longevity on television is the exception.

The regular weekly shows also tended to have a sameness about them that caused much of the early excitement in television programming to disappear. In the season 1954–1955, network television broke loose from this pattern with the concept of the "Special," originally called the "Spectacular," developed at NBC by Sylvester L. Weaver, Jr., who probably influenced the development of television programming more than any other single individual. The Special concept meant a departure from traditional programming practices; it meant big programs, an hour, 90 minutes, or two hours in length, depending upon the needs of the subject matter, and it meant scheduling these programs once a month or sometimes as a "one-shot." The forerunners of the Specials were the two-hour Ford show in 1953 that starred Mary Martin and Ethel Merman and the two-hour Rodgers and Hammerstein show in 1954. The hour-long *Bob Hope Show,* scheduled only a few times a year, also demonstrated the effectiveness of the big, nonweekly program. The largest program budgets in broadcasting history were assigned to the Specials to make it possible to obtain the highest-priced stars, the most elaborate production, and the best scripts. These programs, it was hoped, would break habitual weekly viewing patterns and obtain large audiences through their outstanding quality and special promotional campaigns. In their first season, the Specials recaptured for television the public excitement that had previously made the new medium a "conversation piece."

In the following years, all three networks presented Specials that interrupted the flow of regularly scheduled weekly programs. As the number of Specials mounted, it was inevitable that to some extent they lost their power to evoke unique response. The fact that a program was a Special did not automatically guarantee a high rating or a satisfactory advertising return. The concept of the Special became further refined over the years, and it became possible to develop, with advertising support, a wide range of Special programs, amounting to more than 100 in a single season. These included programs like the National Geographic Specials, the Jacques Cousteau programs, tours of the Louvre and the Kremlin, the Hallmark dramatic Specials, and entertainments built around topflight singers, comedians, or top Hollywood and television stars.

In addition to continuing the presentation of one-time special programs, the commercial networks began experimenting in the mid-1970s with limited series, designed to come to an end after the production of a specific number of programs. This followed a pattern established by the public broadcasting network with its presentation of dramatizations of novels and biographies, most of them produced in Great Britain. *The Adams Chronicles,* produced in the United States for public broadcasting, was also a limited series. Among the notable "mini-series," as they came to be called, appearing on the commercial networks was a TV treatment of Irvin Shaw's novel *Rich Man, Poor Man*. Special programs, such as a dramatization of the biography *Eleanor and Franklin* and a TV version of the book on the Charles Manson case, *Helter Skelter*, were telecast over the course of two different evenings. The most successful program in television's history as far as audience numbers are concerned was also a "mini-series." It was the television treatment of Alex Haley's *Roots*, broadcast on eight successive evenings in early 1977. The ABC Network estimated that 130 million viewers (representing 85 percent of all television homes in the United States) saw all or part of the series and the final episode drew the largest television audience in the history of the medium, some 36 million households or 80 million viewers. (See Table 4–1.)

The importance of the TV version of *Roots* lies in more than the enormous number of people who watched it, however. By giving black people a new understanding and appreciation of their history and by impressing other people with the injustices visited on blacks by the institution of slavery, the series had a profound effect on race relations in the United States. Some felt that the program would increase animosity between the races. Others saw it leading to a greater mutual understanding between them. Meg Greenfield, writing in the February 14, 1977, issue of *Newsweek*, compared the influence of *Roots* to that of *Uncle Tom's Cabin* written by Harriet Beecher Stowe more than 100 years before.

The success of "mini-series" like *Roots* may presage a drastic change in the nature of TV programming. Speaking to an audience of broadcasters in early 1977, Robert Wussler, then president of CBS-TV, said that "never again in the history of TV will we see the same dependence on weekly series."

NETWORK CONTROL OF PROGRAMMING

When radio was the major broadcasting medium, most major series had a single sponsor. This system made it possible for the sponsor either directly or through its advertising agency to control the show and to identify its products with the talent. Most network programs during the radio era were produced by production departments in advertising agencies rather than by the networks, which simply provided their studio and transmission facilities. This system raised the question whether it was good for broadcasting for so much program control to be in the hands of advertisers.

The higher costs of television programming and time charges made it impossible for all but a handful of advertisers to sponsor an entire show. Thus there developed the pattern of alternate-week sponsorships of the same program by two advertisers. From this it was but another step to the "magazine" concept of program sales in which programs were offered for sale to multiple sponsors on an insertion or participating basis. Because so many advertisers were involved in sponsoring one program, none could control its content and the function of program production and control devolved to the networks. Now with the program function back in the hands of the three

Table 4–1. NTI TOP 50 PROGRAMS, 1960 through January, 1977, Average Audience Estimates

Rank	Program Name	Telecast Date	Network	Average Audience (No. of Households) (000)
1	Roots	Jan. 30, 1977	ABC	36,380
2	Big Event Pt. 1 (Gone With The Wind—Pt. 1)	Nov. 7, 1976	NBC	33,960
3	Mon. Night Movie (Gone With The Wind—Pt. 2)	Nov. 8, 1976	NBC	33,750
4	Roots	Jan. 28, 1977	ABC	32,680
5	Roots	Jan. 27, 1977	ABC	32,540
6	Roots	Jan. 25, 1977	ABC	31,900
7	Super Bowl XI	Jan. 9, 1977	NBC	31,610
8	Roots	Jan. 24, 1977	ABC	31,400
9	Roots	Jan. 26, 1977	ABC	31,190
10	Roots	Jan. 29, 1977	ABC	30,120
11	Super Bowl X	Jan. 18, 1976	CBS	29,440
12	Super Bowl IX	Jan. 12, 1975	NBC	29,040
13	Roots	Jan. 23, 1977	ABC	28,840
14	Airport (Movie Special)	Nov. 11, 1973	ABC	28,000
15	Super Bowl VII	Jan. 14, 1973	NBC	27,670
16	World Series Game #7	Oct. 22, 1975	NBC	27,560
17	Super Bowl VIII	Jan. 13, 1974	CBS	27,540
18	Super Bowl VI	Jan. 16, 1972	CBS	27,450
19	ABC Sunday Movie (Love Story)	Oct. 1, 1972	ABC	27,410
20	All In The Family	Jan. 5, 1976	CBS	27,350
21	Bob Hope Christmas Show	Jan. 15, 1970	NBC	27,260
22	Bob Hope Christmas Show	Jan. 14, 1971	NBC	27,050
23	Mon. Night Movie (Godfather—Pt. 2)	Nov. 18, 1974	NBC	26,990
24	Sun. Night Movie (Poseidon Adventure)	Oct. 27, 1974	ABC	26,720
25	Sun. Night Movie (Little Ladies Of The Night)	Jan. 16, 1977	ABC	26,270
26	Sun. Night Movie (Jeremiah Johnson)	Jan. 18, 1976	ABC	26,100
26	Helter Skelter—Pt. 2	Apr. 2, 1976	CBS	26,100
28	The Fugitive	Aug. 29, 1967	ABC	25,700
29	All In The Family	Sep. 15, 1975	CBS	25,540
30	Academy Awards	Apr. 7, 1970	ABC	25,390
31	Sat. Night Movies (Godfather—Pt. 1)	Nov. 16, 1974	NBC	25,350
32	All In The Family	Jan. 8, 1972	CBS	25,270

33	ABC Sunday Movie (True Grit)	Nov. 12, 1972	ABC	25,210
34	Maude	Jan. 5, 1976	CBS	25,130
35	ABC Sunday Movie (Patton)	Nov. 19, 1972	ABC	24,950
36	All In The Family	Jan. 15, 1972	CBS	24,840
37	Academy Awards	Mar. 29, 1976	ABC	24,710
37	The Waltons	Nov. 4, 1976	CBS	24,710
37	Happy Days	Jan. 4, 1977	ABC	24,710
40	Bob Hope Special	Dec. 10, 1972	NBC	24,690
41	Happy Days	Sep. 21, 1976	ABC	24,640
41	Happy Days	Jan. 25, 1977	ABC	24,640
43	Laverne & Shirley	Jan. 27, 1976	ABC	24,500
43	Helter Skelter—Pt. 1	Apr. 1, 1976	CBS	24,500
45	Laverne & Shirley	Jan. 4, 1977	ABC	24,490
46	Heavyweight Boxing Championship	May 24, 1976	NBC	24,360
46	All In The Family	Dec. 22, 1975	CBS	24,360
48	Charlie's Angels	Nov. 3, 1976	ABC	24,140
49	Happy Days	Sep. 28, 1976	ABC	24,070
50	All In The Family	Sep. 29, 1975	CBS	23,940

Courtesy A. C. Nielsen Company.

television networks, there was considerable concern that excessive semi-monopolistic power over programs was held by a few network program executives. This concern was shared by the FCC, which after extensive studies imposed a limitation on the networks by reducing to three hours in prime time the amount of programming television stations in the top 50 markets may accept from a network source. This limitation, which went into effect in 1971, came to be known as the Prime Time Access Rule or PTAR. A waiver was granted to permit network news programming between 7:00–7:30 P.M. provided that it follows an hour of local news. Subsequently PTAR was amended to exempt public affairs, children's programs, and documentaries from the three-hour limitation on network prime-time programming each evening. The networks thereupon offered their affiliates four hours of programming on Sunday evenings, the first hour of which offered exempt programs like *The World of Disney* and *60 Minutes*. On Mondays through Saturdays, however, the networks offered entertainment programs for three hours starting at 8:00 P.M.

In the 1970s the Justice Department entered antitrust suits against the major networks that were designed to limit their production of programs. In 1976 NBC in a consent decree agreed to produce only two and one-half hours of programming per week in prime time and further agreed to limit the time it would control program proposals or pilots. This agreement will have no effect, however, unless the other two networks accept it, and it might not be approved by the court. Moreover, the significance of the agreement is questionable, because the networks produce few entertainment programs. At the time NBC signified its acceptance of the consent decree, it was producing only one hour of prime-time programming a week.

TELEVISION PROGRAM SUPPLIERS

Though the control of programs rests primarily with the television networks, they produce few programs, as we have just noted. There are many sources of television talent and program materials and many ways in which programs are put together. Most programming actually is produced by independent program suppliers, which contract with networks for the production of individual series. A network may invest speculatively in the script and pilot-film development for a series in return for exclusive telecast rights at preset prices. The principal film program suppliers to the networks are the TV subsidiaries of the companies that produce feature films for movie theaters—MGM-TV, Paramount, Twentieth-Century Fox, Universal, Columbia Pictures TV, and Warner Communications. Hanna-Barbara Productions, which specializes in cartoon shows for children, is another major supplier. Many smaller independent production companies have also been successful, among them Talent Associates, QM Productions, Don Fedderson Productions, Lorimar Productions, and companies controlled by star talent and top producers. Production entities controlled by Norman Lear produce *All in the Family, Maude, Good Times, Sanford and Son, The Jeffersons,* and other comedy series. Mary Tyler Moore's company, MTM Enterprises, produced her own series in addition to shows such as *Rhoda, Phyllis,* and the *Bob Newhart Show.* An organization that has specialized in producing audience participation, panel, and game shows is Goodson-Todman Productions. Its programs are seen both on networks and in syndication. Among these programs are *Match Game, The Price is Right,* and *To Tell the Truth.* Networks produce news and public affairs programs and a limited number of entertainment shows.

The performing, writing, directing, and producing talent needed to build and produce successful programs is supplied through talent agencies. Until 1962, by far the largest of such agencies, constituting the single largest force in the entertainment industry, was the Music Corporation of America (MCA). In addition to representing talent, however, MCA through its wholly owned company, Revue, also produced programs. This mixture of production and talent-representation functions in one company permitted a talent bureau to produce a show on one network and book the talent for the show competing against it on another network. The Department of Justice intervened in this anticompetitive situation, and MCA withdrew from the talent-representation business. Among the principal talent representatives now in operation are the William Morris Agency, International Creative Management (ICM), Creative Artists Agency, Chasin-Park-Citron Agency, and Sy Fisher Company and numerous smaller agencies.

THE GROWTH OF FILM AND TAPED SHOWS

The place of film programs in television has been a question of continuing interest to many. Television, with its enormous demands for program material, has made extensive use of film programming of four kinds: 1. the feature-length film made for theatrical exhibition that is released to television after its box-office possibilities have been exhausted; 2. hour and half-hour film series especially produced for television; 3. feature-length films especially produced for television; and 4. filmed mini-series.

The major companies of the Hollywood motion picture industry at first resisted all efforts by television to obtain fairly recent motion pictures for TV showing. In the mid-fifties this resistance began to weaken and some important studios, anxious to produce some quick income, licensed whole blocks of their films to television. Soon most of the other major companies had made similar deals, and films made after 1948, which had been established previously as the cutoff date, began to flood the market. Networks in recent years increased their use of feature films until there was at least one movie being shown every night of the week, and on some evenings two network movies competed for audience attention. The supply of feature films was not adequate to sustain this schedule, however, and the networks reduced the number of "movie nights." A further problem is the fact that many new movies use language and deal with subject matter considered unsuitable for such a home-oriented medium as television. Editing can often solve this problem, however.

Very old feature films are used by individual stations as television's equivalent to the recorded and transcribed music programs that fill up so many radio hours. Many stations close out their late evening schedules with a feature film, and stations without network affiliation may rely chiefly on old feature films for programming, playing as many as four or five a day.

The production of half-hour and hour films for television has become a major activity in Hollywood. As we have noted, many of the companies that make films for theatrical exhibition are major producers in this field, and they are joined by other firms that specialize in the production of TV films. Each half-hour situation comedy- or adventure-film series involves the production of 24 to 30 half-hour films, or the equivalent of about 12 feature-length motion pictures. The hour series requires the production of even more footage. Each half-hour film is usually shot in three days, or two a week. Alternate weeks no films are shot in order to give the performers a rest and a chance to study scripts. In this way four half-hour films are turned out each month. The production of hour films requires turning out a film a week, with occasional weeks when no films are shot. The cost of a film is usually greater than what the network pays for the initial telecast, but the film provides an opportunity for gaining further profits through repeated showings. For these repeat showings, the performers and all others involved in the production receive residual payments at a lower rate than the payments received for the first showing. After successful network runs film series like *Happy Days* are licensed to individual stations via syndication distribution for numerous additional telecasts. The same process is followed with network programs recorded on video tape. Film and tape programs produced specifically for syndication are also available to stations. The *Mike Douglas Show* and *The Lawrence Welk Show* are examples. Another type of syndication involves the distribution not of filmed or video-taped programs but of show ideas or scripts, which are then produced independently by local stations. The formats of *Romper Room* and *Bozo the Clown* programs are licensed on this basis. The persons who serve as hosts of the *Romper Room* programs attend training sessions at national centers to learn the program techniques and approaches that are incorporated in the series design.

PUBLIC AFFAIRS AND SERVICE PROGRAMMING

Public affairs and service programs most clearly demonstrate the use of broadcasting to serve the public interest. In a variety of forms, these programs provide information and understanding about the real world in which we live: they report information and news about activities as different as agricultural marketing and the major league baseball contests; they present direct coverage of important events; they provide a public platform for speeches, press conferences, and discussions of public issues; they dramatize, through documentary techniques, historical events and current social and political problems; they provide a pulpit for religious services; they broadcast practical information for use in homemaking, shopping, family health, and child raising.

Some of these programs, such as religious programs, are broadcast as "sustaining" shows by stations and networks and are not offered for sale to possible advertisers. Other public affairs programs, such as sports and news, are among the most popular of program types and are sponsored. Network television newscasts are far more involved and expensive to produce than most viewers realize. In the programming of a single television news program, CBS calls on the services of more than 250 people including almost 100 regular staff members and more than 150 foreign and domestic camera correspondents, not counting operations, engineering, reference, and other network departments. The broadcasting of special events also requires the expenditure of a great deal of money and the employment of many people. It is estimated, for example, that the coverage of man's first walk on the moon and the launching and return of the Apollo capsule cost the networks from $11 to $13 million and required the services of 1000 people.

CBS's *60 Minutes* is an outstanding example of a network magazine-type public affairs program that competes successfully in prime time with entertainment shows.

The networks also produce documentary programs that deal with social issues, but the style of these documentaries is sharply different from the penetrating exposés that such teams as Edward R. Murrow and Fred Friendly produced for CBS in television's earlier days. Alexander Kendrick, biographer of Murrow, says that "The sharp, shrewd editing of film that enabled a Murrow-Friendly program to make point after point, was replaced by a kind of *cinéma vérité* that substituted impressions for points. . . . Old style, or Murrow-Friendly, documentaries dealt with cause and effect, and tried to show the circumstances that produced the consequences. The new wave offers the viewer a sensory experience rather than a balanced judgment."[2] The first Alfred I. du Pont-Columbia University Survey of Broadcast Journalism

[2] Alexander Kendrick, *Prime Time: The Life of Edward R. Murrow* (Boston, 1969), p. 28.

criticized the networks for the decline in the number of documentaries and for their unwillingness to engage in hardhitting exposés that might be expected to arouse controversy. In its 1977 anniversary issue, *Variety* once more decried the decline of issue-oriented in-depth TV documentaries.

The decline in number and the change in the nature of documentaries are understandable in the commercial world of television. Few advertisers sponsor documentaries: they draw small audiences and the controversy they arouse may alienate prospective customers. Many network affiliates often fail to carry the documentaries that the networks produce, substituting for them entertainment programs that draw a larger audience and provide greater income.

The production of documentaries is not the exclusive province of networks, although the networks, as a matter of policy, generally refuse to telecast public-affairs documentaries that were not produced under their supervision and control. David Wolper, an independent producer, has produced several successful documentary series, most of which have been telecast on a syndicated basis. Local stations often produce relatively inexpensive public-affairs and service programs that achieve excellent results. Interview programs with various authorities, local cooking and shopping programs, simple news and feature programs, discussion and public forum programs with exponents of conflicting points of view, and other program forms are produced locally as well as on networks with good public acceptance. Call-in programs are particularly popular on local stations.

CHILDREN'S PROGRAMS

No area of television programming is more sensitive to public criticism than that of children's programs. Special concern has frequently been voiced about the effect on children of programs dramatizing crime and violence. This concern is often expressed by parents who, in what seems to some to be an abdication of parental responsibility, have turned over their television sets for indiscriminate and unlimited viewing by their children. We know that children watch television on the average of more than 20 hours a week, and that their viewing is not limited to programs intended for children, but extends in the early evening hours to the popular comedy and variety shows. Regardless of parental responsibility, television stations and networks would seem to have positive responsibility for the quality of the programs they present. An organization that has played a leading role in agitating for improved programs for children is the Boston-based group known as Action for Children's Television (ACT). This group filed petitions with the FCC demanding that programs for children be presented without commercials and criticizing the nature of their programs. It did not win all of its objectives, but it did achieve significant changes, particularly in programs broadcast for children on Saturday mornings. The violence in the cartoons was reduced, some cartoons were replaced with live-action shows, and commercial messages were reduced in number and modified in approach.

Another consideration has been the time at which programs are broadcast. In 1975 the broadcasting industry introduced what it called Family Viewing Time, the period between 7:00 and 9:00 P.M. EST, during which only programs suitable for viewing by the entire family were to be telecast. The audience would be alerted by special announcements at the beginning of programs if there were any divergence from this policy and such announcements would also be included in any programs, no matter what time they were broadcast, if their content might be considered suitable for only mature viewers. The future of the family-viewing concept, however, was thrown into jeopardy when a federal court ruled that the method through which it came into being was unconstitutional because it violated the First Amendment. The FCC particularly was criticized in the decision because it brought illegal pressure on the networks to put the family-viewing policy into operation.

Networks and stations have also presented programs like *Captain Kangaroo* that are specifically designed for children. Public television stations have given particular attention to children's needs with such series as *What's New?* and *Misteroger's Neighborhood.* A notable entry in this field was *Sesame Street,* a production of the Children's Television Workshop. Supported by contributions from the Department of Health, Education, and Welfare, various foundations, and the Corporation for Public Broadcasting, *Sesame Street* was designed to prepare preschool children for their first school experiences. It achieved enormous popularity.

SUMMARY

The key function in television and radio is programming. The programming function is characterized by its vastness in scope, its continuous nature, its competitiveness and costliness, its complexity, its tendency to seek stability, its variety of sources, and its speculative quality. Radio programming has changed its program forms under the competitive impact of television, while television had to unburden itself of program forms it inherited from radio before it found its own program strength. The Special concept also played an important role in shaping the development of television programming. Films and tape programs fill the schedules of both network and local station programming. In public-affairs and service programming, networks and stations most directly serve the public interest. Children's programming has been especially subject to public criticism.

Questions For Discussion

1. What are the special characteristics of the programming function?
2. What have been the traditional patterns of radio programming? Why were these patterns changed and what new forms were developed?
3. Compare network radio programming with local radio programming.
4. What is the meaning and significance of the "Special" concept in television programming?

5. Is television fulfilling its proper function in serving as a transmission means for the presentation of motion pictures originally made for projection in theaters?

6. Does it make any difference to you whether a TV program is presented "live," prerecorded on tape, or on film?

7. What is the function of public-affairs and service programming? How have radio and television handled such programming?

8. How do you explain the popular appeal of contest and give-away programs?

9. What role do drama, comedy, and variety play in radio and television programming? What are the relative strengths of each in a program schedule?

10. What is the difference between network presentation of a film and syndication of a film?

11. What is the difference between a "sustaining" show and a commercial show?

12. "TV is the biggest economic revolution in America since the cotton gin, but its monopoly is mediocrity."—statement of Jerry Wald, former Production Chief of Columbia Pictures. Do you agree or disagree with this point of view? Why?

the federal communications commission

5

Only on occasions, as when the Federal Communications Commission authorized color television, or when its chairman makes provocative speeches condemning the quality of radio and television programming, or when it rules on a minority-party candidate's petition for free debate time, or it holds public hearings on the performance of broadcasters, does the FCC come directly to the attention of the general public through front-page newspaper stories. Most of the time its actions are reported only in broadcasting trade journals, and the general public has little knowledge of the Commission's authority and responsibility in the field of television and radio. Yet the FCC is one of the four pillars supporting the structure of American broadcasting: 1. The Federal Communications Commission; 2. stations and networks; 3. advertisers and agencies; and 4. the listening and viewing public. The FCC is the agency of the federal government authorized to carry out the law of radio and television. In this chapter we shall discuss the Communications Act of 1934, which is the basic statute on broadcasting, and the composition and functioning of the Federal Communications Commission.

THE COMMUNICATIONS ACT OF 1934

In Chapter 2 we related how the federal government stepped into radio in 1927 in response to calls for action by the public and the radio industry. Unregulated radio had fallen into a state of chaos and only Congress, under its Constitutional power to regulate interstate commerce, could do anything about it. Congress passed the Radio Act of 1927 and, seven years later, incorporated the law in the Communications Act of 1934. That statute, with certain amendments, still remains on the books. As defined by the Act, the word "radio" is construed to mean television as well as sound broadcasting.

The Communications Act sets forth as its purpose

to maintain the control of the United States over all the channels of interstate and foreign radio transmission; and to provide for the *use* of such channels, *but not the ownership thereof,* by persons *for limited periods of time, under licenses granted by Federal authority,* and no such license shall be construed to create any right, beyond the terms, conditions, and periods of the license. No person shall use or operate any apparatus for the transmission of energy or communications or signals by radio . . . except under and in accordance with this Act and with a license in that behalf granted under the provisions of this Act.

In order to leave no doubt about the matter of ownership of radio frequencies and the right of the government to regulate broadcasting, the law states that no license may be granted "until the applicant therefor shall have signed a waiver of any claim to the use of any particular frequency or of the ether as against the regulatory power of the United States."

The yardstick for issuing or renewing radio licenses shall be the "public convenience, interest, or necessity." The FCC is specifically directed to "encourage the larger and more effective use of radio in the public interest." Congressional judgment that radio must be developed as a medium for free expression of opinion without censorship by the FCC is set forth in Section 326, which states:

> Nothing in this Act shall be understood or construed to give the Commission the power of censorship over the radio communications or signals transmitted by any radio station, and no regulation or condition shall be promulgated or fixed by the Commission which shall interfere with the right of free speech by means of radio communication.

From these provisions we can see that American public policy toward radio and television involves the following key ideas:

1. The airwaves belong to the people.
2. The federal government shall maintain control over all broadcasting channels.
3. Use of these channels is limited to persons licensed by the federal government.
4. Licenses may be issued to persons only when the "public interest, convenience, or necessity" will be served thereby.
5. Licenses are good for limited periods of time only.
6. Radio and television shall be maintained as media for free speech.
7. Use of a radio or television frequency in no way creates an ownership right to that frequency.
8. The regulatory power of the federal government supersedes the right of any individual to the use of a radio or television frequency.

The Act of 1934 created the Federal Communications Commission to carry out the law. The FCC is an independent regulatory commission, quasi-judicial in many of its functions, but primarily administrative and policy-making in its day-to-day operations.

COMPOSITION OF THE FCC

The FCC is composed of seven Commissioners appointed by the President for seven-year terms by and with the advice and consent of the Senate. The President designates one of the Commissioners to be chairman. The Com-

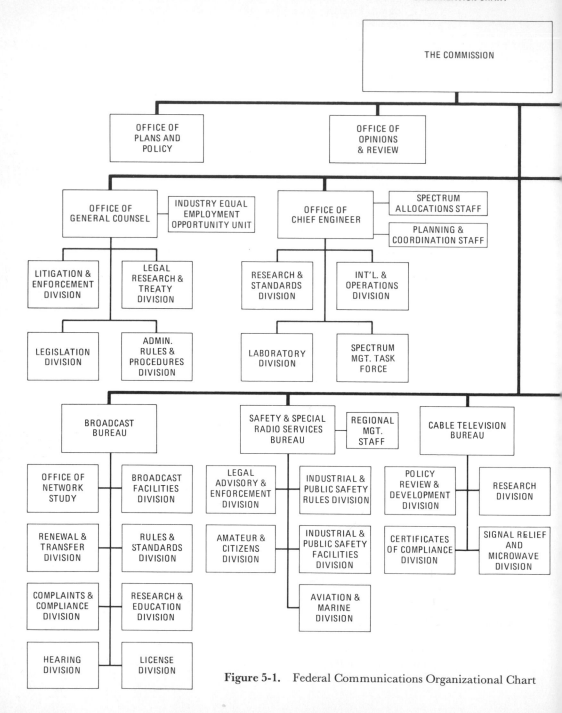

Figure 5-1. Federal Communications Organizational Chart

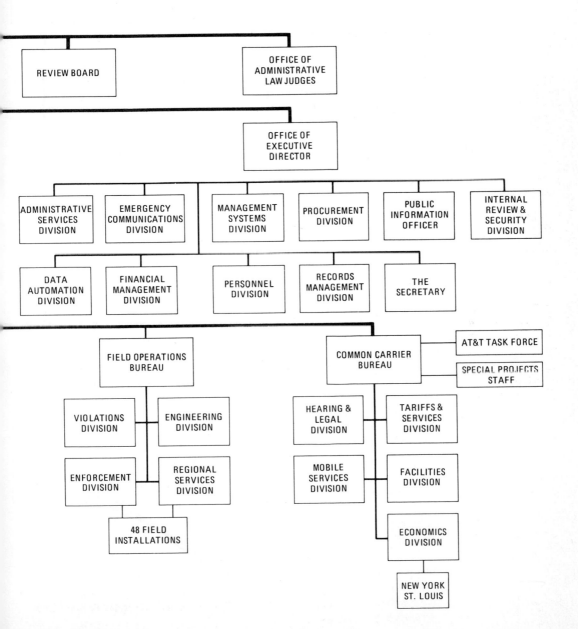

mission functions as a unit, although it often delegates responsibility to boards or committees of Commissioners, individual Commissioners, or the staff of the Commission. Policy decisions are made by the Commission as a whole.

Each member of the FCC must be a United States citizen with no financial interest of any sort in the communications business. Not more than four Commissioners out of the seven may be members of the same political party. Each Commissioner is provided with a personal staff of assistants. The Commission maintains its central offices in Washington and field offices in 24 districts. The Commission's staff is organized in seven offices and in five bureaus. The names of these offices and bureaus and the FCC structure of organization are indicated in Figure 5-1. The annual budget of the Commission is over $40 million, and it employs a staff of approximately 2000 people.

FUNCTIONS OF THE FCC

The FCC has the following general functions pertaining to radio and television:

1. It advises the State Department in negotiating international radio agreements and acts as the agent of the United States in carrying out the American end of such treaties. Radio waves cross international borders, and so there must be coordination and agreement in a master allocation plan on a worldwide basis to prevent mutual interference. Furthermore, nations must agree on which bands to assign airplane communications, distress signals, ship-to-shore radio, etc.

2. It allocates bands of frequencies to various radio and television services. Examples of this allocating function were the decisions, previously mentioned, to use the 88 to 108 megacycle band for FM radio and to add channels 14 to 83 to the television band.

3. It licenses television and radio stations and broadcast operators. The power to issue licenses is supplemented by the power to revoke or renew licenses and to approve or disapprove transfers of licenses. In carrying out these functions, the FCC holds hearings, conducts investigations, and issues decisions in individual cases involving license applications. It also promulgates regulations binding directly or indirectly on the entire television and radio industry.

4. It classifies television and radio stations and prescribes "the nature of the service to be rendered by each class of licensed stations and each station within any class."

5. It assigns bands of frequencies to the various classes of stations and assigns frequencies for each individual station, determining the power which each station shall use and the time during which it may operate.

6. It determines the location of stations and regulates the kind of apparatus television and radio stations may use.

7. It makes regulations "necessary to prevent interference between stations and to carry out the provisions" of the Act.

8. It is authorized to make special regulations applicable to stations engaged in network broadcasting.

9. It requires stations "to keep such records of programs, transmissions of energy, communications, or signals as it may deem desirable."

10. It designates call letters of all stations.

11. It polices the ether to make sure that broadcasters stay on their assigned frequencies and that no unauthorized persons use the airwaves. Volunteer groups made up of such people as radio and television repairmen and amateur radio operators assist the FCC in this work.

12. It encourages new uses of radio, particularly those that will promote safety of life and property.

13. It supervises all common carrier telephone, cable, and telegraph services. The American Telephone and Telegraph Company and other companies whose microwave equipment and telephone lines are used in network broadcasting are regulated by the FCC.

14. In wartime, the FCC coordinates the use of television and radio with the national security program. During World War II, the FCC set up a Foreign Broadcast Intelligence Service that monitored enemy propaganda broadcasts.

LICENSING RADIO AND TELEVISION STATIONS

In licensing radio and television stations when "the public convenience, interest, or necessity will be served thereby," the FCC must also try to allot stations among the various states and communities so "as to provide a fair, efficient, and equitable distribution of radio service to each of the same."

The period for which licenses are good is limited by law to a maximum of three years. The FCC at first issued six-month licenses for standard radio stations; now AM, FM, and TV stations are licensed for three years. There is considerable agitation in the broadcast industry to amend the law to provide for five-year licenses.

Applicants for radio or television stations must file written statements describing their citizenship and character and their financial, technical, and other qualifications to operate broadcast stations. Aliens, foreign corporations, or any corporations "of which any officer or director is an alien or of which more than one-fifth of the capital stock is owned of record or voted by aliens" may not obtain a station license.

An applicant for a license must set forth: 1. the location of the proposed station; 2. the frequency and power he wants to use; 3. the hours of the day during which he proposes to operate the station; 4. the purposes for which the station will be used; and 5. a full statement of his proposed program service.

To preserve competition in radio and television, the law directs the FCC not to grant licenses to applicants when, by doing so, competition would be substantially reduced or commerce restrained. The Commission has ruled that not more than one AM, one FM, and one TV station serving the same listening area may be licensed to the same applicant. This is known as the "duopoly" rule. No more than seven AM, seven FM, and seven TV (five VHF and two UHF) stations serving different areas may be licensed to or controlled by the same persons or corporations. In March 1970 the Commission took an even more drastic step to prevent concentration in too few hands of control over the main avenues of communication when it announced its intention to bar the future acquisition of more than one broadcasting station by the same owner in a single market. Known as the "one-to-a-customer" rule, the new regulation provides that parties now holding an AM, FM, or TV license would not be eligible for further grants of AM, FM, or TV licenses in the same market. Some exceptions to this rule in communities of 10,000 population or less or in transactions involving UHF television stations were permitted, and the rule was later modified to permit certain AM-FM combinations. Later the Commission, with the support of the Justice Department, also acted to break up the existing cross-ownership of publishing enterprises and broadcasting facilities in certain small communities. A further extension of this policy was a move to prevent the transfer intact of radio, television, and newspaper facilities held by a single owner to another single owner. For example, when Washington Star Communications, which included a newspaper, an FM and AM radio station, and a TV station, was sold in 1975, the new owner was ordered to divest himself of either the broadcasting or newspaper properties. In 1976 he sold WMAL-AM-FM to ABC for $16 million, the highest price ever paid for a radio property, and within two years had to dispose of either the *Washington Star* or WMAL-TV.

When the FCC made its original decision in 1975 that an owner should not control both newspapers and broadcast operations in the same city, it made an important exception with a grandfather clause that permitted most cross-ownerships to continue. In 1977, however, a U.S. Court of Appeals struck down the grandfather clause with a decision that ordered the FCC to adopt new rules forbidding joint local ownership of newspapers and TV and radio stations. The Court further ruled that the burden of proving that a joint ownership was harmful should not rest on a citizen group challenging a joint ownership. Rather, the Court said the joint owner should have the burden of proving that "cross-ownership is in the public interest." In the absence of such proof, divestiture should take place.

It is expected that the FCC will appeal to the Supreme Court for a review of this decision, and it may take its case to Congress as well. The cross-ownership question is not likely to be resolved for a long time.

When this policy was announced, more than 200 companies published newspapers or magazines or both and also operated broadcasting stations. If the plan is carried out, it will be one of the most revolutionary and far-reaching actions ever taken by the FCC. The Commission has for many years favored nonnewspaper owners over newspaper owners in issuing licenses if other factors in the situation were equal. Many newspaper owners, however, began operating stations before the antimonopoly policy went into effect. If their service to the community was satisfactory, these newspaper owners were permitted to go on operating stations.

For many years the FCC charged no fee for the privilege of holding a broadcasting license, although it began assessing filing fees in 1964. Early in 1970 the FCC, in addition to increasing the fees charged for filing applications, began to charge an annual license fee in the hope that the funds acquired in this way would pay the Commission's operating expenses. The fees charged each station were based on the amount the station charged for its commercials. The fee schedule was revised in 1975. In late 1976, a U.S. Court of Appeals in response to four suits brought by organizations protesting the institution of these fees ruled that assessing fees higher than the cost of the services rendered by the FCC was illegal and ordered it to refund all fees collected since 1970 that were excessive by that standard. This decision was based on a 1975 Supreme Court decision, which said that the FCC's assessing fees against the cable-TV industry higher than the cost of the service it provided amounted to taxation and the FCC had no power to levy taxes. A fee system comparable to that introduced by the FCC can be reinstituted only by an act of Congress. The FCC decided not to seek legislation that would authorize it to reinstitute a fee system.

The Commission has no direct authority to license or regulate television and radio networks. It does in fact, however, regulate networks through rules directed at stations owned by or affiliated with networks. In 1941, for example, the FCC promulgated a set of regulations designed to reduce network domination of affiliates. These regulations are discussed in Chapter 6. In 1977, the FCC announced its intention to investigate network domination of television to determine whether stations affiliated with networks enjoy alternatives to network programs and the freedom to select these alternatives. It is possible that further regulation of networks will arise from this investigation.

Renewal, Revocation, and Transfer of Licenses

At least four months before the expiration of a license, a station must file a renewal application with the FCC. In this application the station is obliged to provide a statement of the program service it has broadcast in the preceding three years. The FCC may take this record of actual program service and compare it with the statement of proposed program service the station made in its original application for a license. If the FCC is satisfied that performance reasonably matches the promises, it will renew the application. If numerous complaints about the station have been made to the FCC, if the comparison between promises and performance does not show a high correlation, or if a competing application is filed, the FCC may order a public hearing on the renewal application. In this hearing, the applicant bears the burden of proving that renewal of his license will serve the public interest.

In January of 1969, the FCC sent a chill through the broadcasting industry when it failed to renew the television license under which the *Herald Traveler* had been operating Station WHDH-TV on Channel 5 in Boston for a period of 12 years on the ground that the original license grant had been tainted by improper *ex parte* practices. Broadcasters were concerned that it opened the door to assaults on the licenses of other well-established television stations. In 1969 nine other television stations coming up for license renewal were challenged by applicants who promised the FCC that they would do a better job of broadcasting.

In the face of this threat, broadcasters sought refuge in a bill introduced by Senator John O. Pastore of Rhode Island, which would require the FCC to ignore competing applications for licenses until it had decided that the present licensee should be denied renewal. The proposed bill was intended to protect the position of incumbent licensees and virtually freeze the broadcasting industry in the hands of the current station licensees. If a license of a television station is "up for grabs every three years," as one proponent put it, the owner cannot be expected to make a substantial investment or engage in long-range plans. The main argument against the proposal was that it violated the principle set forth in the Communications Act that a station is given the right to use a frequency for a specific period of time but is granted no right of ownership. In the eyes of Nicholas Johnson, a former member of the FCC who vigorously opposed the Pastore Bill, the legislation would, in effect, make station owners perpetual holders of the frequencies on which they broadcast because they would not be subject to effective review or challenge.

As the controversy heightened, the FCC clarified its own position. The FCC pointed out that the WHDH-TV case, because of its special circumstances, was not a precedent for similar action against other stations. In 1970 it also said that the current holder of a license would be granted a renewal if it could show that its service was substantially attuned to meeting the needs and interests of its service area. The United States Court of Appeals in Washington, D.C., repudiated this policy because it would not result in the best possible service to the area and weighted the situation too much in favor of the current licensee. In response, the FCC called for "superior" rather than "substantial" service. The issue will not be resolved, however, until the Congress passes a new license-renewal bill which, in addition to spelling out the conditions under which licenses will be renewed, will also probably extend the licensing period from three to five years.

The FCC has the power to revoke a license when the station fails to operate in accordance with the law or with FCC regulations, or substantially as it said it would in its application. In revocation proceedings, the FCC bears the burden of proving that the station is *not* serving the public interest. The Commission hesitates to use its power of revocation because such extreme action is usually excessive punishment for most violations, and prior to 1952 the Commission usually limited itself to giving a sharp warning to an offending station and waiting until the license-renewal application was submitted before taking further action. In extraordinary cases, such as where the licensee concealed the real ownership of his station by deceptive and misleading statements, the FCC took the final step and denied renewal of the station's license.

In 1952, Congress amended the Communications Act to authorize the Commission to issue "cease-and-desist" orders to erring stations. The stations are obliged to reply to the Commission's charges and formal hearings are provided for, with the burden of proof resting on the Commission. Failure by a station to observe a properly issued cease-and-desist order is made legal grounds for revoking the station's license. The Commission also has the authority to fine stations for infractions of the law or of its regulations.

BROADCAST IDENTIFICATION REQUIREMENTS

The Communications Act states that

> All matter broadcast by any radio station for which service, money, or any other valuable consideration is directly or indirectly paid, or promised to or charged or accepted by, the station so broadcasting, from any person, shall, at the time the same is so broadcast, be announced as paid for or furnished, as the case may be, by such person.

FCC regulations require that whenever stations are furnished scripts or tapes of political discussion programs, an announcement as to the source of such material must be broadcast. Sponsored programs must carry at least one announcement stating the sponsor's name or the name of his product. This regulation seems a bit whimsical, since advertisers seldom need to be pressured into announcing the name of their products; it is designed, however, to prevent deception. Radio and TV stations are also required to broadcast their call letters and location at least every hour unless the continuity of longer programs, such as music or drama broadcasts, would be interrupted thereby.

EMERGENCY BROADCAST SYSTEM

Knowing how vital a role broadcasting plays in America, the FCC has devised a system for making the best use of radio and television during periods of national emergency. It is known as the Emergency Broadcast System (EBS). Under the EBS plan, broadcast licensees, commercial radio and television networks, and other communication services, licensed or regulated by the FCC, participate in the activities of the system. All stations are required to maintain equipment to receive emergency action notifications and to conduct an on-air test of the system once a week. When an emergency situation is proclaimed, every station must take certain prescribed actions. All commercial activity must cease; authorized stations remain on the air broadcasting common programs at the national, state, or local levels; those stations not authorized to broadcast must shut down and remain off the air until the emergency situation is terminated.

SUMMARY

The federal government, acting through the Federal Communications Commission, plays a vital role in American broadcasting. Through its regulatory powers, the Commission grants temporary and conditional access to the airwaves to private broadcasters who pledge to serve the "public interest, convenience, or necessity." Television and radio serve as media of free speech, with the FCC specifically denied any direct power of censorship. The Commission, through license renewal, cease-and-desist orders, fines, revocation proceedings, and its rule-making powers, has supervisory jurisdiction and authority over all broadcasting stations.

Questions for Discussion

1. What role does the federal government play in American broadcasting?
2. What are the key ideas to be found in the Communications Act of 1934?
3. In what ways does the philosophy of the Act of 1912, which required the Secretary of Commerce to grant broadcast licenses to all qualified applicants, differ from the Communications Act of 1934?
4. Under what conditions does a person or group interested in broadcasting acquire the right to use a radio frequency or a television channel?
5. Describe the general composition of the Federal Communications Commission.
6. What steps has the FCC taken to prevent monopoly control of communications?
7. What provision does the Act of 1934 make to preserve free speech on the air?
8. Do you think that networks should operate under FCC licenses as well as the radio or television stations that may be affiliated with them?
9. Can you think of any circumstances under which a sponsor might wish to conceal his identification with a program?
10. Do you believe that a measure similar to the Pastore Bill should be passed to give existing license holders the first right at renewal time to continue using the frequencies assigned to them?
11. What authority does the FCC have over a station's program policies?

networks, stations, and cable tv

Networks and stations are the means by which broadcasting becomes possible. When you turn on your radio or television receiver, you must adjust the set to a particular frequency or TV channel to receive the program. That program comes from an individual station in your reception area. It may be the same program tuned in by an audience 2000 miles away. If so, the explanation is network broadcasting, which connects stations by land telephone lines, satellite, microwave relays, or a combination of these facilities, and furnishes the same program simultaneously to all network stations, which in turn broadcast the program from their individual transmitters. This is what makes possible the use of Hollywood and New York City as the source of most big-time entertainment programming. Stations and networks are therefore vitally important in the structure of American broadcasting.

We have noted that the FCC has the power to classify stations and to issue licenses. In order to make maximum use of the available channels in the broadcast spectrum and to provide an equitable distribution of these channels throughout the nation, the FCC has divided and subdivided many of these channels as far as engineering and policy considerations have allowed.

AM RADIO STATIONS

Generally speaking, AM radio stations are classified in terms of their broadcasting power: 1. small stations—250 watts; 2. medium—500 to 5000 watts; and 3. large—10,000 to 50,000 watts. The importance of a station depends not only on its wattage, however, but on the population of the area in which it broadcasts; a 250—watt station in Boston may actually have a greater audience than a 5000—watt station in Montana. The power assigned to a radio station depends upon the frequency channel on which it is licensed to broadcast.

Classification of Channels

A broadcast "channel" is the band of frequencies occupied by a carrier frequency and two sidebands of broadcast signals. In AM radio, carrier frequencies begin at 535 kilohertz and follow in successive steps of 10 kilohertz up to 1605. This allows for 107 channels, which the FCC has divided into three classes.

1. *Clear channels.* A "clear channel" is one in which a station can broadcast over a wide listening area free from interference from other stations. By international agreement, 60 channels have been set apart for clear-channel broadcasting in North America, and of these 45 have been assigned primarily to the United States. In its original meaning the term "clear channel" meant that only one station operated on that frequency. As the pressure for new stations increased, the FCC gradually gave additional stations the right to operate on clear channels. The FCC took pains, however, to keep the clear channels as free from interference as possible. Under international agreement, the United States is obligated to license at least one high-powered station (a minimum of 50 kilowatts) on each clear channel. As a matter of national policy, the FCC makes the international minimum of 50 kw the maximum for clear-channel broadcasting, so that no stations in this country may now have more than 50,000 watts power.

2. *Regional channels.* A "regional channel" is one on which several stations may operate with power not to exceed 5000 watts. There are 41 of these channels, many of which serve a principal center of population and the contiguous rural area. The primary service area of a station operating on a regional channel may be limited by some interference from other stations.

3. *Local channels.* A "local channel" is one on which several stations may operate with power not in excess of 250 watts. The primary service areas of these stations also may be limited by interference from other stations. There are six local channels for use in the United States. In some instances stations in the same area may share channels.

Times of Operation

The conditions under which radio waves are propagated when the sun is shining are quite different from those prevailing when the sun is down. Standard AM radio stations emit two types of waves—a ground wave that follows the surface of the earth, and a sky wave that goes into the atmosphere. During the day only the ground wave is picked up by radio sets, because the conditions created by sunshine prevent the sky wave from being heard. Thus the range of the station is limited to the distance its ground wave travels. At night, however, the sky wave is reflected to earth by a section above the earth's atmosphere known as the ionosphere, giving the station a far greater range than it has during the day. If interference is to be controlled, it is obvious that all stations operating during the day cannot operate in the same way when the sun is down. Attempts to control interference are reflected in the rules the FCC has laid down regarding the times a station can be on the air. The FCC licenses AM stations according to the following time schedules:

1. *Unlimited time* allows broadcasting around the clock if the station so desires.

2. *Limited time* applies to certain secondary stations operating on clear channels. It permits station operation during the daytime and until local sunset if the second-

ary station is located west of the dominant station on the channel; if the secondary station is located east of the dominant station, it may operate until sunset at
the dominant station.

3. *Daytime only* permits operation solely between sunrise and sunset.

4. *Sharing time* permits operation during a restricted time schedule required by multiple use of the same channel by several stations.

5. *Specified hours* means that the exact operating hours of the station are specified in
the license.

Power and Directional Changes

We have noted that one measure the FCC has adopted to minimize interference among stations at night is to require that some stations cease broadcasting entirely as soon as the sun goes down. A second measure is to require
that some stations broadcasting at night reduce their power at sundown. A
third measure is to require that some stations broadcasting at night operate
on a directional antenna system, a procedure that keeps the signal from going into an area where it would interfere with the broadcasts of other stations. Some stations are required both to reduce their power and broadcast
on a directional pattern as soon as the sun sets.

Call Letters

AM stations east of the Mississippi River have call letters that begin with the
letter "W" and stations west of the Mississippi begin with the letter "K."
Several old stations like KDKA, Pittsburgh, are exceptions to this rule. Applicants for new AM radio stations may choose any arrangement of four letters beginning with the appropriate "W" or "K" provided they are not identical with the call letters of an existing station. Some stations have used the
initials of the owners in choosing their call letters, such as WABC, KNBC,
WCBS, WJLB (for John L. Booth, its founder). The state universities of
Iowa and Ohio call their stations WSUI and WOSU. Other stations have selected pronounceable combinations such as KORN, WREN, and WIND.

Station Operation

The operating function of a station is to produce programs and to sell time
to advertisers for its programs or for programs produced elsewhere and made
available to the station. The staff and mode of operation of an AM radio station depend upon four factors: its location, its authorized broadcast power,
its status as an independent or a network-affiliated station, and its programming and sales concepts.

A 50,000—watt clear-channel station located in a large metropolitan
center and operated independently with aggressive programming and sales
activity will require a sizable staff of programming, sales, technical, and administrative personnel, as well as substantial studio and office space. A station that concentrates on local live programs supported by local advertising

must have a staff of salesmen to bring in business, a commercial department to handle the administration of all sales orders, a program department to plan and produce programs, and an engineering staff. By way of contrast, a small 250—watt AM station operating in the daytime only, with a programming emphasis on news and recorded music, may manage with a staff of five or six people who double as engineers, announcers, salespeople, and bookkeepers. There is also a trend toward automated operation, which reduces even further the need for personnel.

FM RADIO STATIONS

Many FM radio stations are operated as adjuncts to AM radio stations, with the same operating staff running both stations. For many years the FM stations in this situation often carried the same program schedule as the AM station. The FCC first acted to promote diversification of programming by requiring that associated AM—FM stations in markets of 100,000 or more must originate their own programming at least 50 percent of the time. Later it revised this requirement by ruling that by 1979 FM stations in markets of 25,000 or more could duplicate AM programming only 25 percent of the time. In cases where the AM station must sign off at dusk, the FM station may continue on the air through the evening, usually with programs of news and recorded music.

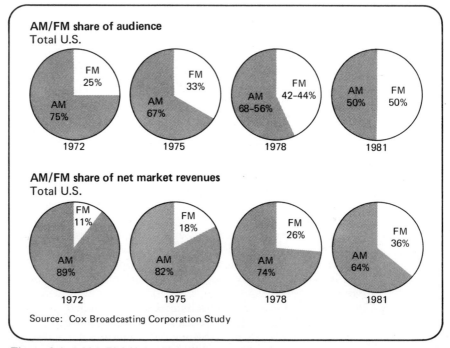

Figure 6-1. AM/FM Share of Audience and Revenue.

FM radio stations owned and operated independently of AM stations are generally run with small staffs and modest budgets. Such stations often provide specialized program services such as background music or certain types of popular and contemporary music. A few stations specialize in broadcasting high-fidelity classical music recordings, which are transmitted with better quality over FM than over AM radio. The FM broadcast band, which ranges from 88 to 108 megahertz, is divided into 100 channels. The lowest 20 channels from 88 to 92 megahertz are reserved for use by non-commercial educational stations.

As noted earlier, FM's share of the radio audience and its share of broadcasting revenues have grown in recent years. A study done by the Cox Broadcasting Corporation documents this growth and predicts that in 1980 FM will share the audience equally with AM (Figure 6–1).

Certain main market FM stations are very successful and outrank most of their competitors in listenership. FM's ability to broadcast in stereo makes it attractive to many people, and many FM stations have broadcast specialized programming that appeals to particular groups.

TELEVISION STATIONS

Television stations are authorized by the FCC to operate in either VHF (channels 2–13) or UHF (14–83). In an overall UHF reallocation in 1966 the FCC generally cleared the upper UHF channels (70–83) of assignments for stations, except for two channels reserved for noncommercial use, to permit consideration of other possible uses for these frequencies. The 12 VHF and the 54 lowest UHF channels now assigned for station use are distributed around the country as follows: 579 VHF and 660 UHF channels for commercial use; 120 VHF and 533 UHF channels reserved for educational use.

In all general business aspects, commercial television stations operate along the patterns established by AM radio stations. The wide difference in programming and production methods between radio and television, however, accounts for the differences to be noted in television station operation. Staff requirements are notably greater in television stations in order to provide cameramen, additional engineers, stagehands and electricians, graphic artists, film technicians, camera directors, floor managers, makeup artists, etc. Space requirements are considerably greater, too, to satisfy television studio needs, construction and storage space for settings, props, and set dressings, film storage, editing, and projection facilities, lighting equipment, cameras, cranes, microphone booms, etc. Some small television stations that draw upon a network affiliation and film features for most of their daily schedule manage to operate with minimal staffs and a single studio for live shows. Large television stations that program aggressively in the local interest have extensive space and personnel requirements and are often housed in several different buildings. In all cases, the establishment and operation of a television station requires many times the capital required for setting up and running a radio station. For example, the capital investment in WTMJ–

TV, Milwaukee, excluding land and the original building, was $630,000, of which $400,000 was spent for operating equipment such as cameras and projectors. An additional $650,000 was required for improvements in transmission facilities. By today's standards, even these costs are small. In an effort to make it financially feasible to operate television stations in small communities, the FCC has authorized the establishment of "satellite" television stations, which are linked with a television station located in another city and simply reproduce the other station's program schedule. In this way, the only operating costs are the rental of the connecting cable, the television transmitter, and a small engineering staff at the transmitter. A satellite station is unable, however, to serve the special needs of the community in which it is established because it has no facilities to originate its own programs. It simply transmits programs furnished by the station to which it is linked.

Group Owned Television Stations

Each of the three national TV networks owns five VHF television stations including New York, Los Angeles, Chicago, and two other major markets. In addition, there are other group-owned television stations of considerable importance: Westinghouse owns VHF stations in Philadelphia, Boston, Pittsburgh, San Francisco, and Baltimore. Metromedia owns VHF stations in New York, Los Angeles, Washington, Kansas City, and Minneapolis, plus a UHF station in Cincinnati. Storer Broadcasting owns VHF stations in Cleveland, Detroit, Milwaukee, Atlanta, and Toledo. Other large group TV station owners include Capital Cities Broadcasting, McGraw-Hill, Scripps-Howard, Corinthian, Taft Broadcasting, Wometco, and Cox Broadcasting.

TELEVISION AND RADIO NETWORKS

Network (or chain) broadcasting is defined in the Communications Act as the "simultaneous broadcasting of an identical program by two or more connected stations." It is accomplished by transmitting the program by cable, usually leased telephone lines in radio and coaxial cables in television, or by microwave relays, from the point of origin to each of the outlet stations of the network. At various points along the network cable, booster stations are operated to maintain the transmission power of the program signal.

Function of Networks

Networks are indispensable to the American system of broadcasting. Networks make it possible for programs to be broadcast throughout the country simultaneously. They are the only way in which live programs can be broadcast nationally, and they are the most efficient way in which recorded and film programs can reach a national audience. Because networks exist, important special events, such as a presidential inauguration, or a major political address, or sporting events, such as bowl games, the Olympics, and the World Series, can be broadcast live throughout the country. The excitement and impact of live television on a national basis, therefore, is possible only through networks.

With programming and production headquarters located in New York and Hollywood, the talent centers of the nation, networks are able to provide major entertainment programs to affiliated stations that could never obtain such programs if they were obliged to depend on local resources only. Because network programs can reach national audiences, they are especially attractive to national advertisers.

Networks, thus, serve both programming and business functions for stations throughout the country, servicing them with programs they cannot produce themselves, and providing income from national advertisers that might otherwise never be spent on television or radio.

National Networks

NBC, CBS, and ABC operate national television and radio networks through stations that regularly carry the programs of a particular network. The Mutual Broadcasting System operates national radio networks on this basis but not a television network. There are also two networks that provide programs for public broadcasting stations: National Public Radio (NPR) and Public Broadcasting Service (PBS). Some organizations calling themselves networks are not actually interconnected but circulate films and tapes.

Each of the permanent networks except MBS owns and operates several radio and television stations (limited by FCC rule to a maximum of seven FM, seven AM, and seven TV), and maintains affiliation agreements with a large number of stations across the country. Under TV affiliation agreements the stations give the networks the right to sell certain hours of the stations' broadcast time at established rates to national advertisers and to provide the programs that the stations will broadcast during those hours subject to "clearance" by the station of the individual program or series. In return, the network agrees to provide these programs without charge to the stations and to give them a portion of the money received from the advertiser (roughly one-third of the gross sum). The network pays all advertising agency commissions and incentive discounts and absorbs any costs involved in the production of programs. In addition, networks produce at their own expense cultural, religious, and public-service programs, which are offered without charge as "sustaining programs" to affiliated stations. Stations supplement their income by the sale of station-break announcements that come at the end, and sometimes in the middle, of network programs.

According to a plan originated by CBS, stations for many years made some of their program hours available to the network on call in return for receiving a certain number of sustaining programs free of charge. Believing that this option over program time gave the networks too much power in broadcasting, the FCC first restricted the number of optioned hours and then prohibited option-time agreements altogether. This action meant that networks must negotiate with their affiliates to carry each program. When a station agrees to carry a program it is said to have "cleared" the program. A program of high popularity like *Happy Days* will be cleared by virtually every station on the network; an informational program may have only half as many clearances as a program of popular entertainment.

Advertisers designate the stations they wish to carry their programs, but the network may require that if the advertiser is to sponsor a particular program, he must use certain stations or a specific number of stations. This requirement is known as a "minimum list." Occasionally a station carries a commercial program without receiving any compensation because it wishes to make a certain network program available to its community. Because the carrying of the program provides a bonus to the advertiser, stations operating under this arrangement are called "bonus" stations.

Leadership in network programming and sales is a matter of vital interest to affiliated stations, not only because the financial compensation received from the network is directly related to network sales, but because top-flight network programming makes it possible for the station to achieve program leadership in its own community and therefore to be able to sell its time periods for announcements preceding and following the network shows. A network affiliation pays dividends to an affiliated station in several important ways: 1. it relieves the station of the cost of producing programs for the nine or more hours each day that the network provides programs; 2. it provides income from national advertisers; and 3. it provides programming leadership that increases the value of the station-break announcements and remaining time periods. For a network it is important to have a good lineup of affiliated stations: a lineup consisting of stations that have good local broadcast coverage and effective local programming, and a lineup large enough to provide effective national coverage.

The networks, themselves, are large corporate enterprises and are highly competitive both among themselves and with other entertainment media for talent and programs. They compete for national advertising money with nonbroadcasting advertising media, such as newspapers and magazines, and with other broadcast sales organizations, such as national spot-sales agencies, which place national advertising on local stations without going through a network. These agencies sell station time during non-network hours for film and tape programs and local shows; they also sell spot announcements that are made between network shows and at various other times.

The National Broadcasting Company. NBC is a wholly owned subsidiary of RCA which is one of the largest manufacturers of electronic equipment in the United States, making transmitters and receivers for all broadcast service. It is also one of the leading producers of phonograph records in the country. It owns and operates AM and FM radio stations in New York, Chicago, Washington, and San Francisco. It operates a nationwide radio network of 232 stations with a broadcast coverage unsurpassed by any of its competitors. NBC also owns VHF television stations in New York, Chicago, Los Angeles, Washington, and Cleveland. At one time it also owned UHF television stations but disposed of them when their operation proved to be unprofitable. Stations in the NBC television network number 212.

CBS, Inc. CBS owns and operates AM and FM radio stations in New York, Chicago, Los Angeles, San Francisco, Philadelphia, Boston, and St. Louis and operates a nationwide radio network of 258 stations. CBS owns VHF television outlets in New York, Chicago, St. Louis, Los Angeles, and Philadelphia. Like NBC, it also gave up its UHF television stations. Its television network numbers 197 stations. CBS is a leading manufacturer of phonograph records, thus competing with RCA in this field, but it discontinued its unprofitable electronics manufacturing division, which manufactured tubes, radios, phonographs, and television sets.

The American Broadcasting Company. ABC started in the broadcasting business in 1943 when RCA was forced to divest itself of the Blue Network. Until 1953, ABC's sole business was broadcasting, but in that year it merged with United Paramount Theatres, one of the largest owners of theaters in the United States. ABC owns AM, FM, and VHF television stations in New York, Detroit, Los Angeles, Chicago, and San Francisco. In addition, it owns an AM and FM stations in Houston and Washington. Up until 1968 ABC operated a single radio network, but in that year it was given permission by the FCC to set up four independent radio networks with services patterned to fit the formats of the stations that became affiliates. The nature of the formats are implied in the names given to these networks: The American Contemporary Radio Network, The American Information Radio Network, The American Entertainment Radio Network, and The American FM Radio Network. With all of these networks in operation, the total number of ABC's radio affiliates is around the 1,000 level, many of these stations that had never carried network programs before. The ABC television network has about 190 primary affiliates and 67 secondary affiliates, many of the latter having primary affiliation with NBC or CBS.

The Mutual Broadcasting System. Mutual operates a radio network of 685 stations, many of which are low-powered. Prior to the introduction of ABC's four networks, Mutual often provided the only radio service available in small towns and areas of sparse population. In addition, the company operates the Mutual Black Network, which provides programs designed to represent the black point of view to 100 affiliates.

Public Broadcasting Networks. The network that distributes programs on a national basis to approximately 250 public television stations is the Public Broadcasting Service. Among the program suppliers are the National Public Affairs Center for Television (NPACT), the Educational Broadcasting Corporation, successor to NET, and a number of the public television stations. Radio programs are fed to noncommercial educational radio stations by National Public Radio (NPR) for immediate or delayed broadcast.

Special Networks. A network that operates in the east, midwest, and south to provide radio programs designed to meet the special needs of black listeners is the National Black Network. It services 78 affiliates. The Hughes Tele-

vision Network and the TVS Television Network do not serve regular affiliates, but contract with stations on a per-program basis to carry coverage of
sports and special events.

Regional Networks

Regional networks are networks created to link stations within certain geographical and marketing areas. Regional networks are attractive to advertisers who market their products in certain sections of the country but not in
others, and therefore would not benefit from the use of the national networks. There are 14 regional television networks that link commercial stations and approximately 112 regional radio networks of commercial stations.
Among the commercial regional networks are:

Alaska Television Network	Lazy K Group
Dakota Giant Network	Lobster Network
All Spanish Network	Mid Atlantic Network
Christian Broadcasting Network	Mountaineer Group

In addition to these commercial regional networks, there are several regional television and radio networks which link public television and public
radio stations.

STATION-NETWORK RELATIONS

Relations between stations and networks are controlled by the Chain Broadcasting Regulations put into effect by the FCC in 1943. After a lengthy investigation of the networks, the Commission concluded that the system of
network broadcasting then in operation was stifling competition and was
contrary to the public interest. In 1938, CBS and NBC alone owned or controlled 23 powerful stations out of the 660 stations then on the air, and more
than 85 percent of the total nighttime wattage in the nation. The FCC
investigated the contractual arrangements between the networks and their
affiliates and concluded that these contracts had "resulted in a grossly ineq-
uitable relation between the networks and their outlet stations to the advantage of the networks at the expense of the outlets."[1] Some of these contracts
forbade affiliated stations to accept programs from any other network and
required the outlet to keep almost all of its time available for the use of the
network. In 1939, Mutual obtained the exclusive right to broadcast the
World Series and offered the program to stations throughout the country, including NBC and CBS affiliates in communities having no other stations.
CBS and NBC immediately invoked the "exclusive affiliation" clauses of
their network affiliation contracts and, as a result, thousands of persons were
unable to hear the broadcasts. The FCC concluded that competition was
being stifled and that outlets were being made the servant of the network
rather than an instrument for serving the public interest.

[1] *Report on Chain Broadcasting* (Washington, 1941), p. 97.

To eliminate these evils, the Commission promulgated the following eight rules, which are in effect today with the amendments indicated:

1. No station-network agreement may be made that prevents the station from broadcasting the programs of any other network.

2. One network affiliate may not prevent another station serving the same listening area (in radio) or the same community (in television) from broadcasting network programs that the first station does not carry; nor may it prevent a station serving a substantially different area or community from broadcasting any of the network's programs. A network affiliate may, however, have "first call" for network programs over other stations in the area or community served by the station.

3. Station-network contracts are limited to two-year periods.

4. A network must give affiliated stations 56 days' notice if it wants to make use of a station's time for network shows, and it may have an option on no more than three hours within each four segments of the broadcast day. As we have noted previously, the FCC later reduced that time to two and a half hours and then eliminated option-time arrangements altogether.

5. Stations must be free to refuse to carry network programs that the station "reasonably believes to be unsatisfactory or unsuitable." With respect to network programs already contracted for, stations must be allowed to reject any program "which, in its opinion, is contrary to the public interest," or to substitute "a program of outstanding local or national importance."

6. Networks may not own more than one station in the same listening area or in any locality where network ownership would substantially restrain competition.

7. Networks may not operate more than one network of stations. (This forced NBC to divest itself of the Blue Network, now ABC. The FCC granted an exception to this rule when it permitted ABC to operate four radio networks and Mutual to operate two.

8. Stations may not enter into contracts with networks that would prevent them from fixing or changing their time rates for nonnetwork shows.

INDEPENDENT TELEVISION AND RADIO STATIONS

Independent television and radio stations operating without any network affiliation are found in cities with more than four radio stations or three television stations. As a rule, stations operate independently only when they are unable to obtain a network affiliation. Independent radio stations have succeeded in making a virtue of necessity, and many are more successful than their network-affiliated competitors. Independent television stations, which must draw all their income from local and national spot advertising and must produce all their own programs, compete with network-affiliated stations under great handicaps. Nevertheless, in markets like Chicago, New York, Los Angeles, St. Louis, and San Francisco, independent television stations have been very profitable.

CABLE TV (CATV)

In 1949 the people of Astoria, Oregon, blocked off by mountains from receiving a television signal directly at their homes, organized a company that built an antenna on a high point and then fed the programs by cable to various homes in the community. Soon after in Lansford, Pennsylvania, a commercial company providing the same type of service started operation. Thus began what is variously referred to as community-antenna television, cable TV, or CATV. The new industry expanded rapidly until in the seventies more than 3000 cable TV systems were providing service to more than 10 million subscribers. It was estimated that 15 percent of the homes in the country received their TV programs by cable.

A number of reasons explain the explosive growth of CATV. 1. A cable could bring TV programs to communities that were denied them either because of natural obstacles or because the population was too small to sustain a station. 2. Communities with limited TV service could expand the range of TV offerings by importing programs through a cable. 3. Even where the number of TV programs is adequate, cable service often improves the quality of reception. 4. Cable companies, in addition to transmitting the programs of a number of TV stations, often originate special services; among them are continuous weather information, minute-by-minute reports of the time, a continuous scan of a news ticker, stock-market reports, cartoon shows for children, and pickups of local sports events or of city council meetings.

The question of who was to regulate the new industry arose early. Where cable companies used microwave relay connections, regulation was clearly the province of the FCC. A number of companies, however, used only cable in transmitting programs. Did the FCC have the authority under the Communications Act to regulate cable-only systems? The Commission decided that it did not and sought specific authority from Congress to regulate CATV. Congress proved to be unresponsive, however, so in 1962 the FCC began a tentative exploration of its powers in the new field. In 1965 and 1966 it issued specific regulations governing CATV operations. Its authority was challenged in the courts, but in 1968 the Supreme Court settled the matter by agreeing unanimously that the 1934 Federal Communications Act, by implication, did give the FCC regulatory power over CATV. With this affirmation of its power, the FCC in 1972 proceeded to issue a comprehensive set of regulations governing the operation of cable systems.

Regulations Governing Cable TV

The development of CATV introduced a number of problems for the regular broadcasting industry and for society as a whole. One concern of the FCC has been to protect existing television stations from undue competition. A single station with a market all to itself, for example, might be overwhelmed if the programs from distant cities were suddenly introduced, and even several stations operating in a single market might experience damaging competition if cable systems were allowed to transmit programs without restraint. One rule designed to protect the local television industry is the requirement that a cable system carry the programs of all local stations. There is also a restriction against the duplication of a program being presented by a station in the listening area.

One of the great fears of the broadcasting industry is that cable TV systems might lure from the regular TV industry programs of high popular appeal by offering higher returns through some form of pay-television. This threat is referred to as siphoning. The FCC has established barriers to siphoning by limiting the freedom under which cable systems may use programs broadcast by TV stations and networks. A cable system, for example, may not present a syndicated program until one year after it has first been broadcast by the regular TV industry and it may not transmit any syndicated program in a community until after the local contract to broadcast that program has expired. Similar restraints restrict the use of movies and other broadcast programs by cable TV systems. A 1977 Court of Appeals decision, however, invalidated the FCC's restriction on the use by cable systems of movies and sports events.

Another concern of the broadcasting industry is the harm that might befall local stations if a cable system imported signals from distant cities to amplify the offerings of the local channels instead of picking them up from nearby cities. This practice is called leapfrogging. The FCC recognizes this concern as a legitimate one and requires that cable systems must generally use the signals of the nearest TV stations to fill out its offerings to cable systems operating in the top 100 markets; however, the FCC does permit the importation of two distant signals. Its purposes in permitting this exception are to widen the program service available in a community, to attract the investment capital needed for the construction of new systems, and, in general, to open the way to the full development of cable's potential.

The CATV regulations indicate that the FCC is concerned not only with the welfare of the broadcasting industry, but also with the welfare of society as a whole. A further reflection of this concern is the regulation that permits or requires cable systems to provide a full range of program services to their clients. There are a number of aspects to this policy. To begin with, cable systems have the potential for providing a 20-to-40-channel service. If the local community does not provide a three-network service, a noncommercial service, an independent station service, and a non-English service, the cable system may bring in signals from outside the community to fill out whatever is missing in the local operation.

At one time the FCC required that cable systems with more than 3500 subscribers must originate regular programs of their own. This obligation was eliminated in 1975 but some production of local programs was still necessary because of another FCC requirement that cable systems make channels available for use by local persons and institutions. One channel, called a public-access channel, must be available to people who wish to use it on a first-come, nondiscriminatory basis. There must also be channels for use by local educational officials and by local government officials. Other channels may be leased for use to local people.

A regulation suggesting the potentialities for future educational and commercial uses of cable TV systems requires the incorporation of a capacity for some kind of return communication on a channel on at least a nonvoice basis. To prevent the domination of communication facilities by one company, the FCC has ruled that the same company may not own TV broadcasting facilities and a cable system in the same community.

One problem outside the regulatory power of the FCC is the right of a cable TV system to retransmit copyrighted material without the payment of royalties. The Supreme Court ruled that under the Copyright Law passed in 1909, cable TV systems were not obligated to pay royalties for the use of copyrighted material. The Congress revised that law in 1976, however, and cable systems must now make royalty payments for the carriage of distant nonnetwork programs.

Problems Presented by Cable TV

The introduction of CATV raised questions that are exceedingly complex and controversial. The answers to these questions are equally complex. The FCC in 1972 found it necessary to publish a document 500 pages long to list and describe its CATV regulations. As an example of the complexity, it propounded rules that vary somewhat depending on whether the cable system is located in one of the 50 largest markets, one of the second 50 largest markets, in a small community, or in an area with no broadcast TV service at all. One difficulty in establishing rules is that the interests of the broadcasting industry, the cable industry, and the public are sometimes in conflict. It is impossible for the FCC to establish regulations that will satisfy all of these interests. There are also continuing questions about the right of the FCC to regulate the cable TV industry. Bills placed before Congress would limit the Commission's authority in the CATV area and would establish regulations that are different from those promulgated by the FCC. But whoever makes the rules, the agitation for change will undoubtedly continue. In considering these demands, the FCC and the Congress face a difficult challenge in establishing a system that minimizes the damage to any sector and provides service that is in the best interests of the public.

No matter what answers may be found to the many questions that surround CATV, it is inevitable that its development will have a profound effect on the broadcasting industry. Already CATV has expanded the range of service and improved the quality of reception for millions of viewers. Enthusiasts foresee the day when CATV will entirely supplant the present system of TV broadcasting, making the spectrum space now reserved for this purpose available for other purposes. Multiple-channel systems are being developed; 20- to 40-channel systems are now in operation, and the number of available channels in one system may rise to 100. With this number of channels the services provided by CATV can extend far beyond those now encompassed by conventional television programs. Some even see the day when CATV will replace newspapers and magazines. Instead of being delivered by the postman or a newsboy, they would roll out from a facsimile set operated by a signal sent over a CATV system. Cable connections also provide the facilities through which pay-TV systems are set up and operated, and a number of companies now have cable subscribers who support the system through the payment of monthly fees.

In 1977 Warner Communications launched an extensive experiment in Columbus, Ohio testing a special system of pay cable utilizing multi-channels and two-way transmissions between the cable headquarters and home subscribers, and offering a wide variety of new services and programs. If this experiment proves economically successful, it is likely that it will set the pattern for future developments in pay-cable TV.

SUMMARY

Networks, stations, and CATV constitute the second pillar of American broadcasting. Stations vary in modes of operation depending upon their power, location, and network affiliation, if any. Networks make it possible to broadcast live programs simultaneously throughout the country; they make national markets available to advertisers and offer stations major entertainment and public service programs. Station-network relations are carefully regulated by the FCC in order to preserve competition. The development of CATV has brought new problems to broadcasters and to the government. It has potentialities for bringing about revolutionary changes in the nature of the industry.

Questions for Discussion

1. What role do networks play in American broadcasting? What would radio and television be like without networks?
2. What is the difference between clear, regional, and local channel AM stations? Is there any special significance to be found in this difference?
3. Compare the major radio and television networks in terms of size, programming, mode of operation, and influence.
4. What are the advantages of a network affiliation?
5. How are network-station relations governed? For what purpose?
6. Distinguish among a network-affiliated station, an independent, and an owned-and-operated station.
7. In what way was the FCC instrumental in the formation of ABC?
8. What is the significance of station call letters?
9. Do you believe that option-time agreements should have been outlawed by the FCC?
10. In what way are CATV systems and television stations in competition, and in what way do they support each other?
11. Do you believe that CATV companies should pay copyright fees for the programs they carry?
12. How do you think CATV will eventually affect the television industry?
13. What are the conflicting interests of television stations and cable television, and how are public interests involved?

Every system of broadcasting requires a sound means of financial support to keep it going. Unless a station has ample funds to maintain a competent staff and facilities and to hire the best talent, its programming will suffer. Various ways have been devised throughout the world to support broadcasting. These include: 1. annual taxes on receivers, similar to our annual state taxes on automobiles; 2. governmental appropriations; 3. endowments, similar to university endowments; 4. subscription broadcasting in which the public pays for individual programs; and 5. the sale of broadcast time to advertisers.

American television and radio are supported predominantly by income from advertising. Indeed, advertising revenue from the sale of time and programs is the only source of income for all commercial broadcasting; the advertisers, therefore, support not only their own programs, but indirectly all sustaining programs, too. The United States, however, also makes use of other methods of financial support. Some stations owned by states, municipalities, and state universities receive their entire support from state or city appropriations. Some stations licensed to private universities are supported by the university's endowed funds; others combine endowed income with advertising support, such as Cornell University's WHCU, which was built originally with endowed funds and since has supported itself by accepting advertising.

Constituting the complete support of almost all television and radio stations, advertising is a fundamental element in our broadcasting scheme. This being the case, let us proceed to three questions: 1. What do advertisers expect from television and radio? 2. How are television and radio advertising managed? 3. What effect does the advertising method of financial support have on television and radio programming?

ADVERTISING AND THE BROADCASTING MEDIA

In evaluating television and radio along with other media of communication, such as newspapers, magazines, billboards, skywriting, weekly supplements, match covers, etc., the advertiser is concerned with the following criteria: 1. circulation; 2. effectiveness of the medium to sell his product; and 3. cost.

Circulation

When advertisers buy time on television or radio, they do so because they are impressed with the wide circulation that television and radio can give to their advertising message. A commercial message delivered on a popular network evening television program usually reaches 20 to 30 million people. Only through magazines such as *Time, Newsweek,* or *Reader's Digest,* or through the purchase of space in many newspapers throughout the country, can the advertiser otherwise hope to reach an audience approaching this size. In local advertising, the advertiser compares the circulation offered by the local television and radio stations with that offered by local newspapers.

Circulation (or "reach" in advertising parlance) relates to the number of people who are exposed to the advertiser's message. In television and radio, circulation is influenced by the potential coverage offered by the station by virtue of its transmitting power, the general programming popularity of the station, the popularity of the program on which the advertising message is presented, the popularity of adjacent programs, and the attractiveness of the advertising message itself. In printed media, circulation is influenced by the number of copies sold, the position of the advertisement within the publication and the attractiveness of the advertisement in terms of its ability to command reader attention.

It is therefore to be expected that advertisers who buy television and radio time will generally seek to have commercial messages appear on programs that reach the largest audience.

Effectiveness

Each advertising medium has its own special characteristics of communication that make advertising in it more or less effective. Some advertising media are better for certain types of advertising than other media. In printed media, for example, four-color advertisements are generally considered more effective in promoting sales than advertisements in black-and-white. Department stores, which desire to list dozens of different items for sale, usually turn to newspapers for this purpose. Brand-name identification is often sought through repeated radio announcements. No advertising medium, however, can show a product to potential buyers as completely or effectively as television. Many advertisers have found that television provides them with an opportunity to demonstrate their product and deliver a sales message to millions of people at the same time instead of to just a few people over the counter.

Moreover, the association of the advertising message with a popular program can give the advertiser additional values: goodwill engendered by the program itself; identification with the program and the program talent that often is used for point-of-sale merchandising purposes; direct sales appeals by the stars; special attention to the advertiser's message through lead-ins designed to invite attention; and strategic placement of the messages.

The development of sophisticated audience research techniques has provided advertisers with information about prospective buyers that helps to guide the selection of programs in which commercials are to be placed. This is known as demographic information. Advertisers are interested, for example, in the age of the people in their audiences. Women ranging in age from 18 to 49 are considered to be the best prospects for buying most of the products advertised on television. Other information of interest to advertisers is the educational level and the occupations of audience members. Advertisers can materially increase the effectiveness of their messages by taking demographic information into account in planning and placing their commercials.

Cost

In evaluating the cost of advertising in relation to its effectiveness, advertisers are often forced to work with variable factors that make it very difficult to arrive at a scientific judgment. Ideally, the advertiser desires to know which method of advertising produces the greatest number of sales of his products at the smallest cost. Because he usually has several different advertising campaigns proceeding simultaneously and because the effectiveness of his own commercial message is not a controlled factor when different media are compared, the advertiser generally contents himself with taking the simple circulation figures, dividing them by a thousand, and dividing that figure into the cost of buying the broadcast time and the program to arrive at a figure representing how much it costs to reach 1000 homes. Thus, a half-hour evening television program that reaches 10 million homes and costs $200,000 for time and program would cost about $20 for each 1000 homes. If the advertiser were entitled to six 30-second commercial messages, the cost per 1000 homes (CPM) per 30-second commercial would be stated as $3.33.

This yardstick is widely used in advertising; in comparing television with other advertising media, it fails to take into account television's special selling effectiveness, which often outweighs simple circulation in influencing the number of purchases made as a result of a commercial message.

RATE CARDS

Commercial television and radio stations and networks generally publish rate cards. These cards state in tabular form the cost of broadcast time over the stations or networks. Rates are based upon historical time-period classifications such as "Class A" hours, which applied to 6:00 to 11:00 P.M., or "Class C" hours, which applied to post 11:00 P.M. nightly and to weekend daytime.

CBS and NBC sell time by listing the applicable Gross Base Hour (or A hour) rate and applying varying percentages to each half-hour sold, ranging from 11 percent to 77 percent per half-hour, depending upon the time of day or night purchased. ABC has fixed gross package prices for each separate half-hour.

The present Gross Base Hour value of the full NBC Television Network of 212 stations is something in excess of $165,000, and an advertister might pay as little as 28 percent or as much as 154 percent of the Base Hour rate for an hour of time on that network. In addition to time costs, advertisers pay production costs for programs and commercials as well as network cable or "integration" charges.

In general, however, most network selling is now done in packages of 30-commercial participations in various shows, with the price of each such commercial position geared to the anticipated (or achieved) circulation (audience size as determined by ratings). Thus, a prime time network advertiser may, through its agency, negotiate for a large dollar volume purchase that would involve placing its 30-second commercials in half a dozen different shows each week.

Local television stations usually make finer distinctions than networks among the varying periods of the day in terms of the audience that can be expected to tune in during a given period. Many stations distinguish six different periods, designating them as "AAA," "AA," "A," "B," "C," and "D." A station lists rates for program periods and for announcement periods. Thus, for a Class "AAA" period a New York City television station that charges $10,700 for an hour may charge $3700 for a 20-second and $2100 for a 10-second station-break announcement, exclusive of production costs. Prime time, the period when the largest audiences are tuned in, is different in radio from what it is in television. People watch television more in the evening than at any other time, whereas they listen to radio more in the morning and afternoon, particularly when they are driving to and from work. These are the periods for which radio charges its prime rates if it differentiates among time periods at all; a number of stations charge uniform rates throughout the day and night.

Rate cards also contain the necessary facts concerning a station's power, frequency, ownership, network affiliation if any, sales representatives, and other pertinent information. *Standard Rate and Data Service,* a regular publication, summarizes the rate cards of all stations and is used by advertisers and agencies in buying television and radio time.

ADVERTISING AGENCIES

The formulation and management of advertising campaigns is distinctively the function of advertising agencies. These agencies are hired by advertisers to advise them on promotional matters and to plan and execute advertising campaigns. The size of an advertising agency depends upon the number and size of accounts it handles. The agency receives its income from the advertising media in which it places its client's advertising. Television and radio stations pay an advertising agency 15 percent of the gross amount of the time

purchase the agency makes in behalf of its client. The agency is also generally entitled to add 15 percent for itself to all bills submitted to its client for
program and production costs. Table 7–1 lists the top 30 agencies most active in radio and TV in 1976, together with their billings.

Agency Organization

Large advertising agencies are equipped to handle all types of advertising in
all the mass communication media. To handle this work, an agency employs
a staff of skilled personnel, among whom are found the following:

1. Account executives, who supervise the activities of major advertising accounts
   and maintain liaison between the agency and the client's advertising manager.
   The account executive is responsible for the general supervision of all advertising
   placed by his agency in behalf of his client.
2. Media specialists, including time and space buyers, who are closely acquainted
   with the availabilities and costs of different advertising media. Specialized media
   services have now come into being that are able to supply spot buying services to
   advertisers and to agencies that do not want the overhead of a media department.
3. Television program buyers, who deal with networks and other program suppliers
   and recommend programs for sponsorship by the agency's clients, and program
   supervisors who read scripts prior to production and seek to protect the interest of
   the agency's clients who sponsor the program. With the increase in participation
   advertising in network television and the decline in program sponsorship by advertisers, this department has been dropped or reduced in size at many agencies.
4. Television and radio production specialists, who prepare and produce television
   and radio commercials and may also participate in the production of major television and radio shows owned by the agency, although the production of shows
   by agencies is now rare.
5. Copy writers, who write the advertisements seen in newspapers and magazines
   and the commercials seen on television or heard on the radio.
6. Art directors, who conceive of layouts for newspaper advertisements and design
   television commercials.
7. Marketing research experts, who evaluate the effectiveness of advertising campaigns and assist in the choice of advertising appeals.

Agency Operation

The agency starts with the client's sales problem and the budget assigned to
advertising. After deciding that television or radio advertising can help to
solve the client's sales problem, the agency recommends, on the basis of an
allocation of the budget, the best use to be made of these media, including
the following considerations:

1. Whether the money should be spent on a network or spot basis, or a combination
   of both;
2. Whether the emphasis should be placed on evening hours or daytime;
3. Whether the client should sponsor a program availability of one of the networks

or should instead develop its own program or buy one from an independent packager and seek air time on one of the networks or obtain station clearance on a syndicated basis.

After buying time and program, the agency must then undertake to supervise the client's interest in the program and to prepare and produce the commercials. To produce television film commercials the agency usually contracts with a specialized film company. Taped commercials are usually produced in recording studios for radio and in a production facility for television.

Table 7–1. Top 30 Advertising Agencies Most Active in TV-Radio
(all figures are in millions)

	Combined Broadcast Billings	Total TV	Total Radio
1. J. Walter Thompson	$347.1	$321.1	$26.0
2. Leo Burnett	302.0	288.0	14.0
3. Young & Rubicam	278.5	248.2	30.3
4. BBDO	247.0	227.0	20.0
5. Grey Advertising	199.3	190.8	8.5
6. Ogilvy & Mather	193.0	180.0	13.0
7. Ted Bates & Co.	187.2	174.3	12.9
8. Benton & Bowles	185.5	178.6	6.9
9. McCann-Erickson	168.0	145.0	23.0
10. Dancer—Fitzgerald—Sample	166.0	156.3	9.7
11. Foote, Cone & Belding	143.8	129.5	14.3
12. D'Arcy-MacManus & Masius	138.0	116.0	22.0
13. Doyle Dane Bernbach	122.0	110.0	12.0
14. Wm. Esty	114.0	102.0	12.0
15. SSC&B	101.0	93.5	7.5
16. Wells, Rich, Greene	99.1	85.4	13.7
17. Needham, Harper & Steers	98.6	92.5	6.1
18. Compton	89.0	87.2	1.8
19. Kenyon & Eckhardt	87.9	80.3	7.6
20. Cunningham & Walsh	85.2	81.0	4.2
21. Campbell-Ewald	79.8	71.3	8.5
22. Gardner Advertising	79.6	74.1	5.5
23. N. W. Ayer	59.0	51.5	7.5
24. Marschalk	53.4	50.0	3.4
25. Campbell Mithun	50.1	40.6	9.5
26. Ketchum, MacLeod & Grove	45.5	38.4	7.1
27. Bozell & Jacobs	45.0	39.0	6.0
28. Norman, Craig & Kummel	41.8	38.7	3.1
29. McCattrey & McCall	37.0	34.5	2.5
30. Tracy-Locke	36.9	34.4	2.5

SOURCE: *Broadcasting*, December 6, 1976, p. 44.

NETWORK ADVERTISING

Advertisers on national television and radio networks in 1976 spent well over three billion dollars for network time and for talent, program, and commercial production costs. Five major product groups were the major advertisers on both network radio and television: food and food products, toiletries and toilet goods; soaps, cleansers, and polishes; automobiles, auto equipment, and accessories; and household equipment and supplies. Table 7–2 shows the leading television network advertisers, with their total expenditures for network time, exclusive of program costs.

THE PARTICIPATING CONCEPT

The great expense of single network sponsorship of weekly television shows as well as the lack of flexibility that single sponsorship provides have contributed to the popularity of the participating concept—the purchase of time for the insertion of commercial messages in network shows. The network supplies the program and the client simply pays for the right to insert his commercial. These participating commercials used to be one minute in length, but in 1971 the three national networks began to sell in 30-second units to make up for the loss in tobacco advertising, which was banned by law. Thirty-second commercials are now used 85 percent of the time. The total amount of time devoted to advertising in prime-time network programs has not increased, but the use of shorter commercials permits more products to be advertised in a given advertising period. An advantage of the participating plan is that advertisers are not required to make long-term commitments, but may buy only one or two participations as they desire. An important change brought about by the participating plan is that it has enabled many more advertisers to use network television. The sponsorship of an entire program was beyond the means of many small companies, but these same companies, some with advertising budgets as low as $250,000, can afford to buy time for network commercials on a participating basis.

NATIONAL SPOT ADVERTISING

National spot advertising, where the advertiser purchases time over selected stations for spot announcements or for complete programs, has certain advantages and disadvantages when compared to network advertising. National spot offers the national advertiser the chance to buy time on the best station in every market he wants to reach. He cannot do this in network broadcasting, since no one network has all the best stations. He can choose the station according to the particular audience it has attracted by its programming emphases. Moreover, spot broadcasting enables him to purchase any length of time from brief announcements to a three-hour coverage of a sporting event. The advertiser may buy time on one station or 500 stations, using only those that suit his advertising needs, free from the requirements to buy time on a basic or supplementary network. The time differentials in-

Table 7-2. Top 40 TV Advertisers

	Total TV	Spot TV	Network TV
1. Procter & Gamble	$261,198,500	$99,969,100	$161,329,400
2. General Foods	136,568,100	52,127,600	84,400,500
3. American Home Products	115,239,000	33,585,000	81,654,000
4. Bristol-Myers	110,090,300	20,377,900	89,712,400
5. Lever Brothers	80,439,800	32,791,400	47,648,400
6. Sears, Roebuck & Co.	73,761,500	22,302,400	51,459,100
7. General Motors	68,959,300	14,169,700	54,789,600
8. Colgate-Palmolive	67,667,700	21,574,300	46,093,400
9. Ford Motor	65,994,800	20,371,600	45,623,200
10. Warner-Lambert	62,309,500	15,032,000	47,277,500
11. Nabisco	61,533,300	12,572,300	48,961,000
12. Gillette	61,253,500	14,582,200	46,671,300
13. Sterling Drug	57,586,400	10,713,000	46,873,400
14. McDonalds	57,544,000	34,498,600	23,045,400
15. General Mills	56,948,100	26,755,500	30,192,600
16. Ralston Purina	47,844,000	11,649,800	36,194,200
17. Hublein	45,880,600	23,545,800	22,334,800
18. Chrysler	45,469,300	10,537,400	34,931,900
19. American Tel & Tel	43,365,000	21,334,000	22,031,000
20. Kellogg	43,032,200	12,920,200	30,112,000
21. Pepsi Cola	41,008,500	21,438,100	19,570,000
22. Coca-Cola	40,138,400	24,824,400	15,314,000
23. Kraftco	38,234,700	17,568,300	20,666,400
24. Nestle Co.	35,807,700	13,674,400	22,133,300
25. Miles Laboratories	35,074,100	10,802,700	24,271,400
26. Schering-Plough	33,991,300	9,212,800	24,778,500
27. Pillsbury	31,918,700	9,661,100	22,257,600
28. Johnson & Johnson	31,180,800	6,383,100	24,797,700
29. S. C. Johnson & Son	30,925,100	4,636,700	26,288,400
30. Norton Simon	29,435,900	11,929,600	17,506,300
31. Morton-Norwich Products	29,243,900	7,142,300	22,101,600
32. Internat'l Tel & Tel	26,614,000	19,349,500	7,264,500
33. Carnation Co.	25,975,700	7,677,100	18,298,600
34. William Wrigley Jr.	25,204,300	23,240,300	1,784,000
35. Bordon	25,029,900	12,579,300	12,450,600
36. Campbell Soup	24,918,700	10,417,200	14,501,500
37. Esmark	24,848,100	4,860,000	19,988,100
38. Mobil Oil	24,804,500	19,730,000	5,074,500
39. Clorox	23,473,800	3,367,200	20,106,600
40. CPC International	23,047,900	14,626,600	8,421,300

SOURCE: *Broadcasting*, May 24, 1976, p. 43.

volved in network broadcasting are also eliminated in spot broadcasting. Furthermore, spot broadcasting is very flexible in time availability, and an advertiser suddenly faced with the immediate need to unload merchandise can have his message on the air in spot broadcasting soon after he has made up his mind to buy time.

There are disadvantages to national spot broadcasting that becloud the picture painted above. The network shows occupy the best broadcast hours. The national spot advertiser is usually obliged to rely on programs that may lack the prestige, publicity, and entertainment value of network shows. Instead of completing negotiations with a single network representative, spot broadcasting involves making arrangements with each station. Program and/or commercial material must be prepared and sent to each outlet.

Generally speaking, advertisers who can afford network advertising attempt first to obtain a good network time period and a popular show. They may also desire to supplement their network advertising with national spot campaigns. Procter & Gamble, for example, the nation's biggest television advertiser, splits its TV budget on a regular basis between network and spot advertising. The McDonald Company spends more on national spot advertising than it does on network advertising. Advertisers who are unable to obtain a good network time period may have no alternative but to undertake a national spot campaign if they desire national exposure. National spot is also used by advertisers to obtain additional advertising in major markets where sales are greatest and where competition with local brands is keenest.

BARTER PLANS

Sometimes an advertiser pays for the production of a program series and then offers it to a network or station free of charge with the understanding that the advertiser may present commercial messages without any payment for them during half of the periods allotted for advertising on the program. The network or station makes the rest of the advertising periods available to other advertisers whose products do not compete with those of the advertiser providing the program. The sale of this time gives the network or station its profit. This system is known as the barter plan.

LOCAL ADVERTISERS

Radio time sales to local advertisers now account for a large portion of all radio advertising. Local television advertising is sought by all stations to supplement their income from network advertisers and to strengthen their relations with the local community.

Local advertisers include all types of local retailers ranging from department stores to gasoline stations. Arrangements for local advertising are usually made by the station's salesmen and the local merchant who is persuaded to buy broadcast advertising. Some retailers, in cooperation with the station, may develop their own music, news, or other type of program which, when broadcast regularly, favorably associates the merchant with the program in the listener's mind. Most local advertising, however, consists of direct sales messages describing products and giving details of prices. This is the very kind of advertising feared by early leaders in radio. But it is the way in which many stations, particularly the independent stations, which have difficulty attracting national advertising, earn their income.

PROBLEMS POSED BY ADVERTISING

Advertising support of broadcasting poses a number of problems for a system of television and radio in which licensees are pledged by law to serve the "public convenience, interest, or necessity" and where broadcasting the best entertainment, informational and cultural programs available is generally considered to be in the public interest.

Advertising Excesses

One of the most common public criticisms of American broadcasting relates to advertising excesses. The Television Code of the National Association of Broadcasters contains rules regarding the amount of time that can be devoted to nonprogram material, most of which is advertising, and the number of times that programs can be interrupted for the insertion of commercials. In prime time, for example, nonprogram material may not exceed nine minutes 30 seconds in any 60-minute period, and program interruptions may not exceed two on any 30-minute program or four in any 60-minute program. No more than four commercial announcements may be scheduled consecutively in any program period, unless the sponsor wishes to schedule more to reduce the number of interruptions, and no more than three commercials may follow one another at station-break periods. Restraints such as these, which have been gradually loosened through the years, do exert some control over advertising excesses, but a person listening to a station that follows these rules may still feel that programs are being interrupted a great many times for the presentation of advertising. Not all broadcasters agree to observe even these limitations. Until 1976 members of the National Association of Broadcasters were not required to operate in conformity with the NAB Code; in that year all stations operating in the top 100 markets were required to observe the code as a condition of membership. That policy is being reconsidered, particularly since a court enjoined the NAB from enforcing the Family Viewing provision in the code. Stations not belonging to the NAB have no obligation to follow code requirements.

The agitation about advertising excesses includes more than a concern for the amount of time spent in presenting commercials, however. There is also the belief in some circles that a few broadcasters have overstepped the bounds in presenting commercials for products that, because of their personal nature, should not be advertised at all on television and radio. A corollary to this problem is the use of techniques that offend good taste in advertising products that might otherwise be considered acceptable.

The use of claims or statements that are untrue or misleading constitutes another advertising problem. In combating this evil, the Federal

Trade Commission plays a significant role. The FTC found, for example, that a TV commercial purporting to show that Listerine was effective in combating the common cold was deceptive and banned the commercial from the air. The manufacturers of the product announced their intention to contest the ban. Claims that Geritol could relieve a tired feeling were also described as deceptive. Where the FTC has found commercials to be clearly misleading, it has sometimes required advertisers to buy comparable time to broadcast corrective informational announcements. As a service to broadcasters, the FTC provides stations and networks with a regular publication called *Advertising Alert,* which contains information about FTC actions or proceedings in progress. The broadcaster can take this information into account in deciding whether to accept advertising for products whose claims or qualities have been brought into question.

Some people wonder whether any advertising at all is appropriate on programs aimed at children. A Boston-based group of mothers known as Action for Children's Television (ACT) filed a petition with the FCC requesting that television stations be required to present at least 14 hours of programming for children each week with no commercials whatsoever. The FCC did not accept this recommendation, but ACT's campaign and the activities of similar groups did bring about a reduction in the number of commercials in network programs for children. The networks also introduced stricter controls on what can be advertised on children's programs, and they softened the selling approaches.

Control of Programs

Another perennial problem in American broadcasting is to decide who is to control the content of programs, the advertiser or the broadcaster. In the period of radio's dominance, most network programs were produced by a department of the advertising agency that represented the client, a situation that permitted maximum control by the advertiser over what was to be presented. When television moved to the center of the stage, networks made valiant efforts to recapture control of programming, and a comparison of the TV situation with what had existed in radio suggests that, to a large extent, they succeeded. Another factor in diluting advertising control over program content was the replacement of the sponsor system with the participation system. When one advertiser sponsored an entire program, that advertiser held a powerful veto over what could be presented. When a great many advertisers buy time for their messages in a single program, one advertiser has little or no power to control specific program content.

Though advertising control of programs has diminished, it has not vanished. Control is exerted indirectly through the willingness or unwillingness of advertisers to buy time. Documentary programs on controversial subjects have difficulty attracting advertisers because advertisers are afraid that they will offend potential buyers of their products. Advertisers may refuse to buy time in dramatic programs involving potentially offensive material for the same reason. Advertisers are also unwilling to pay for time in programs that may be considered wholesome and of high quality if they are afraid that such programs will not attract enough viewers to justify the cost of the commercial time. That is another reason why documentary programs have difficulty attracting advertisers.

At the heart of the problem of advertiser control over programs lies an important question. Is the advertiser's interest in reaching an audience always compatible with the most effective overall program service? If the airwaves are used only by advertisers seeking the largest possible audience, quality programs of necessarily less appeal will find no place on the air. On the other hand, a network may fail in its commercial responsibility if it permits an advertiser to put on a program with limited appeal simply because the advertiser likes that type of program or because it is an inexpensive program that manages, when combined with effective merchandising, to satisfy the advertiser's needs. The responsibility of stations and networks extends to their entire program schedules; they may not delegate to the advertiser or to the advertising agency final say as to what is acceptable on the airwaves. It is the obligation of the broadcaster to work in the interest of both the advertiser and the public.

To a certain extent, the role of the advertiser in deciding whether a program gets on the air or remains on the air cannot be altered. Many seemingly good program series have waited years before getting on the air because they could not attract advertisers willing to finance the broadcast. On the other hand, some good programs have been withdrawn from the air because advertisers, for a variety of reasons related to business needs, withdrew financial support and no other advertisers came forward to replace them.

SUMMARY

Advertising constitutes the sole financial support of most American broadcasting. Television and radio offer the advertiser wide circulation and effectiveness at relatively low cost. Advertising agencies, which buy air time for advertisers and sometimes produce their own programs, play a great role in television and radio. Network, national spot, and local advertising are the main ways in which air time is purchased by advertisers. Among the problems posed by advertising support are advertising excesses and the question of control over programs.

Questions For Discussion

1. What are the various ways in which broadcasting is supported financially throughout the world?
2. What are the main advantages of television and radio as advertising media? How do these advantages compare with those of other media, such as newspapers, magazines, billboards, match covers, etc?
3. What constructive functions do advertising agencies serve? How necessary are they for advertising purposes?
4. What role do the large national advertisers play in television and radio?

5. What are the differences between network advertising and national spot advertising? What functions does each serve?

6. What are some of the problems posed by advertising in television and radio? How can these problems be solved?

7. Do you think that advertising agencies or networks should control the actual production of programs?

8. Do you believe that the sales impact of a program is always related to the circulation it achieves?

9. What is the relationship of cost-per-thousand to the audience rating of a program and the cost of production?

10. What do you think should be done with respect to advertising on television directed at children?

11. Should the advertisers' major interest in reaching audiences 18–49 in age mean that television may rightfully ignore older viewers in designing program schedules?

The effectiveness of television and radio depends ultimately on the willingness of the public to listen to or to view what is broadcast. No broadcasting system, however well intentioned, can survive without public acceptance of the programs it offers. In American broadcasting, where the federal government formulates public policy, stations and networks do most of the programming, and advertising provides the financial wherewithal, the audience is the *raison d'être* of the entire enterprise.

Listeners and viewers express judgments by tuning in and out of programs. Since these acts of judgment take place privately in millions of homes each day, it is impossible to determine with absolute certainty the overall attitude of the audience to a particular program. There is no formal expression of opinion as in political elections. There are no box-office or circulation figures, as with magazines and theaters. Eager to know what the public reaction to any program will be, but handicapped by these limitations, program planners and advertisers have been forced to rely on *a priori* speculations and on available audience research methods.

In *a priori* judgments, program planners, like producers of Broadway shows, venture a guess as to what the public will like on the basis of past experience. They may try to confirm their hunches by pretesting programs on small panels of representative or expert people. The numerous flops on Broadway and on the air testify to the limitations of the *a priori* approach, but the great successes prove that there are also acute and sensitive minds in show business who possess a keen sense of audience tastes. *A priori* judgments are usually related to the best available evidence of audience attitude, but it is common knowledge that the American public frequently acts unpredictably in ways contrary to the most expert forecasts of pollsters.

More scientific in approach are the audience research methods of estimating the size of the audience for particular programs, determining the composition of the audience, and describing general listening or viewing habits. Television and radio audience research, while definitely not as reliable as box-office tallies, constitutes the only scientific means by which we may, with some degree of accuracy, form judgments as to the extent of viewing or listening to any program.

Several caution signs should be erected before we proceed further in this discussion of the role of the public in American broadcasting and the ways devised to ferret out the public's judgments. For one thing, the public does not exercise its judgment independently: television and radio condition the public and establish the scale of values, on the basis of which the public must make its judgments. Furthermore, the so-called *public* is actually made up of many diverse publics, brought together at different times out of common interest. Each such broadcast audience is oriented in terms of the choices offered it now and in the past, as well as in terms of its attitude toward television and radio as a whole. There is evidence, for example, that in some areas where very few TV stations can be seen without "snow," viewers relate their viewing habits not to program quality, but to the comparative strength of the TV signals. Given a choice of three adventure dramas at the same time, the audience's judgments can relate only to the comparative merits of the three adventure dramas, or to adventure dramas as a group, but it cannot indicate preference for other types of programs. A lover of classical music will very likely be pleased if a local station programs good music half an hour daily if it has never done so before, but he will react differently if the half-hour represents a reduction from a previously greater offering of good music.

AUDIENCE RESEARCH

Fan-mail

From the very start of broadcasting, some effort has been made to determine how many people listen to any one program. In amateur shortwave broadcasting, the radio operator often asks people who receive his signal to let him know by sending him a postcard. In the twenties the same request was commonly made over long-distance commercial stations. A letter received from a listener in Alaska would always stir some excitement in a New York station. But such responses proved only that the station's signal could be heard at a certain place at a certain time. It did not provide any information on the size and distribution of the total audience. To get this information, stations at first relied on the spontaneous "fan-mail" they received; listeners who were pleased or excited about a particular program might sit down and write the station a letter to that effect. This was much more common while radio retained the element of novelty. But such fan-mail often proved very misleading. Upon study many of these letters turned out to be the work of the more vociferous members of the audience whom the psychologists call the "lunatic fringe" of the public. There was no way of knowing how representative the letters were of the size or character of the entire audience, so the results had to be used cautiously.

Stations then sought to increase the volume and broaden the makeup of fan-mail by offering inducements to every listener who would send in a letter or a card. To determine the popularity of one program, a free offer of flower seeds might be announced. The requests for the free offer would be tallied and tabulated geographically, and would serve as a fairly crude index of program popularity. The ratio between letter writers and the whole listening audience was still not known, but it was possible with this mail to compare different programs in terms of public reaction and to get an idea of the distribution of the radio audience. If the total number of letters received from the county in which a station was located was assigned the absolute figure 100, it was possible to compute the relative response from the neighboring counties, and estimate the general layout of the audience. Thus, where a neighboring county to the north sent in 60 percent as many letters as the home county, its relative importance as a listening area was indicated by the fact that the county to the south had sent in only 40 percent as many. This type of audience analysis is the least expensive and is still widely used by many stations.

Field-Strength Surveys

A scientific means of establishing the coverage area of a station is the field-strength survey. In making this measurement, engineers take an instrument into the field to measure the strength of the transmitted signal. The area in which this signal is heard with the greatest strength is considered to be the primary area of the station. Where the strength falls below a certain minimum, the listening area is considered to be secondary in nature. Beyond this are the fringe areas where the station signal is heard weakly or erratically. The FCC requires all stations to make field-strength surveys and plot its listening contours. This information is studied to determine coverage patterns throughout the nation and may suggest changes in channel allocations or operational conditions to prevent interference. It should be noted that the coverage patterns established by a field-strength survey indicate only where the station may be heard or received; they do not necessarily show that anyone is actually tuning in the station.

Sampling

The limitations and crudities of the mail-response method of audience analysis created a need for more refined techniques of research. Under the stimulus of new discoveries in the field of social psychology, progress in general public opinion research accelerated, and it soon became apparent that the technique of sampling opinion might be adapted to broadcast audience studies. The sampling technique is a common technique all of us use in our daily lives: we need taste only a spoonful of soup in order to know whether the bowlful is too hot or too salty. The assumption, of course, is that the spoonful is just like the rest of the soup in the bowl—and almost always it is the same. In public opinion research, the technique involves determining the attitudes of a limited number of people who constitute a sample of the larger public, and then projecting the results of the sample to the whole group. Measuring public opinion is more difficult than tasting soup, however. Constructing a sample of population that will accurately represent all the economic, social, and cultural strains, as well as sex and age distributions and family backgrounds of the whole group, is a complicated matter. Commonly used are "probability" or random samples of the population, in which every person theoretically has an equal chance of being selected for the sample. The technique of getting responses by asking questions also involves the possibility of error: questions may not be worded properly, interviewers may be biased, some people may answer questions dishonestly, and the results may be susceptible to various interpretations. Still other problems are those of definition: How long must one tune in to a program to qualify as a listener or viewer? Can the act of tuning in to a station be equated with listening to or viewing that station? How do you determine how many people are watching a single television set? Should out-of-home radio listening be included in computing the size of the audience, and if so, how can this type of mobile listening be measured with any degree of accuracy?

Students of audience measurement research have worked constantly to reduce the possibility of errors; as a result, quantitative sampling now is a respected research technique. Many business firms have specialized in audience surveys, but the output of some of them has been criticized by experts because they do not reveal all the data on which their reports are based or they lack the quality of "disinterestedness" demanded by scientific research.

COMMERCIAL RESEARCH ORGANIZATIONS

With the high premium set by advertisers on the size of the broadcast audience their programs and announcements reach, it is not surprising that a number of commercial firms have been organized especially to gather such information. Television and radio audience research, which aims to gauge station coverage, the size and composition of the audience, and program popularity, has been a highly competitive field, with several different companies, using contrasting research techniques, bidding for leadership. National ratings of network programs are the most difficult to compile because of variations between time zones, differences in urban and rural listening habits, variations in the number of stations carrying a network program, and the variety of competing programs in localities throughout the country. Serious efforts were made in the early thirties to devise reliable rating systems to indicate relative popularity of programs. The Crossley Reports were the first of such national rating devices, followed by the Hooperatings and, more recently, by the Nielsen Radio Index, Nielsen Television Index, and the reports of the American Research Bureau.

Early rating systems like those of Crossley and Hooper used telephone calls in 30-odd cities to question people about what they had listened to before the call was received (Crossley) or were listening to at the very moment the call was received (Hooper). From the replies to these telephone questions three figures were computed that became standard in the audience measurement field: 1. *Rating*. The rating indicates the percentage of the sample who are receiving a particular program. A program with a rating of 22.8 means that out of every 100 homes contacted, 22.8 percent are receiving the program. 2. *Homes Using Television*. This figure indicates the number of sample homes in which sets are turned on. Thus a HUT figure of 44.7 means that out of every 100 homes contacted 44.7 have sets operating. 3. *Share of Audience.* This figure indicates the comparative popularity of programs broadcast over different stations at the same time. Thus, a figure of 51 means that of the homes in the sample with sets turned on, 51 percent are watching a particular program. The share-of-audience is obtained by dividing the program rating by the homes-using-television figure.

The terms described above refer to audience estimates for specific programs. In addition, research organizations report the audiences drawn by stations over specific periods of time. A figure may be calculated, for example, that estimates the number of unduplicated households that tune in a station sometime during a day. Similar cumulative averages are arrived at for a week or for a month. These figures are known in the broadcasting industry as "cumes."

Nielsen

The Nielsen system makes use of the "Audimeter," an electronic device inserted in television sets that makes a continuous record of every moment the set is on and the station to which it is tuned. At first this record was made on film or tape, which was removed every two weeks and replaced with a new roll. This procedure resulted in a long delay between the time a program was broadcast and the time its rating could be determined. Now as many as four different television sets in a single household are connected to a Storage Instantaneous Audimeter (SIA), which collects information about each set's use. If there are more than four sets, a second SIA is used. At intervals the information collected by the SIA is transmitted to a central computing center. It is supplemented with data from diaries in which people in some of the homes equipped with the SIA record their viewing activity and other information. Small cash incentives are provided the sample households to encourage cooperation.

When television became the dominant medium, Nielsen gave up its services to the radio industry to concentrate on the measurement of television audiences. For its national report, known as the Nielsen Television Index, Nielsen uses a sample of homes that is claimed to represent substantially the entire United States, including homes of all significant types—those with telephones and those without, urban, small-town, and farm dwellings—in carefully weighted proportions. In the sample, which consists of approximately 1200 homes, Nielsen accounts for such demographic items as the ages of the people in the sample household, their educational levels, and their occupations.

With the cooperation of families constituting the sample, a Nielsen representative inserts an Audimeter into every television set in a sample home. When any of the sets is turned on, the Audimeter graphically records the time and the station tuned in; in this way, every occasion of dial twisting is noted and made available for analysis. It is possible to determine whether particular announcements caused listeners to tune to different stations or at what point in a program most listeners tuned in. Since the sample of homes used for the survey remains relatively constant (only 20 percent change annually), it is also possible to establish trends in viewing habits. In addition, Nielsen representatives personally visit the sample homes on a regular basis to get reliable information on the advertised brands and commodities actually purchased by each family.

In addition to its national service, the Nielsen Company provides a measurement of local TV station audiences. This service is known as the Nielsen Station Index. The measuring instrument is a diary mailed to people living in 200 different areas in which a record of TV viewing is made and then returned to the company. In Los Angeles, New York, and Chicago a system that ties from 300 to 500 homes into a computer supplements the diary method. This Audimeter system permits the instantaneous recording of viewer activity.

The data gathered by the Nielsen organization enable it to make reports of various kinds. It can determine the number of homes using television (HUT), the ratings of programs, and the shares of audience gained by competing programs. These figures can be translated into national estimates of the number of homes and people viewing a particular program. The minute-by-minute record of viewing on the Audimeter also shows when programs gained or lost audiences and can indicate the size of audience for a particular commercial. Knowledge of the people in the household in which the Audimeter is located and information recorded in diaries provide data of great interest to advertisers about the characteristics of people who view various programs—their age, sex, education, occupation, etc.

The Nielsen company reports the results of its surveys at regular intervals. Reports of the popularity of programs throughout the nation are made in a booklet known as a "pocketpiece," which provides a comprehensive listing of viewing data. The pocketpiece is supplemented by daily reports and by a fast weekly service. Reports on local television viewing are made from three to eight times a year, depending on the size of the viewing area. In addition to providing information about the number of homes using television, program ratings, and the shares of audiences drawn by various programs, Nielsen provides information on other matters. Among them are reports on the demographic characteristics of audiences for particular programs, cumulative audiences for programs and commercials, and the cost-per-thousand-homes for delivering commercials and programs to audiences. Rating services for local areas are also provided, using a diary system.

The advantages of the Nielsen system are self-evident. It avoids the human errors that Hooper had to cope with, it covers rural and urban dwellings, and it records viewing habits by the minute. The Nielsen system is not without its limitations, however. The validity of using a sample of homes in which families know that their habits are under observation and study is open to question. Sample homes that refuse to cooperate have to be replaced with homes willing to cooperate. People often behave differently under a spotlight than when they are left to themselves. Moreover, while the Audimeter accurately records all the channel changes, it cannot tell whether any one is actually listening to a program or whether, for example, a conversation is in progress at the time. Students of public opinion research will also want to know more about the construction of the Nielsen sample to verify its representativeness. Some broadcasting and advertising executives assert that the Nielsen sample is too small to have much value. Nevertheless, despite these limitations and the rather large cost of subscribing to the system, Nielsen has become the most widely accepted national audience measurement system.

American Research Bureau

The basic research tool used by the American Research Bureau (ARB) is the diary, which is used to measure the audience to both radio and television programs. The service for television is known as ARBITRON television. Diaries are mailed to homes in sampling units throughout the country. A new set of homes is selected for each survey by a computer, using lists supplied by the Metro-Mail Advertising Company. A letter is sent to each selected household informing it that a diary will follow, and an interviewer telephones before the diary is mailed to solicit cooperation and to explain that the company wishes a careful record to be made of all television viewing during the survey week. As does Nielsen, the ARBITRON Company provides cash incentives to stimulate respondent cooperation. The interviewer calls again the day before the survey begins to make sure that the diary has been received and to emphasize the importance of keeping a careful record of television viewing. A third call is made a few days later to deal with any difficulties that may have developed and to remind the diary keeper to mail the diary in at the end of the survey. In addition to the record of television viewing, the diaries contain demographic information. All of these elements are analyzed, and reports similar to those made by the Nielsen Company are available to the broadcasting industry. ARBITRON rating reports are prepared three times a year for every television market in the United States, and almost all national spot advertising placements are made on the basis of these survey reports. In 33 of the larger markets, more frequent ARBITRON reports are issued.

Other Research Organizations

More than 60 organizations service the broadcasting industry by conducting research of various types. The Pulse, Inc., rating system uses interviews conducted in the homes of listeners to measure the audiences to broadcasts and to provide data regarding the nature of those audiences. Concentrating mainly on radio in local areas, the Pulse organization uses a roster of programs to help interviewees remember their listening, a technique known as "Roster-Recall." Other companies specializing in audience research are Trendex Inc., which uses a coincidental telephone technique, Videodex Inc., which uses the diary technique to secure information for advertisers, and Alfred Politz Media Studies, which specializes in the study of media contributions to advertising performance. Instead of arriving at estimates of the size of audiences drawn by particular programs, one company, using what it calls a TvQ measure, attempts to rate the "enthusiasm quotient" of television performers and program series currently telecast by interviewing samples of viewers and asking them to indicate the programs they are familiar with and those that are their favorites. From these responses the TvQ prepares a scale indicating the relative familiarity and popularity of different shows, according to age groups of the viewers.

Some companies using research techniques attempt to provide information about the potential effectiveness of programs and commercials before they are broadcast. This is an entirely different type of audience research from audience measurement; it uses different methods and proceeds on the basis of different assumptions. Sample audience groups are tested to make qualitative evaluations of commercials and programs using a competitive preference technique. A device known as the Lazarsfeld-Stanton Program Analyzer is used by CBS to measure the appeal of programs it is considering broadcasting. People in sample audiences are asked to press one button during the time the program interests them, another button when they lose interest, no button at all when they are neutral. Using a similar method, ASI, a Hollywood-based company, pretests pilot programs for NBC and ABC and compares the questionnaire responses of studio audiences with responses to previous programs they have tested. Another technique used in the industry is to describe program ideas to groups of people and ask whether or not they would be interested in viewing the program.

Sometimes advertisers and agencies are interested in finding out whether the programs or commercials for which they contracted were actually broadcast according to the terms of the agreement. Some companies specialize in making recordings of stations' transmissions to answer this need.

CRITERIA FOR AUDIENCE RATINGS

The conflicts between the various rating systems have frequently caused considerable confusion within the broadcasting industry. In the early years, the differences between Crossley and Hooper ratings for the same show aroused concern; later it was the disparity between Hooper and Nielsen ratings that caused confusion. In more recent years, the ratings produced by the Nielsen Company and the American Research Bureau have been the primary contenders for industry attention. Frequently the ARB and Nielsen ratings for the same show differ, sometimes to a marked degree. Merely comparing ratings, however, without taking any other factors into account may lead to inaccurate conclusions about the relative reliability of various systems. A detailed analysis of ratings often shows less conflict than appears on the surface, because different ratings actually measure different things and therefore are not directly comparable. The conflicts do point up, however, the great limitations in using rating information to draw conclusions as to audience size or program popularity without thorough analysis of the rating information.

As a result of concern about conflict over rating systems, a number of committees of audience research specialists have been set up to study the problem and formulate criteria by which the industry may judge the various rating systems. In 1961, a committee on broadcast ratings appointed by the

Regulatory Agencies Subcommittee of the House of Representatives published a report.[1] It recommended no particular rating system, but did make other suggestions. It said, for example, that audience research organizations should go beyond merely establishing ratings to provide more data about the composition of audiences. It also called on the various services to publish more precise information about the methods used in establishing their ratings. In 1963, the FTC persuaded the major rating services to call their ratings estimates rather than accurate measurements.

The broadcasting industry itself set up a research group known as the Committee on Nationwide Television Audience Measurements (CONTAM) to investigate various questions connected with rating services. To date four studies have been reported. The first investigated the validity of sampling theory and concluded that estimates of television audience size obtained from well-drawn samples are unbiased and tend to fall reasonably close to the results obtained from census counts. The second study investigated the potential sources of error in the meter technique used by the Nielsen Company and in the diary technique used by the American Research Bureau. The study compiled a list of things the services were doing that might have caused errors in their ratings. The third study found that families willing to cooperate in providing information to rating services watch television more than noncooperating families do, a fact that inflates nighttime ratings about 3 percent. The fourth study found that improper interviewing in telephone surveys and the failure to get full information or to evaluate busy signals and no answers properly created errors that caused their ratings to be 9 percent lower than those of meter surveys.

INTERPRETATION OF RATINGS

Until an audience measurement system is developed that wins unqualified scientific support for its validity and reliability, it is likely that competitive rating systems will continue to operate in the field of television and radio. These rating systems, despite their limitations, will serve a useful purpose to networks, stations, advertisers, and agencies, provided they are interpreted properly. To use ratings to determine the popularity of any program or the size of the audience reached, we must be sure to take into account the following considerations:

1. No program rating can be evaluated without knowing what rating system is used. To state that a program had a rating of 20 without stating whether it is a Nielsen or ARBITRON 20 makes it impossible to evaluate the rating.

2. No program rating can be properly evaluated without knowing the full context of the rating:

   a. What was the rating of the program that preceded it? The effect of a strong adja-

[1] U.S. Congress, House Committee on Interstate and Foreign Commerce, *Evaluation of Statistical Methods Used in Obtaining Broadcast Ratings,* 87th Cong., 1st Sess., House Report No. 193, March 23, 1961.

cent program can often mislead people into thinking that a program has strong popular appeal when it really is profiting from its fortunate position in the program schedule. One network program that had a good rating actually was tuned out by more people than any other network program. Its strategic position between two very popular shows nevertheless managed to sustain a sizable audience that it would never have attracted at another time on the program schedule.

b. Did the program have strong competition on the air from programs on other stations or networks? If two equally good programs are on the air at the same time, each may get only half as high the rating it would get it if had weak competition. On the other hand, a program that achieves a fair rating against one of the highest-rated shows may actually have more popular appeal than one with a higher rating earned against weak competition.

c. How many stations telecast the program? Network programs telecast over long station lineups (180–200 stations) obviously can win larger audiences, therefore higher ratings, than programs telecast over short lineups (100–150 stations).

d. At what time of day was the rating made? Audiences for television programs are much greater in the evening than in the daytime. For this reason advertisers are unwilling to spend as much money for time and program in the morning or afternoon as they will in the evening. Daytime ratings must therefore be judged within the context of all daytime ratings.

e. To what extent did the rating benefit or suffer from regular listening or viewing habits, special program publicity, etc.? The rating for a program that is broadcast one time only without advance publicity is practically meaningless in judging the program's popularity, because many potential viewers did not know the show was on the air.

3. Ratings must be used not as an absolute measurement, but mainly as a guide to program popularity. The reports of the rating services should be used to modify or reinforce judgments that are arrived at after a consideration of all the factors in the situation. To draw final conclusions about the success or failure of a series solely on the basis of the ratings it attains is to place unjustified and indefensible dependence on these measures.

4. Program ratings must not be confused with advertising effectiveness. Ratings can provide an indication of circulation, but not of sales effectiveness, which may be related to the special relationship developed between the audience and the program, the effectiveness of the commercial messages, or the special kind of audience attracted to the program.

5. Very low program ratings tend to be less reliable as a guide to judging audience size than high program ratings. In low ratings probable errors that may occur through the operations of chance have a great effect in upsetting estimates of audience size. A rating system that has a probable error of plus or minus 2 percentage points means that a rating of 8 may actually be a rating from 6 to 10. An advertiser may want to invest in a show when it reaches six million homes with a rating of 8, but the six million may actually have been reached when the rating was 6 or 7, or may not have been reached even when the rating was 9. With program ratings of 20 or 30, the effect of the probable error does not have a comparable effect upon judgments of a program's popularity.

6. Small rating differences should be discounted in judging comparative program popularity, all other factors being equal. Competitive ratings of 26.2 and 25.7 should be interpreted as indications of equal popularity; the rating systems are not fine enough in their measurements to yield more than approximations.

SUMMARY

Public acceptance of television and radio programming is essential to any system of broadcasting. It is difficult to determine with accuracy what listeners and viewers think about particular programs, but numerous commercial audience research organizations, using sampling techniques, provide program ratings, indications of audience size, information regarding the nature of the audience for various programs, and people's opinions of prospective series and programs on the air. Despite the limitations of the rating methods, program ratings can serve a constructive function to networks, stations, advertisers, and agencies when they are properly interpreted and used.

Questions For Discussion

1. Why may an audience measuring procedure utilizing a sampling technique be more accurate in measuring a program's popularity than a count of fan-mail received by the program?
2. What are the advantages and disadvantages of the Nielsen rating system?
3. What is the meaning of the following terms used in audience measurement: "homes using television," "rating," "share of audience"?
4. How may the rating of a given program be affected by the popularity of other programs?
5. Why do you think the conclusion was reached that a combination of Nielsen's automatic recording device and the use of diaries would be the most reliable method of measuring a program's audience?
6. What role do you think audience ratings should play in determining the fate of radio and television programs?
7. Could we manage without rating systems?
8. What influence can a single individual exert in determining the kind of radio and television fare that is to be available?
9. What has been the effect of audience research on the broadcasting industry?
10. How should ratings be interpreted?

The "public convenience, interest, or necessity," as stated in the Communications Act of 1934, is the touchstone of American broadcasting. But what is the public interest? How is it to be determined? Who shall make the determination? In this chapter we deal with these questions.

The use of a general phrase like "public interest" to embody basic congressional policy in some field of government activity is rather common. In writing a law, members of Congress realize that they cannot anticipate every situation that may arise in carrying out the law. It is customary for Congress to lay down the broad general policy and to appoint some authority to execute this policy and to make administrative interpretations of the law. Anglo-Saxon legal tradition has developed the rule of reasonableness; executive authorities, in their interpretations of congressional policy, must not act arbitrarily or capriciously, but solely in terms of reason. The final decisions as to whether or not they have acted reasonably rests in the hands of appropriate courts to which aggrieved parties may appeal.

This procedural aspect of American government characterizes television and radio regulation. Congress laid down the general policy, with limited specific directives such as equal time for political campaign broadcasts, and it created the Federal Communications Commission to execute the law, to issue administrative rules and regulations, to decide cases, and generally to represent the will of the people. The law contains an elastic clause that the FCC "may perform any and all acts, make such rules and regulations, and issue such orders, not inconsistent with this Act, as may be necessary in the execution of its functions."

With this authority, the FCC has sought to regulate television and radio in the public interest. The Commission itself has not specifically defined what "public interest" means in all instances, but, in various statements and decisions, it has expressed definite judgments as to what the public interest includes and what it does *not* include. Most of these statements are made *ad hoc,* that is to say, in connection with specific cases that come before the Commission in its exercise of the power to grant, renew, or revoke broadcast licenses. There are also FCC rules and regulations, such as the Chain Broadcasting Regulations, which indicate the Commission's interpretation of public policy, and occasional general reports or opinions issued by the Commission. We may also look to the Communications Act itself and its legislative history and to appellate court cases reviewing FCC decisions to determine the meaning of "public interest."

Wherever we turn for light on this subject, we find that in television and radio regulation, as the FCC itself has pointed out, the

> paramount and controlling consideration [is] the relationship between the American system of broadcasting carried on through a large number of private licensees upon whom devolves the responsibility for the selection and presentation of program material, and the Congressional mandate that this licensee responsibility is to be exercised in the interests of, and as a trustee for the public at large which retains ultimate control over the channels of radio and television communication.[1]

BASIC THEORY OF THE PUBLIC INTEREST

In interpreting the public-interest clause, the FCC has at various times set forth the following general principles:

1. The right of the public to broadcast service is superior to the right of any individual to use the ether. The legislative history of the Radio Act of 1927 clearly indicates that "Congress intended that radio stations shall not be used for the private interest, whims, or caprices of the particular persons who have been granted licenses."[2]

2. Broadcasting must be maintained as a medium of free speech for the people as a whole.

3. Television and radio stations have a definite responsibility to provide a reasonable amount of broadcast time for controversial public discussion. In programming such discussions, the broadcaster must avoid one-sidedness and observe overall fairness. The right of the public to be informed of different opinions in important matters of public controversy is the dominant consideration.

4. Licensees must maintain control over the programming of their own stations, and may not surrender their program responsibility by contract or otherwise to networks, advertising agencies, or other program-producing organizations.

5. Television and radio stations must be responsive to the needs and interests of the communities in which they are located. To this end, the Commission has often favored local ownership of stations, integration of ownership and management, and local live programs.

6. Television and radio stations may not be used exclusively for commercial purposes. They must use some of their broadcast time for sustaining programs and must avoid advertising excesses that offend good taste.

7. Television and radio stations are expected to abide by their promises of program service unless exceptional circumstances supervene. Since the Commission grants

---

[1] Federal Communications Commission, *Report in the Matter of Editorializing by Broadcast Licensees,* Docket No. 8516, June 2, 1949.

[2] Address by Wayne Coy, former FCC Chairman, at Yale Law School, January 22, 1949.

licenses on the basis of these promises, the Commission holds that it has the right to determine whether the promises have been kept. The Commission therefore reserves to itself the right to review the overall program service of stations when licenses come up for renewal. (This right is disputed by many prominent broadcasting executives and attorneys.)

8. The Commission favors diversity of ownership of television and radio stations. In approving the sale of the Blue Network by RCA, the Commission said, "The mechanism of free speech can operate freely only when the controls of public access to the means for the dissemination of news and issues are in as many responsible ownerships as possible and each exercises its own independent judgment."[3]

9. The Commission may not censor any television or radio program in advance of broadcast.

In carrying out these principles, the FCC has taken punitive action only in rare instances of extreme abuse by licensees; most of the time it has resorted to mild or indirect chidings of errant stations and it has relied on persuasion to achieve most of its objectives. For many years this failure to act decisively was attributed to the reluctance of the Commission to invoke the death penalty for a station for anything less than the most unmitigated misuse of a license. Until Congress authorized the FCC in 1952 to issue "cease-and-desist" orders and to suspend and penalize stations violating its rules, the problem of making the punishment fit the crime was almost impossible of solution. One of the most useful devices of the Commission, however, continues to be a letter from the Commission requesting a licensee to explain, for example, how his action, in failing to broadcast any political campaign talks during an election campaign, served the public interest. The licensee then bears the burden of justifying his action in terms of the concept of public interest held by the FCC.

GRANTING AND RENEWING LICENSES

In granting and renewing broadcast licenses, the FCC is often obliged to refine its interpretation of public interest. When the Commission has two or more financially and technically qualified applicants where only one license may be granted, the Commission may have no alternative but to base its decision on the "public convenience, interest, or necessity" as expressed in terms of ownership considerations and programming intentions.

Ownership Preferences

Misrepresentation of ownership. Misrepresentation of ownership is sufficient cause for the FCC to refuse to grant a broadcast license or, if the fraud is discovered at a later date, to revoke the license. In the *WOKO* case, decided in 1945, the Commission refused to renew the license of WOKO because it had concealed the real ownership of 24 percent of its stock. The Supreme Court

---

[3] Federal Communications Commission, "Decision and Order in the Matter of RCA, Transferor and ABC, Inc., Transferee," Docket No. 6536, October 12, 1943 (mimeo).

upheld the FCC, even though the station's programming service was not held to be unsatisfactory.[4]

Multiple ownership. Seeking to achieve as much diversity of ownership as possible, the Commission has set limitations on the number of stations that may be licensed to the same person or corporation. Seven is the maximum number in FM stations, seven in TV (5 VHF, 2 UHF), and seven in AM. Furthermore, under the FCC's "duopoly" rule, one owner may not have two television or two AM or FM radio stations serving substantially the same listening or viewing area. This regulation is designed to prevent a recurrence in broadcasting of what is often the case in the newspaper business: the same publisher owning two local dailies and operating without competition.[5] As we have noted previously, the Commission has stiffened its multiple-ownership rules to permit one organization to operate only one major medium of communication—a television station, a radio station, or a newspaper—at least as far as new acquisitions are concerned. This proposed regulation has been called the "one-to-a-customer" rule.

Special-interest groups. Before World War II, the FCC was reluctant to issue broadcast licenses to special-interest groups like religious organizations and labor unions. The Commission felt that these groups would tend to use a station to advance their own political, economic, or religious ends. The Commission preferred to issue licenses to applicants whose organizational affiliations would not tend to make them favor any one group. By and large, this remains the Commission's policy. Since the war, however, with the huge increase in the number of AM and FM stations, the Commission has licensed radio stations to special-interest groups in some metropolitan areas. Labor unions holding licenses have agreed to program their stations for the general public and not merely for their members.

Newspaper ownership. During the late thirties, newspaper publishers in great numbers applied for broadcast licenses. In 1931, less than 15 percent of all radio stations were licensed to publishers, but by 1938, a third of all stations were newspaper-owned. The FCC became disturbed about this situation, and in 1941 it ordered an investigation into the propriety of joint ownership of newspapers and radio stations in the same area. After many hearings and deliberations, the Commission dismissed the proceedings, and newspapers were authorized to apply for broadcast licenses. If the one-to-a-customer rule is sustained, of course, newspaper owners will not receive licenses in the future to operate broadcasting stations.

One principle followed by the FCC in assigning licenses is to select nonnewspaper applicants if their qualifications are at least equal to those of competing newspaper applicants. In 1954 the FCC seemed to violate this criterion when it awarded Channel 5 (WHDH) in Boston to the owners of the

---

[4] *Federal Communications Commission* v. *WOKO, Inc.,* 329 U.S. 223.

[5] The FCC, however, has made an exception to its "duopoly" rule by granting some educational groups the right to use a UHF channel even though they were already licensed to use a VHF channel, thus permitting an expansion of services to schools.

Boston Herald Traveler, even though there were local applicants of apparently equal worth who did not own newspapers. Allegations that the FCC was subjected to undue influence in reaching its decision further beclouded the situation. The victory of the *Herald Traveler* in this case was not clear-cut, however. The FCC never awarded it the conventional three-year license but limited the license period to one year. After renewing the *Herald Traveler's* license yearly until 1969, the FCC finally took Channel 5 away from the newspaper on the ground that there had been improper *ex parte* contacts with various commissioners during the original proceedings and awarded it to a nonnewspaper applicant.

Since then other moves have been made to diminish the crossownership of broadcasting facilities and newspapers. In 1974 the Justice Department petitioned the FCC to deny license renewals to five stations owned by companies that publish newspapers in the same area, a move that sent shock waves through the broadcasting industry. Other petitions of a similar nature followed. The FCC, responding to these petitions, announced a plan to break up cross-ownership in sixteen small-market situations in the next five years. It further announced that it would no longer approve the sale of both broadcasting facilities and newspapers to new ownership in the same market unless a special waiver were granted.

Types of ownership preferred. The Commission favors local ownership and integration of ownership and management over absentee ownership. In evaluating the qualifications of an applicant, the Commission considers it in the public interest to investigate the applicant's background and personal and business reputation. If the applicant has had brushes with the law, his standing before the Commission will be less favorable than that of competing applicants without such a record.

Character of the licensee. In the *Edward Lamb* case, on which hearings were held in 1954 and 1955, the Commission proposed to deny renewal of a broadcasting license on the ground that the licensee was untrustworthy, and it ordered a hearing. The specific allegation in support of this charge was that the licensee had knowingly signed a false affidavit to the Commission stating that he had never been a member of the Communist Party when, the Commission charged, he had in fact been a member of the party. The licensee denied the truth of the allegation. After many months of hearings, an FCC trial examiner rejected the charge against the licensee as unfounded and recommended renewal of the broadcasting license. The authority of the Commission to deny a license for material untrustworthiness of the licensee, if established after appropriate hearings, seems beyond dispute.

Programming and Related Activities

Public interest vs. private interest. The FCC has always required applicants for broadcast licenses and renewals of licenses to submit detailed statements of their proposed program policies. The decision to grant or deny the application has been based in part on a determination of whether the proposed programming was or was not in the public interest.

The authority of the Commission to follow this procedure has been upheld by the courts in several important cases. In the *KFKB Broadcasting Association* case, the Commission denied renewal of a license after finding that the station's owner had used his facilities to prescribe treatment for patients whom he had never seen, basing his diagnoses on letters from them.[6] In the *Trinity Methodist Church* case, the station was owned by a minister who used it for sensational broadcasts that contained false and defamatory statements and vilified other religious groups. On one occasion the minister announced that he had certain damaging information against a prominent unnamed man whose name he would disclose unless a contribution of $100 was immediately forthcoming. As a result, he received contributions from several persons. The Commission refused to renew the station's license and the decision was upheld by the courts.[7] Both of these cases made the point that "the interest of the listening public is paramount and may not be subordinated to the interests of the station licensee."

Programming and community interests. A number of cases involving the public's interest were considered by the FCC in the sixties. In 1962, it refused to renew the license of a Kingstree, South Carolina, station, WDKD, on the grounds that the station had presented broadcasts by a disc jockey who regularly indulged in obscene and indecent remarks. A further count against the station was what the examiner called "horrendous" overcommercialization, a charge supported by an analysis that showed 1,448 commercials during a composite week. Another license-revocation case involved KWK in St. Louis, Missouri, charged with deceiving the public by advertising that it had hidden a prize that it did not actually hide until a few hours before the contest was scheduled to end. In 1962, the FCC refused to renew the license of KRLA in Pasadena, California, because it had failed to make programming proposals in good faith, had indulged in fraudulent contests, and had changed its logs to misrepresent its actual programming record. In 1972, the Commission denied a license renewal for Station WEBY in Milton, Florida, because its owner misrepresented to the FCC the content of an editorial that had attacked a political candidate. In 1976, the FCC revoked the licenses of four stations owned by the same company, KOIL-AM and KEFM-FM in Omaha, WIFE-AM in Indianapolis, and KISN in Vancouver, Washington, alleging that their owner had run phony contests on the air, billed advertisers twice, slanted news broadcasts, and given free time to some political candidates.

The FCC also has the power to apply penalties for undesirable practices that are less stringent than a refusal to renew a station's license. It may reprimand a station for engaging in a certain practice and call on it to cease and desist, or it may go further and fine a station as a means of enforcing operation in the public interest. As an example, the FCC in 1970 fined an edu-

[6] *KFKB* v. *Federal Radio Commission* (App. D. C.), 47 F. 2d, 670.

[7] *Trinity Methodist Church, South* v. *Federal Radio Commission* (App. D. C.), 62 F. 2d, 850.

cational FM station, WUHY-FM in Philadelphia, for allowing obscene language to be broadcast during a taped interview with the leader of a rock-music group.

Petitions to deny license renewals. In recent years a number of stations have been forced to respond to petitions from groups that challenge the station's right to a renewal of its license because of its failure to meet the needs of the community. This trend began when Reverend Everett Parker, a minister of the United Church of Christ, accused WLBT in Jackson, Mississippi, of presenting programming that was racist in tone and demanded that the FCC deny a renewal of its license. The FCC rejected the demand and granted the station a renewal of its license. Reverend Parker then took his case into the courts. In a 1969 decision written by Warren Burger, later Chief Justice of the United States, the U. S. Court of Appeals for the District of Columbia castigated the FCC for not being more responsive to public complaints and ordered it to make the frequency available to other applicants.

The challenger's victory in the WLBT case encouraged a great many other groups to question the right of many stations to continue broadcasting. In the flood of challenges that suddenly burst forth, some addressed legitimate complaints, but a number were capricious in nature and others seemed plainly designed to harass. In the light of these developments, the FCC served notice that it would give heed only to reasonable and substantial complaints when it rejected a petition that would have denied license renewal to Station WMAL-TV in Washington, D.C., because the station, serving a city that was 70 percent black, had not provided programming that was 70 percent black in orientation. The FCC rejected the petition because the complaint was too general, and because WMAL-TV served a far larger area than the city of Washington, to which the petition specifically referred. In 1972, the Court of Appeals upheld the FCC decision, an action that brought great relief to the broadcasting industry.

TELEVISION AND RADIO AS MEDIA OF FREE SPEECH

In its concern over maintaining television and radio as media of free speech, the FCC has been required to consider a number of difficult questions involving the nature of free speech and censorship. Freedom of speech for whom? The idea of unlimited freedom of speech, such as we generally think of when we mention the soapbox, is impossible in television and radio because of the limitations of frequencies and broadcast time. Since not everyone who wants to speak on the air can be given the chance to do so, someone had to decide who shall speak, when he shall speak, and for how long.

One point of view holds that "The broadcast licensee should be given complete and exclusive control over program content, including the sole right to determine who shall speak, and the right to censor any material intended for broadcast."[8] This position gives rise to several questions. Does

---

[8] Hearings before a Subcommittee of the Committee on Interstate and Foreign Commerce, U.S. Senate, 80th Congress, 1st Session, on S. 1333 (1947), p. 314. This was the testimony of a representative of the National Association of Broadcasters.

freedom of the air mean freedom for the licensees to use their stations as they please? Or does it mean freedom of expression for the persons who broadcast on the station? Is it an act of censorship to restrict the licensees' freedom to make unfair use of their stations? Is it an act of censorship when licensees review in advance scripts intended for broadcast over their stations? What constitutes unfairness in denying air time or censoring a script, and who shall make the final decision? Should the licensees be permitted to use their stations the way publishers use their newspapers, broadcasting their own editorials and supporting political causes and candidates? Should they deny time on the air to a point of view because it is a minority and perhaps an unpopular point of view? Should licensees be required to make time available for political campaign talks between elections? Should licensees be required to make time available for the discussion of controversial issues of interest in the community served by the station? Does freedom mean that the licensees are free to run these discussions as they see fit, or must such programs be designed so that the public has a reasonable opportunity to hear different opposition positions?

In a number of important rulings and opinions, the Commission has expressed itself on these questions.

THE FAIRNESS DOCTRINE

In 1941 the FCC came face-to-face with the question whether it is consistent with the public interest for licensees to utilize their facilities to present their own partisan ideas on vital public issues to the exclusion of opposing viewpoints. The case came up when the Mayflower Corporation requested that it be assigned the license of station WAAB in Boston, which was up for renewal. In reviewing this request the FCC discovered that it had been the station's policy to broadcast editorials urging the election of various candidates for political office or supporting one side of various questions in public controversy, with no pretense at objective or impartial reporting. "It is clear," the Commission observed in a decision that came to be known as the *Mayflower Case,* "that the purpose of these editorials was to win public support for some person or view favored by those in control of the station." The Commission renewed the license in 1941, but at the same time it issued a *dictum* prohibiting such editorializing in the future, saying: "A truly free radio cannot be used to advocate the causes of the licensee. It cannot be used to support the candidacies of his friends. It cannot be devoted to the support of principles he happens to regard most favorably. In brief, the broadcaster cannot be an advocate."

The *dictum* did not, however, expressly limit the editorial freedom of commentators whom the station hired.

The Commission's ruling was criticized by groups and individuals who felt that station licensees were being denied a right newspaper publishers had without restriction; that the increase in number of stations made it possible to allow editorializing without fear that all points of view would not be heard; that licensees would be able to play more active roles in their communities if allowed to editorialize; and that the prohibition was an unconstitutional restraint of the licensee's freedom of speech.

Those who supported the Commission's ruling pointed out that licensees should be umpires of public controversy and not public advocates; that it would be unfair and potentially dangerous to allow licensees to make use of the prestige and goodwill of their stations for editorial purposes; that no constitutional question was involved since broadcasting was, by its nature, a regulated medium; and that it would be impossible to police all stations to make sure that fair treatment was provided all points of view by a licensee who had already committed himself publicly to one side.

In 1948, the FCC held public hearings on the issue in the *Mayflower* decision and, a year later, it issued a new opinion modifying the earlier one. Licensees are now allowed to editorialize in the name of their station provided they maintain an overall fairness. The Commission, which now actually encourages stations to editorialize, stated that "the identified expression of the licensee's personal viewpoint as part of the more general presentation of views or comments on the various issues" may be broadcast.

> But the opportunity of licensees to present such views as they may have on matters of controversy may not be utilized to achieve a partisan or one-sided presentation of issues. Licensee editorialization is but one aspect of freedom of expression by means of radio. Only insofar as it is exercised in conformity with the paramount right of the public to hear a reasonably balanced presentation of all responsible viewpoints on particular issues can such editorialization be considered to be consistent with the licensee's duty to operate in the public interest. For the licensee is a trustee impressed with the duty of preserving for the public generally radio as a medium of free expression and fair presentation.[9]

The point that the public is entitled to hear a reasonably balanced presentation of all responsible viewpoints on particular issues came to be known as the fairness doctrine. This doctrine was embodied in federal statutes in 1959 when the Congress, in excluding news programs from the application of the equal-time requirement, added the proviso that "nothing in the foregoing sentence shall be construed as relieving broadcasters . . . of the obligation imposed upon them . . . to afford reasonable opportunity for the discussion of conflicting views on issues of public importance." During the sixties the FCC refined its interpretation of what it meant by fairness. It made clear that the doctrine did not require that equal time be provided for every view, nor was it necessary to permit a spokesman for every side to be heard. The station met the requirements of the doctrine if in its overall programming it provided a reasonable exposure to the various points of view on a controversial issue. The FCC did lay down some specific rules with respect to certain types of programs, however. If the honesty, integrity, or character of a group or person were attacked in connection with the discussion of a controversial issue, the FCC required that the subject of the attack be notified of the date and time of the broadcast, be sent a tape, script, or summary

---

[9] Federal Communications Commission, *Report in the Matter of Editorializing by Broadcast Licensees,* Docket No. 8516, June 1, 1949.

of the attack within seven days, and be afforded a reasonable opportunity to reply. If a station endorsed a political candidate, it was required to notify opponents within 24 hours and provide an opportunity for replies by spokesmen for the other candidates. If the endorsement took place within 72 hours of the election, other candidates had to be notified prior to the broadcast.

The application of the fairness doctrine aroused much opposition in the broadcasting industry, and from the controversy two notable cases emerged. One involved the advertising of cigarettes. In 1967 a young man named John Banzhaf III wrote a letter to the FCC, arguing that since cigarette commercials constituted persuasion in favor of smoking cigarettes—a controversial position—stations under the fairness doctrine were obligated to present arguments against cigarette smoking. The FCC in a unanimous vote accepted Banzhaf's point of view, and from that time on required stations to broadcast antismoking messages. This continued until Congress, in 1971, barred the broadcasting of cigarette commercials altogether.

The other case involved station WGCB, a Pennsylvania station, operated by the Red Lion Broadcasting Company, which broadcast a talk by Reverend Billy James Hargis impugning in several respects the integrity and character of Fred J. Cook, who had written books critical of J. Edgar Hoover and Barry Goldwater. When Cook heard about the broadcast, he demanded that the station give him an opportunity to reply, a privilege the station was willing to grant if Cook would pay for the time. Cook refused this offer and took his complaint to the FCC, which ordered the station to grant Cook air time, whether or not he was willing to pay for it. The decision was appealed to the Court of Appeals, which upheld the FCC, and then to the Supreme Court. There, as the *Red Lion* case it was combined with an action taken by the Radio Television News Directors Association to overthrow the fairness doctrine as a violation of freedom of speech.

In June 1969, the Supreme Court voted unanimously to uphold the FCC in its application of the fairness doctrine, arguing in a decision written by Associate Justice White that because broadcasting frequencies are not available to all, the right to freedom of speech guaranteed by the First Amendment cannot apply with the force that it does in other situations. In the words of Justice Byron White:

> Although broadcasting is clearly a medium affected by a First Amendment interest . . . differences in the characteristics of new media justify differences in the First Amendment standards applied to them . . . . The right of free speech of a broadcaster . . . does not embrace a right to snuff out the free speech of others . . . . Where there are substantially more individuals who want to broadcast than there are frequencies to allocate, it is idle to posit an unbridgeable First Amendment right to broadcast comparable to the right of every individual to speak, write, or publish.[10]

Though the Supreme Court decision would seem to settle the matter, agitation about the fairness doctrine continues. In responding to attacks, its defenders argue that the doctrine is necessary to make certain that broadcasters will discharge fairly their responsibility to cover controversial issues.

[10] *Red Lion Broadcasting Co.* v. *FCC*, 395 U.S. 367, 386–88.

It is argued further that it is important to give people with minority opinions on issues some opportunity to reach the public with their ideas. One person who defended the fairness doctrine with great vigor was Richard Wiley when, as Chairman of the FCC, he said that the elimination of the doctrine would be "the worst single thing to happen in the whole history of journalism."

A person who attacks the doctrine with equal vigor is Senator William Proxmire, who has introduced a bill to abolish it. His argument is that it denies radio and television broadcasters their right to freedom of speech. Former Senator Sam Ervin expressed a similar point of view when he said that the fairness doctrine is an affront to the First Amendment. Fred Friendly, a former president of CBS News and a former producer of documentaries for that network, points out that the doctrine has been used by government officials to harass radio and television station owners who disagreed with them.[11]

On the face of it, the requirement that broadcasters be fair in their coverage of controversial issues seems reasonable and straightforward, but in practice the word "fair" seems to be imprecise and the requirement is difficult to enforce. What should be done, for example, when a President of the United States announces a controversial decision on television, as President Nixon did in 1970 when he told the nation that American troops had been sent into Cambodia? Should all the people who flood the networks on such occasions with demands for broadcast time to express their opinions be accorded that privilege? Should all those who argue that their views have been misrepresented or not represented at all when a news program or documentary treats a controversial issue be given the right to reply?

The development of the fairness doctrine has confronted the FCC with difficult problems. After every controversial broadcast it is deluged with demands for air time. In 1973 and 1974, for example, it received 4300 such requests; it dismissed out of hand 97 percent of them. Its enforcement of the fairness doctrine is not without teeth, however. In 1970 it denied station WXUR in Media, Pennsylvania, controlled by the conservative preacher Dr. Carl McIntire, the right to continue broadcasting because of the station's "blatant and continuing unfairness." These actions suggest that the Commission will be flexible in its enforcement of the fairness doctrine, according stations and networks a good deal of freedom in the treatment of controversial issues, but will act with vigor when unfairness appears to be obvious, deliberate, and systematic.

The *WHKC* Case

In the WHKC case, in 1945, the issue was whether it is in the public interest for a licensee arbitrarily to limit certain types of organizations from securing time on the station to express their opinions on vital issues, or to restrict the manner or method in which they present their views.

---

[11] Fred Friendly, *The Good Guys, the Bad Guys, and the First Amendment: Free Speech vs. Fairness in Broadcasting* (New York, 1976).

The case developed out of the policy of many stations not to sell radio time to labor unions on the grounds that discussion of labor affairs was inherently controversial and therefore not suitable for broadcast on sponsored programs. The president of a national network testified that he would not sell time to the American Federation of Labor to sponsor a symphony orchestra, but that he would sell the same time to an automobile manufacturer. Corporations might hire commentators to editorialize on the air, but unions were not permitted to buy time for their commentators.

The situation came to a head when the Congress of Industrial Organizations petitioned the FCC not to renew the license of WHKC, Columbus, Ohio, because the station had stringently censored remarks scheduled to be delivered on a United Automobile Workers program. Upon the request of both parties, the Commission dismissed the action, WHKC having promised the union a reasonable opportunity to be heard. In its order, however, the FCC denounced the policy of refusing to air labor discussions on the basis of their controversial nature. The Commission asserted that the public interest requires licensees, as an "affirmative duty," to make reasonable provision for broadcast discussions of controversial issues of public importance in the community served by the station.[12]

The *Scott* Case

The *Scott* case, in 1946, presented a crucial test to the Commission because it involved a complaint by a member of a group holding a viewpoint contrary to that shared by a majority of the population, that certain stations had refused to afford him or persons sharing similar views any opportunity to state their position, although time was given to representatives of groups holding contrary positions.

Scott, a self-professed atheist, filed a petition with the FCC to have the licenses of three California stations revoked because they flatly refused to give him any time whatsoever for a discussion of atheism. He claimed that these stations carried many broadcasts of religious services which openly attacked atheism and that therefore he was entitled to time to present an opposite point of view. He also complained that some stations had refused him time on the ground that any broadcast on the subject of atheism was contrary to the public interest.

The Commission denied Scott's petition, but it issued an important opinion which said, in part:

> We recognize that in passing upon requests for time, a station licensee is constantly confronted with most difficult problems. Since the demands for time may far exceed the amount available for broadcasting, a licensee must inevitably make a selection among those seeking it for the expression of their views. He may not even be able to grant time to all religious groups who might desire the use of his facilities, much less to all who might want to oppose religion. Admittedly, a very real opportunity exists for him to be arbitrary and unreasonable, to indulge his own preferences, prejudices, or whims; to pursue his

[12] *United Broadcasting Co. (WHKC),* 10 FCC, 515.

own private interest or to favor those who espouse his views, and discriminate against those of opposing views. The indulgence of that opportunity could not conceivably be characterized as an exercise of the broadcaster's right of freedom of speech. Nor could it fairly be said to afford the listening audience that opportunity to hear a diversity and balance of views, which is an inseparable corollary of freedom of expression. In making a selection with fairness, the licensee must, of course, consider the extent of the interest of the public in his service area in a particular subject to be discussed, as well as the qualifications of the person selected to discuss it.

Every idea does not rise to the dignity of a "public controversy," and every organization, regardless of membership or the seriousness of purposes, is not *per se* entitled to time on the air. But an organization or idea may be projected into the realm of controversy by virtue of being attacked. The holders of a belief should not be denied the right to answer attacks upon them or their belief solely because they are few in number.

The fact that a licensee's duty to make time available for the presentation of opposing views on current controversial issues of public importance may not extend to all possible differences of opinion within the ambit of human contemplation cannot serve as the basis for any rigid policy that time shall be denied for the presentation of views which may have a high degree of unpopularity. The criterion of the public interest in the field of broadcasting clearly precludes a policy of making radio wholly unavailable as a medium for the expression of any view which falls within the scope of the Constitutional guarantee of freedom of speech.[13]

The Scott decision did *not* say that every time a radio station carries religious broadcasts, atheists are entitled to time for the expression of their views. It did say, however, that licensees in exercising their judgment as to what is a controversial issue, should not deny time for the expression of a particular point of view solely because they do not agree with that point of view.

The *Morris* Case

The *Morris* case, in 1946, raised the issue whether the licensee's obligation for overall fairness in the discussion of controversy extends to advertising messages for products that some listeners consider detrimental.

Sam Morris, a prohibitionist, asked the FCC not to renew the license of a Dallas station because it sold choice time to beer and wine interests and refused to sell time for abstinence messages. The Commission denied Morris' specific request, but it extended the fairness requirement to cover advertising matter by saying that "the advertising of alcoholic beverages over the radio can raise substantial issues of public importance" inasmuch as the question of the sale and consumption of such beverages is often a matter of controversy.

What is for other individuals merely a routine advertising "plug," extolling the virtues of a beverage, essentially no different from other types of product

---

[13] "In re Petition of Robert Harold Scott, Memorandum Opinion and Order," FCC Release No. 96050, July 19, 1946 (mimeo).

advertising, is for some individuals the advocacy of a practice which they deem to be detrimental to our society. Whatever the merits of this controversy . . . it is at least clear that it may assume the proportions of a controverted issue of public importance. The fact that the occasion for the controversy happens to be the advertising of a product cannot serve to diminish the duty of the broadcaster to treat it as such an issue.[14]

FCC STATEMENTS OF POLICY

In early 1945, the Federal Communications Commission announced a policy of a more detailed review of broadcast station performance in passing on applications for license renewals. A year later, the Commission issued a lengthy, much-publicized, and much-controverted report entitled *Public Service Responsibility of Broadcast Licensees,* commonly referred to as the *Blue Book.*

In the *Blue Book,* the FCC examined the logs of several stations and compared them with the promises the stations had made when they filed their license application. KIEV, Glendale, California, had devoted 88 percent of its program time in a sample week to transcribed music and less than 3.7 percent to local live talent whose availability in the community had been the chief argument made by the station in applying for its license. The station's programs were interspersed with spot announcements on the average of one every five-and-a-half minutes. A total of 1042 spots were broadcast during the sample week, of which 1034 were commercial and eight were broadcast as a public service. WSNY, Schenectady, New York, broadcast transcriptions for 78 percent of its air time, although it had promised a maximum of 20 percent in competing with another applicant for the same station license. WTOL, Toledo, had been given permission to engage in full-time broadcasting on the ground that local organizations needed to be heard. It promised to devote 84 percent of its evening time to such broadcasts, but the record showed the actual percentage was 13.7.

The Commission expressed concern over the amount of time devoted to commercials, the undue length of individual announcements, and the piling up of commercials. In a wistful vein the Commission said, "The listener who has heard one program and wants to hear another has come to expect a commercial plug to intervene. Conversely, the listener who has heard one or more commercial announcements may reasonably expect a program to intervene." But the Commission discovered that there were many occasions when a listener might be obliged to listen to five commercial announcements between two programs. Poor taste and propaganda in commercials, the middle commercial in newscasts, and intermixing programs with advertising also disturbed the Commission. "A listener is entitled to know when the program ends and the advertisement begins," the report asserted.

At the end of the *Blue Book,* the Commission announced its future policy with regard to the public-interest aspects of broadcasting. Among the factors the Commission said it would consider in evaluating a station's public-service contribution were the proportion of time devoted to sustaining

[14] *Petition of Sam Morris,* 3 Pike & Fischer, Radio Regulations, 154.

programs, the number of local, live programs, the amount of time spent in discussing public issues, and the avoidance of advertising excesses.

While it did not have the force of a formal Commission regulation, the *Blue Book* stood for many years as the most comprehensive FCC interpretation of the "public convenience, interest, or necessity" clause of the Communications Act. In the period immediately following the issuance of the report, some license renewals were held up for hearings, and new licenses were issued on the basis of *Blue Book* criteria, but as the years went by and membership of the Commission changed, many observers felt that the *Blue Book* had become a dead issue in broadcast regulation.

In July of 1960 the FCC, for the first time since the publication of its *Blue Book,* issued a general *Report and Statement of Policy* regarding the obligation of broadcasters for programming. This report did not arouse nearly as much controversy as had been provoked by the *Blue Book*—one reason, perhaps, being that its pronouncements were somewhat less specific and less restrictive than those of the previous publication. It did, nevertheless, provide firm programming criteria for the guidance of broadcasters. In one passage, for example, it stated:

> The broadcaster is obligated to make a positive, diligent and continuing effort to determine the tastes, needs and desires of the public in his community and to provide programming to meet those needs and interests. The Commission does expect its broadcast licensees to take the necessary steps to inform themselves of the real needs of the areas they serve and to provide programming . . . for those needs and interests.

The Commission further listed 14 major elements of programming usually necessary to meet the public interest, and it placed entertainment at the bottom of the list. These elements included 1. opportunity for local self-expression, 2. development and use of local talent, 3. programs for children, 4. religious programs, 5. educational programs, 6. public affairs programming, 7. editorials by licensees, 8. political broadcasts, 9. agricultural reports, 10. news, 11. weather and market reports, 12. sports, 13. service to minority groups, and 14. entertainment programming. One significant change from the *Blue Book* was that the Commission no longer distinguished between sustaining and commercially sponsored programs in evaluating station performance.

In the years since the issuance of the 1960 statement of policy, the FCC has refined its position on what constitutes acceptable programming and has described in greater detail the elements involved. Five years after the statement, the FCC published a primer on the ascertainment of community needs, emphasizing responsibility of applicants for licenses and renewals to discover information about community problems rather than to collect information about suitable programs. The devising of programs aimed at meeting these community problems would then follow. The process of ascertaining community needs has become one of the most critical elements in a licensee's application for renewal or in a new applicant's request for a license allocation.

One problem that grew steadily more acute during this period was the question of what to do when the FCC was faced with competing applications at renewal time. In 1970 the FCC issued a policy statement saying "that if the applicant for renewal of a license shows in a hearing with a competing applicant that its program service during the preceding license term has been substantially attuned to meeting the needs and interests of its area, and that the operation of the station has not otherwise been characterized by serious deficiencies, he will be preferred over the newcomer and his application for renewal will be granted." When this policy was tested in the courts, however, it was repudiated because the Commission had unreasonably weighted the situation "in favor of the licensees it is meant to regulate, to the great detriment of the listening and viewing public." The court argued further that the policy would "in effect, substitute a standard of substantial service for the best possible service."

The FCC later changed the term it used from "substantial" to "superior" and defined in detail what it considered superior service to be. One measure it advanced was to establish the percentage of news, public affairs, and local programming broadcast in relation to the entire programming schedule.

Congressional committees have also struggled with this problem of comparing a station's performance with the promises of competing applicants as they have considered license-renewal bills over a number of years. No great changes are expected if and when final action is taken. It is likely that incumbent licensees who provide reasonably satisfactory service to a community will continue to have a significant advantage in receiving a renewal of their licenses over those competing applicants who seek to wrest it from them. Another change Congress is considering is to increase the licensing period from three to five years.

In addition to considering official documents of the FCC, the broadcasting industry must take into account the unofficial statements of individual members of the Commission. In May of 1961, Newton Minow, who had been recently appointed Chairman of the FCC by President Kennedy, alarmed broadcasters when he characterized most TV programming as a "vast wasteland" and implied that if the industry did nothing to improve programming, the FCC would enforce higher program standards. In more recent years, Nicholas Johnson, a member of the Commission, angered and alarmed broadcasters with virtually every speech he made. He criticized broadcasters for their failure to live up to their public-service responsibilities, he opposed the Pastore Bill, much favored by broadcasters, which would protect them against applications for their licenses until the FCC had first denied them renewals, and he attacked the way in which government policy worked to concentrate power over communications media in a very few hands.[15] In 1974, the chairman of the FCC met with the heads of the three networks to urge adoption of policies that would reduce violence in programs telecast before 9:00 P.M. The "Family Viewing Time" policy, labeled the "prime-time censorship rule" by the Writer's Guild, followed these meetings. Later a court ruled that the policy was unconstitutional because it violated First Amendment rights.

[15] See Nicholas Johnson, *How to Talk Back to Your Television Set* (Boston, 1970).

THE CONSTITUTIONAL QUESTION

The right of the Federal Communications Commission to engage in any kind of program review, even on an overall basis, has been frequently challenged in court on the ground that such action violates the censorship section of the Communications Act and constitutes an abridgment of the freedom of speech and press guaranteed by the First Amendment to the Constitution.

The FCC has defended its regulatory acts by arguing that television and radio, as licensed media of communication, are not in the same status as the press. The Commission holds that the purpose of the Communications Act is to maintain the control of the United States over broadcasting and that the law explicitly states that the right of free speech by television and radio shall not be impaired. To suggest that persons who are granted limited rights under licenses to run stations may, by their action, make television and radio unavailable to others as a medium of free speech is, in the opinion of the Commission, contrary to the intention of the law.

Wayne Coy, former chairman of the FCC, once said:

> If freedom of radio means that a licensee is entitled to do as he pleases without regard to the interests of the general public, then it may reasonably be contended that restraints on that freedom constitute acts of censorship. If, however, the freedom of radio means that radio should be available as a medium of freedom of expression for the general public, then it is obvious enough that restraints on the licensee which are designed to insure the preservation of that freedom are not acts of censorship.[16]

It is interesting to note that when the issue of constitutionality of radio regulation was raised 46 years ago, Secretary of Commerce Hoover commented, "We can surely agree that no one can raise a cry of deprivation of free speech if he is compelled to prove that there is something more than naked commercial selfishness in his purpose."[17]

These issues must ultimately be decided by the Supreme Court. Leading cases so far seem to support the Commission's position. Among the significant Supreme Court decisions, the *Sanders,* the *Network,* and the *Red Lion* cases are perhaps the most important guides for deciding the extent of Commission authority over programming without committing an unlawful act of censorship.

The *Sanders* case, decided in 1940, concerned whether the FCC was obliged to consider the economic injury that might result to existing stations in determining whether it shall grant or withhold a license to a new station. The Supreme Court concluded that there was no such obligation.

> An important element of public interest and convenience affecting the issue of a license is the ability of the licensee to render the best practicable service to the community reached by his broadcasts. That such ability may be assured

---

[16] Address by Wayne Coy at the Yale Law School, January 22, 1949.

[17] Address by Herbert Hoover before the Fourth National Radio Conference, Washington, 1925.

the [Communications] Act contemplates inquiry by the Commission, *inter alia,* into an applicant's financial qualifications to operate the proposed station. But the Act does not essay to regulate the business of the licensee. The Commission is given no supervisory control of the programs, of business management, or of policy. In short, the broadcasting field is open to anyone, provided there be an available frequency over which he can broadcast without interference to others, if he shows his competency, the adequacy of his equipment, and financial ability to make good use of the assigned channel . . . . Plainly it is not the purpose of the Communications Act to protect a licensee against competition but to protect the public. Congress intended to leave competition in the business of broadcasting where it found it, to permit a licensee who was not interfering electrically with other broadcasters to survive or succumb according to his ability to make his programs attractive to the public.[18]

In the *Network* case, NBC challenged the Commission's authority to issue the Chain Broadcasting Regulations on the ground, among others, that the regulations abridged freedom of speech under the First Amendment. The Supreme Court upheld the Commission's regulations and spoke as follows:

. . . we are asked to regard the Commission as a kind of traffic officer, policing the wave lengths to prevent stations from interfering with each other. But the Act does not restrict the Commission merely to supervision of the traffic. *It puts upon the Commission the burden of determining the composition of that traffic* . . .

The Commission's licensing function cannot be discharged . . . merely by finding that there are no technological objections to the granting of a license. If the criterion of "public interest" were limited to such matters, how could the Commission choose between two applicants for the same facilities, each of whom is financially and technically qualified to operate a station? . . .

We come, finally, to an appeal to the First Amendment. The regulations, even if valid in all other respects, must fail because they abridge, say the appellants, their right of free speech. If that be so, it would follow that every person whose application for a license to operate a station is denied by the Commission is thereby denied his constitutional right of free speech. Freedom of utterance is abridged to many who wish to use the limited facilities of radio. Unlike other modes of expression, radio inherently is not available to all. That is its unique characteristic, and that is why, unlike other modes of expression, it is subject to governmental regulation.[19]

In the *Red Lion* case, mentioned earlier, the Supreme Court upheld the FCC's fairness doctrine. These interpretations by the Supreme Court stand as the ruling cases today. In a series of other decisions in the District of Columbia Circuit Court of Appeals, the right of the Commission to consider various aspects of program policy or plans of the applicants for station licenses has been upheld.[20] The Supreme Court itself has cited, in a related

---

[18] *Federal Communications Commission* v. *Sanders Brothers' Radio,* 309 U.S. 470, 475 (1940).

[19] *National Broadcasting Company* v. *United States,* 319 U.S. 190 (1943).

[20] *Bay State Beacon* v. *Federal Communications Commission,* App. D.C., 171 F. 2d, 826; *Kentucky Broadcasting Co.* v. *Federal Communications Commission,* App. D.C. 174 2d, 38; *Johnson Broadcasting Co.* v. *Federal Communications Commission,* App. D.C., 175 F. 2d, 351; *Easton Publishing Co.* v. *Federal Communications Commission,* App. D.C., 175 F. 2d, 344.

case, its prior decisions in the *Sanders* and *Network* cases in further ruling that "Although the licensee's business as such is not regulated, the qualifications of the licensee and the character of its broadcasts may be weighed in determining whether or not to grant a license."[21] Nevertheless, the view persists among some important leaders in the broadcast industry that the public-interest clause of the Communications Act of 1934 cannot constitutionally enlarge the function and authority of the FCC beyond that of being a traffic cop of the airwaves without violating the First Amendment to the Constitution.

Another aspect of this overall issue came into focus in 1969 when an organization known as the Business Executives Move for Vietnam Peace requested that station WTOP in Washington, D.C., sell time to present editorials opposing the involvement of the United States in the Vietnam war. When the station refused, the organization complained to the FCC that its First Amendment rights were being violated. It was joined in that action by the Democratic National Committee, which hoped to purchase time for editorials favoring its cause in the next election. The FCC rejected the complaint because in its view the public interest was being served by the fairness doctrine, which provided for the airing of various views on controversial issues.

The U.S. Court of Appeals in Washington, D.C., reversed the action of the FCC on the grounds that a station's refusal to provide paid editorial time when other sorts of paid commercials were accepted did violate the First Amendment, and it ordered the FCC to establish regulations governing the selling of time for editorials.

The matter, with additional parties joining the action, was then brought before the Supreme Court, which issued its decision in 1973. The Supreme Court reversed the Court of Appeals and supported the original decision of the FCC.[22] Among the arguments the Court advanced in support of its decision were 1. that under the fairness doctrine licensees had broad journalistic discretion in the area of the discussion of public issues; 2. that neither public-interest standards nor the First Amendment required broadcasters to accept editorial advertisements even though they accepted commercial advertisements; and 3. that the FCC was justified in concluding that the public interest would not be served by a station's affording a right of access to broadcasting facilities for paid editorial advertisements because such a system would be heavily weighted in favor of the financially affluent and would jeopardize the operation of the fairness doctrine.

SUMMARY

The touchstone of broadcast regulation in the United States is the public interest. The Federal Communications Commission has tended to interpret the public interest in piecemeal fashion, proceeding from case to case, but in

---

[21] *Regents of Georgia* v. *Carroll,* 338 U.S. 586, 598.

[22] *Columbia Broadcasting System* v. *Democratic National Committee,* 412 U.S. 94 (1973).

some instances it has expressed a broader interpretation in such documents as the *Blue Book,* the *Mayflower* opinion, and the 1960 *Report and Statement of Policy.* The authority of the Commission to review overall program service to decide whether the public interest is being served has been upheld by various courts.

Questions for Discussion

1. What does freedom of broadcasting mean?
2. How can we decide whether a station is serving the public interest?
3. Why does the obligation to operate in the public's interest apply more to the owner of a TV station than it does to the owner of a newspaper?
4. How has the FCC interpreted the "public interest" clause of the Communications Act?
5. How can we reconcile the prohibition against censorship and the FCC's practice of overall program review in considering license renewals?
6. Should a fixed limit be maintained on the number of stations controlled by the same licensee?
7. What should be our policy toward newspaper ownership of television and radio stations?
8. Should the owner of a station "be given complete and exclusive control over program content, including the sole right to determine who shall speak and the right to censor any material intended for broadcast"?
9. What issue was involved in the *Mayflower* and *Red Lion* cases?
10. Should station owners be held responsible for programs broadcast by their stations but originated by a network?
11. Cite two types of violation of the public's interest that have caused the revocation of broadcasting licenses.
12. What important principle was enunciated by the FCC in its decision on the *Scott* case?
13. Do you think that the criticisms of radio station programming included in the FCC's *Blue Book* still apply to broadcasting?

10

Of all the facts that make television and radio important institutions in our society, probably the most imposing is the opening of private homes for the purpose of conveying political messages, either directly in the form of political presentations, or indirectly through the coverage of political events. Political programs are important because it is clear beyond all doubt that listeners and viewers at home are influenced by what they see and hear.

It has been demonstrated experimentally, for example, that even a single 15-minute radio talk can influence significantly our attitudes on political issues, and these shifts in attitude can still be observed two weeks after the talk. Our first dramatic evidence of the political effectiveness of radio came in the 1930s, when it was a common broadcasting practice to allow the air to be used for political exhortation. The effectiveness of radio in inducing specific political action was demonstrated on an extraordinary scale in 1935 when Father Charles E. Coughlin, a Detroit priest, denounced the World Court in a radio talk and 200,000 telegrams tied up the wires of Western Union. Again in 1938, Father Coughlin, in opposing a bill pending in Congress, appealed to his listeners by saying, "The immediacy of the danger insists that before tomorrow noon your telegram is in the hands of your senator." By the next day, 100,000 telegrams had piled up on congressional desks, and thousands were still pouring in when the time came for a vote.

THE DEVELOPMENT OF POLITICAL BROADCASTING

Radio first became a significant factor in politics in 1924, when the Democratic and Republican convention proceedings were broadcast gavel-to-gavel, but its influence in the campaign of that year was slight because few people had sets and there were no permanent networks. As broadcasting facilities expanded, so did radio's role in politics. By 1932 it had become the nation's most important means of political communication, a function it maintained until television took over the major responsibility 20 years later. Radio's effect on the results of elections is difficult to assess, but some believe its influence was profound. The Democratic campaign manager of 1936, James Farley, felt that radio, by offsetting the almost total opposition of the country's newspapers to Franklin Roosevelt's reelection, was the major factor in Roosevelt's landslide victory over his Republican opponent, Alfred Landon.[1] Radio's decisive effect may have come from its power to persuade people to vote, according to Angus Campbell, Director of the Survey Research Center at the University of Michigan. He found that "Roosevelt's great majority in 1936 was based not so much on defecting Republicans as on citizens who had not previously voted."[2]

When television replaced radio as the major means of political communication in 1952, reducing radio to a supporting role, the impact of broadcasting on political events and procedures increased. The trends that had developed in the radio age were accentuated. The costs of campaigning, which had grown greatly when radio time had to be purchased, were multiplied many times over by the much higher charges for television time. The result was that a lion's share of campaign budgets went for the purchase of television and radio time. Changes in convention procedures that had begun in the radio era were hastened by television. One change now fully in effect is to schedule the most important events when the largest television audience can be expected to receive them. Thus the acceptance speeches of candidates, the first volleys of the campaign, are now carefully scheduled for delivery during prime evening hours instead of occurring by chance as they had before. Harry Truman's acceptance speech in 1948, for example, was given well after midnight, long after most people had turned off their sets and gone to bed. Since then acceptance speeches have been given when most people are awake except in 1972 when, in a convention that was generally chaotic, the Democrats lost control of the schedule and George McGovern did not appear to make his acceptance speech until the early morning hours. Jimmy Carter, vowing not to repeat that error, maintained a control of the convention in 1976 that brought him before the TV cameras to accept the nomination in prime time. The Republican Convention in 1976 took longer than was expected to nominate a Vice-President, but Gerald Ford still managed to begin his acceptance speech well before the midnight hour.

Another adaptation to television is the elimination or modification of certain political exercises that the average viewer finds dull or meaningless. The polling of delegations now takes place out of camera range, and demonstrations and seconding speeches are severely limited in time and number. Before these restrictions were introduced, demonstrations and seconding speeches went on interminably. In 1936 there were 56 seconding speeches for Franklin Roosevelt's nomination.

The wide use of television and radio in campaigning has also forced candidates to change the nature of their presentations to meet the requirements of effective broadcasting. A greater emphasis has been placed on brevity in sustained speaking, greater informality of delivery, and there is an extreme concern for personal appearance. Interviews and discussions have been widely substituted for the formal address.

[1] James Farley, *Behind the Ballots* (New York, 1938), p. 319.
[2] Angus Campbell, "Has Television Reshaped Politics?" *Columbia Journalism Review*, 1 (Fall, 1962), p. 11.

One of the most significant changes introduced as politicians became broadcasters was the entry of advertising agencies into the political arena. Agencies first began working behind the scenes in 1936, but not until 1944 did the parties acknowledge their services. There was some reticence at first in merchandising candidates in the same way that products such as soap and beer are advertised on television and radio, but as the years went on this reticence decreased until by 1952 it vanished altogether. In that year General Dwight Eisenhower became the first presidential candidate in our history willing to appear in television and radio commercials. The saturation campaign of spot announcements that came in the two weeks before the voters cast their ballots was considered by some to be a vital factor in his election. Despite this success, the commercial approach to electioneering was not adopted immediately by all candidates, but by 1968 it seemed that both the Democratic and Republican candidates were willing to appear in 30- and 60-second spots without any hesitation.

Television and radio have had another significant effect on politics: they have brought nationwide recognition to relatively obscure politicians almost overnight. Radio performed this service as early as 1924 when it helped make Calvin Coolidge a national figure after he was catapulted from the obscurity of the Vice-Presidency into the Presidency by the death of Warren Harding. In 1952 Adlai Stevenson, the relatively unknown Governor of Illinois, faced the internationally renowned war hero Dwight Eisenhower. Stevenson's appearances on television won him millions of adherents who had never heard of him before. John F. Kennedy, who decided that he would run for President after the 1956 convention, used television to make his name and face known to the country. In the years that followed, television was used more and more for the same purpose.

Whether the use of television has decisively influenced the outcome of a presidential election is an intriguing question, difficult to answer. The Eisenhower victories would probably have been won without the aid of broadcasting—in the 1952 election because of his fame as a victorious general and in 1956 because he was the incumbent,—but in the presidential campaign that followed in 1960, television may have played a decisive role in determining the outcome as John F. Kennedy and Richard M. Nixon met each other in four "great debates." During the period of these TV and radio meetings, the research firm of Sindlinger and Co. found that the eventual winner, Kennedy, gained ground with the voters. Some saw this as the factor that made his narrow victory possible.

There were no more debates between presidential candidates until 1976, when the incumbent Republican President Gerald Ford met the Democratic candidate Jimmy Carter in three televised confrontations. (There was also one meeting between the candidates for Vice-President, Democrat Walter Mondale and Republican Robert Dole.) The effect of these debates on the election result is as difficult to assess as the effect of the 1960 debates. At least one person, however, considered their role crucial—Jimmy Carter, the victorious candidate. He felt that without them he would have lost the election to Gerald Ford. The debates, Carter believed, helped to establish him as "a respectable person" and left the American people reassured that at least Jimmy Carter had some judgment in areas such as foreign affairs and national defense.

The use of the broadcast media for political purposes is not restricted to national candidates, of course. In 1960, in addition to regular radio and TV appearances by state and local office-seekers, the example of the presidential joint appearances inspired similar meetings between candidates for mayor, governor, congressman, and senator. In the years since, candidates have continued to meet each other on occasion before the TV cameras. The prediction of Jack Gould, former television editor of *The New York Times,* seems indisputable: "There is no question that hereafter TV and politics will be inseparable as never before."

Outside the formal campaign periods, television and radio are used to foster political causes and personalities. Congressmen use television and radio to "tell the folks back home" how matters stand in Washington. Government administrators broadcast reports to the public, and parties out of power just as frequently seek air time to reply, when controversial matters are at stake. Labor and management spokesmen make regular use of the air to win support for particular legislative programs. Some politicians who appear on discussion or press interview programs claim that a supposedly nonpolitical appearance before a camera can be just as effective in winning friends, if not more so, than a straight political appearance. The numerous news summaries broadcast throughout the day with their news reports of important political statements and addresses also serve as vehicles for political messages to the public. Indeed, experienced politicians release copies of their addresses for news coverage prior to the actual delivery of the speeches. Thus we often hear in an early evening newscast what a politician is scheduled to say to an audience later in the evening; several hours later newscasts repeat what he did say. In this way many politicians obtain double news coverage of addresses that are actually delivered before an audience of only a few hundred people.

THE LAW AND POLITICAL BROADCASTING

In writing the Communications Act of 1934, Congress made no bones about the power of the federal government to impose upon broadcasting stations, despite the First Amendment to the Constitution, a rigid standard of fairness it has never imposed upon newspapers. Section 315 of the Act provides in part:

> If any licensee shall permit any person who is a legally qualified candidate for any public office to use a broadcasting station, he shall afford equal opportunities to all other such candidates for that office in the use of such broadcasting station, and the Commission shall make rules and regulations to carry this provision into effect: Provided, That such licensee shall have no power of censorship over the material broadcast under the provisions of this section. No

obligation is hereby imposed upon any licensee to allow the use of its station by any such candidate.

The charges made for the use of any broadcasting station for any of the purposes set forth in this section shall not exceed the charges made for comparable use of such station for other purposes.

This provision means that television and radio stations must offer free time or sell time on an equal basis (including identical discounts) to all legally qualified candidates for the same office during a political primary or election campaign. Under the original law a station could choose to offer or sell no time at all to any of the candidates but a later Act of Congress requires that stations accept advertising by political candidates.

Four problems have arisen in connection with this section of the Communications Act. The first derives from the fact that although we tend to have a two-party system in politics, there are usually, especially in national elections, as many as 18 very small parties that put up legally qualified candidates for office and are therefore entitled to equal opportunity with the candidates of the major parties to obtain air time. If a television station invited the presidential candidates of the Democratic and Republican parties to appear on one of its programs, it was obligated to extend similar invitations to all other candidates for the Presidency.

The second problem stems from the conflict between the ban against censoring political campaign broadcasts and the requirements under state laws that libel shall not be voiced on the air. The FCC has ruled that once a station has agreed to broadcast a political campaign speech, the station must go through with it even though the station manager may consider the speech libelous in part or in whole. The FCC reasoned that fear of libel would be a convenient excuse for a station operator to refuse to carry attacks on his political friends. Many state legislatures passed laws relieving stations from responsibility for libel contained in speeches delivered under this provision of the Communications Act. The final step came in 1959 when the Supreme Court, recognizing that stations could not censor political broadcasts, made stations immune from any liability for defamatory statements contained in speeches broadcast by legally qualified candidates for public office.

A third problem arose when Lar Daly, running for Mayor of Chicago in the late fifties against the incumbent, Richard Daley, argued that reports of the Mayor's activities on TV news programs constituted political coverage under Section 315 and demanded that he be given equal time. The FCC, deciding that Daly was right in his interpretation of the Act, ordered that he be given the same coverage in newscasts that the Mayor was being given. Although the FCC was undoubtedly right in its assessment of the way that Section 315 as then written should be applied, its action probably meant that from that point on political campaigns would no longer be covered in news programs. Considering this development unfavorable to the democratic process, the Congress in 1959 amended Section 315 to exempt newscasts, on-the-spot coverage of news events, news interview programs, and certain types of documentary programs from the equal-time provisions. It was this provision that permitted the networks to broadcast the 1976 debates between

Jimmy Carter and Gerald Ford without providing time for debates involving the candidates of the minor political parties. The debates were arranged by the League of Women Voters and under the law the networks simply covered them as a "bona fide" news event. This means of circumventing the requirements of Section 315 was considered a sham by many observers and was challenged unsuccessfully in court by minor party candidate Eugene McCarthy. The 1960 debates between John Kennedy and Richard Nixon were broadcast under a different set of circumstances. In that year the Congress passed a temporary amendment to the equal-time provision of the Federal Communications Act that permitted the broadcasting of debates between the presidential candidates of the Democratic and Republican parties without incurring the obligation of providing time for the candidates of the minority parties.

The fourth problem that arose in connection with Section 315 concerned the practice indulged in by some stations of charging more than regular broadcast rates for political programs. Following a particularly glaring case of excessive time charges during a congressional by-election campaign in Pennsylvania in 1959, Congress amended the Communications Act to require stations to charge only standard rates for political broadcasts. In the Campaign Communications Reform Act of 1971, the Congress went even further by requiring that stations charge only their lowest unit rate for commercials or programs in which political candidates appear. In addition to preventing broadcasters from exploiting candidates by charging excessive rates, the Congress put pressure on stations to afford reasonable access to their facilities for political candidates by threatening those who failed to provide such access with license revocation. The term "reasonable access" is subject to varying interpretations. Broadcasters respond to it in a number of different ways, but the responsibility of making their facilities available for some political messages by candidates seems inescapable. Station WGN, in Chicago, for example, refused to accept political messages less than five minutes in length because it argued that the explanation of a political position required at least that much time. The FCC forced it to abandon that policy by requiring it to sell time for 30- and 60-second commercials in which political candidates appeared.

In a later action the Congress tightened its requirement that stations accept advertising by political candidates by making it illegal for them to refuse to provide no time at all. It was under this provision that Senator James Buckley demanded that the educational TV stations in New York provide him time for campaign messages.

The Congress has demonstrated that it believes the use of broadcasting facilities for political messages to be in the public interest, but it has shown concern for preventing domination of the media by those able to afford it. It is the belief of many that the permissiveness that permitted the Richard Nixon campaign organization to raise vast sums of money to finance his re-election was at the root of the Watergate scandal in 1972. Nixon spent some $20 million to win renomination by his party even though he faced no serious Republican contenders, and it is estimated that he spent $60 million overall to win the presidency a second time. To control political expenditures, the Congress passed a law providing for federal financing of presidential campaigns. Under this law, primary candidates could receive $5 million from the government and could spend an additional $5 million. Even with these restraints, expenditures by the primary candidates in 1976 amounted to $70 million. In the election campaign that followed, Ford and Carter each spent approximately $21.8 million provided by the federal government, plus some $3 million raised by the parties.

One reason for the high cost of campaigning is the tremendous expenditure required for television time. To control this factor, the Congress ruled that funds spent for the broadcast media may not exceed 60 percent of the total media costs permitted. This restraint requires careful planning by the candidates. President Ford in his 1976 election effort decided to save a substantial amount of the money he could use for television to purchase time in the last two weeks of the campaign. In the opinion of some observers, this saturation strategy helped to overcome much of the gap that, according to pollsters, originally separated him from his opponent Carter, though it did not succeed in winning Ford the election.

TELEVISION AND IMAGE PROJECTION

Some people have wondered whether the marriage of television and politics is really good for our democracy. One of the dangers cited is that television appears to give the advantage to the candidate who can project the most favorable image to the voters rather than to the one who may have the best qualifications for the office. The impression people have of a candidate has always been a significant factor in politics, of course. As far back as 1840, William Henry Harrison was elected President because of the victorious image he had as the winner of the battle of Tippecanoe. Unfortunately, that battle had been won 30 years before and Harrison, who was ordered by his managers not to say a single word about his political principles during the campaign, lived barely long enough to survive his inauguration. But television has placed an importance on image projection that it has never had before. According to some, image now is all that matters. One's qualifications for office or his stand on the issues are no longer important. What counts is not what the candidate is but what he can be made to appear to be. Recent events suggest that there may be some truth to this disturbing view of the way in which voters make their choices.

In the 1952 election General Eisenhower was portrayed in radio and television commercials as a victorious general who could "clean up the mess in Washington." In both of his campaigns his image as a good family man was constantly reinforced by his references to his wife, Mamie. His Democratic opponent Adlai Stevenson was divorced and lacked the enhancement of image that a successful marriage can contribute. At one period he tried somewhat pathetically to acquire this image anyway by appearing on television with his son, Adlai, Jr., and his daughter-in-law in a setting that was depicted as their "happy home." As far as the majority of voters was concerned, it appeared that General Eisenhower won the battle of the images in the 1952 and 1956 campaigns.

Marshall McLuhan, a writer on media effects, believes that Kennedy won the "great debates" of 1960 not because of the arguments he advanced but because he won the battle of the images. In McLuhan's view, television was "a disaster for a sharp intense image like Nixon's and a boon for the blurry, shaggy texture of Kennedy."[3] Nixon, looking back on the campaign of 1960, seemed to realize himself that he had failed to perform on television in a way that took full advantage of the medium. In his book *Six Crises* he wrote: "I believe that I spent too much time in the last campaign on substance and too little on appearance. I paid too much attention to what I would say and too little to how I would look."[4]

In 1968 Richard Nixon, having learned his lesson, pursued a course far different from the one he had followed in 1960. He did not repeat the promise he had made that year to visit personally all the fifty states, a pledge that wasted his energies and his time, for some of the states he visited were inevitably his or were inevitably his opponent's. Such a tactic, he realized, was a relic of the past. Televison could now take over the job of personal visitation. For that reason Nixon decided to build his campaign around the use of television. To make sure that he would use it in the most effective way, he recruited a group of people who were most familiar with television—men from the advertising and broadcasting industries.

The way these men planned and carried out Nixon's campaign was recorded in meticulous detail by a young newspaperman, Joe McGinniss. In his book *The Selling of the President 1968,* he reports that the first step was to plan the parameters of the candidate's image. The sharp cold Nixon of 1960, who seemed to be a little too hungry for public office, was to be replaced by the image of a warm, human man who cared deeply about people. It was decided that the main instrument for projecting this image would be a series of regional telecasts in which Nixon would answer questions put to him by a panel that was carefully balanced among various ethnic and occupational groups.

The selection of panel members would be further controlled to insure that the questions would be challenging, but not so hostile as to make the candidate's position untenable. Nixon's willingness to stand up and answer questions in this type of situation added the further dimensions to his image of coolness, courageousness, and youthful vigor. This part of the campaign was backed up by a series of spot announcements that featured excerpts from Nixon's acceptance speech illustrated with still pictures and films.

An advertising agency also played a major role in the campaign of Nixon's opponent, Hubert Humphrey, but we have no record of its activities to match McGinniss' record of the Nixon campaign. The broadcasts in which Humphrey appeared seem to be rougher and less controlled than Nixon's, but perhaps that was a conscious technique designed to project the image his agency had planned.

How well did the Nixon image-building approach work? There is no way of knowing for certain. His initial lead over Humphrey, according to

[3] Marshall McLuhan, *Understanding Media: The Extensions of Man* (New York, 1964), p. 287.

[4] Richard M. Nixon, *Six Crises* (New York, 1962), p. 371.

the polls, gradually dwindled during the campaign, but this may have been caused by unknown factors. The important point was that he won the presidency, and that alone will cause those who seek public office to pay close attention for many years to come to the techniques Nixon used in his campaign.

In the campaigns that followed, television continued to play the dominant role in presidential politics. Although it did not win his election in 1972, George McGovern gave television most of the credit for providing him with the public recognition he needed to win the nomination of the Democratic Party. In 1976 television projected the image of a peanut farmer from Georgia who promised to wield presidential power free from the corrupting influence of Washington politics. The projection of that image was a major element in Jimmy Carter's victorious primary campaign. Ronald Reagan's skillful use of television brought him close to achieving what many considered to be an impossible task, the denial of his party's nomination to an incumbent President, Gerald Ford.

There is not sufficient evidence yet to indicate the ultimate effect television's image-building powers may have on our political processes, but there are two possibilities that cause concern. First, television may have the capacity to project an image of a politician that is a false representation of his true character. Sometimes this representation may be beneficial to a candidate, at other times it may be damaging. Barry Goldwater, the Republican candidate for President in 1964, suffered as a result of television exposure. Early in the primary campaign he came through on television as a warmonger who believed in nuclear bombing and as a heartless rich man who was against social security. That image followed him through the campaign and helped destroy any chance he might have had to win the election.

A second problem with television is that it may be the medium of communication best adapted to selling a candidate to the public for reasons that are irrelevant to his qualifications for the office. His appearance, his demeanor, and his style may count more heavily, for example, than his political principles. Can anything be done to minimize these dangers? The outlook is not hopeful. It would be naive to expect that campaigners seeking political prizes of immense worth would refrain from exploiting the powers of television to their maximum possible advantage. If the nation adopts a constitutional amendment to elect the President by direct popular vote, television may become virtually the only means used to reach the public in national elections. Our expectation must be that candidates will continue to be merchandised like packaged goods and that image manipulators will continue to play a major role in politics.

Some recent studies, however, have thrown some doubt on television's power to build favorable images. Edward Diamond in his book *The Tin Kazoo* pointed out that in the 1970 elections many candidates who employed high-priced image makers were defeated. Thomas Patterson and Robert McClure have carried out research indicating that TV commercials may be severely limited in what they can do for candidates (reported in their book, *The Unseeing Eye*). They found, for example, that political commercials have almost no power to change people's preexisting views of candidates and parties. They discovered also that although commercials may provide voters with information about issues, they have little influence on how they vote. Generally, they found that television news coverage is no more influential than newspaper coverage in affecting the voters' response to candidates.

It might be noted that using television to create favorable images for candidates has virtually eliminated the half-hour set speech delivered in a formal setting. Now the emphasis is on the short commercial—which, despite the finding just cited, most candidates believe to be vital to the success of their cause. In addition to commercials, candidates gain a great deal of television exposure from coverage by news programs and appearances in television interviews. Though face-to-face meetings with voters still have some importance, the main reason candidates campaign in the various states is to gain news and interview coverage, which comes to them free of charge.

Television was also used in 1976 for a purpose quite different from that of image making. In that year Ronald Reagan spent $100,000 for a speech on national television in which he asked for contributions to support his campaign. His investment won him a 1500 percent return, as $1,500,000 flowed in. Similar appeals on national television by Senator Frank Church generated four times as much money as they cost when the influx of additional federal matching funds was counted. Television was used therefore not only in the hope that it would build favorable images but also to raise money.

TELEVISION COVERAGE OF POLITICAL EVENTS

In addition to feeling concern about television as a political image builder, many worry about whether television can be trusted to convey a political situation as it really is. It is well known that tape or film shown on television can be edited to distort the truth or even give a totally false impression. The best example of such distortion is that accomplished by editing words on a tape. Gene Wyckoff in his book *The Image Candidates* mentions that a statement made by General Eisenhower in 1960 endorsing Henry Cabot Lodge for the vice-presidency was edited in 1964 to make it appear that the General was endorsing Lodge for the presidency. But editing may not only rearrange words, it may also reorder a sequence of events or juxtapose happenings that occurred entirely separately. The crowds one sees in a film appearing to cheer a candidate may never have seen him; they may have assembled for another reason altogether—a football game, perhaps. It is not just tape or film that may distort an audience's view of an event, however. Even the live transmission of a situation may project a false impression of what is taking place. Seeing an event on television, in other words, is not quite like being there.

Some cite the televising of the events connected with the 1968 Democratic Convention in Chicago as a prime example of the distortion that can result from selective transmission. In particular, broadcasters were accused of concentrating on the reactions of police to the mobs in the streets without showing the provocation that caused those reactions. The result was that the police seemed to be making unprovoked assaults on mere onlookers. The broadcasters, of course, defended themselves vigorously against this charge, asserting that they did convey a complete picture of the violent street happenings that took place in Chicago in 1968. Similar criticisms are made of the way in which television broadcasters cover events within the convention halls. They are accused of pursuing the dramatic rather than following events that may be duller but are more significant. Broadcasters are even accused of generating rumors that have no basis in fact simply to make broadcasts more intriguing. They are also charged with creating synthetic excitement by encouraging convention delegates to make inflammatory statements, and they are accused of doing everything they can to stir up controversy. Some have noted that the mere presence of TV cameras tends to provoke incidents that would not have happened had they not been there.

A crucial limitation of television is that it cannot present everything that is taking place. The exclusion of certain happenings from the television broadcast may distort the viewer's perception of the total situation. The focus of the television camera on certain elements in the situation may also result in distortion.

Another important limitation arises not from any inherent flaw in the medium, but from the way in which television has been mainly used in our society. It has become primarily an instrument of entertainment, which networks and stations use to draw as large an audience as they can for their offerings. When conventions are being broadcast by more than one network, the competition between them to win the largest share of the audience becomes most intense. In such a situation a network tries to make its version of the proceedings as attractive as possible by injecting drama and excitement that in some instances may be developed somewhat synthetically.

What can be done to modify the limitations just described? Some have suggested that political conventions should be broadcast as United Nations' sessions have been, by keeping the cameras focused on the official speakers and proceedings and saving comments and interpretation until the convention goes into recess or is adjourned. If this suggestion were followed, correspondents who roam the floor seeking interviews would be kept in check until the session was over. The nature of the interviews should also be changed, it is argued. Instead of being designed to provoke excitement and controversy, they should be aimed at providing the viewer with maximum enlightenment about the situation. To avoid competition between networks for audiences it has been suggested that only one network broadcast the full proceedings at any one time, with the various networks taking turns at this assignment. Thus the temptation to inject synthetic drama into the events might be minimized. A step in this direction was taken in 1968 when the ABC-TV network decided for its own reasons not to broadcast the convention proceedings gavel-to-gavel but limited itself to presenting a 90-minute roundup of the main events. It continued this practice in the elections that followed.

In addition to covering national political conventions, television provides national exposure for many other political events. For many years the Senate has permitted television coverage of its committee sessions. The Ervin

Committee's hearings on the Watergate scandal in 1973 permitted the nation to hear the testimony of the principal actors in this political drama. The following year the House of Representatives permitted television coverage of its Judiciary Committee as it considered the impeachment of President Richard Nixon. One of the most dramatic moments in all of television's history occurred when the Committee in a session filled with emotion voted to recommend to the House that the President of the United States be impeached.

Many people have urged that television cameras move from the Committee rooms into the halls of the House and Senate. If this suggestion is adopted, the people nationwide will be able to see members of Congress debate and act on legislative proposals.

THE EFFECT OF EARLY ELECTION PREDICTIONS

One other problem connected with broadcast coverage of political events has aroused some concern. This problem stems from the growing sophistication of computing equipment and statistical procedures, which permit broadcasting organizations to predict the winners of political contests even before everyone has voted. During the 1964 presidential election, for example, a network forecast the victory of Lyndon Johnson over Barry Goldwater four hours before the polls had closed in California. How does this prediction affect those who have not voted? Do some of them decide not to vote, feeling that they no longer have a role to play in determining who is to be President? Do some switch their votes, either to the apparent winner or to the one who appears to be the underdog? Concern about such questions became particularly intense in the period just after the California Republican Presidential primary of 1964, in which Barry Goldwater and Nelson Rockefeller were the main contenders. Thirty-six minutes before the polls closed in the San Francisco Bay Area, a center of Rockefeller strength, CBS made a flat prediction that Goldwater would win the primary. There were reports that on hearing this prediction a number of people lined up to vote concluded that the race was over and left without voting. It is true that Goldwater did win the primary, but he won by a very narrow margin. If the reports about people dropping out of the voting lines were true, the defections may have cost Rockefeller the California primary—and perhaps the nomination and the presidency. A victory in California would have immensely strengthened him in his fight for the Republican nomination; his defeat virtually wiped out any chance he had of becoming Johnson's opponent.

To test the effect of early predictions on voting, a man-and-wife team of sociologists, Kurt and Gladys Lang, studied the behavior of a group of people who had not yet voted before the prediction was made that Johnson had won the 1964 election. The results of their study are reassuring. Of the 364 people they interviewed, the Langs discovered that only one decided not to go to the polls after he had heard the prediction. Furthermore, the Langs found no evidence of voter switches, although they did discover that the intentions of some people to vote for one or the other of the two candidates were crystallized when they heard the prediction. The results, of course, were clouded by the fact that the presidential race was only one element in the election situation. Even though these people may have known who was to be President, they did not know who was to be their Mayor or their Senator, and they would go to the polls to help decide those races.

Although the results of the Langs' study suggest that we have less to worry about than we thought with respect to the effect of early predictions on voting behavior, the Langs remind us that their results do "not mean that the broadcast of returns before polls closed had no effect upon voters, or that there will be no effects in the future."[5] The practice of making early predictions may have unfortunate consequences that have not yet been discovered. In 1968 and 1976 the problem did not arise because the closeness of the race between Nixon and Humphrey and between Ford and Carter prevented networks from making firm predictions until all the polls had closed. Some have proposed that broadcasting organizations be prevented from making forecasts about election outcomes until the polls have closed throughout the nation. The trouble with this suggestion is that it denies the right of people to know crucial and exciting information as soon as it can become available. A second suggestion, principally propounded by Frank Stanton, former President of CBS, is to establish a 24-hour uniform voting day during presidential elections, which would begin and end throughout the nation simultaneously. Because the polls would all close at the same time, vote-counting would not begin until everyone had voted. Under this plan early predictions could still be made, but there would no longer be any expectant voters to influence. There is no indication that this plan will be adopted, however. Our assumption must be that the people's desire to know election results as soon as they are available will discourage any attempt to keep them back until everyone in the country has voted.

SUMMARY

Radio began playing an important role in politics as soon as it became established as a public medium. The development of television expanded the influence of broadcasting on politics as a result. The costs of campaigning greatly increased, and long-standing political procedures were modified. The equal-time requirement in the Communications Act constitutes an important control over political broadcasting. A number of important questions have arisen in connection with the role of politics in broadcasting: Should conventional advertising techniques be used in campaigns? Is there too much emphasis on image projection? Does television transmit a true picture of political events? Do election predictions influence the results?

Questions for Discussion

1. Do you feel that political advertising has affected your judgment about candidates?

[5] Kurt Lang and Gladys Engel Lang, *Politics and Television* (New York, 1968), p. 283.

2. "While it is true that a great man, a modern Pericles, with television can be a thousand times more effective, it is also true that a slippery demagogue, a modern Alcibiades, can also be a thousand times more effective . . . It is useless and foolish to deny that this medium offers certain dangers to civilization. It adds a tremendous premium to personality as distinguished from intellectuality . . . I know that this thing is social dynamite that in the hands of a fool or a knave is capable of doing a vast amount of damage."—Gerald W. Johnson. Discuss the implications of this statement.

3. Do you believe that control over the amount of money a candidate can spend on television advertising is proper? If not, what type of control would you favor?

4. Do you believe that the broadcasting industry has a responsibility to present programs about political matters even though the programs might not be sponsored?

5. If you were a candidate for public office, how would you use television in your campaign?

6. Does the "equal-time" restriction serve a legitimate purpose, or should it be abandoned?

self-regulation in broadcasting

11

In addition to formal regulation by the Federal Communications Commission, there exist in television and radio written and unwritten codes of regulation promulgated within the industry itself—the nationwide television and radio codes of the National Association of Broadcasters, the broadcast standards of the networks and of various stations, the rules of certain groups of professional broadcasters, and informal but no less effective standards of talent and program acceptability by advertisers, agencies, networks, program production companies, and stations.

As communications media that deal directly with the public, television and radio are especially sensitive to the currents of public opinion. The fields of book and magazine publishing and motion picture production similarly are subject to public pressures related to the public ideas of acceptablity in tastes, morals, and politics.

Television and radio enter our homes in such a way that we cannot fully anticipate what will come out of the loudspeaker or will appear on the television screen. Subject to the limitations of the Communications Act, stations and networks have the responsibility for deciding what programs may be broadcast in keeping with the public interest and the moral standards and tastes of the community. It is obvious to everyone that some precautions are necessary to prevent libel and breaches of common decency on the air. In areas beyond libel and decency, such as the moral values of television dramas and the effect of violence on the audience, there has been great dispute in recent years over the proper use of broadcasting's powers of self-regulation. The principles and practices of self-regulation, however interpreted and applied, play a great role in influencing the content and manner of presentation of television and radio programs.

THE NAB

The main channel of self-regulation in television and radio is the national trade association of the industry—the National Association of Broadcasters (NAB), which acts as a general clearinghouse for the broadcasting industry and has formalized a code of self-regulation.

148

The National Association of Broadcasters was organized in 1922 to resist pressures for royalties from the American Society of Composers, Authors, and Publishers (ASCAP), which controls important music copyrights. The association developed during the course of years to service the needs of the broadcasting industry—to provide professional advice to members on employee regulations, to formulate engineering standards, to represent the industry before Congress and the public, to engage in research to show the public and commercial importance of television and radio, and to develop acceptable programming and advertising standards. With the development of television the association's name was changed in 1951 to the National Association of Radio and Television Broadcasters, but in 1958 it returned to its original name. The NAB includes 2350 AM stations, 1631 FM stations, 526 television stations, 5 radio networks, and 3 television networks. Members pay annual dues based on their net income. In addition to regular members, there are almost 300 associate members, among them film producers and syndication companies.

Of greatest interest and importance to the public are the codes of broadcast practice promulgated by the NAB. The organization, seeking to establish uniform practices throughout the industry, has drawn up codes of self-regulation. A first tentative "Code of Ethics" in 1929 banned the broadcast of commercial announcements between 7:00 and 11:00 P.M., but the restriction was ignored, and when the first industrywide standards of practice were adopted for radio in 1937, this restriction had disappeared. The first television code went into effect in 1952. Both codes have been revised at regular intervals.

The problems discussed by the codes range from proper handling of news, controversy, and religion, to children's and mystery programs, advertising standards, and contests. In general the codes represent compromises between the demands of network and station managers, who sought stringent rules to prevent advertising and programming abuses that caused public criticism of radio and television, and those managers who felt that more stringent codes would seriously injure the economic standing of the industry. Some critics believe the codes effected some compromises by linking high aspirations with mild restrictions.

Here, in full, is the Television Code of the NAB. A close reading of the Code reveals the wide range of problems faced by the industry and the ways in which the NAB has attempted to meet those problems. The official purpose of the Code, as set forth in its regulations and procedures, "is cooperatively to maintain a level of television programming which gives full consideration to the educational, informational, cultural, economic, moral and entertainment needs of the American public to the end that more and more people will be better served."

Television Code of the NAB

Preamble

Television is seen and heard in nearly every American home. These homes include children and adults of all ages, embrace all races and all varieties of philosophic or religious conviction and reach those of every educational background. Television broadcasters must take this pluralistic audience into account in programming their stations. They are obligated to bring their positive responsibility for professionalism and reasoned judgment to bear upon all those involved in the development, production and selection of programs.

The free, competitive American system of broadcasting which offers programs of entertainment, news, general information, education and culture is supported and made possible by revenues from advertising. While television broadcasters are responsible for the programming and advertising on their stations, the advertisers who use television to convey their commercial messages also have a responsibility to the viewing audience. Their advertising messages should be presented in an honest, responsible and tasteful manner. Advertisers should also support the endeavors of broadcasters to offer a diversity of programs that meet the needs and expectations of the total viewing audience.

The viewer also has a responsibility to help broadcasters serve the public. All viewers should make their criticisms and positive suggestions about programming and advertising known to the broadcast licensee. Parents particularly should oversee the viewing habits of their children, encouraging them to watch programs that will enrich their experience and broaden their intellectual horizons.

Program Standards

I. Principles Governing Program Content

It is in the interest of television as a vital medium to encourage programs that are innovative, reflect a high degree of creative skill, deal with significant moral and social issues and present challenging concepts and other subject matter that relate to the world in which the viewer lives.

Television programs should not only reflect the influence of the established institutions that shape our values and culture, but also expose the dynamics of social change which bear upon our lives.

To achieve these goals, television broadcasters should be conversant with the general and specific needs, interests and aspirations of all the segments of the communities they serve. They should affirmatively seek out responsible representatives of all parts of their communities so that they may structure a broad range of programs that will inform, enlighten, and entertain the total audience.

Broadcasters should also develop programs directed toward advancing the cultural and educational aspects of their communities.

To assure that broadcasters have the freedom to program fully and responsibly, none of the provisions of this Code should be construed as preventing or impeding broadcast of the broad range of material necessary to help broadcasters fulfill their obligations to operate in the public interest.

The challenge to the broadcaster is to determine how suitably to present the complexities of human behavior. For television, this requires exceptional awareness of considerations peculiar to the medium.

Accordingly, in selecting program subjects and themes, great care must be exercised to be sure that treatment and presentation are made in good faith and not for the purpose of sensationalism or to shock or exploit the audience or appeal to prurient interests or morbid curiosity.

Additionally, entertainment programming inappropriate for viewing by a general family audience should not be broadcast during the first hour of network entertainment programming in prime time and in the immediately preceding hour. In the occasional case when an entertainment program in this time period is deemed to be inappropriate for such an audience, advisories should be used to alert viewers. Advisories should also be used when programs in later prime time periods contain material that might be disturbing to significant segments of the audience.

These advisories should be presented in audio and video form at the beginning of the program and when deemed appropriate at a later point in the program. Advisories should also be used responsibly in promotional material in advance of the program. When using an advisory, the broadcaster should attempt to notify publishers of television program listings.

Special care should be taken with respect to the content and treatment of audience advisories so that they do not disserve their intended purpose by containing material that is promotional, sensational or exploitative. Promotional announcements for programs that include advisories should be scheduled on a basis consistent with the purpose of the advisory. *(See Television Code Interpretation No. 5.)*

II. *Responsibility Toward Children*

Broadcasters have a special responsibility to children. Programs designed primarily for children should take into account the range of interests and needs of children from instructional and cultural material to a wide variety of entertainment material. In their totality, programs should contribute to the sound, balanced development of children to help them achieve a sense of the world at large and informed adjustments to their society.

In the course of a child's development, numerous social factors and forces, including television, affect the ability of the child to make the transition to adult society.

The child's training and experience during the formative years should include positive sets of values which will allow the child to become a responsible adult, capable of coping with the challenges of maturity.

Children should also be exposed, at the appropriate times, to a reasonable range of the realities which exist in the world sufficient to help them make the transition to adulthood.

Because children are allowed to watch programs designed primarily for adults, broadcasters should take this practice into account in the presentation of material in such programs when children may constitute a substantial segment of the audience.

All the standards set forth in this section apply to both program and commercial material designed and intended for viewing by children.

III. *Community Responsibility*

1. Television broadcasters and their staffs occupy positions of unique responsibility in their communities and should conscientiously endeavor to be acquainted fully with the community's needs and characteristics in order better to serve the welfare of its citizens.

2. Requests for time for the placement of public service announcements or programs should be carefully reviewed with respect to the character and reputation of the group, campaign or organization involved, the public interest content of the message, and the manner of its presentation.

IV. Special Program Standards

1. Violence, physical or psychological, may only be projected in responsibly handled contexts, not used exploitatively. Programs involving violence should present the consequences of it to its victims and perpetrators.

Presentation of the details of violence should avoid the excessive, the gratuitous and the instructional.

The use of violence for its own sake and the detailed dwelling upon brutality or physical agony, by sight or by sound, are not permissible.

The depiction of conflict, when presented in programs designed primarily for children, should be handled with sensitivity.

2. The treatment of criminal activities should always convey their social and human effects.

The presentation of techniques of crime in such detail as to be instructional or invite imitation shall be avoided.

3. Narcotic addiction shall not be presented except as a destructive habit. The use of illegal drugs or the abuse of legal drugs shall not be encouraged or shown as socially acceptable.

4. The use of gambling devices or scenes necessary to the development of plot or as appropriate background is acceptable only when presented with discretion and in moderation, and in a manner which would not excite interest in, or foster, betting nor be instructional in nature.

5. Telecasts of actual sports programs at which on-the-scene betting is permitted by law shall be presented in a manner in keeping with federal, state and local laws, and should concentrate on the subject as a public sporting event.

6. Special precautions must be taken to avoid demeaning or ridiculing members of the audience who suffer from physical or mental afflictions or deformities.

7. Special sensitivity is necessary in the use of material relating to sex, race, color, age, creed, religious functionaries or rites, or national or ethnic derivation.

8. Subscribers shall not broadcast any material which they determine to be obscene, profane, or indecent.

Above and beyond the requirements of law, broadcasters must consider the family atmosphere in which many of their programs are viewed.

There shall be no graphic portrayal of sexual acts by sight or sound. The portrayal of implied sexual acts must be essential to the plot and presented in a responsible and tasteful manner.

Subscribers are obligated to bring positive responsibility and reasoned judgment to bear upon all those involved in the development, production, and selection of programs.

9. The presentation of marriage, the family and similarly important human relationships, and material with sexual connotations, shall not be treated exploitatively or irresponsibly, but with sensitivity. Costuming and movements of all performers shall be handled in a similar fashion.

10. The use of liquor and the depiction of smoking in program content shall be deemphasized. When shown, they should be consistent with plot and character development.

11. The creation of a state of hypnosis by act or detailed demonstration on camera is prohibited, and hypnosis as a form of "parlor game" antics to create humorous situations within a comedy setting is forbidden.

12. Program material pertaining to fortune-telling, occultism, astrology,

phrenology, palm-reading, numerology, mind-reading, character-reading, and the like is unacceptable if it encourages people to regard such fields as providing commonly accepted appraisals of life.

13. Professional advice, diagnosis and treatment will be presented in conformity with law and recognized professional standards.

14. Any technique whereby an attempt is made to convey information to the viewer by transmitting messages below the threshold of normal awareness is not permitted.

15. The use of animals, consistent with plot and character delineation, shall be in conformity with accepted standards of humane treatment.

16. Quiz and similar programs that are presented as contests of knowledge, information, skill or luck must, in fact, be genuine contests; and the results must not be controlled by collusion with or between contestants, or by any other action which will favor one contestant against any other.

17. The broadcaster shall be constantly alert to prevent inclusion of elements within a program dictated by factors other than the requirements of the program itself. The acceptance of cash payments or other considerations in return for including scenic properties, the choice and identification of prizes, the selection of music and other creative program elements and inclusion of any identification of commercial products or services, their trade names or advertising slogan within the program are prohibited except in accordance with Sections 317 and 508 of the Communications Act.

18. Contests may not constitute a lottery.

19. No program shall be presented in a manner which through artifice or simulation would mislead the audience as to any material fact. Each broadcaster must exercise reasonable judgment to determine whether a particular method of presentation would constitute a material deception, or would be accepted by the audience as normal theatrical illusion.

20. A television broadcaster should not present fictional events or other non-news material as authentic news telecasts or announcements, nor permit dramatizations in any program which would give the false impression that the dramatized material constitutes news.

21. The standards of this Code covering program content are also understood to include, wherever applicable, the standards contained in the advertising section of the Code.

V.   Treatment of News and Public Events

General

Television Code standards relating to the treatment of news and public events are, because of constitutional considerations, intended to be exhortatory. The standards set forth hereunder encourage high standards of professionalism in broadcast journalism. They are not to be interpreted as turning over to others the broadcaster's responsibility as to judgments necessary in news and public events programming.

News

1. A television station's news schedule should be adequate and well-balanced.

2. News reporting should be factual, fair and without bias.

3. A television broadcaster should exercise particular discrimination in

the acceptance, placement and presentation of advertising in news programs so that such advertising should be clearly distinguishable from the news content.

4. At all times, pictorial and verbal material for both news and comment should conform to other sections of these standards, wherever such sections are reasonably applicable.

5. Good taste should prevail in the selection and handling of news:

Morbid, sensational or alarming details not essential to the factual report, especially in connection with stories of crime or sex, should be avoided. News should be telecast in such a manner as to avoid panic and unnecessary alarm.

6. Commentary and analysis should be clearly identified as such.

7. Pictorial material should be chosen with care and not presented in a misleading manner.

8. All news interview programs should be governed by accepted standards of ethical journalism, under which the interviewer selects the questions to be asked. Where there is advance agreement materially restricting an important or newsworthy area of questioning, the interviewer will state on the program that such limitation has been agreed upon. Such disclosure should be made if the person being interviewed requires that questions be submitted in advance or participates in editing a recording of the interview prior to its use on the air.

9. A television broadcaster should exercise due care in the supervision of content, format, and presentation of newscasts originated by his/her station, and in the selection of newscasters, commentators, and analysts.

Public Events

1. A television broadcaster has an affirmative responsibility at all times to be informed of public events, and to provide coverage consonant with the ends of an informed and enlightened citizenry.

2. The treatment of such events by a television broadcaster should provide adequate and informed coverage.

VI.   Controversial Public Issues

1. Televsion provides a valuable forum for the expression of responsible views on public issues of a controversial nature. The television broadcaster should seek out and develop with accountable individuals, groups and organizations, programs relating to controversial public issues of import to his/her fellow citizens; and to give fair representation to opposing sides of issues which materially affect the life or welfare of a substantial segment of the public.

2. Requests by individuals, groups or organizations for time to discuss their views on controversial public issues should be considered on the basis of their individual merits, and in the light of the contribution which the use requested would make to the public interest, and to a well-balanced program structure.

3. Programs devoted to the discussion of controversial public issues should be identified as such. They should not be presented in a manner which would mislead listeners or viewers to believe that the program is purely of an entertainment, news, or other character.

4. Broadcasts in which stations express their own opinions about issues of general public interest should be clearly identified as editorials. They

should be unmistakably identified as statements of station opinion and should be appropriately distinguished from news and other program material.

VII.   Political Telecasts
   1. Political telecasts should be clearly identified as such. They should not be presented by a television broadcaster in a manner which would mislead listeners or viewers to believe that the program is of any other character. (Ref.: Communications Act of 1934, as amended, Secs. 315 and 317, and FCC Rules and Regulations, Secs. 3.654, 3.657, 3.663, as discussed in NAB's "Political Broadcast Catechism & The Fairness Doctrine.")

VIII.   Religious Programs
   1. It is the responsibility of a television broadcaster to make available to the community appropriate opportunity for religious presentations.
   2. Programs reach audiences of all creeds simultaneously. Therefore, both the advocates of broad or ecumenical religious precepts, and the exponents of specific doctrines, are urged to present their positions in a manner conducive to viewer enlightenment on the role of religion in society.
   3. In the allocation of time for telecasts of religious programs the television station should use its best efforts to apportion such time fairly among responsible individuals, groups and organizations.

Advertising Standards

IX.   General Advertising Standards
   1. This Code establishes basic standards for all television broadcasting. The principles of acceptability and good taste within the Program Standards section govern the presentation of advertising where applicable. In addition, the Code establishes in this section special standards which apply to television advertising.
   2. Commercial television broadcasters make their facilities available for the advertising of products and services and accept commercial presentations for such advertising. However, television broadcasters should, in recognition of their responsibility to the public, refuse the facilities of their stations to an advertiser where they have good reason to doubt the integrity of the advertiser, the truth of the advertising representations, or the compliance of the advertiser with the spirit and purpose of all applicable legal requirements.
   3. Identification of sponsorship must be made in all sponsored programs in accordance with the requirements of the Communications Act of 1934, as amended, and the Rules and Regulations of the Federal Communications Commission.
   4. Representations which disregard normal safety precautions shall be avoided.
   Children shall not be represented, except under proper adult supervision, as being in contact with or demonstrating a product recognized as potentially dangerous to them.
   5. In consideration of the customs and attitudes of the communities served, each television broadcaster should refuse his/her facilities to the advertisement of products and services or the use of advertising scripts, which the

station has good reason to believe would be objectionable to a substantial and responsible segment of the community. These standards should be applied with judgment and flexibility, taking into consideration the characteristics of the medium, its home and family audience, and the form and content of the particular presentation.

6. The advertising of hard liquor (distilled spirits) is not acceptable.

7. The advertising of beer and wines is acceptable only when presented in the best of good taste and discretion, and is acceptable only subject to federal and local laws. *(See Television Code Interpretation No. 4.)*

8. Advertising by institutions or enterprises which in their offers of instruction imply promises of employment or make exaggerated claims for the opportunities awaiting those who enroll for courses is generally unacceptable.

9. The advertising of firearms/ammunition is acceptable provided it promotes the product only as sporting equipment and conforms to recognized standards of safety as well as all applicable laws and regulations. Advertisements of firearms/ammunition by mail order are unacceptable. The advertising of fireworks is unacceptable.

10. The advertising of fortune-telling, occultism, astrology, phrenology, palm-reading, numerology, mind-reading, character-reading or subjects of a like nature is not permitted.

11. Because all products of a personal nature create special problems, acceptability of such products should be determined with especial emphasis on ethics and the canons of good taste. Such advertising of personal products as is accepted must be presented in a restrained and obviously inoffensive manner.

12. The advertising of tip sheets and other publications seeking to advertise for the purpose of giving odds or promoting betting is unacceptable.

The lawful advertising of government organizations which conduct legalized lotteries is acceptable provided such advertising does not unduly exhort the public to bet.

The advertising of private or governmental organizations which conduct legalized betting on sporting contests is acceptable provided such advertising is limited to institutional type announcements which do not exhort the public to bet.

13. An advertiser who markets more than one product should not be permitted to use advertising copy devoted to an acceptable product for purposes of publicizing the brand name or other identification of a product which is not acceptable.

14. "Bait-switch" advertising, whereby goods or services which the advertiser has no intention of selling are offered merely to lure the customer into purchasing higher-priced substitutes, is not acceptable.

15. Personal endorsements (testimonials) shall be genuine and reflect personal experience. They shall contain no statement that cannot be supported if presented in the advertiser's own words.

X.   *Presentation of Advertising*

1. Advertising messages should be presented with courtesy and good taste; disturbing or annoying material should be avoided; every effort should be made to keep the advertising message in harmony with the content and general tone of the program in which it appears.

2. The role and capability of television to market sponsors' products are

well recognized. In turn, this fact dictates that great care be exercised by the broadcaster to prevent the presentation of false, misleading or deceptive advertising. While it is entirely appropriate to present a product in a favorable light and atmosphere, the presentation must not, by copy or demonstration, involve a material deception as to the characteristics, performance or appearance of the product.

Broadcast advertisers are responsible for making available, at the request of the Code Authority, documentation adequate to support the validity and truthfulness of claims, demonstrations and testimonials contained in their commercial messages.

3. The broadcaster and the advertiser should exercise special caution with the content and presentation of television commercials placed in or near programs designed for children. Exploitation of children should be avoided. Commercials directed to children should in no way mislead as to the product's performance and usefulness.

Commercials, whether live, film or tape, within programs initially designed primarily for children under 12 years of age shall be clearly separated from program material by an appropriate device.

Trade name identification or other merchandising practices involving the gratuitous naming of products is discouraged in programs designed primarily for children.

Appeals involving matters of health which should be determined by physicians should not be directed primarily to children.

4. No children's program personality or cartoon character shall be utilized to deliver commercial messages within or adjacent to the programs in which such a personality or cartoon character regularly appears. This provision shall also apply to lead-ins to commercials when such lead-ins contain sell copy or imply endorsement of the product by program personalities or cartoon characters.

5. Appeals to help fictitious characters in television programs by purchasing the advertiser's product or service or sending for a premium should not be permitted, and such fictitious characters should not be introduced into the advertising message for such purposes.

6. Commercials for services or over-the-counter products involving health considerations are of intimate and far-reaching importance to the consumer. The following principles should apply to such advertising:

a. Physicians, dentists or nurses or actors representing physicians, dentists or nurses, shall not be employed directly or by implication. These restrictions also apply to persons professionally engaged in medical services (e.g., physical therapists, pharmacists, dental assistants, nurses' aides).

b. Visual representations of laboratory settings may be employed, provided they bear a direct relationship to bona fide research which has been conducted for the product or service. *(See Television Code, X, 11.)* In such cases, laboratory technicians shall be identified as such and shall not be employed as spokespersons or in any other way speak on behalf of the product.

c. Institutional announcements not intended to sell a specific product or service to the consumer and public service announcements by nonprofit organizations may be presented by accredited physicians, dentists or nurses, subject to approval by the broadcaster. An accredited professional is one who has met required qualifications and has been licensed in his/her resident state.

7. Advertising should offer a product or service on its positive merits and refrain from discrediting, disparaging or unfairly attacking competitors, competing products, other industries, professions or institutions.

8. A sponsor's advertising messages should be confined within the framework of the sponsor's program structure. A television broadcaster should avoid the use of commercial announcements which are divorced from the program either by preceding the introduction of the program (as in the case of so-called "cow-catcher" announcements) or by following the apparent sign-off of the program (as in the case of so-called trailer or "hitch-hike" announcements). To this end, the program itself should be announced and clearly identified, both audio and video, before the sponsor's advertising material is first used, and should be signed off, both audio and video, after the sponsor's advertising material is last used.

9. Since advertising by television is a dynamic technique, a television broadcaster should keep under surveillance new advertising devices so that the spirit and purpose of these standards are fulfilled.

10. A charge for television time to churches and religious bodies is not recommended.

11. Reference to the results of bona fide research, surveys or tests relating to the product to be advertised shall not be presented in a manner so as to create an impression of fact beyond that established by the work that has been conducted.

XI.   Advertising of Medical Products.

1. The advertising of medical products presents considerations of intimate and far-reaching importance to consumers because of the direct bearing on their health.

2. Because of the personal nature of the advertising of medical products, claims that a product will effect a cure and the indiscriminate use of such words as "safe," "without risk," "harmless," or terms of similar meaning should not be accepted in the advertising of medical products on television stations.

3. A television broadcaster should not accept advertising material which in his/her opinion offensively describes or dramatizes distress or morbid situations involving ailments, by spoken word, sound or visual effects.

XII.   Contests

1. Contests shall be conducted with fairness to all entrants, and shall comply with all pertinent laws and regulations. Care should be taken to avoid the concurrent use of the three elements which together constitute a lottery—prize, chance and consideration.

2. All contest details, including rules, eligibility requirements, opening and termination dates should be clearly and completely announced and/or shown, or easily accessible to the viewing public, and the winners' names should be released and prizes awarded as soon as possible after the close of the contest.

3. When advertising is accepted which requests contestants to submit items of product identification or other evidence of purchase of products, reasonable facsimiles thereof should be made acceptable unless the award is based upon skill and not upon chance.

4. All copy pertaining to any contest (except that which is required by law) associated with the exploitation or sale of the sponsor's product or service, and all references to prizes or gifts offered in such connection should be considered a part of and included in the total time allowances as herein provided. *(See Television Code, XIV.)*

XIII.   Premiums and Offers

1. Full details of proposed offers should be required by the television broadcaster for investigation and approved before the first announcement of the offer is made to the public.

2. A final date for the termination of an offer should be announced as far in advance as possible.

3. Before accepting for telecast offers involving a monetary consideration, a television broadcaster should be satisfied as to the integrity of the advertiser and the advertiser's willingness to honor complaints indicating dissatisfaction with the premium by returning the monetary consideration.

4. There should be no misleading descriptions or visual representations of any premiums or gifts which would distort or enlarge their value in the minds of the viewers.

5. Assurances should be obtained from the advertiser that premiums offered are not harmful to person or property.

6. Premiums should not be approved which appeal to superstition on the basis of "luck-bearing" powers or otherwise.

XIV.   Time Standards for Non-Program Material

In order that the time for non-program material and its placement shall best serve the viewer, the following standards are set forth in accordance with sound television practice:

1. Non-Program Material Definition:

Non-program material, in both prime time and all other time, includes billboards, commercials, promotional announcements and all credits in excess of 30 seconds per program, except in feature films. In no event should credits exceed 40 seconds per program. The 40-second limitation on credits shall not apply, however, in any situation governed by a contract entered into before October 1, 1971. Public service announcements and promotional announcements for the same program are excluded from this definition.

2. Allowable Time for Non-Program Material:

a. In prime time on network affiliated stations, non-program material shall not exceed nine minutes 30 seconds in any 60-minute period. Prime time is a continuous period of not less than three consecutive hours per broadcast day as designated by the station between the hours of 6:00 P.M. and midnight.

b. In all other time, non-program material shall not exceed 16 minutes in any 60-minute period.

c. Children's Programming Time—Defined as those hours other than prime time in which programs initially designed primarily for children under 12 years of age are scheduled.

Within this time period on Saturday and Sunday, non-program material shall not exceed nine minutes 30 seconds in any 60-minute period.

Within this time period on Monday through Friday, non-program material shall not exceed 12 minutes in any 60-minute period.

3. Program Interruptions:

a. Definition: A program interruption is any occurrence of non-program material within the main body of the program.

b. In prime time, the number of program interruptions shall not exceed two within any 30-minute program, or four within any 60-minute program.

Programs longer than 60 minutes shall be prorated at two interruptions per half-hour. The number of interruptions in 60-minute variety shows shall not exceed five.

c. In all other time, the number of interruptions shall not exceed four within any 30-minute program period.

d. In children's weekend programming time, as above defined in 2c, the number of program interruptions shall not exceed two within any 30-minute program or four within any 60-minute program.

e. In both prime time and all other time, the following interruption standard shall apply within programs of 15 minutes or less in length:

5-minute program—1 interruption;
10-minute program—2 interruptions;
15-minute program—2 interruptions.

f. News, weather, sports and special events programs are exempt from the interruption standard because of the nature of such programs.

4. No more than four non-program material announcements shall be scheduled consecutively within programs, and no more than three non-program material announcements shall be scheduled consecutively during station breaks. The consecutive non-program material limitation shall not apply to a single sponsor who wishes to further reduce the number of interruptions in the program.

5. A multiple product announcement is one in which two or more products or services are presented within the framework of a single announcement. A multiple product announcement shall not be scheduled in a unit of time less than 60 seconds, except where integrated so as to appear to the viewer as a single message. A multiple product announcement shall be considered integrated and counted as a single announcement if:

a. the products or services are related and interwoven within the framework of the announcement (related products or services shall be defined as those having a common character, purpose and use); and

b. the voice(s), setting, background and continuity are used consistently throughout so as to appear to the viewer as a single message.

Multiple product announcements of 60 seconds in length or longer not meeting this definition of integration shall be counted as two or more announcements under this section of the Code. This provision shall not apply to retail or service establishments.

6. The use of billboards, in prime time and all other time, shall be confined to programs sponsored by a single or alternate week advertiser and shall be limited to the products advertised in the program.

7. Reasonable and limited identification of prizes and donors' names where the presentation of contest awards or prizes is a necessary part of program content shall not be included as non-program material as defined above.

8. Programs presenting women's/men's service features, shopping guides, fashion shows, demonstrations and similar material provide a special

service to the public in which certain material normally classified as non-program is an informative and necessary part of the program content. Because of this, the time standards may be waived by the Code Authority to a reasonable extent on a case-by-case basis.

9. Gratuitous references in a program to a non-sponsor's product or service should be avoided except for normal guest identification.

10. Stationary backdrops or properties in television presentations showing the sponsor's name or product, the name of the sponsor's product, trademark or slogan should be used only incidentally and should not obtrude on program interest or entertainment

Time Standards for Independent Stations

1. Non-program elements shall be considered as all-inclusive, with the exception of required credits, legally required station identifications, and "bumpers." Promotion spots and public service announcements, as well as commercials, are to be considered non-program elements.

2. The allowed time for non-program elements, as defined above, shall not exceed seven minutes in a 30-minute period or multiples thereof in prime time (prime time is defined as any three contiguous hours between 6:00 P.M. and midnight, local time), or eight minutes in a 30-minute period or multiples thereof during all other times.

3. Where a station does not carry a commercial in a station break between programs, the number of program interruptions shall not exceed four within any 30-minute program, or seven within any 60-minute program, or 10 within any 90-minute program, or 13 in any 120-minute program. Stations which do carry commercials in station breaks between programs shall limit the number of program interruptions to three within any 30-minute program, or six within any 60-minute program, or nine within any 90-minute program, or 12 in any 120-minute program. News, weather, sports, and special events are exempted because of format.

4. Not more than four non-program material announcements as defined above shall be scheduled consecutively. An exception may be made only in the case of a program 60 minutes or more in length, when no more than seven non-program elements may be scheduled consecutively by stations who wish to reduce the number of program interruptions.

5. The conditions of paragraphs three and four shall not apply to live sports programs where the program format dictates and limits the number of program interruptions.[1]

The Radio Code, a shorter document, is similar in content to the one governing television. In addition to the Codes, the NAB from time to time issues advertising guidelines and clarifications expanding on provisions of the Codes. Among the subjects that have been covered are alcoholic beverages, acne products, arthritis and rheumatism remedies, bronchitis products, cigarettes, disparagement of competing products, hallucinogens, hypnosis, men-in-white testimonials, time standards, toys, and weight-reducing products.

[1] *Reprinted from the Television Code, published by the National Association of Broadcasters, Nineteenth Edition, June 1976.*

For many years adherence to the codes was not a condition of membership in the NAB. Those who wished to abide by the rules signified their intention by becoming subscribers to the Code and were thereupon permitted to display NAB's "Seal of Good Practice" or to announce that they were following Code principles. Later, the NAB moved toward requiring adherence but was forced to withdraw when a court ruled the "Family Viewing" provision to be unconstitutional.

ENFORCING THE CODES

The principal responsibility for enforcing the Codes is assigned to a Code Authority Director who is appointed by the President and Board of Directors of the NAB. He carries out a continuing review of radio and television broadcasting through the monitoring of stations and the examination of their logs. He is assisted in this responsibility by an executive staff, which operates in major broadcasting centers in the United States. Any alleged breach of the TV Code is reported to a Television Code Review Board, a body made up of not more than nine members, appointed from subscribers to the Code by the NAB. If the Review Board decides that a violation has taken place, the matter is brought before the TV Board of Directors, which makes the final decision regarding the suspension or revocation of the accused subscriber's right to display the "Seal of Good Practice." In the case of radio, the Code Authority Director may suspend or revoke a subscriber's membership if he discovers a violation, but his decision may be appealed to a Radio Code Board, an 11-man body appointed by the NAB, and then to the Radio Board of Directors.

In addition to his enforcement duties, the Code Authority Director is responsible for administering and interpreting the Codes and for making recommendations regarding revisions. He is assisted in this latter responsibility by the Television Code Review Board and the Radio Code Board. Final authority for making revisions in the Codes rests with the TV Board of Directors and the Radio Board of Directors of the NAB.

NETWORK AND STATION CODES

Because the NAB codes do not go into much detail or take a firm stand on many questions that arise in connection with putting programs and commercials on the air, networks and stations have formulated their own standards of broadcast practices that are generally compatible with the NAB code but may spell out network and station policy in specific situations. For example, the NBC *Manual on Radio and Television Broadcast Standards and Practices* contains 20 pages that set forth network policy on acceptable program and advertising content and operating procedures of the Broadcast Standards Department, which screens all programs for the network. As a general operating practice, compliance is obtained voluntarily through frank discussions with program producers and advertising agencies. Self-regulation normally works quietly and effectively and achieves little or no publicity. Prepared scripts are reviewed in advance of broadcast by the Broadcast Standards Departments of stations and networks. Statements or words that violate broadcast standards may be removed from all except political campaign talks. The fact that the movie industry can be much freer than television in its use of language and portrayal of situations has created some special problems. Extensive editing is necessary before some films are acceptable for television. In some instances two versions of the same film are made, one for exhibition in theaters, the other for showing on television.

If a subject is very controversial, a speaker may be advised of station requirements before he writes his script, and he is checked against the prepared script during broadcast. Advertising copy that breaches the station's rules is returned to the agency for revision. Constructive suggestions are often advanced to show how a script may be changed to conform to policy. Staff announcers and commentators are informed of station policy and then entrusted with observing it in their broadcast remarks. Extemporaneous or ad-lib interviews, quizzes, and forums are checked during taping or live broadcast. Although a flip of a switch by a director can cut short an off-color remark before its completion, such action is only rarely necessary. It is the unintentional slip of speech or unexpected recalcitrance by a performer or speaker that causes difficulty. In large television variety shows, a representative of Broadcast Standards often attends dress rehearsals to check on costumes, dances, and physical action that has been indicated in the script. The NBC manual states that the network considers there are two general standards in judging entertainment programs for broadcast acceptability: 1. Is the subject matter acceptable? 2. Is the treatment consonant with good taste?

> NBC believes that the proper application of these standards should not preclude the presentation of programs of genuine artistic or literary merit dealing with valid moral and social issues even though they may be challenging or controversial, or present realities which some people might wish did not exist. The test is whether such material is treated with dramatic integrity, rather than for purposes of sensationalism; and whether it seeks to develop genuine moral and artistic values, rather than to shock or exploit audiences or appeal to prurient interest or morbid curiosity. Nothing should be presented to mislead or deceive the audience.[2]

UNWRITTEN CODES AND PRESSURES

The formal codes and declarations of principles do not, however, tell the full story of self-regulation in broadcasting. Much of the self-regulation in television and radio is conducted in an unofficial and unwritten way. The broadcasters, working in a context of conflicting political, economic, and social forces, are under continual pressure from influential majority and mi-

[2] Quoted by permission of NBC.

nority groups that want to ban certain speakers, performers, writers, or topics from the air. Religious, racial, professional, political, and trade organizations may request a station or network not to carry programs which, in their opinion, reflect unfavorably on them. Some of these groups hope to bring about social improvement by working for the elimination of unfavorable racial stereotypes or provocative themes and actions. Lawyers, policemen, teachers, and workers in other specialized fields frequently object to the way a member of their profession is portrayed in a dramatic presentation. Some religious groups in certain areas have sufficient influence to persuade a station not to carry discussions of controversial questions, although representatives of that religion may have been invited to participate in the discussion.

The desire to avoid becoming the object of public controversy of any sort is possibly the most influential factor in the unwritten codes of self-regulation. Charges have been made repeatedly that advertising agencies and networks have secret blacklists of performers and writers who have been deemed to be "controversial" and therefore unacceptable because of their political or personal associations.

In 1950, the sponsor of a program series in which a well-known actress was to be featured, received a number of protests that she was a Communist. Despite the actress' vigorous denials that she had ever been a Communist or had Communistic leanings, the sponsor withdrew her from the program on the grounds that she had become a "controversial personality" whose presence on the show might adversely affect the sale of the advertiser's products.

In late 1962, the appearance of Alger Hiss on an ABC news documentary program evaluating the investigative career of Richard Nixon aroused a storm of protest. An unusual apsect of this incident was that the sponsor of the news program did not object, but the sponsors of some other programs on the ABC TV network expressed their indignation and announced that they were withdrawing from the sponsorship of further programs on that network.

At one time a publication named *Red Channels* listed the names of people in the entertainment industry who, the publication alleged, were suspected of Communist affiliations or sympathies. Some broadcasting officials, concluding that the mere appearance of an individual's name in this list made him a controversial figure, immediately banned that person from the air. Many critics who agree that television and radio performers must be acceptable to the public strongly objected to the use of such lists to determine whether a performer was qualified to go on the air without evaluating the accuracy or significance of the charges against the performer or providing even the semblance of a hearing. Thus, Jack Gould, former radio-TV critic of *The New York Times,* stated: "With *Red Channels* the business community in broadcasting simply abdicated its citizenship in as dismal an hour as radio and TV ever had."[3] Still others argued that networks and agencies are not competent to evaluate political affiliations of performers, and that the acceptability of a performer for broadcast work should be related solely to competence in performance. This is a tangled and difficult question, extend-

[3] *The New York Times,* June 6, 1954, Section X, p. 11.

ing beyond the area of politics and Communism to the general moral acceptability of performers and writers. In 1962 this problem was brought to the
attention of the public when John Henry Faulk, a radio and television performer, won a libel action against an organization known as Aware Inc. because it had unjustly accused him of Communist sympathies.

The doctrine holding that a person against whom charges are made,
regardless of his actual innocence or the irrelevance of the charges, is thereby
made "controversial" and unacceptable for broadcasting purposes has also
produced the unintended result of rendering controversial the very people
who make the charges or publicly approve the doctrine and actively support
it. To a large extent, the problem with which broadcasters, advertisers, and
performers contended was a reflection of national tensions in a difficult
world situation, particularly during the period of McCarthyism in the 1950s.

Other events have also illustrated the way in which pressures from outside the industry can influence what is broadcast. In 1968 the assassination
of Senator Robert Kennedy caused a nationwide revulsion against the violence that seemed so prevalent in our society. Much of the criticism was
aimed at violence in television programs, although no connection was ever
made between the assassin's act and what he might have seen on television.
The attempted assassination of George Wallace while he was campaigning
for the presidency in 1972 roused new concerns about the prevalence of violence, and once more the spotlight focused on television as a significant factor in the situation. A series of studies by Professor George Gerbner of the
University of Pennsylvania, which catalogued violence in television programs, demonstrated that violent acts played a major role in many broadcasts. Though no one has yet been able to prove a definite causal connection
between violence on television and the violence committed by those who
watch it, there was still an understandable concern about its effect, particularly on children. Former Senator John Pastore was one of the most vocal
critics of the violence in TV programming. His voice was listened to with
particular attention by the broadcasting industry because he headed the
Senate subcommittee drafting the legislation that would establish the regulations for licensing stations. Richard Wiley, when he was Chairman of the
FCC, was also listened to closely when he asked the broadcasting industry to
take the initiative in correcting the problem.

The agitation against violence presents the broadcasting industry with
a cruel dilemma. It fears, on the one hand, that removing all violence from
programs would strip them of an element that makes programs exciting and
thus attractive to listeners. To refuse to do anything, on the other hand,
might invite restrictive government regulations. In response to the demands
the industry took two major steps. First, it sharply reduced the violence in
the children's programs broadcast on Saturday mornings by replacing a
number of the cartoon shows with other types of entertainment and by tem-
pering the violence in the cartoon shows that remained. Second, it established the Family Viewing Period from 7:00 to 9:00 P.M. (in the Eastern
zone), during which only programs suitable for viewing by the entire family
were to be broadcast. As part of this move, it further required that audiences
were to be warned about possibly offensive or disturbing material in pro-

grams no matter when they were broadcast. The attempt to establish a family viewing period was largely negated when a court ruled that requiring adherence to this practice was unconstitutional.

The decision by broadcasters to eliminate cigarette advertising from radio and television also came about because of pressure from the public. The broadcasters resisted this pressure, for the revenues obtained from cigarette advertising amounted to more than $200 million a year or more than 9 percent of all their income. But people and members of Congress asked more and more insistently how an industry that by law was required to operate in the public interest could possibly encourage the sale of a product that mounting medical evidence showed to be a threat to both health and life. Finally, the industry acted to phase out the advertising of cigarettes on those radio and television stations and networks subscribing to its Code by September 1973. The broadcasting industry's fear that the government will act if the industry fails to respond to public pressure demanding an end to undesirable practices was well founded in this case. Deciding that the broadcasters were reacting too slowly, Congress passed legislation that made all cigarette advertising on radio and television illegal after January 1, 1971.

One of the most direct criticisms of broadcast content ever made by a politician came from Vice-President Spiro Agnew in 1969 when he attacked network commentators for finding fault with President Nixon immediately after the President had finished a speech on the Vietnam war. The Vice-President's speech was particularly threatening to broadcasters because he referred to the fact that they operated under government licenses, and he demanded that networks be made more responsive to the viewers of the nation. Both comments seemed to contain an implied threat of government censorship. Network spokesmen responded sharply that they would not buckle under to this coercion but would continue to exercise their right to speak freely on government policies. But Walter Cronkite, who stated firmly that he would not be intimidated, conceded that after the Vice-President's speech, some network commentators were not as strong as they could have been in evaluating presidential statements. There was also an effect on local stations. A number announced that thereafter they would return to their regular programming as soon as the President finished speaking, thus depriving their viewers of any network commentary that might follow.

As the years went by, the fear of retaliation lessened. After a period of self-evaluation, the networks returned in some degree to their practice of analyzing speeches and events after they were broadcast. Yet, though Vice-President Agnew who made the threat and President Nixon who motivated it both resigned from office, some broadcasters are warier than they used to be about criticizing incumbent political leaders.

PROFESSIONAL ASSOCIATIONS AND UNIONS

A number of professional broadcasting associations concerned with the working standards of their members have been established. These include the Academy of Television Arts and Sciences, International Television and

Radio Society, the Radio-Television News Directors Association, the American Federation of Television and Radio Artists, the Writers Guild of America, the Screen Actors Guild, the Directors Guild of America, The National Association of Television Program Executives, the National Association of Farm Broadcasters, and the Society of Motion Picture and Television Engineers.

PROFESSIONAL ASSOCIATIONS AND UNIONS

A number of professional broadcasting associations concerned with the working standards of their members have been established. These include the Academy of Television Arts and Sciences, International Television and Radio Society, the Radio-Television News Directors Association, the American Federation of Television and Radio Artists, the Writers Guild of America, the Screen Actors Guild, the Directors Guild of America, the National Association of Television Program Executives, the National Association of Farm Broadcasters, and the Society of Motion Picture and Television Engineers.

SUMMARY

Stations and networks are charged with the responsibility for everything that is transmitted on the air. They guard against libel, obscenity, breaches of good taste, and other matters that will offend the public, through established continuity-acceptance procedures. The radio and television codes of the National Association of Broadcasters are influential forces for self-regulation in broadcasting. These codes are supplemented by individual station and network standards of practice. Unwritten codes and pressures toward self-regulation reflect orthodox attitudes and the interests of dominant political, economic, and social groups.

Questions For Discussion

1. Why is there a need for self-regulation in broadcasting?
2. How successful has self-regulation been in maintaining standards of decency and good taste in programming?
3. What was the original reason for the organization of the broadcaster's association that was the predecessor of the NAB?
4. State some of the basic purposes and functions of the NAB.
5. Why do you think that radio and television broadcasters both belong to the same service organization, the NAB, even though they seem to be competitors for the same audience?
6. Why do you think that there is a restriction in the TV Code against the simulation of news or special events in television drama?
7. What are the fundamental values expressed in the TV Code of the NAB?

8. In a dispute between a station and a sponsor on the definition of commercial time, who must take the responsibility for the final decision?

9. The FCC at one time indicated that it might not renew the licenses of stations that failed to conform to the provisions in the NAB Codes governing advertising. Do you think that such a step would be justified?

10. Are the limitations placed on radio and television advertising adequate?

11. Do you believe that a newscaster should be asked to present the commercials for the sponsor of the program?

12. What is a blacklist, and how did it function in the broadcasting industry?

13. What should be the standard for determining whether radio and television performers and writers are acceptable to the public and should be permitted to work in programs?

14. How do private pressure groups act to regulate broadcasting? What is the effect of such pressures?

15. How well do you think commercial broadcasters have lived up to the principles expressed in the TV Code regarding children's programs?

16. Can you think of specific practices by radio or television stations that in your opinion are undesirable?

comparative broadcasting systems

12

Broadcasting has developed in practically every country throughout the world. The structure of each nation's broadcasting system depends on the educational level of the populace, the wealth of the nation, its form of government, and the availability of radio and television frequencies. Other factors are the customs and traditions of the country and the cultural and linguistic differences within its borders. Canada, with a French- and English-speaking citizenry, and the Soviet Union, encompassing more than two hundred different cultural groups, obviously cannot rely on a single broadcast service to appeal to all listeners. Countries suffering from extreme shortages of consumer goods can scarcely expect advertising to support broadcasting.

In poor and illiterate countries, television and radio receivers are beyond the financial reach of most people. Some European countries use cable broadcasting and radio relay exchanges to make radio reception available to people who cannot buy their own receivers. A relay exchange, located in a key point in the community, receives programs through the air and then, over specially adapted telephone lines and circuits, transmits the programs to loudspeakers in individual homes. Cable broadcasting is much cheaper than using individual receiving sets; moreover, it eliminates much of the static and fading typical of cheap receivers. The programs, however, are limited to the ones the relay exchanges make available. Cable broadcasting is especially useful in mountainous regions and in towns where direct reception is poor; it is widespread in the Soviet Union where the government, for political reasons, favors collective listening. Cable broadcasting has developed in Great Britain, too.

INTERNATIONAL ALLOCATION OF FREQUENCIES

International treaties and multilateral agreements allocate the broadcast spectrum to various countries and continents in order to prevent interference. The administration of the agreements is carried out by an agency of the United Nations, the International Telecommunications Union (ITU), a successor to the International Telegraph Union, which was organized in 1865 by 20 member nations. The ITU gave its first attention to radio in 1906 in a conference held in Berlin, attended by the representatives of 27 nations. This conference originated the first regulations regarding the assignment of call letters to the nations of the world. Conferences were held at regular intervals from that time on to decide what uses were to be made of the various parts of the broadcasting spectrum and to allocate frequencies. In the 1930s the band of carrier frequencies from 540 to 1600 kilocycles was allocated to AM broadcasting. An international conference to consider the reallocation of broadcast frequencies is scheduled for 1979. Within the American and European continents further allocations of frequencies and powers of transmission were necessary to avoid interference between adjacent countries in heavily populated areas. Allocations were made for Europe in the Copenhagen plan of 1948, and in the Western Hemisphere by the North American Regional Broadcast Agreement (NARBA), drawn up in Havana in 1937, and revised at general conferences several times since then.

One problem with an international agreement is that it is effective only so far as the individual nations who sign it are willing to abide by its conditions. Complicating the situation is the fact that there is not enough space in the broadcasting spectrum to satisfy the demands of all nations. A single frequency may have five applicants. The resulting competition sometimes leads to violations of the agreements by nations that seize a more favorable space in the spectrum than those they have been able to achieve by negotiation. The exercise of national and international policies through broadcasting is another cause of violations. The jamming of radio programs from the free nations by the Soviet Union is an example. The failure by some nations to follow agreements reached in international conferences has caused some deterioration in the quality of broadcasting, but so far violations have not taken place on a wholesale scale. It is well that they have not, for such a development would make both internal and external broadcasting by adjacent nations impossible.

TYPES OF BROADCASTING SYSTEMS

Broadly speaking, four systems of broadcasting are used by countries around the globe:

1. Official ownership and operation of stations by the government, which runs broadcasting as a state service. This system, found in all totalitarian states, has proved a convenient means for helping to dominate a nation. The control of broadcasting usually rests with the ministry of education or propaganda, which "clears" all broadcasting personnel and censors all program material. Hitler perfected this system of broadcasting as a propaganda arm of the German government. A prominent present-day example is the U.S.S.R. Government-operated broadcasting is not limited to dictatorships, however. During the period when Charles De Gaulle was President of France, that country, even though a democracy, stifled the expression of political opposition through broadcasting and made the radio and television services virtual mouthpieces for government propaganda. Public tax money, supplemented in many instances by license fees, supports state systems.

2. Private ownership and operation of stations by individual broadcasters or corporations, educational institutions, and religious or labor associations, subjected to limited governmental regulation. This system is financed by the sale of time for advertising, by endowments, or by tax money. American television and radio come under this category.

3. Ownership and operation of stations by public or private corporations given a monopoly of broadcasting by the government. These corporations are subject to limited governmental supervision, making possible a degree of independence in programming. Income is derived from license fees, taxes, or advertising, or a combination of the three. Great Britain, Austria, Italy, and Luxembourg have systems that come within this classification.

4. Ownership and operation of some stations by a public nonprofit corporation chartered by the government in conjunction with privately owned and commercially operated stations. The best example of this system, which combines the features of types 2 and 3 above, is found in Canada. A modification of this system is used in Great Britain. In these countries, commercial stations supported by advertising are usually located in thickly populated urban areas. Without a nonprofit broadcasting system supported in some way by the government, thinly populated areas that cannot support a profitable commercial system would be entirely deprived of broadcast service.

Of these systems of broadcasting, study of those used in Great Britain and Canada has most value for American students of broadcasting. We shall therefore discuss British and Canadian radio and television in some detail and then briefly describe interesting systems in use in several European countries, Mexico and Japan.

RADIO AND TELEVISION IN GREAT BRITAIN

The development of radio and television in Great Britain is of special interest to Americans because the British, with a similar cultural background, took a broadcasting road that was considerably different from the one followed in the United States. Until September 1955, radio and television were run as a chartered monopoly, were financed directly by the listeners and viewers, and carried no advertising. The monopoly was held by the British Broadcasting Corporation, which was created by a royal charter on January 1, 1927, as a public nonprofit corporation. The operations of the BBC were periodically examined in the years that followed. One demand heard with increasing frequency was that the BBC monopoly of all broadcasting in Great Britain be broken. In 1954 the Parliament finally responded to this agitation by passing a Television Act, which authorized the establishment of the Independent Television Authority to operate competitively with the BBC in the field of television. In 1973 the Parliament took what many considered to be an obvious second step when it changed the name of the Independent Television Authority to the Independent Broadcasting Authority and commissioned it to set up a system of radio broadcasting that would compete with the BBC's.

The British Broadcasting Corporation

The BBC is a public nonprofit corporation that operates under a Royal Charter. The present charter was issued in 1976. The corporation is controlled by a Board of Governors of 12 members appointed for five-year terms by the monarch on recommendation of the government in power. A Director-General charged with the administration of the BBC is its chief executive officer.

The BBC is relatively independent of the government-of-the-day by virtue of its chartered status, but its chain of responsibility to Parliament is maintained through a license and agreement with the Secretary of State for the Home Department, who is the ultimate authority for broadcasting in Great Britain. The license lays down regulations governing the building of transmitters, the heights of aerials, the frequencies and power to be used, and other technical requirements. It prohibits the BBC from broadcasting commercial advertisements or sponsored programs, and it retains for the Secretary of State the right of veto over programs.

The only general restriction imposed through this veto power has been a ban upon the broadcasting by the BBC of its own opinion on current affairs. Government departments can, upon request, insist that their special announcements be broadcast, but the BBC may tell its listeners that the broadcast was made on demand of the government. The BBC is also directed by the license to "broadcast an impartial account day by day by professional reporters of the proceedings in both Houses of the United Kingdom Parliament." There is provision for government control of radio during national emergencies, but this power has not been invoked, even in wartime.

People who own only a radio set no longer pay any license tax; those with a monochrome TV set pay £8 per year for a license to operate their sets; those with color sets pay £18 per year. Under the British system, the household is licensed and the possession of additional TV sets does not add to the cost of the license. The license revenue (less administrative costs) is turned over to the BBC to finance its domestic broadcasting operations. In recent years the net income received by the BBC from license fees has approximated £146 million. Overseas broadcast services are financed by annual grants from the Treasury, much as the "Voice of America" is supported by Congressional appropriations.

BBC Radio

Like U.S. networks, the BBC aims to win mass audiences with good entertainment, but unlike its American counterparts, it has been assigned a definite cultural responsibility, frankly paternalistic in nature, to elevate public tastes and standards. At the end of World War II, the BBC established three program services designed as a broadly based cultural pyramid through which listeners might move from popular programs to those that, in the opinion of the BBC's Governors, were more worthwhile, being led from good to better by curiosity, liking, and growth of understanding. At the base of the cultural pyramid was the Light Programme, broadcasting a frothy schedule of quiz, audience participation, variety and comedy shows, light music, children's adventure stories, and serial dramas; this service captured about two-thirds of the BBC radio audience. At the center of the pyramid was the Home Service, which aimed "to appeal to a wide range of tastes and to reflect the life of the community in every sphere." The Third Programme, at the apex of the cultural pyramid, was dedicated to broadcasting the best music, literature, and talks under the best possible conditions, free from the demands of mass appeal and the tyranny of rigid time schedules.

The attempt by the BBC to teach people to discriminate in favor of programs it considered to be worthwhile incurred a great deal of resentment. Moreover, it was not broadcasting the popular programs for which many people hungered. They began tuning in increasing numbers to radio programs originating outside of the country, particularly to those by Radio Luxembourg, which beamed a powerful signal that covered most of Great Britain. Its program fare of light popular music interlarded with commercials paid for by British advertisers sometimes drew larger audiences than the three BBC radio services combined.

In 1963 a new program service began competing with BBC radio for daytime audiences in the heavily populated southeast part of England. Its source was a so-called "pirate" ship, which anchored in international waters off the coast. This ship appropriated a frequency in violation of international agreements and began broadcasting a program of popular music, similar to that of Radio Luxembourg. British advertisers who bought commercials also supported the activities of this pirate ship and several others that soon joined it. At first the British government moved to eliminate this illegal competition by legislation, but it withheld action when it discovered that such a move would outrage millions of English people who listened to the broadcasts of the pirate ships. It was soon realized that the BBC would have to provide an equivalent service before the public would accept suppression of the pirate ships. The introduction of the new BBC service was finally accomplished in 1967, at which time the government eliminated the pirate ships by making it illegal for them to be serviced by British subjects.

The radio service designed to provide the type of popular music broadcast by Radio Luxembourg and the pirate ships was named Radio 1. The existing radio services in keeping with this designation were renamed Radio 2, Radio 3, and Radio 4. Radio 2, the Light Programme, continues to provide the light music and entertainment that it had featured previously. At times Radio 1 and Radio 2 carry the same programs, particularly in the evening. Radio 3 is the source of good music, drama, talks, and poetry of the Third Programme and it also carries a service known as the Music Programme, special programs of an educational nature, and sports on Saturdays. Radio 4 carries the programs of the Home Service. Special attention is given to news, but the service also offers a wide range of other program types: plays, music, comedy, and quizzes.

The radio services of the BBC are primarily national in nature in that most of the programs are heard simultaneously throughout the British Isles. Some modification of this national approach is attained through the broadcasting of occasional programs designed for particular regions, but not until

1967 did Great Britain have anything similar to the local radio service that is so common in the United States. In that year the BBC in cooperation with local authorities established three stations in English communities, and more have been added since. These stations aim primarily to provide local news, information, and discussions of area events, paying particular attention to local industrial and commercial affairs even though they do not carry commercials. Records requested by listeners, coffee-break interviews, and local music and drama are other program ingredients. Local residents often participate in the programs on a "do-it-yourself" basis. The BBC pays all expenses from the income provided by license fees.

AM radio frequencies throughout Europe were allocated by the Copenhagen Convention and Plan of 1948, which went into effect in 1950. When stations started to operate on the newly assigned frequencies, interference developed between stations in Great Britain and those on the Continent. The situation became worse when some nations began using frequencies not assigned to them or increased power beyond the limits granted them in the Convention. The result was that AM radio reception greatly deteriorated in quality in Great Britain. To help solve this problem, the BBC decided to begin making use of FM frequencies (referred to in England as VHF), intending at first to shift all of its radio operations to the FM band. It now seems unlikely that the AM frequencies now being used for domestic broadcasts will be abandoned, but since the first FM broadcast in 1955, there has been a considerable development of this form of broadcasting. Programs on FM are now available to most of the people in Great Britain. FM frequencies are used for the local radio stations, and they also provide a second source for the national radio services that are mainly available on AM. Stereophonic broadcasting on FM frequencies is also taking place in Great Britain.

BBC Television

"The BBC offers some of the most superlative television in the world. . . . In really going out and reporting the world, the BBC runs rings around American TV. . . . Its documentaries are exceptionally fine. Its best drama is good indeed and its concern with the educational value of TV is often thoroughly rewarding on the screen itself." Thus wrote Jack Gould, *The New York Times* radio and television critic, during a visit to Britain in 1955.[1] Many visitors to Great Britain since that time have expressed similar opinions.

The BBC began television operations in 1936 and televised the coronation of George VI less than a year later. With the beginning of World War II in 1939, it ceased operations, resuming seven years later in 1946. Until 1964 the BBC provided a single TV service, but in that year a second TV service began in the London area and in the years that followed was gradually extended through the nation. This second service, named BBC-2, the first service becoming BBC-1, was established to provide alternative programs for British viewers. The offerings of the two networks are planned together to

[1] *The New York Times,* September 22, 1955.

make certain that a choice is available. Thus when BBC-1 is televising sports, BBC-2 may offer light entertainment or drama. When one service is offering a serious documentary, the other may provide music or a feature film.

All British television programs are now broadcast in color, employing the 625-line standard used in most European countries. UHF transmitters carry these broadcasts to 95 percent of the United Kingdom. The BBC originally employed a 405-line standard, and some broadcasts are still being presented on VHF frequencies using that standard, but its use will shortly be phased out. Ninety percent of British homes are now equipped to receive the 625-line broadcasts. BBC made a careful study of the three main color systems, NTSC (used in the United States) and two systems developed in Europe, PAL and SECAM. It had hoped that a single system would be adopted throughout the world, but when that aim appeared beyond reach, it decided on the PAL system because of its technical qualities and because it was the system most European countries had decided to adopt. Color broadcasting began in July of 1967 and in the first year, 30 percent of BBC-2's programs were transmitted in color. Now two out of five British homes are equipped to receive the all-color service.

Television programs in Great Britain neither begin as early nor do they continue as late as they do in the United States. Telecasting is concentrated in the late afternoon and evening hours and usually ceases before midnight. Some broadcasting is done during the day, but the programs are mainly specialized or educational in nature, many designed for children in school. The steady diet of television entertainment available to American housewives during the day is not available in Great Britain. At one time there was a restriction against the broadcasting of programs between 6:00 and 7:00 in the evening so that young children could be put to bed without interference, but it was finally abandoned.

BBC television, with a coverage of 99 percent of the British population, has carried over into television the same basic programming philosophy that has characterized its radio operation. This means that its objective is not merely to appeal to the tastes of the mass audience but, in addition, to provide programs for minority interests and, in general, to upgrade the appreciations and understandings of all who may tune in, an aim that has caused both its enemies and its admirers to refer to it sometimes as "Auntie BBC." This approach, however, has been somewhat modified by the competition with the commercial television network, which in its early years outdrew its BBC rival by a ratio of 2 to 1. In an effort to attract more viewers, BBC television did lighten its schedule somewhat, a move that was successful in winning a greater share of the available audience, but it has by no means abandoned its original purposes. For example, it schedules more programs for minority interests during prime listening hours than does the commercial network, and its program fare in general is somewhat more serious and substantial. It is particularly distinguished for its television dramas, a number of which have been seen in the United States through the facilities of both educational and commercial TV stations. Outstanding imports from BBC were the serial drama adapted from John Galsworthy's novel sequence *The Forsyte Saga* and the comedy series, *Monty Python's Flying Circus.* Programs produced in the United States have also found their original inspiration in BBC programs, among them *All in the Family* and *Sanford and Son.* In return the BBC broadcasts a number of programs produced in the United States. BBC television activity has also been marked by excellent coverage of the great events in public life such as the coronation of monarchs, the Silver Jubilee of Queen Elizabeth II, the investiture of the Prince of Wales, and parliamentary and political happenings.

BBC Publications and Special Enterprises

In addition to producing radio and television programs, the BBC also publishes magazines, pamphlets, and books. Its *Radio Times,* which prints the weekly program schedules and carries advertising, has a regular circulation of more than three and a half million copies per week, the largest weekly circulation of any periodical in Great Britain. The *Listener,* which publishes outstanding BBC talks, has a more modest circulation of 38,000 copies a week. The BBC also publishes many booklets especially in connection with its school broadcasts and further education programs. A number of special enterprises provide income for the BBC. Among them are the sale of its radio and television programs to other nations and the sale to its own nationals of phonograph records of programs.

Commercial Television

The Television Act of 1954 created the Independent Television Authority (ITA) to operate competitively with BBC television. The ITA, with the operation of the independent radio service added to its functions; has now become the Independent Broadcasting Authority (IBA). It is governed by a board of directors, which appoints a Director General as the Chief executive. Whereas the BBC produces its own programs, as well as owning and operating studios and transmitting facilities, the IBA owns and operates facilities, but its programs are supplied by privately financed companies known as program contractors with which the IBA has made exclusive broadcasting agreements. The IBA is responsible for seeing that the programs maintain a proper balance and for regulating all commercial aspects of the operation. Advertisers and agencies may not produce programs or be identified as sponsoring programs; they may simply buy spot announcements during various time periods, and they may not choose the precise time or program in which their announcement will appear. Advertising on television is limited to an average of six minutes in an hour with three breaks in the program for advertising; on radio nine minutes per hour of commercials are permitted; commercial announcements must be clearly differentiated from the program. Strict rules govern their content and method of presentation, particularly those directed at children, and those that advertise medicines and treatments or deal with financial offers. The Television Act bans commercials by or for any religious or political group or cause, and any commercial related to a labor dispute. The Television Act is very specific in describing acceptable commercial practices:

Nothing shall be included in any programs broadcast by the Authority whether in an advertisement or not, which states, suggests, or implies, or could reasonably be taken to state, suggest or imply, that any part of any program broadcast by the Authority which is not an advertisement has been supplied or suggested by any advertiser.

When the ITA began telecasting in September 1955, it had made agreements with several different program contractors. The ITA began its telecasts over a single station in London in September of 1955. Stations were then added in rapid succession to cover the Birmingham and Midlands area, Lancashire and Yorkshire, Central Scotland, Wales, Northern Ireland, and other heavily populated areas in Britain. Low-power satellite stations were added to improve reception in various areas. Finally, the ITA had transmitters that reached virtually all of the British people. News programs are produced by a single program-packager—the Independent Television News Company—which supplies news programs to other program contractors.

The program contractors receive their income from selling spot announcements on their programs. From these revenues the contractors pay the IBA for the rental of its transmitters and further sums based on the amount they earn from advertising. The IBA, in turn, pays for its operations from these revenues and, in addition, pays large amounts each year to the British Exchequer. When Independent Television broadcasting began, it faced, like UHF stations in the United States, the technical obstacle that most sets were not equipped to receive its programs. To encourage people to spend the $30 necessary to buy a multichannel tuning device, the program contractors embarked on what they hoped was attractive programming. They arranged for outstanding British stars to appear in favorite plays and interspersed these offerings with popular American programs. In general, their offerings were lighter than those of the BBC and most of the time they attracted larger audiences than their rival. They were also successful in producing some programs that became popular in the United States, among them the series broadcast on public television stations—*Upstairs-Downstairs.*

News and Public Affairs Programs

BBC radio and TV newscasts, prepared by a large staff of news editors in what are among the most active newsrooms in the world, are marked by an impartiality and reserve bordering on dullness. Emotionally loaded words are stripped from all copy, and announcers are instructed to avoid sensationalism or coloring in delivery. The BBC has won wide recognition for reliability and fairness in the handling of news. During World War II, BBC news became the voice of truth for Europe and had a tremendous and intensely loyal listening audience. Radio 2 and Radio 4 broadcast news bulletins at regular intervals and also offer discussion and comments on news events. The other radio services provide occasional news coverage. BBC-1 presents a daytime news program, and both BBC-TV services broadcast news during the evening hours. In addition there are other daily TV programs that provide extensive news features and interpretation.

The news broadcasts of the Independent Television News Company (ITN), which provides all of the national coverage for the Independent Television contractors, are somewhat brighter in tone than those of the BBC, resembling more closely news programs produced in the United States. This competition, in fact, forced the BBC to put more snap into its coverage of the news. ITN also produces other programs that interpret news happenings.

Political broadcasts by party members are handled under an arrangement designed "to remove from the party in power the temptation to use the state's control of broadcasting for its own political ends." Ministers of the government broadcast from time to time on noncontroversial matters, but if a minister is inadvertently controversial, the Opposition has a right to reply. There are several official party broadcasts each year, apportioned according to the total votes cast for each party at the last general election. A similar plan is followed in allocating radio and television time to the representatives of the various political parties during the periods when election campaigns are actually in progress.

Until 1959 the BBC and ITV contractors, interpreting their mandate to be impartial in the strictest possible way, did not cover election campaigns in their news bulletins except to report the results. During the campaign the only coverage of the issues came from the party political broadcasts. In the campaign of 1959, however, the campaign speeches of the contenders were reported on broadcasts, and this practice has continued in election campaigns ever since. In that same year Harold MacMillan became the first British Prime Minister to answer questions on a popular television program. Even though BBC and ITV broadcasters never take a position on the issues, they do not hesitate to analyze them, and their quizzing of political aspirants is far more biting and probing than the questioning to which American politicians are subjected.

British documentary programs, emphasizing the "actuality" technique and featuring original scripts by leading writers, have won wide acclaim. The dramatized documentary, produced in a studio and dealing either with a current issue or an exploration into a historical subject, also remains an important item in British program offerings.

Educational Broadcasting

One of the features of broadcasting in Great Britain is the special attention given to the production of programs for schools, a venture in which both BBC and Independent Television companies participate. More than 200 television series are broadcast during a year, and many programs receive two or more transmissions to make them readily available for school use. BBC programs are utilized by 88 percent of primary schools and 62 percent of secondary schools. In addition to programs broadcast on a national basis, both BBC and IBA companies produce additional programs especially adapted to regional needs.

The broadcasting of radio programs for schools began in Great Britain in 1924 and has continued on a national and regional basis ever since, with the programs being used by 97 percent of the primary schools and 60 percent of the secondary schools. A special type of program known as "radiovision" utilizes a radio program in conjunction with a filmstrip projector operated by the teacher.

The broadcasting companies are aided in preparing the programs by national and regional advisory councils that provide evaluation and advice. In addition, both BBC and the ITV companies maintain an extensive network of school liaison officers, who keep in constant touch with the consumers of the programs and report their reactions and evaluations to the producers.

BBC also produces educational programs for further and adult education. In addition, it broadcasts for the Open University of Great Britain, a university that accepts all applications and does its teaching through correspondence and a wide range of audiovisual equipment. The BBC has supported some 78 Open University courses with specially prepared radio and television broadcasts. This activity is paid for by a grant from the Open University.

The BBC is now experimenting with a special technique for using television for educational purposes. Called CEEFAX, it permits the display on a television screen of written or printed information. A comparable IBA service is called ORACLE.

BROADCASTING IN CANADA

Broadcasting in Canada has taken an unusual form because of the special geographical and cultural makeup of that country. Canada encompasses five different time zones, and is larger than the United States, but it has a population of only 23 million. Most Canadians speak English, but some speak only French. Great distances separate the large metropolitan centers. The cost of a national radio service linked by land lines is prohibitive for independent commercial networks. Advertisers, quite naturally, are interested in reaching heavy concentrations of people and cannot undertake to finance broadcasts that reach only scattered listeners.

When radio got under way in Canada in the twenties, most stations were located in densely populated areas where profitable advertising markets could be tapped, and sparsely populated farming areas were virtually excluded from broadcast reception. It soon became clear that if radio were to be made available to all Canadians, commercial broadcasting could not do the job by itself, but not until 1936 was definitive action taken by the Canadian Parliament. In that year it created the Canadian Broadcasting Corporation. Under this act, the CBC was given two basic responsibilities. First, it was directed by Parliament to "carry on a national broadcasting service" and for this purpose was authorized to "maintain and operate broadcasting stations." Second, it was given the power to supervise the programming and operation of privately owned stations, which were permitted to operate and compete for listeners with the stations owned by the CBC. Unlike the BBC, the stations and networks of the CBC accepted advertising, and the income derived from this source provided substantial revenue. It was not nearly enough, however, to pay for all CBC operations. To supplement this income, a license fee of $2 per year was levied on all radio receivers in operating condition, and the Corporation also received the fees paid by private stations for their operating licenses. In 1937 the listener's license fee was raised to $2.50, and in 1953 it was supplanted by a 15 percent excise tax on the sale of new radio and television receivers. In 1952 the government, which had previously provided loans to the CBC, began supplementing its income with annual grants. In 1958 it was decided to discontinue assigning excise tax and broadcast license revenues directly to the CBC and to replace them with annual appropriations for operation and capital needs. These appropriations, together with revenues derived from the sale of advertising, which provide about a fourth of its income, support the CBC. Privately owned stations had to exist entirely on the revenues they could gain from the sale of advertising.

Owners of these privately owned stations were understandably restive under the provisions of this act, for they found themselves being regulated by the very organization that competed with them for both listeners and advertising. Their organization, the Canadian Association of Radio and Television Broadcasters, agitated vigorously for a revision of the Act that would remove privately owned stations from what they considered to be the discriminatory control of the CBC. An oft-cited example of this discrimination was the fact that CBC not only competed for advertising accounts with privately owned stations, but it also regulated the amount of advertising that these stations could carry. Other complaints were that the CBC reserved to itself the sole right to operate networks and that the system endangered freedom of speech. The introduction of television broadcasting further exacerbated the situation. The principal objection was to the rule by the CBC that in the six major cities of Canada it was to have no competition in the television field from privately owned stations. In the eyes of the private operators, this exclusion from these major markets effectively isolated them from their best opportunities for making profits from advertising. In response to this agitation, the Parliament appointed a commission to study the entire radio and television situation and after receiving its report, passed a new law governing broadcasting that went into effect in 1958.

Under this law, the CBC was shorn of its regulatory powers, and a newly created agency, the Board of Broadcast Governors, was given general powers of regulation and control over all of broadcasting. In most respects it was comparable in authority to the Federal Communications Commission, although, unlike the FCC, it did not actually license stations; this authority remained in the hands of the Minister of Transport, where it had been placed under the original act. CBC stations pay nothing for the privilege of receiving a license, but privately owned stations pay a considerable license fee based on the gross income of the station.

The basic character of Canadian broadcasting, established when the CBC was the regulatory authority, was maintained under the administration of the BBG, but some important changes took place. One of the most significant was the elimination of the CBC's monopoly in television broadcasting in Canada's six major cities. The CBC's previous restriction against the operation of any privately owned TV station in any city where the CBC had a

TV station meant that in such large cities as Toronto and Montreal there was only one Canadian TV station. The BBG not only permitted the establishment of competitive privately operated stations in these and other cities, but it also permitted them to be linked into a network. Thus, the CBC-TV Network, which was formerly the only Canadian TV network, now competes for listeners with the privately operated Canadian Television (CTV) Network, which has 15 regular affiliates and three supplementary affiliates. Like the CBC, the BBG established regulations that maintain control over program standards, advertising content, and the use of broadcast facilities for political purposes.

An important aim of the BBG was to diminish the influence of the United States on Canadian broadcasting. This objective is in keeping with a general Canadian effort to establish and maintain a distinctive national culture and to avoid being annexed culturally by the United States. As far as broadcasting is concerned, the problem is exceptionally difficult, for many Canadians, living close to the border of the United States, can tune in American stations as easily as they can Canadian ones. No walls can be erected against signals that come through the air, but the BBG took decisive steps to prevent Canadian stations from merely picking up American programs and relaying them to Canadian listeners. To this end, they ruled that 55 percent of all broadcasts must be Canadian in content and required that in the prime listening hours from 6:00 P.M. to midnight, stations must broadcast Canadian programs at least 45 percent of the time. Another weapon in the fight to keep broadcasting in the hands of Canadians was the BBG regulation that no more than 20 percent of Canadian broadcasting facilities could be owned by foreigners.

Parliament in 1968 passed a new broadcasting act, which replaced the Board of Broadcast Governors with a regulatory body called the Canadian Radio-Television Commission. Its powers are similar to those of the BBG except that it now has the authority previously held by the Minister of Transport to grant broadcasting licenses. The CRTC has generally followed the practices initiated by its predecessor of enforcing rules that will assure a broadcasting service that is predominately Canadian in content and character. It raised the required Canadian content to 60 percent. In compliance with a provision in the new act that "the Canadian broadcasting system should be effectively owned and controlled by Canadians" it moved to force foreign owners of broadcasting stations to sell their facilities to Canadian citizens. A further evidence of the desire to counter the influence of the United States in Canadian life was CRTC's requirement that commercials in American programs being relayed by certain Canadian cable companies be deleted, and a bill was introduced in the Canadian Parliament to deny Canadian companies the right to deduct as a business expense the money they spent to pay for advertising on American radio and television stations. The Canadian Government has also announced its intention to prevent Canadians from hearing American FM programs.

Despite the elimination of its regulatory power, the CBC still remains the most important single element in Canadian broadcasting. It is the primary source of Canadian programs, serving as well as a distributor of some

American programs. As the one organization that maintains both radio and TV networks extending from coast to coast, it provides Canada's only truly national broadcasting service. The Board of Directors of the Corporation consider that their most important responsibility is to provide leadership in the setting of national standards of quality in Canadian broadcasting. That this quality was attained primarily through the contribution of Canadian talent is supported by the CBC's proud boast that in a single year the work of almost 20,000 Canadian writers, speakers, and performing artists was seen and heard over CBC facilities. This activity is supported by budgets, moreover, that by United States standards are relatively modest. The total budget of the CBC for a single year's activity is just under $400 million. Approximately 80 percent of this amount is provided by grants from public funds; the rest is gained from the sale of time to advertisers and from miscellaneous sources.

Canadian Radio

Using its own stations as focal points, the CBC operates two radio networks, one in English and one in French. The English Network is made up of 26 CBC stations and 59 affiliated stations that are owned privately. More than 200 relay transmitters provide further coverage. The French Network, which provides programs for French-speaking people in all parts of Canada, includes 14 CBC stations, 19 affiliated stations, and some 80 relay transmitters. A northern service provides radio programs for people scattered through the northern territories. In addition to AM networks, the CBC operates an English FM stereo network of eight stations and a French FM stereo network of four stations. Radio service of some type is now available to 99 percent of the Canadian population through the operation of CBC and privately operated stations.

Radio in Canada has declined in importance with the development of television, but it has not yet been demoted to the completely subordinate role it now occupies in the United States, where television is at the center of the spotlight. A considerable amount of effort and money is still being expended in Canada to produce radio programs of quality and distinction including comedy, drama, and live music, forms that have almost disappeared from American radio networks.

In addition to providing programs for listeners in Canada, the CBC is also active in international broadcasting. An Armed Forces Service provides radio programs for Canadian servicemen abroad. This service operates under Radio Canada International, which also broadcasts in 11 languages to Europe, Africa, Latin America, the Caribbean, Australasia, and North America.

Canadian Television

Television came to Canada in 1952 after a period of watchful waiting. The basic plan for the development of CBC television has been similar to the plan of CBC radio: a combination of stations owned and operated by the CBC operating in conjunction with privately owned stations, many of which serve as affiliates in the CBC networks. As is now the case in radio, there are two of these networks, one for the English-speaking people of Canada, made up of 17 CBC stations and 28 privately operated stations, and a second network for the French-speaking people made up of eight CBC stations and seven privately operated stations. A large number of relay and rebroadcasting stations amplify the coverage of both the English and French TV networks. As mentioned previously, there is now a third TV network owned and operated by a private enterprise known as the CTV Television Network. In Canada about 98 percent of the population can receive TV programs. Color TV was introduced in 1966, and now virtually all programs are broadcast in color. Television in Canada is largely restricted to VHF channels, although a few stations operate on UHF channels.

Canada, striving to prevent cultural domination either by its mother country or by its populous American neighbor, has evolved a broadcasting system that follows the pattern of neither country completely, but combines features of both the British and American systems. In establishing a public broadcasting corporation, supported in part by public funds, and in keeping it free from the domination of the party in power, Canada was following the example of Great Britain. In permitting a privately owned system to operate side by side with the public system, both of which receive support from advertising, and in administering all of broadcasting through a national regulatory organization, Canada was following the example of the United States.

OTHER BROADCASTING SYSTEMS

Some form of broadcasting has developed in almost all parts of the world. In Europe, for example, every country except tiny San Marino and Liechtenstein has a radio broadcasting service, and they are served by broadcasts from their neighbors. Television developed more slowly in many parts of the world than it did in the United States, but with the rapid growth of television facilities in recent years, most populated areas now have some kind of television service. In Europe only San Marino, Liechtenstein, Andorra, and Vatican City lack a television system of their own. Different governmental forms, cultural traditions, and national aspirations have given rise to the various types of broadcasting systems. Since there is not space to describe all of them here, we shall note only those systems that are of particular interest— either because they are excellent representatives of a particular approach or because they diverge in a significant way from conventional patterns.

The Soviet Union

A distinctive example of a radio and television system operated by and for the state is the one in the Soviet Union. Responsibility for broadcasting is vested in a state agency headed by an official who is a member of the government. In addition to this central agency located in Moscow, committees are set up in the independent republics of the U.S.S.R. to provide broadcasts that have a regional orientation. The Russian people pay no license fees to receive broadcasts; funds to support radio and television are provided through state subsidies and from money obtained through the sale of programs and the presentation of concerts. About half the radio receivers in Russia operate on relay systems. The television system operates on a 625-line standard and the color system is the same as that used in France—SECAM. As one might expect, the Communist Party exercises strict control over broadcasting and sometimes through its Central Committee publishes criticisms of what is being done. The result is that the radio and television services are major avenues for political propaganda. The loudspeakers and TV screen do not spout politics continually, of course, for if they did people would soon stop listening. Music is presented 50 percent of the time, and many programs offer other distinguished artistic and cultural experiences. Most of Russia's satellite nations have developed broadcasting systems similar to that of the Soviet Union.

France

Even though French radio and television operate under a public corporation that in many respects is similar to the BBC, the French did not follow the British example of preventing domination of the broadcasting media by the government in power. The result is that the French system more closely approximates the Russian system of state control than it does the British. This was particularly true during the regime of Charles DeGaulle. Protesting that such domination was alien to democratic principles, groups in France agitated for the removal of the broadcasting organization from the influence of the Ministry of Information. In 1964 this demand was answered with the replacement of Radiodiffusion—Television Francaise (RTF) with the Office de Radiodiffusion Francaise (ORTF), which no longer was controlled by the Minister of Information but operated under an Administrative Council with private as well as government members. Until DeGaulle retired, this change seemed to make little difference, but since that event there has been an increase in the freedom with which French broadcasters discuss public affairs. The long tradition of state control is difficult to erase, however. It seems likely that the government in power will continue to exercise more influence over broadcasting than is the rule in other democratic nations such as Great Britain and the United States.

France differed from most other European nations in using a TV transmission system with an 819-line definition, but it recently introduced a second system using the 625-line system prevalent in the rest of Europe. It also diverged from its neighbors to join Russia in using the SECAM color system instead of the PAL system adopted in Great Britain and most other European countries. The activities of ORTF, which has a monopoly of broadcasting in France, are supported primarily by the payment of license fees, but financial stringency has forced the French to experiment with advertising support of television.

Italy

In Italy all radio and television activities are carried on by a private company, which has been granted a monopoly of broadcasting by the government. The company, Radio-televisione Italiana (RAI), receives its income from license fees and the sale of advertising. Even though RAI operates as a private company, the government maintains firm control over its activities by holding a majority of its stock and by requiring that its program plans be approved by the Ministry of Posts and Telecommunications. This agency is guided by a committee that helps to determine cultural, artistic, and educational policies. At one time another private company challenged the monopoly of broadcasting enjoyed by RAI. The government rejected this challenge, but it did underline the principle that a company with a monopoly must be careful to provide equal treatment for all. Some have complained that the influence of the government is too great, but Burton Paulu, a perceptive observer of the European broadcasting scene, concludes that the system works well, pointing out that in the wide range of offerings many political and controversial programs are broadcast that the government could suppress if it wanted to.[2] Italy has two television networks and three radio networks. One feature of television in Italy is the use of the medium to bring education to children and adults who would otherwise be deprived of organized educational experiences. Other nations with broadcasting systems similar to Italy's are Sweden and Switzerland.

Luxembourg

A tiny country, Luxembourg wields an influence in broadcasting out of proportion to its size because it has specialized in providing programs for foreign listeners. Its radio programs are regularly heard in Great Britain, Germany, France, and the Netherlands, and its television programs are designed for viewers in France and Belgium. Most of the program fare provided by the broadcasting service on both radio and television is popular in nature, but it does present some educational programs and it prides itself on the accuracy and objectivity of its news broadcasts. Radio Luxembourg—a private company granted a monopoly of broadcasting by the government—is supported entirely by commercial revenue, much of it obtained from advertisers in the various countries to which it directs programs. License fees go directly to the government.

Mexico

The broadcasting system in Mexico is similar to the one in the United States in that it is mainly privately owned and depends in large measure on advertising revenues for its support. It differs from the United States system, however, in that the Mexican government plays a greater official role in actual broadcasting than the United States government does. Mexican law requires that radio stations carry 30 minutes of information from the government every day and a special National Hour, produced by a government agency, every Sunday evening. The only way a Mexican station can escape this latter obligation is to go off the air during the period of the broadcast. The National Hour, which presents music, drama, editorials from newspapers, read-

---

[2] Burton Paulu, *Radio and Television Broadcasting on the European Continent* (Minneapolis, 1967), p. 79.

ings from the Mexican constitution, and government information and propaganda, has been on the air since 1937. Mexican law also calls for the
establishment of noncommercial stations designed to present educational
and cultural programs. Most of these stations are operated by universities.
The emphasis in Mexico, however, is on the entertainment the commercial
radio stations provide over transmitters that in some instances broadcast
with 250 thousand watts, far more power than is allowed in the United
States. According to one observer, the commercial content of Mexican radio
programs is also greater than it is in the United States.[3] Television broadcasting, which has been carried on almost entirely by one company, is
mainly commercial and popular in nature. One educational television
station is in operation and a few educational programs are presented over
commercial TV facilities, but television has been generally neglected as an
educational tool in Mexico.

Belgium, West Germany, The Netherlands, Japan

The broadcasting systems in some other countries have unusual features that
are worth noting. Belgium, a nation split into major language groups—
French and Flemish—has responded by creating two public broadcasting
corporations made up of three autonomous institutes responsible respectively
for broadcasts in French, Flemish, and German. This latter institute is also
responsible for foreign-language broadcasting. Belgium is unusual too in
being the only European free nation that still prohibits advertising on radio
and television.

Organization on a state rather than a national basis is the distinguishing feature of broadcasting in West Germany. Most of the German
states or *Länder* have set up separate and independent broadcasting corporations. There are also two federal public radio corporations and a public
television corporation. A national committee coordinates the activities of the
various state corporations and provides for network broadcasts that are
heard on a national basis. Support for the corporations comes from license
fees and advertising.

The unusual feature of broadcasting in the Netherlands is the power
wielded by private societies of a religious and political nature. Five of them
first obtained radio concessions in the 1920s, and they have continued to
play a significant role in broadcasting ever since. In 1947 they formed a
coordinating organization to administer jointly their buildings, studio and
technical equipment, and program resources. Television began under the
same type of arrangement, and one national organization now coordinates
both radio and television broadcasting. The number of participating organizations has now grown to seven. In 1965, while maintaining dominance of
the original broadcasting societies, the government did move to open broadcasting to other groups and to require that different points of view be expressed. Support comes from the funds of the various societies, license fees,
and advertising.

[3] Walter Emery, *National and International Systems of Broadcasting* (East Lansing, 1969), p. 33.

Japan was marked by a faster development of broadcasting facilities than occurred anywhere else in the world. Two television stations in 1953 grew to more than 1200 stations in the next 15 years, more stations than in the United States. Japan was also one of the first nations in the world to begin TV color broadcasts. Another distinguishing feature of Japanese broadcasting is its emphasis on education. Hundreds of Japanese radio and television stations operate as educational stations. There are two systems of broadcasting in Japan—a public system (NHK) and a private system in which a number of corporations participate. The public system exists mainly on the revenue derived from license fees; the private system is supported by advertising. The influence of the United States can be seen in the adoption of the 525-line system and the NTSC color system and in the broadcasting of many programs produced in America.

SUMMARY

Practically all nations now engage in radio and television broadcasting. Systems of broadcasting now in use include government-operated radio and television; monopoly broadcasting by public or private corporations; combinations of government stations and privately owned stations; and completely commercial operation of almost all stations with a minimum of government intervention. Some nations, because of unusual conditions or traditions, have developed unique features in their broadcasting systems. In most nations revenue from both advertising and license fees supports broadcasting.

Questions for Discussion

1. What is the difference between a relay exchange and a broadcasting system?
2. Describe the basic national systems of broadcasting.
3. Upon what factors does the structure of a country's broadcasting system usually depend?
4. What factors must be considered in evaluating a national system of broadcasting?
5. How does British broadcasting compare with American broadcasting in terms of structure, programming, and regulation?
6. In what ways does the Canadian broadcasting system combine features of the British and American systems, and in what ways is it unique?
7. What value, if any, would there be in having an interchange of information and programs among different national broadcasting systems?
8. How does Great Britain handle the problem of broadcasting by political parties?
9. Why do you think that advertising in Great Britain came to television before it came to radio?

international broadcasting

13

"The story of radio in international affairs is part of the story of power politics," write Professors Childs and Whitton.[1] Broadcasting has no equal as a means of international communication. Instantaneous in transmission, it penetrates national frontiers and spans the walls of censorship that bar the written word. Broadcasting can be used to foster international amity, but it has been used mainly to wage psychological warfare on people.

GROWTH OF INTERNATIONAL BROADCASTING

As early as World War I, when radio was still in its "wireless" stage, international broadcasting was used for espionage and intelligence. The Allies dropped Marconi senders in enemy territories to get reports from secret agents. Radio was also used to communicate with neutral countries across telegraph and mail blockades; the belligerents themselves used radio to send out "peace feelers" and to conduct preliminary armistice negotiations. Not until the middle twenties, however, were efforts made to use international broadcasting to influence public opinion abroad. These early efforts were not systematic and were limited to isolated issues and occasions, such as the "radio war" that broke out between Radio Berlin and the Eiffel tower station in Paris during the invasion of the Ruhr in 1923.

The Bolshevik masters of the newly constituted government of the Soviet Union were among the first to make effective use of radio to spread world revolutionary propaganda. Moscow waged a radio war with Rumania over Bessarabia in 1926, and revolutionary appeals were broadcast to German workers in the critical year preceding Hitler's assumption of power in 1933.

But not all early efforts at international broadcasting were unfriendly in intention. Nations exchanged good broadcast programs and occasionally linked their facilities for programs of common interest. The International Broadcasting Union was formed in 1927 to bring radio's warring parties to-

[1] Harwood I. Childs and John B. Whitton. *Propaganda by Short Wave* (Princeton, 1942), p. 3.

gether and to obtain agreements to abstain from hostile propaganda and to avoid mutual interference. Fear of possible attack, however, caused the nations of Europe to expand their radio "defenses." This meant the construction of more radio transmitters, since retaliation or "jamming" operations are the only defense a nation has against enemy broadcasts.

Holland, Britain, France, Belgium, and Portugal used international broadcasting to reach their colonies in the late twenties. The broadcasts were directed not to the natives, but to nationals residing in the colonies, or to the ruling emissaries. With its colonies spread around the globe, Great Britain decided to set up regular Empire broadcasting on a round-the-clock basis in 1932. In the same year, the League of Nations formed its own radio facility in Geneva, to transmit international messages to individual countries and to communicate information to its far-flung representatives.

The first use of radio as a weapon of direct warfare appears to have been made by Japan with its broadcasts to enemy armies and civilians during the Manchurian invasion of 1931. The Japanese were not content with using radio merely to win a speedier victory. After the conquest, "broadcasting was organized in Manchukuo to instill new loyalties among the conquered and cut them off from Chinese influence."[2] To do this, free receivers were distributed among the people. In 1935, Japan began shortwave broadcasting overseas to consolidate her new empire.

Radio was immediately exploited by Hitler when he assumed power in Germany. The Nazi government used shortwave transmissions to reach distant countries and broke into the medium-wave band to attract listeners in neighboring European countries. A thorough radio propaganda campaign helped prepare the people of the Saar basin for German reentry in 1935. Hitler's next triumph took place in Austria, where a combination of military threats, radio propaganda, and conspiracy by secret agents won a reported 99.75 percent of the total Austrian vote to approve the country's incorporation within the German Reich. In the days that preceded the plebiscite, the Nazis distributed 100,000 radios among the Austrians.[3] The German government's next step was to set up a shortwave broadcast service to spread Nazi doctrine to its friends and potential supporters overseas. Foreign audiences of German birth or ancestry were organized into clubs for group listening.

From 1936 to 1939, during the Spanish Civil War, radio got a dress rehearsal for World War II. Childs and Whitton write that "By virtue of . . . diabolically clever propaganda the democracies were split internally from top to bottom and were not only neutralized into 'nonintervention' for the duration of the war, but for years to come were politically paralyzed by the formation of 'appeasement' parties hostile to any action against Fascism."[4] In actual combat, Franco used radio to keep in touch with his fifth column in Madrid and to direct a propaganda barrage against the civilian populace.

---

[2] *Ibid.,* p. 10. This account of the growth of international broadcasting is drawn mainly from Childs' and Whitton's discussion.
[3] *Ibid.,* p. 18
[4] *Ibid.,* p. 24.

Advised by German and Italian propaganda experts, Franco used vituper-ation, threats, sadism, and braggadocio in his radio propaganda campaign. A weary Spanish republic, split from within by communist machinations and left without support from friendly democracies, finally succumbed.

Benefiting from its own successes and the Spanish experience, Germany launched a propaganda war against the Czechs before fomenting the Mu-nich crisis of 1938. Radio laid down a "drum-fire barrage of terror and prop-aganda," which continued even after the crisis was temporarily resolved and did not come to an end until the Czechs surrendered completely the next year. By the time German troops were ready to enter Prague, the Czech radio had capitulated along with the government, announcing the German occupation at five-minute intervals and warning the people not to offer resistance.

In early 1939, the western European democracies awakened to the dan-ger of unanswered German propaganda and began a vigorous radio counter-offensive. An all-out effort was launched to reach European populations in their native tongues. The BBC set up a European service which, by the out-break of war, was broadcasting in 16 foreign languages. Nazi reaction was violent. The German people were warned not to listen to the "false" foreign radio propaganda maligning German leaders, and heavy penalties were im-posed for such listening or for spreading news heard on foreign broadcasts. The German who harbored a shortwave radio receiver in his home did so at grave personal peril.

During these turbulent years, the United States took no official part in international broadcasting. Private organizations—World Wide Broad-casting Foundation, CBS, NBC, Crosley, Westinghouse, and General Elec-tric—had, however, undertaken regular shortwave broadcasting.[5] CBS set up a "Network of the Americas," hoping to build up a profitable operation in Latin America, and NBC joined the international business soon thereafter. By the time of Pearl Harbor, there were only 13 international voice-broad-casting transmitters in the United States.[6] Until 1940, the United States Army paid scant attention to psychological warfare, and in the years from 1925 to 1935 not one full-time officer was assigned even to study the subject.[7]

The reasons for such limited activity in international broadcasting and propaganda by this country are clear. The United States was in a period of isolationist thinking, and the failure to use international broadcasting more fully was merely a reflection of the general political outlook. Business inter-ests in radio also opposed government intervention in any broadcasting out of fear that a precedent would be established for state interference in broad-casting at home. Commercial broadcasters had no motivation to undertake shortwave broadcasting themselves on a regular basis because there was no profit to be made from it.

[5] Forney A. Rankin. *Who Gets the Air?* (Washington, 1949), p. 35.

[6] Charles A. H. Thomson, *Overseas Information Service of the United States Government* (Wash-ington, 1948), p. 3.

[7] Paul Linebarger, "Psychological Warfare in World War Two," *Infantry Journal,* 60 (1947), 32n.

RADIO IN WORLD WAR II

World War II saw the full flowering of broadcasting, both domestic and international, as a vehicle for propaganda. The objectives of each belligerent were the same: 1. to demoralize enemies by confusing, terrifying, and dividing them; 2. to maintain the friendships of neutral countries by broadcasts justifying war aims and inviting cultural exchanges; 3. to stimulate the morale of its own fighting forces and civilian populace. Nations constructed transmitters to send out their own programs and set up listening posts to monitor enemy broadcasts in an effort to turn up clues to future enemy policy and to provide ammunition for counterpropaganda. By the war's end, there were more than 360 transmitters manned by thousands of skilled linguists and script writers in more than 50 different countries, sending around the world more than 2000 words a minute in 40-odd languages.[8]

Perfecting what has been called the "strategy of terror," the German government took early leadership in the radio propaganda war. Raising the image of defeat and subjugation, the Nazis followed up their Czech success with an incessant torrent of words against Poland, and later against France, Holland, and Norway. By 1941 Germany was using 88 of its own shortwave transmitters plus those it took over in occupied countries. It created radio personalities like Lord Haw-Haw and Axis Sally to conduct their English broadcast propaganda. At home, the Nazis clamped heavy penalties on shortwave listening and fed the German people a steady list of misinformation, which caused no problem as long as news of military victories continued to roll in, but which began to wear thin as the prospect of defeat loomed.

Operating through the Overseas Service of the BBC, Great Britain relied on regular newscasts to point out the lies of the German leaders. To the occupied peoples of Europe, the voice of the BBC, broadcast in 50 different languages, came as a heartening sound in the world of darkness. An old lady in Holland wrote during the Nazi occupation, "Nowadays I believe nothing but the BBC and the Bible."[9] The BBC developed the "V for Victory" slogan, which became the most effective propaganda symbol of the war. At home, the British used radio to sustain the morale of factory workers and civilian defense personnel, with "music-while-you-work" programs and "actuality" broadcasts from microphones set up in canteens and air-raid shelters.

The Soviet Union disclosed great technical ability in countering German radio propaganda. Ingenious technicians and quick-witted broadcasters learned how to track down and wreck German "newscasts" by transmitting on the same frequencies as the German stations. Soviet broadcasters heckled the German announcers, filling in pauses between German news bulletins with caustic comments on their probable falsity, and even mimicked Hitler. Within the U.S.S.R., "Russian foreign propaganda concentrated on denigrating the Allies and celebrating Russia's lone role in the war."[10]

---

[8] Llewellyn White and Robert D. Leigh, *Peoples Speaking to Peoples* (Chicago, 1946), p. 11.

[9] T. O. Beachcroft, *British Broadcasting* (London, 1946), p. 20.

[10] Thomson, *op. cit.,* p. 99.

Japan used shortwave broadcasting to hold together its scattered empire of islands and primitive populations, and to wage propaganda warfare against American troops and native populations outside its domain. Tokyo Rose broadcast to American troops, hoping to make them more homesick and to sap their fighting ambition. Utilizing racist propaganda, Japan sought to weld a binding tie among yellow-skinned peoples and to turn them against the lighter-skinned Occidentals. The fly in the ointment of this propaganda was China, a nation of inhabitants with pigmentation similar to the Japanese, but with different national aspirations.

With the attack on Pearl Harbor, the United States changed its orientation toward international broadcasting. Although, according to Wallace Carroll, President Roosevelt had little interest or understanding of psychological warfare, he authorized the establishment of the Office of War Information under the direction of Elmer Davis to run America's propaganda efforts at home and abroad.[11] The OWI was empowered to "plan, develop, and execute all phases of the federal program of radio, press, publication, and related foreign propaganda activities involving the dissemination of propaganda." Davis was responsible only to the President, but he seldom had access to him.[12]

The OWI, with 11,000 employees, was divided into two main operations: 1. The domestic branch, which channeled governmental information to the American people through press and radio, and coordinated the publicity efforts of official bureaus; and 2. the overseas branch, which waged the "strategy of truth" through the "Voice of America."

During the four years of its operation, the OWI sent out from its New York offices as many as 2700 broadcasts a week in 25 languages and dialects, and an additional 1200 programs in 22 languages from its San Francisco headquarters. About 700 people were employed for this work. News, news features, analyses, and entertainment constituted the main program fare. In the early stages of the war, emphasis was placed on spot military and political news, but later on more use was made of round tables, special events, interviews, and commentaries. Entertainment consisted of drama, music, poetry, and talks on noncontroversial subjects.[13] At the end of the war, the OWI had a world communications system of 36 transmitters in continental United States and 14 overseas.

The OWI overseas branch did not broadcast to Latin American countries, which were assigned to the Office of Inter-American Affairs headed by Nelson Rockefeller. The OIAA carried on its own schedule of shortwave programs to our Latin American allies.

To sustain morale among soldiers and sailors overseas, the Army and Navy set up a joint broadcast operation called Armed Forces Radio Service, which provided entertainment and information for troops stationed in Europe and in the Pacific areas. Small stations were built at headquarters or advanced bases to broadcast recorded music, news, transcriptions of the best

[11] Wallace Carroll, *Persuade or Perish* (Boston, 1948), pp. 6–7.

[12] *Ibid.,* p. 7.

[13] Thomson, *op. cit.,* pp. 55–56.

network shows with the commercials deleted, and especially prepared AFRS shows.

In 1944, the American Broadcasting Station in Europe (ABSIE) was set up in London.

> to broadcast both locally originated and New York programs to the people of Europe as required by the immediate necessities of the invasion and the liberation of the continent. One of the great prizes of the European campaign from the propaganda point of view was the capture of Radio Luxembourg practically intact.[14]

In addition, psychological warfare units were established in the Army and Navy to make use of the latest techniques of strategic and combat propaganda. The most notable use of this weapon during the war was the broadcast talks of Navy Captain Zacharias to the people of Japan.[15]

To detect drifts in Germany policy, the Federal Communications Commission established the Foreign Broadcast Intelligence Service, with a staff of 300 linguists and technicians who recorded and transcribed almost a million words a day of Axis propaganda broadcasts. These scripts were carefully studied for clues to enemy thinking, and daily analyses were prepared for State, War, and Navy department officials.

It is hard to evaluate the total effectiveness of all these efforts at radio propaganda and counterpropaganda. Judging by the large sums and effort expended on radio by Germany, Britain, and the Soviet Union, it would seem that the military and diplomatic leaders of those countries firmly believed that radio was playing an important part in the war. Isolated instances of surrenders by defeated soldiers, which were attributed to specific radio broadcasts, bolstered the belief in radio's power. From subjected peoples in occupied countries came surreptitious but eloquent testimony to the psychological value of international broadcasting, and from underground agents, communicated with by radio, came evidence of specific military value. At the end of World War II, General Eisenhower said:

> . . . I am convinced that the expenditure of men and money in wielding the spoken and written word was an important contributing factor in undermining the enemy's will to resist and supporting the fighting morale of our potential Allies in the occupied countries. . . . Psychological warfare has proved its right to a place of dignity in our military arsenal.[16]

INTERNATIONAL BROADCASTING SINCE WORLD WAR II

International broadcasting, which received such impetus during World War II, continued in peacetime on a far greater scale than it had before the war. The various armistice agreements had not actually terminated the hostilities.

---

[14] *Ibid.,* p. 54.

[15] Ellis M. Zacharias, *Secret Missions* (New York, 1946).

[16] The Psychological Warfare Division, Supreme Headquarters, Allied Expeditionary Force, *An Account of Its Operations in the Western European Campaign, 1944–1945* (Bad Homburg, Germany, 1945), frontispiece.

The war merely took a new form—the Cold War—in which propaganda, instead of bullets and bombs, became the main tool of battle. In that kind of war, broadcasting was obviously qualified to play a major role. The Cold War became a battle of ideologies in which most of the adversaries of World War II shifted into new alignments that placed them either with the Communist bloc nations or with the free nations of the world. Of the 80-odd nations that now engage in international broadcasting, almost all in some measure used their programs as weapons in the Cold War. As the years went by, the development of new tensions—the break between Russia and China, for example—increased the use of radio for hostile purposes. China bombards its Russian neighbor with 300 hours of programs a week, and the Soviet Union has doubled its broadcasts to China.

Although most international broadcasts are designed to influence world opinion in favor of the nation that originates them, some have friendly purposes: to give information or to provide educational or cultural experiences. Great Britain uses some of its programs to maintain relations with British Commonwealth nations around the world. The overall aim of even these friendly broadcasts, however, is to promote national policies. Their ultimate purpose is to develop the kind of world opinion that will enhance the attainment of the nation's political and social objectives.

International Broadcasting by the United States

The leading international broadcaster in the world is the United States. Its four international services, the Voice of America, RIAS, Radio Free Europe, and Radio Liberty broadcast more than 2000 hours of programs per week. The transmissions made for the armed forces add many more hours to this total.

The Voice of America. Shortly after the Japanese surrender was announced in August 1945, President Truman abolished the domestic bureau of the OWI and transferred the functions and personnel of its overseas branch to the Department of State. There it remained until Congress, feeling that the commercial radio industry should handle overseas broadcasting, divested the State Department almost completely of its authority over the Voice of America by requiring that 75 percent of the broadcasts be prepared and produced by NBC and CBS on a contractual basis. After a series of embarrassing incidents involving several scripts that irked some Congressmen, this arrangement came to an end in the spring of 1948, much to the relief of the networks, which had not wanted the job. The United States Information and Educational Exchange Act of 1948 effected this change. The law committed the United States for the first time in our history, in time of peace, to engage in international broadcasting, and assigned the Voice of America to the State Department.

In 1953, after another investigation of our overseas information program, the Voice of America was transferred from the State Department to the newly created United States Information Agency, an independent government agency.

The work of the Voice of America is "to submit evidence to the peoples of other nations . . . that the objectives and policies of the United States are in harmony with and will advance their legitimate aspirations for freedom, progress, and peace." The VOA is obligated under the law to provide a news service that is consistently reliable and authoritative and to project a comprehensive picture of American thought and institutions. It operates 41 powerful shortwave transmitters in the United States, which beam its programs worldwide, and 72 other transmitters located in various countries also transmit VOA programs. This distribution system is augmented by the relaying of VOA broadcasts by the radio stations of friendly nations. Most of the broadcasts originate from 23 studios in Washington, where 80 programs can be recorded simultaneously. In 1976 the VOA operated on a budget of $60 million and employed 2272 people.

The Voice of America now broadcasts 24 hours a day, producing 932 program hours a week in 36 languages, a production rate that ranks it third after Radio Moscow and Radio Peking. The broadcasts consist of news, news analysis, and features including commentaries, press reviews, documentaries, discussion, and special events. There are 253 newscasts daily. All of these broadcasts are designed to provide the people of other nations with information about world events and to promote better understanding of the United States. Even material that does not necessarily reflect credit on the United States is included in the programs as a means of building up the credibility of the service with its worldwide audience; listeners can expect to hear the truth whether or not it specifically helps the American cause.

Establishing the number of people who listen to VOA broadcasts is difficult. It is known that there are about 600 million radio receivers in the world, of which about 200 million are equipped to receive shortwave transmissions. The best estimate is that 50 million adults listen each week to VOA broadcasts. An audience study conducted in a number of countries showed that from .5 percent to 10 percent of the adults listen regularly to VOA broadcasts. Assessing the overall effectiveness of the VOA is even more difficult than measuring its audience, but some indications of its value are available. Foremost is the attempt by the Communist nations of the world to jam VOA broadcasts. The Soviet Union and most of the nations of Eastern Europe carried out jamming operations from 1948 to 1963. The U.S.S.R. resumed jamming after the Soviet invasion of Czechoslovakia in 1968 and continued until 1973. Bulgaria ceased its jamming in 1974, the last Eastern European nation to do so. Cuba has also jammed broadcasts from the United States, particularly during the 1961 missile crisis, and the People's Republic of China continues to jam VOA Chinese-language broadcasts.

In addition to the radio services of the Voice of America, the United States Information Agency (USIA) also produces some 275 films and television programs each year for use in theaters and television stations in other countries. Some programs are made as coproduction ventures with foreign media units. Some 300 other films and television programs are acquired for distribution abroad.

Radio Free Europe. The broadcasts of RFE are directed to the Eastern European nations—Czechoslovakia, Hungary, Poland, Rumania, and Bulgaria—which are usually considered to be satellites of the Soviet Union.

From broadcasting headquarters in Munich, Germany, it presents programs built around news that provide information about the world outside the satellite countries and news about the satellites themselves that may have been suppressed by their communist governments. It is estimated that about 30 million people listen to the broadcasts at least once a month, or half the adult population. Many of the programs are prepared and presented by defectors from these countries. Though ostensibly a private institution, RFE was supported financially by the United States through the CIA and carries out policies consistent with those of the United States.

Radio Liberty. Similar in nature to Radio Free Europe in set-up, programming policy, and financial support, Radio Liberty broadcasts 24 hours a day in 18 languages to the Soviet Union. It is estimated that 35–40 million adults hear its programs each month.

The American Forces Network. To provide servicemen and their families with entertainment and information, the Armed Forces operates facilities that make radio and television programs available wherever service personnel may be located. Around the world, 800 radio stations and 230 TV stations transmit AFN programs. The main shortwave facilities are located in Washington, D.C. AFN produces its own programs, often in local studios by servicemen assigned to this duty, and also makes use of the programs presented by American networks. A major policy of the AFN is to provide a free flow of news and information to service personnel without censorship, propagandizing, or manipulation. The service also provides full coverage of sports and broadcasts programs featuring music and other types of entertainment.

BBC External Services

Ever since Great Britain awakened in 1938 to the needs of regular international broadcasting as an instrument of foreign policy, the BBC External Services division has been a leader in the field and now offers one of the most active shortwave schedules in the world. The broadcasts are supported by an annual grant-in-aid that comes to about one-quarter of the money spent by the BBC in running its domestic radio services. The External Services division beams an elaborate schedule of programs in 39 languages round-the-clock to meet the political, cultural, and geographical needs of different regions and countries throughout the world. Included within the shortwave operations of the BBC, which presents approximately 720 hours of programs a week, are broadcasts intended for Europe, the Middle East, Asia, Africa, and the Americas. More than 50 nations help in the distribution of these programs by rebroadcasting them. One of the special services provided by the BBC for its external listeners is lessons in English, which have been broadcast on radio for more than 25 years. In 1962 this service was supplemented by a television series that is broadcast in all but one country in western Europe and in 40 countries outside Europe. In addition the sale of tapes and transcriptions provides a world audience for television and radio programs made for British domestic use.

Estimating the number of listeners to BBC external broadcasts is difficult, but there is evidence that the listening is substantial. One of the best indications that the broadcasts are heard is 280,000 letters sent in every year by listeners from abroad. Audience studies have shown that the BBC has one million listeners a day in India, almost a million a week in Germany, and two million a week in Italy.

Radio Canada International

Canada inaugurated the CBC International Service toward the close of World War II. Its purpose is "to present an honest, objective, colorful picture of Canada and Canadian life through information talks, commentaries, news, and entertainment programs." The International Service is operated by the CBC for the Canadian government and is financed by a Parliamentary grant of funds. It is part of an External Services Division, which also includes export sales functions. The Canadians broadcast on shortwave to Europe and Africa about 150 hours a week. The main emphasis is on news and commentary, but the programs also include music, sports, and miscellaneous material. Canadian influence is further felt around the world through the sale to foreign countries of many CBC radio and television programs.

International Broadcasts by Communist Nations

Among the most active international broadcasters are the communist nations, led by the Soviet Union, which presents more than 1900 hours of programs a week, closely followed by Communist China, which broadcasts more than 1300 hours of programs a week. The satellite nations add considerably to this amount. Communist nations as a group broadcast in twice as many languages as the noncommunist nations do. The Soviet Union alone originates programs in 79 different languages. A particular focus of communist attention has been the nations of Latin America and the emerging nations of Africa, but other parts of the world are not being neglected. The North American Service, for example, is aimed directly at the United States and Canada, and from 10 different transmitters it provides programs continuously from 6:00 P.M. to 1:00 A.M., EST. An example of the careful adaptation to its audience that characterizes this service is the use of general American speech in presenting news broadcasts to the United States, whereas the same news broadcasts will be presented in British dialect to areas where that is the prevailing speech. The Soviet broadcasters have also adopted the informality of language that is characteristic of American broadcasts. A varied group of programs is presented, including Russian classical music, American popular music, interviews with American visitors to the Soviet Union, answers to questions sent in by American listeners, and news and commentary every hour. The news presented is usually accurate, but it is carefully selected to support Russian propaganda themes. Because there are very few shortwave receivers operating in the United States and because the Soviet signal is usually weak and erratic, it is estimated that the audience for these broadcasts is extremely small.

INTERNATIONAL BROADCASTING ORGANIZATIONS

International Organizations Dealing with Facilities

In order to make broadcasting possible on either a domestic or an international basis, it is necessary to have international agreements regarding the use of frequencies and cooperation in the development of facilities. Two organizations are the main contributors in these areas.

The International Telecommunications Union (ITU). Formed in 1865 to provide for the extension of telegraph lines across national boundaries, the ITU, which now operates as an agency of the United Nations, is concerned with all wired and wireless communications. As far as broadcasting is concerned, it has two major functions: 1. to allocate frequencies; and 2. to help provide for the most efficient and orderly use of the broadcasting spectrum. The General Secretariat of the ITU and its offices are located in Geneva.

The International Telecommunications Satellite Consortium (INTELSAT). This international organization provides for cooperation among nations in the development and operation of the satellites that make it possible for people around the world to watch the same television program simultaneously. The agreement establishing INTELSAT was signed in 1964 by 19 nations, and the consortium has now increased in number to more than 90 nations. The international organization is particularly concerned with the establishment of earth stations that will help nations to take advantage of the programs and other communications relayed by the satellites.

International Organizations Dealing with Programs

Broadcasters in various parts of the world have established organizations dedicated to promoting program exchanges and to setting up the facilities needed for this purpose.

The European Broadcasting Union (EBU). This organization, founded in 1950, with headquarters in Geneva, has a number of different objectives: 1. to support the interests of broadcasting organizations; 2. to develop information regarding broadcasting and to disseminate it; 3. to seek the solution of differences; and 4. to encourage adherence to international agreements. In pursuit of these objectives, the organization publishes the *EBU Review* to provide information about developments in broadcasting. The EBU's most dramatic activity, however, is the operation of Eurovision, a network of more than 1000 television stations in the countries of western Europe which permits programs produced in one country to be seen simultaneously by residents in all the other countries. There were some tentative exchanges of television programs between Great Britain and France in 1950, but it was not until 1954 that Eurovision was set up on a permanent basis with technical headquarters in Brussels. As television was introduced into the various nations of western Europe, the network gradually expanded until it linked an area from Sweden to Italy and from Northern Ireland to Austria. When Greece, the last European nation to adopt television, joined Eurovision, the network was complete. In reaching this goal many different types of problems had been solved—the different line standards used by the member nations, geographical obstacles such as mountains, and language barriers. One way that Eurovision solved the language difficulty was to program those events in which speech is not a major factor. Thus, Eurovision concentrates on sports 40 percent of the time and also transmits special events such as coronations, space exploration, and funerals, which can be understood visually. For the same reason ballet has been a frequent subject of Eurovision transmissions. The development of satellite relays has made it possible for Eurovision to bring world events to its viewers as they happen. The first transatlantic "live" transmission between the United States and Europe took place in 1962. Many nations outside of the European area belong to the EBU as associate members.

The International Television and Radio Organization (OIRT). This organization, a counterpart of the EBU in eastern Europe, began as an all-European organization with headquarters in Brussels, but when the Soviet bloc of nations tried to make it an instrument of communist propaganda, the western nations withdrew in 1949 to form the EBU, and OIR, as it was known at that time, moved its headquarters to Prague. The organization sought members around the world and soon enrolled many nations outside of Europe that had communist governments or were friendly to the Soviet Union and its satellites.

The stated aims of OIRT are similar to those of the EBU. As one of its activities it operates a network among the 13 Soviet bloc nations in eastern Europe. Known as Intervision, it operates much as Eurovision does in western Europe. There have been occasional contacts between the two networks, particularly in the broadcasting of sports and state events, but regular connections between the two must undoubtedly wait until international tensions have eased.

The United Nations and radio. When the United Nations was established, there were high hopes that international broadcasting might be turned into an instrument of peace and understanding. In October 1946, the UN Radio Division was set up on a meager basis with one studio and some recording facilities for radio correspondents. The next year the UN asked the CBC and the United States Department of State to make available to it their shortwave transmitters to disseminate programs of the UN. Since those modest beginnings UN radio has developed a worldwide network, presenting broadcasts in the principal languages of the world from shortwave transmitters placed so as to give coverage of important areas of the world. Its programs are rebroadcast daily in many countries and its recorded programs are played on thousands of stations, including many in the United States. They are now being utilized by approximately 142 countries and territories.

The United Nations offers a wide range of services to enable radio stations around the world to cover its activities. The main services are as follows: 1. The provision of facilities to correspondents; 2. shortwave broadcasts of meetings of major UN bodies; 3. shortwave broadcasts of news summaries

and news programs in some 31 languages; 4. the supply of ready-for-broad-
cast feature programs transcribed on tape or disc, or fed by line if feasible;
and, 5. the provision of a selection of audio material from UN archives when
specifically requested by national organizations for use in their coverage of
UN activities.

One problem the UN faces in preparing its radio programs is to avoid
taking sides on issues that divide nations. It must concentrate on telling the
UN story rather than becoming a vehicle for the dissemination of a particular national point of view. The antipathies that exist among nations often
create serious obstacles to providing complete and unbiased consideration of
issues. Arab delegates, for example, will not appear on the same program
with delegates from Israel, and Russian delegates have participated very
little in UN broadcasts.

Other international organizations. A number of international organizations designed to promote broadcasting have sprung up in various areas of the
world, most of them modeled after those in Europe. Among these organizations are the Asian Broadcast Union (ABU), the Union of National Radio
and Television Organizations of Africa (URTNA), and the Inter-American
Broadcast Association. Another organization of this type is the International
Television Federation (INTERTEL), established to facilitate the exchange
of programs among such organizations as the British, Canadian, and Aus-
tralian broadcasting corporations and public broadcasters in the United
States.

COMMUNICATIONS SATELLITES

A development that enormously increased the reach of man's communication potentialities was the deployment in the 1960s of communications
satellites in stationary orbits around the earth. The satellites now in place
make it possible for people all over the world to view the same television program simultaneously. But this development is important for more than its
advancement of global television; it is bringing about a change in the way in
which television programs are distributed within a given country.

The communications satellite era began in July 1962, when the American Telephone and Telegraph Company engaged the National Space
Agency to launch Telstar, a satellite that made the first live transmissions between Europe and the United States possible. Telstar did not permit continuous transmissions, however, for as it dropped below the horizon in its 158-
minute elliptical orbit around the earth, the relaying of the signal abruptly
ceased. Keeping a satellite in sight of the transmitting and receiving station,
a requirement for maintaining continuous operation, would have required
from 20 to 40 satellites of the Telstar type constantly orbiting the earth. The
problem was solved when the Hughes Aircraft Company developed a type of
satellite that, shot into space 22,300 miles above the equator, orbits at a
speed synchronized with the rotational speed of the earth. The result is that
it seems to hang motionless in space, always remaining in line-of-sight contact with the transmitting and receiving stations.

The first synchronous satellite, Early Bird, was successfully launched in February 1965, making possible continuous transatlantic television transmission. Since that time a number of other synchronous satellites with greater power, more circuits, and a greater life expectancy than Early Bird have joined it in space. Simultaneous reception of the same television program is now possible throughout most of the world. The development of satellites has also greatly increased the facilities for international telephone communication.

The operation of the satellite system is an international venture in which some 90 nations participate as members of the International Telecommunications Satellite Consortium (INTELSAT). The Soviet Union did not join INTELSAT but established its own organization, Intersputnik, in 1971, which serves the U.S.S.R. and the other communist nations of the area. The first Russian nonsynchronous satellite, Molniya, was launched in 1965, and other similar satellites followed it into space. A synchronous Russian satellite called Orbita is now operating. There have been some common transmissions on the INTELSAT and Intersputnik systems, but there is no connection on a regular basis.

In 1974 Western Union launched WESTAR I, the first satellite designed to provide domestic telecommunications relay service, and later it launched WESTAR II. Public broadcasters are planning to make use of the facilities of these satellites and comparable ones to provide network links for radio and television programs. RCA placed SATCOM I in orbit in 1975 and plans to launch SATCOM II. Comsat plans to launch two COMSTAR satellites in 1978, each with 14,400 voice circuits. Since 1973 Canada has been using a domestic satellite system as a means of bringing "live" television programs to residents in its northern territories who are now beyond the reach of network facilities. Many other countries with large areas, such as Indonesia, whose people are scattered over 3000 islands in a vast stretch of the Pacific, would benefit from the establishment of a national satellite system. Satellites may eventually eliminate the need for television stations entirely.

The communications satellites' role in global and television communications as a means of relaying programs is now well established, though it is unlikely that satellites will be used to send programs directly to homes, at least in the immediate future. On an experimental basis, however, a satellite has been used to beam educational programs to regional earth receiving stations in the Rocky Mountain, Appalachian, and Alaskan areas of the United States. After a year of service for these areas, the satellite was moved to provide educational broadcasts for 5000 villages in India. In 1976, transmission via satellite was first used to link widespread cable television systems in the United States to receive the same programs simultaneously, including movies and athletic events.

SUMMARY

International broadcasting enables nations to communicate information and propaganda across territorial borders instantaneously and without censorship. Propaganda by shortwave was perfected by Nazi Germany as a political weapon of terror, deception, and demoralization. World War II saw the full flowering of radio as a weapon of psychological warfare. Since the war, international broadcasting, as an instrument of foreign policy, has been continued on a large scale through the Voice of America, the BBC Overseas Service, the CBC International Service, and other broadcasting activities. The development of international satellites permits the reception of the same program simultaneously on a worldwide basis, and satellites are now being used in domestic TV transmission.

Questions for Discussion

1. What advantages does international broadcasting have over other means of communication across international frontiers?
2. How were international broadcasts used to accomplish what might be called "unfriendly purposes" before World War II?
3. In what way were international broadcasts used before World War II to develop good will?
4. How was international broadcasting used in the thirties to influence world public opinion?
5. How was radio used to achieve victory in World War II?
6. What should be the programming policy of the Voice of America to promote better understanding of the United States throughout the world?
7. How does Radio Free Europe differ from the VOA?
8. How can the effectiveness of VOA or RFE broadcasts be measured?
9. How is international telecasting carried out, and what are the problems that must be solved to make it possible?
10. Do you think that receiving broadcasts on home receivers directly from satellites would have advantages over receiving them from TV stations?

educational and
public broadcasting

14

Of all the uses to which television and radio have been put, none has commanded more enthusiasm and at times led to as much disappointment as the educational uses. No other means of transmitting knowledge broadly, whether by the printed book, the classroom lecture or discussion, or the magazine article, would seem nearly as effective as television and radio, which allow a single teacher to address an educational message to audiences of thousands and, at times, of millions of people. Nevertheless, for a variety of reasons, television and radio have not displaced, and probably never will, traditional means of education; instead, they have been used on a limited scale to supplement and enrich traditional modes of education. In certain instances, where traditional devices have been found seriously wanting, they have served to fill previously untended needs.

THE EDUCATIONAL PROGRAM

What makes a television or radio program educational? Few questions in the field of broadcasting have been subject to more dispute. Answers have ranged from the view that any broadcast program constitutes an experience in itself and therefore is educational to the listener or viewer, to the opposite extreme that holds a program to be educational only if it is presented by an educational institution. Neither extreme position is tenable. To equate education with all human experiences, without regard to the nature of the experience and the effect it has on the individual, is to ignore the realities of human life; the advances of civilization were made possible only by the classification of knowledge and the interpretation and evaluation of significant human experience. To say that only educational institutions can teach is to ignore another reality; many other social institutions participate in the educational process in various ways and with various degrees of effectiveness.

We know that certain programs are educational to some and not to others, depending upon the state of their interests, knowledge, and learning capacities. In other words, a television or radio program, like a book or magazine article or lecture, is educational only to the extent that it has an educational effect upon an audience. This effect may be of several types: 1. it may involve adding to the significant knowledge of the audience—knowledge that can be applied for constructive individual and social purposes; 2. it may involve training in and understanding of significant skills; 3. it may involve extending the range of the cultural experience of the audience, with a view toward developing an appreciation of artistic expression and a refinement of artistic tastes; 4. it may involve an exploration of the materials and bases of social and political values and human judgments, toward the end that these values and judgments will be in accord with facts and supported by reason.

To achieve any one of these educational effects, the educational program, like the effective lecture or the well-written book, must capture the attention of the intended audience and hold attention throughout the presentation. Although it is obvious to all that a class that is not paying attention is not learning from its teacher, teachers who engage in broadcasting sometimes ignore the equally obvious fact that listeners and viewers whose attention is not captured will turn to another station or turn off their receivers. In television and radio the techniques of commanding attention are referred to as "showmanship," although the process involved is fundamentally identical to that found in the classroom of effective teachers. To qualify as educational, a television or radio program must combine showmanship with the objective of achieving one or more of the educational effects described above. A successful educational program is one that achieves its objectives to a significant extent.

ADVANTAGES OF THE EDUCATIONAL PROGRAM

Several unique characteristics make television and radio especially useful for educational purposes. Among them are 1. ease of communication; 2. a sense of reality; 3. technical assets available through the media; 4. timeliness; 5. special motivation.

Ease of Communication

Through radio, and even more so through television, it is possible to communicate knowledge quickly to large groups of people situated at different points throughout the country or in small geographic areas. Although the distances may be great in terms of the number of miles between the teacher and the audience, the communicative bond between the two always remains intimate and direct. Through television or radio, thousands of students can be brought into intimate contact with great teachers. The general public need not leave their living rooms to make contact with great minds.

A Sense of Reality

Educational television and radio programs may use as their subject matter real people and the materials of life in a way that is beyond the capacity of the classroom teacher or the writer of books. For example, to explain the governmental process, it becomes possible on television and radio to interview public officials, to observe them in debate, to observe public ceremonies; to discuss art, it becomes possible to bring a masterpiece into the classroom via television. Emotional reactions and attitudes toward people and institutions are also conveyed through television and radio. A "feeling with" peoples of other areas and other races and creeds is inspired when students are transferred by sight and sound to distant places and come into contact with strange people through presentations of their music, art, and literature.

Technical Assets

The television and radio media themselves offer certain technical assets to teaching that are not otherwise available except through the use of motion picture film or recordings. For example, color television demonstrations of surgery via live or tape closed-circuit transmission or via cassettes have made it possible for large numbers of medical students to obtain a front-row view of operations through the camera close-up. Television and radio dramatizations of significant subject matter also contribute to better understanding and learning, as do documentaries that present facts and interpretations in a dramatized fashion.

Timeliness

Textbooks are often behind the sweep of world events. Even magazines are a step or two removed from the actual events. Special events, news programs, and lecture material refreshed with the latest developments in related fields make it possible for television and radio presentations by experts to keep teachers and students in the classroom up-to-date in various subject fields.

Special Motivation

Because of the special way in which television and radio programming has captured the public imagination, all communication via these media tends to benefit by the public excitement and to motivate the audience more easily than many other forms of communication. This additional element of special motivation on the part of the student often can make the difference between the attentiveness necessary to learn from a presentation and the boredom that forestalls all learning.

LIMITATIONS OF THE EDUCATIONAL PROGRAM

Together with these assets one finds a number of important shortcomings in the educational uses of television and radio. These are: 1. lack of a reciprocal relationship; 2. lack of flexibility; 3. lack of regularity and system; 4. limitation in the physical senses utilized.

Lack of a Reciprocal Relationship

Doubtless the gravest shortcoming to the educational use of television and radio is the lack of a reciprocal relationship between the teacher and the student. There is no way for the student at home or in the classroom to ask questions of the studio teacher during the broadcast. Nor is it possible for the teacher to read the students' faces to determine how well the material is being understood and whether or not another example or analogy is required to clarify any particular point. The unseen, albeit perceived, student remains much of a mystery to the teacher; to the student the broadcaster remains distant and unapproachable. In an effort to simulate a true reciprocal educational relationship, some educational broadcasters have brought small groups of students into the studio to serve in place of the unseen broadcast audience. It is generally agreed, however, that only the teacher physically present in the classroom or in the personal teaching situation can fully round out the educational experience.

Lack of Flexibility

Instruction via television or radio contends with the problem of a single fixed presentation for an audience that in many ways is heterogeneous in interest, knowledge, and learning capacities. This is especially true in the case of broadcasts directed to the general adult audience, although such broadcasts do tend to draw more homogeneous audiences than programs of pure entertainment.

Lack of Regularity and System

Effective education generally depends upon an organized presentation of subject matter in a graduated and systematic fashion. The transmission of miscellaneous data and information on an irregular basis rarely results in anything approximating genuine education. Except in school broadcasting situations, such as those described later in this chapter, educational television and radio almost always suffer from a lack of regularity and system in the presentation of material to a constantly changing audience of whom some have attended the previous program in the series and others have not. There is no way of insuring attendance at each presentation in a sequence.

Limitation in the Physical Senses Utilized

The ability to command attention and to communicate meaning and emotion is usually closely related to the variety of physical senses through which the meaning and emotion can be reinforced and restated. One of the main handicaps of radio, like the limitation of the printed page, is its use of only a single physical sense to convey meaning. Certain subjects like music suffer much less by this limitation of radio than other subjects such as geography. On the other hand, color television, combining motion, color, and sound, is extremely effective in communicating chemical demonstrations or works of art.

TYPES OF EDUCATIONAL PROGRAMS

Several major types of educational programs have been developed that work within the limitations of television and radio and capitalize on the unique characteristics of the media. They are: 1. direct classroom teaching; 2. supplementary classroom teaching; 3. intraschool broadcasting; 4. informal preschool and out-of-school education; 5. formal adult education; 6. informal adult education; and 7. integrated education and entertainment.

✓ Direct Classroom Teaching

Educational programs on television and radio have been used for direct classroom teaching in various public school systems, colleges, and universities, and by United States military organizations. One of the leaders in the use of television for direct instruction is the school system of Hagerstown, Maryland, which has linked a large number of schools with a closed-circuit installation and telecasts many courses for elementary and secondary school classes. More than 1000 school systems use similar closed-circuit systems. In South Carolina ETV stations broadcast programs that reach 95 percent of the state's children. A number of special TV libraries provide tapes and cassettes of elementary, secondary, and university courses to ETV stations and to individual public school and university systems and institutions. Among the organizations that provide such services are the Great Plains Instructional Television Library, the Agency for Instructional Television, and the International ITV Co-op.

On the college and university level there has been a great deal of experimentation to test the potentialities of television in direct instruction. Pennsylvania State University and New York University were pioneers in this effort, and the United States Army also conducted a number of early studies. More than 1000 colleges and universities are using television for instruction in courses that enroll a half-million students. This instruction is carried out through the broadcast facilities of educational TV stations and commercial stations or by means of closed-circuit installations. Complete courses as well as special parts of courses can be taught via television. Medical and dental schools use television to bring close-up views of clinical procedures to students, and television is also being used in many science classes to enlarge the students' views of laboratory experiments.

Supplementary Classroom Teaching

Radio has been used very little for direct instructional purposes, although the Cleveland Public Schools did use it for many years for this purpose. The major use of radio has been as a supplement to regular instruction. In the state of Wisconsin, for example, for over 40 years hundreds of public elementary schools have made a regular practice of incorporating a systematic schedule of educational radio programs into their regular curriculum. At one time the national radio networks broadcast many programs for schools, but the time-zone differences throughout the country made it extremely difficult to broadcast programs for schools on a national basis, and the programs were finally abandoned. Many school systems and educational TV stations broadcast television and radio programs on a local basis that are designed not to teach directly, but to enrich the educational experiences of students. A unique example of closed-circuit TV permits students at the University of Michigan Law School to observe all public sessions of the court in an adjunct to the court located in the Law School. Some 3000 school systems use television for direct and supplementary instruction, and many public television stations devote a substantial part of their daytime schedules to programming designed for schools.

Intraschool Broadcasting

Schools of all levels carry on intraschool broadcasting, a simulated form of broadcasting using public-address sound systems or closed-circuit TV systems that permit simultaneous reception in all or a select number of classrooms in the school. This practice provides many opportunities to integrate various class activities. Student interest increases when the "home folks" do the broadcasting. The disc-jockey program has been used for news of school events, public-service announcements about school safety and charity drives, and for interviews with teachers and administrators about school traditions and regulations, sandwiched in between the playing of popular music records during lunch or home-room periods.

↙ Informal Preschool and Out-of-School Education

Some educational programs are intended for listening and viewing by youngsters at home—those too young to go to school and those who have returned home from school. *Romper Room,* a syndicated program for preschool children, is presented on a number of local stations throughout the country. *Captain Kangaroo,* designed for the same age group, has been broadcast on CBS for many years. Another program for preschool children broadcast by PTV stations is *Sesame Street,* which is designed to prepare youngsters for their first school experiences. This program, underwritten by a number of organizations including the Ford and Carnegie Foundations and the Corporation for Public Broadcasting, has attracted larger regular audiences than any series ever broadcast by PTV stations. Other programs broadcast by PTV stations for children at home are *The Electric Company, Zoom,* and *Misteroger's Neighborhood.* Commerical networks and stations also present some programs of this type.

Formal Adult Education

The use of television and radio for transmitting formal adult education has been limited mainly to credit courses given over local broadcasting facilities by the extension division of various universities. These broadcasts are, of course, available for listening or viewing by anyone; they cannot be limited to the students, who register by mail and pay an enrollment fee for the receipt of study materials, reading lists, syllabi, and a final examination which they must take in person, usually on the university campus. Western

Reserve University, Michigan State University, the University of Michigan, and other institutions have experimented with the telecast of college courses for credit. The University of Houston has telecast regular undergraduate lecture courses, which resident students may view in their rooms instead of at the college lecture hall. The state universities of Wisconsin, Ohio, Illinois, and Minnesota broadcast by radio many university courses, many directly from the college classroom and others from radio studios, ranging freely, yet systematically, over the arts and science curriculum. Listeners at home are at liberty, however, to tune in only when they desire to, and there are no certificates of completion of instruction. One organization that did offer certificates was the Chicago Board of Education, which in 1956 began offering on television a complete junior college course leading to the degree of Associate in Arts. Some twenty years later it was estimated that some 150,000 students had benefited from this instruction, and 2000 students had actually earned Associate of Arts degrees, mainly from courses taken at home by means of television.

Informal Adult Education

The most common type of educational television and radio program is devoted to informal adult education. It seeks a broad appeal, it usually has interesting subject matter, and it generally lacks a systematic and graduated plan of instruction. Each program generally stands by itself and is evaluated independently. Discussion and documentary programs such as *Meet the Press, Face the Nation, Issues and Answers,* and network news specials usually offer informal adult education.

Integrated Education and Entertainment

It has been said that people obtain their greatest satisfaction from programs that not only entertain them but also give them a feeling of having been enriched by the experience. Such is certainly the case with great dramatic and documentary presentations. In many popular entertainment programs a conscious effort is made to integrate items of some educational significance, whether it be an operatic aria in a popular music program or a commentary on college activity in connection with the pickup of a football game. Such educational efforts, while they reach large audiences, often suffer from the complete lack of system in presentation and represent only a miscellaneous kind of education. With careful treatment, however, integrated education and entertainment on a large scale over a substantial period of time can leaven popular tastes and create demand for better things.

EDUCATIONAL (PUBLIC) RADIO STATIONS

Much of the solid work in educational radio programming has been done in a number of separate geographical areas across the country by a group of educational noncommercial radio stations operated by universities, school systems, and municipalities. These stations are financed by allocations of state or municipal tax money and by endowments and special grants from philanthropic organizations. The stations operate modestly but earnestly and often very effectively with a singleness of purpose—the rendering of a public service through the broadcast of programs of education, information, and constructive entertainment. The educational programs consist of the types mentioned above; the informational programs consist mainly of news, consumer and marketing information, public-health guidance, government reports, etc.; the entertainment usually concentrates on wholesome children's programs, classical music recordings and occasional live performances, and dramatizations of literary works.

During the first decade of radio broadcasting, there were a large number of educational radio stations, but most of them were concerned primarily with experimenting with the physical and engineering aspects of the broadcast medium. During the 1930s and early 1940s, a hard core of some 20-odd educational radio stations broadcast in the AM band. Some of these stations, like those affiliated with the state universities of Wisconsin, Iowa, Minnesota, Illinois, Ohio, and Oklahoma, as well as WNYC, the municipally owned and operated station in New York City, competed successfully with the networks in winning awards for superior educational programming. After World War II, with the development of FM radio and the allocation by the FCC of the 88–92 megacycle band for educational use only, it became possible for many other state universities, school systems, and local schools to establish their own FM radio stations, many of them low-powered, with transmission power limited to 10 watts to provide coverage within a small community area. There are now more than 400 educational radio stations operating in the AM and FM bands. There are also more than 500 carrier-current stations operated primarily by university students for people who live in the campus areas. Many of these stations are members of the Intercollegiate Broadcasting Stations (IBS).

EDUCATIONAL (PUBLIC) TELEVISION STATIONS

From 1948 to 1952, during the freeze on new television broadcasting licenses, of the 108 television stations in operation only one, WOI-TV, in Ames, Iowa, was owned by an educational institution (Iowa State College). Because it was then the only station serving a substantial population in Iowa, WOI-TV carried commercial network entertainment programs in addition to its own educational offerings. During the course of FCC hearings on the issuance of a new television allocation plan, support was developed throughout the country in behalf of a reservation for educational use of as many as 10 to 25 percent of the broadcast channels to be made available for television. In a rare demonstration of coordinated educational effort, under the leadership of the NAEB and a new organization called the Joint Committee for Educational Television (JCET), located in Washington, 76 important witnesses appeared before the FCC in support of educational reservations, and formal statements from 838 colleges, universities, school systems, and public service agencies were filed with the Commission. The New York State Board of Regents filed a voluminous brief in behalf of its request that the FCC allocate

11 television channels in New York State for an educational television network. In the FCC's "Sixth Report and Order" issued in 1952, 242 television channels out of a total of 2053, or slightly more than 11 percent, were reserved temporarily for application by educational groups only. The number of reservations for education was later increased to 653 (120 VHF and 533 UHF).

Following the favorable Commission action, there was a groundswell of activity in educational circles to bring new educational television stations into being. Supported by grants of money from the Fund for Adult Education of the Ford Foundation and with leadership provided by the JCET, educational television seminars and institutes were convened throughout the country to alert educational leaders to the needs and promise of educational television and to draw up plans for action in various states and communities throughout the country. Some of these plans failed to materialize, others were blocked by political obstruction, others failed for want of proper organization and adequate finances, and others succeeded in putting on the air a number of educational television stations that now occupy a permanent and important place in the American system of television.

Although opposition developed in certain states, in other areas educational television was advanced with the cooperation of community, business, and educational leaders. A National Citizen's Commission for Educational Television was organized to mobilize public opinion in behalf of the movement. Positive results were soon observed in cities like Houston, Texas, where the first postfreeze educational television station went on the air May 25, 1953. In Oklahoma a three-station educational television network was authorized by the state legislature, which floated public bonds to finance the enterprise. Despite the failure of one UHF station that went on the air and then returned its license, a total of 15 educational television stations were on the air three years after the FCC allocated the channels. Since then the growth has been rapid. In 1962, 71 educational television stations were on the air: their number continued to grow steadily, nearing the 275 level in the middle 1970s. In the same period they came to be known as public television (PTV) stations instead of as educational television stations. As the number of stations rose, so did the number of people who tuned in to their programs. It is estimated that people in 20,500,000 American homes tune to PTV stations at least once a week. In Chicago more than half the homes tune in on PTV broadcasts at least once a week. From 1974 to 1976 the public TV audience increased by more than 50 percent.

American PTV stations are independent and locally operated. Four types of owners predominate: colleges and universities; nonprofit community groups; state educational agencies; and local school systems.

The following statement of program policy of Station WCET, in Cincinnati, is fairly typical of educational or public television programming intentions:

Program Policy of Station WCET, Cincinnati

WCET believes that the proper and adequate use of television is an important adjunct to existing educational processes. In Cincinnati the Educational Television Foundation through its membership calls upon all educational systems and institutions to use this station as a means of extending the cultural and civic benefits of the community to each and every citizen.

Thus, WCET is the voice of organized education in Greater Cincinnati, and with this in mind the station's program policy has been formulated to carry out the following objectives:

1. Systematic programming for children of preschool age;

2. Programs which will enrich the classroom experiences for children in the elementary and secondary schools;

3. Constructive programs for out-of-school hours for children of all ages;

4. Courses in formal education in high school and college subjects for youths and adults;

5. Programs for the home viewer to improve skills and earning power; to better understand civic and community problems and projects; to demonstrate new developments in science, art and international affairs;

6. Music, drama, and other programs in the field of the arts, that are both entertaining and self-improving;

7. Programs which will add to the store of personal values which may contribute to better family life, and the long-range welfare of the community and the country.

INSTRUCTIONAL TELEVISION FIXED SERVICE (ITFS)

To supplement the channels reserved for ETV stations in the VHF and UHF bands, the FCC in July of 1963 opened 31 channels in the 2500–2690 megahertz range for use by educational institutions in presenting instructional, cultural, and other types of educational material. Unlike the school programs broadcast by regular ETV stations, the ITFS signals cannot be picked up by regular television sets in homes but are available only to receiving stations in schools that have specially designed sets. There is no limit on the number of ITFS stations a particular institution may be licensed to operate, but it is allowed to use only four channels in one area, and the power of the station is controlled to permit a signal that travels from 5 to 20 miles. The ITFS system is a boon to educational organizations of limited resources because it permits them to present television instruction more economically than is possible over regular ETV stations. The availability of four channels also makes a flexible broadcasting arrangement possible in which specific programs can be repeated many times to achieve maximum utilization.

THE PUBLIC BROADCASTING CONCEPT

For many years those who have been engaged in what is generally known as "educational" broadcasting have been unhappy with the term because to many it connotes both dullness and forced feeding. Early in its existence the National Broadcasting Company reacted to this stigma by renaming its Education Division the Public Service Division. In 1959 officials of what was then the National Educational Television and Radio Center tried without success to devise a term that would make it possible to eliminate "educational" from their institution's name. They considered using the term the FCC uses in referring to channel reservations—"noncommercial"—but rejected it because it was awkward and negative in tone. Not until 1967, when the Carnegie Commission on Educational Broadcasting made its report, was the right expression found—one that harked back to the NBC solution—namely, public broadcasting. Educators rushed to embrace the term, and commercial broadcasters, although arguing somewhat ruefully that they also were presenting programs for the public, seemed willing to let the term be used for this special purpose.

In its report[1] the Carnegie Commission on Educational Television distinguished among three types of television: *commercial television,* which seeks to capture large audiences with programs mainly designed to relax and entertain; *instructional television* or ITV, which presents programs of instruction calling upon the viewer's instinct to work, build, learn, and improve and asks him to take on responsibilities in return for a later reward; and *public television,* which includes all that is of human interest and importance that is not at the moment appropriate or available for support by advertising, and which is not arranged for formal instruction.

The Commission urged immediate action to extend and strengthen instructional and public television, including as main points in its proposal: 1. the establishment of a federally chartered, nonprofit, nongovernmental corporation to be known as the "Corporation for Public Television" (later changed to the Corporation for Public Broadcasting to include radio), which would be empowered to receive and disburse governmental and private funds in order to extend and improve public television programming; 2. the support of two national television production centers for the preparation of public television programs; 3. the provision of federal funds for the support of the Corporation through the establishment of an excise tax on television sets (beginning at 2 percent and rising to a ceiling of 5 percent); 4. the provision of additional funds through the Department of Health, Education, and Welfare for basic equipment and operating funds; and 5. the establishment of studies to develop better insights into the use of television in formal and informal education.

The proposal of the Commission was marked by a number of noteworthy recommendations. One concerned the nature of the funds needed to support public television. It estimated, for example, that the Corporation it recommended establishing would require $104 million in annual revenues to operate properly. It also recommended that the Corporation be freed from dependence on annual Congressional appropriations by designating funds from a specific source—an excise tax on television sets—to be held in trust for public television purposes. This procedure was necessary, the Commission argued, to free the Corporation from the overseeing of its day-to-day operations by Congress that would be the natural consequence of annual budgeting and appropriations procedures. When the Congress established the Corporation for Public Broadcasting, it did not follow the Commission's recommendations on this point; the Corporation for a number of years depended for most of its support on annual appropriations by the Congress. The Commission's fears that this procedure might lead to some degree of political control seemed to be justified by an incident that happened early

[1] *Public Television—A Program for Action* (New York, 1967).

in 1970. A Congressman who was shocked by an NET program featuring the civil-rights activist and comedian Dick Gregory wrote the president of NET saying that if that organization continued to produce such programs, he would vote against any further funds for public television. In 1975 the Congress finally abandoned its year-by-year allocations when it appropriated funds to support the Corporation for the next five years.

It should be noted that other proposals for supporting public television from designated sources have been made. The Ford Foundation advocated the substitution of domestic satellites for the present system of microwave relay and coaxial cables as a means of providing network connections. The savings it said would result from this change could be used to support public television. A second proposal is to tax the commercial television industry a certain percentage of its gross revenues for the support of public television. Other proposals include the institution of a license tax on TV receivers; the use of advertising; a pay-TV system; and a tax on cable-TV companies. Before the Commission's report, the Congress had made a significant contribution to the development of ETV. In the 1962 Educational Facilities Act it appropriated $32 million for disbursement by HEW to the various states for the establishment or upgrading of facilities, the maximum granted to any one state being $1 million.

In addition to its stand on the way in which public television should be supported, the Carnegie Commission took strong positions on other matters. Although it recognized the importance of program production by national organizations, it also emphasized the importance of local production both for the local area of the station and for regional or national use. Also by implication it suggested that the networking function for national programs be separated from the production function. The public television network system, it argued further, should be used primarily for the distribution of programs that could be recorded and played later by stations, rather than for live interconnection, although such interconnection should be used when the nature of the programs demanded simultaneous national reception.

ORGANIZATIONS IN PUBLIC BROADCASTING

The Corporation for Public Broadcasting

In November of 1967 President Johnson signed the Public Broadcasting Act, which established the Corporation for Public Broadcasting, an organization designed to promote noncommercial television and radio broadcasting. It was structured largely along the lines recommended by the Carnegie Commission. The Congress established four guidelines for the Corporation: 1. to develop programs of high quality from diverse sources; 2. to develop a system of interconnection for the distribution of the programs; 3. to strengthen and support local stations; and 4. to carry out its functions in a manner that assures maximum freedom of these stations from interference with or control of program content or other activities. Included in the law is a prohibition against editorializing by public TV and radio stations.

The Corporation for Public Broadcasting has a board of directors of 15 persons appointed by the President. It maintains a staff of 140. Its administrative costs are financed by the allocation of ten percent of the sums appropriated by Congress to underwrite PTV programming.

The Corporation also received support from private institutions, notably the Carnegie Foundation and CBS, each of which granted it $1 million, but the support from Congress fell far below that recommended by the Carnegie Commission. Only $5 million was appropriated in the first year and only $15 million was appropriated in the second year. The Carnegie Commission's hope that a trust fund supported by revenues from a specific source would be established was also lost for the time being. As noted earlier, however, Congress in 1975 did authorize funds to support public broadcasting for the following five years—a sum of $634 million.

In its first year CPB spent its revenues in a variety of ways. It supported local television and radio programming for local areas and for national distribution; it contributed to the production of programs by NET; it issued direct grants to most of the ETV stations; it provided money for fellowships in educational broadcasting; and it supported instructional television through grants for programs and research.

Public Broadcasting Service

To carry out its responsibilities for establishing interconnection services for public television, the CPB established as a separate entity the Public Broadcasting Service with its own president and board of directors, made up of representatives from PTV stations. PBS does not produce any program, restricting its activities to distributing programs acquired from a variety of sources. The distribution has taken place through conventional coaxial cable and microwave facilities, but there are plans to provide network connections through the use of satellites operated by the Western Union Company. Some PBS programs are broadcast simultaneously by stations throughout the nation; others are recorded by stations as they are fed by the network and then broadcast at a time of the station's choosing. This national service is supplemented by regional TV networks such as the Eastern Educational Network and the Central Educational Network in the Midwest. There are also state networks of PTV stations operating in various parts of the country. In 1976, a long-simmering dispute between the CPB and PBS over the control of funds for underwriting programs broke out in the public press, and a temporary accommodation was reached.

Subsequently the administration of President Carter proposed several major changes in the organization and operation of the CPB and its working relationship with the PBS, as well as substantially increased federal funding.

National Public Radio

To provide a public radio networks service comparable to that provided in television by PBS, the Corporation for Public Broadcasting established National Public Radio (NPR). Unlike PBS, it does produce programs and, in addition, distributes programs, many of which are produced by its affiliated stations.

Program Suppliers

Through the years an organization now known as NET has been a principal supplier of programs to educational and public television stations. Founded in 1954 by the Ford Foundation, NET has become a part of the Educational Broadcasting Corporation, which also operates New York City's public television station WNET. In the beginning, NET was envisioned as a central organization through which ETV stations could exchange their best programs and series. The organization soon began contracting with ETV stations and other organizations to produce programs and series specifically for national distribution. There was no interconnected network, however, until PBS was established. Distribution was accomplished by mailing films and tapes to stations. NET no longer acts as an exchange center, that function having been taken over by other organizations, but it continues to supply programs, which it either produces itself or contracts to have other organizations produce.

Other major program suppliers are WETA-NPACT in Washington, D.C., which specializes in public affairs and news-related programs, the Children's Television Workshop, producers of *Sesame Street* and the *Electric Company,* and the Maryland Center for Public Broadcasting. PTV stations also produce or obtain programs that are distributed nationally by the PBS network, among them WGBH in Boston, WTTW in Chicago, KCET in Los Angeles, and KQED in San Francisco. It may be noted that support for the production of many programs broadcast nationally comes from funds donated by American corporations. *Masterpiece Theater,* for example, has been supported by grants made by the Mobil Oil Corporation and *Misteroger's Neighborhood* by the Sears-Roebuck Foundation. The underwriting companies receive acknowledgment in the form of on-the-air credits.

In the instructional television area an organization located on the campus of Indiana University in Bloomington serves as a national clearinghouse for programs broadcast to schools. Known as the Agency for Instructional Television, it obtains instructional programs for use by stations that contribute to its support, and it also creates series of its own. The programs it provides are shown in 40 states and in three Canadian provinces. Another center of this type is the Great Plains Instructional Television Library in Nebraska. The Nebraska Educational Television Council for Higher Education distributes instructional programs designed for use in college and university classrooms.

NAEB

One of the oldest organizations in educational broadcasting is NAEB, which has now adopted as its official title the acronym derived from its former name—the National Association of Educational Broadcasters. The organization came into being in 1925 as the Association of College and University

Broadcasting Stations. The purpose of the NAEB is to provide direct and indirect services to the institutions of educational broadcasting, including educational television and radio stations, program agencies, teaching units, and the users of educational programs. It also serves individuals in the field. With its main offices in Washington, one of its principal responsibilities is to represent educational broadcasters in dealing with Congress and other governmental agencies. At one time NAEB circulated tapes of educational radio programs, but this function has now been taken over by National Public Radio. In the same way the distribution and exchange of educational television programs formerly carried out by NAEB is now administered by the Public Television Library in association with the Public Broadcasting Service. The NAEB continues to publish a journal known as PTR—which stands for *Public Telecommunications Review.* The NAEB also fosters research in educational broadcasting, holds regular institutes and a yearly convention, and operates a placement bureau for people seeking positions in the field.

The Ford Foundation

One of the most influential organizations in educational broadcasting and particularly in television is the Ford Foundation, whose grants made possible much of the early development of ETV. Indeed it is difficult to see how the movement could have gained momentum without the assistance the Foundation provided. It helped in two important ways: it made grants to the early stations that permitted them to establish facilities and initiate a program service, and it supported the NET national program service. In addition, it helped to underwrite a number of programs, among them the enormously successful series designed for preschool children, *Sesame Street.* It is estimated that the Ford Foundation has contributed $300 million to support the development of educational television.

COURSES IN BROADCASTING

A great many colleges and universities now offer courses in broadcasting. Of these, 204 offer a course of study that leads to a major in television and radio on the undergraduate level. On the graduate level, 99 schools offer a master's degree in broadcasting; 27 offer a doctorate. Many other institutions, although not offering majors, have a substantial number of courses in broadcasting.

Many institutions teaching broadcasting courses are affiliated with the Broadcast Education Association (BEA), which operates as a part of the National Association of Broadcasters. The BEA holds a yearly meeting at the time of the NAB Convention, publishes a quarterly, the *Journal of Broadcasting,* and provides its affiliated institutions with regular information about developments in radio and television.

Some of the facilities for teaching broadcasting courses are rudimentary, being made up of simple public-address systems, tape recorders, homemade sound-effects trucks, and simple manual sound-effects equipment.

Their production material consists of student-written scripts supplemented by scripts available in published anthologies. These workshops make it possible for students to develop elementary broadcasting skills and to set up intraschool broadcasting operations. Many of the low-powered educational FM radio stations were developed from simple broadcasting workshops. Often coupled with the production activity of a workshop are simple audience-research studies and the full range of on-the-air broadcast offerings.

A number of college and university workshops have a full complement of professional color TV equipment, three or four camera chains, film cameras and projectors, video-tape recorders, portable videotape camera systems, mobile trucks, staging, construction, and storage rooms, and other basic facilities.

SUMMARY

To be successful, educational broadcasting must effectively combine showmanship and valid educational content. Despite certain inherent limitations, television and radio possess special characteristics that make them very useful for various educational purposes. Educational programs can be used for direct and supplementary classroom teaching, intraschool broadcasting, education for preschool children, for youngsters out of school, and for adults. Integrated education and entertainment describes the effort of commercial broadcasters to incorporate educational materials into the popular entertainment programs. Noncommercial educational AM, FM, and TV stations serve the special purpose of rendering a public service through the regular scheduling of programs of education, information, and constructive entertainment. With the report of the Carnegie Commission the term public broadcasting came into general use to describe the programming of noncommercial stations. Institutions that play significant roles in the area are CPB, PBS, NAEB, the Ford Foundation, and BEA.

Questions for Discussion

1. How can we best define an educational program?
2. How can television and radio be used effectively by the teacher in the classroom? What is required besides listening to or viewing the program?
3. How do the limitations of television and radio as educational media compare with their advantages as means for conveying information and education?
4. What types of programs are especially useful for educational purposes?
5. What functions, if any, can noncommercial educational stations serve that are not already served by commercial stations?
6. What kinds of programs should a public broadcasting station broadcast? How broad an appeal should a public broadcasting station make in its effort to win an audience?
7. How do educational programs over commercial outlets compare with educational programs over educational stations? Can you supply examples?

8. To what extent can we hope to develop better discrimination in listening and viewing through the classroom study of broadcast programs?

9. Compare the relative advantages and disadvantages of educational broadcasting by means of radio and by means of television.

10. Should educational broadcasts be limited to educational stations?

11. Should public broadcasting stations be prohibited from editorializing when commercial stations are encouraged to do so by the FCC?

standards of criticism

15

On what bases should television and radio programs be judged? By their popularity or by their artistic quality? By the amount of useful information they convey or by their effectiveness as vehicles for advertising?

Confusion over standards of criticism is not limited to the field of broadcasting but is also found in other forms of practical and artistic communication. In the field of literature, for example, the popularity of novels can be measured by the number of copies sold, but their comparative quality as novels is never judged by their popularity. Judgments of quality are made by critics who have read a great many books and who make their evaluations on the basis of criteria involving intrinsic literary merit. In arts like painting, music, and poetry, the enduring judgment is never based upon immediate popularity. Many works of art make an excellent first impression, but soon wear thin, owing to an essential superficiality; other works, of more enduring if less immediate popularity, encounter initial public and critical resistance, but manage to win increasing favor with the passage of time. In the field of practical communication, the newspaper or magazine with the largest circulation (manifestly the most popular publication) is not necessarily the "best" newspaper or magazine. In the legitimate theater, plays adjudged by professional critics to be of superior quality often fail to win immediate popular appeal, while plays considered by the critics to be inferior occasionally become box-office hits. It is clear that the standards of immediate popularity and of inherent quality, both of which tend in casual conversation to be assimilated into a single critical concept of "good," are often quite different judgments—one made immediately by the public to which the communication or work of art is addressed, and the other by individuals of professional repute who, through long and discriminating exposure to various forms of communication and works of art, have developed critical standards of judgment. When an immediate popular success is also a critical success, there is general satisfaction. In the course of time, popular and critical judgments are often revised; the ultimate test of quality is usually a single judgment representing enduring popular and critical esteem.

This cleavage in critical standards between immediate popularity and intrinsic quality is probably more evident in television and radio than in most other fields of practical and artistic communication. In broadcasting, the pressure for immediate popularity is overwhelming. Each program competes for an audience with programs broadcast simultaneously over other stations and networks. The elements of immediate enjoyment and breadth of appeal usually determine which program obtains the largest audience. On the other hand, each program, whatever its form—drama, comedy, documentary, or audience participation—achieves a certain qualitative standard of performance in terms of its form and the potentialities of its material. In the day-to-day judgments of television and radio programs these conflicting considerations often spill over and confusion results. "That was a terrible show," remarks one person, to which another replies, "Not so, it had a great rating." Only through an understanding of the broadcasting media and a clarification of the criteria for criticism can we hope to remove some of this confusion.

We have said that television and radio programs in America are used to serve three fundamental purposes: 1. to conduct commerce; 2. to provide entertainment; and 3. to provide public service. Failure to acknowledge the validity of these purposes results, of course, in widely different judgments of an enterprise that involves business, artistic, and educational considerations. The critic who fails to appreciate the financial problems imposed on television and radio by virtue of their competitive nature and their sources of available income is reasoning from faulty premises no less than the broadcaster who looks upon his station solely as a means of making a personal fortune. Proceeding from opposite assumptions, it is easy to see how an advertiser might not be satisfied until his commercial message had been flaunted throughout an entire program, and how a sensitive writer or performer, on the other hand, might be unwilling to have his artistic presentation associated in any way with a commercial product.

COMMERCIAL STANDARDS

A common form of criticism of television and radio relates to the number and quality of commercial announcements on broadcast programs. Through long exposure the American people have come to accept commercial messages as the price they pay for programs they like to see or hear. The code limitation for prime time of 9 minutes and thirty seconds of nonprogram material in each 60-minute period appears to be within the tolerance of the American public. Raucous, unduly repetitive, and often stupid commercials do, however, arouse critical hostility that appears to many persons to be amply warranted. Inasmuch as clever commercials are not only tolerated but often enjoyed by the public, the question has been raised as to whether advertising agencies should spend more time, effort, and imagination to improve the quality of their commercial announcements. The question of whether stations and networks should protect the public not only from misleading and inaccurate advertising but also from grossly irritating advertising has also been raised. In order to avoid losing their audience, the broadcasters, who now pass judgment on the quality of all programs proposed by advertisers, may eventually be obliged to apply more rigorous standards of quality to the commercials as well. Clients who mistakenly believe that their commercials are more important than the program must be educated to the truth that their advertising is wasted without the circulation that can be provided only by effective programming. Broadcasters who mistakenly believe that their license to broadcast may be used solely for the production of quick profit to the exclusion of public service must also be educated to the truth of their public responsibility. In the long run, however, only those stations that operate in a successful business manner can provide the financial resources necessary to program effectively in the public interest.

ENTERTAINMENT STANDARDS

Most television and radio programs aim to entertain, but the overwhelming concentration on this one objective has been questioned. A number of research projects have been carried out to determine what people think about television and to analyze what they are seeking when they turn on their sets. Not to anyone's surprise, it has been discovered that most people watch television for relaxation and enjoyment. This is particularly true of those whose education ended with their graduation from high school or before. They may wish vaguely that television could be more informative and educational, but they tend to accept its offerings uncritically and are generally satisfied with the range of entertainment that is provided.

Those in the audience whose education has extended through college may be more critical of television than the average viewer and they may be somewhat more concerned with selective viewing, but when they turn on their sets they usually seek light entertainment also. Although they may express a wish for more informational programs, they actually watch few of them. The big difference between these two groups is not how they use television, but how they feel about it.

It would seem, therefore, that in making television primarily a vehicle for entertainment, broadcasters are meeting the public's demand. The question remains whether they are satisfying the public's needs. Some attempt has been made to provide programs that appeal only to minority tastes, but broadcasters are reluctant to present programs that few people view when they can gain larger audiences with programs of more general appeal. The result is that most programs of specialized appeal are broadcast in marginal time periods, such as Sunday afternoon, when program competition is less keen, although a few have been presented in prime-time periods.

The quality of the production in television and radio entertainment is likewise a subject of much concern. Owing to the enormous volume of programs and the great expense of production, it is impossible to assign to every program all the creative talent and the production facilities necessary to produce a top-quality show. In television the rate of production of the finished product has been faster than the rate at which quality raw materials have been developed. Nevertheless, there have been enough demonstrations of first-rate productions in all entertainment and informational forms to establish standards of qualitative judgment. Criticism of program quality must be based, however, on an understanding and acceptance of television and radio as media for the presentation of art forms of their own. It is no more justified to withhold praise from a television drama on the ground that it would not hold up as a two-hour Broadway play, than to withhold praise from a Broadway play on the ground that it would not make a good movie, or to condemn a short story on the ground that it would not make a good novel. The qualitative judgment should always be based on fundamental criteria such as, in the case of a television drama, the following: Did the production excite interest? Was the situation believable? Were the characters real and were their actions adequately motivated? Was the subject matter worthy of the time given to it? Was the production technically competent? Was the total effect emotionally and intellectually satisfying? In the case of informational programs, the criteria would be somewhat different: Was the subject matter worthy of a program? Was the information presented clearly? Was interest sustained? Was the material presented with sufficient effectiveness to cause the audience to remember the main points?

PUBLIC-SERVICE STANDARDS

The obligation of broadcasters does not end, however, with the provision of entertainment. The people must be kept informed, and the broadcasting industry has a critical role to play in reaching this objective. In their concern over entertaining the public, many broadcasters often forget that their audience is made up of human beings and citizens upon whose political and social judgments depends the fate of our country. By virtue of the public license they hold, it seems hard to dispute that broadcasters have an affirmative responsibility to see that the television and radio media are used for purposes of good citizenship through the dissemination of information and opinion on matters of public importance. Criticism of the public-service performance of television and radio is usually related to four aspects: 1. the accuracy of broadcast information and the qualifications of those who comment on the news and express opinions on controversial matters; 2. the balance of fairness in the presentation of controversial points of view; 3. the quantity of public-service programs in relation to the need for them; and 4. the broadcast time allotted to these programs. These are seemingly valid critera. At CBS William S. Paley established the following standards for news and public-affairs programs:

> In news programs there is to be no opinion or slanting, the news reporting must be straight and objective. In news analysis there is to be elucidation, illumination, and explanation of the facts and situations, but without bias or editorialization.
>   Opinion broadcasts must be labeled for what they are. In particular, opinion must be separated from news. The listener is entitled to know what he is receiving, news or opinion, and if it be opinion, whose opinion. When opinion is expressed in any type of information program—excluding news and news

analysis where opinion is not allowed—opportunity for reply is given to the person with whom issue has been taken, or to a responsible spokesman representing an opposite viewpoint.

An advertiser who sponsors any type of information program produced by us does not thereby purchase, or in any way gain, any rights to control the contents of the program.

In an effort to break loose from the concentration of public-service programs on Sunday afternoon and their exclusion from other, more desirable places on the broadcast schedule, the national networks have succeeded in arranging their commercial sales contracts so that they may from time to time broadcast important public-service programs in prime evening time periods. News, documentary, and "actuality" Specials are also telecast during these periods.

THE RESPONSIBILITY FOR LEADERSHIP

Midst all the concern for programs that will immediately win broad popular appeal, there nevertheless abides with television and radio broadcasters a positive responsibility for leadership in the development of new creative talents and new program forms, in raising popular tastes, eliminating popular ignorance, and advancing public understanding of the world in which we live. To concentrate solely on the immediate problem of giving the public only what the largest single segment of the public currently wants is, in the opinion of some critics, equivalent to engaging in a form of cultural demagoguery that betrays the future of broadcasting and the promise of American life. Many people have argued that the broadcaster has a responsibility not only to satisfy tastes as they exist, but to work constantly to improve them. This is similar to the credo enunciated by John Reith, first Director General of the British Broadcasting Corporation, who said that the BBC must lead not merely follow the public taste. A similar ideal was expressed by the American critic Gilbert Seldes when he said that broadcasters cannot be satisfied simply because their audience is satisfied. He argued that broadcasters are obligated to give people the best product they can develop even before they ask for it.

Frank Stanton, who for many years served as President of CBS, recognized the responsibility of broadcasters to present a wide range of programs, but he maintained that the public must be the final judge of what ultimately is to be broadcast. In an address given at the University of Pennsylvania, he said:

Chief among these fundamental problems is the arrival at standards for programming. Whose standards should they be? How should they be determined? Can you trust the people to know what is good for them? Or must they be told by some authority? Despite the diversity of taste, somebody has to set standards. Broadcasters have turned to the general public. Should we meet the standards set by *most* of the people *all* of the time? I think that the answer to that is clearly no. We must be constantly aware that ours is a most varied population, with a wide range of degrees of sophistication, of education, of interests, of tastes. We must make an effort to accommodate that endless variety. But we must do it with some sort of scale and balance in mind. . . .

I think that it would be a misuse of the air waves, for example, to carry very esoteric, avant-garde material that experienced observers know would be meaningless to all but a handful of the initiated. On the other hand, there is a great and restless potential in the American people to broaden their cultural horizons. Television can, and does, play an enormous role in stimulating that potential. . . .

We watch very carefully how the people react, because their acceptance or rejection influences our next move—and ought to influence it. We must remain primarily the servant of the majority, but at the same time, recognize the interests and values of significant minorities. We have to serve both. The people, whatever their temporary errors or inadequacies, are, in the long run, the best judges of their own interests, and they will make themselves heard.

PROFESSIONAL CRITICISM

While it was true several years ago that there was a "woeful dearth" of professional radio criticism in the United States, the situation has changed considerably since the advent of television. Although publishing media have not yet accorded professional television and radio criticism the same status or space accorded book, theater, or motion picture reviews, the trend is in that direction. Television programs and developments are reviewed regularly in national news magazines and in *TV Guide,* and they receive some attention in the small-circulation magazines that deal with literature and the performing arts. In the early days of television, audiences had no opportunity to read reviews until after the programs had been broadcast. These reviews could therefore play no role in helping listeners to determine what they were going to watch. Now reviewers are being given opportunities to see programs before they are broadcast and can get their comments into print in newspapers the night a particular program is scheduled. These previews may be written by critics operating on a national level, whose comments are syndicated to newspapers throughout the country, or they may originate with local critics who are assigned by their newspapers to preview programs.

Professional criticism of television and radio is also conducted through the issuance of various awards of merit. Among the more esteemed are the Peabody and "Emmy" citations awarded yearly to programs and personalities.

Still another form of criticism is that offered by organizations and committees specifically created for the purpose of evaluating programs. It is not uncommon for local parents' associations to set up television committees to review local children's programs. The Wisconsin Association for Better Radio and Television and the National Association for Better Radio and Television in Los Angeles are typical public councils whose stated purpose is, among other things, "to encourage the development of high individual standards of radio and television appreciation both in the schools and in the home, to encourage a cooperative attitude between the radio and television industry and the listening public, and to create and maintain patronage for sponsors who broadcast programs meeting with the standards recommended by the organization."

SUMMARY

Informed and intelligent criticism is essential to the advancement of the broadcasting media. Criticism must take into account the complex operation of television and radio as business enterprises, and as media for the communication of art and public service. The conflict between immediate popularity and broad appeal on the one hand, and inherent program quality on the other, is a fundamental problem in formulating useful standards of criticism. Television and radio programs should be judged in terms of the aesthetics of the broadcast media and the potentialities of the program forms. Broadcasters have an affirmative responsibility for raising public tastes.

Questions for Discussion

1. How do you react to commercials in general? Do you like them, finding some better than the programs? Are you willing to put up with them in order to receive the programs? Or would you prefer a radio and television system without commercial?
2. On what bases should television and radio programs be judged?
3. Compare the practice of literary criticism with the criticism of television and radio programs.
4. Is there any difference between the concepts of "good" and "effective" in evaluating broadcast programs?
5. To what extent can we use audience ratings as a guide to the critical evaluation of programs?
6. Can we reconcile the conflict between artistic and business considerations in broadcasting? How?
7. How high a level of professionalism do we have a right to expect in television and radio programs?
8. What responsibility, if any, do broadcasters have for raising public tastes?
9. Do you think that cultural standards and tastes can be raised by broadcasting programs that may be considered to be of high cultural value but that do not interest the large mass of people?
10. Do you think that the public should be given the kind of programs it wants or the kind of programs it should have?

11. TV networks have been criticized for failing to present enough public information programs and for failing, in general, to provide for the interests and needs of minorities in the mass audience. Do you think that this criticism is justified?

12. What special problems, if any, are involved in the commercial sponsorship of programs covering political conventions, election results, and official ceremonies, such as the proceedings incidental to a presidential inauguration?

part two

television and radio in the studio

inside the station

16

The power to make or break a star, to keep a program on the air or to take it off, to enable a station to operate in the black or in the red, rests with individual viewers or listeners at home and what they decide to do with the tuning devices on the set. Program popularity, station circulation, and sales curves depend upon audience interest and reaction. Consequently, what comes out of the loudspeaker and is shown on the screen is the result not of "happenstance" but of definite planning and organization designed to meet the needs and interests of the audiences.

Let us tune in some stations briefly and observe what is being offered. Then we can draw some conclusions about the people and plans involved, and go behind the program transmission into the stations to learn about the organization and functions of the station personnel.

It is morning. Programs are available to us from clear-channel radio stations across the state; from both a radio and television station owned by the same company in the next county; and from a small local radio and television station in our own community. Several programs we can tell are specifically to interest the farmer. Included are complete weather reports, market information, news of exhibitions and demonstrations, Department of Agriculture reports, an on-the-spot tape-recorded interview with a nearby farmer who has been particularly successful with crop rotation, films from the state land-grant college on silo construction, and sound-film interviews with winners in 4-H Club competition. The people handling the broadcasts are authoritative and experienced farm directors, they present the farm machinery and feed commercials in persuasive manner, the visual devices used are clear and informative, the filmed sequences have a professional touch, and commercials between programs are widely varied—from straightforward messages to elaborate filmed cartoons. There is a program of the general "wake-up" type with bright popular music and chatter, five-minute world and local news summaries, and weather reports. Here is a program consisting of morning devotions, hymns, and Bible readings. Another program is a relay of a network TV presentation featuring well-known personalities who conduct informal interviews with people in the news or from the entertainment world, together with news summaries and live and filmed features from around the nation and world. And another is designed to entertain small

231

children with cartoons and studio banter between the program host and puppet characters.

Later in the morning, we hear a newscast from the nation's capital by a single newscaster who engages in personal expressions of opinion about actions of certain legislators "on the Hill." "Progressive rock" music on records is coming from one of the stations. A film feature popular 10 to 15 years ago has started; a "Breakfast at Home" man-woman interview program has a prominent regional novelist as its guest of the day; homemaking hints are given; reducing exercises are demonstrated; a telephone quiz on American history is in process; a rebroadcast of an instructional series on the psychology of the child is being projected via film or video tape; midmorning reruns of situation comedies and game shows are competing for attention; and the late-morning television daytime serials enter the competition for viewers.

This listening and viewing during a brief two- or three-hour period is such a simple matter that few people stop to ask what type of organization and planning permits the smooth flow hour after hour, day after day, week after week, on a split-second schedule of programs and announcements, varied in content, style, origination, and personnel.

STATION ORGANIZATION

While the particular organizational details may vary according to the size and type of station, affiliation or nonaffiliation with a network, and an active or static program policy, the procedures and the jobs to be done are such that the basic functional organization of a station is fairly well standardized throughout the country. Figures 16–1 and 16–2 show how a Detroit AM-FM combination and its associated TV station are organized.

Determination of Station Policy

As explained in earlier chapters, each station operates on the basis of a license issued by the Federal Communications Commission. Usually the license is held by a corporation especially formed for the business of operating the station. The board of directors of the corporation is the final authority on station policy; it is responsible to the stockholders on the one hand for efficient management and to the FCC on the other hand for operating to serve "the public convenience, interest, or necessity." Stations may also be owned by individuals or partners. In some instances the corporation owning a station may be engaged primarily in other types of business, such as newspaper publishing, insurance, radio and television manufacturing, or wholly unrelated activities. Other stations, usually noncommercial, may be owned by colleges or universities, municipalities, public corporations, and religious groups.

General Manager

The person chosen to interpret in detailed fashion station policy as determined in general form by the board of directors is called the general manager or station manager. The manager has supreme authority in running the

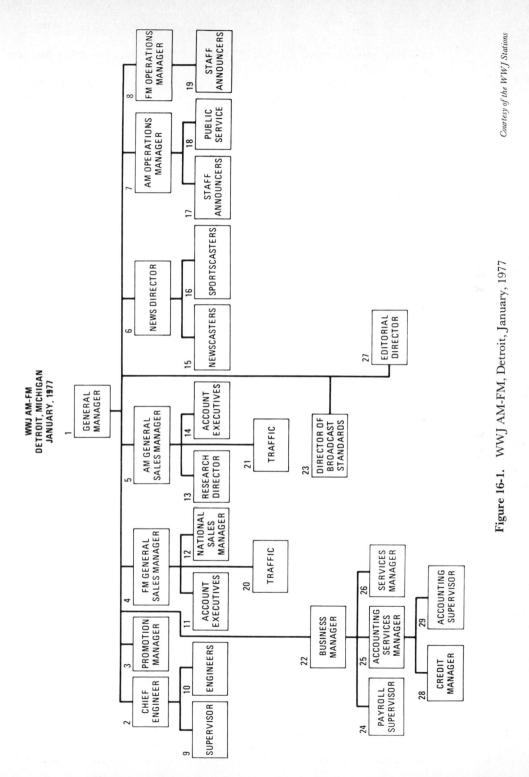

**WWJ AM-FM
DETROIT, MICHIGAN
JANUARY, 1977**

1 GENERAL MANAGER

2 CHIEF ENGINEER
3 PROMOTION MANAGER
4 FM GENERAL SALES MANAGER
5 AM GENERAL SALES MANAGER
6 NEWS DIRECTOR
7 AM OPERATIONS MANAGER
8 FM OPERATIONS MANAGER

9 SUPERVISOR
10 ENGINEERS
11 ACCOUNT EXECUTIVES
12 NATIONAL SALES MANAGER
13 RESEARCH DIRECTOR
14 ACCOUNT EXECUTIVES
15 NEWSCASTERS
16 SPORTSCASTERS
17 STAFF ANNOUNCERS
18 PUBLIC SERVICE
19 STAFF ANNOUNCERS

20 TRAFFIC
21 TRAFFIC
22 BUSINESS MANAGER
23 DIRECTOR OF BROADCAST STANDARDS
27 EDITORIAL DIRECTOR

24 PAYROLL SUPERVISOR
25 ACCOUNTING SERVICES MANAGER
26 SERVICES MANAGER

28 CREDIT MANAGER
29 ACCOUNTING SUPERVISOR

Figure 16-1. WWJ AM-FM, Detroit, January, 1977

Courtesy of the WWJ Stations

233

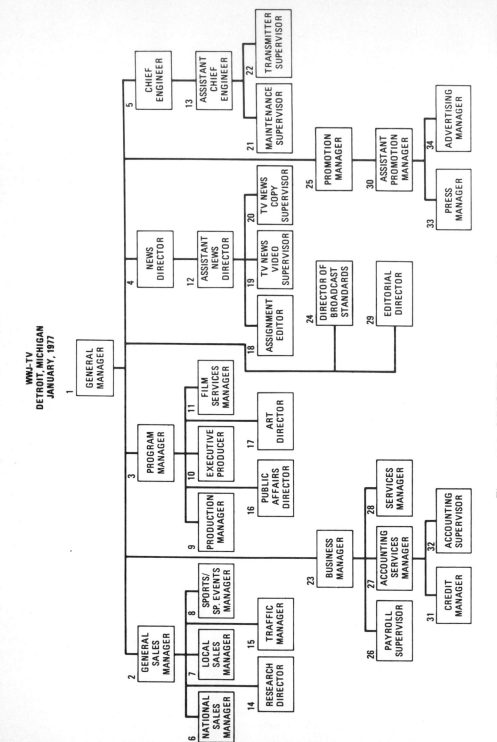

WWJ-TV
DETROIT, MICHIGAN
JANUARY, 1977

1 — GENERAL MANAGER

2 — GENERAL SALES MANAGER
6 — NATIONAL SALES MANAGER
7 — LOCAL SALES MANAGER
8 — SPORTS/SP. EVENTS MANAGER
14 — RESEARCH DIRECTOR
15 — TRAFFIC MANAGER

3 — PROGRAM MANAGER
9 — PRODUCTION MANAGER
10 — EXECUTIVE PRODUCER
11 — FILM SERVICES MANAGER
16 — PUBLIC AFFAIRS DIRECTOR
17 — ART DIRECTOR

4 — NEWS DIRECTOR
12 — ASSISTANT NEWS DIRECTOR
18 — ASSIGNMENT EDITOR
19 — TV NEWS VIDEO SUPERVISOR
20 — TV NEWS COPY SUPERVISOR
24 — DIRECTOR OF BROADCAST STANDARDS
29 — EDITORIAL DIRECTOR

5 — CHIEF ENGINEER
13 — ASSISTANT CHIEF ENGINEER
21 — MAINTENANCE SUPERVISOR
22 — TRANSMITTER SUPERVISOR

23 — BUSINESS MANAGER
27 — ACCOUNTING SERVICES MANAGER
26 — PAYROLL SUPERVISOR
31 — CREDIT MANAGER
32 — ACCOUNTING SUPERVISOR
28 — SERVICES MANAGER

25 — PROMOTION MANAGER
30 — ASSISTANT PROMOTION MANAGER
33 — PRESS MANAGER
34 — ADVERTISING MANAGER

Courtesy of the WWJ Stations

Figure 16-2   WWJ-TV, Detroit, January, 1977

station and, in many instances, serves as a member of the board of directors or as an officer in the corporation. The success or failure of stations depends in large measure on the administrative skill of managers in selecting and supervising an efficient staff, on the quality of their day-to-day programming judgments, and on their sense of responsibility to the community in fulfilling the obligations laid upon the holders of broadcasting licenses. This is a big order. There are no hard-and-fast rules for winning public favor. Television and radio combine show business, advertising, and public service. Programs must be interesting and entertaining to get audiences and to sell the goods and services advertised on the station. The manager must be aware of the likes and dislikes of the community; not only the existing likes and dislikes, but the potential ones.

Some kind of "station personality" must emerge. For example, to be effective in one area, a station may have to highlight a succession of disc jockeys, another station may find its place in the sun with an active farm schedule, a third may depend chiefly upon telephone talk shows, a fourth upon feature films, and a fifth upon news and sports. The primary responsibility for selecting and developing this station personality and winning acceptance for it in a highly competitive industry is usually in the hands of the general manager.

To carry out the operation of broadcasting, the general manager hires executive assistants to supervise the various departments set up in the station. In the average station these departments are program, engineering, and sales. Each executive has a staff to carry out the particular duties of the department. In a smaller station the general manager may "double in brass" either as the program director or as the sales manager. In larger stations the persons who hold these positions are often vice-presidents.

In instances of single ownership of both television and radio stations, management policy may call for separate television and radio departments. However, considerable intermixture of personnel may exist. Other companies may integrate one department and separate others. Considerable variation exists throughout the industry.

Program Department

It is the function of the program director and staff to plan and present the programs in a manner satisfactory to the management, the sponsor, and the audience. The program director supervises the following divisions: announcing, sports, news, film, staging, art, music, transcriptions and records, continuity, production, and talent. It is the responsibility of the program director to suggest ideas for new programs; to be informed on all program availabilities to the station from the various distribution sources; to work with the sales department in suggesting program ideas for the various advertisers on the station; and to keep a close check on the quality of production and overall balance of the station's program structure.

Announcing division. In a small 250-watt local radio station, three or four announcers may handle the entire day's schedule, relief announcing being taken care of by other members of the staff. As stations grow larger and more complex, the announcing staff may increase to eight or ten and be headed by a chief announcer who has supervision over them. The staff may be supplemented by special announcers handling news and sports. It is desirable, for more effective showmanship, to schedule the announcers so that a person selected to handle a program will fit in with its format and style. A slangy, disc-jockey program conducted by a restrained announcer will annoy listeners.

The program director, aided by the chief announcer, tries to build a staff with different specialties and a range of vocal variety. Alternating announcers for consecutive programming is desirable. In many stations the announcers also handle the studio controls and play the records, tapes, and cartridges. When the same management operates both television and radio stations, announcers often are scheduled for assignments on both media.

Recalling the programs mentioned earlier in this chapter, we can note the parts played by the various announcers. They introduce the farm director, broadcast the news, present popular music with a light touch and serious music with a dignified one, chat with the cooking specialists, act as hosts for live introductions to film features, introduce the feature commentators and interviewers, conduct the quizzes with spirit and verve, and during station-breaks and programs, present commercials ranging in subject matter from farm machinery to soap.

Announcers may be classified according to their main duties:

1. Introduction of featured program talent.
2. Master of Ceremonies (MC).
3. Featured personalities in their own right.
4. Effective salespersons.

Many announcers, in addition to being good performers before the microphone, must also be adept in carrying out the production techniques employed in transferring sound to automated systems.

News division. The news has to be prepared in the station's news room for the newscaster or announcer. Preparation of the news may take nothing more than "scissors and paste" as the staff announcer tears off copy from the press association wires. The preferable practice is to have an experienced news editor prepare the copy with the particular area to be served in mind. In small stations, the news editor may also be a part-time staff announcer. In large television and radio stations several writers, still and motion picture camera operators, audio-and video-tape technicians, and audio-tape, video-tape, and film editors may be employed to cover local events, process and rewrite the news dispatches, and select and edit newsfilm and taped material. Video and audio tape recorders, press cameras, and silent- and sound-film and TV cameras are available for on-the-spot coverage.

The people who prepare the news may deliver it themselves. However, the general trend is for trained broadcast journalists to write the news for presentation by announcers with a flair for effective delivery and with an attractive television personality, when that medium is used. "Name" newscasters who prepare their own copy, however, may be featured in their own right. Such persons usually are broadcasters with either local or national reputations who acquire personality value for the station.

Music division. Music is a very important part of the programs presented on radio. Most music is broadcast from records, tapes, or cartridges, but a few large stations still present some music performed "live" by soloists and small music combinations. Television stations do not use much music as basic program material. Large stations have a music director who has overall responsibility in connection with the music played on various programs. The director is assisted by a music librarian who maintains the transcription and record library and is responsible for overseeing the copyright and clearance problems and for maintaining the records of music use necessary to determine payment to special music licensing agencies.

Continuity and script division. In the early days of radio, most of the words heard on programs were written down ahead of time and were read from scripts. Now radio relies much of the time on announcers who *ad lib* their remarks from notes. Large stations occasionally employ one or two staff or free-lance writers to prepare music continuity and other special programs.

In radio, a script may be read without the audience's being aware of the prepared nature of the presentation. In television the situation, of course, is quite different. Several methods of presentation may be used: 1. read from the script even though the audience is able to see the performer: 2. read from script when "off camera" and memorize material for "on camera" appearances; 3. rely upon "cue cards," large pieces of cardboard containing a word-for-word script or an outline, which are held at the side of the camera and thus within the performer's line of sight; and 4. refer to "TelePrompter" or similar devices mounted on cameras or placed around the studio that reveal in large type several lines of the script in synchronization with the speed of delivery.

In cooperation with the sales departments, the continuity division may be called upon to prepare commercials. In small markets the local merchants may not have advertising agencies handling their accounts. The salespersons who service these accounts relay to the staff writer suggestions from the sponsor for the commercials. Often the continuity writers personally visit the merchants for consultation and ideas. It is not unusual in some small stations to find one of the announcers doubling as a continuity writer and assuming responsibility for preparing commercials. In large stations the continuity division has no responsibilities for writing commercial copy. Advertising agencies send the scripts, slides, and recorded, video-taped, and filmed commercials directly to the commercial department.

Production division. With the concentration in most radio stations on news and recorded music, the production function has almost vanished. Such programs do not need the directing and producing that were necessary when radio stations were presenting "live" music, dramatic, audience participation, and variety programs. Documentary programs, which some stations still present, are now produced with tape recorders on location rather than in studios. When studio direction is needed in radio, it may be handled by an announcer or engineer. Because television production is far more complex and important, direction is required. Even though some programs presented by local stations are not rehearsed before they are presented, they must be carefully planned, and they must be directed every second of the actual broadcast. Television stations generally rely upon full-time personnel as producer-directors or as studio directors. Many administrative details on programs may be delegated by management to producer-directors. Program talent may be selected and fees arranged, program ideas conceived, staging properties and film budget allocations determined, scripts edited, and script writers supervised. A producer-director also is in direct charge of rehearsal and air presentation. Studio directors in television have no primary budget or administrative responsibilities, but they supervise the various details encountered in putting a program together, the staging, graphics, music, costumes, properties, editing script, tape, or film, blocking action, conducting camera rehearsals, and finally "calling" the camera shots on the air or for taping.

Additional personnel involved in the presentation of a television program in the production division are the stage managers, also referred to as floor managers. They are the representatives of the director on the studio floor. They relay signals to the performers and are in charge of the studio crew, the program assistants handling properties and title cards, stagehands moving sets, and other technicians changing lights and producing sound effects.

The directors may have other persons assisting them in the rehearsal and presentation. Assistant or associate directors time the program, make notes about performance and technical details that must be attended to before the broadcast, and render general assistance during the telecast such as reminders about camera movement, lighting effects, and upcoming signals. Some stations call these people "script" or "production" assistants. Some stations consider that the TV camera operators are a part of the production division. On simple programs such as a local service program the camera operator may double as floor manager. In small stations announcers often act as stage manager or camera operators or direct programs during their schedule. In the larger stations the camera operators are generally considered part of the technical department.

Few TV or radio stations are active enough to require a full-time person in sound effects. When the sounds of newspaper presses, jet planes, or thundering herds of cattle are needed, records with these sound effects are played by the same person who is handling the recorded music. If the special effects are to be done in the studio, such as the closing of a door or a pistol shot, colleagues in the program department are pressed into service.

A card file, with photographs, audition reports, and other information about available talent, is maintained in the production division for ready reference when actors, vocalists, dancers, talented youngsters, animal acts, baton twirlers, hog callers, bagpipe players, one-man-band acts, etc., are needed. One or two versatile performers may be put on staff. Generally such persons are employed as specific programs require their services for definite periods of time, ranging from a single appearance to a 26-week or a year's contract.

Film and tape division. Television stations rely heavily on film and video tape of all types: full-length, 90-minute features; half-hour dramas; cartoons; travel shorts; documentaries; brief, filmed inserts; commercials; and educational or public-service programs. One to four persons are employed to keep close track of film and video tape, to screen them for technical quality and standards of good taste, to schedule them for broadcasting, and to do what editing is necessary for insertion of commercials and correct timing. The persons who thread up the film projection equipment and supervise the actual telecast details are generally a part of the engineering department. The photographers, video-tape technicians, and film camera operators who shoot film and stills for station use may be a part of the film and tape division or attached to another division such as news, or be employed on a free-lance or "assignment" basis.

Art division. In television programs there is a great variety of prepared "visual aids": weather maps, charts to show farm prices, charts to indicate baseball standings, title cards at the opening and closing of programs that carry the cast and production credits, station identification slides, simple animated devices, cartoon-type drawings, commercial slogans on the rear wall of the set, and even humorous or "cute" slides to tell the audience about the difficulties when the station loses its sound or network transmission gives a poor picture. These "visuals" are prepared in the art division. If a station prepares slides for local sponsors or is at all active in studio programming, at least two staff artists are needed.

Staging and facilities division. Many individual programs have their own distinctive settings—ranging from realistic kitchens to abstract arrangements of light patterns on the floor and draped backgrounds. The responsibility for designing and building the sets, securing large and small properties such as furniture, tables, vases, getting the studio ready for use by putting up the scenery and placing the properties, and changing sets while on the air is given to the staging division. Lighting the sets may also be handled by staging, although the general industry pattern is to look upon lighting as a function of engineering.

Specialties in the program department. 1. Public-Service Division. An important division of the program department is the public-service division, which deals with education, religious programming, political campaigns, public issues and safety, health, and bond-drive campaigns, United Way, Red Cross, and similar appeals. Announcements and interviews are scheduled, special interviews and documentaries prepared and presented, and taped or filmed programs from the organization's national headquarters presented. Some of this material is included in sponsored programs and some is donated by the station and presented on a sustaining basis. Everyone at the station may be involved in public-service programs as an addition to regular duties. One person, however, may be designated the coordinator or director of public service for convenient approach by outside organizations. In small stations this person is often the general manager; in somewhat larger stations the program director has charge of this division; and in a few of the very large stations a specialist is hired. If a political campaign is in progress, the purchase of time by the various political party television and radio chairpersons will be handled as any other commercial broadcasts, but the programs are supervised by a key person familiar with the FCC regulations on political broadcasting. Stations differ greatly in the amount of public-service programming and in the choice of person to run the division.

2. Sports. Here again we find a great difference among stations. Some very small stations specialize in sports, with one or two people doing nothing but that. In metropolitan areas, an independent station may secure a consistently high rating whenever it carries play-by-play reports of sporting events, studio recaps, taped and filmed interviews with visiting sports celebrities, or sports news periods. If the station does not have a separate division for sports, one or two of the announcers will usually be chosen to handle the programs.

3. Farm Programs. Many programs are especially designed to assist the farmer with complete weather and market reports, agricultural news, and information about new farming methods and refinements of old methods, by presenting authoritative talks, demonstrations, and interviews featuring government officials, state agricultural college professors, experiment station workers, and successful farmers. Many stations include some agriculture programs in their schedules and some make the farm audience their prime consideration. It is a very common practice to have attached to the program department a farm director who is an expert in agricultural matters. The press, taped, and film releases of the U.S. Department of Agriculture, State Agricultural Boards, and Agricultural Colleges are available to the station for programming purposes, but an effective series conducted by a farm director will include far more than these releases. The usefulness of a portable tape recorder and film cameras is never more evident than in farm broadcasts. News film and on-the-spot interviews with successful farmers, exhibitors at county and state fairs, and groups conducting various demonstrations are easy to obtain, providing the station's budget permits the farm director and technical personnel to attend these functions. Often farm directors operate the tape recorder or film camera by themselves.

4. Women's and Children's Features. Some stations may present programs designed to have special appeal to women at home. These programs are prepared and presented in various ways. In small stations a regular staff member may be assigned this function. Medium and large stations may hire a specialist to handle the women's features. In newspaper-owned stations the women's editor may double as the station's women's specialist.

Children's programs fall into several types. One is a children's talent revue. Another emphasizes narrations of favorite stories, a clown or other distinctive personality introducing cartoon features or engaging in banter with puppets who dance to records or dramatize stories, or a "kindergarten" type of show with stories and games.

Another favorite juvenile program is the quiz or stunt program, handled by a staff announcer or special-events person. A recent addition to a number of station's schedules is the teen-ager MC handling a record show especially aimed toward the junior and senior high school audience.

Engineering Department

Although the members of the home audience are often unaware of the engineering department, a moment's consideration makes it apparent that this department is a vital link in station operation. It is headed by the chief engineer and is usually divided into studio and transmitter divisions.

Radio. If a station has the transmitter and studio together at one location, a smaller staff is possible. Frequently the two are separated, sometimes by as much as fifteen miles. The studios may be located in the center of town and the transmitter outside the city limits. In a small station the studio engineer may be stationed in master control, while announcers take care of announce-booth equipment, such as cartridge machines, and recording turntables. The process may be further simplified by having combination announcer-engineers in a control room overlooking two other studios. In some large stations, engineers may play tape cartridges and records, but there is considerable variance in this practice. Many station managers feel that since records are a part of the program department, they should be played by someone in that department, usually the announcer.

Studio engineers are also responsible for transferring commercials on transcriptions to station tape cartridges and cassettes, splicing tapes, and servicing tape-recording equipment. Whenever a "nemo" or remote (a program away from the studio) is broadcast, an engineer or combination announcer-engineer is in attendance with the remote amplifying equipment and microphones. Since the FCC prescribes definite rules and regulations for maintenance of technical standards, it is the responsibility of the engineering department to follow these rules and regulations, to anticipate the replacement of obsolete transmitter, monitor, and studio equipment, and to maintain the required broadcast logs. Engineering staffs vary in number from four in small stations to over 20 in some of the large ones.

Television. Many more engineers are required in television station operation. Some organizations that own both radio and TV stations may employ three times as many engineers in the TV operation as they do in the radio operation. All of the duties required of radio engineers are present also in television. Added to these are the responsibilities for camera operation in the studio, camera switching in the control room, making video tapes, and regulation of the video controls in the control room, master control, and remote truck. The film projectionists and lighting supervisors may also be engineers. Keeping all of the complex electronic equipment in working order requires considerable time as well as personnel who have extremely high levels of technical knowledge.

COMPARISON OF RADIO AND TELEVISION PROGRAM PRODUCTION

Without dipping too deeply into the techniques of television production for the moment, let us observe the same program in both radio and television studios in order to make a comparison.

Radio. Here is a consumers' program, an everyday affair. In the studio at a table, ready for the radio broadcast, are the commentator, the guest for the day (a celebrated chef) and the announcer. The commercial announcements on the program are in the script together with the notes for the interview. In the control room is a studio engineer. Such production-direction as is needed is taken care of by the announcer who gives simple three-, two-, and one-minute warnings before the show ends. Two production or program people therefore are sufficient to handle the broadcast.

Television. In the studio we find the commentator, the guest, and the announcer, but added to the group are two camera operators, one for each of the two cameras, who move the cameras into position and change camera shots as instructions come from the control room over the telephonic communication system; one stage manager, to relay signals from the control room to the talent and to coordinate on-the-air activity; one studio assistant, who handles the lights required to illuminate merchandise displays, talent, and the settings (which consist of a comfortable living room set for part of the program, and a kitchen set for the interview); and one studio assistant, in charge of properties, who manipulates the title cards at the opening and closing of the program, places the proper piece of merchandise in its place for an effective camera shot during a commercial, and assists behind the scenes during the salad-tossing demonstration by the chef. In the control room we find the same engineer handling the audio equipment, turning on the microphones and supervising the voice levels throughout the broadcast, but there is also a video engineer who handles control units for both cameras and controls picture quality; a second video engineer or technical director (abbreviated TD) who communicates with the cameramen in the studio on camera placement and lens selection for long shots, medium shots, medium or big close-ups as instructed by the director, and who does the actual switching from camera to camera; and the director, who is responsible for coordinating the entire operation in the most effective manner. In another room is still another technician who, on cue from the technical director in the program control booth, runs the commercial films or video tapes used by some of the sponsors on this shopper's guide.

In the case of the radio broadcast, two people were sufficient in the immediate area to put the commentator's program on the air. In the telecast of the same program 11 were used. The production of the television program could be more elaborate with an additional camera and camera operator, special engineers to maneuver the dolly camera and boom microphone, more studio assistants for special effects and sets, and an assistant director. When one tries to televise a simple production like this with a bare minimum of personnel, it may be possible to cut down on studio people from six to five or even to three (announcer and two camera/operators) and to reduce the control room personnel by letting the director do the switching, but you will still have a minimum of four or five contrasted to radio's two.

Staff requirements also increase for remote television broadcasts, in contrast to radio pickups of the same event. Whereas an announcer and an engineer, with an occasional production director to supervise the unit, are quite satisfactory in radio, the remote crew for television, on a minimum basis, will generally consist of:

1. *Two camera operators,* one for each of two cameras, stationed to overlook the event being telecast.
2. *One audio engineer,* whose duties are much the same as those of the radio engineer mentioned above.
3. *One video engineer,* to control picture quality on the two cameras.
4. *One announcer,* whose general duties are similar to those in the radio counterpart, although different techniques are used.
5. *One director,* who coordinates the production, monitors the camera not on the air, and calls the shots to be telecast.
6. *One TD,* or "switcher," who supervises the technical aspects of the video pickup and the microwave relay transmitter and does the actual switching from camera to camera.

Sales Department

The sales department is the revenue-producing department. Station-break announcements and program commercials result when a representative of the sales department obtains a contract covering the presentation of a sponsor's message over the station's facilities. The two major sources of advertising contracts available to independent stations are local advertising and national spot advertising; network-affiliated stations have an additional source of revenue: network advertising. The sales manager with the assistance of one salesperson may handle all sales negotiations for a small station. Medium-sized and large stations keep a full-time sales force of three to six salespersons.

The salespersons and sales manager work closely with the program department in building or acquiring programs and writing copy. In small stations the salesperson may also be a part-time announcer. To have information available on time-periods open for sponsorship, and to schedule the announcements and programs correctly according to the terms of the contracts, stations rely on a traffic division, generally a branch of the sales department although in some organizations it comes under the program department.

The traffic manager and assistants are responsible for preparing the final program log, which itemizes exactly what is to be broadcast for which client, at what time, in which studio, by which announcer, and indicates what facilities are to be available, necessary switching cues, and which directors are to supervise. Each member of the station's staff concerned with operations, as well as the executives, receives the program log for ready reference throughout the broadcast day.

Many stations have installed automation equipment into which the program log is fed and which then controls the daily schedule. In radio, tape recordings, cartridges, and cassettes provide the program and commercial elements. In television they are provided by films, slides, and video tapes. The development of the television cassette, containing program and commercial elements recorded on film or video tape, has simplified automatic broadcasting processes for television stations and cable-TV systems.

Before the compilation of the final log, the program director supplies information to the traffic department, listing programs to be logged, indicating if originations are local (live or recorded) or network, and necessary production coverage. The sales manager supplies bookings for commercial announcements and programs according to contractual agreements. Specific transcriptions, tape cartridges, slides, tapes, or films are noted. Before or after the final typing or duplication of the log, the chief announcer names the announcers to handle the specific announcements and programs. The chief engineer assigns personnel to cover the programs according to technical needs. A master book of a loose-leaf notebook style, containing all copy to be read on the air, is assembled in chronological order corresponding to the program log. Transcriptions, films, cartridges, tapes, and slides are made ready. After the broadcast, the announcer signs the announcing copy in the master book and the final "as-broadcast" program log. The traffic department uses these records to bill clients and advertising agencies. Figure 16–3 shows a portion of the program log of KTTV, Los Angeles.

Another function of the traffic department is to work out analyses of program types when required by the FCC. The sales department also includes the bookkeeping or accounting division, which enters accounts, renders statements, makes out the station payroll, and pays bills. Some stations have computerized both traffic and accounting procedures.

Promoting the station's program schedule and individual programs is an essential part of station operation. This is handled by the promotion department, which often reports directly to the general manager. Promotional announcements on the air, billboard, transportation and newspaper advertisements, direct mail, window displays, booklets, blotters, book matches, bread wrappers, collars on milk bottles, movie trailers, listing in the newspapers and magazines, public relations work with organizations, publicity campaigns in the press, and talent appearances before local clubs are standard methods for promoting program schedules.

Projects and Exercises

1. Tune in the radio and television stations that are received well in your immediate area. On the basis of this observation, estimate the staff organization each station needs. Each student should take a different period in order to survey varied hours of station programming.

DAILY PROGRAM LOG

KTTV

6/06/77

MON TUE WED THU FRI SAT SUN

TIME ON HR:MIN:SEC	DURATION MIN:SEC	VID SOURCE A	AUD SOURCE A	LOG SEQ NO	RANDOM SLIDE NUM	EVENT DESCRIPTION	ADVER NUM	VIDEO NUMBER	AUDIO NUM	CONTRACT NUM	LINE NUM	ELEM PROG	FCC PROG SCE TYPE
10:17:38	00:30	V2	V2	8130		VAUDEVILLE						C	
10:18:08	00:00	R3	M3	8140		00.10/NEWS TEASER		X166/3				C	PA
10:18:18	08:37	V3	V3	8130		PART 9—MERV		A107/9				C	PA
10:26:55	00:00	R3	M3	8160		00.15/NEWS TEASER						C	
10:27:10	00:30	V4	V4	8170		00.30/KRUGERRAND GOLD COIN	46374	3L0725A01	1101	20759	11	C	PA
10:27:40	00:30	V4	V4	8180		00.30/BLOCK DRUG POLIGRIP	09975	3L0789A02	1202	23240	3	C	SA
10:28:10	00:30	V4	V4	8190		00.30/GARNEAU BOLLA WINE	31271	3L0193A03	1303	23018	2	C	SA
10:28:40	01:10	M3	V3	8200		PART 10—MERV		A107/10				C	SA
10:29:50	00:06	V4	A1/V4	8210		00.10/ID/CART/MARY HARTMAN	X210	1Z0016A04	1404			B	PA
10:29:56	00:04	V4	V4	8220		SAME—CART		04	1404			B	ID
10:30:00	00:00	R3	M3	8230		00.30 ** METRO NEWS **						N	NL
10:30:00	00:00	R3	B	8240		OPEN BILLBOARD/NEWS							
10:30:00	00:00	S5	M3	8250	0001	TITLE SLIDE		708	2105				
	00:30	V4	V4	8260		00.30/LINCOLN MERCURY	49055	3A0910A05	2105	67456	16	C	SA

AUTOMATION COMMANDS

ACTUAL TIME OR SIGNATURE

Figure 16–3. Portion of Program Log, KTTV, Los Angeles

2. Visit one or more stations for "behind-the-scenes" tours. Ask a representative of the station to discuss the actual organization. Discuss later how nearly correct your estimate of the organization staff was.

3. If a class tour is not possible, invite a representative of the station to come to the school and speak.

technical aspects of radio

17

Radio communication involves the transmission of sound through space to a point of reception not connected by wires to the point of origin. To accomplish this, microphones are used to convert sound waves into patterns of electrical energy. This energy is amplified and modulated by transmitting apparatus and broadcast on radio frequencies into the air. At the point of reception, the electrical patterns are converted back to sound waves, which emerge from the loudspeaker.

For an elementary understanding of the technical aspects of radio, it is helpful to examine each stage of this process and to describe the equipment that makes radio communication possible.

MICROPHONES

The Nature of Sound

Sound consists of waves of air particles in motion. When one speaks, the air expelled by the lungs passes through the vocal folds, which set up vibrations of the air particles. These are amplified by resonators in the head and throat, and the resultant product emerging from the mouth and nose is called voice. Musical sound is produced in a violin by vibrating a string with a bow, using the box of the violin as the resonator. Thus sound is a physical product, brought into being by physical energy, and limited in its radius of transmission by the physical strength of the sound and the existence of intervening barriers. Sound produced by a violin or the human voice is usually periodic, or regular in pattern, and thus pleasing to the ear; often, especially among younger violinists or persons with vocal defects, aperiodic sounds are heard; these are irregular and unpleasant, and to them are ascribed such qualities as rasping, noisy, and scraping. Sound is perceived through the ear; the physical movement of air particles caused by the sound vibrates the membrane in the ear, which then transmits the pattern to the brain where, through various complex nervous processes, meaning is given to the perception of sound.

The sound itself has a frequency, which we perceive as pitch, determined by the number of its vibrations—the greater the number per second,

247

the higher the pitch; a regularity or irregularity of vibrations—with simple to complex patterns—which we perceive as quality; amplitude of vibrations which we perceive as intensity or loudness; and has an existence in time which we perceive as duration. Figure 17–1 shows the frequency range of some common musical instruments and the human voice.

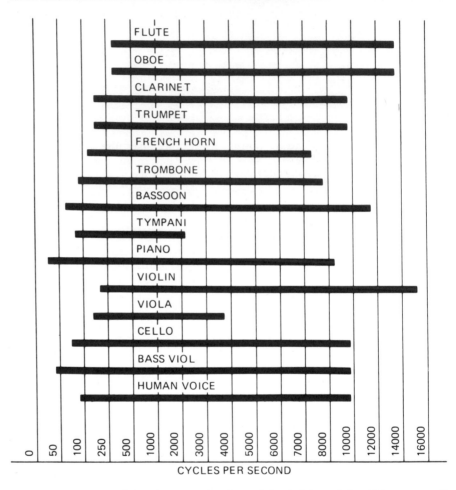

CYCLES PER SECOND

The more sensitive the reproduction of the full sound, in all its range of frequencies, quality, intensity and duration, the fuller and more satisfying will be the experience of hearing.

Microphone Fundamentals

The purpose of the microphone is to convert sound waves into electrical impulses as faithfully as possible. There are four general types of microphones: 1. pressure or dynamic, 2. velocity or ribbon, 3. combination pattern; and 4. condenser. Microphones may also be classified by their pickup of sound: 1.

nondirectional or a 360-degree area of pickup; 2. unidirectional or a pickup on one "live" side, 3. bidirectional or a figure-eight pickup area, two opposing sides being "alive," and 4. polydirectional, in which the area of pickup can be adjusted in various ways. These adjustments for the polydirectional microphone give three, or six, or twelve variable patterns based upon the first three basic response patterns, nondirectional, unidirectional, and bidirectional.

Pressure or Dynamic Microphone

The dynamic microphone receives sound vibrations on a diaphragm and translates them into electrical impulses in a moving coil. The moving of the coil in the magnetic field, proportional to sound pressures acting on the diaphragm, generates a small electric current. Dynamic or pressure microphones used in many stations include the RCA BK 1A "Commentator"; the Electro-Voice RE series, a unidirectional microphone; and the Electro-Voice 635A, a nondirectional microphone. Common characteristics of these microphones are ruggedness of construction, small size, light weight, good frequency response, and relative freedom from the effects of wind and moisture, which makes them very useful for remotes. Many stations use them for studio work as well, particularly as announce microphones.

Velocity or Ribbon Microphone

This microphone has been widely used in the past for studio work because of its high fidelity, though its use is now declining. It is live in two directions and dead in two others. This bidirectional characteristic provides opportunities for subtle shadings of sound perspective as performers move around the microphone, a technique that is useful in the production of radio commercials. The velocity microphone consists essentially of a thin duraluminum ribbon suspended between two magnetic poles. Small electric currents are developed when the ribbon is set in motion by sound vibrations.

Combination Pattern

Another type of microphone now declining in use combined a ribbon and a dynamic unit to provide the characteristics of both the velocity and the dynamic microphone. These microphones could be adjusted to provide three types of pickup: unidirectional, bidirectional, or nondirectional, and in the first two of these settings provided a wide heart-shaped pickup pattern, in contrast with the narrow beam of the velocity microphone, a characteristic that caused some people to refer to them as cardioid microphones.

Condenser Microphone

The condenser microphone was used in the early thirties, but its lack of ruggedness imposed certain limitations. Recent improvements have eliminated this difficulty, making it the type perhaps the most widely used today. It comes in various directional patterns, or in a variable pattern, does not distort under sudden blasts of sound, and has excellent frequency response. Some of the best condenser microphones are manufactured in Germany, Austria, and Japan, among them the German Telefunken and Neumann, the Austrian AKG, and the Japanese Sony ECM-5. The Altec and Electro-Voice companies are the chief manufacturers of condenser microphones in the United States. In addition to being widely used in radio broadcasting, the condenser microphone is the one most often used for making high-fidelity recordings.

Public Address (PA) and Tape-Recorder Microphones

Broadcast microphones are generally not used with inexpensive public address and portable tape recorders. "Crystal" and low-cost dynamic microphones are commonly substituted. These microphones are "high-impedance" in character, matching the PA and tape-recorder amplifiers. However, the high-impedance microphones are not only subject to hum, but they also lose high frequencies when long microphone cables are used. Therefore, when a high-fidelity (and expensive) public address system is installed, transformers may be included so as to permit use of comparable high-fidelity broadcast (low-impedance) microphone pickups. Some models of tape recorders are designed to allow either a high-impedance or a broadcast microphone to be used. In the latter instance a transformer is included in the recorder.

STUDIOS

As radio programming in the television age was reduced mainly to the presentation of music recordings and news, the elaborate studios that large stations and networks built when they were producing dramas, music, and variety shows were no longer necessary. In those days studios were built to "float" as a room within a room to prevent transmitting shocks and noises generated in other parts of the building. Special acoustic treatment was applied to assure optimum production of sound, and some studios even received variable acoustical treatment that resulted in more reverberation at one end of the studio than at the other. Programs could then be produced in the live end or the dead end depending on the acoustical environment that was most favorable to them. These studios have now been converted to other uses. What used to be the main studio of a Detroit station, for example, serving as the source of a constant stream of music, variety, drama, and documentary shows in the 1930s and 1940s, is now the station's newsroom. Radio broadcasters now use a combination studio and control room in which records are played, announcements are made, and news is presented. Some stations operate a separate studio for news broadcasts, and a few large stations, which produce some live music and interview programs, maintain studios separate from control rooms from which to originate these broadcasts. But elaborate radio studios and control room setups have virtually disappeared. They can still be found, however, in music recording studios, which flourish in cities like New York, Los Angeles, Detroit, Nashville, and Chicago.

A sound lock, or indirect entrance to a studio or control room, designed to prevent the pickup of unwanted sound, originated in radio and still survives. This plan of construction places a small entrance or foyer between the studio or control room door and the corridor doors. The doors are of extra heavy construction and fit tightly. In entering, the corridor door closes before the studio door is opened, thus preventing the seepage of corridor noise into the program. To prevent control-room noise from entering a studio, the same device can be used; the windows between the two are made of double panes of glass with space between, a method of construction that prevents sound from going in either direction through the window area.

CONTROL ROOM

The next step in tracing the broadcast circuit is in the control room. The microphone in the studio or control room turns the sound into minute electric waves (audio current), which travel through a special microphone cable to the control-room console. Here a preamplifier strengthens the weak audio current and it passes through a gain control known as a "fader," "pot," or "mixer," which regulates the volume of the audio current. At the point on rotary-knob faders where the numeral 7 would be on a clock, the fader is closed and no audio current from that microphone will pass. If the fader is turned clockwise, audio current is passed according to the distance the fader is turned. *Fading up* the microphone means that the control console fader connected to that microphone "channel" is turned clockwise or *on; Fading down* or *off* is the reverse. Faders are also commonly seen in linear form; *fade up* and *fade down* then correspond to the up-and-down sliding action of the fader control handle.

The console contains a number of faders, located in parallel series near the bottom, convenient for easy manipulation by the engineer or announcer seated at the console. Each input into the console has its corresponding fader; microphone, turntables for playing records, tape player, and tape cartridges. The operator is responsible for maintaining the appropriate level of volume on these various inputs, a technique known as "riding gain." The console also has audition speakers that permit the cueing of records before they are broadcast. A speaker in the control room lets the announcers hear what is being broadcast when they are not actually on the air. Found as supplementary equipment in some control rooms are jack panels with their associated patch cords. These are used to extend the flexibility of the console by terminating the inputs and outputs of all amplifiers on the jack panels. This allows rapid rerouting of the signal in case of trouble, variation in distribution of the various channels, or the use of filter or echo devices to change the quality of the signal.

In addition to the individual faders the usual console has a master fader, shortened to "master," which has overall control of the other faders. With the master, the engineer can fade up or down all the component parts of the program at the same time.

From the microphone faders, the audio signal goes through additional amplification to strengthen the signal enough to boost it along the wire to

Radio Control Room Showing Control Board and Cartridge Players.

the master control room or directly to the transmitter. There must be enough amplification for proper transmission, but not so much that the equipment will be overloaded and the sound distorted. A volume indicator, on the face of the console, translates visually the amount of signal being sent. This is a meter displaying a needle that moves across the scale to indicate modulation percentages in black figures from 0 to 100 and volume units in decibels shown in red figures from minus 20 to plus 3. *The more gain or volume being sent, the more to the right the "needle" moves across the meter scale in direct proportion to the variations in strength of the signal.* This instrument is referred to as the VU (for volume units). If the incoming level is too low for proper amplification and transmission, so that the listener at home will not be able to understand it easily, the engineer "riding gain" will turn the fader up; if the VU needle "peaks" over 100 to plus 1, 2, or 3 consistently, the level is too high and the fader has to be turned down; otherwise, distortion will result as automatic compressors in the transmission equipment go into action to prevent overloading.

Announcers who work in a control room as disc jockeys (DJs) must have great dexterity as well as considerable talent. Their duties include cueing up records, operating the tape cartridge system, making announcements, answering the telephone, and in some stations they are even required to keep the program log. At the same time they must maintain effective communication with their audience. Many stations require that they do all of these things without permitting the constant flow of sound to be interrupted by a single moment of silence. Only the highly skilled can meet this challenge.

MASTER CONTROL ROOM

Stations that originate all their programs from a single point find a master control room unnecessary. Where the operation is more complicated, however, the master control room serves as a coordinating center. Here the various studio outputs, or program feeds, are received and amplified. The master control room may range from a simple extension of the control room to an extremely complex arrangement with relay racks lining the walls. These racks contain power supplies, program and monitor amplifiers feeding several speakers, and jack panels for routing any channel in a countless variety of ways. They also have equipment for receiving and equalizing network and remote channels and sending them into the appropriate studio at the right time, and to the transmitter; and elaborate systems of preset switches, push buttons, signal lights, and countless other pieces of equipment known only to the technicians who expertly and calmly make the necessary adjustments for smooth operation.

TELEPHONE NETWORK

The reference to network channels coming into the MCR or master control room should be supplemented by a brief description of how network programs get from origination centers to stations affiliated with them. It could be more descriptively termed a "telephone network" because of the thousands of miles of specially leased telephone lines that are used in network broadcasting. Programs go from the network master control room by special telephone circuits to the "Long Lines" division of the American Telephone and Telegraph Company, where they are routed north, east, south, and west. Booster amplifying equipment is located along the lines or at microwave relay stations and at switching centers to keep the volume at proper level. Upon receiving the signal in its master control, each radio station relays the program to its respective transmitter by similar high-fidelity telephone lines. The telephone network can reverse the circuits to receive program feeds from affiliated stations along the network and redistribute the programs in regular fashion.

It is anticipated that more and more use will be made of communication satellite circuits for television and radio network distribution. For example, National Public Radio expects to have a four-channel stereo service transmitted to its affiliates by means of a communication satellite in the year 1980.

RECORDINGS

The radio industry today relies for most of what it broadcasts on recordings. Recordings are of two main types.

Disc Recordings

Most of the music broadcast today is produced from recordings that are also sold in music stores. Many stations receive regular supplies of the latest releases from record manufacturers, who hope that the station will help to make a particular record popular. These records are of two types: the 12-inch albums that contain a number of selections and play at 33⅓ rpm and the singles, 7-inch records, that play at 45 rpm.

In addition to these sources, radio stations also play transcriptions that are produced for broadcast use only. These transcriptions, some of them 16-inch records, mainly contain music programming or commercials and play at 33⅓ rpm.

Tape Recordings

The radio industry is a major user of tape recordings, either the regular type that run from one reel to another at 7½ or 15 inches per second, or tape cartridges containing commercials and program elements, which can be cued instantaneously. Most stations also make tape recordings for use on programs and produce tape-cartridge material for insertion into programs, particularly newscasts and commercial announcements.

The development of tape recording after World War II brought many advantages to the broadcasting industry. The mechanism is so arranged that succeeding recordings wipe off previous ones. In addition, the tape can be spliced quite easily, so that changes can be made in the program before it is played on the air, without loss of fidelity. This opportunity to "edit" a program, eliminating faults in production, the portability of the equipment, and the convenience of making tape recordings ahead of scheduled broadcast times have induced most stars and program producers to "tape" their programs. Less expensive tape-recording methods are available to schools and universities.

Turntables

Transcriptions at 33⅓ rpm and commercial recordings at 33⅓, 45, and 78 rpm are played on turntables similar in function to phonographs. Turntables must be carefully designed and constructed with special filter controls and extremely light pickup arms. At least two tables are needed to enable the operator to "cue" one record while the other is on the air.

Remote Pickups

When programs originate away from the studios, a special telephone circuit is ordered from the telephone company. This circuit goes from the point of pickup to the master control of the station. An engineer uses portable remote amplifiers similar in design and function to the control-room console. Suitable microphones are placed for the best pickup of the program, and the engineer mixes and balances the microphones and sends the program along the special telephone circuit to master control. A second circuit may be ordered for communication between the control room and the engineer at the point of pickup. After a period of test transmission, time signals are given up to the time the program is due to go on the air. The control room at the station may give a "take-it-away" cue, or the remote may start on a time basis or immediately following a prearranged word cue included on the program.

For special remote pickups that cover fast-breaking news stories, reporters may use regular telephones for live voice reports, or they may attach tape recorders to telephones. When telephone service is not available, a shortwave transmitter is used instead. The announcer follows the action, using a portable "walkie talkie" to broadcast to a mobile truck, which sends the signal by special shortwave transmission to master control.

TRANSMISSION

The equipment at the transmitter sends out radio waves according to the licensed power and frequency of a station. The methods of transmission are Amplitude Modulation (AM) and Frequency Modulation (FM).

The Broadcast Spectrum

Let us compare radio and sound waves. Radio waves are caused by electrical vibration or "oscillation," whereas sound waves are air particles set in motion by physical action. Radio waves travel, as do sound waves, in all directions, similar to the familiar illustration of water waves activated by a stone, but they go faster than sound, with the speed of light, or 186,000 miles per second (300,000 kilometers per second) instead of the sound-velocity rate of 1090 feet per second (332 meters per second), and, of course, can travel much farther than sound, to the moon and back, for instance. Whereas sound to our human ear varies in frequency from approximately 16 cycles to 20,000 cycles, various broadcasting services utilize radio frequencies beginning at 10 kilohertz (10,000 cycles) and rising to 1000 megahertz (1,000,000,000 cycles). [The term "hertz" is now used to designate a cycle per second in honor of Heinrich Hertz, the German physicist who helped to develop the science of radio. A kilohertz (kHz) is 1000 cycles and a megahertz (MHz) is 1,000,000 cycles.] The broadcast spectrum is illustrated in Figure 17–2.

With a receiving set possessing no frequency discrimination, a listener would receive a jumble of signals due to the great use of these radio waves for communication: control tower to airplane, ship to shore, amateur to amateur, and commercial and governmental messages, for example. As we have seen, different frequency bands are assigned to various kinds of communication services by the Federal Communications Commission. The standard broadcast or AM carrier-frequency band extends from 535 to 1605 kilohertz. The United States, following international allocation agreements, has available a total of 107 channels in this band.

Below the standard band are various communication services. The very low frequencies, from 10 to 100 kilohertz, are useful for long-distance

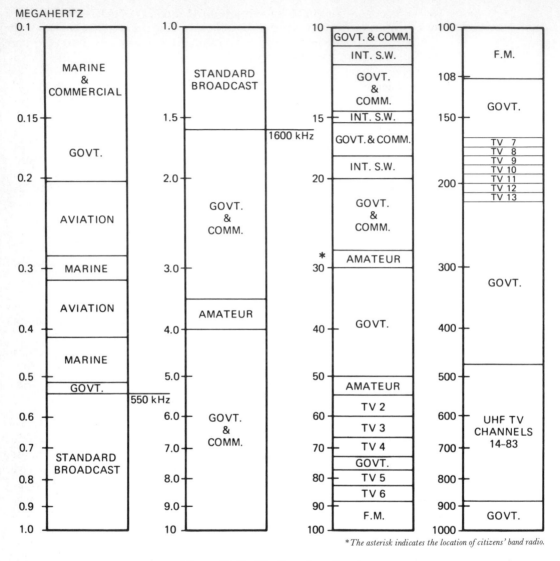

MEGAHERTZ

*The asterisk indicates the location of citizens' band radio.

Figure 17-2   The Broadcast Spectrum

communication; those from 100 to 500 kilohertz are used for distances up to a thousand miles. Above the standard band are other communication services, international shortwave, FM and television, and radar and experimental research bands. The VHF television band, numbered for convenience, ranges from an assigned frequency of 54 to 88 megahertz for channels 2–6 (in channels of 6 megahertz each) and from 175 to 216 megahertz for channels 7–13. The FM bands, ranging from 88 to 108 megahertz, are in between the television channels. The UHF band ranges from 470 to 890 megahertz.

The FCC is now no longer assigning stations the uppermost 13 channels in the UHF band.

Transmitter and Antenna

Modern transmitters arc almost entirely self-operated. Engineering science and manufacturing skill provide instruments to insure accuracy and sustained transmission. Except for some small stations, transmitters and antennas are usually located in outlying areas. This is due to intense radiation of energy from the antenna, which tends to "blank out" listener reception in the immediate area, and the need for extensive ground systems consisting of thousands of feet of copper wire buried from six to twelve inches deep. Another important consideration is the electrical interference when the transmitter is located in a thickly populated district.

Transmitters have two functions:

1. Generation of a powerful radio wave initiated by a vacuum-tube or transistor oscillator and amplified until it reaches the assigned power of the station. This wave is termed the carrier wave because it carries with it on its path the audio signal produced in the studio.

2. Modulation or superimposure of the audio signal upon the carrier wave. A homely illustration is that this process is like putting oil into a truck and having the truck carry it to your home. The two methods used for this process are:

   a. Amplitude modulation or AM. The power or amplitude of the carrier wave is varied. The frequency is the same.

   b. Frequency modulation of FM. The frequency of the carrier wave is varied. The amplitude remains the same.

Unless one possesses a great deal of engineering knowledge, a discussion of AM-FM methods of transmission is confusing. A preferable method for nontechnical people is to consider the effect of the two types of transmission. Reception of a wider range of frequencies is possible in the FM system. Lightning, summer heat storms, electrical appliances in the neighborhood, building elevators, and other such disturbances do not interfere with FM reception. As a result the fuller frequency range makes the program seem more lifelike. This is especially true with live music. Another characteristic of FM transmission is a decrease in station coverage, due to the tendency for FM to travel in "line-of-sight" paths instead of following the earth's curvature as does AM transmission. The sky wave does not normally reflect in FM, with the resultant decrease in station interference; more stations, therefore, may be assigned to the same FM channels than is possible with AM. In reaching remote and rural areas, however, AM is the only satisfactory method as yet developed.

The antenna tower serves as the jumping-off place for the modulated carrier wave. It may be a single symmetrical tower reaching hundreds of feet up into the sky with the upper portions containing TV and FM extensions; or it may be a series of vertical spires so placed as to complement or interfere with each other in order to change the pattern of radiation. The latter, referred to as a "directional antenna," is used to prevent an overlap of coverage with another station on the same frequency, or to direct transmission away from a section of land or water the station does not care to reach, in order to intensify the strength of its coverage in another area.

RECEPTION

The next and final step in the broadcast process is the reception by the home receiver. The radio waves sent out by the transmitter via the broadcast antenna are received at home on whatever antenna system is used. The receiver amplifies the weak signal, separates the audio signal modulation from the carrier, amplifies it, and projects it from your loudspeaker as sound waves, with relatively the same characteristics they had when they entered the microphone as voice or music in the studio. The "oil truck" has delivered the oil. The entire process is completed with great speed. The transmission of radio waves through the air takes place at the speed of light; the audio waves going through lines and amplifiers travel somewhat more slowly, but the entire process occurs so rapidly that a word uttered into a microphone is heard instantaneously by a listener tuned in to a radio set.

STEREO AND AUTOMATION

A relatively recent development in broadcasting is the presentation of stereo programs on FM. This type of broadcasting requires dual channel consoles, special turntables and tape recorders, and special microphone techniques. The two stereo signals are transmitted by means of a supersonic or subcarrier signal superimposed upon the main program channel. Special FM receivers are required for reception of the program as a stereo broadcast, although regular FM receivers will pick up the two stereo signals and present them to the listeners as a blend. Experiments to develop quadraphonic broadcasting and AM stereo are also being carried out.

Another trend in station operation is the use of equipment that permits a station to broadcast for an entire day on an automated basis. This is accomplished through the use of tape machines that provide the program elements to be transmitted by the station. The signals from these program tapes are interspersed with signals from other tape machines that carry the commercial messages, which are usually inserted into the machine in the form of cartridges. The operation of the various tape machines is accomplished automatically through the use of tones on the tapes. These tones, which cannot be heard by the listening audience, act as cueing signals to stop tapes and start tapes when the program elements or commercial messages recorded on them are scheduled for the station. Specialized clock mechanisms or small computers regulate insertion of station-break announcements at appropriate times. It is possible through the use of these automatically cued tapes to broadcast an entire day's schedule without involving an announcer or engineer. A station featuring news or weather reports could not, of course, depend on a completely automated system if it wished to present up-to-date reports, but a large share of its program day could be broadcast automatically.

Projects and Exercises

1. Classify the microphones in your studio according to their respective areas of pickup—nondirectional, bidirectional, unidirectional. Conduct experiments to determine the operational characteristics of your microphones that give the best results. Use different speakers and musical instruments.

2. See whether it is possible for your class to visit a radio station to observe a "disc jockey" at work. If the equipment in your control room permits it, set up and announce a disc jockey program of your own.

3. Practice "riding gain" on a single voice. Then practice on two voices and move into riding gain on two or three microphones. Open and close faders on cue or script markings. Follow hand movements by instructor in fading up or down to acquire dexterity in manipulation of the faders. Play a professional recording and observe the VU meter readings.

4. Practice "patching up" the various combinations possible in your control room. Clear the board after each try for the person who follows.

5. Play a recording and listen to it critically for fidelity and balance as it is patched first through a highly sensitive loudspeaker and second through a small "home-type" speaker. Compare the results and draw conclusions about the differences in quality and perception that influence control-room operation. Compare, for example, the difference in level for a sound effect of night noises needed to assure clear-cut recognition over the small speaker as contrasted to the level needed when heard over the more sensitive speaker.

6. Observe and practice recording technique using the equipment available at your studio.

7. Make a field trip to several station transmitters.

technical aspects of television

18

Television involves two simultaneous operations: the transmission of sight and of sound. The audio (sound) part of a television program is transmitted as a frequency-modulation signal; the video (sight) part is transmitted as an amplitude-modulation signal. The audio that accompanies video in television follows the path traced in the preceding chapter, utilizing the upper one-half megahertz in the assigned frequency band (channel). Turning to video, let us first explain the television process from camera to home and then analyze elements in the "program chain."

GENERAL EXPLANATION

At one time motion picture theaters featured song sessions in which the audience was invited to participate. To help them keep time, audience members were shown one line of the song at a time with a little white dot moving across that line from left to right indicating which words the audience was to sing, and how long the word was to be held. When it reached the final word at the right, the dot jumped back quickly to the left side of the screen to start again with a new line of lyrics now in view. This is a very rough illustration of the first step in the telecast journey: The electronic camera, moving as the white dot from left to right but at a constant speed, scans the object or scene to be televised.

The scene in front of the camera is focused by means of a lens on a light-sensitive surface. In this way the optical image is converted into a pattern of electronic charges. Where the light is brighter in the studio scene, the electrical charge is stronger; where there are shadows, the electrical charge is weaker. An electron gun sends a scanning beam across the pattern of charges at the amazing speed of 525 lines from top to bottom every one-thirtieth of a second (a frame). The scanning beam is altered by the pattern of charges in terms of scene brightness—the result being the video signal. At this point it is very weak and must be amplified many millions of times on its journey to the control room, transmitter, and receiving set. A number of different types of light-sensitive pickup tubes are used in contemporary television, among them a lead-oxide tube called the Plumbicon® (registered trademark of the N.V. Philips Company of Holland, the inventor of the tube), the vidicon, and the image orthicon.

The television receiving system consists of a special antenna, a combination of tuning and amplifying circuits in the set to select and strengthen the signal, and a kinescope, a picture tube, on the face of which the original scene is recreated by a reverse process of the original action by the camera in the studio. Here an electronic beam scans the inner surface of the picture tube at the synchronized rate of 525 lines every one-thirtieth of a second. The image is thus reassembled in the home receiver for direct view or projection on a screen.

As noted earlier, the very-high and ultrahigh frequencies used for FM and television transmission do not normally permit much more coverage than "line-of-sight." The station antennas therefore are as high as possible, utilizing skyscrapers in metropolitan centers or nearby heights of land, in order to reach as much area as possible.

The telephone lines used for network radio broadcasting cannot carry the television signal. Special coaxial cable, capable of doing so, has been developed. In conjunction with such cables automatic microwave relay stations are used extensively to provide television network service throughout the country. The original signal is picked up by one relay, amplified and directed in a straight air line to the next point, and so on until the destination is reached. These relays generally are no farther apart than about 25 miles. Satellite reception and transmission systems are also being developed for use in connecting stations into networks.

"Organized chaos" might be the reaction of a casual observer visiting a studio scene during the progress of a program of moderate complexity. The observer would see a great variety of types of lighting combined to create a blaze of light; massive movable platforms or "dollies," which support boom microphones, moving left or right and extending forward or drawing back as the operators follow the action; additional cameras with pedestal bases being moved around by the camera operators, tilted up and down or swinging right or left; a huge camera crane electrically raised up and out in space like a steam shovel ready to take another mouthful of dirt; stage settings, special device mechanisms, and props; milling performers and production personnel; camera, light, and mike cables, and intercommunication wires covering the nonplaying area like a mass of snakes. However, upon becoming more familiar with the details of program production, the observer realizes that there are definite reasons for the patterns of activity and the various elements and soon becomes aware of the highly skilled team play that is in operation.

What primary technical facilities are required for television? They are:

1. Studios
2. Microphones
3. Cameras
4. Staging
5. Control room
6. Film, slide, and video tape
7. Master control
8. Transmitter and antenna

An introductory discussion of these facilities follows, excluding staging, which is treated in a separate chapter.

STUDIOS

Many early television studios consisted of converted radio studios, many of them in downtown office buildings high above the ground floor. As program schedules expanded, the required equipment, cameras, microphone booms, sets, lights, and numbers of people involved demanded more and more space. Makeshift expansions into halls and adjoining offices became the rule. Numerous difficulties and excessive expenses were encountered in transporting large props and sets up narrow stairs or small service elevators. Although these conditions still prevail, stations generally have recognized the need for specialized design of television studio buildings.

One key principle developed is that of *horizontal* (ground floor) rather than *vertical* planning in order to permit easier and more economical movement in and out of raw stock, finished sets, equipment, and properties. A display of automobiles in the studio is simple when cars may be driven through doors directly into the studio. Station WBAP-TV in Fort Worth has a novel "video-land" feature that permits movement of autos, trucks, elephants, and even "herds of cattle" across its large studio right before the cameras. Two huge doors (15 x 12 feet), one on each side of the studio, facing each other, open directly to the outside of the building. The Budweiser commercial that utilized an 80-foot-long wagon and team of horses was presented "live" in the studio. With the increased use of video tape and film, however, the use of studios for such purposes has declined. The scenes are now usually shot on film or recorded on tape in locations more appropriate than a television studio.

Another highly important principle is *traffic flow* or *circulation.* "Such close scheduling of TV broadcasts is necessary, in order to make maximum use of the costly space and equipment, that circulation assumes paramount importance," writes J. P. Allison in the *Architectural Record.* "People and things must flow through the building; control is essential." Functional design is essential to keep the various kinds of groups from interfering with each other as they move in and around the studios. Figure 18–1 lists the types of people and things to be considered. Effective design for plant utilization should provide not only for separation of these groups but also for the shortest possible interior traffic paths. Engineering workshops close to the technical areas, news machines near studios used for news programs, directors' offices near control rooms, and set construction space adjacent to studios are examples of this type of design.

The third key principle in studio design is a provision for *expansion.* It is a commonplace experience for many stations that additional space is needed before the building is finished. Many architects and building consultants recommend an advance overall, step-by-step development that permits flexible growth in stages as the station increases its program production. Such a master plan may avoid haphazard space additions as temporary expedients that impose serious limitations on future program production requirements.

Studio buildings are generally constructed on the outskirts of cities in order to secure adequate ground space at less expense and to provide ample parking facilities for station personnel and guests. When existing structures are secured for remodeling, the search for needed space has led officials to

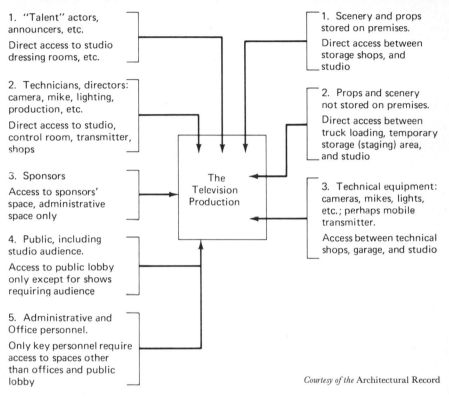

FIVE KINDS OF PEOPLE

1. "Talent" actors, announcers, etc.
Direct access to studio dressing rooms, etc.

2. Technicians, directors: camera, mike, lighting, production, etc.
Direct access to studio, control room, transmitter, shops

3. Sponsors
Access to sponsors' space, administrative space only

4. Public, including studio audience.
Access to public lobby only except for shows requiring audience

5. Administrative and Office personnel.
Only key personnel require access to spaces other than offices and public lobby

The Television Production

THREE KINDS OF THINGS

1. Scenery and props stored on premises.
Direct access between storage shops, and studio

2. Props and scenery not stored on premises.
Direct access between truck loading, temporary storage (staging) area, and studio

3. Technical equipment: cameras, mikes, lights, etc.; perhaps mobile transmitter.
Access between technical shops, garage, and studio

Courtesy of the Architectural Record

Figure 18–1   Circulation Problem in a TV Studio

take over such buildings as riding academies, dance halls, creameries, garages, motion picture sound stages, theaters, armories, and, as the University of Michigan did, a mortuary and a lens-grinding factory.

The size and number of the studios depend in large measure upon program activity. A station relying basically upon network schedules may have only one small studio approximately 15 x 30 feet with a 12- to 14-foot ceiling, permitting some local live programming and advertising display. The controls may be placed in the master control room to conserve on the number of personnel required. The next step may be for a separate control room, then substitution or addition of a larger studio. A combination of one good-sized studio 50 x 80 feet and a smaller studio 25 x 35, with 14- to 18-foot ceilings, seems to be adequate for a station planning a fair amount of local live or tape productions that include some programs with studio audiences. It is implicit that such a two-studio arrangement must also have allied storage, workshop, dressing room, and rehearsal areas.

Figures 18–2 and 18–3 show two-floor and one-floor TV operations.

Second Floor

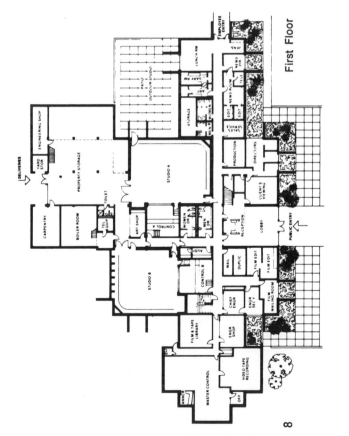

First Floor

Figure 18-2 Two-Floor TV Operation.

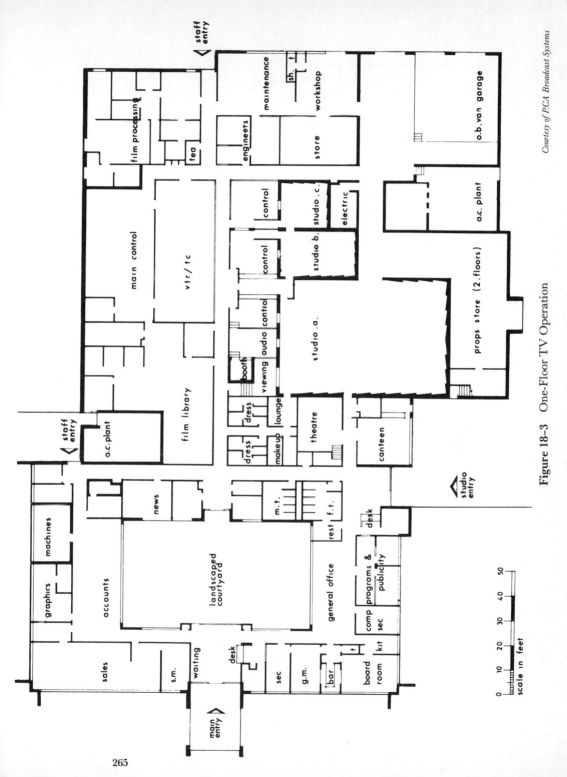

Figure 18–3 One-Floor TV Operation

The acoustical requirements of television studios differ from those for radio. Size and shape and wall and ceiling treatment are important factors in radio studio acoustics. In television, however, these factors are reduced in importance, owing to the many different sets that occupy portions of the studio. Unlike radio, in television there is a necessity for a great deal of physical movement of personnel, properties, and equipment as sets are struck and erected and cameras and microphone booms are changed in position during the actual airing of the program. This activity causes incidental noise. Since microphones are usually kept out of camera range, they are farther from talent and may pick up such undesirable noises. As a consequence, television studios should be "deadened" through use of draperies and considerable sound-absorption material on walls and ceilings. Brightness and reverberation, when required, are frequently obtained through the use of "echo" chambers or electronic devices.

The avoidance of noises from the outside is needed in television as in radio. Similar sound locks and floating-type construction of studios may be employed. Location of studios in suburban areas decreases the traffic noise, but unfortunately sometimes increases the airplane noise potential.

MICROPHONES

In radio the performers move, but the microphones remain stationary; in television the usual pattern is for the microphones to follow the talent. The two microphones used most generally for this suspended and flexible boom operation are the RCA BK 5A and the Electro-Voice RE series. The unidirectional pattern is preferred in order to eliminate as much of the incidental studio noise as possible. RCA introduced its Uniaxial BK 5B as a microphone primarily designed for television. The standard microphone boom permits continuous variations in length. It may be extended forward 17 feet into the set and retracted 10 feet; it may be swung in an arc from side to side to follow action; and a special attachment enables the boom operator to rotate the microphone itself in any direction. The latter feature is useful when two persons who are separated in the set are talking to each other. The operator directs the boom to the person speaking. If both are speaking, the distance between is divided and the boom is adjusted so that the beam covers both. Counterbalancing permits easy movement of the microphone down to the floor and up above the heads of the performers. The boom is usually mounted on a large boom dolly which is movable, has a platform for the operator and a device for raising the boom pivot position vertically from a height of 6½ feet to 9½ feet. A lighter-weight combined boom-and-tripod base, which is less flexible but which may be moved physically around and in and out of the set, is used in many smaller studios and for supplemental microphone pickups in larger studios.

The same types of microphones used in radio are available for off-camera musical accompaniment, announcing, and narration. In the early days of television, it was assumed that microphones must always be out of sight. With maturity and more critical attention to improvement of the audio portions, it became fashionable to show microphones in discussions or forums where a number of microphones were needed, on news programs and interviews, for MCs, and for occasional vocal selections. Smaller and less conspicuous microphones have found favor with producers. Some of those frequently selected are the RCA BK 1A and 6B pressure types, and the Electro-Voice 635A dynamic. The RCA BK 6B and the Electro-Voice 649B and Sony ECM-5 are used as lavaliere microphones. Microphones concealed in hollowed-out books, flower bouquets, false telephone bases, behind stage properties, or tucked away in costumes may also be used. Wireless microphones are also being developed for use in television.

CAMERAS

Those engaged in black-and-white programming used the image orthicon camera, but as color broadcasting increased, the "orth" has gradually disappeared from the broadcasting scene. The original television camera image tube was the iconoscope, which Dr. Zworykin invented in 1923. Until the end of the 1940s the iconoscope was the basic camera tube of television. Now the basic studio camera is a three-tube color instrument using lead-oxide tubes. These tubes are particularly well adapted to color broadcasting because they provide an accurate representation of color brightness and intensity.

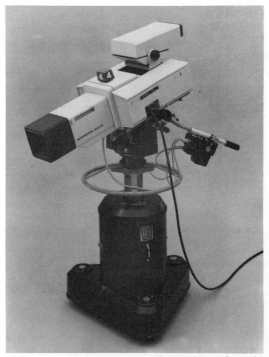

Ampex BCC-1 Studio
Camera on Pedestal.

Courtesy of Ampex Corporation

Another type of television camera tube, the vidicon, although not used in normal studio operation, is widely employed in industrial and military work and for closed-circuit laboratory instruction. A number of schools and colleges have turned to these smaller and less expensive versions of studio cameras for teaching television techniques. A few TV stations have used them in the studio or for "remotes." Special electronic synchronizing equipment is required for such broadcast use. One of the most important uses of the vidicon is in film projection.

Earlier cameras used a number of lenses of fixed focal length. The camera lens turret could be switched to various lens positions during the course of the program. Now cameras use zoom lenses that permit an infinite variety of focal lengths and image sizes.

Factors affecting mobility and flexibility of cameras in the studio are 1. smooth floor, usually asphalt tile floor covering over carefully leveled concrete; 2. camera pan and tilt mechanism that enables the operator to tilt the camera up and down and swing (pan) in a wide horizontal arc; and 3. camera support units with wheels, tripods, pedestals, and cranes.

In addition to cameras designed for studio operation, there are now small television cameras, usually called "minicams," designed for use outside studios. Weighing only 11 pounds, they can be carried easily into areas where news or special events are taking place. The picture and sound can either be sent back "live" by phone lines or microwave relay systems for immediate transmission or be recorded on portable equipment for future use. All three networks used minicams to cover the political conventions of 1976 and are gradually replacing film cameras with portable TV minicams for use in

Ampex BBC-2 Portable Camera (minicam) in Operation.

Courtesy of Ampex Corporation

news programming. Many local stations are making the same transition to electronic news gathering (ENG).

The tripod is rather difficult to maneuver smoothly, but it is inexpensive. Many stations have all or some of their cameras mounted on tripods. Camera height is fixed. Tripods are used most frequently on remotes. Special platforms, operated electrically, allow the tripods with cameras to move along the sidelines with the action to permit ground-level pickups of football games. Another type of camera mount is the pedestal. Called the "workhorse of the studio," it was especially designed for television work. Like the tripod, it may be handled by only one person. The camera, however, can be steered easily in any direction while on the air through the synchronous alignment of all wheels. It may be raised and lowered between 37 to 60 inches above the floor by a hand crank (earlier model) or by pressure on the steering ring. Networks and larger stations also use crane dollies, which were adapted from the movie prototypes. The one most frequently encountered has a small camera boom or "tongue" extending out from a turntable on the base of the dolly and which may be swung in a complete circle. The camera operator may ride the boom or pull the tongue to the side and stand on the platform or studio floor. The services of a dolly pusher who wheels the unit in the desired direction are required. The crane ranges in height from 23 to 74 inches. Other more elaborate cranes are made. The largest one utilizes electric motors to move the unit and is large enough to let the camera operator be seated with a camera on a special platform extending out from the end of the crane. Two or three dolly assistants are needed to maneuver the "monster." Only the largest studios can accommodate this crane, but when ceiling height and floor space are ample, it is very flexible. Camera lens height ranges from 2 to 10 feet, and 360-degree rotation of the crane boom is possible.

CONTROL ROOM

The control room is often referred to as the nerve center in television program production. The persons gathered here are responsible for unifying the many separate elements into a smoothly blended program.

The selection of the particular camera shots is determined by the director of the program. The director monitors each camera that is in use by looking at monitor screens, one of which is assigned to each camera. The director, therefore, is able to see what is to be telecast before the picture is sent out. Final "preview" adjustments in focusing and framing the picture and changes in the shading and quality may be made, together with any rechecking of the lens for the proper shot and shifting of angle of pickup. The major work, for such directorial duties, should have been accomplished during the camera rehearsal, with only refinements remaining to be made during the actual telecast. This does not apply, of course, when the director and technicians are ad libbing or "winging" the program, that is, doing a production without previous rehearsal, or in emergencies when one camera blanks out or develops "bugs" and goes out of commission, leaving one less camera available.

Courtesy of RCA Broadcast Systems

Combination Director-Switcher in a Small Station.

The director calls for the desired camera by using such expressions as "take one," "super slide over three," or "dissolve to two." The technical director (TD) manipulates the controls at the video switching console to accomplish the desired effect. Bright tally lights placed on studio cameras and on control-camera monitors indicate which camera is "hot." A final check of the program is possible by reference to another screen, the line monitor, on which appears the picture actually being telecast. A preview monitor may also be available for aid in setting up special effects before they go "on the air." Occasionally an "off-the-air" monitor also is available for inspection. The process of camera-shot selection is similar to motion picture editing in principle, but quite different in execution.

The camera controls, with viewing picture tubes and oscillograph tubes that reproduce the picture in signal-wave form, are operated by the video engineer; and the audio controls, consoles, and audio-tape recorders are handled by the audio engineer. An assistant or associate director (AD) may also be in the control room following the script closely, checking timings and giving warnings of upcoming shots and prearranged switches. The AD relieves the director of the need to look for every detail in the script.

Constant communication is necessary between the control room and the technicians in the studio as well as with film projection, video-tape room, announcer's booth, audio control, and master control room during the telecast. Such commands by the director or TD as "roll film," "roll tape," "stand by to zoom back when guest enters from right," "cue announcer," "flip

TV Station Control Room.

card," "show him camera three," "boom in the shot" must be made to appropriate technicians. Special wired telephone (PL) circuits with clamp-on headsets and mouthpieces or walkie-talkie radios are used to reach the studio floor, and various types of public address intercommunication or private telephone lines (PAX) are utilized for reaching film projection, video tape, announcer's booth, and master control. A talk-back speaker arrangement used in rehearsals for general studio directions has a cutoff switch to prevent use during the broadcast.

The control room may be situated so that it looks into the studio. In other instances, directors may work from a "blind control room" or from a remote van where they must depend entirely on what they see on the monitors. The size, location, and design of control rooms differ from station to station, with no generally accepted pattern. Many people favor the separation of audio from the rest of the personnel and equipment units, believing that the engineer then may maintain a more critical evaluation of the audio portion. Some stations that operate with small staffs eliminate the TD, permitting the director to do the switching, and consolidate the video and audio engineering positions. The use of master control as a studio control room allows for a minimum technical staff. Some stations have only audio, monitors, and switching facilities in the control room with the video controls in MCR. A two-level design with director, TD, and audio engineer on a raised level overlooking the video controls is perhaps the most common approach. However, if a separate bank of monitors for the director is not provided, they must be shifting position constantly and craning their necks to view the monitors. Much more space in the TV control room is required than for ra-

Control Room in Mobile Unit.

dio. It is obvious that far more primary operating personnel are required as well as a much greater amount of equipment. Additional program personnel such as script secretaries, lighting directors, costume and makeup supervisors, choreographer, graphics supervisor, together with writers, producers, agency representatives, and observers are frequently present.

PROJECTION AND VIDEO TAPE

The area where a majority of films, slides, and opaques start on their transmission path is referred to as the "telecine" or film projection room. The various equipment items found most generally in the telecine area are as follows:

16mm TV Film Projector

The 35mm width film has been standard for use in theaters for many years. Although the networks and a few stations have 35mm TV projectors, and the networks still require film series to be shot on 35mm film, the television industry has established the 16mm width as its standard. Many large film-production companies shoot with 35mm and reduce the width to 16mm for prints distributed to stations. Lower cost of equipment, raw stock, and processing, together with the existence and availability of many documentary,

RCA TK-28 Telecine Unit.

educational, and industrial films in the 16mm width, were important factors in establishing the 16mm standard.

Specialized film-projection equipment has been designed to improve the picture and sound quality for 16mm television transmission. Film that is to be projected has been exposed at 24 frames per second. This simply means that the camera shooting the scene has a mechanism that causes the film to pause 24 times a second as it goes past the lens for a series of individual exposures. A shutter keeps the light from the film during the move to the next frame. When the strip of 24 still pictures or frames per second is presented at home or in the theater, it is projected a frame at a time via a "pull down" mechanism. However, it has been noted earlier that television transmission in this country operates at 30 frames per second. This rate is due to the need to synchronize with the standard 60-cycle AC electrical power supply. Normal film projection at 24 frames—television transmission 30 frames! The conversion of 24 frames into the TV 30-frame system is accomplished by the special TV film projector, which scans each frame in multiples of 2 and 3 in sequence in order to arrive at the first common denominator of 24 and 30, 120. Thus the first film frame is scanned two times, the next frame three times, the next twice, etc.

TV Film Camera

At one time the camera most frequently used for the televising of film, slide, and opaque materials employed the iconoscope tube. This tube was large enough to permit focusing the picture from the lens of the projection machine directly onto the positive surface (mosaic) of the camera tube. The iconoscope tube was replaced by the vidicon tube for projection purposes, and the smallness of the vidicon tube, with its ½ x ⅜-inch face as compared with the iconoscope's 3 x 4-inch face, makes it difficult to focus from the projection machine directly onto the face of the tube. Instead the picture from the projection machine is focused on an intermediate field lens from one side and the vidicon is focused on this lens from the other side. The vidicon tube, unlike the iconoscope, can be used for color transmissions. The camera transmits color by using three vidicon tubes, one for each of the primary colors. Other advantages of the vidicon tube are its excellence of half-tone reproduction and freedom from the necessity of constant shading by a technician.

In closed-circuit installations where broadcast quality is not required, the regular studio camera may be used as a film camera. A special film projector is placed in the studio. The film is projected through a boxed enclosure (a shadow box) on a small translucent screen. The TV camera picks up the picture from this screen and transmits it.

Slide Projector

Many slides are used in the day's operation. A varied assortment of models are available for purchase by stations from the inexpensive 2 x 2-inch projector as used in classrooms to elaborate automatic devices permitting remote operation, dissolves from slide to slide, and accommodations for 3¼ x 4-inch lantern slides as well.

Opaque Projector

The equipment is often referred to as the "telop" or "balop." Small opaque cards containing lettering, art work, or credit "crawls" are projected on the air from the telop instead of using the live studio cameras. Stations also employ the telop to show the face of an actual clock in operation during time-signal commercials, as well as to project Polaroid news pictures, book illustrations, map sections, news ticker-tape, and small objects. Stations may construct homemade opaque projectors or order models specially designed for TV work. The use of mirrors permits horizontal placements of cards and objects in the telop.

Video-Tape Recorders And Playback Machines

A machine that has assumed a position of paramount importance in television is the video-tape recorder (VTR). Prior to its introduction in 1956, the only means of recording television programs was through the use of what was called a kinescope process, which involved the use of a film camera to

RCA Two-Inch Video-Tape Recorder and Video-Tape Cartridge Recorder.

capture the program as it appeared on the receiving tube. The resulting film projected a picture of poor resolution. When the video-tape process came into being, it provided programming indistinguishable in picture quality from live programming and quickly displaced the kinescope process. The kinescope is used now only for special purposes.

In addition to its high picture quality, the video-tape has other advantages over the kinescope. Because the making of a video-tape recording of a television program is entirely an electronic process, the intermediate step of film processing that is necessary in the production of a kinescope is not required. This means that the video-tape recording can be played back as soon as it is made. Moreover, a video tape can be used, erased, and used again a number of times. It can also be edited easily using an electronic system.

Adaptations of the video-tape recorder have been developed for special uses. One is the video disc, which keeps a constant recording of the last several seconds of a sports event. If a goal is shot in hockey, a home run is hit in baseball, or a touchdown is scored in football, the disc can instantly replay that section of the event. It can also slow down the action or freeze it into a still picture.

One video-tape machine can both record and play back commercial and program material, but stations have more than one machine so that recording and playing back can go on simultaneously. In some stations the

Ampex Video-Tape Cassette—Closed.

Courtesy of Ampex Corporation

video-tape machines may be installed in the same room with projection equipment, or they may be in a separate space.

The video-tape recorder contributes greatly to the flexibility of station operation. Programs and commercials can be video-taped when studios and personnel are most conveniently available and then presented at the scheduled air time from the recording. Network programs that come at the same time as a local program can be recorded and presented later in the same way. Many syndicated programs are now supplied to stations on video tape.

A useful development is the production of TV material packaged in containers called either cartridges or cassettes. In the operation of TV stations, an automated computerized cassette or cartridge system is used to eliminate human errors in split-second timing during groupings of announcements at station-break times. Cassettes can also provide short segments of program material for TV stations. Because of their convenience, video-tape cassettes are commonly used to preview programs.

Film programs are often recorded on video tape by networks for color correction and ease of editing. Two playback machines are used for actual air presentations, the reserve machine being used as a backup in the event of trouble with the primary video-tape playback equipment. Local stations may but usually do not transfer film to tape for air presentation except when news film segments are transferred to tapes.

Outside the broadcasting industry, the primary users of cassettes have been institutions such as hospitals, which use programs recorded on cassettes

Ampex Video-Tape Cas-
sette—Open.
Courtesy of Ampex Corporation

to entertain patients, and educational institutions and corporations, which use the cassettes for educational and training purposes.

At one time it was thought that video cassettes would be used as a direct source of home entertainment. This use has not materialized in a significant way, though cassette machines that permit householders to record TV programs for later viewing are now being marketed. Another development is the video disc system, which some people believe will become commonplace in homes in a few years. Such systems make use of a plastic disc similar in size to a long-playing phonograph record, but revolving much more rapidly. There are a number of different systems, each with its advantages and disadvantages, but all exhibit high picture quality and can easily be attached to home TV receivers.

MASTER CONTROL, TRANSMITTER AND ANTENNA

As in radio, the master control room is needed when more than one studio and announcing booth are used. MCR takes care of rerouting of the output from studios, tape, and film projection, amplifies the signals, and makes additional checks on the quality of the pictures. Occasionally the video controls, instead of being in the studio control room, are located in MCR. The transmitter and antenna perform the same function as in radio: transmission of the video and audio signals into the air. In an effort to obtain as much

TV Station Master Control Room.

height as possible, thus increasing the coverage area, transmitting towers ranging from 300 to 400 feet upward to 2000 feet have been constructed to support the antenna. In some instances several stations may share the same location or tower, each with its separate transmitter and antenna. Equipment for receiving microwave signals from remote pickups may be located on the tower.

COLOR TELEVISION

In 1953, compatible color television was authorized for commercial telecasting. Compatible color means that the color programs can be received in black and white on standard black-and-white television sets without special adapters or modifications. Figure 18–4 diagrams the transmission and reception of compatible color.

The cameras used in color television productions have not one but three pickup tubes, one for each primary color: red, green, and blue. They are larger than monochrome cameras. The light from the original scene reaching the camera lens is separated into the three primary colors with the aid of reflective mirrors or prisms and color filters and directed to the corresponding color-sensitive pickup tube. The action of scanning and amplification in each tube is similar to the process described earlier. The video signals from the tubes have separate electronic controls available on the corresponding camera control in the control room. Technicians adjust and regulate the

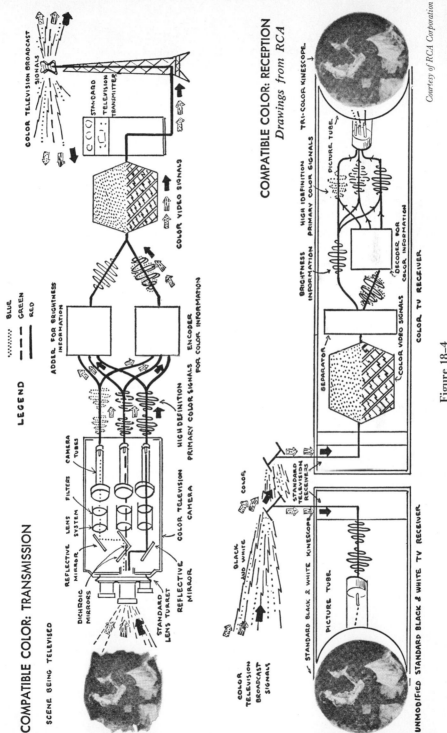

COMPATIBLE COLOR: TRANSMISSION

SCENE BEING TELEVISED

DICHROIC MIRRORS

REFLECTIVE MIRROR

LENS SYSTEM

FILTERS

CAMERA TUBES

STANDARD LENS TURRET

REFLECTIVE MIRROR

COLOR TELEVISION CAMERA

HIGH DEFINITION PRIMARY COLOR SIGNALS

ENCODER FOR COLOR INFORMATION

ADDER FOR BRIGHTNESS INFORMATION

LEGEND

BLUE
GREEN
RED

COLOR VIDEO SIGNALS

STANDARD TELEVISION TRANSMITTER

COLOR TELEVISION BROADCAST SIGNALS

COLOR TELEVISION BROADCAST SIGNALS

COLOR

BLACK AND WHITE

STANDARD TELEVISION RECEIVERS

COMPATIBLE COLOR: RECEPTION

Drawings from RCA

BRIGHTNESS INFORMATION

HIGH DEFINITION PRIMARY COLOR SIGNALS

TRI-COLOR KINESCOPE

PICTURE TUBE

DECODER FOR COLOR INFORMATION

SEPARATOR

COLOR VIDEO SIGNALS

COLOR TV RECEIVER

STANDARD BLACK & WHITE KINESCOPE

PICTURE TUBE

UNMODIFIED STANDARD BLACK & WHITE TV RECEIVER

Courtesy of RCA Corporation

Figure 18-4

separate signals before they are merged by the encoder (colorplexer) into a composite color signal for actual transmission over the air and reception on home receivers in color or in black and white.

Virtually all network programs have been broadcast in color since 1967. Local stations not only carry network color but also have color cameras, color tape, and color telecine equipment.

Projects and Exercises

1. Visit a television station for a behind-the-scenes tour.
2. Clip and post on a bulletin board television-programming pictures from magazines and newspapers. Compare studio, microphones, camera types and placement, and control-room design.
3. Arrange for committees or class-viewing periods at television studios for reports to the class. Discuss and comment on camera shots, editing techniques employed, and use of slides, telop cards, and film.

elements of
television production

19

As a visual medium, television calls on a whole range of theatrical services that are wholly foreign to radio. Program production in television can be a complex operation, as in a major network musical Special, involving as many as 400 people for one program, or a relatively simple operation, as in a local station's interview program involving perhaps 5 to 8 people. Whether the program is large or small, however, certain basic functions are essential to television production. This chapter explains these functions in an introductory way, so that the specific production problems discussed in later chapters will be understood more clearly.

"ABOVE-THE-LINE" ELEMENTS

There has developed in television a convenient division of program production services into "above-the-line" and "below-the-line" elements. This division, suggestive of a bookkeeping arrangement, serves to distinguish production elements for budgetary and cost purposes and for matters of artistic control. Above-the-line elements refer primarily to writing, performing, and producing talents, usually including the following:

Star performers
Supporting cast, including actors, singers, dancers, and speciality acts
Executive producer
Producer
Associate producer
Production assistants
Script handler
Director
Writers
Script editor
Choreographer
Choral director

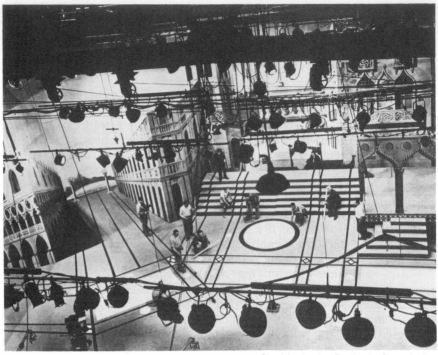

Staging a TV Show.

services. Among the main elements included in staging services are the following:

1. Set design. The services of a scenic designer are required to design the physical layout of the show, just as in the legitimate theater and in motion picture production. The scenic designer is a creative artist who works closely with the writer, director, and producer. In addition to conceiving the settings for the production and preparing floor plans and elevations to indicate how the sets should be installed, the designer also supervises all activities involved in preparing the sets and orders the furniture, draperies, and set dressings required for the show.

2. Construction of scenery. On the basis of the instructions received from the scenic designer, carpenters construct scenery. Whenever possible, scenery already in stock is adapted to the designer's orders. As in theatrical production, "flats" or "wings" are the basic elements of most sets. Flats are sectional framed units, covered with muslin or canvas duck, with a standard width of five feet, nine inches. For dramatic, comedy, and musical shows, sets are usually quite elaborate and considerable special construction is involved.

3. Painting of scenery. Scenic painting is used to suggest perspective and to simulate natural or man-made textures as part of a decorative or definitive background. The work of the scenic painter ranges from flat "lay-in," a priming coat of paint which dries without any special texture, to various devices such as stippling, glazing, and stencilling.

4. Draperies, drops, and cycloramas. For staging purposes, scenic designers also make extensive use of draperies, drops, and cycloramas. Draperies may be used to decorate a set or, in the form of a painted drop, may serve as the background for a scene. "Scrims," drops made from gauze, are useful because, with properly adjusted lighting, they can be made transparent or opaque. Studio cycloramas are curved drops suspended from pipes or a curved track. They can be used to suggest the sky or simply as a neutral background, depending upon their color and the way they are lighted.

5. Properties and set dressings. Whether the set is a simple kitchen with decorative trivets on the wall or an elaborate imaginative setting for a music program, furniture and set dressings of some sort are required. Even a simple television discussion program requires a table and several chairs. Most properties and set dressings are rented from commercial warehouses or are taken from stock at the station or network. Hand props, such as special-type telephones, firearms, dummy packages or letters, and innumerable other small items required by the script are rented, purchased, borrowed, or constructed in the prop shop. Large network shows often have a unit property person to obtain the necessary props for each week's show.

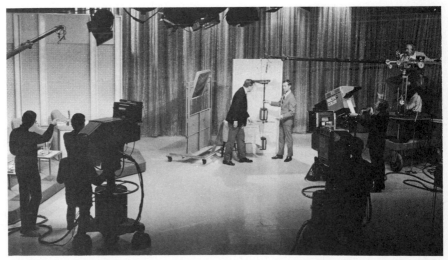

Courtesy of National Broadcasting Company, Inc.

Video-Taping in a Studio. Studio scene: The *Tonight* show with Johnny Carson and Ed McMahon. Note the desk and sofa at the left and the prompting devices on the cameras in the foreground.

6. Trucking. Sets, draperies, furniture, set dressings, and properties often represent considerable bulk volume that must be transported from warehouses and scenic construction shops to the studio and then returned for final disposition. Because of the heavy trucking expenses involved in these movements, production companies and stations prefer whenever possible to have their construction shops in the same buildings that house their studios.

7. Stagehand labor. Of key importance in any television show are the stagehands in the studio. Three groups of craftsmen comprise stagehand labor: carpenters, property people, and electricians. The carpenters and property people set up the show under the direction of the scenic designer; the electricians arrange the lighting for the show according to the instructions of the lighting direction engineer. While the show is on the air, the property people hand the props to performers off camera as instructed by the stage manager.

8. Graphic arts. Graphic artists are employed to prepare special art work or lettering required for a show. On most shows this includes, at the minimum, the art work for the title of the show and for the closing credits. This may appear on special "flip" or art cards usually 11 x 14 inches in size, on 2 x 2-inch glass slides, on long vertical or horizontal "pan" cards, and on "crawls," long vertical sheets of black paper. The flip cards are placed on flip stands (easels with loose-leaf type binders at the top) and the art cards are placed on easels. In both instances two flip stands and two easels are usually used so that with two cameras it becomes possible to cut or fade directly from one card to the next. Slides are handled by slide projectors in a projection room. If a show has obtained projection facilities for another purpose, using slides instead of flip cards frees the studio cameras from having to cover the opening titles and the closing credits. With pan cards, the studio camera simply pans horizontally or vertically to reveal the credits. A crawl is fastened to a drum and is slowly revolved, either manually or electrically, in front of a studio camera. Stagehands operate the crawl and handle flip cards.

Graphic artists are also used to prepare special visual materials, such as identifying slides that can be used to establish a locale (e.g., a doctor's nameplate set against a representation of brickwork sets the scene for a doctor's office), nameplates that can be used to identify members of a panel, and visuals such as maps, sketches of persons or scenes for rear projection or electronic insertion on news programs.

9. Costume design. Big dramatic and variety shows usually require the services of an expert costume designer to design special gowns and period costumes for star performers. Most shows, however, cannot afford special costume design and manage instead with a fashion consultant who arranges to borrow gowns without charge from leading retail outlets in return for a credit on the show.

10. Wardrobe handlers. To help performers in and out of costumes male and female wardrobe handlers are employed. The handlers also are responsible for packing and unpacking costumes used by the show. On nondramatic shows and on dramatic shows not requiring period costumes, actors wear their own clothing whenever the clothing is appropriate to the part; in those instances wardrobe handlers are unnecessary.

11. Makeup development. Special makeup is occasionally required on dramatic shows, such as the makeup used to portray Cicely Tyson changing from youth to old age in "The Autobiography of Miss Jane Pitman." When elaborate makeup creations are involved, as in that program, a makeup development artist is needed.

12. Makeup artists and hair stylists. More common than the preparation of special makeup is the application to performers of standard and character makeup. This is handled by makeup artists. Hair stylists are employed when unusual hairdos are involved.

13. Assistant directors and stage managers. During rehearsal the assistant director works closely with the director of a show, assumes responsibility for timing the show, lays out positions for actors on the rehearsal floor, and performs similar related duties. While the show is on the air, the assistant director sits next to the director, notes cues coming up, checks the timing of the show, and stands ready to take over direction should the director be suddenly indisposed. The stage manager, on the studio floor, receives direct communications from the director over a special battery-operated shortwave radio receiver or over wired telephone circuits (PL). The stage manager cues the performers and directs the stagehands.

14. Sound effects. Television production requires sound effects in the same way that radio production does. As needed, a sound-effects technician with a sound-effects truck works in an out-of-the-way spot in the studio, with a special on-the-air monitor to show the action that must be supported with sound.

15. Prompting devices. On most programs prompting devices are used. These may be no more than "cue cards," large white cardboard cards on which the script is printed in large letters. Another device is the electrically operated "TelePrompter" system described earlier. TelePrompters are mounted on each camera and are remotely controlled by a special operator. The script, which appears in large type on TelePrompter, is advanced according to the rate at which the performer reads the lines.

16. Special effects and devices. Special effects refer to such matters as producing rain, snow, and fog, or simulating a burning fire in a fireplace. There are other devices, such as the "H-R Cellomatic," which produces effects of semi-animation through the use of transparencies. Real-projection (RP) is another device commonly used in television production. With slides or moving pictures projected on the rear of a latex or lucite screen, it becomes possible to establish a locale or to suggest motion without constructing expensive sets or actually moving on stage. Most scenes set in a moving automobile are actually shot in a stationary car with an RP screen, seen through the rear window, showing traffic in action. With appropriate sound and lighting effects, the impression conveyed to the audience is that of a moving automobile.

All of the below-the-line services described here do not, of course, figure in every television production. Simple television shows require a minimum of production elements; large musical shows require a vast number of services. Most of the below-the-line personnel are union craftsmen: the stagehands, makeup artists, and wardrobe handlers are members of the International Association of Theatrical and Stage Employees (IATSE); engineers are usually members of NABET, IBEW, or IATSE. A strict union shop applies to television production in New York, Hollywood, Chicago, and other important television centers.

Projects and Exercises

1. Observe closely a television panel quiz program and a television musical variety program. Compare the production elements utilized in each, in terms of facilities and personnel.
2. Watch a daytime soap opera, which is produced in a television studio, and a drama produced on film and compare the two in terms of production values and the production techniques that you observe.
3. Observe in a succession of television programs the various ways in which closing credits are handled. Which ways seem most effective?

20

Announcers play many parts. To many people they are the station's spokesmen. Behind the scenes at the studio they have other duties and responsibilities. They are, of course, performers, doing straight announcing, presenting commercials and demonstrating products, newscasting, acting as MC or as foil to a comic, handling sports, interviews, discussions, quizzes, and narration. In addition, in evening hours they may be the studio manager; they are frequently writers, preparing their own material except for commercials; and they may put to effective use supplemental skills such as cartooning or puppet manipulation. The announcers in radio stations are often in charge of program production and, in conjunction with announcing assignments, often act as technicians, handling the controls, placing microphones, joining and breaking away from the network, producing material for automated systems, and playing records, tapes, and transcriptions. Announcers in small local television stations may also assist the director by serving as stage manager, operating a camera, or handling the boom microphone when they are not actively performing on the air. In this chapter, however, we shall concentrate primarily on the announcer as a performer. In this area there is much in common between the work of the announcer in radio and the announcer in television.

The station announcer may join the staff through a "front or side entrance." The procedure at most stations is to audition prospective announcers with varied copy of music continuity, commercial announcements, news, descriptive material, and extemporaneous or ad-lib assignments. Versatility, salesmanship, ability to respond quickly, and basic vocal equipment are judged in this way. Aptitude for on-camera effectiveness may be evaluated in the initial interview or by observation during the microphone audition. Tryouts before the cameras are usually reserved for those applicants who have satisfied all other requirements.

A "side entrance" may be used when a member of a station staff regularly employed as a salesperson, engineer, clerk, elevator operator, or writer, to mention but a few, becomes interested in performance and demonstrates an aptitude for announcing. An occasional brief appearance on commercials or variety programs may lead to regular assignments. Persons originally hired for positions involving techniques akin to announcing, such as acting or singing, may also enter announcing through a side entrance. These people may decide to change their professional capacity because of new interests or recognition by program officials of their particular talents.

AN ANNOUNCER'S KIT OF WORKING TOOLS

Voice

The basic equipment needed by an announcer is a good voice. A clear, resonant, and relaxed speaking voice is desirable. A low pitch range, the lack of which automatically excluded many candidates from consideration as announcers, is no longer the chief consideration. The intimacy of the broadcasting medium does favor relatively low, rather than high, pitches in the overall range of an announcer's voice, but clarity and resonance are more important than pitch alone. Unpleasant qualities such as hollowness, harshness, or marked nasality limit opportunities for announcing work. Training and exercise may enable one to increase vocal range and gradually lower average pitch. If extensive work is required for these changes, it should be supervised by a competent voice teacher.

Courtesy of the WWJ Stations

Control Board and Studio on an All News and Information Radio Station.

Attitude

The keynote of an announcer's personal attitude should be confidence. Announcers must be poised and confident on the air. Audiences quickly detect nervousness or uncertainty. When attention is focused on the way one speaks instead of on what one is saying, effective communication ceases. Leadership in the announcer-listener relationship must be assumed by the announcer, who must be a dominant, not a retiring, personality. Everything about the delivery must give the listener or viewer the feeling that the announcer is confident of the product's ability to live up to the claims for it, and of the talent's ability to be as good as the announcer claims. Broadcasting has no place for the timid, "Why am *I* here today?" announcing approach. What the announcer does and says from "The following was recorded earlier for broadcast at this time," to "Shop at Blanks and Save!" must be spoken with assurance and dominance. *A note of caution:* When this confident and self-assured manner becomes exaggerated and merges into a bullying, shouting, and superior style, with an undercurrent thread of "See how good I am" running through it, then one has become afflicted with "announceritis," a swelled head. Controlled confidence is the desired goal.

Style

This may be referred to as the announcer's "air personality." One announcer may have sincere warmth and vitality and seem like an interested friend; another may capitalize on a homey approach, talking as one neighbor to another over the back fence; another may rely on a quiet authoritative assurance, apparently unruffled by anything or anybody; another has worked out a bouncy, breezy manner. Other approaches are those of the soft, professional sympathizer; the circus barker or pitchman; the staccato, human machine gun; and the naive "It's-simply-wonderful" style. This list could be extended and modified, but it illustrates the impressions listeners receive. Each announcer has to determine the particular style best suited to him or her. An added responsibility of a station-staff announcer is to develop a multiplicity of styles or approaches according to the various programs handled. It is in flexibility and adaptability that many young announcers fail. To be familiar and jocular on a popular music show, then serious and sincere on a hymn period, then informal and kidding in an audience-participation period, and then dignified and authoritative on a classical music program requires skill and concentration. Conversely, the demand for general adaptability, a program "chameleon," may be dangerous to an announcer concerned with a long-term professional outlook. The better paid network and free-lance positions call for specialists with distinctive "air" personalities. If individuality, or show-business "color," is lacking, audiences may accept the message without remembering the person. *Again a note of caution:* The style should not become so important that communication suffers.

Understanding

It is possible for announcers to present their material without actually understanding its meaning. If they do deliver a script as a mechanical mouthpiece, they may get by in less critical situations. Announcers should, however, strive to understand the significance of the material they are reading. They should not become absorbed with the mechanics of the vocal process, listening to their own voice and speaking with a pride in how they are saying it, but should "think the thought" instead.

Pronunciation

There are many discussions on "correct" pronunciation among network personalities and in stations throughout the country. So much attention is given the subject because these people know they are considered authorities by listeners. Broadcasting is effective, along with the movies, in furthering a trend toward standardization of American pronunciation. Even station personnel in regional areas tend to follow the lead of their contemporaries on the networks, and to eliminate their regional speech habits. The type of pronunciation labeled "General American" appears to be the standard radio and television speech, with individual differences according to the regional background of announcers. It is an accepted custom among many announcers to check the latest complete dictionary recommendations, keeping in mind that the dictionaries record the prevailing usage deemed best by social standards; to compare these recommendations with actual pronunciations by personalities in the public eye who might be considered "authorities"; and to double-check by their own reactions the appropriateness of the pronunciation for them as individuals, and for the program.

Foreign place names and proper names create special problems. The press services and the networks compile word lists as the names appear in the news. The general practice is toward Anglicizing foreign names. Two reference volumes, other than recognized dictionaries, that are of special value are *NBC Handbook of Pronunciation* and CBS's *World Words*. These volumes are consulted by many announcers.

Which of several pronunciations is "right" cannot always be decided with finality. The pronunciation "preferred" by the reference works, by public figures, and by co-workers should guide an announcer. When you choose a pronunciation, use it with assurance and confidence. *Caution:* Overly precise, pedantic pronunciation will cause the audience to react negatively to the announcer and to the message.

Articulation

Articulation is concerned with the utterance of vowels, consonants, and diphthongs. Good articulation aids in effective communication. Articulation must be distinct and pleasing without calling attention to itself. Consider again the position of the listener or viewer in relation to the person on mike. The microphone is only a few inches away from the speaker. The person at home is really just as close to the speaker, owing to the electrical increase in speaker volume. Very few people, except relatives and intimate friends, ever get as close to a person as a microphone does. The microphone reveals much about speech and personality that is hidden by distance. As a microscope brings out minute flaws and rough spots in material that to the eye is apparently flawless, the microphone highlights what might be disregarded in other situations. The amplifying system serves to bring the voice to us in magnified detail for "microscopic" *sound* examination. Listeners do not expect a high degree of careful articulation from the casual performer, but they are quick to detect slovenliness and indistinctness in indifferent or untrained announcers.

Good articulation demands: 1. an ample supply of air, 2. a relaxed throat, 3. the use of head, throat, and chest resonators in correct proportion, and 4. the strong and agile movement of lips, tongue, and jaw. You may be familiar with the announcer who uses *dubya* for *double u* or *git* for *get, probly* for *probably, godder* for *got to, kuz* for *because, jest* for *just, gonna* for *going to, l'll* for *little,* and *in'* in *ing* endings. You may be familiar too with the over-articulation of "stage-trained" or "platform-minded" announcers who carry over speech habits from their activities in fields where it is necessary to project to the rear of a theater without electrical amplification.

Both sloppy and exaggerated articulation adversely affect judgments of an announcer's personality. When one is as frequent a caller in the home as is an announcer, minor faults of articulation may grow into major irritations.

The following appears frequently in announcer's audition copy. Try it as a challenge:

> SHE: (TO PLUMBER) Are you copper plating those pipes?
> HE: No Mum! I'm aluminuming 'em, Mum!

Or, for a change of pace, five standbys:

> 1. "Is this the sixth sister's zither?"
> 2. The seething sea ceaseth, and it sufficeth us.
> 3. He thrusts his fists against the posts and still insists he sees the ghosts.
> 4. The green glow grew, a glowing gleam, growing greener.
> 5. Geese cackle, cattle low, crows caw, cocks crow.

And an announcement which completely threw an announcer when he read it at sight:

Rome wasn't built in a day . . . and you can't serve a good cocktail or good punch in a minute . . . that is, not unless you serve Piccadilly Cocktail or Piccadilly Punch, the bottled cocktail and punch that the famous house of Old Nobility has made available to smart hosts everywhere. Old Nobility Piccadilly Cocktail and Old Nobility Piccadilly Punch come bottled . . . ready-prepared for you to chill and serve in a jiffy. Your neighborhood dealer has Old Nobility Piccadilly Cocktail and Old Nobility Piccadilly Punch at only $1.45 a large bottle.

Emphasis

The announcer uses emphasis to point out for the audience the important and unimportant ideas in the spoken material. A platform speaker, of course, uses gestures to give emphasis and clarity to ideas, but radio listeners cannot see an index finger pointed at them on the sentence, *"This* is important news for *you,"* or *"Shop* at *Blanks* . . . and *save!"* accompanied by a nod of the head and a smile of satisfaction on *save!* Television, of course, permits the viewer to see the gestures. However, a radio announcer may profit by using gestures, even though they are not part of the audible code. Speaking with gestures is very common in good conversation; incipient radio announcers who avoid gestures break their conversational speaking patterns and risk a dull and lifeless presentation of their material.

One method of emphasis is vocally to underscore key words:

Your tea is easier to **make,** more delightful to **taste,** more **flavorful** and **satisfying.**

Another method is to separate key words or phrases with appropriate pauses:

The orchestra plays a favorite of yesterday . . . **Lady Be Good.**
Remember the address . . . **Main and Second.**

Climactic emphasis may be achieved by increasing or decreasing force.

It's priced to save you money. **Don't delay—buy today!**
It's **mild** . . . mild . . . mild.

A note of caution to the announcer: An emphatic and enthusiastic treatment is acceptable if it is in keeping with the product and the program, but if the announcer resorts to "shouting" or "barking" for emphasis, the audience may be "turned off".

Word Color

Word color is closely related to emphasis. Emphasis is concerned primarily with volume, and word color with quality of tone and emotional undercurrents. Not only the generally accepted denotations, but associated impressions, attitudes, and mood are communicated.

Consider the narrative setting for Hawthorne's "Ethan Brand": "Within the furnace were to be seen the curling and riotous flames, and the burning marble, almost molten with the intensity of the heat . . . while outside, the reflection of the fire quivered on the darkness of the surrounding forest." This selection requires care and skill in setting a mood through word color.

In musical continuity, word color is the announcer's stock in trade:

Hold on to your hats, here's Jimmy Lunceford's treatment of "Runnin' Wild."

An Irish medley . . . first a lively jig . . . "The Irish Washerwoman" . . . then, the tenderly nostalgic "Danny Boy" . . . and finally "Come Back to Erin."

Majestic, resplendent with regal beauty and appeal, the orchestra's interpretation of "Pomp and Circumstance."

Music Sweet . . . Music Hot . . . the Rhythm Parade!

In announcing commercials, consider the implicit meanings brought out in word color by:

The **lowest-priced** . . . The car of the year . . . Blank pipe tobacco: smokes **sweet** and **fragrant** . . . It's **smart** to wear a Blank suit.

Rate

Two factors are involved in rate. One is the overall pace, the line rate or number of words per minute; the second is the speed with which individual words are spoken. Announcing requires variety in pacing. Mood and pace are closely related. Consider the following:

Jones leads with a right to the jaw. Brown brushes it off before it reaches him
. . . Jones gives him a left hook . . . there's another left hook . . . and now Jones
is following Brown . . . a short jab by Jones a right to the jaw . . . Brown blocked
it . . . There's a clinch . . . they're apart . . . Now Jones gives a left to the stomach
. . . another left . . . a straight right lead—and a powerful . . . but powerful left
hook.

With variations in pacing, an impression can be given of a slow, extremely
tense, or a fast bout.

The choice of pace can influence the degree of comprehension. Consider this narrative description of ways of detecting counterfeit money:

NARR 1:   The best way to recognize illegal money is to know what genuine
          bills look like. Open your purse—that's right—now take out a dollar
          bill. Go ahead—there—hold up the side with Washington's portrait
          . . . now look at the numerals in the upper corners.
WOMAN: Why they're set against a pattern of fine lines—it's almost like a lace
          doily. And—the lines are traced along the entire border.
NARR 1:   The tracing is much more complicated than most of us realize from a
          quick glance. Made by a skilled craftsman using a geometric lathe.
NARR 2:   This type of geometric lathe is a special engraving machine capable
          of cutting precise lines into a steel die—the designs it makes are so
          involved they can never be reproduced. These machines were
          developed solely to defeat counterfeiters.
NARR 1:   Now look at the portrait of Washington. This part was done by hand.
          Those fine lines—even the ones around the eyes and mouth—were
          cut into hard steel by the skilled hand of an expert engraver. A
          counterfeiter cannot produce work of such high quality. If he could
          he would demand a legitimate job at very high pay.
NARR 2:   Actually there are only about twenty-five men in the world who
          could be called competent in this work. These engravers must have
          the delicate touch of an artist and the sense of precision of an
          engineer.
NARR 1:   If you ever see a bill where the portrait is dark—or the eyes dull—or
          the hair lines blurred—that bill is a counterfeit.[1]

If this selection is read at a fast clip, it will communicate nothing. The
auditors must feel close to the narrator, as though they were right at his or
her shoulder examining the same bill in the same intimate manner they
might learn from a golf professional how to grip a club. Knowing when to
slow down, how to capitalize upon contrast in rhythm and how to use pauses
are refinements and subtleties that give announcing professional flavor.

[1] Courtesy of the author, Rollin Quimby, and University of Michigan Department of
Speech.

EXAMPLES OF TELEVISION NARRATION

"Those Thrilling Days of Yesteryear"[2]

The following passage is the opening narration from a television program about the *Lone Ranger* series. The tone of the writing is conversational and nostalgic: in reading it, the narrator should attempt to communicate his or her own appreciation of the golden days of radio with the aim of stimulating a similar response among those viewers who remember the series to which the narrator refers.

NARRATOR: (IN SET WITH OLD RADIOS OF DIFFERENT TYPES—CRYSTALS, CONSOLES, TABLE MODELS, CAR RADIOS)

   Radio drama is more than a part of the past. It began and developed into a true art form in America, crossing three decades. It affected every facet of our lives. It helped us laugh our way through the worst depression in history; and became our chief source of entertainment. It helped the housewife forget her problems for a while and escape into the world of soap operas; through radio we all were able to travel around the world with Jack, Doc, and Reggie in **I Love a Mystery;** we could swing through the jungle with Tarzan; cloud men's minds so they could not see us with The Shadow; and of course we rode the plains with the Masked Man and his faithful Indian companion, Tonto. We, as the listeners, took part in developing those dramas. We saw the handsome hero, the pretty heroines, and the vicious villains. We saw the old west, the steaming jungle, or bustling city. We saw it all on our own bigger than life, full color screen of imagination. Regardless of whether we listened on a crystal headset, a table model, car radio, or a beautiful console, the only boundaries came from the ability to let our imagination soar.

"Vincent Van Gogh: A Self Portrait"[3]

The narrative passages in this special program were prepared to be voiced over pictures and films and over paintings produced by Van Gogh and other artists. This material, written in a poetic style, calls for the utmost in professional skill for effective presentation. The program, written and produced by Lou Hazam, won Peabody and "Emmy" awards. It was produced under the auspices of NBC News.

[2] Courtesy of Jack R. Stanley and the University of Michigan Television Center.

[3] Courtesy of Lou Hazam and NBC. The letters quoted first appeared in *The Complete Letters of Vincent Van Gogh* (Greenwich, Connecticut, 1958), 3 volumes; and subsequently appeared in *Van Gogh: A Self-portrait, Letters Revealing His Life as a Painter,* selected by W. H. Auden (Greenwich, Connecticut, 1961).

AUDIO	VIDEO
NARRATOR:	
This is he,	DISSOLVE TO (PHOTO)
Vincent Van Gogh—	VINCENT
Eighteen now,	
But soon—at twenty-three—	START ZOOM INTO EYES
Desperate to be a preacher.	
He does not know it	
(He cannot know it)	
But upon reaching that decision,	
He will have left	
Only fifteen years of life	
Wherein to shape a totally	
different career.	
His story best begins	DISSOLVE TO (PHOTO)
When—	YOUNGER VINCENT
As a boy—	
He wandered the moors of his	
father's parish	
In Zundert, a little village in the	
south of Holland . . .	
MUSIC: ZUNDERT VARIATION UNDER	DISSOLVE TO L. S. FIELDS,
	CHURCH IN BACKGROUND
VAN GOGH:	
"Zundert, I can see again the	
radiant blue sky with the white	
clouds in it . . . Every path . . . The	PATH THROUGH FIELD
views of the fields outside . . . The	BROOK AND FIELD
church . . . The graveyard."	CHURCH TOWER—PAN DOWN
MUSIC: FADE OUT UNDER	TO GRAVE
NARRATOR:	
Yes, especially the graveyard.	WALKING SHOT TO GRAVE
For when as a child,	
He passed these monuments	
On his way to church,	
He looked down upon this grave	
Bearing his own name—	CU GRAVE
SOUND: BELLS UP LOUD AND FULL	
(NARRATOR—CONT.)	
The grave of his elder brother,	CU GRAVE—PULL BACK
Still-born	
A year before himself,	
The same day of the same month—	MONTAGE GRAVE AND
March thirtieth	CHURCH BELL
SOUND: BELLS DOWN UNDER	
(NARRATOR—CONT)	
And because of his parents' grief	HOLD ON GRAVE
The living Vincent—	
All during his early years—	
Lived in the shadow of	SLOW PAN CU NAME ON
The dead Vincent	STONE
Beneath this tombstone.	

MUSIC: BELLS, AND OUT

MUSIC: ENGLAND THEME, IN AND DOWN	DISSOLVE TO ESTABLISHING SHOTS OF ENGLAND

(NARRATOR—CONT)
It was here in England,
As a young man
In pursuit of the love of God,
That—Vincent
At Isleworth, up the Thames,   PAN DOWN TOWER OF
Took his place in this church,   CHURCH
And—
As he ecstatically wrote his   PAN ESTABLISHING SHOT
    brother Theo . . .   ISLEWORTH

MUSIC: ORGAN, REVERENTLY, IN
           AND UNDER FAINTLY

VAN GOGH:
"Theo, your brother preached for
the first time last Sunday!"

VAN GOGH (ECHO):   INTERIOR CHURCH FROM
"Let us not forget that we are   PULPIT
strangers on earth, but we have a
God and father who preserveth
strangers, and that we are all
brothers. Amen".
    "When I was standing in the   PULPIT
pulpit, Theo, I felt like somebody   ZOOM INTO STAINED GLASS
who, emerging from a dark cave
underground, comes back to the
friendly daylight."

    MUSIC: ORGAN, UP AND OUT FULL.
           ORCHESTRA, IN WITH
           PROGRESS THEME AND
           UNDER

NARRATOR: DISSOLVE TO ROAD TO
In December of 1878,   BORINAGE
After a three-month course
At a school for evangelists,
    in Belgium,
Vincent set out along this road
To the coal mining district of the
    Borinage,
On probation as a lay minister.
From this point on,   DISSOLVE TO CU LETTER
Vincent's letters—
Among the most remarkable in
    literary history—
His letters to the one person on
    earth
To whom he felt close,
His younger brother Theo—   DISSOLVE (PHOTO) THEO
Who was commencing a career as an
    art dealer in Paris—

These letters
Are Vincent's only bridge with life
As normal men knew it.

    MUSIC: SEGUE MINING PASSAGE
        UNDER

DISSOLVE AND
ZOOM INTO LETTER

VAN GOGH:
    "Dear Theo—here in the
Borinage, Life goes on underground
instead of above. One might live
here for years and never know the
real state of things unless one
went down into the mines."

DISSOLVE TO MINE TOWER

ELEVATOR RISES
FACES

    "I should like to make rough
sketches of the things I meet on
the way, but it would probably keep
me from my real work."

TOWER, PAN DOWN TO
MINERS
MINERS WALKING

    MUSIC: ORCHESTRA JOINS AND
        UNDER

NARRATOR:
In such a setting
Vincent plunged wholeheartedly
    to work.

HIGH SHOT BORINAGE

But soon the whole district buzzed
With his extraordinary behavior . . .

STREET SCENE
CU HOUSES

He gave up his warm room,
Moved to a hut meaner than the
    miners' . . .

HIGH SHOT HUT
MEDIUM SHOT HUT
CU ROOF

And—amid the ash heaps—
Lived on scraps . . .
As he nursed the sick,
Comforted the lowly.

MS BUCKETS OF ASHES
CU BUCKETS OF ASHES

(NARRATOR—CONT)
These reflections
Were made later,
After he was dismissed by the
    missionary society

DISSOLVE TO (PAINTING)
WOMEN CARRYING SACKS

For "Carelessness in dress and
    bearing . . .
Want of dignity."

(DRAWING) MINERS TO
WORK

    MUSIC: FADE OUT

VAN GOGH:
    "Theo . . . It is not merely the
question of dress, it is a much
more serious question I assure
you . . . It is simply that I have
different ideas."

(DRAWING) MAN WITH
SHOVEL

    MUSIC: SAD, IN AND
        UNDER

DISSOLVE TO MARSH, PAN TO
HOUSE OF DECRUCQ

Inflection

The English language has its own characteristic melody patterns. An incident widely quoted in the broadcasting industry illustrates this. On a dramatic broadcast from Hollywood, the usual practice was to have a star reappear after the play, to give an "oral trailer" about the program to come. This continuity sometimes did not get rehearsed, owing to exigencies of time or late confirmation of broadcast details. A prominent star began the following trailer in good form. It read:

Next week this program will feature in the starring role the very **talented** and **brilliant** young actor, John Blank!

Just as he was about to give the name of the person he was lauding, the star saw it for the first time. His amazement and horror at such praise for this particular actor of little standing or prestige was perfectly reproduced by the melody pattern, a questioning snort, with which he uttered the words: "John . . . Blank?" He had never spoken a more expressive phrase in his entire acting career.

Students of speech should be familiar with the drills in variation of meaning and emotion: saying "Oh" or "Yes" in many different ways. The physical "nearness' of the auditor to the broadcaster permits extensive use of inflection to signify minute shades of thought and feeling. The attitude of announcers toward the product they are talking about, toward the talent, musical selections, and the personalities mentioned in the news broadcasts, are revealed in the melody patterns of their speech. Their state of health, their poise or confidence in their ability, and clues to their personality are suggested by their vocal inflections. It might be well to mention three very common melody patterns that are particularly distracting: 1. a mechanical, transitional vocal hold, 2. singsong, and 3. recurrent up-or-down patterns.

Mechanical, transitional vocal hold. This is the result of the working conditions in many radio studios. The announcer, in addition to reading copy, may be cueing in records while one turntable is on the air, filling out a program and announcement log, editing news for the next program, checking outgoing program levels, auditioning microphone placement for a studio program, pulling records from the transcription library, and answering the phone. In television studios they may have some of these same duties together with giving signals for taped or film projection and watching the monitor as copy is read. With all of this responsibility and activity, announcers may not have sufficient time to rehearse their continuity and commercial announcements. They may be obliged to read from sight. Therefore, to insure themselves enough time to glance ahead quickly and get some general sense of the copy, announcers may fall into the habit of mechanically lifting their voices at ends of phrases and holding the final note. While holding this note they may look aside to check a title or the console controls. After a time the habit is firmly established. Consider the following:

> You know, Mothers, every child going to school needs lots of energy to do good work. If your child comes home after school feeling tired and worn out maybe it's because he's not getting the right kind of food at lunch. Now **bread** is a very important part of any lunch . . . and it's important that the bread you use . . . be full of all the food energy that children need so much.

This is a straightforward commercial announcement. It needs a direct and friendly approach. An announcer who has fallen into the mechanical, transitional vocal hold habit may read it very unevenly. The emphasized words below indicate the trouble spots for such announcers.

> You know, Mothers, every child going to **school** needs lots of **energy** to do good work. If your **child** comes **home** after **school** feeling **tired** and worn **out** maybe it's because he's not getting the right **kind** of **food** at **lunch** . . . and it's important that the **bread** you **use** . . . be full of all the food **energy** that **children** need so much.

The habit of separating phrases and sentences by three and five dots used indiscriminately by some copy writers, tends to encourage this faulty reading style. The announcer is never certain where the end of the thought comes unless the script is studied carefully.

Singsong. This is sometimes referred to as "ministerial" pattern. Translating the announcement into singsong style, indicating pitch levels and relative stress, we might get something that looks like this:

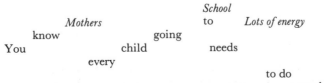

Recurrent up-or-down patterns. Another melody trap is present when the performer gets past the word-by-word style of delivery and into the word-combinations phase. With a close correlation to breathing rhythm, usually short half-breaths, the inflections always go up, or always go down, at ends of phrases and sentences. The melody curve can be plotted if one follows it with a pencil in hand. The same announcement is read:

You know Mothers..........every child going to school....................

need lots of energy............to do good work.

Or, the curve may be just reversed and will go up instead of down. This style leads to monotony.

Resourcefulness

Adroit ad-libbing by the announcer may be needed when unforeseen contingencies arise in radio or television. A notable example occurred during the initial "live" appearance of a woman announcer substituting for a vacationing colleague on a top network TV dramatic program. One of the characteristics of the new-model refrigerator being advertised was the ease with which it opened when the homemaker was laden down with packages. One of those horrible and frustrating nightmare situations resulted. The woman described its "finger-tip" opening action and confidently pressed the door plate. Nothing happened. The woman tried again and again, but the refrigerator door refused to swing open. The remainder of the announcement dealt with the features inside the refrigerator. Without apparent discomfiture the woman announcer ad-libbed a vague reference to the fact that the refrigerator power outlet had been disconnected after the show rehearsal, and went on to point out desirable features of specific areas behind the closed door which the viewers *would* have seen. Moving slightly away from the stubborn machine she continued to talk smoothly about the refrigerator while the camera moved in on a close-up. At the conclusion of the announcement, upon signal from the stage manager that the refrigerator was tractable again (without permitting the audience to see that she had received such a signal), she moved back to the refrigerator door, gave it only the slight pressure she had mentioned as required, and, with the viewers, watched the door swing ajar. Never once did she lose her poise.

STRICTLY TELEVISION

Appearance

This factor has no bearing on effectiveness in radio or in those phases of TV announcing where one is not seen on camera. Much TV and film work by station staff announcers never demands personal appearances. However, as soon as the announcer moves into specialized and feature assignments on camera, mainly the reading of commercials, appearance becomes extremely important. In the early days of network telecasts one prominent male announcer who was completely bald except for side fringes worked a transformation in his appearance by the purchase of a series of toupées, each with a gradual increase in the amount of hair until he attained the "well-groomed" look. It was first assumed that announcers would need to have the "Hollywood" gloss, and program producers attempted to hire announcers on appearance alone. Agencies handling photographer's models were approached. The casting files of agencies handling performers for motion pictures were examined. Men who looked handsome and distinguished, women who were striking and glamorous, were in demand.

Soon, however, the absence of the many other factors that make for effectiveness became apparent when these persons were entrusted with responsibilities for persuasive broadcast salesmanship. A study by the National Association of Broadcasters of the viewpoints of station managers regarding jobs in television points out that "most TV station managers have found that the great majority of their radio announcers are sufficient on this count [appearance] to handle a TV job. Most TV station managers feel that an honest sincere pleasant face will stand up best over the long haul."

Related to appearance are good grooming, naturalness of posture, facial expression, gesture, and movement. Announcers must not possess irritating facial or gesture mannerisms distracting to the viewer, and they must sit and move gracefully. Since much of the camera shooting will be in close-ups, extreme gestures, where hands and arms are extended towards the camera, may lead to considerable distortion as well as to distraction. Crossing one's legs towards the camera may exaggerate their length and size. The appearance of the announcer is, of course, also related to age. Many radio announcers are quite young. Their vocal qualities alone may give an impression of maturity. When these announcers appear on the screen, however, the viewing audience takes its primary cue from what it sees. As a result, many advertisers and program producers prefer announcers who "look" as well as "sound" mature. Announcers may compensate somewhat for their "youth" by paying careful attention to their choice of clothing and of hair style.

A minor yet specialized aspect of appearance is in the "freeze" of the facial expression following the conclusion of the announcement. The director frequently will hold a closing shot of the announcer for a few seconds before taking the next shot or ordering a slow dissolve. The announcer must not move or take on a "sickly" self-conscious or "blank" look during this period. A break in mood might completely ruin the effect of the message just concluded. This subtle yet professional skill takes practice to acquire.

Memorization

Commercial announcements and program continuity are sometimes committed to memory, although this practice is now much rarer than it was in the early days of television. When material is memorized, any mental struggle to remember specific words must be concealed from the audience.

Since pictures and words must be synchronized, a process that requires careful camera work, the announcer should present the commercial on the air in the exact sequence as rehearsed. The announcer usually depends on automatic prompting devices for recall of the material, or on cue cards that display the copy to be presented. The announcer should try to use these aids without making the audience aware of their use. Accomplishing this objective demands considerable practice and may, in fact, require that the announcer have the content practically memorized by broadcast time.

Synchronization

We have said radio announcers must imagine that the listener is close beside them when they read descriptive narration. In television, in contrast to radio, the viewer is guided primarily by the picture on the screen. It is as though the announcer is beside the viewer: both are examining a photo album or a sales leaflet as the announcer comments on each. The announcer must know what is actually being shown in order to direct the attention of the viewer and, through nuances in delivery, to emphasize certain points. Thus, it is clear that television announcers have much less freedom than radio announcers in determining their rate of speech. If they read the credits at the close of the drama faster than the names are displayed on the scroll, if they are enthusiastic about the excellent taste of the salad before the actress has tried it, if they refer to action or details not being captured by the camera and seen on the home screen, the mismatch of words and pictures results in confusion that may be comic or otherwise. Effective communication of mood or message has been lost. Constant reference to a monitor in the studio or announce booth must be made during this type of announcing assignment.

Studio Signals

A number of standardized signals or cues, useful when on the air, for control-room to studio communication, or for intrastudio work, are described in Table 20–1.

Table 20–1. Studio Signals

MEANING	*CUE OR SIGNAL NEEDED*
1. Get ready—or stand by for signal to come.	One or two hands raised—palm toward studio.
2. Start your portion, go ahead *now*.	Index finger pointed at respective performer using whole arm motion; or, a head nod towards performer. This latter signal used frequently by announcer or engineer in simple productions.
3. You're speeding. Slow down. Stretch it out. *(Not abruptly but gradually.)*	Drawing hands apart as if pulling taffy or rubber band.

4. You're too slow. Pick it up. Increase rate. (*Gradually.*)	Circular motion of hand with index finger extended. Action goes to right similar to dialing a phone, except it's a larger circle.
5. More energy. More volume. (*Do it gradually.*)	Moving hands up, palms up. One or two hands.
6. Less energy. Less volume. (*Gradually.*)	Moving hands down, palms down. One or two hands.
7. Move closer to microphone. Get in *on-mike*. For TV, close up distance between you and other scene element, person, or object.	Hold hands up, a few inches apart, palms toward each other. Move hands toward each other, repeating gesture—or—bring hand toward face, palm in.
8. Move farther from microphone. Get *off-mike*.	Push hand away from body or face, palm out.
9. Look at other camera.	Wave hands toward correct camera with wide sweeping but slow gesture and end up pointing at camera lens.
10. Watch director for cue to come.	Tap forehead next to eye.
11. Time going as planned. Don't worry. Relax.	Touch nose.
12. Time left.	Hold up appropriate number of fingers—three, two, one—for minutes left. For 30 seconds, show half of forefinger. For 15 seconds, show clenched fist. In TV, show cards marked 3, 2, 1, 30 seconds, and "wrap" (for 15 seconds). Show cards in view of talent below lens of appropriate camera.
13. Stop or cut. Use a natural ending such as close of sentence if not pre-arranged. Also means microphone is dead.	Slash throat with index finger or edge of hand. In TV, show card marked "cut."
14. Good going. Everything is all right. Thanks for what you did.	Circle with thumb and forefinger together, other fingers extended.

PLANNING MUSIC PROGRAMS

In the role of "disc jockey" (DJ) announcers are often responsible for selecting the music they present. If they are working for a station that offers an unvarying schedule of the same type of music—country and western, hard rock, or soul music, for example—the task may involve merely selecting music of a particular type that is enjoying the greatest popularity at the moment. In some instances, disc jockeys make no choices at all, but merely play selections chosen by the music director. If the station format is less set, however, DJ's may have considerable leeway in building programs. In such cases, the selection process should involve certain considerations.

The first factor to take into account in selecting music is the basic program format of the station. Stations tend to present music and other material of a particular type in an effort to attract the segment of the audience that prefers that type of music and material. An important factor in making this decision is the array of formats available from competing stations. A station may deliberately restrict its potential audience by specializing in a type of program that appeals to a minority because that particular minority interest is not being served by any other station and because the audience for formats with a more general appeal might have to be shared with a number of competing stations. Selecting a format is one of the most critical decisions a station manager must make. Stations may change formats in an effort to draw a larger proportion of the audience. The various formats broadcast by stations are designated by brief descriptive initials, words, or phrases. In 1976 Arbitron Radio conducted a survey in the first 50 markets to determine which formats were the most popular. Table 20–2 lists the 25 most popular formats and the number of stations of the 500 surveyed that were following each format.

Table 20–2. The Top 25 Formats in Radio

Format	Number of stations
1. Contemporary	135
2. Beautiful Music	88
3. MOR (middle-of-the-road music)	68
4. Country	45
5. News	20
6. MOR/Talk/News	23
7. Talk/News	13
8. Contemporary/AOR (album-oriented rock)	20
9. Black	24
10. MOR/Contemporary	18
11. AOR	17
12. Talk	5
13. Golden Oldies	6
14. Spanish	5
15. Mellow Rock	2
16. News/Beautiful Music	2
17. Contemporary/MOR	1
18. Country/MOR	1
19. Disco	1
20. Classical	1
21. Hawaiian	1
22. Religious/Black	1
23. Contemporary/Talk	1
24. MOR/Beautiful Music	1
25. Band	1

Courtesy Arbitron Radio.

Copyright Regulations

An important factor in planning music programs is to know which numbers can be played without danger of copyright violations. Musical selections, like written works, come under the copyright laws. Copyrighted works of any type are protected from unauthorized performances during the creator's lifetime and for a period of 50 years after the creator's death. After the copyright period has expired, material is considered to be in the public domain and can be performed without authorization. An important point to remember is that arrangements of public-domain numbers may be protected by copyright. A station, therefore, must be certain that the music it broadcasts is either an original public-domain (PD) version, or one it is permitted to use under a license agreement with representatives of holders of the copyright.

The oldest and largest licensing organization is ASCAP (American Society of Composers, Authors and Publishers), founded in 1914 by Victor Herbert, Gene Buck, and others to protect themselves from widespread violations of copyright. The organization serves all affiliated authors, composers, and publishers and allocates payment to them from the license fees it collects. It has agreements with similar foreign licensing groups in order to permit performances in this country. Licenses to play ASCAP music are covered by agreements negotiated by the broadcasting industry with ASCAP, and payments are made on the basis of those agreements. BMI (Broadcast Music Inc.), a competitor of ASCAP, was organized in 1939 by the radio industry as a protest against an increase in licensing fees by ASCAP.

Program Formats

The next step is to decide on the idea for a particular program and work out the format. This is where imagination, showmanship, and knowledge of audience tastes enter into the picture. The specific period of time and day of the broadcast, the availability of music, the commercial arrangement, the balance in the schedule, and the competition must all be considered.

Here are some questions that should be raised in planning a series of musical programs:

1. *Where is the spotlight?* Is the audience to pay particular attention to the disc jockey's comments, the program idea, or the talent? For whom is the program a showcase? What ingredients will attract the listeners? The impact of an imaginative and clever program idea or the pull of an accustomed and familiar idea may also be utilized.

2. *Does the series have unity?* Audiences live by the clock—they are used to tuning in for a specific program type. A program that presents a hard rock number for the first selection, a symphony movement for the second selection, a vocal quintet for the third, and concludes with a soft waltz, does not attract a loyal audience. Grab-bag routining is ineffective.

3. *Does the program have variety?* A program without this ingredient makes for dull listening. Extreme variations are not necessary, but changes in mood and style of arrangements, instrumentation, featured vocalists and vocal groups, rhythm, and tempo, are desirable.

4. *Does the series need a new twist or "gimmick"?* Two dress designers have the same basic ingredients to work with, but one prepares a "creation" while the other has an acceptable but ordinary costume. We use the term "invention" to describe the process of reassembling existing items in a new pattern. Effective program building requires invention. It may be just a slight flourish, as a salad may be distinctive because of the carrot curls framing it, and nothing more. The addition of sound effects of a crowd applauding soloists after vocal choruses and at the completion of numbers has given a new twist to many radio record shows; singing along with the artist puts another disc jockey out in front.

New "gimmicks" are not easy to devise. Invention is not simple, which may explain why in the need to program so many hours of the day, every day, every week, stations tend to copy and repeat formulas that have been developed elsewhere. To copy an existing program and yet give it a new angle is a regular assignment for many program directors. This process may actually result in the new program's possessing individuality of its own. This does not mean that every music program must be "hypoed" by tricks. Some programs may be just pleasant listening interludes.

5. *What happens on the twenty-seventh program?* Many excellent programs are developed that run for the first 13 weeks' cycle and even manage to get through the next 13. The real test for a program is what happens the twenty-seventh week. Almost without exception, the first program series planned by a newcomer will be a "Musical Journey" format. "How easy it is, you have 'Music of England' the first week, then 'Music of Spain' the second, and so on. A fine series!" With this "chestnut" idea the program builder has limited himself to only as many programs as there are countries with indigenous music. The format must be elastic and not too restrictive in application.

EXAMPLES OF RADIO CONTINUITY

Music comments are usually spoken extemporaneously by announcers, but when programs are carefully designed, continuity may be written and read by an announcer. The following examples provide practice in this type of presentation.

---

1. "Your Concert Hall" and 2. "Meet the Artist"[4]

YOUR CONCERT HALL

TIME: 59:30

ANNCR: (STATION/SPONSOR)...........presents ... YOUR CONCERT HALL
MUSIC: ESTABLISH THEME: ANDANTE FROM SYMPHONY NO. 5 IN C
        MINOR (Opus 67) FADE AT 0:40   (Beethoven/PD)
ANNCR: This is a program of concert music for your listening pleasure ...
        recorded melodies to enjoy, brought to you by (STATION/SPONSOR) ..
MUSIC: THEME UP - OUT AT 1:00

[4] Courtesy of Broadcast Music Inc.

ANNCR: Perspective on an artist's development is often gained by reviewing his earliest efforts. Beethoven's (BAY-toh-ven) FIRST SYMPHONY admirably foretells the growth in creative powers that was imminent.

For cogency of idea and intensity of expression this work is unique. Now on YOUR CONCERT HALL we hear Beethoven's SYMPHONY NO. 1 IN C MAJOR.

MUSIC: SYMPHONY NO. 1 IN C MAJOR, OP. 21 (Beethoven/PD)

VICTOR LCT 1023

ANNCR: Opening YOUR CONCERT HALL Arturo Toscanini (ar-TOO-roh tos-cah-NEE-nee) has conducted the NBC Orchestra in Beethoven's FIRST SYMPHONY. To continue our concert we hear a FLUTE CONCERTO by Mozart (MOH-tsart).

During his second trip to Paris in search of work and a secure position, Mozart wrote several compositions for the flute, on commission from "a gentleman of means and a lover of all the sciences."

In the CONCERTO NO. 1 IN G MAJOR FOR FLUTE, we hear John Wummer (WUM-mer) as soloist - with Pablo Casals (PAH-blow cah-SAHLS) conducting the Festival Orchestra.

MUSIC: CONCERTO NO. 1 IN G MAJOR FOR FLUTE, K. 313 (Mozart/PD)

Columbia ML 4567

ANNCR: On YOUR CONCERT HALL John Wummer has played Mozart's FIRST FLUTE CONCERTO IN G MAJOR.

Regarding his own work, a prominent contemporary composer has said: "After studying many pages of a certain composer, I sense his musical personality and, like a detective, reconstruct his musical experience."

In hearing our next selection, which is called SCENES DE BALLET (SENN duh b-LAY), we discover that our prominent tune-detective is none other than the great Igor Stravinsky (EE-gor stra-VIN-skee).

MUSIC: SCENES DE BALLET (Stravinsky/Schott-AMP)

COLUMBIA ML 4047

ANNCR: The New York Philharmonic has performed Stravinsky's SCENES DE BALLET - with the composer conducting.

MUSIC: FADE IN THEME - PLAY IN B.G.

ANNCR: . . . And so we come to the end of another of YOUR CONCERT HALL programs. (STATION/SPONSOR)......................invites you to tune in again..........at..........for another program of recorded concert music dedicated to your listening pleasure. Your commentator has been ....

MUSIC: THEME UP FOR TIME
59:30

MEET THE ARTIST

TIME. 14:30

ANNCR: (STATION/SPONSOR).....invites you backstage to MEET THE ARTIST!

THEME: "DANSERO" - HAYMAN-MERCURY 70166 - B&F MUSIC ESTABLISH - FADE AT :15 FOR:

ANNCR: Would you like to know more about your favorite recording artists? Well . . . MEET THE ARTIST puts the spotlight on the stars . . . America's most popular music-makers. Come with us now as we take you backstage into the lives of those YOU have made famous. Today, let's get acquainted with one of America's most popular singers and Academy Award winning actor . . . FRANK SINATRA.

THEME: "DANSERO"

UP AND OUT

MUSIC: "THIS LOVE OF MINE" - SINATRA - VICTOR/EMBASSY ESTABLISH - CUT AT A SUITABLE BREAK FOR:

ANNCR: Yes, that's the million dollar voice, and we'll hear more of it after this message.

(INSERT COMMERCIAL HERE)
ANNCR: And now to officially meet Sinatra. You know, in this business, we play a lot of records and hear a lot of success stories.

But I don't think there's been anything to equal Frank Sinatra's fabulous rise to fame. In 1943, he hit the headlines like a comet and has been shooting upwards ever since. From a fifteen dollar a week singing waiter to a twenty-five thousand dollar a week national idol. That's what can happen in show business! So let's listen to one of Frank Sinatra's own compositions. "This Love of Mine," originally recorded with Tommy Dorsey, and which has since become his theme song.

MUSIC: "THIS LOVE OF MINE."

ANNCR: If there ever was such a thing as an average American boy, it was probably Frank Sinatra! Born December 12th, 1917, in Hoboken, New Jersey, he did all the things expected of a normally active youngster . . . including getting his head caught in the roof of a carousel! Needless to say, Frankie lost most of his hair and the carousel had to be torn apart to get him out!

A few years later, while in High School, he was burning a path as a track star. He was a great swimmer, and a member of a championship basketball team. Sure, Frankie sang too! At the Demarest High School, he was with both the school band and the Glee Club. After school he worked on a delivery truck of the Hudson Observer, which gave him ambitions to be a newspaperman.

That was Frank Sinatra - a nice average kid. But more about that episode in a moment. Right now, a song for lovers, young and old. Frank Sinatra suggests "VIOLETS FOR YOUR FURS."

MUSIC: "VIOLETS FOR YOUR FURS." - SINATRA - CAPITOL/EMBASSY

ANNCR: Can you believe that a man who sings like that was once a newspaper copy boy and sports editor? Well, that's exactly what Frank Sinatra was upon leaving High School. But it didn't last long. One day he went to a local movie and saw a Bing Crosby show. Overnight, Frankie decided to be a professional singer. He did it too . . . as a fifteen dollar a week singing waiter at a roadhouse near Hoboken! The next break came in 1938 when he was signed with Harry James at seventy-five five dollars a week, then with Tommy Dorsey at one hundred and fifty a week. Teen-agers began to swoon and the Sinatra legend swept the nation! The rest of Frank Sinatra's story is sweet music whichever way you look at it. He was booked at New York's Paramount Theatre at a thousand a week and broke all records. For his return engagement he got over seven thousand dollars. Yet, for all this, Sinatra is a nice guy . . . unassuming, friendly, and a hard worker. And, as he proved in the movie "From Here to Eternity" and in many movies since . . . he can act too! Now here is Frank with one of his biggest hits . . . "YOUNG AT HEART."

MUSIC: "YOUNG AT HEART." - SINATRA - CAPITOL/SUNBEAM
(INSERT SECOND COMMERCIAL HERE)

THEME: "DANSERO"

   ESTABLISH - FADE FOR:

ANNCR: Today, MEET THE ARTIST featured FRANK SINATRA.

THEME: "DANSERO"

   UP APPROXIMATELY :15 - FADE FOR:

ANNCR: Listen again......................at.......when (STATION/SPONSOR)..........
............invites you along to MEET THE ARTIST, a special radio feature which brings you the interesting and unusual stories about today's most popular recording artists.

THEME: "DANSERO"

   UP TO TIME.

14:30

COMMERCIALS FOR ANNOUNCING PRACTICE[5]

1. Kraft Foods

VIDEO	AUDIO
PULLOUT FROM CORNBREAD COOLING ON OVEN DOOR TO SHOW OLD-FASHIONED COUNTRY KITCHEN, INCLUDING SET TABLE.	HERLIHY: Farm kitchens observe the seasons and try to use foods when they taste best and cost least. In that spirit, here are Kraft's recipes for a farm-wise supper.
BEAUTY SHOT POT ROAST & GRAVY.	At the center is a good, substantial pot-roast—browned and seasoned with CATALINA Salad Dressing. CATALINA gives the meat and vegetables a subtle spicy taste. One bottle does all the flavoring for you, and later turns into a tasty gravy.
POUR CATALINA OVER MEAT IN DUTCH OVEN. SEE VEGETABLES.	
SET DOWN DRESSING BOTTLE. I.D. CATALINA (NEW BOTTLE).	
SPOON GRAVY OVER POT ROAST AND VEGETABLES ON PLATTER.	
I.D. CASINO MONTEREY JACK. SEE PEPPERS, CORN MEAL, FLOUR, ETC.	Then, to celebrate the Fall Cheese Festival, CASINO BRAND Monterey Jack Cheese baked into cornbread. This fine, natural cheese is mixed in with the cornmeal batter and layered on top with pepper rings. This makes a moist cornbread that's full of good Southwestern flavor.
ADD SHREDDED CHEESE TO DRY INGREDIENTS.	
TOP CORNBREAD MIXTURE WITH CHEESE. BEAUTY SHOT WITH PIECE CUT OUT.	
ADD GRAPES TO SHREDDED CABBAGE IN BOWL.	Cabbage and grapes are in season, so we've combined them for a new kind of cole slaw. Include KRAFT Miniature Marshmallows for a sweet touch, and dress it all with MIRACLE WHIP Salad Dressing. Some people say that cole slaw isn't cole slaw without MIRACLE WHIP.
ADD MINIS TO CABBAGE–GRAPE MIXTURE. I.D. MINIATURE MARSHMALLOWS.	
ADD MIRACLE WHIP TO SLAW. I.D. MIRACLE WHIP. SEE INGREDIENTS.	
BEAUTY SHOT.	
BEAUTY SHOT BREAD PUDDING WITH PITCHER OF CREAM.	Finally, sensible bread pudding transformed into a rich dessert. Here are plenty of eggs and milk, juicy autumn apples and golden caramel.
ARRANGE APPLE SLICES OVER BREAD CUBES IN BAKING DISH. SEE EGGS, MILK, APPLES, ETC.	KRAFT Caramels melt so smooth that it's easy to add old-fashioned caramel flavor.
POUR CARAMEL SAUCE OVER BREAD PUDDING MIXTURE. I.D. CARAMELS.	
RECIPE FOLDER OPEN.	Look for these recipes in tonight's listing section of TV Guide Magazine, or at the special Kraft display at your store.
HAND CLOSES FOLDER TO SHOW COVER.	

PULL OUT TO SHOW KITCHEN TABLE WITH FINISHED DISHES.	Here's a supper that's farm-wise and also absolutely delicious. Good taste and good value with good food and good food ideas—all from Kraft.

Courtesy of Kraft, Inc.

[5] Further commercials for announcing practice appear in the chapter on "Commercials," and there are feature talks, which can be used for practice, in the chapter on "News and Feature Programs."

2. Rockwell International—"Monsieur Cugnot"

OPEN ON LONG SHOT OF VEHICLE. WE SEE FULL FRAME OF REPLICA OF CUGNOT VEHICLE COMING AT CAMERA. CUT TO SIDE VIEW. WE SEE SPOKESMAN AT CONTROLS.	This is a replica of the first self-propelled road vehicle invented over two-hundred years ago by Nicholas Joseph Cugnot of France. (LOUDER TO BE HEARD OVER SOUNDS)
VEHICLE PASS BY. CU OF SPOKESMAN.	Today, Monsieur Cugnot, transportation is a science and Rockwell International is very much a part of that science. Two out of three heavy-duty trucks ride the Rockwell Line of axles, springs, brakes, plastic assemblies, or U-joints. Rockwell also builds a variety of parts for passenger cars and recreation vehicles.
CARS AND TRUCKS BEGIN TO PASS SPOKESMAN.	
BUS BEGIN PASSING CUGNOT VEHICLE.	
CUGNOT VEHICLE PASSES ROCKWELL AIRCRAFT—A TWIN AND A SABRELINER.	And over the years, Rockwell has built more kinds of flying machines than anyone . . . from Commander and Sabreliner business aircraft to spacecraft that helped carry men to the moon.
SHOW BOTH PLANES IN BACKGROUND.	
DISS. TO VEHICLE COMING TO STOP ON PARKING DOCK.	They're even using space technology for down-to-earth transportation . . .
WE SEE HYDROFOIL IN BKGD. BOAT JETS OUT OF HARBOR. WE SEE SEVERAL DRAMATIC BOAT SHOTS VIA HELICOPTER.	(ROAR OF ENGINES—UP, THEN UNDER TO FINISH) this hydrofoil boat is powered by a propulsion pump that came directly from Rockwell's rocket research.
CUT BACK TO SPOKESMAN GETTING OFF OF CUGNOT VEHICLE. HE TAPS VEHICLE, THEN WALKS TOWARDS CAMERA.	Merci, Monsieur Cugnot, you sure got things moving. The science of transportation is one of the sciences of Rockwell International, where science gets down to business.
CUT TO LOGO ENDING. Rockwell International, where science gets down to business.	

Courtesy of Rockwell International and Campbell-Ewald Company

3. "Color Copier"

SONGS SUNG IN ORIGINAL ERA STYLES

"Grey Slippers"
"Baa Baa Grey Sheep"
"Grey River Valley"
"I Dream of Jeanie"

ANNCR. VO: There are lots of things in this world that are sorely in need of a little brightening up. Not the least of which is the world of business. That's why we spent so many years developing our new copier. One that takes the grey out of the business world. It's the new Xerox Color Copier. Now you can actually make copies in colors. Colors to enhance, colors to attract attention, colors to make a point, colors to help communicate. The new Xerox Color Copier. It can brighten your life.

"Grey skies are gonna clear up, put on a happy face."

Courtesy of Needham, Harper and Steers Advertising, Inc. and Xerox Corporation

4. "Cheez-Whiz"

(Sung)
Glorious cheese
What could be more delicious
More fun to eat
So good in lots of dishes.
And America spells cheese K-R-A-F-T.
Glorious cheese, glorious cheese
Have some more-ious cheese.

WOMAN:
When fall arrives, my motto becomes "Good Hot Lunches." Good thing I have CHEEZ WHIZ pasteurized process cheese spread for help. For instance, I may take a can of tomato soup and stir in some CHEEZ WHIZ. Or add CHEEZ WHIZ to hot macaroni for a hearty lunch. Right from the jar, CHEEZ WHIZ makes a creamy golden topping that turns an open-faced sandwich into a knife-and-fork meal. This Fall, count on Pimento, Jalapeno Pepper, and Regular CHEEZ WHIZ—the little glass jars full of ideas—from KRAFT.

(SUNG)
Any time of day the taste is so inviting,
Creamily smooth, lively and exciting.
And America spells cheese K-R-A-F-T.

Courtesy of Kraft, Inc.

Projects and Exercises

1. Assign announcer's copy found in the chapter and in scripts elsewhere in the text. Study these announcements before presentation in class. Class criticism, evaluation, and drill.

2. Tune in stations in your area and report on the work of the announcers. Compare radio and television styles.

3. Prepare brief pronunciation check lists on the basis of such observation. Each student should bring in 10 words heard on the air with their pronunciations as given. Discuss "correctness" of presentation.

4. Prepare a practical announcer's audition for another student. Include:

   a. An ad-lib assignment to reveal ease of delivery without script and appearance on camera.

   b. News copy to reveal general ability in reading from script and style together with the auditionee's command of pronunciation of foreign and domestic place names.

   c. Musical continuity to reveal familiarity with composers and selections. Do not select the very obscure composers or too technical terminology.

   d. Voice-over narration to check on ability to synchronize delivery with film. Still pictures may be used instead of film.

   e. Commercial copy.

Alternate presentations of audition material. Criticize delivery and material.

21

In this chapter we consider the function of the actor, a term we use to refer to both male and female practitioners of this art. An actor has two tasks: to sell and to create. The selling of an actor's ability takes place in the audition, where a casting director or producer passes judgment on the quality of the performance. Selected for a part, the actor then performs before a television camera in a studio or before a film camera in a studio or on location. Microphones, of course, pick up the audio portion of the performance. With the virtual disappearance of radio drama, the chances of practicing the acting art entirely through the voice have seriously diminished, but the ability to project a character only through a microphone is still needed in the production of radio commercials and in recording characters for cartoons or for postproduction audio tracks. In all these situations the actor is circumscribed by the complex equipment necessary to transmit picture and sound.

AUDITIONS

General auditions give actors an opportunity to present capsule versions of their skill in portraying different roles. The actor's own evaluations of personal strong points should influence the choice of material. When an actor is being considered for a specific part, special auditions are often held. The casting director may request a number of actors "to read for the part" in order to determine which one is best suited and is most responsive to directorial suggestions. Instead of working alone, the actor may be given a partner. Appearance in costume or on camera may be checked. Short screen or tape tests may be made when an actor is being appraised for a film role. The calls for special auditions or readings may be awarded to actors on the basis of past credits, personal observation by the director, recommendations by an agent, or results of the general audition.

1. The first step in preparing for auditions is the selection of material. For many, this seemingly simple task takes on the dimensions of a tremendous obstacle. Since the audition is to enable actors to be heard and viewed in the characterizations they feel most capable of performing, they should choose first from the roles they have played elsewhere, provided they

did a commendable job. The advantage of this procedure is familiarity with the material. It is usually desirable to avoid Shakespeare, Greek tragedy, and other classical plays, because TV does not have many such programs. They should also be avoided because very few actors can do them well. To be avoided, too, are the excerpts for drill that appear in acting manuals. These have been used so many times by so many candidates that directors are unable dispassionately to hear them again.

2. The customary time allowed for an audition is from five to eight minutes. Three selections of two-and-a-half minutes each should be sufficient. The next step is the arrangement of the selections.

Study the agency or production company. If it does nothing but a certain type of commercial or drama, then you should concentrate on performing parts that will fit that style. Don't attempt roles you cannot handle. If you cannot do crooks well, but can play lawyers (the so-called "professionals"), present characters of that type doing different things and in different moods: an excited lawyer, a lawyer cross-examining a witness, a lawyer delivering an emotional plea for the life of a client, etc. If you cannot do dialects authentically and with assurance, avoid them. Dialects require a keen ear, close observation of physical mannerisms, and memory of rhythm and melody patterns. Even if you played numerous character roles in a college or community theater, remember that in professional television you are facing competition from established character actors with many years of experience who do not need elaborate makeup to look the age of a character.

If you are giving a general audition instead of trying out for a specific part, it will be well to select material that will give the director an idea of the range of roles you can portray. One selection should present a straight or neutral character fairly close to your own age; a second should reveal your ability to play character roles. Your material should also provide you with an opportunity to show how well you can develop a climax or communicate intense emotion. If you are a specialist in accents or comedy roles, or a combination vocalist-actor, your material should be selected to reveal those talents.

3. The third step is the actual presentation of the audition. Identify the selection briefly by general type: "The first is a straight lead, from *Mister Roberts.*" This enables the director to check your performance against what you think you are doing, without falling into the very human habit of attempting to guess the particular play and the role. In auditioning, work 6 to 12 inches away from the microphone; work slghtly farther away for a dynamic delivery. Avoid stage projection and overly precise articulation. Voice alone must communicate the character and the meaning. This does not mean that you should refrain from bodily action. Let your body help you in the portrayal of the roles. In television, as in radio, remember that there is an intimate relationship between the actor and the audience. Physical movement and facial expressions will be seen by an audience, which may be thought of as being present on the stage with you.

4. Next, the director evaluates the audition. What are the standards of judgment? What does the director look for? The first reaction may be a general one: "This actor isn't up to desirable standards." And from the director's

point of view, that may be the final reaction—a big "No" on your card. However, we may probe a little deeper and examine some of the specific things considered in arriving at a judgment.

One of the first items is the positiveness of attack. This is a signpost of professionalism. The characterization may be faulty, the interpretation muddy, but the poise and the assurance with which the actor proceeds is important. *Caution:* There is no direct correlation, however, between frenetic activity or great volume and positiveness of attack.

Another key item brought into focus by the demands of television is the reality of the presentation: whether the characters seem real or seem artificial or exaggerated. The microphone and camera show quickly where technique overshadows meaning, where actors are more conscious of how they are "doing a part" than what the scene means in a real flesh-and-blood situation. We must observe the actor thinking, reacting, and feeling, not reciting.

In arriving at a judgment, also considered are a number of other factors, many of which are essential in the art of acting: control of voice and body, portrayal of emotion, meaning of phrases and sentences, timing of physical action and lines, ability to pause and express nuances for emphasis.

A SCRIPT FOR PRACTICE

Even though prospective actors may now find few jobs that require radio performance, practice before a microphone can help them tremendously in polishing their general acting skills. The advantages are numerous; they can practice material without having to memorize it; they can record it over and over to note what needs to be done to improve their performance; they can hear all of the nuances and gradations in their vocal effort, for the microphone provides a close-up of audio performance. A small recording machine can be a valuable tool in helping actors to polish their performance.

A radio script, "Aesop: Fables for Today and Tomorrow," is included here for laboratory study. This script is extremely useful because of its vignette construction. The individual scenes lend themselves to performance by separate groups, and provide opportunities for doubling roles.

Home Is What You Make It[1]

Episode # 139, Greece, "Aesop: Fables for Today and Tomorrow,"
by Lou Hazam

(MUSIC: ACCENTS EACH COUNTRY WITH A STING)

1. NARR: (ECHO) Canada . . . China . . . England . . . France . . . (FADE) Greece . . . Denmark . . . India . . .

[1] Courtesy of Lou Hazam and the National Broadcasting Company.

(MUSIC: SWELLS TO COVER)

2. ANNCR.   For a better and more tolerant understanding among nations and the promotion of enduring peace . . .

(MUSIC: UP A TONE TO HAND FOR)

3. ANNCR.   HOME IS WHAT YOU MAKE IT, brought to you weekly by the National Broadcasting Company and its affiliated independent stations, presents in its eighth program in its summer series devoted to the contribution of the peoples of the world to American culture and homelife! Today, we acknowledge our debt to—

4. VOICE: Greece!

(MUSIC: SALUTE AND OUT)

5. ANNCR.   "Aesop-Fables for Today and Tomorrow!"

(MUSIC: THEME IN AND UNDER)

6. ANNCR.   Here is your narrator, Ben Grauer . . .

7. NARR: To Greece we Americans can bow for many things. For some of the greatest works of sculpture that have ever been born of the hands of man. For a style of architecture by which we have built public buildings in virtually every city of our nation. For the drama of Aristophanes . . . for the wisdom of Aristotle and Plato. Indeed, for the very way in which we govern ourselves—for Greece was the first democracy. But today, we choose to salute a lesser appreciated inheritance from ancient Greece—a man whose **ideas** have been just as enduring as Greek art and wisdom, Aesop! (CHANGE NOW TO MORE INFORMAL TONE) Yessir, Aesop of the famous fables.—We don't know very much about Aesop, my friends. They say he was a slave, who—discharged by his master—rose to play an important part in the political life of his day. The story goes that somebody finally framed him and he ended up condemned to be thrown from a high cliff.—But this much we do know. The fables which bear his name pack just as much of a wallop today as they ever did—are just as filled with meaning to guide our future actions. To prove it—to show how the fables of Aesop can be readily applied today to individual matters, family matters and national affairs—we've corralled two extremely versatile actors. Here first is Miss Mitzi Gould.

8. WOMAN: How do you do.

9. NARR: And Joe De Santis.

10. MAN: How do you do.

11. NARR: Well now, here's what these two, Miss Gould and Mr. De Santis, are going to do. They are going to perform a variety of typical scenes from our present day life—and then defy me to find an Aesop fable that applies to each scene. In short—to see if the

scene literally strikes a bell in my mind and I can make with the appropriate message. So lend us your ears, my friends, and listen for that bell—for remember what Aesop said:

(MUSIC STING)

(ECHO)

He who refuses advice may some day vainly seek it.

(MUSIC: IN AND UNDER)

12. NARR: First we have a typical "family" scene. Hubby is just coming home from work . . .

(SCREEN DOOR OPENING AND CLOSING)

13. MAN: (AS HUSBAND; GAY AND CHIPPER) Oh, hello, darling . . . and how's my lovey dovey wife tonight?

14. WOMAN: (ON VERGE OF TEARS) Hello . . . Jim.

15. MAN: Hey—what's the matter? What's wrong?

16. WOMAN: (BETWEEN SNIFFLES) Junior . . .

17. MAN: (QUICKLY) What's he done?

18. WOMAN: He wanted to eat early . . . but he left the table . . . he wouldn't eat his spinach.

19. MAN: What! How dare he do a thing like that? Where is he?

20. WOMAN: He went out. He said he wouldn't touch the . . . the darn stuff.

21. MAN: He did, did he? Well, I'll fix him. Who does he think he is around here? . . .

(OPENING THE SCREEN DOOR)

(CALLING FORCEFULLY) Junior! (ANGRILY) Junior! (SORE AND GRUMBLING) Not wanting what's good for him. How does he expect to grow up into anything, answer me that! (CALLS) Junior!

22. WOMAN: (ALMOST WEEPING) I don't know what to do with him.

23. MAN: I'll show him who's boss around here. When I say eat spinach he'll eat it and like it, by gosh!

(CALLS) (DOOR OPENS) Junior! Jun-ior! (DOOR BANGS SHUT) (TURNING TO WIFE) By the way what's for dinner for **us** tonight?

24. WOMAN: Steak, potatoes 'n—spinach.

25. MAN: Spinach? Me? Good heavens, Grace, you know I can't abide spinach! Open a can of peas or something—(CALLING, AS IF HE SEES HIM NOW), Oh, there you are, Junior—Junior—come and eat your spinach!
    (BELL)

26. NARR: Yessir it rings a bell with me right off. I am reminded of Aesop's fable which goes like this.

(MUSIC: SNEAKS UNDER)

Once a mother crab and her son were taking a walk on the sand. Said the mother crab—"Child, why do you walk so ungracefully crooked? Walk straight my child, without twisting." "Pray, mother," said the young crab—"do but show me the way and I will follow you."—Moral . . .

(MUSIC: STOP)

(ECHO)

Example is the best precept.

(MUSIC UP AND OUT)

27. NARR: Score one for Ben Grauer. And now an office scene.

(INTERCOM BUZZER; SWITCH)

28. MAN: (BOSS, BIG, BLUSTERY TYPE) Yes?

29. WOMAN: (AS SECRETARY, FILTER) I finally got Miss Wilson, sir. She's waiting to see you.

30. MAN: Well, it's about time! Send her in.

31. WOMAN: (FILTER) Yessir.

(SWITCH)
(DOOR OPEN AND CLOSE)

32. WOMAN: (AS STENO; TIMIDLY) Did . . . Did you want to see me, Mr. Merriam?

33. MAN: Of course I wanted to see you or I wouldn't have sent for you! . . . Where have you been?

34. WOMAN: Well, I . . .

35. MAN: Sit down.

36. WOMAN: Yessir.

37. MAN. Look here, Miss Wilson. I run an office here, not a country club. I notice from your time card that you've been late twice this week. And three times this week your typing has shown errors.

38. WOMAN: Well, I . . .

39. MAN: Now, Miss Wilson. We pay you what we believe to be a fine salary. We naturally expect a proper return for that salary.

40. WOMAN: If you'd only let me explain, Mr. Merriam—

41. MAN: I can't understand why you're not cooperating. After all I don't
              treat you unfairly.—Now, what is your explanation?

42. WOMAN: I . . . I'm awfully sorry about it all, Mr. Merriam, but you see—
              my mother's been awfully sick. I've had to do a lot of things at
              home that I wouldn't ordinarily do and that's what made me
              late. As for typing mistakes, I've been so worried about her—
              well, really, Mr. Merriam, I shouldn't be at work at all . . . I
              should be home taking care of her. I asked to have my vacation
              moved up, but I was told—

43. MAN: You were told it was impossible and it **is** impossible. While we
              sympathize with you, Miss Wilson, you can't expect us to run
              an office to conform to home emergencies.—I can't understand
              you people I employ here. I don't seem to be able to get
              anything but the most average work out of the whole lot of you!

              (THE STRIKING OF A BELL)

44. NARR: Well that incident reminds me of Aesop's fable of the Wind and
              the Sun. Remember?

              (MUSIC: SNEAKS UNDER)

              Once the Wind and the Sun had an argument about which one
              was stronger. "I know how we can tell who is the stronger,"
              said the Sun. "Look down there at the traveller walking along
              the road. Let's test our strength by seeing who can cause him
              to remove his cloak." The Wind tried first. It blew as hard as it
              could . . .

              (WIND IMPRESSION)

              But the harder it blew, the tighter the traveller held his cloak
              about him. At last the Wind gave up in despair. Then the Sun
              began to try.

              (WIND FADES—BIRDS)

              It warmed the air and calmed the breeze. It shone pleasanter
              and pleasanter upon the traveller. At first he loosened his
              cloak and then finally he removed it entirely.—Which all goes
              to show . . .

              (MUSIC: STOP)

              (ECHO)

              Kindness brings better results than severity.

              (MUSIC: UP AND OUT)

45. NARR: So far, so good—we continue. Along a main highway a nice
              looking woman stands staring dejectedly at a flat tire on her
              car. Along comes a kind motorist. . . .

              (CAR PULLING UP TO A STOP)

46. MAN: Can I help you, madam?

47. WOMAN: Oh dear . . . I would be so obliged! Looks like I've gone and got a flat tire.

48. MAN: Oh yes . . . well . . . Let's see what I can do with it.

(CAR DOOR CLOSES AS HE CLIMBS OUT)

49. WOMAN: So kind of you to stop.

50. MAN: Not at all . . . not at all, madam.—There was something about your face that reminded me of my sister.

51. WOMAN: Oh, how nice.

52. MAN: (EXAMINING TIRE) I think I can fix this for you in a jiffy. Shouldn't be hard at all.

53. WOMAN: Oh, how wonderful . . . It really is so sweet of you . . .

54. MAN: Not at all. Not at all . . .

55. WOMAN: May I hold your coat and vest—so you won't get them dirty?

56. MAN: Oh,—well, that's real thoughtful of you—

57. WOMAN: Hate see a man soil his suit—particularly a nice one like yours.

58. MAN: (EFFORT) Here 'tis. Thanks. Yes—well, I'll get my stuff out of the back of my car and get to work on this tire right now. (FADE) Won't take long . . .

(MUSIC: BRIDGE)
(SOME LAST FEW BANGS. PERHAPS THE JACK)

59. MAN: (JOB FINISHED) There you are.—I think that will be all right now.

60. WOMAN: Oh, I can't tell you how very grateful I am!

61. MAN: That's all right. Don't mention it.—Here, I'll open the door for you.

(CAR DOOR OPENING)

62. WOMAN: (EFFORT) Thank you again. I really appreciate it a whole lot!

63. MAN: You're quite welcome.

64. WOMAN: Here's your coat and vest.

65. MAN: Thank you.—Goodbye.

(CAR DOOR CLOSES)

66. WOMAN: Goodbye.

(CAR STARTING UP, AND MOVING OFF)

67. MAN: (TO SELF, AFTER CAR SOUND FADES OFF) Sweet woman.—
(CHANGE) Well, I've been delayed. Wonder what time it is?
(PATTING POCKETS) (PAUSE; THEN A STARTLED
EXCLAMATION) My watch! Gone!—(THEN, AFTER A QUICK
CHECK, GIVES OUT WITH A SHRIEKING) **MY WALLET!**

(BELL . . .)

68. NARR: Aesop could have warned that man—with his fable of "The Wolf
in Sheep's Clothing." It goes like this.

(MUSIC: IN AND UNDER AS B.G.)

There was once a greedy wolf who had trouble catching sheep.
So one day he decided to disguise himself. He found a sheepskin
and covered himself with it. Then he went in and mingled with
the flock. One at a time, the young lambs who belonged to the
sheep whose skin he had taken, followed him away . . . And so
soon as they had gone a little apart from the flock, he pounced
upon them and ate them.—Proving—

(MUSIC: STOP)

(ECHO)

Appearances are deceptive.

(MUSIC: UP AND OUT)

69. NARR: Score three for Grauer.—Onward and upward with Aesop!

(MUSIC: FANFARE)

Our scene now—an office to the back of a night club . . .
Attendez!

70. MAN: O.K., Trixie . . . What's it about . . . Why did you want to talk to
me?

71. WOMAN: (NITE-CLUB TYPE; ARGUING AND PLEADING) Listen, Mr.
Bragato . . . I don't see why you don't give me a break. After all I
been workin' for this run-down honky-tonk for two years now
. . .

72. MAN: But, Trixie—I already give you a break. You're the hit of the
floor show. You come out last draped in that white mink
sarong with the red spotlight.

73. WOMAN: But I wanna sing!

74. MAN: You're beautiful, Trixie. People who come want to look at you,
not hear you. You're the most beautiful showgirl in New York!

75. WOMAN: But I'm tired of being the most beautiful showgirl in New
York.—I wanna **sing!** Listen to me, Mr. Bragato, I can sing . . .
Listen!

76. MAN: No no, please, Trixie, no no . . .

77. WOMAN: (BURSTS OUT SINGING A BLUES NUMBER)

78. MAN: (OVER SINGING) Please, Trixie . . . please . . .

79. WOMAN: (CONTINUING UNDETERRED)

(MUSIC: PICK UP REFRAIN AND CURTAINS)

(BELL)

80. NARR: Believe it or not, I've got an Aesop that hits **that** one right on
             the nose!—Stand by, folks, for "The Peacock and Juno . . . "

(MUSIC: IN AND UNDER AS B.G.)

Once upon a time there was a peacock who, in spite of all his
attractions, was not satisfied with his fate. So the peacock went
to the goddess Juno and petitioned her that she add to his
endowments the voice of a nightingale. Juno refused. But the
peacock persisted. He reminded Juno that he was her favorite
bird. But Juno wouldn't listen. Finally, when Juno could
stand no more, she turned upon the peacock and said:

(MUSIC: STOP)

(ECHO)

**Be happy with your lot in life. One cannot be first in
everything.**

(MUSIC: UP AND OUT)

81. NARR: Next scene, Anytown, U.S.A.

(CAR SPEEDING)

Mrs. Peyton Smith speeds along the highway with scarcely a
glance in her rear view mirror until . . .

(MOTORCYCLE COP'S SIREN)

82. WOMAN: Oh dear . . .

83. MAN: (OFFICER: CALLING) Pull over to the curb. Where do you
             think you're goin'?

(CAR HALTING)

84. MAN: (COMING ON) You must be mighty late for that bridge game.

85. WOMAN: But, officer . . . I didn't do anything. I can't imagine why you
             stopped me!

86. MAN: You weren't doin' anythin'—but 50 miles an hour, madam—in a
             25 mile zone!

87. WOMAN: But, officer, that's ridiculous! Your speedometer must be
             wrong.

88. MAN: (SIGHING) Sure and that's a new one, that is. Now I've heard everything. You tell that one to the judge, man—he gets tired, he does, of the same stories all the time—

89. WOMAN: (PROTESTING) But, officer—!

(MUSIC: BRIDGE)

(GAVEL—TWO BANGS)

90. MAN: (JUDGE) Next case—Mrs. Peyton Smith. Charge, speeding, Main Street off Taylor Avenue.

91. WOMAN: Your Honor . . . it's all a mistake.

92. MAN: (BORED) Do you plead guilty or not guilty, Mrs. Smith?

93. WOMAN: Not guilty, of course!

94. MAN: The officer's report says you were going fifty miles an hour in a twenty . . .

95. WOMAN: (INTERRUPTING) But I **couldn't** have been doing that, Your Honor! I **never** speed. I must ask you to take my word as the wife of a leading citizen of this community. I'm a great believer in respecting traffic laws. I never go beyond the speed that's posted. I've driven down Taylor Street a million times and turned on to Main and never been stopped before!

96. MAN: **Down** Taylor Street, Mrs. Smith?

97. WOMAN: That's right—time and time again!

98. MAN: You're fined ten dollars for speeding . . . and ten dollars for wrong-way driving!

99. WOMAN: But, Your Honor!

100. MAN: Taylor Street, Mrs. Smith, which you've driven **down** a million times, is a one-way street—**going up!**

(BELL)

101. NARR: Alas, poor Mrs. Peyton Smith. She should have read Aesop's "The Mole and Her Mother," and been forewarned . . .

(MUSIC: SNEAK UNDER)

It seems that once a young mole cried out to her mother: "Mother—I can see!" To try her, the mother found an onion and held it before the young mole's face. "What is it, my child?" she asked. "A stone," cried the young one eagerly ". . . a stone!" "Alas, my poor child," said the mole, "Not only are you blind, but you cannot even smell!"—Remember then—

(MUSIC: STOP)

(ECHO)

Brag, and you betray yourself.

(MUSIC: UP AND OUT)

102. NARR: Now we give you two lovers—who are able to keep in touch with each other only through the grace of a certain A. G. Bell . . .

(TELEPHONE RINGING, RECEIVER PICK-UP)

103. WOMAN: Hello?

104. MAN: (FILTER, THROUGHOUT) Oh hello, honey.

105. WOMAN: (THRILLED, BUT CAUTIOUS) Oh, it's you. (CHANGE, AS SHE'S IN EARSHOT OF HER FATHER) I'm sorry you troubled to call, Mildred, I won't be available this evening.

106. MAN: (DEFIANTLY) Won't be available? Why not?

107. WOMAN: Well, Dad thinks I'd better stay in and hit the hay early.

108. MAN: You mean your father's home and hears what you're saying?

109. WOMAN: Yes.

110. MAN: But I've got to see you, Betty . . . I haven't seen you for two whole days!

111. WOMAN: Er . . . aha . . . I know it is, Mildred. I feel the same way.

112. MAN: Isn't the old bozo going out this evening?

113. WOMAN: Well . . . Dad is going out in a little while to the club meeting . . . but I've promised to stay home tonight and get some badly needed rest.

114. MAN: What time is the meeting? . . .

115. WOMAN: Yes, I saw the gang at nine o'clock. They're all carrying on pretty much the same way—nothing new.

116. MAN: You mean he's driving?

117. WOMAN: Yes.

118. MAN: Well, I'll be parked around the corner, out of sight. When I see him go by I'll drive around and come on up.

119. WOMAN: So you're going to buy a new dress! Well, I'd be real careful if I were you. I always preferred a real dark color for evening . . .

120. MAN: Don't worry . . . I'll pick out a dark spot where he won't see me.

121. WOMAN: Goodbye, Mildred. I'm glad you called. I can't wait to see how you look—

122. MAN: And me, to see you, honey. Gosh, it'll be like heaven again. See you soon.

(MUSIC: BRIDGE)

123. MAN: Darling!

124. WOMAN: Oh, Wilbur! You had me so worried. I was sure you'd bump into him!

125. MAN: Missed him by a mile. I'm too smart for him!—How about a kiss?

126. WOMAN: (GIGGLES) (STOPS)

127. MAN: (PAUSE) Darling. Gosh, I dont see how I can live another day without you!

128. WOMAN: Sweetheart!

    (OFF, DOOR OPENING AND SLAMMING)

129. MAN: (QUICKLY) Who's that—

130. WOMAN: I don't know unless—he forgot something and—

    (STOPS THEN, AS IF HE'S JUST COME IN THE ROOM) Dad!

131. MAN: (AN ESCAPING WORRIED SIGH) Oh me!

    (BELL)

132. NARR: No, the fabulous Aesop didn't forget advice for you lovelorn, either. He made up a fable especially for people in your predicament called—"The Lion in Love" . . . listen—

(MUSIC: SNEAKS UNDER)

A lion once fell in love with a woodcutter's daughter, and went to the father to ask for his daughter's hand in marriage. The woodcutter did not care for the match, but he was afraid to decline the ferocious King of the Beasts. So he said to the lion, "Very well, I give you my consent. But, good lion, my daughter would not like your sharp claws and big teeth. She'd be frightened of you. Why not have your claws and teeth removed and come back tomorrow. Then the wedding can take place." So enamoured of the daughter was the lion that he went at once to rid himself of his teeth and claws. When he returned, there was the woodcutter awaiting him with a club. And since the lion could no longer defend himself, he was driven away!—Heed this moral, lovers all—

(MUSIC: STOP)

(ECHO)

Beware lest the eagerness of love bring your undoing!

(MUSIC: UP AND OUT)

133. NARR: That makes six down and I haven't failed yet to match an Aesop fable—containing a practical message—to every scene!— But let's see what we have next, here . . .

(TYPEWRITER UNDER)

134. WOMAN: (BEFUDDLED SECRETARY) Dear Mama: Just thought I'd take my typewriter in hand and let you know how I'm doing on my new job. Up until yesterday, I **liked** working for Wheeler, Webster and Wiggin. But yesterday—jeepers—everything seemed to go wrong. First it was Mr. Wheeler. He decided that from now on I was to type all office memorandum in small type. Said it saved paper and paper was scarce. But when I sent the first memorandum through that way, Mr. Webster—he's the second partner—came out fit to be tied! He said what did I think his eyes were—magnifying glasses? He said he couldn't read the small type. I told him Mr. Wheeler told me to use the small type, but he said he didn't care **what** Mr. Wheeler told me, I was to type things so's people could **read** them. So I started to use the large type again when what should happen but out should come Mr. Wiggin—he's the third partner. He said that his secretary and I were to switch typewriters. Hers was too noisy, he said, and it disturbed him and mine was a noiseless. Then Mr. Wiggin gave me her typewriter, which—as you can see from this letter—has **medium** type!

Now if I send office memorandums through on medium type, why Mr. Wheeler will say it's too big, Mr. Webster will say it's too little, and only heaven knows what Mr. Wiggin will say!— Mama, what should I do?

(BELL)

135. NARR: (WITH A LAUGH) Do? Why open a book of Aesop's fables, of course, and read the story of "The Man and His Two Wives."— Don't you know it?

(MUSIC: SNEAKS UNDER)

Back in olden days, when men had more than one wife, there was a middle-aged man who had two. One wife was old and the other was young. Each of them loved him a great deal, and wanted him to appear as each desired him. His young wife did not like to see his hair turning grey. So every night, as she combed his hair, she plucked out the grey ones. The elder wife was grey herself. So every night she combed his hair she plucked out all the **black** hairs she could find. This went on and on until the man, who tried to be pleasing to both wives, found himself **completely bald!**—Which is to say—

(MUSIC: STOPS)

(ECHO)

Try to satisfy everyone and you'll satisfy no one.

(MUSIC: UP AND OUT)

136. NARR: We have time for just a few more. We let you listen, next, to a telephone conversation . . .

(PHONE RINGING; RECEIVER PICK-UP)

137. MAN: (PLEASANT, UNCONCERNED TYPE) Hello.

138. WOMAN: (FILTER THROUGHOUT ... UPSET AND DETERMINED) Mr. O'Hare?

139. MAN: Yes, this is Mr. O'Hare.

140. WOMAN: I'm Mrs. Lawson ... a couple of blocks up the street.

141. MAN: Oh yes, Mrs. Lawson ...

142. WOMAN: I'm calling to complain about your son, John.

143. MAN: Oh yes? What's Johnny been doin'?

144. WOMAN: He's been constantly annoying my Albert, that's what he's been doing. This morning he actually whipped my Albert because Albert said his catcher's mitt was better than Johnny's pitcher's glove.

145. MAN: (BELITTLING) Well ...

146. WOMAN: Apparently, Mr. O'Hare, you son's idea of solving an argument is to whip anybody who disagrees with him!

147. MAN: Well I'm sure that—

148. WOMAN: And another thing—

149. MAN: Yes.

150. WOMAN: Yesterday, Albert lost his baseball and your Johnny found it and absolutely refused to return it, claiming it was his. Now that's downright stealing, Mr. O'Hare, and I think—

151. MAN: (LAUGHING IT OFF) Oh come, come, now, Mrs. Lawson. You're letting yourself get too excited. Boys will be boys, you know.

152. WOMAN: I think it's a far more important matter than just "boys will be boys," Mr. O'Hare! Bullying and stealing are not my idea of—

153. MAN: (BORED, CUTTING IN) Well, I'll speak to him about it, Mrs. Lawson—

154. WOMAN: I should think that's the **least** thing you'd do. I should think you'd be interested in seeing that—

155. MAN: (CUTTING HER SHORT) Thank you very much, Mrs. Lawson. Goodbye.

               (Cradling phone)

               (SIGHS WEARILY) Women! Cackle, cackle, cackle just like hens! Probably nothing but a chronic complainer ...

               (BELL)

156. NARR: So Mr. O'Hare does nothing about Johnny's youthful transgressions. Oh, if he'd only known Aesop's story of "The Thief and His Mother".

(MUSIC: SNEAK UNDER)

There was once a young man who was caught stealing. Upon being condemned to death, he asked if he couldn't see his mother. His wish was granted and they brought his old mother to him. He leaned over his mother, as if to whisper in her ear. Suddenly, instead of whispering, he almost bit her ear off! The court attendants jumped upon him and pulled him away, horrified at such inhuman conduct. "Why do you bite your own mother!" they cried. "So that she may be punished," he said. "When I was a child, I began stealing little things and bringing them home. My mother, instead of punishing me as she should, laughed and said it would not be noticed. It is because my mother did not punish me then that I am condemned to die today!"—For . . .

(MUSIC: STOP)

(ECHO)

Evil should be nipped in the bud.

(MUSIC: UP AND OUT)

157. NARR.   We might call the next one a summer scene. Engrossed in the travel section of the Sunday paper, Madam wife looks up to Mr. Husband and exclaims—

158. WOMAN: (THRILLED) Bermuda! . . . The magic Caribbean! Gentle trade winds . . . velvet seas! . . . (EAGERLY) Why can't we go to Bermuda on our vacation?

159. MAN: (IRRITABLE TYPE) Are you insane Gladys?

160. WOMAN: Of course I'm not insane! What's so impossible about going to Bermuda?

161. MAN: (BLUNTLY) The expense.

162. WOMAN: Oh, ridiculous. You know we can afford the trip.

163. MAN: I refuse to concede any such thing.

164. WOMAN: Look, dear. **Before** the war, we were too busy to go anywhere . . . **during** the war it wasn't patriotic. But **now** there's no reason on earth why we can't—

165. MAN: (FINISHING IT FOR HER) **Stay put.**—I can't see any point in going travelling half way around the world just to—

166. WOMAN: But it isn't half way around the world to Bermuda! It's just a few hours by plane, or we can make a cruise in—

167. MAN: (FIRMLY) The answer is no!

168. WOMAN: It would be wonderful for the children—education and everything and—

169. MAN: My dear. I do not intend to spend my life making money only to squander it on vacation trips.

170. WOMAN: But you've done remarkably well this year—it wouldn't cripple our bank account at all!

171. MAN: We'll go to Oxyboxo lake, like we always do . . .

172. WOMAN: Flies! Mosquitoes!

173. MAN: We can get a cottage there for next to nothing.

174. WOMAN: Mud instead of sand!

175. MAN: I can commute to work.

176. WOMAN: The same old faces in the same old places!

177. MAN: (CONCLUDING) We'll **save money.**

               (MUSIC: SNEAK UNDER)

178. NARR: There was once a miser, says Aesop, who buried a bag of gold under a tree. Each day he would come and look at it. One day a thief saw the miser dig in the earth, take out his bag of gold, fondle it and put it back again. When the miser had gone, the thief dug up the gold and put in its place a bag of stones. The next day the miser returned and when he saw his bag of gold was gone, and in its place was a bag of stones, he raised such an outcry that all his neighbors came running to him "My gold is stolen," he cried. "Stolen!" "What did you do with the gold when you had it?" asked one. "Why, I, came each day and looked at it," replied the miser. "In that case," said the other, "come each day and look at the bag of stones. It will do you just as much good."—In other words—

               (MUSIC: STOP)

               (ECHO)

               Wealth unused may as well never exist.

               (MUSIC: UP AND OUT)

179. NARR: We have time for just one more, my friends. So far Aesop has taught us—
               Kindness brings better results than severity . . . Example is the best precept . . . Appearances are deceptive . . . Be happy with your lot . . . Brag and you betray yourself . . . Beware lest the eagerness of love bring your undoing . . . Try to satisfy everyone, and you'll satisfy no one . . . Evil should be nipped in

the bud . . . Wealth unused may as well never exist.—Yes, each scene from our present day life has struck a bell in my mind and I haven't failed yet to match it with an ancient fable! Now let's see how I make out on the last one . . . The scene, a large hall crowded to the rafters—with an arm-waving speaker holding forth from the state—

(CROWD SNEAKS IN ABOVE)

180. MAN: (SLIGHT ECHO—POLITICIAN, SHOUTING) And so I say to you, my friends . . . far from finding peace and justice in the United Nations, we can only find trouble! Let us, then, sever this artificial connection with foreign nations! . . . . Let us turn to the solution of our own problems in our own individual way! Let us show the world that **we** can get along without the help of other countries, even if they cannot! I propose that we devote our total energies not to the United Nations—no no!—but to one nation—our own—the **American** nation!

(APPLAUSE)

181. NARR: Oh-oh . . . That one's got me stumped—no bell! (WORRIED) Let me see now—surely Aesop couldn't have failed us on the most important principles in international life! . . . What did that speaker say, now . . . (MUMBLING) Sever connections with other nations . . . go on our own way alone . . . —(SUDDENLY) Wait a minute, now, it's coming . . . its' coming!—

(THE CLANG OF THE BELL . . . CONTINUING EXCITINGLY FAR EXCEEDING THE PREVIOUS EFFECTS)

Ah, I **knew** it . . . I knew it! I knew Aesop wouldn't let us down.—(HURRIEDLY) Listen to this . . .

(MUSIC: SNEAK UNDER)

182. NARR: There was once a father who had a family of sons who were always quarreling. When his exhortations failed to stop them, he determined to give them a practical lesson in the evils of disunion. One day, he instructed his sons to bring him a bundle of sticks. When they did so he gave each one in turn the bundle and told them to break all the sticks **at the same time.** Each of his sons tried with all his strength, but was not able to do so. Next the father separated the sticks, one by one, and again put them in their hands. This time each son broke the sticks with ease.—Then said the father to his sons . . . "Remember, my sons—

(MUSIC: STOP)

(ECHO)

In unity, there is strength!

(MUSIC: UP AND CURTAIN BIG)

183. NARR: To Greece, then, my friends . . . not only for its sculpture, architecture, drama and philosophy . . . but for the enduring fables of its one-time slave, Aesop —fables which are packed today with as much significance to the individual, the family, the nation as ever . . . fables by which we can help shape our future—to Greece, "thank you."

(MUSIC: THEME IN AND FADE OUT UNDER)

184. ANNCR: You have just heard the 139th program of HOME IS WHAT YOU MAKE IT, and the eighth in the summer series, devoted to contributions of other peoples to American culture and home-life. The program saluted Greece and was entitled "Aesop—Fables For Today and Tomorrow!"—speaking of Aesop, did you know that in his fable "The Clock and The Dial" he makes this significant point.

(MUSIC: STING)

(ECHO)

No person can do without help.

185. ANNCR: That's one reason why HOME IS WHAT YOU MAKE IT has prepared for its listeners, a handbook on the Family.

186. NARR: Tell us about it, Ray . . .

187. ANNCR: It's fifty-six pages long, Ben—packed with all sorts of information not readily available to homemakers elsewhere.

188. NARR: For instance?

189. ANNCR: Such information as—What Families Are For—Doing Things Together—Getting and Spending the Family Income—Families Alive to Religion.—Copies of this useful handbook can be secured by simply sending 25 cents—the non-profit price—to NBC, Box 30, Station J., New York 27, New York. The address again—for the family handbook, send 25 cents to NBC, Box 30, Station J., New York 27, New York. Act now, for again remember what Aesop said—

(ECHO)

We often forget what is most useful to us.

(MUSIC: THEME IN AND UNDER)

190. ANNCR: HOME IS WHAT YOU MAKE IT is presented as a University of the Air feature by the National Broadcasting Company and its affiliated independent stations—in cooperation with the American Home Economics Association, the General Federation of Women's Clubs, the National Congress of Parents and Teachers and the United Council of Churchwomen. Your narrator was Ben Grauer. Music was by Jack Ward. Mitzi Gould and Joe DeSantis were featured.

(MUSIC: UP AND DOWN)

HOME IS WHAT YOU MAKE IT is written by Lou Hazam. The series is directed by Garnet R. Garrison. Be sure to listen next week when we will present the ninth dramatization in the new summer series—A Salute to Poland, entitled, Paderewski—Pianist and Patriot.

This is Ray Barret, and

THIS IS THE NATIONAL BROADCASTING COMPANY.

TELEVISION ACTING

A few generalizations should be borne in mind as students begin practice and work in television acting:

1. There are two techniques for producing television shows. Using one technique, filmed shows and some taped shows are shot in short sequences, which are then edited into the completed program. This production method does not require the memorization of a complete script, but it is still important to know the lines in the scenes to be shot on a given day to avoid expensive retakes. Using the second technique, the script is rehearsed in its entirety through a period of several days and is then recorded on tape in long se-

Photograph Courtesy of Columbia Pictures Television

Janice Lynde in Close-Up Scene in Daytime Serial *The Young and The Restless.*

quences, often before an audience. The recording may be interrupted to permit scene and costume changes, but the actors must have memorized the complete script before the session begins. It is generally advisable to memorize words and actions simultaneously. Faulty memories can cause acting careers to be very short lived.

The television actor should be quick in memorizing the role. The brief time available for rehearsals does not allow the cast much time to learn lines. One director of an hour dramatic series requested that his actors have their lines completely memorized by the second rehearsal, 48 hours after the first meeting of the cast. A background in stock company acting is valuable because of the experience one gains in quick study.

2. Never look directly at the camera lens unless specifically directed to do so. This is completely opposite to the style used by announcers and speakers.

3. Don't drop out of character at any time during scenes, even when off-camera, or at the tag of a scene, until released by the stage manager. Something may go awry with the cameras, and instead of close-ups or medium shots that exclude you, you may be in the scene. Staying in character also helps other actors playing opposite you by giving them some degree of interaction and response. A "freeze" at the end of a scene is difficult to do and yet stay in character. However, the director may have difficulty in lining up the next shot and may have to keep the cameras on you. It may seem ages to the actor who is on camera before the release comes from the stage manager. One should not break the freeze until the signal is received.

4. Learn to take cues from the stage manager without looking directly at the source of the cue. It is distracting to have a scene appear on the air and catch the actor just standing motionless, staring in a fixed direction, then spring into action. Directors should issue cues for action before the camera takes, but often they cannot. Actors should be in character and whenever possible be engaged in some movement suitable to the character and situation slightly ahead of the camera take.

5. Actors should become proficient in "hitting the mark." Chalk marks or masking tape on the studio floor are used to guide actors where they are to stand for certain effects. The director may want a small light spot beamed up from a floor stand to illuminate the actor's eyes, or a tight over-the-shoulder shot may have been plotted. Just the slightest error in position by the actor may spoil the effect. If marks are not used, the actor may be told where to stand in reference to properties or furniture. Freedom of movement is not one of the television actor's prerogatives. It takes considerable practice to learn how to attend to hitting the mark while performing on camera without revealing the techniques to the audience.

6. Television is a close-up medium. Actors should work for mobile facial expressions. The camera is frequently focused on faces of actors who are not speaking, but are listening and reacting. Television, like film, emphasizes the effect of speech and action upon others in the scene. An impassive "deadpan" look conveys to an audience little of the thoughts and emotions that should be mirrored on the face. *A note of warning:* do not make the error of gross facial movements or "mugging," which irritate and distract when seen

in close-up. The intimacy of the medium calls for naturalness in bodily action. What appears as natural to the television viewer, however, may have come about as the result of long arduous practice by actors. Gestures must not be aimless or unrestrained. An arm extended toward the camera may be distorted out of correct proportions if the scene is being shot on a 35mm wide-angle lens. A close-up of a handclasp may be blurred if performed in a vigorous up-and-down hand-pumping manner. Shifting of weight from foot to foot can be distracting in a tight waist (from the waist up) shot because the actor may appear to weave from right to left of the screen. Working with other actors while standing or sitting only inches apart is difficult for some to learn. Scenes played "nose to nose" in the studio may be strangely uncomfortable to the actors but appear "natural" when viewed on the small television screen.

7. Actors should become proficient at pantomime. Often a narrator describes the setting or action while actors are performing in pantomime. Prerecording thoughts is a technique frequently utilized. Actors are seen without lip action while the recording of their thoughts is being played. A loudspeaker in the studio permits the actor to hear the recording. If the camera is on a close-up, resorting to extremes of facial expressions in an attempt to reflect the emotional undercurrents or "inner speech" may distract the viewers. An impassive, "poker face" may be almost as bad.

8. The audio side of television cannot be ignored. It is true that, in contrast to radio, where the actors move to and from the microphone, in television the microphone follows the actor. However, TV actors also must be aware of microphone pickup patterns. Actors who move from one portion of the set to another may have to time their delivery so that they do not speak while they are crossing an area not covered by a boom microphone. In studios where only one boom microphone is available, actors may have to make adjustments. For example, if the microphone is covering a conversation between one actor on the set at camera right and another across the set on the left, each must project more than if the same conversation were taking place with both seated together on a couch. It may be advisable for actors not to speak when turned away from the beam. Sometimes an actor may have to engage in "stage business" to invest a pause with significance and meaning—the pause being necessary to permit the microphone to be swung around into position for the next speech.

9. Actors should be prepared to begin or end a scene alone. Scenes may have to start or conclude with a character supposedly talking to another person in the scene when actually the second character is not physically present. The audience must not be aware that this is the case. Camera shots exclude the missing actor. It takes considerable poise to talk in convincing manner to someone who isn't there.

10. Actors must act, and act well, even though they may conclude that they are only a piece of machinery at the mercy of technicians. They are pushed here, then there, started and stopped by the wave of a stage manager's hand, huge cameras are pointed at them, lights shine in their eyes, microphones weave in and out and up and down, just above their heads, scenery and costumes are changed all around them—and all this without a

live audience to listen to them, to give them "feedback," to respond to their acting! Actress Judith Evelyn made an observation some time ago that is still applicable. She felt the restrictions upon the player are "out of all proportion to reason. . . . It is a nerve-wracking ordeal, for example, to be playing a violent love scene with one's brain, voice and body, and at the same time having to keep one eye in constant vigil to see which camera is taking the picture at which particular point."

COMMERCIALS FOR ACTING PRACTICE

---

1.   "Put Your Money — Movies"

VIDEO	AUDIO:
OPEN ON LYNNE AND BETTY ENTERING MOVIE THEATRE, CARRYING SHOPPING BAGS.	**LYNNE:** You know, Roy used to treat me like a movie star . . . now he doesn't **look** at me.
CU OF LYNNE AS SHE SHOWS BETTY A LARGE EARRING.	But these'll help . . . $30 earrings! **BETTY:** Terrific . . . now try Close-up. **LYNNE:** Oh, that's just toothpaste. Maybe another bracelet?
LYNNE HOLDS UP HER ARM, SHOWING SEVERAL BANGLE BRACELETS. SHE JIGGLES THEM.	
BETTY THRUSTS CLOSE-UP TUBE TOWARD CAMERA.	**BETTY:** Lynne . . . put your money where your mouth is. Whiter teeth and fresh breath'll get him back.
EMERGENT GEL.	**LYNNE:** Looks like mouthwash.
	BETTY: There's mouthwash **in** it . . . for your breath.
TWO-SHOT OF GIRLS.	**LYNNE:** Does it whiten your teeth?
CU OF BETTY, SHOWING TEETH.	**BETTY:** White as they can be. How's Roy?
DISSOLVE TO GIRLS AT MOVIE AGAIN, THIS TIME WITH DATE.	**LYNNE:** We're co-starring again!
ZOOM INTO LYNNE'S SMILE. MATTE PACKAGE AND SUPER: "PUT YOUR MONEY WHERE YOUR MOUTH IS".	**ANNCR: (VO)** Put your money where your mouth is. Buy Close-up.

Courtesy of J. Walter Thompson Company and Lever Brothers

---

2.   "Iggy—Alka 2"

VIDEO	AUDIO
OPEN ON MAN AT DINNERTABLE TALKING TO CAMERA WHILE HIS MOTHER AND AUNT PLY HIM	Oh what a night! Momma's stuffed zucchini with garlic sauce, Aunt Fanny's Flaming Swedish

WITH FOOD, CHILDREN ARE FIGHTING IN B/G AND COUSIN IGGY IS DANCING AROUND WITH A LAMP.	Meatballs. And three minutes of conversation with my nitwit cousin Iggy. Such a heartburn! I need relief. And make it fast.
CUT TO PACKAGE OF ALKA 2 ROLLING INTO SCENE	**(SFX OF SPEED)** **ANNCR (VO)** Alka 2 gives you fast relief. It chews fast. And it works fast too.
CUT TO HAND PICKING UP ROLL. CUT TO MAN TAKING A TABLET OUT OF ROLL AND LOOKING AT IT.	
CUT TO CU ALKA 2 TABLET. TABLET CRACKS, FALLS APART AND DISINTEGRATES.	Alka 2 is built to fall apart fast.
CUT TO MAN HOLDING UP ROLL OF ALKA 2 WITH MOTHER AND AUNT ON EITHER SIDE OF HIM NODDING IN AGREEMENT. SUPER: READ AND FOLLOW ALL LABEL DIRECTIONS.	Cool and creamy. Not as chalky, not as gritty.
CUT TO CU OF ALKA 2 ROLLING INTO SCENE	**(SFX OF SPEED)** **MAN** Alka 2. When you need relief from heartburn, make it fast.
MORTISE MAN AND COUSIN IGGY ABOVE ROLL OF ALKA 2.	

Courtesy of J. Walter Thompson Company © by Miles Laboratories, Inc., 1976.

EXAMPLE OF A TV SERIES PRODUCED ON FILM.

THE WALTONS - The Legend[1]

"The Waltons" has been a most popular and award winning series. In addition to the consistently high quality of the writing, directing and production, the acting by members of "the family" and those who appear in guest acting roles has been outstanding. Act I of "The Legend" follows. The script format is that used for film production.

THE WALTONS

"The Legend"

ACT ONE

FADE IN:

1   EXT. WALTON'S MOUNTAIN—DAY (STOCK)
It is early morning and the sunlight is warm on the Mountain.

[1] "The Legend" written by John McGreevey, Copyright (C) MCMLXXII Lorimar Productions, Inc. All rights reserved. From the television series "The Waltons".

JOHN-BOY'S VOICE (AS A MAN)

Usually, each family has its own
special folklore—stories and
anecdotes polished smooth with
the telling. The setting for most
of our family myths was Walton's
Mountain.

2   EXT. WALTON HOUSE AND YARD—ESTABLISHING SHOT—DAY

ELIZABETH and JIM-BOB in swing.

JOHN-BOY'S VOICE (as a man)

But one favored part of our
folklore took place far from the
Mountain—when my father had
served overseas in what was then
called the Great War. To us
children, my father's stories of
the places he'd seen and the men
he'd known were endlessly
fascinating—And then one day
a legend came to visit us—

3   ANOTHER ANGLE

A breathless MARY ELLEN comes running in from the direction
of the chicken shed closely followed by a loudly BARKING
RECKLESS. Mary Ellen disappears into the house leaving
Reckless to continue BARKING.

After a beat, the door opens and JOHN, OLIVIA, JOHN-BOY,
JASON, ERIN, BEN, JIM-BOB, ELIZABETH and Mary Ellen
stream out and head toward the chicken-shed escorted by
the ecstatically barking Reckless.

4   ANGLE ON CHICKEN-SHED

Mary Ellen rushes in, followed by the others, and points
dramatically to a window in the side of the shed where
the screen which covers it has been pushed out. On the
ground beneath are a scattering of chicken feathers.
The family clusters in at the scene of the tragedy.

OLIVIA

It's that fox again!

John moves in to examine the screen and is assisted in
his temporary repairs by John-Boy. Reckless continues
to BARK.

JOHN

Busted right through this screen.

Olivia stoops and picks up a few feathers.

OLIVIA

And here's all that's left of
one of my prize pullets.

ELIZABETH

Did the fox gobble up the
chicken right here?

JOHN-BOY

No. He took it home to his
wife and children.

X

X

MARY ELLEN

They're sitting down to
chicken and dumplings right
about now.

Reckless is racing around BARKING.

OLIVIA

Reckless! Hush!

JIM-BOB

He's excited cause he smells
the fox.

OLIVIA

We could use a little less
barking the morning after and
a little more while the fox is
on the premises!

JOHN (finishing with the screen)

There. That'll discourage most
critters—

OLIVIA

But not that fox.

JOHN

I'll take care of him—

JASON

Are you going to track him down,
Daddy?

JOHN

Can't do it today. Too many
logs waiting to be sawed. Maybe
you and I'll go hunting tomorrow,
John-Boy.

JOHN-BOY

All right, Daddy.

JASON

How about me going along, too?

JOHN

Well, Jason—I don't know—

JASON

Can't there be a place for
next-to-oldest some times?

OLIVIA

Now what kind of question is
that?

JOHN

Hunting is something you have
to grow into—

JASON

Maybe I'm not up to it, Daddy.
But maybe I am. How'll I ever
know if I don't get a chance to
try?

                         JOHN
             We'll see.

He starts away toward the house.

                         OLIVIA
             Mary Ellen, you can finish
             gathering the eggs.

Mary Ellen nods and moves to the chicken-pen. Olivia,
Erin, Elizabeth, Ben and Jim-Bob follow John toward
the house. John-Boy and Jason hang back slightly.

                       JOHN-BOY
             Jason—far as I'm concerned,
             you can go in my place.

                         JASON
             I don't want to take your place,
             John-Boy. I just want a place
             of my own.

Jason moves off and John-Boy moves thoughtfully after
him.

5   INT. WALTON KITCHEN—DAY

The family is just about to begin lunch. John-Boy is
absent.

                         JOHN
             Not like John-Boy to be late
             for lunch.

                         OLIVIA
             He went to Ike's for the mail.

                         JOHN
             Just have to start without him.
             Grandpa.

All join hands as Grandpa begins the blessing.

                        GRANDPA
             Master Jesus, we thank thee for
             this food and for all the blessing
             you have seen fit to bestow upon us.

During the following, John-Boy enters and bows his head
respectfully, but it is plain that he has news he is
desperate to impart.

                   GRANDPA (continuing)
             We thank you for the riches you
             have given us: these children,
             this land, our toilsome days,
             our nights of rest.

Grandma feels the blessing is getting too lengthy and
nudges Grandpa.

                        GRANDPA
             I even thank you for this old
             woman who thinks I ought to cut
             this short. Amen.

There is a chorus of Amens and a reprimanding look
from Grandma, then:

                       JOHN-BOY
             Daddy, would you look?

                    JOHN
          What am I supposed to look at?
                  JOHN-BOY
          On top of the mail—it's a
          telegram!

He puts the mail on the table and all react:

                    JOHN
          I don't believe it. Who'd be
          sending me a telegram?
                   OLIVIA
          Want me to open it?
                    JOHN
          No. I'll do it.

He gingerly picks up the telegram and opens it. He
stares suspiciously at it and then he lets out a
whoop!

                   OLIVIA
          John—what is it?
                    JOHN
          Do you know who sent me this
          telegram?
                  GRANDPA
          No—but we'd like to.
                    JOHN
          My old Army buddy—Theodore
          Roosevelt Harrison!
                 MARY ELLEN
          Tip Harrison!

The other kids react in excited disbelief.

                    JOHN
          Wouldn't you know Tip would be
          the one to send me the first
          telegram I ever got?
                   OLIVIA
          What's the telegram say?
                    JOHN
          "Tenshun—Corporal Cootie-Bait."

The kids react, giggle delightedly.

                    JOHN
          "Tenshun—Corporal Cootie-Bait.
          Stop. The caissons will be
          rolling through your sector
          tomorrow. Stop. Would like
          to share your bivouac for an hour
          or two. Stop. We will win the
          war all over again. Stop.
          Always your buddy . . . Tip."
                   OLIVIA
          He's coming to visit!
                 MARY ELLEN
          We'll really get to see him!

The kids are agog.

ERIN

I can't believe it! Tip
Harrison . . . here!

JOHN

I can hardly believe it myself.
Been a lot of years since Tip
and I were discharged from the
Army.
(looks at telegram)
But he sure sounds just the same.

JOHN-BOY

Tell about how he took over
the train, Daddy—

BEN

No. I want to hear about Tip
and the carrier pigeon—

ELIZABETH

First tell why he's called Tip . . .

JOHN

All right. All right!

The kids settle happily for a familiar and cherished
ritual.

JOHN (continuing)

Well, right from the first day
at Fort Dix, this fellow
Harrison was . . . different.
Everybody else griped about Army
chow. Harrison—he fixed it
up with a local restaurant to
serve him an eight course dinner
right there in the mess hall—

ERIN

Silver platters—

MARY ELLEN

Steam tables—

JOHN-BOY

A flaming dessert—

JOHN

The rest of us wrote letters to
the girls back home. Harrison
invited eight Ziegfield girls to
an evening in the barracks.
Everybody else was singing
"K–K–K–KATY"—

JASON

—but Harrison was singing
"It's a Long Way to Tipperary"—

JOHN

So we started calling him
"Tipperary"—

JIM-BOB

But that was too long a name—

                    ELIZABETH
—so you settled for "Tip".

                    JOHN-BOY
Now tell about how he borrowed
the railroad train—

                    BEN
No—I want to hear about the
time he captured the town—

The kids are all plugging for their favorite.

                    JOHN
Hey, hey! You kids know all the
stories better than I do—

                    MARY ELLEN
But we like to hear you tell
them, Daddy—

                    JOHN
Run on now. You can hear them
from the man himself tomorrow.

Olivia has picked up the telegram and studied it.

                    OLIVIA
You won't even have to wait til
tomorrow—

                    JOHN
What do you mean, Livvy?

                    OLIVIA
This telegram's been a long
time getting here. Tip Harrison
will be "rolling in" here some
time today!

As everyone reacts to this startling news—

6   INT. WALTON LIVING ROOM—DAY
Grandma is dusting a table. Grandpa is reading/dozing.   X

                    OLIVIA
Have you seen John?

                    GRANDPA
He went through here a little
while ago—

                    GRANDMA
I believe he headed upstairs.

This surprises Olivia but she moves to the stairs, goes up.

                    GRANDPA   X
You already dusted that table.

                    GRANDMA   X
All this talk about the war sets
me remembering. Those were
terrible days, worrying about
John and the others, wondering if
they'd come home. Thank heaven
there won't ever be another war
like that one.

7   INT. JOHN AND OLIVIA'S BEDROOM—DAY

John has dragged a footlocker out of the closet and from
it is trying on his World War I uniform: the jacket,
trousers, puttees, cap, helmet. Olivia enters. John
looks up just a mite sheepishly.

> OLIVIA
>
> I'd forgotten you still had that.

> JOHN
>
> I'm not just sure why I saved
> it—

> OLIVIA
>
> You wore it well.

John holds up the jacket.

> JOHN
>
> To tell you the truth, I was never
> all that comfortable in it. Now
> Tip—you'd've sworn he was born
> wearing it—but everything about
> soldiering just came natural to
> him.

> OLIVIA (teasing)
>
> So I've heard.

> JOHN
>
> I do go on about old Tip, don't
> I? It's just that in my whole
> life, Livvy, I've never known
> anybody quite like him—not
> afraid of anything or anybody.

> OLIVIA
>
> Doesn't seem to me you're a
> man who scares easy.

> JOHN (shakes his head)
>
> Tip's special. You don't mind
> his coming—?

> OLIVIA
>
> Of course not. I'm glad to be
> meeting him. Those months you
> were away during the War—that's
> a time in your life I don't know
> anything about—except for those
> funny stories you tell the children.
> It's like you had a little separate
> life that I hadn't any part of.

> JOHN
>
> Hey, now! What's worth knowing
> about John Walton you know—
> better than anyone else—and the
> best part of the war was coming
> home to you—

John kisses her lightly. She smiles, nods.

> OLIVIA
>
> I hope Mr. Tip Harrison likes
> plain home cooking—

                    JOHN
          He will. Don't you worry.
                    OLIVIA
          If he doesn't, I guess he can
          always fix it with some restaurant
          to serve him his 8 course meal.

They laugh. Olivia moves to the door. John grins at
his reflection in the mirror. Just for a moment, he
DOES seem a stranger. Olivia EXITS.

8   EXT. WALTON HOUSE AND YARD—ANGLE ON PORCH—DAY

Grandma and Grandpa are sitting on the porch. The
children: John-Boy, Jason, Mary Ellen, Erin, Ben,
Jim-Bob and Elizabeth are lined up—waiting. John-Boy
is half-heartedly reading but the others are mostly
just impatiently staring off.

                  GRANDMA
          Why are you children all mooning
          around the porch. Run and play—
                    BEN
          We're waiting for Tip Harrison.
                    ERIN
          I want to see him the minute he
          gets here.
                  GRANDPA
          All this fuss! You'd think it
          was President Roosevelt stopping
          by—
                  GRANDMA
          More likely to be **Mrs**. Roosevelt.
                  ELIZABETH
          Maybe he can't find our house—
                 MARY ELLEN
          Tip Harrison can find ANYTHING.
                  JIM-BOB
          He got lost once in France—
                    JASON
          Tip Harrison knew where HE was.
          Everybody else was lost.
                  JOHN-BOY
          If Mr. Harrison does come—
                    ERIN
          Of course he's coming—
                  JOHN-BOY
          Just remember he's here to
          see Daddy—so don't you children
          be pestering him all the time—

As John-Boy speaks, there's the RUMBLE of an APPROACHING
CAR. Everyone slowly turns and stares o.s. in
disbelief. They are stunned, speechless.

9   ANOTHER ANGLE

A glittering Pierce-Arrow touring car is just pulling

to a stop in front of the Walton house. At the wheel
of this magnificent machine is TIP HARRISON—handsome,
dashingly dressed. Lohengrin and his swan . . . The Lone
Ranger astride Silver never made a more perfect
entrance. As Tip brakes to a stop, all of the Waltons
move slowly from the porch and house to stand in an
awed semi-circle around the dazzling chariot and its
driver. There's a moment's silence. And then Tip
opens his door and steps out:

> TIP
>
> "Lafayette—we are here"!

> JOHN
>
> Tip!

And they are shaking hands, pounding each other on the
back as the family looks on in delight.

> TIP
>
> John Walton—you ornery backwoods
> son of a gun! How are you?

> JOHN
>
> Never better. And I don't have
> to ask how YOU are! You look
> great. And what a buggy!

He gestures to the gleaming auto, lights a cigarette.   X

> TIP
>
> Easier to handle than that Army
> Mule you and I shoved halfway
> across France.

John remembers the family. He turns Tip around.

> JOHN
>
> Tip—this is my wife—Olivia.

> OLIVIA
>
> Mr. Harrison—

She offers her hand. Tip takes it, brushes it with
his lips.

> TIP
>
> John always did have more than
> his share of the luck—

> JOHN
>
> My mother and father—

> GRANDPA
>
> Pleasure—

> GRANDMA
>
> That telegram you sent didn't
> get here till this morning—

> TIP
>
> I knew I should've sent it by carrier pigeon!

This reminder of a favorite story sends the kids into
giggles.

> JOHN
>
> Our children—

                    TIP
No need to ask what you've been
up to!
                    JOHN
This is the oldest—John-Boy . . .
Tip Harrison.
                    JOHN-BOY (they shake hands)
Mr. Harrison—
                    TIP
Call me "Tip"—
                    JOHN
Jason . . . Mary Ellen . . . Erin . . .
Ben . . . Jim-Bob . . . Elizabeth.
It'll take you awhile to sort
them out—
                    ELIZABETH
I'm Elizabeth—the Youngest.
                    TIP
I never would have guessed. I
didn't know how many children
you had, John—how old they
might be—whether they were boys
or girls—so I decided a little
candy would be the safest kind of
present.—

He lifts out a couple of enormous boxes of candy. The
kids react in pure pleasure.

                    OLIVIA
Now you children be sensible—

The children chorus thank you's. Tip smiles at them
and then turns and lifts a basket with three bottles
of champagne from the car.   X

                    TIP
For the rest of us . . . champagne!
                    GRANDPA
Champagne!

One momentary negative reaction from Olivia, then she
smiles agreeably.

                    JOHN
This is a special occasion—
                    TIP
A very special occasion—
                    GRANDPA (singing)
"Should auld acquaintance be
forgot—"
                    TIP & GRANDPA (joining in)   X
"—and never brought to mind."
                    JOHN & TIP & GRANDPA
"Should auld acquaintance be
forgot and days of Auld Lang Syne."

                        JOHN

        Remember my very first taste of
        French Champagne?

                        TIP

        Crouched in a bombed out wine
        cellar near Chateau-Thierry—

                    MARY ELLEN

        You drank it out of a German
        Helmet—

                    JIM-BOB

        —it tasted like vinegar—

                    JOHN-BOY

        And Mr. Harrison said: "Oh, well,
        John—it wasn't a very good year."

                        TIP

        Somebody's been telling stories!

The children all laugh and look pleased.

                        JOHN

        You're staying the night at least—

                        TIP

        Well, I don't know, John—

The children groan in disappointment.

                        JOHN

        That help you make up your mind?

                    TIP (grins, nods)

        I'll stay.
        (takes Elizabeth's hand)
        I never could stand to
        disappoint a lovely lady.

                        JOHN

        John-Boy—bring Tip's luggage.

                    JOHN-BOY

        Right, Daddy.

Tip moves toward the house completely surrounded by the
enthralled family.

                        TIP

        John Walton—you old cootie-
        bait! I haven't felt this
        high since we danced a hoe-down
        in the middle of the Champs-Elysee!

10   ANGLE FEATURING PIERCE-ARROW

John-Boy opens the car to remove the two pieces of
elegant cowhide luggage from the back-seat. He is
marveling at the beauty of the car's interior. He
sets the luggage on the ground and turns for a closer
inspection of the front seat, special steering wheel.
This leads him to the registration slip in a celluloid
cover on the steering wheel. John-Boy reacts in
surprise.

11   INSERT: REGISTRATION SLIP

The Registered owner is listed as HAROLD T. HARRISON.   X

12   BACK TO SCENE

John-Boy stares at the registration slip a moment and then gets out of the car. He shuts the door. He starts to pick up the luggage. He stares at it.

13   INSERT: LUGGAGE

The luggage tags read: HAROLD T. HARRISON.   X

14   BACK TO SCENE

John-Boy's puzzlement deepens. He picks up the luggage and with a last look at the glistening car, moves thoughtfully toward the house.

15   INT. LIVING ROOM—DAY

John is looking out the window to the porch. The SOUND of children's delighted giggles can be heard.

16   EXT. PORCH—JOHN'S POV—DAY

Tip is the center of all the Walton children. He is playing a game of checkers with John-Boy and telling a story at the same time. The kids—especially Mary Ellen and Erin hang on every word.   X

17   INT. LIVING ROOM—DAY

Olivia joins John at the window. The SOUND of laughter from the porch continues.

> JOHN
>
> He hasn't changed a whit.
>
> OLIVIA
>
> In all these years, that doesn't seem natural.

18   EXT. PORCH—JOHN'S POV—DAY

The children are laughing helplessly, eyes on Tip.

19   INT. LIVING ROOM—DAY

John turns from the window.

> JOHN
>
> Anyway—the children know now I haven't been stretching the truth about Tip Harrison—
>
> OLIVIA
>
> He could charm the birds out of the trees.
>
> JOHN
>
> Only man I've ever known to be that sure of himself and never take a fall—   X

There's another BURST of LAUGHTER.

20   EXT. PORCH—DAY

Mary Ellen, Erin, Elizabeth, Ben, Jason and Jim-Bob are convulsed. John-Boy is studying the checkerboard to make his move.

> TIP
>
> The only sound was this heavy breathing—
> (demonstrates)
> So I whispered: "Mademoiselle—s'il vous plait . . . n'avez pas   X

peur." Miss—please—do not
be afraid. Heavy breathing. I
moved closer. "Please, cherie—
say something." Heavy breathing.
I leaned nearer. Suddenly—
there was a flash of light—

                    MARY ELLEN

A Very shell—

                    TIP

And I was gazing tenderly into
the warm brown eyes of my
"Mademoiselle"—a very solemn
and completely indifferent French
cow!

The kids react appreciatively. John-Boy makes his move.

                    JOHN-BOY

Your turn, Mr. Harrison.

Tip regards the board. He is NOT pleased. He is a
"winner" in all things large and small.

                    TIP

I better pay attention to my
game—

                    BEN

John-Boy's good—

                    ERIN (adoringly)

But not as good as you, Tip
Harrison—

                    TIP

Thanks for that vote of
confidence—

                    ELIZABETH

Tell us about **your** children—

                    TIP

I don't have any—yet. One
of these days, I'm going to
settle down and have at least
a dozen.

Tip makes his move. Like lightning, John-Boy counter-
moves. The trap has closed. Tip is even more nettled
though he tries to hide it.

                    TIP (continuing)

Looks like I'm going to have
to send for the Marines.

                    JOHN-BOY

Give up?

                    TIP

Never! We may have lost a
battle but we haven't lost
the war! You'll see my strategy
in a minute here—

                    JOHN-BOY

What kind of business are you
in, Mr. Harrison?

                    TIP

          Business? Oh . . . investments . . .
          and John-Boy, please, call me
          Tip.

                  JOHN-BOY

          Is that stocks and bonds and
          such?

                  TIP (a little edgy)

          Investments—of all kinds.

Tip's anger at his apparent loss of the checker game
is coming close to the surface. Elizabeth leans in
closer.

                  ELIZABETH

          When will I see your strategy,
          Tip Harrison?

Tip uses Elizabeth's move to screen himself as he
deliberately upsets the checkerboard.

                    TIP

          Careful, honey. Oooooops!

The checkers go rolling.

                  JOHN-BOY

          Don't worry. I know where the
          pieces go—

                  TIP (rising)

          No point in setting it up again,
          son—

                  JIM-BOB

          But John-Boy was winning—

                  TIP (stretching)

          Two more moves and I'd have
          swept the board—

                  JIM-BOB

          I don't see how—

                  TIP (slightest edge)

          Take my word for it.

John appears in the doorway to save the moment:

                    JOHN

          Hey, Tip! Chow-line's forming
          in here!

                    TIP

          Chow line! That's one place
          you'll always find Tip Harrison
          up front.

Tip goes IN, followed by Mary Ellen, Erin, Ben, Jason
and Elizabeth. John-Boy looks thoughtfully after Tip.

                                        FADE OUT.

END OF ACT ONE

Projects and Exercises

1. Prepare and present an acting audition for the following:

   a. University radio station.

   b. A television audition for a production agency specializing in daytime serials.

   c. A television audition for a production company holding general auditions.

   d. A television audition for a situation comedy series being held by the package agency in charge of production. After each audition, the class should offer criticism of the material selected by the student and the presentation.

2. Divide into groups to prepare and present the scenes from "Aesop's Fables" script.

3. Bring in brief scenes from script collections that may be rehearsed outside of class by each group.

4. Record actual persons of all ages and dialects speaking naturally. Prepare a written transcript and then record the same material as delivered by a class member. Compare the two.

5. Film or tape the face of a classmate as he or she reacts to some emotional speech presented by a fellow student. Project the film or tape for the class and see if the class can tell which emotion is portrayed on the screen. Project the same footage for different age groups and secure their reactions. Evaluate results.

6. Evaluate the acting you hear on some radio commercials and report to the class.

7. Report on your reactions to the acting you have observed on some TV programs.

22

The person who takes the script from the writer and actively guides its progress until it has been brought to life through performance is the director. The producer of a series may also direct the program in addition to his executive work. This chapter deals with the directorial responsibilities and techniques.

The director must be able to view the material being prepared for performance in enlarged detail, as through a microscope, in order to suggest specific recommendations to members of the cast on aspects of their performances, but must also see the material as a whole to make qualitative judgments on general aspects of the production.

The director is obliged to supervise many details in putting together a broadcast or telecast. The need to decide which details require attention first and which are of lesser importance led one network to give the following dictum to newly hired directors: "There are *fifty* specific things you need to do before recording a show or broadcasting it, but the rehearsal time allotted makes it possible to do only *twenty-five* out of the fifty. The choice of which twenty-five you do makes the difference between a good showmanlike production and a poor one which may have polish in unimportant details but misses fire."

Experience proves the soundness of this statement. No one can set down ironclad recommendations as to what any individual director should do. In mathematics the figure four is always four, but not so in directing. What works today with one actor, one engineer, one camera operator, one sound technician, may not work tomorrow. The pattern changes with people, script, studio, and time of day. Directors should adjust to these changes and vary their techniques accordingly.

RADIO

The only radio material generally being broadcast these days that needs specific direction is the commercial that uses voices, sound effects, and music in a variety of combinations. The bulk of radio programming—news and recorded music—is presented by the performer without the aid of a director.

The production of complicated radio commercials, on the other hand, requires skilled directors. The techniques they use are those developed during the days when radio drama was being produced. The suggestions that follow apply specifically to the production of commercials, but they can also be applied to the production of radio drama for those schools that still carry out this activity.

Before Studio Rehearsal

1. Read the script through without interruption to get an overall impression of it. First impressions are important, because the audience receives nothing but first impressions.
2. Study the commercial carefully, observing its details. Determine the general type of treatment it requires. Estimate its length, for commercials must be timed to the half-second. Decide on the kind of actors you will need and the nature of the sound effects and music.
3. To guide your direction of the commercial, write notes into the script regarding such items as the perspective of a line or sound, writing "off-mike" when they occur at a distance from the center of the scene, or the points when you will give cues to actors or other members of the crew.
4. Schedule a music conference with the organist, composer, or the person who is to obtain the records. Indicate where music is to "sneak," "stab," "fade out," the length of bridges, the flavor of desired music and other such details. Welcome suggestions from your musical adviser, but remember that you must make the final decisions. Do the same with your sound-effects technician.
5. Cast the actors. Do this on the basis of past experience, audition cards, by consulting other directors, or by special voice tests for the program. Be sure to audition on microphone. A large character man may not sound as virile on microphone as he looks on stage.

    In addition to suitability for the part, consider the actors' own personalities and the balance of their voices with others in the cast. Actors who like to direct others, or fool around, or think they are above direction may destroy the necessary sense of a cooperative "in-group" feeling.
6. Order whatever is necessary in manpower and equipment for the script. Reserve the studio, request the engineer for a particular time, sound effects, and such things as filters, echo chambers, platforms, screens, turntable, etc.

First Read-Through—Off-Mike

1. Distribute scripts, assign parts, and allow time for the actors to mark their scripts.
2. Briefly explain the treatment you are going to follow in the script, outlining in general terms, describing the characterizations as you see them at this point. Don't be too specific or long-winded.
3. Have the actors read aloud through the script from beginning to end. Allow time for sound and music bridges. Cue as you have planned for the recording. This gives the actors time to establish a habit of waiting for a cue.

4. Determine whether the script runs overtime. If so, make the cuts you tentatively marked. The reading rehearsal usually takes less time than the actual perform-ance, so you usually can cut with impunity.
5. Correct any characterizations that are completely "off." Approve those that are on the right track.

Production Rehearsal on Mike

1. Forget timing during this rehearsal unless you have an assistant. Work in the con-trol room.
2. Start at the beginning and continue to the end of the commercial. Sound effects are included and music, too, if an organist or recorded music is being used. Or-chestra rehearsal is usually separate and concentrated for budget reasons. In nor-mal practice, rehearsal of the orchestra would come at the end of the production rehearsal period.
3. Work carefully on each sequence before going on to the next. This is the creative period. Sound patterns are introduced and integrated with the dialogue. With the sound-effects technicians, try different levels and microphone positions for manual effects. Experiment with different records.
4. Work on characterization and interpretation. Before hammering away on indi-vidual interpretation, correct the overall attack. Vary the approach to each actor. One actor may react best to the short, succinct, "More speed here," or "Don't ham this line." Another actor may resent this as a mechanical approach, and want suggestions of another type: "This person is frustrated here . . . See if you can give me a bit more of an inner resentment against the world which takes the form of irritation with this poor clerk in the department store." One actor may re-spond best to gentle chiding, another to bluntness. Use whichever attack is needed to build and set the character and interpretation. The director must be a good practical psychologist.

During this period work closely with the engineer, who will be marking a script along with you. Check the levels with the engineer and always re-main aware of the problems that may develop. You cannot expect any per-son to use more than two hands in making board fades, bringing in effects, and controlling multiple microphones. The usual number of microphones consists of one cast mike or possibly two, if there are many people on mike at the same time; one sound mike, one filter or echo, and one music mike. Don't have the engineer run the turntables if you are using recorded music, be-cause in that event there will be difficulty in riding gain. Be cooperative and respect the engineer's advice, but keep the control of the show in your own hands. Weigh seriously the advantages of getting good "presence" out of a close pickup against those of working farther away from the mike, which permits less supervision of the VU but carries less impact. Work with your actors to get intensity without blasting, but don't let them get too far back. In scenes where the actors are shouting or projecting a great deal, move them back. Experiment with relative placement of actors on-mike. Having both

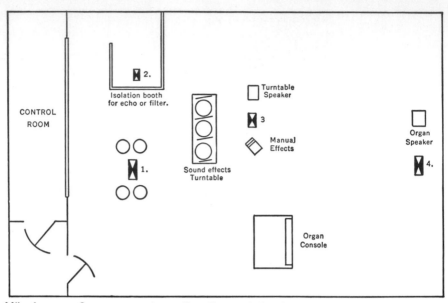

Mike 1, actors; 2, actors on echo or filter; 3, recorded and manual sound effects; 4, organ speaker.

Figure 22-1   Microphone Placement for a Radio Commercial

people in a conversation at the same distance may give a flatness of perspective—move one back a few inches or to the edge of the beam. Microphone placement is illustrated in Figure 22-1.

Dress Rehearsal

1. Run through the complete performance. Make careful note of the timing.
2. Jot down reminder notes on performance and production points. Put these in the left margin. Make them simple and specific enough to jog your memory in the final discussion before broadcast. Such as "Hit wrong word," "Too close," "Watch me for fade," "Tag final speech," "Sound in too soon," "Four stings, not three."
3. Warn engineer of upcoming fades, sudden sounds, shouts, filter mike, etc.
4. Listen to the show as a whole with the perspective of the radio listener who will hear the commercial for the first time.
5. After the run-through, see what time adjustments need to be made.
6. Re-rehearse any difficult sequences, tricky sound synchronization, crowd backgrounds, etc.
7. Do not change actors' characterizations at this point. You had your opportunity earlier.
8. "Take Five!" Relax. Even if you don't feel like it, relax outwardly for the sake of company morale and confidence.

During the Recording

1. Cue clearly as previously rehearsed. Follow the script, looking ahead to warn the engineer and to check that the cast is ready for the next sequence.
2. Keep close contact with the members of your cast. Watch them, as well as your script, and encourage and commend them by visible expressions of your interest in their performance. There should be a close bond between cast and director. *Live* the script with the performers, if you can, and react to the presentation. It is not only discourteous, but distracting for a performer on microphone to look into the control room and see a director looking bored or disgruntled, or talking with others in the control room.
3. Play the tape to make sure that you have achieved the type of production you have sought. If mistakes have been made, or if you can see an opportunity to improve the commercial, record another tape. The show may also be improved by judicious editing.

Following the Recording

1. Thank the cast. Give compliments sincerely when they are deserved. A reassuring smile is in order when the members of the cast have done their best. This is no time for recriminations.
2. Fill out any reports and talent sheets.
3. Leave the show in the studio. Don't brood over the mistakes. Don't direct it again at night before going to sleep. Evaluate your work another day.

Applications to the directing of radio drama. The techniques and procedures described above can be applied to the directing of radio dramas, but there would need to be an expansion of those techniques to meet the demands of the longer dramatic forms. Even though a 30-second radio commercial is often a complicated piece of material, its brevity eliminates some problems that face a director of longer material.

1. A commercial is likely to come from an advertising agency in the exact form in which it must be produced. A drama script, on the other hand, may usually be changed to some extent by the director. He or she should therefore read the script carefully to determine what changes are desirable. If the writer is available, these changes should be made in consultation with the writer.
2. A long script with many characters may require doubling by actors. This factor must be taken into account in casting.
3. Timing a brief commercial is relatively simple, but the timing of a long script is a complicated process. The director should estimate the length of the script on the first read-through, remembering that solid narrative takes longer to perform than short-sentence dialogue. Cuts should be made immediately if the script is obviously too long. Further cuts should be planned in case they are needed so that you will not have to use rehearsal time deciding what to cut. In the first read-through by the cast check the timing, and during the dress rehearsal make timing

notations every 30 seconds in your script. These notations can then be used as reference points while the script is being recorded or broadcast. Music can sometimes be shortened or lengthened to adjust timing, and the cast can be given tentative cuts that can be introduced during the production if the script runs long. In estimating time remember that professionals often stretch on the air, and amateurs often read more hurriedly on the air than they do in rehearsal.

4. In directing a long script, the pacing of the whole show should not be neglected while the director is concentrating on the details. One scene may furnish the necessary balance between scenes of tension and action. One may be the climactic scene for the first half. Establish the tempo for each scene before moving on to the next. Compare scene-by-scene timing with the first timing.

DIRECTING TELEVISION

In the early years of television, programs were produced live in a television studio. Later the live program was replaced by programs recorded on video tape. Using film and video tape makes it possible to produce the program in segments, which are then assembled in an editing room into a complete program.

The first imperative for a TV director is to know what cameras and other technical equipment can do in creating the picture aspect of the pro-

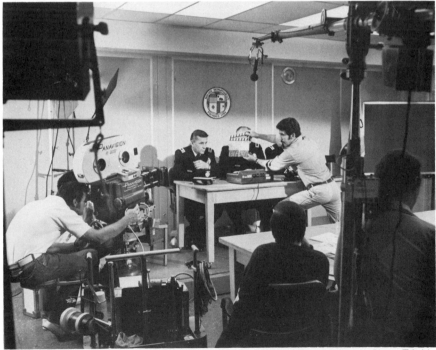

Photograph Courtesy of Columbia Pictures Television

Just Before A Take in a TV Filmed Drama.

gram. The director must understand how this equipment can be used to provide dramatic emphasis, clarity, and visual variety. The basic shots and editing techniques available to the TV director are discussed briefly below.

1. Distance Between Viewer and Scene May Be Varied

Three general types of camera shots may be classified in this category: "long shot," "medium shot," and "close-up." An overall perspective of the setting for the viewer is supplied by the long shot, sometimes referred to as an orien-

Photograph Courtesy of Columbia Pictures Television,

Director Guiding an Actor in A Filmed Drama. Scene performed by Robert Forster and Wynn Irwin.

tation or establishing shot. It aids in indicating "the lay of the land" and the relationship of the various elements. It informs in general terms how many people are on the panel and whether we are in a Western frontier bar or a modern office in New York City. When the audience is comfortable, knowing where it is and who are involved, it is ready to draw closer and join the group. The long shot cannot give much detail, being restricted by the size of the screen on a home receiver. The close-up shots are used to single out details, focus the attention, clearly inform, and heighten dramatic emphasis. A combination of a close-up and long shot is often seen. A vocalist, in close-up,

Shooting an Interior Scene in a Video-Taped Drama.

might occupy a portion of the screen with a dance group in the background. A new character might enter the side of the frame close to the lens while the camera is on a long shot. The new character can dominate the scene because of his or her larger size in comparison to the rest of the group. Interesting composition effects may result from such combination arrangements. The medium shots ranging between the two extremes have many graduations. They are utilized heavily in following the action of the main characters and permit arrangements of people and things in good pictorial composition to enhance the mood. It has been estimated that in dramatic programs, medium shots are used about 70 percent of the time.

Directors, in actual practice, use descriptive functional requests for desired camera pickup areas, such as a "three shot," which will frame as much of the setting needed to include the three performers on the set, "cover shot" to include all of the specific set or action, or "one shot" for a pickup of a single person. When a shorter distance between viewer and character is wanted, terms such as "waist shot," "bust shot," "knee shot," or "shoulder shot" indicate where the bottom edge of the picture frame is to be. "Head shot" or "close-up of hand on the dagger" are examples of pinpointed directions to bring segments of the scene into "big close-up."

2. Position of Viewer May Be Modified by Camera Movement

We are standing in an exhibit hall dedicated to American Business and Industry. On the floor is sketched an outline of the United States with symbols indicating outstanding contributions by the various cities and states: an **auto** in Michigan, oil derricks in the South and Southwest, motion picture studios in California, grapefruit in Florida, salmon and lumber in the Northwest, etc. Directly ahead, lining the wall, are tables containing working models of new machines. At the left are salon photographic prints of industrial scenes. On the ceiling is a huge mural depicting famous inventions. Our physical actions in walking directly forward to one of the models is, in terms of camera movement, a "dolly in" or "zoom in"; if we stop and look down to the outline on the floor the head action corresponds to a "tilt down"; looking up to see the mural would be a "tilt up"; as we turn slowly, keeping the same physical position, looking at the working models and then the photographs, it is a "pan left"; or if we walk along the tables of the working models, looking at each in turn as we walk, it is a "truck shot." The mobility of the television camera permitting a duplication of the freedom of movement by a spectator is one of the medium's unique characteristics. The director is able to guide the viewer's field of view for desired interpretation and emphasis. The sweep of movement also gives to the viewer an emphatic sense of "belonging," of being an active participant and intimately involved in the proceedings.

3. Position of Viewer May Be Modified by Camera Angle

The direction from which the viewer observes the scene may be changed by placement of cameras. The discussion of the various camera-support units described the extent of vertical movement by pedestals and cranes. Variations from the normal eye-level, horizontal plane to "low-angle" and "high-angle" shots may be called for by the director. The use of two or more cameras also permits the easy shifting of direction of view in a horizontal plane. Angle shots from left or right of the subject may be chosen for variety and psychological effect. When two cameras are shooting the scene at approximately 180 degrees, as is frequently done in dialogue scenes between two characters, the shots are referred to as "reverse-angle," "over-the-shoulder," or "tight-cross-two-shot."

4. Camera Switching Methods May Be Varied

In addition to the almost infinite number of different camera shots available through various patterns of distance, movement, and angle, the selection of different transitional techniques or switching methods may also affect visual impressions, tempo, and mood. The "cut" or "take" is most frequently employed during dialogue within a scene in drama and for sports, interviews, news, and forums. The change from one camera to another is instantaneous. Care must be taken to keep the audience from becoming aware of the transition from picture to picture. An unusual difference in distance or angle between the shots, a mismatch in focus, or different light intensity may jar the viewer. Cutting in the middle of a sentence or vocal phrase calls attention to the shift.

The classic example of an unwanted, disorientation shock effect through poor cutting occurred during a network coverage of a horse race in the early days of television. One camera was located in the grandstand, the other on the track infield directly opposite. As the horses came down the homestretch, the director called for cutting from one camera to the other. The horses apparently reversed direction, running first one way then the other, with each cut. An amazing effect, but one that unfortunately was extremely distracting. A "dissolve," the fading of one picture out as the other fades in, is a common technique in variety and music programs during the performance of a vocal or dance selection, in commercial demonstrations, and in dramatic programs, to indicate a shift in locale or the lapse of time. Such dissolves may be extremely fast, approximating a cut, or take a number of seconds to execute. The latter type is sometimes called a "lap dissolve." The rhythm of the dissolve is easier, slower, and smoother than the cut. Sometimes a "matched dissolve," going from one object to a similar one such as from an alarm clock to a factory time-machine clock, is used to bind two scenes tightly together. The "fade-out" and "fade-in" are generally used to indicate a definite break in the progression of the program. The fade-out has been compared to the use of a curtain in the theater to end an act or to indicate a lapse in time. In variety programs this switching method is a standard transition between program segments and commercials.

5. Special Electronic Effects Are Possible

The director may have many effects at his disposal through specialized equipment in the control room. The "superimposure" is used most frequently. A "super" is achieved by making two cameras "hot" at the same time. One signal is superimposed over another. A similar effect is obtained by electronically "keying" one picture into another, using the capabilities of modern video switchers. The keying technique has virtually replaced the supering technique. Many opening and closing titles and credits are supered over or keyed into the setting or action. Commercial announcements use supers or keys to emphasize the price or particular qualities of the product. Trick dramatic and novelty effects are feasible through utilization of these techniques in dream sequences, appearances of ghosts and "magic people," transformation of a vocal trio into a sextet, close-up of a tap dancer's feet simultaneously with his entire body, rain and fog, an apparent reduction in a person's size to only two or three inches in height when compared to other people or objects in the scene.

"Split screen" describes the effect achieved when separate camera images are not superimposed, but actually occupy adjacent portions of the same screen. An example of dramatic usage is the showing of two people in a telephone conversation. Dialogue between a newscaster or MC in one location and other people in another city is an example of nondramatic usage. In picking up four correspondents from different parts of the country, for an election coverage, a network generally uses a four-way split screen. When one picture replaces the other in a horizontal, diagonal, or vertical direction, this action is called a "wipe." Corner or specially shaped "inserts" allow one picture to replace a portion of the screen. Using this technique, a figure can be inserted into a scene. Thus a figure of Andy Williams, previously recorded on a video-tape machine, can be inserted into a scene in which Andy Williams is singing, giving the impression that Andy is singing to himself.

The titles and credits of many television programs are created by the use of an electronic system known as a character generator. This typewriterlike device, based on computer technology, generates electronic signals that may be keyed into studio camera signals and thus create high-quality lettering and other patterns solely by electronic means. No art work is required and no slide camera is involved.

The physical location of the director during the rehearsal and actual performance on the air has been described in the chapter on "Technical Aspects of Television." When one is located in the confines of a control room, surrounded by people (engineers, production assistants, associate directors, agency representatives, and observers) and equipment, (camera and film-chain monitors, oscilloscopes, preview monitors, line monitors, switching panel, talk-back microphones, audio panels, loudspeakers, amplifiers, power supplies, turntables, tape decks, etc.) and somewhere "out there" is the studio with more people and more equipment, one realizes the loss in direct personal contact between the director and his company. The director turns to the stage manager to take care of the cueing and signals to cast and production personnel in the studio; turns to the technical director (TD) to transmit instructions to the members of the technical team if the director is not permitted by union regulations to do so directly; and turns to the AD for timing cues and reminders of upcoming directorial instructions.

The number of personnel connected with the production increases the responsibility for coordination and leadership by the director. Some of the problems that face the motion picture or stage director are about the same in television. In the planning of scenery, design of costumes, procurement of properties and furniture, and the like, the routine is similar. The basic and highly important differences are: 1. a compressed rehearsal period; 2. closeness of contact between cast and home audience; and 3. the 4-to-3 aspect ratio and small size of the TV screen.

The Director's Responsibilities

As the person who is responsible for determining the way a show will look to viewers and how it will sound, the director is one of the most important elements in the production process. The director has the assistance of other highly talented and skilled associates—performers, designers, associate directors, technical directors, lighting directors, and other assistants—but the guidance necessary to integrate their contributions into a program that has unity, clarity, and artistic impact must come from the director. A skilled and imaginative person in this role can do a great deal to enhance the quality of a show that might otherwise be routine; on the other hand, a stolid director can frustrate the accomplishment of the artistic values that may be inherent in a script.

If directors are to draw out the highest values existing potentially in the various program elements, they must possess certain qualities and attitudes. First of all, they must conscientiously prepare for the program. This preparation must include such practical needs as casting the show, planning with the designers such elements as scenery and costumes, working out floor plans, deciding on the movements of performers and cameras, and setting up a practical rehearsal schedule. Most important of all in this preparation phase is to arrive at a program concept whose achievement is the focus of all the rehearsal activity.

Second, directors must be masters in dealing with people. Actors are sensitive individuals whose performances can be greatly affected for good or ill by the way in which they are handled. Other members of the production team, in the same way, may respond crisply or sloppily depending on directors' methods of giving instructions and the attitude they communicate regarding expectations.

Third, directors must be able to maintain absolute control over complicated production situations. They must respond with split-second accuracy to the show's requirements and they must keep cool no matter what happens. During rehearsal periods and actual productions, something is almost bound to go wrong. Directors must be able to respond to these emergencies with flexibility and imagination.

In programs for television certain axioms should be followed:

1. Make a greater use of close-ups than you would in preparing a film for presentation in a theatre: television is a close up medium.

2. Design shots that fill the frame. A loose, empty frame is visually boring.

3. Search for details that can be inserted into a shot to improve its clarity or to make the scene more interesting and dramatic.

4. Move cameras to avoid presenting a dull, static show.

5. Use visual angles creatively.

6. Select camera positions with attention both to practical considerations and to artistic values.

7. Check the audio constantly to make sure that in perspective and quality it is properly related to the scene.

One of the most important artistic responsibilities of the director is to determine the composition of the various shots. The check list that follows describes the most important criteria.

Check List on Composition

a. Group the figures into some form or pattern instead of a haphazard arrangement. Stress simplicity of form. The triangle grouping is considered more pleasing than squares, T forms, circles, or rectangles. The triangle may be formed vertically with differences in height and levels, in depth on a horizontal plane at varying distances from the camera, or by a combination of both. Attention is usually directed to the apex of the triangle, making that figure dominant.

b. Avoid formal balance. The key subject should be located above, right or left of center. Objects such as furniture, wall paintings or decorations, or other people may be placed in the other areas of the frame for more pleasing informal balance. Reverse-angle (over-the-shoulder) shots and facial close-ups should be in slight profile. Keep away from camera shots that have a vertical or horizontal line in the background, dividing the picture symmetrically.

c. Including another person or object in the foreground of a shot tends to give a more interesting perspective, a feeling of depth to the scene. Examples are shots through a door frame, a window, or stairway rails. A camera may be on a close-up of an object in a room as a scene opens, pulling back to reveal actors in the scene but with the object remaining in the foreground for a period of time. Sometimes a shot is taken of subjects through openings framed by arms or legs of other characters. A full-face view of one actor shooting across the face of another actor is quite common.

d. Shots that have too much empty space on the margins or between figures are dull. The director must remember also that the framing of the picture as seen in the viewfinder or control-room monitor is not the same as received at home. There may be considerable loss of the transmitted picture, up to one-sixth of width or height as viewed on the home TV set. This comes about by some loss in transmission, but more importantly from errors in centering and the adjustment of picture size. Various controls at the back of the set regulate the framing. Often the owner attempts such adjustments during regular broadcast hours when no test pattern is being transmitted. When directors place key subjects too close to the side margins, not only may poor composition result, but the figures may be completely out of the frame.

e. The angle of the camera shot affects composition. Looking down tends to weaken the subject; looking up gives the subject more strength and power. Placing people in a shot so that there is difference in height as the camera shoots up slightly to include them makes the taller people dominant. Sets, properties, or furniture may be handled in the same way. Actors can be reduced to insignificance when placed deep in the set under a high arch as the camera is angled down shooting from a high position. If they are moved closer to the camera so that they appear larger in relationship to the arch, which is now behind them, and the camera is moved down so that the angle of shooting is up toward the actor, they will then appear dominant.

f. Not only the static relationship between people and objects must be considered as in a still photograph or in painting, but also their relationship in motion—the movement of actors within the frame, the movement of cameras (giving the audience the impression of shifting position), or the simultaneous movement of both cameras and actors. Generally speaking, movements across the screen towards or from the camera on straight or diagonal lines are more interesting than horizontal movements across the screen.

g. Space or mass occupied in the frame affects dominance and audience identification. A long shot of an actor in a scene tends to submerge the individual and to make the audience feel that they are spectators. Closer shots tend to involve the audience in a more personal relationship and to highlight the subject of the close-up. When movement is added, such as dollying in from long shots to close-ups, dramatic impact is increased on two counts—the personal involvement of the audience and the focus of attention. A dolly back reduces the involvement and diffuses attention. This technique is often applied to "draw the curtain" at the conclusion of a scene. Sudden moves in or out may disturb the orientation of the audience, even producing a shock effect.

Production Methods

Television programs may be produced live, on tape, or on film. Live programs, which are actually broadcast while being produced, are now rare. The only programs regularly done live are sports, special events, and news programs. The director's responsibilities vary somewhat, depending on which method of production is being used.

Filmed programs are usually shot in segments, which are then edited into the final production. Within each segment, the various scenes are filmed many times to provide variety in the composition of the shots and the number of people included in them, since only one camera is in operation at any one time. An actor, for example, may be required to perform a given sequence ten or more times to provide the required number of shots. These sequences—a close-up, a medium shot, a long shot, etc.—are called set-ups.

The film director rehearses a scene, films it in a variety of set-ups, and then goes on to rehearse the next scene. The script is almost never rehearsed in its entirety and the scenes are rarely, if ever, filmed in the order of their appearance in the final program. Scenes that follow one another instantly in time may actually be filmed several days apart. The director must be careful therefore, to maintain continuity—for example, to see that actors appearing in such scenes are wearing the same costumes.

Directors usually rehearse the scene on the set with the actors. They instruct the camera operator regarding the shot they want and then stand beside the camera while the scene is being filmed. Regularly scheduled television series are generally filmed from early summer to the beginning of the new year. This is an intense period of activity in which all involved in the production work long hours, often from five in the morning until midnight. Hour-long dramas—which actually run 50 minutes—are usually shot in seven days. This requires that seven minutes of completed program must be completed each day.

The directors of programs broadcast live or recorded on tape work in control rooms during part of the rehearsal process and are there throughout the actual production of the show. In front of them are a series of monitors that show the input from each camera being used on the show, the inputs from the projection room and other areas, the shot being recorded or broadcast at any given moment, and the shot the director has selected to be broadcast or recorded next. Directors must be conscious of what is appearing on the "line" or air monitor, they must be aware of the shot on the "preview" monitor that is to be shown next, they must be alert to what is appearing on all the other monitors so that they are ready to make the best selection of shots, and they must listen to the audio to make certain it is being properly produced. The technical director switches the show from shot to shot on the director's orders, and the associate director provides information about timing and other matters.

There are two basic methods of recording programs on tape for future broadcast. In one process the program is recorded on tape in one unbroken sequence, just as it would be were it being broadcast live. This is often referred to as the live-on-tape process. A number of the daytime serials, also known as soap operas, are recorded in this fashion. Rehearsal for an episode may begin early in the morning and conclude at the end of the day with the recording of the program. The script is rehearsed in its entirety before this point is reached; lines for the entire show must be memorized by the actors; the director, his assistants, and crew must be prepared by production time to record the program without interruption.

In the second process the program is recorded in segments and then is edited into the complete program on a master tape. In some instances the segments are very short and are generally produced out of sequence, with rehearsal preceding the recording of each segment, following the pattern used in film production. Most musical variety programs are now produced in this way. The final timing of the program takes place, not during production, but during the editing phase.

A more common technique is to rehearse the production in its entirety and then tape it in long segments during one recording session. Often an audience is present in the studio for the taping of the dress rehearsal and the final show, and their responses are recorded as part of the program. At first this technique made use of a number of film cameras to pick up the action, but TV cameras are now used almost exclusively. Among the programs employing this technique are the Norman Lear productions "All in the Family" and "Maude."

In an article in the *Journal of Broadcasting* (Summer 1973) James Lynch described the production schedule for a typical *All in the Family* episode. The entire process takes seven days, with the editing of one show overlapping the preliminary rehearsals for the next show. Three days are spent in what is called "dry run"—rehearsal without the use of TV facilities. On the fourth day the cast rehearses in the studio, and on the fifth the cast rehearses in the studio once more and then at the end of the day performs the program before an audience. This performance takes place in long segments, interrupted only for major changes of costume or scenery. The editing process takes place on the sixth and seventh days. Both the rehearsal and the final performance are taped, and during editing the best segments are selected from these two recordings for the final tape. In addition, further shots of specific phases of the action are taped for use in case they are needed. These individual shots are called "pickups."

In contrast, music and variety programs may be taped using a combination of the two methods just described. Short segments may be recorded in a studio without an audience present. Major production numbers and sketches, on the other hand, may be recorded before an audience one after the other, with breaks between for costume and scene changes. The short takes and the larger segments are then edited into the final program.

Usually two master tapes are made at the same time during recording sessions in case one is damaged. In addition, a third tape may be made that records the input from cameras other than those being recorded on the master tapes. This third tape permits a greater selection of shots for the final program tape during the editing process. It is called an "iso" tape because it is isolated from the master tape and its production requires the services of a second director, who decides which shots are to be incorporated into it.

The recording of programs in long segments before audiences confronts directors with problems essentially the same as those facing directors of live programs. Though they do not have an air time when the program must be ready for presentation, the time when the final recording must begin is almost as absolute. Some slight flexibility exists in case problems arise, but rehearsal periods cannot be extended in any significant way.

THE NATURE OF TELEVISION DRAMA

Much that has been said thus far about directing television has specifically referred to television drama. Beyond a knowledge of these specific techniques, however, the director also needs to understand the basic nature of television drama and particularly how it compares to drama in other media. Various aspects of TV drama are discussed briefly below as they compare to those aspects in theater and film.

Locale or Play Area

Theatrical drama is influenced by the physical stage or playing area and the location of the audience. Most modern theaters have a proscenium arch. Some plays such as *Our Town, Death of a Salesman,* and *Equus* use different areas and levels together with special lighting and staging devices in attempts to achieve a degree of freedom from the "picture-frame" stage. Most stage plays, however, adhere to a conventional stage setting with an open "fourth wall" through which the audience can see the play. Television drama does not have the same freedom as radio drama, but it does make use of "detail sets," "limbos," rear-screen projection (RP), electronic matte effects, video-tape or film inserts, and unit or multiple sets to increase its range of movement. The television camera becomes a moving proscenium arch that extends the audience's horizontal range of vision to all possible angles within 360°; it offers an adjustable vertical range and practically unlimited variations in depth, from extreme close-ups to long shots limited only by the visual requirements of the relatively small television viewing screen. The ability to direct the viewer's attention to specific detail by appropriate camera shots has great significance in television drama. Directors may place the emphasis where they see fit. The filmed show has this same opportunity to focus and, in addition, it has much more flexibility in the selection of locale than television drama produced in a TV studio and much more flexibility in this area than theater. Outdoor or on-location scenes, chase sequences, and spectacles, such as huge crowds, battle scenes, and picturesque exteriors, are limited only by time and budget.

Audience Orientation

In the theater each member of the audience watches the performance from the same fixed position. In contrast, both film and television have great flexibility in changing audience orientation. The cameras move in and around—we look into back corners of the locale—we can see how the characters appear to each other from their respective locations. We can become very close to the characters when we move from a cover view, as though we were in the fourteenth row, right up to the players "on stage." This change of audience orientation may account for the emphasis in film and television upon *reaction* as well as on *action*. Observe, as you watch film or television, how many times the camera directs your attention to a character other than the one speaking in order to show you the effects of the words or action.

The ability of the camera to move around, taking the viewer with it and changing the view as it moves, and the ability to cut from camera to camera so that a viewer can be far away, a little distance away, or very close, in front or behind, below or above, are distinctive elements of film and television drama. Intensification of emotion may be accomplished by the moving camera, the angle of camera shots, self-identification (empathy) with a character, and cuts from one camera to another. In some television dramatic scenes, a camera may stand in for a character. The camera simulates the eyes of the person as he or she looks around the scene and moves toward and away from other actors. The way the world of the grownups appears to a youngster has been suggested by shooting from the youngster's eye level up toward the adults. How a scene appears to one who is losing consciousness is often portrayed by having the camera gradually lose focus or by lens rotation or other camera tricks. This "subjective-camera" technique, however, should be used sparingly. It is mentioned here because it illustrates vividly the contrast between audience orientation in the theater and what may be accomplished in television and film.

Dialogue

Stage plays depend primarily upon dialogue to accomplish their effects. It is true, of course, that action, setting, lighting, costumes, and physical appearance of the actors are very important, but because of the physical limitations of the playing area and the fixed location of the audience the playwright usually turns to dialogue to set forth the problem, to develop the conflict, to proceed to a climax, and to state the resolution.

The editing of camera shots plays an important role in both television and filmed dramas. The tempo of different sequences in a drama is established by the length of time each shot is held and the speed of switching from shot to shot, whether by fast cuts, slow dissolves, or fast dissolves. An identical scene shot in one tempo and then shot in another will differ strikingly in mood. Consider how a series of fast cuts would dissipate the suspense of the slow tortured crawl of a badly wounded man across the floor toward a time bomb set to go off momentarily.

Narration

Although it was an important element in radio drama, narration is relatively unimportant in the other dramatic media. Feature films for theatrical release generally do not use narration except to identify dates or locale or to give the audience some background information. Some pictures are produced with a character narrator. Half-hour dramatic films for television tend to use narration in order to pack as much story as possible into the brief time period. Television dramas may employ program narration—through title cards or words to be read by the viewer or by an announcer's speaking over camera shots of the opening scene. The use of character narration has increased as television dramatic writers have moved away from the more rigid techniques copied from stage plays in the first days of television and have reached for greater freedom of form. It should be stressed, however, that in any medium an excessive reliance upon narration instead of on dramatic action and dialogue usually weakens a play.

Commercial for Directing Practice

1 "Two Pens"

AS PRODUCED
MOOD THROUGHOUT IS DRAMATIC. SPOTLIGHTED, RED LIMBO SET.

VIDEO	**AUDIO** **SFX: ON INSTRUMENT OR** **QUARTET**
OPEN ON CU 2 PENS. METAL ON LEFT, WOOD ON RIGHT. HAND IS NEXT TO PENS, RAPPING TABLE INDECISIVELY.	**ANNCR (VO):** What you see before you are two fine pens.
HAND TOUCHES METAL PEN.	One is metal.
HAND TOUCHES WOOD PEN.	And one is wood.
HAND PICKS UP METAL PEN. PUTS PEN BACK DOWN.	Now pick them up. The metal feels cold.
HAND PICKS UP WOOD PEN, CARESSES IT, ROLLS BARREL AROUND BETWEEN FINGERS PUTS PEN DOWN.	The wood feels warm, grained, natural.
HAND PICKS UP SILVER PLATE THEN GOLD PLATE.	This pen is available in silver plate or gold plate.
HAND PUTS EACH WOOD INDIVIDUALLY DOWN ON TABLETOP IN FAN DESIGN.	This one, in cordia, tulipwood, rosewood, teak, wenge, or walnut.

HAND PICKS UP METAL PEN, SHOW TO CAMERA.	This pen will always look the same.
HAND PICKS UP WOOD PEN.	But this one gets more beautiful with age . . .
FINGERS RUB OVER WOOD GRAIN, PLACE PEN BACK DOWN.	because the oils from your hand polish the grain.
HOLD ON CU BOTH PENS.	There. Now what do you see before you?
HAND COMES IN, MOVES METAL PEN OUT OF FRAME.	One pen,
HAND PICKS UP WOOD PEN, SHOWS IT TO CAMERA.	And one intensely personal possession.
DISS TO HAND PLACING PEN INTO CASE NEXT TO MATCHING PENCIL.	The wooden writing instrument from Hallmark.
	When you care enough to send the very best.

Courtesy of Foote, Cone & Belding Advertising, Inc. and Hallmark Cards, Inc.

Example of an "As-Broadcast" Television Drama Script[1]

The excerpt that follows is the first half of a script in the CBS-TV series, *Maude.* Hal Cooper, who is an executive producer as well as the director, has reproduced his original directorial markings. He explains:

> First of all, let me say that there is no *one* way to mark a script. The glyphs and chicken scratches have never been absolutely formalized. While a group of us (circa 1948) were inventing a given symbol to fulfill a need at CBS . . . another group of directors at NBC were evolving another symbol to fulfill the same need. Hence, what follows is simply *my* way of marking. The important thing is for those working with the director to understand what his markings mean. At best they are an approximation—an *indication* of the composition of a shot, of the timing of a cut, or of the tempo of a zoom. It is in rehearsal that the director refines the Tight-Cross-Three-Shot aesthetically, or instructs the cameraman to include the dagger on the table in the bottom of his frame. The script marking may indicate a camera cut on a given word. But the director, in performance, may snap for that cut before, during, or after that word.
>
> Following is an explanation of my markings:
>
> The pencil line drawn across the page starts, at the left, approximately where the camera cut will take place; The small circled number on the left side of

---

[1] Courtesy of Hal Cooper.

this line is the number of the camera shot. This saves a great deal of time in camera rehearsal. You need only announce to your crew, "We'll go back and pick up the scene at shot 27," and everybody knows exactly where he is. If, in rehearsal, you find you need to add a couple of shots after 27, you simply insert them as 27A and 27B, etc. Each cameraman usually has a list of his shot numbers and their content.

The center of the line carries the description of the shot. I have used more longhand here than I usually do. Naturally, the longer you work with a crew the more shorthand you can employ (i.e., K for knee figure, W for waist figure, etc.).

⟶ means a move toward, either a dolly move or a zoom.

⟵ means a move away from, or widening a shot.

MCU is Medium Closeup (Chest figure).

CU is Closeup (Head).

ECU is Extreme Closeup (Face).

TX2 is a Tight-Cross-Two-Shot. It is cutting across the back or profile of the character nearest the camera to the one farthest away. Obviously, TX3 or TX4 simply means the shot contains 3 or 4 characters. If the shot is described as an FGBG shot, it means that the characters are standing quite far from one another and the shot is a Foreground-Background shot.

Hold means that the cameraman keeps exactly the same composition as he had when the director cut away from him.

The large number at the extreme right side of the page is the number of the camera that will take that shot. If the number is preceded by the symbol ⟫, it means you will dissolve to that camera. Otherwise, all the shots are "cuts" or "takes."

" FINAL DRAFT "
12/20/76

MAUDE

"Maude's Desperate Hours"

Directed by

HAL COOPER

Produced by

CHARLIE HAUCK

Written by

ARTHUR JULIAN

Executive Producers   EPISODE: #0517

   ROD PARKER   TAPE   : 12/21/76
      and
   HAL COOPER   AIR   : TBA

        A
BUD YORKIN-NORMAN LEAR
 TANDEM PRODUCTION

MAUDE

#0517

<u>CAST</u>

MAUDE FINDLAY........................ BEA ARTHUR

VIVIAN HARMON....................... RUE McCLANAHAN

ARTHUR HARMON....................... CONRAD BAIN

DETECTIVE BRONSON.................... PHILIP STERLING

DETECTIVE KENNEDY.................... ROBERT DO QUI

<u>SETS</u>

FINDLAY LIVING ROOM

FINDLAY KITCHEN

MAUDE

TENTATIVE REHEARSAL & TAPING SCHEDULE

#0517

<u>MONDAY, DECEMBER 20, 1976</u>	<u>STAGE 4</u>
CAST LINE READING	9:00 AM - 9:30 AM
DRY BLOCK IN SET W/ALL PROPS	9:30 AM - 11:00 AM
E.S.U.	10:00 AM - 11:00 AM
FAX	11:00 AM - 1:00 PM
LUNCH	1:00 PM - 2:00 PM
FAX	2:00 PM - 4:30 PM
RUN THRU W/COMPLETE WARDROBE	4:00 PM - 4:30 PM
DISMISS CREW, DIRECTOR'S NOTES W/CAST	4:30 PM -

<u>TUESDAY, DECEMBER 21, 1976</u>	<u>STAGE 4</u>
MAKEUP & HAIR CALLS	(TO BE ADVISED)
DIRECTOR'S NOTES W/CAST	1:00 PM - 2:30 PM
E.S.U.	1:30 PM - 2:30 PM
FAX	2:30 PM - 4:30 PM
RUN THRU	4:00 PM - 4:30 PM
CAST NOTES, MAKEUP & WARDROBE	4:30 PM - 5:30 PM
VTR/FAX (DRESS W/AUDIENCE)	5:30 PM - 6:30 PM
MEAL BREAK, NOTES W/CAST (CONF. ROOM)	6:30 PM - 7:30 PM
VT CHECK IN	7:30 PM - 8:00 PM
VTR/FAX (AIR W/AUDIENCE)	8:00 PM - 9:00 PM
PICK-UPS	9:00 PM -

<u>MAUDE</u>

ACT ONE

FADE IN: _____ ①   *Knee figure, Maude*   X3

INT. FINDLAY LIVING ROOM - EVENING   *Slow zoom→ to MCU*

(MAUDE IS ON THE TELEPHONE)

                    MAUDE

...that's right, Walter Findlay...He

hasn't checked into the hotel yet...?

Well, the minute he arrives, give

him this message...it's urgent. Tell

him his wife called and said would he

please hurry home -- someone is going

to kill her...thank you.

(MAUDE HANGS UP THE PHONE; PACES DOWNSTAGE)   *←DOLLY with her, MCU*

SFX: DOORBELL   ②   *Knee figure, Maude* _____ /

(MAUDE GOES TO THE DOOR, UNLOCKS IT, BUT   *pan her, left, to door,*

LEAVES CHAIN LOCK ON IT, AS SHE OPENS IT   *and ——→ to MCU*

A CRACK AND PEEKS THROUGH)

Who's there?

                    MAN'S VOICE (O.S.)

Police Department.

                    MAUDE

May I see your identification, please.

(MAN HOLDS POLICE I.D. THROUGH CRACK IN DOOR.

MAUDE LOOKS AT IT)

Oh, thank God, you are police.

(TO UNLOCK CHAIN, CLOSES DOOR ON MAN'S ③   *Full figure Maude* 2

HAND. AS HE REACTS, HE DROPS I.D.)   *(see wallet on floor)*

②

          MAN (O.S.)

OW!

          MAUDE

Oh, I'm sorry.

(SHE REACHES DOWN, RETRIEVES I.D., OPENS ④   *hold MCU Maude*   1

DOOR A CRACK, HANDS IT BACK)

Here...

(CLOSES DOOR ON MAN'S HAND AGAIN)

          MAN (O.S.)

OW!

          MAUDE

Will you please take your hand out of

my door - you're making me nervous!

(HE RETRIEVES HAND, SHE CLOSES DOOR, UNLOCKS

CHAIN AND OPENS DOOR. DETECTIVES ENTER) ⑤   *TX 3 shot*   4

          BRONSON   *x Maude to detectives*

Mrs. Findlay?

(MAUDE NODS)   ⟵ *with detectives*
                   as they enter

I'm Detective Bronson, and this is

Detective Kennedy.

          MAUDE
           (xs to camera rt.)

Come in. I'm sorry about the hand and

asking you for identification, but you ⑥   *MCU Maude*   1

don't look like the fuzz. ⑦   *TX3 to detectives*   4

          KENNEDY

We're plainclothesmen.

          BRONSON

Now, Mrs. Findlay, the report says you

believe a man is out to kill you, is

that right? ⑧   *hold MCU Maude* 1

(1)

MAUDE

That's right. He's called me three

times today and made threats. He keeps

saying, "Tonight is the night." (9)   *bold* TX3   4

KENNEDY

Do you have any idea who he is? (10)   *bold* MCU *Maude*   1

MAUDE

He's a painter...you see, last Tuesday

I hired him to paint our den and (11)   *bold*   4

bedroom, and I...

BRONSON

Can you give us a description? (12)   MCU *Maude*   2

MAUDE
(*looking downstage*)

Well, the bedroom is chocolate brown,

and I was going to do the den in burnt

orange, but the drapes...   (13)   *bold*   4

                                          (*ready to* ← *with Maude*
                                          to bar. Detectives follow.
                                          Keep T X3)

BRONSON

A description of the suspect, Ma'am.

MAUDE

Oh, well, he's in his early thirties,
(*x to bar*)
about six feet tall, around a hundred ←

and eighty pounds, swarthy complexion

...black hair...fiery brown eyes... (14)   MCU *Maude*   2

make that piercing brown eyes...and

when he takes off his tank top — which

is often -- he has something sexy in

Greek tattooed on his chest. (15)   MCU *Bronson*   3

BRONSON

Did he tell you what it meant? (16)   *bold*   2

②

MAUDE

Constantly. _____ ⑰ _____ *hold* TX3 _____ 4

KENNEDY

What is the suspect's name?

MAUDE

Zorba Apodopolis.

BRONSON

Oh, he's Greek. _____ ⑱ _____ TX3 _____ 2

MAUDE   X Detectives to Maude

Yes, and very hot tempered. I know it

sounds crazy. I mean, a man comes to

paint in my house, is overcome with

passion and says if he can't have me,

nobody will. And now I sit here, ⑲ _____ *hold* _____ 4

terrified. I feel like Helen Hayes in ⑳ _____ TX2 _____ 1

a Movie of the Week...make that   X Kennedy to Maude

Elizabeth Montgomery.   ㉑ _____ T2 shot _____ 4
                                      Detectives

BRONSON

You know, Ma'am, sometimes these things

are somewhat exaggerated. We have

found that women very often imagine

that workmen in the house are making _____ *hold* _____ 2

advances.   ㉒

MAUDE

I assure you, it was not my imagination.

At first, I was willing to chalk it up

to the fact that maybe he was a little

high on the paint fumes... or the wine. ㉒A *hold* _____ 4

(4)

            KENNEDY
He brought wine to work? (22B)   *hld* T×3   *2*

            MAUDE
No, I gave it to him. (23)   *hld* T2   *4*

            KENNEDY
(MAKING NOTATION)
    Gave him wine?   (24)   T×2   *1*
            MAUDE   X *Kennedy to Maude*

Of course...you can't serve a man feta

cheese and Greek olives without red   *4*

wine.   (25)   T×3
            BRONSON   X *Maude to Detectives*

Do you always do things like this for

workmen in your house?   (25A)   MCU *Maude*   *1*

            MAUDE
Only painters.   (25B)   *hld*   *4*

(DETECTIVES NOD)

    You've got to keep painters happy. (26)   *hld*   *1*

Especially if you change the color on

the wall three times in one day... I

kept him happy, but I did not show him

a good time.   (27)   *hld*   *4*

            BRONSON
You're sure you didn't do anything

to encourage him.   (28)   T×3   *1*
                              X *Detectives to Maude*

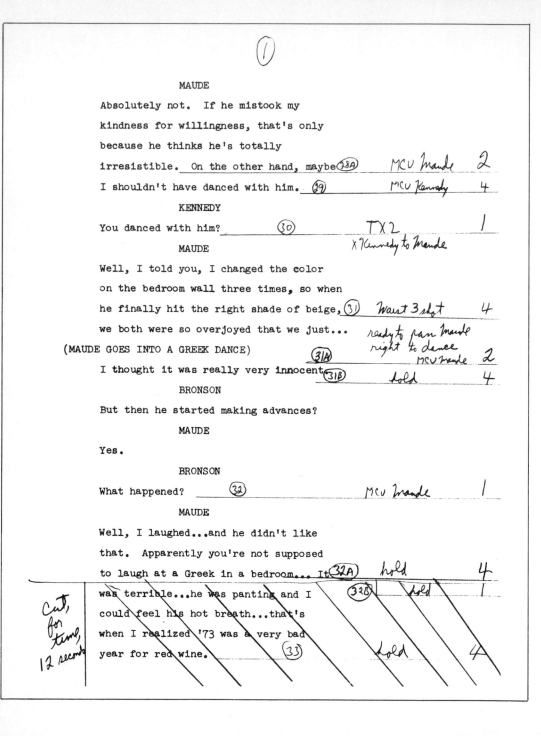

(1)

MAUDE

Absolutely not. If he mistook my kindness for willingness, that's only because he thinks he's totally irresistible. On the other hand, maybe (28A) MCU Maude 2

I shouldn't have danced with him. (29) MCU Kennedy 4

KENNEDY

You danced with him? (30) TX2 X Kennedy to Maude 1

MAUDE

Well, I told you, I changed the color on the bedroom wall three times, so when he finally hit the right shade of beige, (31) Waist 3 shot 4

we both were so overjoyed that we just... ready to pan Maude right to dance

(MAUDE GOES INTO A GREEK DANCE) (31A) MCU Maude 2

I thought it was really very innocent. (31B) hold 4

BRONSON

But then he started making advances?

MAUDE

Yes.

BRONSON

What happened? (32) MCU Maude 1

MAUDE

Well, I laughed...and he didn't like that. Apparently you're not supposed to laugh at a Greek in a bedroom... It (32A) hold 4

was terrible...he was panting and I (32B) hold 1

could feel his hot breath...that's

when I realized '73 was a very bad

year for red wine. (33) hold 4

Cut, for time, 12 seconds

④

KENNEDY

What time does your husband get home

from work, Mrs. Findlay? 3↓

MAUDE

That's my problem...he's gone to New

York on business. I've left a message

at his hotel.   34A

KENNEDY

Well, I'm sure he'll come home as soon

as he gets the message. 35

MAUDE

Right. But until then, I think we can

handle this with two policemen at the

front door and two at the back, and

inside here, maybe just a little S.W.A.T.

team.   36

BRONSON

Mrs. Findlay, I'm afraid all we can

do is have a patrol car drive by every

once in a while.   37

MAUDE

A patrol car? Don't you understand?

A man has threatened my life. Not

twenty minutes ago he phoned and

said tonight's the night. 37A

KENNEDY

I'm sorry. A patrol car is the best

we can do.

Handwritten annotations (right column):

1 REPO FAR LEFT

Medium 3 shot   2
head-on

Let Bronson exit shot

T X 3   4
X Maude to Kennedy
(Ready-then x to door)

T X 3   1
X Detectives to Maude
(← DOLLY as they x to door)

T X 3   4
X Maude to detectives

hold   1

Waist 3 shot   3
(favor detectives)
Let Kennedy exit shot

T X 2   4
X Maude to Bronson

④

BRONSON

If you're this frightened, Mrs. Findlay,

why don't you ask someone to sleep over

tonight?   ㊴   *TX2*   *1*

                                              X Bronson to Maude

MAUDE

Someone's already sleeping over. My

neighbor, Vivian Harmon. Her husband's

a doctor and he's on emergency duty

tonight, and she's afraid to be alone.

Why don't you gentlemen join us? We ㊵   *TX3*   *4*

cut for time could have dinner, play a little bridge   *X Maude to Detectives*

...watch T.V....do you like pot roast?   *Zoom* *as Kennedy Xo in*

KENNEDY

Mrs. Findlay, believe me, you're not

in any danger. I can only remember

one case where a man carried out his

threat. About three years ago...some ㊶ *T2 shot*   *2*

guy murdered a waitress when she turned   *Detectives, lead on*

him down.   *(ready to pan rt to MCU Maude)*

BRONSON

I remember that. The guy they never

caught. He strangled her at the

Acropolis Cafe.   *— PAN RT.*

(MAUDE REACTS -- REACTS -- REACTS) ㊷   *hold*   *4*

Listen, Mrs. Findlay, we'll have a

patrol car make periodic checks. Just

bolt the doors, lock the windows, and

pull down the shades.

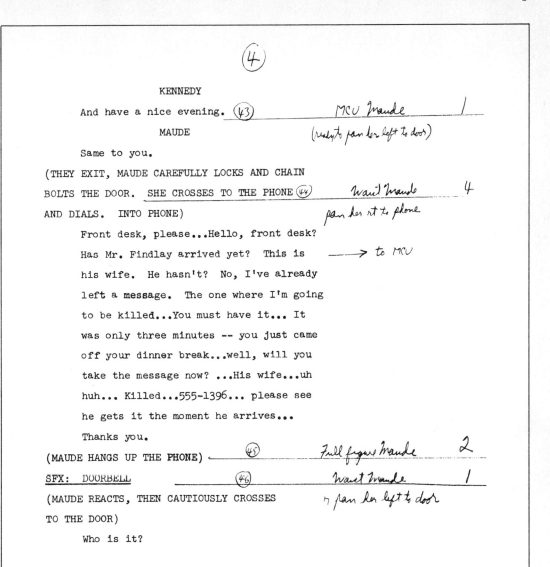

④

KENNEDY

And have a nice evening. ㊸   MCU Maude   /

MAUDE   (ready to pan her left to door)

Same to you.

(THEY EXIT, MAUDE CAREFULLY LOCKS AND CHAIN

BOLTS THE DOOR. SHE CROSSES TO THE PHONE ㊹   Waist Maude   4

AND DIALS. INTO PHONE)   pan her rt to phone

　　　Front desk, please...Hello, front desk?

　　　Has Mr. Findlay arrived yet? This is   ⟶ to MCU

　　　his wife. He hasn't? No, I've already

　　　left a message. The one where I'm going

　　　to be killed...You must have it... It

　　　was only three minutes -- you just came

　　　off your dinner break...well, will you

　　　take the message now? ...His wife...uh

　　　huh... Killed...555-1396... please see

　　　he gets it the moment he arrives...

　　　Thanks you.

(MAUDE HANGS UP THE PHONE) ————— ㊺   Full figure Maude   2

SFX: DOORBELL _____ ㊻   Waist Maude   /

(MAUDE REACTS, THEN CAUTIOUSLY CROSSES   ⌐ pan her left to door

TO THE DOOR)

　　　Who is it?

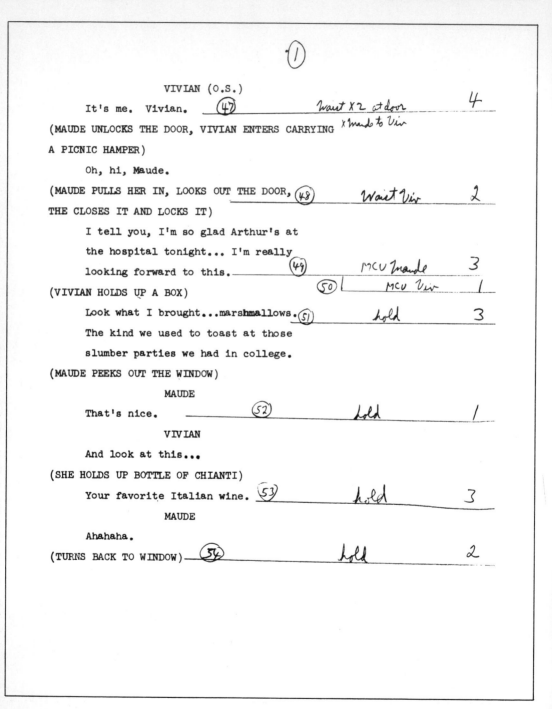

①

VIVIAN (O.S.)

It's me. Vivian. ㊾   *Wait X2 at door*   4

(MAUDE UNLOCKS THE DOOR, VIVIAN ENTERS CARRYING *X Maude to Viv*

A PICNIC HAMPER)

Oh, hi, Maude.

(MAUDE PULLS HER IN, LOOKS OUT THE DOOR, ㊽ *Wait Viv*   2

THE CLOSES IT AND LOCKS IT)

I tell you, I'm so glad Arthur's at

the hospital tonight... I'm really

looking forward to this. ㊾   *MCU Maude*   3

⑤⓪   *MCU Viv*   1

Look what I brought...marshmallows. ⑤①   *hold*   3

The kind we used to toast at those

slumber parties we had in college.

(MAUDE PEEKS OUT THE WINDOW)

MAUDE

That's nice.   ⑤②   *hold*   1

VIVIAN

And look at this...

(SHE HOLDS UP BOTTLE OF CHIANTI)

Your favorite Italian wine. ⑤③   *hold*   3

MAUDE

Ahahaha.

(TURNS BACK TO WINDOW) ⑤④   *hold*   2

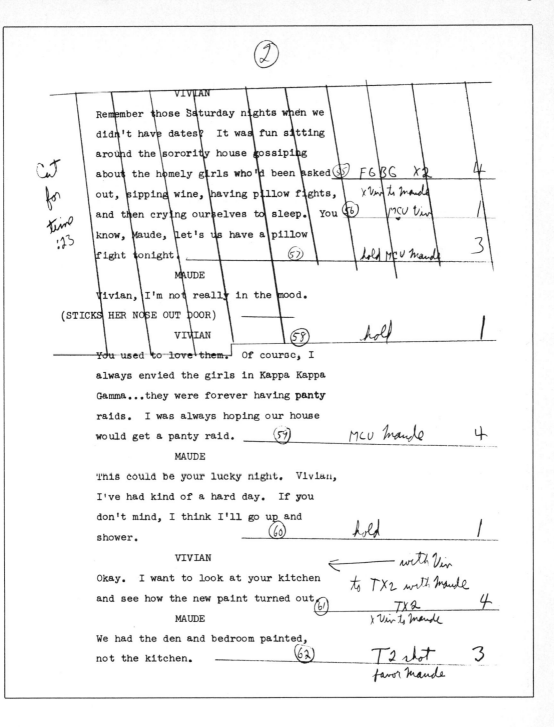

②

VIVIAN

Remember those Saturday nights when we
didn't have dates? It was fun sitting
around the sorority house gossiping
about the homely girls who'd been asked ㉟ F G BG ✗2 ┃ 4

out, sipping wine, having pillow fights, ✗ Viv to Maude
and then crying ourselves to sleep. You ㊱ MCU Viv ┃ 1
know, Maude, let's us have a pillow
fight tonight. ㊲ hold MCU Maude ┃ 3

Cut for time :23

MAUDE

Vivian, I'm not really in the mood.

(STICKS HER NOSE OUT DOOR)

VIVIAN ㉟ ⑤⑧ hold ┃ 1

~~You used to love them.~~ Of course, I
always envied the girls in Kappa Kappa
Gamma...they were forever having **panty**
raids. I was always hoping our house
would get a panty raid. ㉟ MCU Maude ┃ 4

MAUDE

This could be your lucky night. Vivian,
I've had kind of a hard day. If you
don't mind, I think I'll go up and
shower. ㊳ hold ┃ 1

VIVIAN

Okay. I want to look at your kitchen   ⟵ — with Viv
and see how the new paint turned out. ㊶   to TX2 with Maude
                                              TX2   4
MAUDE   ✗ Viv to Maude

We had the den and bedroom painted,
not the kitchen. ㊷ T2 shot 3
favor Maude

③

VIVIAN

I guess I was thinking of Sheila Hackett's

kitchen. You know what? That same Greek ⑥③   TX2   1

man painted her house, too, and Sheila   X'maud te Viv

said he made rude advances toward her. ⑥④   TX2   4

                    MAUDE   XViv te maude

No.

                    VIVIAN

Yes.

                    MAUDE

What did she do about it? ⑥⑤   hold   1

                    VIVIAN

She refused, of course. ⑥⑥   hold   4

                    MAUDE

Did he bother her after that? ⑥⑦   hold   1

                    VIVIAN

I don't know. I haven't seen Sheila

in weeks. I've called, and stopped

by, but she's never around. It's like

she just disappeared off the face of

the earth.   ⑥⑧   MCU maude   4

                    MAUDE

Vivian, would you give me a hand with ⑥⑨   Waist 2 shot   1

this chair?

(MAUDE CROSSES TO LARGE WHITE CHAIR)   pan them left
                                                  to chair, then to
                    VIVIAN   door

What do you want to do with it?

(1)

                    MAUDE

        Just help me push it over to the door.

(THE TWO WOMEN PUSH THE BIG CHAIR OVER TO THE

DOOR, BLOCKING IT)

        Thanks, Viv.

                    VIVIAN

        Why do you want the chair there?

                    MAUDE

        I've been thinking of rearranging the

        room. I rather like it over there.

                    VIVIAN

        What about the front door?

                    MAUDE

        I haven't decided where I'll put that

        yet. I'll **think** about it after my

        shower.   (70)   *wide 2 shot*   *3*

(MAUDE GOES TO THE STAIRS, VIVIAN TO THE   *← with Viv*

TELEVISION SET AND TURNS IT ON)   *to FG BG 2 shot*

                    VIVIAN   *X TV set to stairs*

        A shower? That reminds me. My favorite

        movie is on T.V.

                    MAUDE

        What's that?

③

                        VIVIAN
    "Psycho."   ⑦   _Full figure Maude_   2
(MAUDE COMES DOWN THE STAIRS)   _on stairs_
    I hope I'm not too late for the shower   ⑦② ⌐   _hold_   3
scene.
(VIVIAN LOOKS AT SCREEN AS TUBE WARMS UP,
MAUDE CROSSES TO HER)
    You remember that scene, **Maude?** When
    Janet Leigh is going to be stabbed
    behind the shower curtain?
                        MAUDE
    I remember it well, Vivian. I don't
    think you should watch it.
(SHE PUNCHES BUTTON OFF)
                        VIVIAN
    Maude...I want to watch "Psycho."
(VIVIAN PUNCHES BUTTON ON)
                        MAUDE
    I said no, Vivian!
(SHE PUNCHES IT OFF)
                        VIVIAN
    Maude, I want to!
(SHE PUNCHES IT ON, GRABS MAUDE'S HANDS)
    What's wrong with you, anyhow? ㉓   _T x 2_   4
                        MAUDE   _x Viv to Maude_
    All right, Vivian...I didn't want to
    have to tell you this, but I had the
    same experience with Zorba that
    Sheila had.   ㉔   _T x 2_   /
                                          x Maude to Viv

①

VIVIAN

You mean he made rude advances? ⑦⑤   *hold Tx to Maude*   4

MAUDE

Yes! And when I refused him, he was

enraged. He's threatened my life, Vivian! ⑦⑥   *hold Tx to Viv*   1

VIVIAN

Oh, Maude!   ⑦⑦   *VT X 2*   4

MAUDE   *X Viv to Maude*

Vivian, he called me three times today.

He says tonight's the night. *(Turn to door)* Any minute ⑦⑦A   *VT 2 shot*   1

now, that crazy, wild Greek might come

through that door and try to kill me!

(VIVIAN STANDS WITH HER MOUTH OPEN. SUDDENLY

THERE IS A LOUD SCREAM. MAUDE PUTS HER HAND ⑦⑧   *T 2 shot*   3

OVER VIVIAN'S MOUTH BUT THE SCREAM CONTINUES.   *head on*

MAUDE LOOKS AROUND, REALIZES IT CAME FROM THE

T.V., TAKES HER HAND OFF VIVIAN'S MOUTH) ⑦⑧A   *hold*   1

VIVIAN

That was Janet Leigh's scream... This

is mine --

(VIVIAN SCREAMS, MAUDE CLAMPS HAND OVER HER ⑦⑧B   *hold*   3

MOUTH)

~~THE THEME PLAYS~~

FADE OUT:

END OF ACT ONE   *X Black*

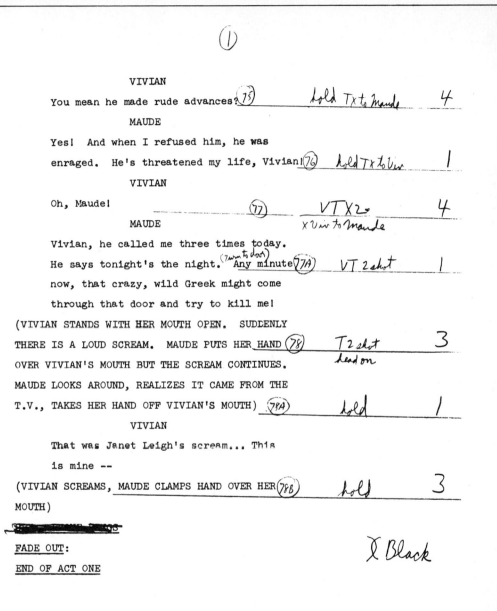

RADIO

The production of radio drama has undergone severe curtailment during the period that television has been on the rise. Radio drama on the networks is now rare. In the 1970s CBS did introduce a nightly radio mystery series and later an adventure series after a long period when no radio drama was available on any network, but none of its competitors followed its example. There is still some radio drama being broadcast by local stations, mainly recordings of network drama produced during the "golden age of radio," and some educational institutions and public broadcasting stations are producing some drama, but it seems doubtful that the form will survive in any significant way.

Many who remember radio drama when it flourished regret its demise, for it had a number of unique qualities. The absence of sight made possible a radio theater of the imagination. The listeners, in their own way, were cooperating playwrights. Each listener provided the setting for the play in his or her mind; with mental imagery the listener gave visual characterization to the participants in the play. Radio drama drew its aesthetic form from the following: 1. the intimacy of the medium, which made the audience feel it was on stage with the performers, 2. the absence of sight, which meant that setting, characterizations, and plot had to be conveyed through dialogue, narration, sound effects, or music, and 3. the complete freedom of locale, time, and characterizations made possible by the absence of sight and limited only by the extent to which one's imagination was stimulated.

DIRECTING INTERVIEWS AND GAME SHOWS

The informality and ad-lib factors in many interviews, quizzes, and audience participation broadcasts do not permit much rehearsal before air time. This precludes advance timing. Adjustments must be made during the performance.

General Considerations

Timing an interview program depends in large measure on interviewers. They follow a studio clock or a stopwatch and conclude at the time agreed upon prior to the broadcast. "Stretch" material should be available for use during the closing period. This material may be a recapitulation of the setting of the interview, or the background of the guest. A director or stage manager gives signals to indicate the time left—three minutes, two minutes, one minute, and "wrapup" when 15 seconds remain.

A quiz or audience participation broadcast is prepared in blocks or units. A timing sheet is worked out prior to the broadcast, indicating in studio-clock times the completion times of each unit. Such timings are "ideal" and never work out exactly as marked; however, they provide guideposts. If the first round goes quickly, a stretch signal to the MC can call for more chatter with those in the second round. The MC's script is also marked with the clock timings for the completion of each unit of a quiz show, and contraction or stretch of the various units continues during the broadcast. With audience participation broadcasts the timing sheet gives approximations of time for individual game units. These times may be completely off in some instances, so that standby units are necessary. Timing deadlines in early portions should not be considered as absolute deadlines. If a particular contestant is exceptionally entertaining, it would be bad showmanship to cut him or her down. It is well to cut short the dull participant as diplomatically as possible.

Since many interview segments have little actual camera rehearsal, but are directed ad lib, preplanning is highly important. The director cannot stop the broadcast to change the background set from a busy one to a plain drape because of the elaborate frock worn by a participant, to change the microphone from the boom to the desk for the guest who has a weak delivery, or to order an extreme camera close-up of a rare postage stamp. The opportunity to make such changes has been lost. The staging requirements must be kept simple when ad-lib programs are presented. If only one camera is to be used, rapid shifts in the size of the picture to be transmitted should be avoided. Even the most professional camera operators should not zoom in from a three-shot to an extreme close-up of a piece of jewelry on a coffee table during the space of these short sentences by the guest: "See this bracelet. Notice the intricate carving!" Such a spurt of movement back and forth would tend to upset the viewer. The director needs to talk with the guests about the objects to be displayed ahead of time in order to preplan camera direction. Considerable practice is required in order to hold objects in the air for tight camera close-ups. Slight variations in position may move the object out of camera range. The director can save trouble by showing the guest before the broadcast how to place the objects on a table or platform at the same location each time. In this way the director may be ready to cut to a close-up of the object at the appropriate time. Few details of this sort should be left to chance.

Off-camera rehearsals should be held whenever possible. Stand-ins for contestants on an audience participation program may be helpful while running through the program. Rehearsals should be on the same set used on the air. Homework by the director on movements and shots is just as essential as for a dramatic broadcast. Timing procedures are worked out before the broadcast. Instead of a stopwatch being given to the interviewer, the stage manager relays the information through cards or hand signals. Run-down or timing sheets are also prepared. In addition to the usual "stretch" material that is included in the script outline and rehearsed, television utilizes the timing of the closing credits as a "cushion." The title drum, flip cards, or telops may be speeded up or slowed down as desired.

Camera Direction

The shots that are basic for most interview programs include the two-shot: a close-up of the interviewer and of the guest. Changing camera pickup angles and distance, such as starting with a close-up of the MC and pulling back to reveal the guest, adds visual variety. The placement of the interviewer and guest side-by-side on a couch is frowned upon by most directors; this grouping makes it difficult to secure full-face shots. If the person speaking turns away from his companion and looks straight ahead in order to provide a full-face shot, the conversational flavor of close communication between the two participants is broken. People usually look at each other when they converse. Restricting this impulse in order to play to the camera results in artificiality. If naturalism wins out, the television audience can see only "half a face." Instead of this horizontal grouping many directors favor putting chairs at an angle or placing the people at adjoining sides of a table. As the two persons talk, cameras may be moved to left and right to catch full-face close-ups as they look at each other.

A general principle to follow is: "Never force lay people to assume the role of professional talent." Instead, the director should plan to place them so that the cameras can shoot them effectively without making them aware of the technique employed. Often the tally lights on cameras are disconnected to keep from revealing to guests which camera is on the air. Some directors feel that static grouping of some interviewers may be lessened by taking a close-up of the interviewer, and then following as he or she moves into another area of the set where the guest is waiting. Visuals, charts, pictures, objects, etc., may be handled by the interview participants and shown to the camera, or be beside the group for direct reference through word or by a pointer, or be shot "wild." Shooting wild means that the visual is placed in another set or another area of the same set, but away from the group. This technique is often used to control the lighting and to insure effective close-ups. Errors that may be avoided by this technique include photographs shown by the guest to the wrong camera, or tilted in such a manner as to reflect the light from a studio spotlight, thereby causing undesirable glare. Sometimes duplicate material is used. A guest may show a small card to the audience. Instead of moving one of the cameras forward and trusting that the guest will not spoil the shot, a duplicate card is held by a stagehand elsewhere in the studio in the correct position for the close-up. Some directors keep cameras on two-shots for overly long periods of time. This often causes attention to be shifted away from the guest's answers and be directed instead to the random movements by the interviewer, such as glancing toward the stage manager for time signals or looking at notes or cue cards. The interviewer should be careful not to engage in distracting movements, but to look at and listen to the guest. The director can help direct the viewers' attention by use of close-ups of the guest alone. Other directors go to the opposite extreme and call for many cuts back and forth from interviewer to guest, as questions and answers proceed. Cut to interviewer for the question; cut to the guest for answer; cut back to interviewer for the next question; cut to guest for the next answer, etc., with never a two-shot to vary the pace. This staccato cutting technique of camera direction is extremely annoying to the viewer during ordinary conversational interplay. And all too often the camera may be on the wrong person as the director attempts to outguess the participants.

Directors of programs where panels are employed seldom use long shots showing both the panel and MC. The more general camera shots employed are close-ups of MC and an alternating cover shot of the panel, with close-ups of individual panel members who speak. Occasionally the person seated next to the panel member who is answering is included to show his or her facial reactions. A pan to other members of the panel is easily made from such a two-shot. Since the formats of game shows differ greatly, the method of camera direction also varies. One general principle is usually followed. Since contestants and MC may move quickly without warning during the ad-lib portions, the director attempts to keep one camera available with a wider-angle or cover shot during close-ups on another camera.

DIRECTING VARIETY PROGRAMS

Television has utilized the variety format to a great degree. When it became possible for the audience to see as well as hear broadcast programs, many more types of entertainment became available to program producers, including "sight" gags, pantomime, and slapstick routines in comedy; circus and vaudeville specialties, such as jugglers, acrobats, magicians, bell ringers, trained animals, etc.; scenes from operas with costumes and staging; semi-dramatized or production vocal numbers; singing and dancing choruses; and dancers, dancers, dancers. *Laugh-In*, one of the most successful shows in the history of television, innovated a new form of variety show made up of short tape segments, some running only two or three seconds, edited into a continuous sequence of comedy, dance, and amusing routines.

Several versions of the variety format have been developed. One of the most successful is the revue—the succession of different acts. Instead of the signs posted at either side of the vaudeville house listing the name of the act to appear on stage, an MC introduces each act. The MC may also be starred in performance portions of the program. When this format is employed, fewer separate and distinct acts are programmed. Comedy, songs, and dances are stressed.

Variety shows use other forms, however, than the revue:

1. A theme is chosen as a "peg" on which to hang the frame. Composers such as Irving Berlin or Burt Bacharach may be "saluted"; a general locale, country, or city such as New Orleans, Mexico, etc., may serve as a springboard; a cavalcade of tunes and dances may be associated with a colorful period of history, the showboat days, for example; a reenactment of the rise to fame by a star may be the unifying device, e.g., "The Judy Garland Story," or the background in making a movie may be presented.

2. A story line similar to the "book" of Broadway musical comedy is utilized to highlight a comedy star or comic team. This approach stresses the "plot" and eliminates many of the individual specialty acts. Comedy, music, and dancing are woven into the continuity. If the story line takes the star to a Central American fiesta, for example, the dancers may be dressed in appropriate costumes; if the star visits a nightclub, the usual showgirl parade and dancing chorus appear; or if the star plays herself in simulated attendance at a rehearsal of the program,

the dances and music may be presented with the company dressed in informal practice clothes and with backstage properties and sets. Instead of "stand-up" comedy monologues, the laughs come from lines that are delivered in character and arise out of situations.

3. Combination sketches and variety acts. Some programs combine one or two longer sketches that have a story line with music numbers and dances or guest spots. The "Bob Hope Show" is an example of this type. A monologue by the star is followed by sketches enacted by Hope and his guest stars, interspersed with dances and songs, sometimes performed by the name stars, sometimes by specialty artists.

The effectiveness of variety programs depends upon *a.* the ability of the acts and stars; *b.* the balance of the overall production with placement or routing; *c.* creativity and imaginative writing and staging. Program producers turn to nightclubs, Broadway musicals, and movies, or tour other countries in search of talent. In variety programs heavy reliance is placed upon music. The traditional routining of vaudeville acts, with the acrobats or an animal act in the opening spot and the star "next to closing," is rarely followed now. Competition with the programming on opposition stations has increased the demand for getting off to a good start with a top act. Producers generally attempt to give audiences a contrast between successive specialties. Two short acts one after another are usually avoided. A fast and bouncy act may well be followed by a "smooth" romantic ballad or flowing dance act.

The dance numbers must be staged with the limitations of the medium

Shooting a Musical Program, *American Bandstand.*

in mind. Cover shots of large groups spread out over huge areas of the studio make the dancers appear mere specks when seen on the average home receiver. Complicated movements by dancers who swirl back and forth and in and around each other may result in a blur when the director attempts any close-ups. TV choreographers tend to emphasize these principles: careful blocking to confine movements to small areas; hold to relatively small groups, eight usually being the maximum for an ensemble; plan movement diagonally or in straight lines to and away from the camera to reduce the need for broad sweeping pans to follow extreme horizontal movement; and stress an interpretative or story-line theme.

Rehearsals of variety programs are spread out over three or four days for an hour show. Music, of course, is an important part of most variety shows. Not only are vocals spotlighted but dance routines, specialty acts, and a number of comedy routines have the support of music backgrounds. Orchestral introductions and playoffs also frame the units. A piano is used for preliminary workouts of vocals and dance numbers; the orchestra is not called in until the program rehearsals are well under way. Comedy sequences are rehearsed with walk-throughs and preliminary on-camera work without the orchestra. The separate elements are not put together until the first camera run-through. A timing sheet has been used during this period of individual unit rehearsals.

Programs with comedy sequences must rely on estimates of "spread" to compute timing. Most programs of this type are recorded before a live audience, and laughter and applause are expected. Program directors must allow for the time consumed by audience reactions. Another unknown factor is the rate of delivery of stars. Most comedians read their lines faster in rehearsal when no audience is present than in performance on the air. Action and business play faster in rehearsal. The directors must evaluate by past experience how much slower the lines will be delivered, how much laughter, how much the performers will "milk" the comedy bits when the show "hits the air." A common practice is to add an arbitrary percentage of rehearsal time to a sequence for spread. This figure may range from 20 percent to 100 percent. A five-minute sequence by rehearsal timing, therefore, is marked down on the timing sheet as six minutes if the lower percentage is taken, as ten minutes if the higher, or somewhere in between.

The ways in which a comic works, whether or not he or she tends to ad-lib and expand a routine, or whether the sequence is likely to induce slight chuckles or hilarious "show-stopping" gales of laughter, are all taken into account in determining the percentage for spread. Since the best guesses are not always correct, a cushion sequence is inserted, which may be included or cut according to time. This cushion may be an introduction to the final number in short and long versions, a section of the final comedy sequence that may be omitted, a final dance "theme" sequence, an extra song by one of the stars, additional choruses of a scheduled song, or a talk by the MC or star about "coming attractions." Sometimes the timing may be off and a stretch in the final moments is needed. The MC or star may bring back the guests of the program for an interview about future plans and another exchange of pleasantries. The director may pan across the audience applauding the program, or run the credits through as slowly as possible. Pre-broadcast electronic editing of "live-on-tape" programs is now used to solve timing problems.

SOUND EFFECTS AND MUSIC

Sound effects were of crucial importance in radio drama. They are used less in television than in radio, but they still assist materially in drama, documentaries, and comedy programs. The usefulness of music in radio drama and in film has been well established. Television has incorporated music in accordance with practices developed in radio. The dramatic writer, director, or producer should be thoroughly acquainted with the possible uses of sound effects and music and should seek to discover new ways to weave imaginative spells with sound and music. The desire to experiment with and exploit these tools should not, however, overshadow the more important objective of telling a story clearly and sincerely.

Sound

A number of different functions can be performed by sound effects. 1. They can help to establish or reinforce a locale or setting. 2. They can help to advance the action of the script. 3. They can tell time. 4. They can reinforce the mood of the script.

An important point to remember is that sound cannot be depended on to identify itself. This is an all-important factor in radio production where the cause of the sound cannot be seen. Sound that accompanies action before the camera can easily be identified, but the audience often needs assistance in identifying sound that takes place off camera.

Sound effects may either be produced live by an actor or a sound-effects technician or from a recording. A number of sound effects are best produced live—a knock on a door, for example. Others must be recorded ahead of time because they cannot easily be produced in a studio—an explosion, for instance, or the sound of an automobile.

Recorded effects may be introduced into a program from discs played on control-room turntables or a studio sound truck or from tape cartridges played from a tape deck in the control room. The use of a sound truck (Figure 22–2) permits great variation in the characteristics and qualities of individual sound effects:

a. The normal speed may be varied. The steady auto effect may be changed to give the impression of stopping by slowing down the turntable to zero speed. Increase of turntable speed gives an impression of increase in speed of auto. Other records may be varied for different impressions.

b. One continuous effect may be made to run longer than the record itself by using a second pickup arm. The arms are located in such a manner as to permit two arms on any one turntable. An airplane in flight may run for the entire sequence if needed.

c. One effect may be reinforced by the use of the sound pickup arm. Two horses can

Figure 22–2

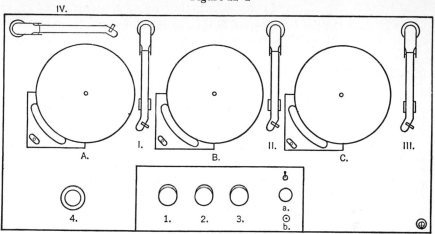

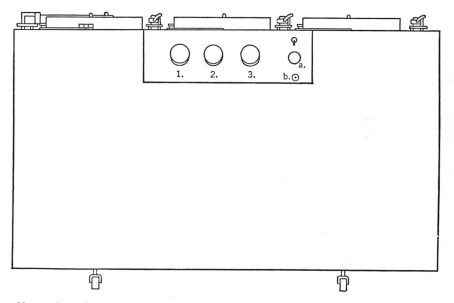

Above, view of sound truck from top. Volume controls 1–4 for pickup arms I–IV. A, B, C, turntables; a, record scratch filter; b, phone jack for headset monitoring. *Below*, view of sound truck from front. Volume controls 1–3, panel sloping.

appear to be in motion from the sound-effects record of one, or one car can be made to pass another by manipulation of the volume controls on a single record.

d. Blending of two or three records gives a great variety of impressions. A continuous tire skid may be blended in with the sound of a running car motor for a short corner skid, a wide sweeping skid, or in between. A third record of a crash can write a tragedy ending.

e. Effects other than those listed in the catalogues and on the labels may be secured by playing records at varying speeds. Eerie and strange or comical and fantasy impressions may be obtained this way. A wolf howl, surf, or Big Ben turn into interesting and useful impressions.

f. Cutting out the highs or lows changes the quality of sounds. A simple switch of a continuous train from regular tone to filtered position may, with correct timing, give the impression of walking from one car to another.

g. Any of the above techniques may be modified by a change in volume. Fading-in a sound or the reverse may help indicate movement by the actors. For example, with appropriate dialogue the fading-in of a church bell can create the picture of movement towards the church.

Imagination and experimentation by the sound-effects technician are needed for full realization of the flexibility of recorded effects.

The great advantage of using sound effects recorded on tape cartridges is ease of cueing. They can be inserted into a program with split-second accuracy merely by pushing the start button on the tape deck. They have two disadvantages, however: the sound effects cannot be modified as they can be when played from a sound truck, and they cannot be instantly set up again for further use, but must be played through to the end before they are ready for introduction into the program again.

Music

Mood music for broadcast drama is a direct heritage from the movies of another generation. The old-time piano players who improvised as they liked during a show would hardly recognize their craft as broadcast media have developed it. Present masters of cue music were thoroughly trained in basic musical education at the finest schools in Europe and America. Composers of music for dramatic programs must combine soundness in musical knowledge with versatility, imagination, and ability to produce fine work in a brief time.

The cue music can ruin a production if the accompaniment is not subordinated to the paramount dramatic idea. "When the audience says, 'The orchestra is playing,' the music director of the program has failed," Bernard Herrmann warns. "Attention is distracted from the drama and the whole aim of the cue music is defeated."

Not every network program and no local station programs can afford the luxury of a specially composed score. Instead recorded music must be used. There are two cautions: avoid music that is too familiar, and avoid mixing instrumentations, symphony for one bridge, small concert orchestra for another, organ for a third.

Music can perform a number of functions, some of them similar to those performed by sound effects: 1. it can provide a theme that identifies a series; 2. it can suggest setting or time; 3. it can provide a transition effect; 4. it can be a powerful agency for reinforcing the atmosphere or mood of a program.

Often music suitable for programs can be found on standard recordings available in music stores. Most of the music listed in Table 22–1 has been composed relatively recently by modern composers. Older music of the classical type is generally unsuitable for bridge or background music because of its familiarity to many listeners. A good source of music for dramas is the recorded sound tracks of movies, a number of which are listed in the table. Most sound-effects companies also issue specially composed and recorded bridge and background music.

Table 22–1. Sample Listing of Recorded Cue Music

Title	Composer	Title	Composer
Adagio for Strings	Barber	*The Incredible Flutist*	Piston
Age of Gold (ballet)	Shostakovich	*La Mer*	Debussy
Appalachian Spring	Copland	*Les Preludes*	Liszt
Anatomy of a Murder	Ellington	*London Again Suite*	Coates
Ballet Mecanique	Antheil	*Louisiana Story*	Thomson
Ben Hur	Sound track	*Mark Twain Suite*	Kern
Billy the Kid	Copland	*The Moldau*	Smetana
Carnival of the Animals	Saint-Saëns	*Night on Bald Mountain*	Moussorgsky
Caucasian Sketches	Ippolitov-	*Nocturnes*	Debussy
	Ivanov	*Pacific 231*	Honegger
The Comedians	Kabalevsky	*Peer Gynt Suite Nos. 1 & 2*	Grieg
Concerto in F	Gershwin	*Pictures at an Exhibition*	Moussorgsky-
Damnation of Faust	Berlioz		Ravel
Daphnis and Chloe	Ravel	*Pines of Rome*	Respighi
(ballet)		*Quo Vadis*	Sound track
Death and Transfiguration	Strauss	*The Plow that Broke the*	
El Salon Mexico	Copland	*Plains*	Thomson
Escales	Ibert	*The Planets*	Holst
Exodus	Sound track	*Rite of Spring*	Stravinsky
Fall River Legend	Gould	*Rodeo*	Copland
Feste Romane		*Romeo and Juliet (ballet)*	Prokofiev
(Roman Carnival)	Respighi	*Scythian Suite*	Prokofiev
Filling Station (ballet)	Thomson	*Serenade Melancolique*	Tchaikovsky
Firebird Suite	Stravinsky	*Sorcerer's Apprentice*	Dukas
Fountains of Rome	Respighi	*Spartacus*	Sound track
Four Squares of		*Spellbound*	Sound track
Philadelphia	Gesenway	*Symphony Fantastique*	Berlioz
Giant	Sound track	*Till Eulenspiegel*	Strauss
Háry János	Kodály	*Victory at Sea*	Rodgers
Interplay for Piano			
and Orchestra	Gould		

Projects and Exercises

1. Divide the class into groups of three or four. Alternate as director for each round. When each member serves as the director of the group, he or she may select a five-minute portion of a radio or television play in one of the published collec-

tions. The script should suit the actors available. Rehearse and present it for class criticism.

2. Work with assigned actors in scenes from the TV excerpts included in the text. Assign different groups to the same scene. Compare the presentations. If cameras are not available, describe the camera shots as the scene is presented.

3. Distribute to each student a copy of the identical television script. Assign students in pairs. One student should sketch out in rough form the staging to be recommended. The other plans the action and camera shots. Report to class the decisions that have been reached by each pair. Class discussion of different approaches.

4. Watch a television play. Report on composition and shot patterns used by the director.

5. Hand out two sound-effects records to each member of the class. Each student writes a melodramatic scene (2 to 2½ minutes) incorporating at least three of the sounds contained on these records. This exercise is to focus attention on the selectivity-of-sound principle; how script techniques can identify sound when identification is needed; and how sound effects establish locale, advance action, and create mood. Produce these scenes exactly as written for class criticism.

6. Play over and classify possible future uses of the music albums at hand. Prepare a file catalogue listing your recommendations.

7. Enlist the services of a college music major and experiment with original scores for dramas.

8. Audition class members and friends for a live talent-variety program and present it for the class.

23

For many years most of the evening shows presented on television were produced on film, as were a large percentage of the programs available on local stations. Though the growth of electronic recording techniques has reduced this proportion to some extent, it is likely that the filmed show will remain an important element in network and station schedules. A significant component in this group is the motion picture originally produced for theatrical exhibition. At one time such features were presented by networks virtually every evening of the week. Their number has declined in recent years, though they still appear regularly in network schedules and at times attract enormous audiences. A good example was the telecast in two parts of the classic motion picture *Gone With the Wind*, which NBC estimated drew a cumulative audience of 110 million people. Feature films are also important elements in the schedules of local stations, particularly those that operate without network affiliation.

SOURCES OF FILM FOR STATIONS

Features

Stations may secure films produced originally for release in motion picture houses. Some pictures are leased on an individual basis for one-time projection only. More generally a "package" or group of films is leased to a specific station. A station may elect to purchase a feature film library that permits multiple runs for each film over a period of years. Some libraries permit unlimited showings during the rental period. Different clients may sponsor an individual film in turn as it is scheduled during this period. Instead of one sponsor taking the entire feature, individual spot announcements are inserted to advertise the products of a number of different companies. Almost all motion picture features are now broadcast under participating sponsorship. The insertion of commercials requires an interruption of the picture at regular intervals. It is common for feature pictures to be interrupted every 10 or 15 minutes to present commercial messages.

A film and art department layout is illustrated in Figure 23-1. The sta-

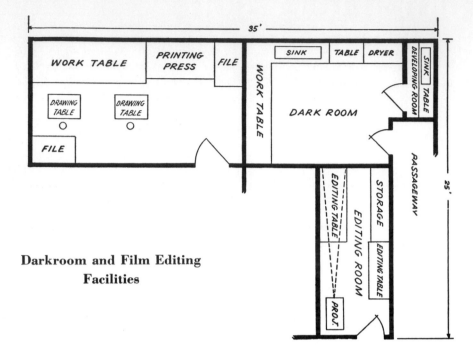

**Darkroom and Film Editing
Facilities**

**Offices and On-Air
Projection Facilities**

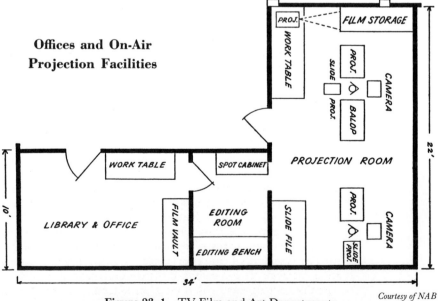

Figure 23–1   TV Film and Art Departments

Courtesy of NAB

tion's film department is responsible for screening carefully all the film received by the station to check sound and picture quality. Features may arrive with defective splices, objectionable scratches, or even missing or reversed reels. Viewers have been startled to see a drawing room romance suddenly shift into a chase across the plains as the U.S. Cavalry rushes to rescue a wagon train. Someone in the film department failed to check the order of the reels.

The films also must be screened in order to determine the best places to insert commercials as well as for editing to meet program time requirements. When a Western was found to be several minutes short, one ingenious film department clipped out a chase sequence from a different picture and made a continuous film loop out of it. At an appropriate place in the scheduled picture the additional chase sequence was faded in on a second projector and the "bad cowboys" kept running after the "good men" round and round through the brush and hilly terrain for the required minutes needed to meet the time limits. The film department claims that no one suspected anything amiss!

Industrial, Governmental, and Audio-Visual Films

An examination of any catalog of films distributed by a university or school audio-visual center reveals a great variety of short films prepared by business firms. American Airlines, the Ford Motor Company, General Motors, and Greyhound Bus prepare many travel shorts. Trade associations and national organizations, such as the National Association of Manufacturers and the American Petroleum Institute, have films available for general distribution. Various governmental agencies, such as the Public Health Service, Department of Agriculture, and different branches of the Armed Forces, maintain active film production units. Most films of this type are supplied free of charge to television stations either by the producers or by companies that collect films from a number of different sources and distribute them to stations.

Information services of the different states and of foreign countries have many films available. For example, the British Information Services produced "English Farm," a film that describes activities of a typical small farmer in southern England. A number of companies such as the Encyclopaedia Britannica Films and Coronet specialize in the distribution of films for general audio-visual use. University audio-visual centers produce and distribute films. The University of Minnesota produced "Youth and the United Nations," which reported the highlights of a pilgrimage to the U.N. by a group of high school students. There are numerous other films of this kind.

Many of these films are available to TV stations without charge. Usually they must be presented in their entirety. If rental charges are required, they are generally quite reasonable. Station program directors often relegate these films to "filler" or fringe-time segments in the day's schedule. The factors that rule against widespread use of audio-visual film material are: 1. the time required for separate negotiations with various companies; 2. poor quality of prints, which are used indiscriminately on a variety of non-broadcast projectors; 3. the informational rather than entertainment nature of the majority of the films; 4. absence of "name" personalities; and 5. lack of continuity between films.

Syndicated Series

Series on film or video tape may be produced expressly for use by local stations on a syndication basis, or they may be filmed or video-taped series that have been telecast originally over a network and are now seen as reruns, under either their original titles or new ones. Film departments in stations usually handle the receipt, screening, and shipment of both video-taped and filmed series.

Miscellaneous Sources

Stations also need film to incorporate into live programs. A film of waves dashing upon a rocky shore may be effective for rear-screen projection behind a vocalist in a popular music program; a view of heavy highway traffic may add atmosphere to a documentary on traffic safety; the producer of a sports program may require an opening montage of scenes from different athletic events for a standard introduction; or the writer of a foreign policies series may feel that a succession of one shot after another of various heads of state involved in negotiations can result in visual reinforcement of the comments and greater dramatic effect.

Stock shot footage from a film library is an answer to such needs. There are companies that specialize in historical newsreel film, and others maintain libraries of stock footage covering every conceivable subject. Networks and stations may also maintain their own libraries of this type. When a station or network uses film footage from another company, it pays the cost of processing plus a specific use charge for each foot of film. Subjects included in a stock footage library might be lumped under the letter "C" as shown in Table 23–1.

Table 23–1. Stock Footage List

cabarets	Christmas	cooks
California	circuses	corpses
camps	cliffs	Costa Rica
Canada	clouds	counterfeiters
canneries	coal	cowboys
capital cities	Coast Guard	crops
C.A.R.E.	colleges	crossbows
castles	collisions	crowds
cattle	confetti	cruisers
caverns	Congress of United States	cyclones
children	conventions	Czechoslovakia

The film department also receives regular shipments of TV film or video-taped commercials from advertising agencies for use on air time purchased by the agency. National organizations such as the Girl Scouts, Red Cross, etc., send public-service spot announcements. Two-by-two-inch slides (35mm film transparencies mounted in glass or cardboard frames 2 inches square) are sometimes used instead of film for commercial or public service spots.

It should be apparent from the number of different sources of film and tape that the film department of a station has an extremely complex operation to handle. Detailed records and well-established routines are necessary in order to see that the right film is received, screened for quality, accurately timed, commercials inserted, correctly marked and taken to the projection room prior to the scheduled time of broadcast, and then to disassemble the film reels following the broadcast, to package, label, and send out the different prints according to plan.

INTERNAL SOURCES OF FILM

Many stations supplement their external sources of film by establishing their own film production units, particularly for news shows. This is an expensive operation, however, and not all stations can afford it. In very small markets, stations may have to rely for news coverage on still pictures shot with "instant" cameras, although their use is rare. Still pictures, however, can be a satisfactory substitute for news film in situations where students in a laboratory are learning to produce news and documentary programs. A step up from the still film is the silent film, which can be shot and processed more inexpensively than a sound film and can be shown with live voice-over narration.

Stations that engage in limited film production may also elect to do their own film processing. Automatic machines that develop and process up to several hundreds of feet per minute are available. A station will usually not install the equipment required to make extra prints, special photographic effects such as dissolves, wipes, fades, animation, and superimposures. Film laboratories specializing in such services are utilized.

Film editing equipment is required whether processing is done on or off the premises. A minimum equipment list includes a viewer, a splicer, a footage counter, and a set of rewinds. Particular shots or sequences intended for broadcast may be selected from the rough footage, cut out, and spliced together. "Leader" must be spliced onto the first shot to be projected. This special strip of film is marked with a "test-pattern" design and large numerals indicating the seconds left until the start of the picture. The final three seconds are blank. The leader permits the video engineer to adjust the shading and enables the projectionist to cue up the film. During the final three seconds of blank film the picture is faded in. Thirty-six feet of 16mm film take one minute to project. Reference to a table of conversion (Table 23–2) tells the editor or writer how long a particular length of film will take on the air.

Table 23–2. Partial Film Conversion Table

Time	16mm Film	Words of Copy (Approximate maximum— usually runs less)
1 second	24 frames	2
5 seconds	3 feet	11
10	6	23
15	9	35
20	12	46
30	18	70
1 minute	36	140
2 minutes	72	270
14:30	522	—
29:30	1062	—

Large metropolitan stations utilize film in a more extensive fashion. They not only add more still cameras, silent-film cameras, specialized lenses, and more elaborate editing gear, but they usually purchase film sound-recording equipment. Newsreel or simple documentary pickups may be accomplished by the "single-system" sound camera, which records the voice and picture on the same film while using only one camera. Lip sync, exact matching of lips and tongue action with words as heard, is assured. Economy of operation is possible because one camera operator alone can handle an assignment if time or budget requires it. This system is also excellent for "deadline" shooting. Only the one strip of film needs to be developed. Speed and economy, however, are counterbalanced by two negative factors. First, it is difficult to do fine editing, although simple editing is quite possible if proper precautions are taken during the shooting, such as having the speaker pause at the beginning of paragraphs. A second disadvantage of the single system is that, since the one strip of film with both sound and picture has to be developed in the same chemical solution, some compromises have to be made in the formula used in the processing machine. This compromise results in some degree of deterioration in audio quality. Even this disadvantage can be eliminated, however, if the audio track is replaced with a magnetic recording stripe to pick up the sound. The sound is then recorded and played back in the same way as a radio tape recording.

An alternate method of recording sound is by "double system." A film camera and separate sound-recording equipment are "locked together" by synchronizing devices. The sound is recorded either optically on a separate roll of film or on magnetic tape. If tape is used, the sound is later transferred to film. The double system has greater flexibility in editing and gives higher audio fidelity. On the other hand, it requires more laboratory time and it is much more expensive, because it uses more equipment and personnel in both filming and editing. Nevertheless, the superior quality of the results obtained and the flexibility of editing are of great importance to producers of feature films, documentaries, and commercials. Hollywood film studios use the double system exclusively.

The film stock used by station production units may be classified as "negative" or "reversal." When negative stock is employed, the original strip of film, following exposure and processing, remains negative; that is, the values of the original scene are reversed. The negative is then used for making separate prints, which are positive. These prints are referred to as "release" prints. As many as needed may be made from the original negative. In films being produced for syndicated or theatrical distribution the original negative is retained in special storage, "dupe" (duplicate) negatives, made from a "fine-grain master positive" taken from the original negative, serve as the source for the many release prints.

Reversal stock is the most commonly used type for color TV film and it is also widely used in amateur photography. The film is exposed in the camera and then processed. The same piece of film is now available as a positive print. No negative exists. The photographer has only the one copy. If the positive print is damaged in any way, the scenes are lost. Stations may not desire extra prints, especially for news programs, and may use the print once or twice and then file it in the film library. If additional "release" prints are desired, the original positive print is handled by film processing companies instead of by the station's film department.

The various stages and alternate methods in the filming process are summarized in Table 23–3. It should be emphasized that all stations and film production units do not follow standardized procedural steps. The chart illustrates some general methods followed.

Table 23–3. Stages in Film Process

→ refers to steps in processing

— — — refers to editing

PICTURE-ONLY OR SINGLE-SYSTEM SOUND AND PICTURE (1, 2, 4, or 5)

1. Reversal stock → — — — positive projection film
    (Color or B & W)
2. Reversal stock → positive original — — — → reversal release print
    (Color or B & W)
3. Reversal stock → positive original → work print — — —
    (Color or B & W) edited original positive → dupe negative → release print
4. Negative stock → negative original — — — → release print
5. Negative stock → negative original → work print — — —
    edited original negative → release print
6. Negative stock → negative original → work print — — —
    edited original negative → master positive →
    dupe negative → release print

SOUND FOR DOUBLE SYSTEM METHOD

Original magnetic sound — — — final magnetic sound mix →
optical sound negative → release print

Projects and Exercises

1. Examine the television station program schedules carried by newspapers and magazines and report on number and types of film used by the stations.

2. Select class representatives to visit station film departments. Request that these representatives observe the procedures followed in screening, choosing appropriate places for insertions of commercials, and checking film in and out. Have representative report on station equipment and staff used for shooting and processing its own film.

3. Tune in television stations and prepare reports on the editing techniques used on news reels and film features.

4. Screen representative nonentertainment films obtained from an audio-visual department. Discuss the techniques employed. Suggest alternate treatment for live or tape television coverage of same subject.

5. Screen footage that has not been edited. Prepare individual editing rundown sheets listing the timing and order of each shot to be used.

6. Have someone demonstrate film camera operation and editing equipment. Practice loading and holding camera. Splice scrap footage.

7. Divide the class into groups of three. Each group plans a two-minute voice-over silent film feature. After a shooting script is roughed out, each person shoots approximately one minute of film. After the film is processed, edit the footage, prepare final script, and present the feature for class criticism. If no film facilities are available, distribute shooting scripts of group projects to the class for group analysis and discussion.

24

The television and radio commercial occupies "center stage" while it is being presented. Unlike advertising in newspapers and magazines, it does not compete against distracting program features for the listener's or viewer's attention. When the sponsor's commercial is presented, the newscast has stopped, the dramatic scene has faded out, the star comic has completed a routine. The broadcast commercial therefore, while it is being presented, commands the spotlight.

This position presents an exceptional opportunity to attract attention, arouse interest, stimulate desire, and impel action. If commercials are ingenious and interesting, are sincerely and honestly related to the audience's personal needs and interests, and are presented in vivid and meaningful fashion, they are generally accepted and widely acted upon by the audience. That is why television, with its enormous "reach" in terms of the numbers of people who watch, is often called a "selling machine."

This very spotlight also explains why poor commercials are experienced as especially irritating or offensive: they are inescapable.

Commercials are placed within and around programs, and during scheduled "breaks" (IDs) when networks and stations identify themselves. Most in-program television commercials are now 30 seconds in length (they used to be 60 seconds) and generally appear in one- or two-minute clusters during appropriate intervals within a program. (There are also "piggy-back" commercials, where the advertiser works a second product into a single commercial.) Commercials are often rotated by stations and networks within one or more programs or within certain time blocks of the day. Individual stations may sell "orbits" at specified rates; these indicate the time periods within which the advertiser's commercials will be rotated. There remain, however, a limited number of programs—usually programs of a special nature—that are solely or jointly sponsored by one, two, or three advertisers, where special commercials are produced for that program and where the length of the individual commercial may be extended to as long as two minutes. In radio, commercials have become shorter and, consequently, more numerous within any one time period than is the case in television.

Hour and half-hour break points are generally used for station identifications and the insertion of 10- and 20-second commercials. These commercials are sold only by the individual stations and not by the networks; they represent a large portion of a network-affiliated station's income in television. These "adjacencies" are particularly valuable when they precede or follow very popular network programs.

As a result of these various practices of in-program and station-break commercials, the number of commercials telecast in any one day over a television or radio station, although limited in number and time for the various day-parts by the code of the National Association of Broadcasters, is enormous.

FORMS OF RADIO COMMERCIALS

No matter which type of commercial is being used, form must be considered. The time available governs the choice of form, but it does not rule out any of the following. Combinations of the different forms may be used:

1. Straight selling or description
2. Testimonial
3. Educational
4. Multivoice
5. Dialogue
6. Humorous
7. Musical

Straight Selling or Description

This is the most common and most widely used. Principal advantages are directness and the unified development of a single appeal. It depends on the announcer and "copy for the ear." A question often raised is: "Should announcers give the commercial as a personal recommendation?" The practice on most stations is for announcers not to do so in regular staff work, but they may be permitted to do so on "personality shows." Statements such as "Come to *our* store" and "*We* have been doing business in the same location" tend to confuse the station-and-sponsor relationship. The usual practice is to avoid them unless they are phrased as quotations from the sponsor.

Testimonial

This may be a personal recommendation by the program star, announcer, or guest, or a quotation from a celebrity or "satisfied user." Testimonials can impart additional impact, owing to the feeling of gratitude many listeners have. They may try a product recommended by a radio "friend," the announcer or the star. If this appeal is not tactfully presented, it may induce a negative reaction. The indirect method is used by many comedians.

Educational

This form may be used when the writer is using "long-circuit" or "reason-why" appeals. A writer on advertising, Albert W. Frey, says that educational commercials "provide information for the consumer who does deliberate before he makes a purchase, comparing values and weighing pros and cons. . . .

They are most used in the advertising of products which are rather high in price . . . and consumed only over a relatively long period of time."

Multivoice

This may consist of a series of alternate voices in a climactic arrangement; a question-and-answer frame that permits an abrupt beginning; a device for pinpointing attention on a slogan or phrase; or reinforcement through repetition.

Dialogue

These commercials may be simple in form or little productions complete with sound effects and music. An announcer may engage in conversational banter with the performer. Some sponsors use the playlet idea by incorporating the "boy-meets-girl, boy-loses-girl, boy-wins-girl!" formula into the commercials. Dialogue commercials win attention and interest, but listeners resent commercials that are too farfetched or too glowing in the claims made for the product. The humorous form is an outgrowth of dialogue technique.

Humorous

There has been an increasing use of humor in commercials of recent vintage. The main reason for humor is to make the commercial as palatable as possible for the audience. Even commercials that are serious for most of their length often end with a humorous twist.

Musical Commercials

Musical commercials are widely used. Some of them have original melodies; others are based on popular songs or themes from the classics. The audio tracks of filmed and taped television musical commercials are sometimes used as radio commercials.

WRITING COMMERCIAL COPY

In writing radio commercials seven points should be kept in mind: 1. gain attention quickly, 2. rococo in language should go, 3. use simplicity in sentence style, 4. repeat with skillful rephrasing and restatement, 5. build word pictures, 6. talk it out, and 7. "stick to your own last." In writing commercial copy you may be writing announcements to be read by someone other than yourself. If so, familiarize yourself with that person's air personality.

The basic appeal to be used for motivating acceptance and purchase of a commercial product is the first thing to be decided by the writer. One or more appeals may be chosen from our basic and impelling motives: the desire for good food and drink, comfortable surroundings, escape from pain and danger, sexual satisfaction, social prestige, and pride.

After choosing your basic appeals, consider the makeup of the audience that will hear the announcement. Note the time and day of the broadcast, and the age and buying habits of potential listeners. Examine the station's programming profile and select the appeal for individuals who may be attracted by such offerings. Study any marketing surveys that have been made for the station. People have local habits, likes and dislikes: in some areas brown eggs are preferred, white eggs in others. Your community may rank high in home ownership, another in apartment rentals. There may be differences in shopping habits. Different areas and different groups respond to different motive appeals. Whereas "style for social prestige" may be the best appeal for a college set, "long wear and economy" may be the best for low-income or rural areas. The specific individual in a special environment must be considered in selecting the appeal.

The particular product must also enter into the selection of appeals. A copywriter may have to prepare copy for a shoe store that wants to stress a certain line of men's shoes. "Style" and "price" appeals are usually used in such copy, but in an area where there are poor transportation facilities and walking long distances is common, "feel" and "fit" appeals stressing comfort may be more effective. Questions like the following should be answered: "Is this product a new and unfamiliar one?" "Is it a luxury or necessity?" "Is it an inexpensive product bought on impulse or one purchased after considerable thought and planning?" "Is it seasonal or all year round?" "Who purchases it, men or teen-age boys?"

An example of the type of consumer analysis helpful to a copywriter is the classification of women into sales-approach types published by the Printz-Biederman Company of Cleveland, a women's clothing manufacturer. The analysis is included here to indicate how a station-staff writer may get away from stock appeals in preparing spot announcements.

1. *The young unmarried woman:* She is very sensitive about the opinion of others. She is susceptible to offense where the fatness of her own or her family's pocketbook is in question. If the girl is in business, she can be talked to on the topic of durability, but beware of allowing her to feel that you have the least idea that her life outside her business hours is not as frivolous and full of pleasure as that of her idle sisters.

2. *The young married woman, without children:* She wants becomingness and style. She wants to look more attractive than anyone else to her husband and wants the other young matrons with whom she spends her time to see that her husband can and does give her as beautiful, if not more beautiful, things than any of them have.

3. *The young married woman, with children:* She is less concerned about becomingness and style and more concerned about price and durability. She still has her youth and her little vanities, but she is beginning to plan for a family as well as to be a charming young lady. This makes her wiser, more practical, and more careful in her purchases.

4. *The middle-aged unmarried woman:* She is interested in dressing in such a way as to appear still young. She is usually interested in quality and fit. If she

is of the slender- or heavy-figure type, she wishes to minimize her bad points and make the most of her good ones.

5. *The middle-aged married woman, without children:* Appeal to her is very much the same as to the unmarried woman of her age group, but with less emphasis on price and rather more on style, fit, and becomingness as factors that tend to increase her own self-esteem and her husband's pride in her.

6. *The middle-aged married woman, with children:* The main consideration is price. She must make those dollars go as far as she possibly can and still not be a disappointment to her children and their friends.

7. *The elderly unmarried woman:* She is appealed to by becomingness, workmanship, and in some cases by style. Quality appeals more and more strongly to her as she grows older, especially if she has grown older gracefully and dresses with dignity and real beauty.

8. *The elderly married woman, without children:* Women of this age group are apt to have unusual figures. These customers must never be made to feel that they are ugly and impossible to fit. Garments should be sold to them that minimize stooped shoulders or other ungraceful features. If the customer is in an income group below the average, more stress must be laid on the price factor. And where the individual is socially prominent, more emphasis is put on style.

9. *The elderly married woman, with children:* She is keenly interested in the way she appears to her children. For this reason more money is often spent and more care taken in the choice of the garment than is the case where only she and her husband need be pleased.

10. *The unmarried professional or business woman:* She has a healthy curiosity about the workmanship and about processes of manufacture.

11. *The married professional or business woman:* In addition to the interests of the unmarried professional woman she is also interested in becomingness for the sake of the husband. She has greater confidence in the article if she is taken behind the scenes a little and is shown the whys and wherefores.

WRITING TELEVISION COMMERCIALS

In the preceding section we stressed selecting the proper appeals for the theme of the radio commercial in order to relate the announcement to the needs and wants of the consumer. The proper choice of effect is equally important in writing television commercials. Information from marketing studies to determine *who* the potential customers are, *where* they live, and *when* they buy are also needed in preparing television copy. In planning and writing the actual commercial, one must avoid the error of thinking that the pictures on the screen merely illustrate and reinforce the spoken copy. The commercial must be approached with primary consideration for what can be shown on the screen. Words should not be used to describe what can be easily demonstrated visually.

When sight was added to sound in broadcasting, it brought with it the variety and flexibility provided by action, staging, costumes, cards, still photographs, special graphic devices, slides and moving pictures. Many new and different ways of presenting announcements resulted. The contrast between various advertising media has been described by the well-known advertising man, Fairfax M. Cone, as follows:

> Advertising in magazines and newspapers always has presented the limitations of space. You can't have a dramatic picture of a boy eating a piece of pie, *and* a huge mouth-watering photograph of the rest of the pie from which the boy's piece was cut, *and* a recipe for making the pie, *and* a striking illustration of your product that makes the pie look and taste so good, *and* the several convincing reasons why—*all* the way you want them in any affordable space unit that I know.

He points out that in print it may be possible either to picture the boy's satisfaction or the pie and that in radio you may only talk about the picture or product. However, in the television commercial *all* elements may be included.

The Television Story Board

The story board is a series of drawings, or "roughs," which show the sequence of picture action, optical effects, settings, and camera or shooting angles, with caption notations indicating what words, sound effects, and music are to be heard as the sequence is presented. The story board resembles the layouts used extensively in agencies preparing advertisements for print. This technique has had its widest use in television filmed commercials, but it is becoming increasingly important for taped commercial presentations as well. When the commercial is completed, it is often converted into a series of stills, which with the accompanying audio copy is called a "picture board." Since the commercial is presented on a visual medium, the use of the story-board technique is helpful because from the beginning it requires the copywriter to think in terms of the pictures. In addition, those who have to approve the commercial—agency executives and the sponsor—have an opportunity to appraise the visualization of the copy. Without the story-board, different people reading a script may have markedly different impressions of what will actually be seen on the air.

The cost of rehearsal does not allow much leeway for experimentation and basic changes during the final stages of production. It is better, therefore, to check and recheck any questionable details in the commercial during the story-board stage. In order to anticipate any possible shooting problems, the director for the commercial usually is given an opportunity to review the story-board. In this way, the director can eliminate impractical or impossible action and staging. Besides acting as a check against possible errors, the story-board technique makes it possible for creative artists connected with the production to suggest to the writer small changes or touches that will increase the impact of the commercial. Various agencies and production firms utilize different formats for their story-boards. Some examples appear on pages 421–432.

FORMS OF TELEVISION COMMERCIALS

The forms of television commercials roughly approximate the forms of radio commercials discussed earlier; straight selling, testimonial, dialogue, etc. Because the method of presentation is so varied and flexible, however, it seems wise to classify the forms of television commercials with the elements of variety and flexibility in mind.

Studio Production—Live or Taped—with Talent in View

An announcer or specialized talent is usually seen during the commercial. The amount of time on camera varies considerably. The spokesperson may be on the screen for practically the entire period, standing by the product if it is large, such as a car, or holding the package if it is small, such as a box of cereal. Charts of cutaway sections may be shown, action may be demonstrated, or main features may be indicated. Key words, specific prices, and slogans may be superimposed, electronically inserted, or shot full-screen. When the announcer handles the display of the product or the demonstration, his or her personality is presumed to add to the overall persuasive appeal of the commercial. Such a presentation carries with it a personal endorsement, implicitly or explicitly conveyed. Consequently, this form of commercial is often employed on programs in which a star can act as a spokesperson.

Studio Production—Live or Taped—Voice-Over

This method of presentation focuses attention on the visual aspects of the product display and the demonstration. Several subdivisions may be noted:

1. Talent may be seen as they display the product or demonstrate, but the audio comes from off-camera.
2. Slides, photographs, or cards may be shown on the screen. This is a common method used for local station-break commercials and promotional announcements.
3. Silent film footage or tape may be used. Many product displays and demonstrations cannot be produced live in the studio; film or tape is used instead. Stations may employ this method to aid local accounts through the use of their film equipment or video-tape camera and recorder. A cover shot and a slow pan, showing many used cars, may serve, together with appropriate audio commentary, as an effective commercial for a used-car dealer. Stock footage such as shots of scenic views in the West may be used for a lead into a local travel-agency spot.

Film or Tape—Realistic Action

Essentially the same approaches are used as those described for the live commercials. Film or tape insures that the commercial will be presented in an approved form without the danger of slips of tongue or errors in production.

When talent forgets lines, stumbles over the name of the product, or gives the competitive product's name, or when demonstrations fail to work, all of which have happened on the air in live commercials, the take is discarded. Only the "right" takes are used. Film or tape increases flexibility and permits effects that cannot be attained in live presentations. An example is the contrast between "before" and "after" in a shampoo commercial.

Film or Tape—Nonrealistic Action

Many different production techniques are available to those who create commercials: dancing, electronic effects, cartoons, puppets, animation, and stop-motion photography. These commercials usually have music, vocals, signature melodies or music to reinforce the mood, and backing for words and action. Many humorous announcements use this form. Detailed explanations of a technical nature may be presented in an entertaining and informative manner. New ways may be explored to express commercial messages visually. John Baxter of the Earle Ludgin Advertising Agency, says that

> Writers of television commercials should be as concerned about the pictures as they are about words. When we planned a series for Manor House, practically all the TV commercials for instant coffees presented their case to the public in pretty much the same manner. They had a picture showing how easy this product was to use. Invariably, the announcer put a spoonful into a cup, added hot water, and stirred. This was usually followed by a lip-smacking picture to indicate how good the product tasted.
>
> This posed quite a problem for us.
>
> To avoid the usual pictorial clichés, we sought for new ways to bring our message to the public visually. It was this kind of thinking that led us into the present series which employs abstract patterns to illustrate words rather than the usual literal picture.

Combination

Commercials, live or taped, often employ more than one of the different forms of presentation. Many different combinations may be observed on the air. For example, the announcer may be seen for a few seconds, followed by film. Realistic action may be framed with a filmed cartoon opening and closing. Some of the commercials, especially film commercials, are designed to permit the extraction of a short station-break announcement from the matrix of a longer version. A combination of "live-style" and film techniques is found when commercials are video-taped in advance of broadcast and use improved editing devices and special electronic effects.

Check List for Increasing Effectiveness of TV Commercials

Some years ago NBC released the findings of a special Schwerin Research Corporation study dealing with television commercial effectiveness. The results are applicable in a discussion of television announcements. A brief summary of the key points follows:

1. Correlate audio and video. Failure to observe this simple rule was often found to have been overlooked. A commercial for baking mix which stressed quality of ingredients was discovered to have greater impact when the video showed the items which went into the mix, milk, eggs, etc., at the same time each item was mentioned, as contrasted to the identical audio message delivered while the video showed a housewife merely using the mix. The double sensory impression fixed the sales point more firmly.

2. Demonstrate. . . . Demonstrate. . . . Demonstrate. People are more likely to remember advertiser's claims when they see them proved by demonstrations. A sales idea in a cleanser announcement was that the product makes it easy to clean greasy pans. One approach, which showed the housewife holding a cleanser in one hand and the cleaned frying pan in the other, was not as effective as an alternate approach, in which the TV audience followed the process as the housewife started with a greasy pan and used the cleanser to demonstrate its speed, ease, and efficiency of operation. The research study emphasis is that farfetched demonstrations or those which smack somewhat of the sleight-of-hand are less successful than realistic demonstrations.

3. Keep it simple. The number of elements and the way in which they are to be presented should be kept as simple as possible. When cause-and-effect sequences were utilized, it was found that when the effect was described first followed by the cause, it was usually more effective. A clear recapitulation of the sales points aids the impact. Tricky camera effects may be effective, but often a complicated approach may weaken the results. When the effects strengthen the sales point, however, they may reinforce the sales point. An illustration of this was found in the reaction to one commercial in which the announcer held a product while he explained what it was not. Results were poor. However, an alternate approach utilizing stop-motion photography was very effective. The camera focused on a row of products clearly identifiable as a soap, a cream, a lotion, and finally the advertised product. When the announcer said the product wasn't soap, the bar of soap disappeared; when the announcer explained it wasn't a lotion, the bottle of lotion was eliminated. When the announcer finally said that the product was absolutely unique, there was nothing on the screen but the product itself.

4. Use the right personality. The person who is chosen to represent the product and present the idea should be compatible with the product or idea, and the person's identity and function should be clearly conveyed. Voice-over audio appeared to be less effective than when the presenter talked directly to the viewers or identified himself or herself and introduced the commercial message prior to the voice-over. The Schwerin findings indicated that, when appropriate, the use of an "authority" increases impact. The person selected by the advertiser as the authority, however, may not be regarded by viewers as the person best qualified to present claims for the product. Thus, in several deodorant commercials the use of a white-coated druggist as the authority was not clearly as effective as the testimony of a typical woman. The misuse of authority may weaken the sales point. The sales theme for commercials of a prepared baking mix was that the mix makes it simple to achieve perfect baking results. In one commercial the authority was a chef in a test kitchen who was shown pulling some pastry out of an oven and explaining how simple it was to insure consistent baking success by using this mix. It was not as effective as a second commercial

in which the same sales point was made by a little girl, who was exceedingly proud of the pastry she had just made with the product.

Certainly the professional chef outranked the child as a culinary authority. But in this instance the chef was too expert for the advertiser's purpose. What was simple for the chef might not be easy for the average housewife. The chef was, therefore, not nearly as desirable a spokesperson for the advertiser's sales point as the little girl. If she could use this product and get good results with it, obviously any housewife would be able to obtain the same results.

Distractions of any kind reduce the sales effectiveness of a commercial. A scantily clad model diverted attention away from a sales message. The advantages from the use of the star of a program were not clear-cut—the results depended on how he or she was used. The mere presence of the star holding the advertised package did not automatically insure greater impact. The star has to seriously assume the role of a commercial spokesman.

5. Keep the setting authentic. Every element in the setting should contribute to the impression the advertiser wishes to make. Commercial personalities who were out of place in the setting such as a program MC attempting to demonstrate a baking mix were less effective than a beaming mother bringing muffins (made with the advertised mix) to the family group at the table. Additional sensory impressions should be used when possible to increase impact. In a commercial for a pancake flour, a steaming plate of hot-cakes was shown being brought to the table. The dialogue was full of praise for the color, lightness, and taste of the hot-cakes. The setting was right. However, an extra setting, a camera shot of the pancake just about done on the griddle, was inserted ahead of the sequence noted above and increased the impact through another favorable sensory impression—hotcakes on the griddle.[1]

EXAMPLES OF DIFFERENT FORMS OF COMMERCIALS

1.   "Mr. Coffee"—A TV Commercial Featuring a Straight Selling Approach

This commercial is shown in three different forms—as a storyboard, as a script and as a picture board.

[1] Courtesy of National Broadcasting Company, abstracted from "How to Increase Effectiveness of Television Commercials."

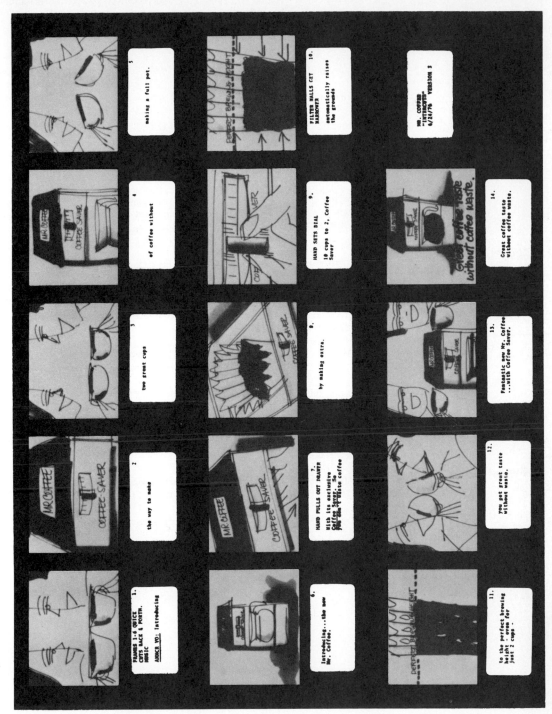

b. Script

VIDEO	AUDIO
FRAMES 1–6. QUICK CUTS BACK AND FORTH FROM MAN AND WOMAN WITH COFFEE CUPS TO COFFEE SAVER.	ANNCR:VO Introducing the way to make two great cups of coffee without making a full pot.
FRAME 6. FULL SHOT MR. COFFEE COFFEE-SAVER MACHINE.	Introducing the new Mr. Coffee.
FRAME 7–8. HAND PULLS DRAW OUT AND WE MOVE IN ON CLOSE UP OF COFFEE-SAVER FEATURTES.	With its exclusive Coffee Saver. So you don't waste coffee by making extra.
FRAME 9. CLOSE UP COFFEE SAVER DIAL.	10 cups to 2, Coffee Saver
FRAMES 10–11. CLOSE UP FILTER WALLS NARROWING.	automatically raises the grounds to the perfect brewing height—even for just 2 cups—
FRAME 12. CLOSE UP MAN AND WOMAN DRINKING COFFEE.	you get great taste without waste.
FRAME 13. CLOSE UP MAN AND WOMAN WITH MACHINE.	Fantastic new Mr. Coffee . . . with Coffee Saver.
FRAME 14. CLOSE UP MACHINE SUPER: GREAT COFFEE TASTE WITHOUT COFFEE WASTE.	Great coffee taste without coffee waste.

1. (MUSIC THROUGHOUT) ANNCR: (VO) Introducing

2. a way to make

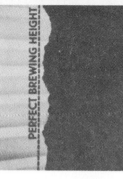

3. two great cups of coffee without making a full pot.

4. Introducing the new Mr. Coffee...

5. with its exclusive Coffee Saver.

6. So you don't waste coffee by making extra.

7. Ten cups to two, Coffee Saver automatically raises the grounds

8. to the perfect brewing height.

9. Even for just two cups,

10. you get great taste without waste.

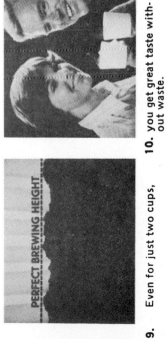

11. Fantastic new Mr. Coffee with Coffee Saver.

12. Great coffee taste without coffee waste.

Courtesy of Ted Bates Advertising and North American Systems

2 "Short and Sassy"—TV Commercial Featuring a Testimonial

ANNCR VO:	Dorothy Hamill for Clairol's Short & Sassy.
D.H. OC:	The longest it was about . . . to the top of my shoulders . . . (laughs) . . . straight bangs and . . . I used to pull it back like this . . .
D.H. VO:	Now with short hair, I need more body. So I use Clairol's Short & Sassy, the conditioner for short hair.
SHOTS OF D.H. SKATING.	Even after blow-drying, Short & Sassy makes it shiny . . . and gives it body. And let's face it, without body, short hair is just short hair.
ANNCR VO: PRODUCT SHOT	Clairol's Short & Sassy, with twice the protein of the leading conditioner.
D.H. OC:	For the Short & Sassy look.

Courtesy of Young and Rubicam, Inc. and Clairol

3 "The Fixer"—A TV Commercial Featuring a Company Spokesperson

1. PATRICK ROSS: I'm
   Patrick Ross,

2. President of the B.F. Goodrich
   Tire Company.

3. No matter how tuff tires
   look on TV

4. in real life they can
   still go flat.

5. But now we've invented a
   new tire called The Fixer,

6. that's actually designed to
   seal most punctures in the
   tread up to 1/4" in diameter.

7. The Fixer, the first steel
   radial designed to fix itself.

8. From Goodrich.

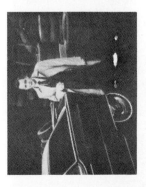

9. Not Goodyear.

10. It's going to make our name
    a lot easier to remember.

Courtesy of Grey Advertising, Inc. and the B.F. Goodrich Tire Co.

4 "We Still Read You, Professor"—A TV Commercial Featuring an Educational Approach

OPEN ON CU OF COOKE/ WHEATSTONE TELEGRAPH. WE SEE MAGNETIC NEEDLES POINTING OUT MESSAGE.

SPOKESMAN: (VO) Y . . . E . . . S.

PULL BACK TO REVEAL SPOKESMAN STANDING NEXT TO TELEGRAPH IN 1800-VINTAGE RAILROAD STATION.

(OC) Yes, we still read you Sir William Cooke and Professor Charles Wheatstone. This invention of yours spelled out the beginning of communications as we know it today. It became the world's first commercial telegraph when installed by a British railway in 1838. Through the inventiveness of people like Cooke and Wheatstone and companies like Rockwell International, communications has become a science.

CONTINUE PULLBACK TO REVEAL MORE OF THE STATION.

CUT BACK TO CU OF SPOKESMAN. HE WALKS TOWARD CAMERA.

REVEAL ADMIRAL COLOR TV IN FGD. HE TURNS ON TV.

A science that brings voices and pictures from around the world . . . even from Mars . . . right into your home. Rockwell is very much a part of that science with products like Admiral television sets, Collins satellite communication systems and air traffic control and Avionics equipment. They also build Collins government and business communications systems like this one, that use microwaves instead of wires.
(PAUSE)

WE SEE SHOT OF COLLINS PARABOLIC ANTENNA ON TV SCREEN. SUPER: Simulated TV Reception.

CUT TO AIRPORT SHOT. WE SEE JET LANDING (OR TAKING OFF) ON TV SCREEN.

CUT TO SPOKESMAN STANDING ALONGSIDE RAILROAD TRACKS.

HE GESTURES UP TO MICROWAVE TOWER.

SUDDENLY A TRAIN ZIPS PAST SPOKESMAN.

(SOUND OF TRAIN, HOLD TO CLOSE) (LOUDER TO BE HEARD OVER TRAIN)

CU OF SPOKESMAN.

SPOKESMAN:
We still read you Sir William and you Professor . . . Communications is one of the sciences of Rockwell International . . . where science gets down to business.

CUT TO LOGO ON BLACK BACKGROUND. SYMBOL AND WORDS: Rockwell International . . . where science gets down to business.

Courtesy of Rockwell International and Campbell-Ewald Company

5   "Toll Booth"—A Radio Commercial Featuring A Humorous Approach

TOLL TAKER:	Good morning, sir.
MOTORIST:	You know I've come through this toll booth 4–500 times and never ever . . .
T.T.:	Sir?
MOT.:	I forgot my wallet.
T.T.:	Sir.
MOT.:	. . . the whole thing—don't have a penny.
T.T.:	Just pull over there and go to the office.
MOT.:	See—that's the worst part. I'm in this fantastic hurry for a board meeting.
T.T.:	Just fill out this form.
MOT.:	I'm late. Look! Here. Take my watch for security.
T.T.:	(LAUGHS) I can't do that.
MOT.:	Cost $1500. Tells you when you're at sea level.
T.T.:	Just pull over there sir.
MOT.:	I, I don't have time. Oh, yes I do. You can take this brand new TIME Magazine.
T.T.:	The form's in the office sir.
MOT.:	You're gonna love this week's theater section. Or look, how about science?? Look at what's in science.
T.T.:	Just pull over there sir.
MOT.:	Think how much fun it'll be reading TIME Magazine out here where it's lonely.
T.T.:	Sir . . . ?
MOT.:	It's bright and exciting. It makes your whole day go—and when people come by you can say things.
T.T.:	All right. I'll take it.
MOT.:	Hey, thanks a lot. I'll be back through here 5:30. Pick up my TIME Magazine.
T.T.:	Oh wait. I get off at 4.
MOT.:	I'll come to your house. Where do you live.
T.T.:	I'll draw you a map OK. Just pull over there. To the office.
MOT.:	I appreciate this.
V.O.:	TIME makes everything more interesting, including you.

Courtesy of Young and Rubicam, Inc. and Time, Inc.

6 "Creety"—A TV Commercial Featuring a Humorous Approach

1. MIDAS MAN 1: I don't believe it.

2. It's Old Man Creety.

3. CREETY: Howdy boys.

4. MIDAS MAN 2: We haven't seen you since...

5. CREETY: ...Since I got this guarantee.

6. Says Annabell gets a free muffler.

7. MAN 1: Aren't you ever going to sell this car?

8. CREETY: No. I wouldn't stop giving you boys the business.

9. SPOKESMAN: At Midas we guarantee

10. to replace our mufflers free for as long as you

11. Even if it's forever.

12. CREETY: See you again, boys.

7 "Monks"—A TV Commercial Featuring a Humorous Approach

1. (MUSIC UNDER BARO-
QUE) (MONKS CHORUS
UNDER)

2. ANNCR: (VO) Ever since
people started recording
information,

3. there's been a need to duplicate it.

4. (MUSIC)

5. (MUSIC)

6. (MUSIC)

7. (MUSIC)

8. (MUSIC)

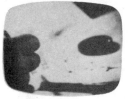

9. FATHER: Very nice
work, Brother Dominick.

10. BROTHER DOMINICK:
Thank you. FATHER:
Very nice.

11. FATHER: Now, I would
like 500 more sets!

12. (MUTTERING PAIN-
FULLY TO HIMSELF
AS HE WALKS AWAY.)

13. (SFX: CLOSES DOOR)

14. (SFX: BUS)

15. (SFX: STREET NOISE)

16. (SFX: OFFICE NOISE)
STEPHENS: Brother
Dominick. How are you?

"Monks" continued.

1. BROTHER DOMINICK:
   Could you do a big job
   for me?

2. ANNCR: (VO) Xerox has
   developed an amazing
   machine that's unlike anything we've ever made.

3. The Xerox 9200 Dupli-
   cating System.

4. It automatically feeds
   and cycles originals ...

5. Has a computerized pro-
   grammer that coordinates
   the entire system.

6. Can duplicate, reduce and
   assemble a virtually limit-
   less number of complete
   sets ...

7. And does it all at the in-
   credible rate of 2 pages per
   second.

8. The Xerox 9200 Dupli-
   cating System.

9. BROTHER DOMINICK:
   Here are your sets,
   Father.

10. FATHER: What?
    BROTHER DOMINICK:
    The 500 sets you asked
    for.

11. FATHER: (GLANCES UP-
    WARD) It's a miracle!

12. (MONKS CHORUS)

Courtesy of Needham, Harper and Steers, Inc. and Xerox Corporation

8 "Eastern Places"—A TV Commercial Using an Announcer (VO) with Music Under

1. (MUSIC UNDER)
   ANNCR: (VO) Come fly
   with us to Eastern's places.

2. CHORUS: Feel the
   seconds.

3. Feel each minute.

4. As the day goes by, feel
   yourself in it.

5. It's a good day to up
   and fly away,

6. it's so easy to do.

7. Eastern's got the right
   time

8. and the right place for
   you.

9. Every minute, every day,

10. an Eastern plane is on the
    way.

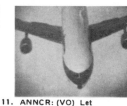

11. ANNCR: (VO) Let
    Eastern Airlines be your
    wings

12. with over thirteen
    hundred flights a day,

13. to more than a hundred
    cities.

14. The people of Eastern

15. have the right time

16. and the right place for
    you.

17. CHORUS: So up and
    fly away. It's so easy
    to do.

18. Eastern's got the right
    time

19. and the right place for
    you.

20. (MUSIC OUT)

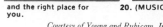

Courtesy of Young and Rubicam, Inc. and Eastern Airlines

9 "Hospital Bed"—A TV Commercial Using Animation

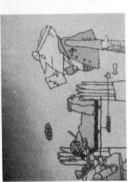

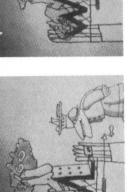

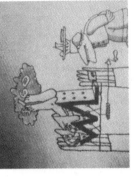

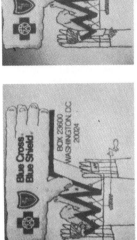

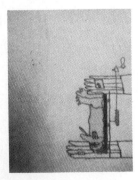

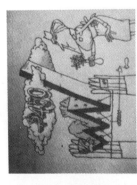

1. (SFX: FOOTSTEPS THROUGHOUT) ANNCR: (VO) The cost of health care has been rising ...

2. till everyone feels the crunch. (SFX: CRANK)

3. Hospital costs are climbing. (SFX: CRANK)

4. We need more planning ...

5. closer review of treatment.

6. To avoid unnecessary care and costs. (SFX: CRANK)

7. If present trends continue ...

8. (SFX: CRANK)

9. ...a room in a local hospital will cost $450 a day by 1980.

10. Blue Cross and Blue Shield need your help to keep this trend down. (SFX)

11. Help us take the squeeze out of getting well.

12. (SFX) Write us to learn how.

Courtesy of J. Walter Thompson Company and Blue Cross/Blue Shield of Washington, D.C.

PUBLIC-SERVICE ANNOUNCEMENTS

Noncommercial announcements may be prepared by staff writers or be received from governmental agencies or local and national organizations. These public-service announcements may be of any type and form listed in the discussion of the commercial announcements. They are broadcast during local and national drives for funds. Many of the same techniques and appeals are used. Reminders to vote, tolerance notes, traffic safety suggestions, information on special community events, and what to do to meet disaster emergencies or epidemics come under this classification.

Stations also face the problem of keeping old listeners and attracting new ones. Promotional "on-the-air" announcements are prepared to acquaint the audience with the start of a new series, or to "billboard" coming program features. Variety in approach is necessary. One method frequently utilized is to assign a definite period for these announcements and work them into a program format. Interviews with personalities heard on the station is one device for entertainment "bait."

A radio announcement first in a 60-second form and then in a 30-second form.

1   Prudence Crandall"—60-second Form

SFX:	SCHOOL BELL
ANNCR:	In 1833, Prudence Crandall, a young Quaker, opened a school for Black girls in Connecticut.
SFX:	NOISE, INCLUDING BURNING OF FIRE
ANNCR:	The villagers tried to burn it. They refused to sell her food or medicine. Still, Black children from all over New England came to the school. Then, the state passed a law prohibiting the establishment of Negro schools. Miss Crandall disobeyed and was sent to jail. (**JAIL DOOR CLOSES**) The law didn't stop Blacks from learning. And it didn't stop others from helping, despite the danger. Thanks to a continuing tradition of support, the United Negro College Fund has been able to help Black students change the course of their lives. Fortunately, supporting Black education won't cost your life or liberty anymore. Today, it just costs money. Please continue a great American tradition. Support the United Negro College Fund. A mind is a terrible thing to waste.
ANNCR. #2:	A public service message of this station and The Advertising Council.

Courtesy of Young and Rubicam, Inc. and United Negro College Fund Campaign

2 "Prudence Crandall"—30-second Form

SFX:	SCHOOL BELL
ANNCR:	In 1833, Prudence Crandall, a young Quaker, opened a school for Black girls in Connecticut. (**NOISES, INCL. CRACKLING OF FIRE**) The villagers tried to burn it. The state passed a law against it. Miss Crandall disobeyed and was sent to jail. (**JAIL DOOR SHUTS**) Supporting Black education won't cost your freedom anymore. Today, it just costs money. Please continue a great American tradition. Give to the United Negro College Fund. A mind is a terrible thing to waste.
ANNCR. #2:	A public service message of this station and The Advertising Council.

Projects and Exercises

1. Visit an advertising agency for a "behind-the-scenes" tour. Request one of the account executives to discuss a current advertising campaign.
2. Tune in a station for an assigned period. Report on the general motives appealed to, and specific forms used in the radio and television commercials.
3. Discuss the relative effectiveness of the above commercials.
4. Using the Printz-Biederman classification prepare commercials for women's clothing suitable for a local department store:
    a. Straight radio announcement for a sale on inexpensive cloth winter coats.
    b. Educational 150-word television commercial for live presentation on an expensive fur coat.
    c. Commercial for a woman's participation program for introduction of a new line of smartly tailored classic suits. Alternate radio and television presentations.
    d. Twenty-second jingle for station-break announcement that may be used on both radio and television. Suggest visual treatment for the television commercial. The subject should be inexpensive evening gowns.
5. Follow a specific program to become familiar with it. Then prepare appropriate radio or television commercials in harmony with the program and its current advertising campaign.
6. Prepare seasonal 60-word radio station-break announcements, using actual companies and products in your area, as follows:
    a. A toy store in the first week of December.
    b. A florist in the week before St. Valentine's Day.
    c. A sale of snow shovels by a local hardware store in November.
    d. A dry cleaner two weeks before Easter.
    e. A garden supply store in the spring.
    f. A soft drink in the middle of summer.
    g. A used-car dealer's sale in September.

7. Prepare television commercials for the same companies. Presentations should be live or voice-over. Discuss how film might be used.

8. Prepare musical commercials based upon public domain songs or current popular melodies.

9. Outline or sketch out in rough form a commercial story board.

interview, personality, and game shows

25

Many programs depend for their effectiveness on verbal exchanges taking place among participants without detailed scripts. Among the shows that include this type of spontaneous exchange as an important element are NBC's *Today*, ABC's *Good Morning, America*, NBC's *Tomorrow*, personality shows, game shows that feature participation by celebrities and audience members, and telephone interview programs. Interviewers or MCs on such programs must not only think of themselves and their presentations but must always consider the answers and actions of those in the studio with them. Something may happen that makes the next question inappropriate; a contestant may become frightened or blurt out censorable material; a telephone call may not go through as planned; the correct identification of a mystery voice may occur before it is expected; a long-winded answer may upset the timing. All of these "surprise" factors must be anticipated in some degree and handled smoothly.

INTERVIEWS

Interviews may be classified in three general types: 1. opinion, 2. information, and 3. personality. Some interviews include more than one of these aspects. A personality, for instance, may offer an opinion on a subject or provide information.

Opinion Interviews

The opinion interview is a feature of many radio stations that broadcast conversations between talk-show hosts and audience members who telephone in. The hosts state a subject that they invite members of the audience to discuss. Often they stimulate discussion by presenting their own opinions on the subject. They may actually argue with those among their callers who disagree with them. The telephone interview has largely replaced the "man on the street" broadcast, in which an interviewer stationed himself on a busy street corner to query passersby about subjects in the news. The opinion interview occurs in television in such programs as that conducted by William Buckley,

Copyright, American Broadcasting Companies, Inc.

Shooting a Sports Interview with a Minicam.

who makes a point of interviewing individuals who are controversial in their backgrounds and their views. The opinion of an expert is often as pertinent to the audience as the information provided.

Information Interviews

Many interviews seek to elicit information from a person who is an authority on some subject. A series that specializes in this type of interview is NBC's *Today* show. The "peg" on which the interview often turns is the fact that the individual has just written a book on the subject on which he or she is being questioned. A great many other programs also use this type of interview as a means of getting information to the audience.

Information interviews used to be scripted before broadcast, but now they are almost always delivered extemporaneously after thorough preparation and research by the interviewers or their assistants. In fact, many go on the air at the moment the interviewer and the guest meet for the first time. On public broadcasting stations interview programs may be rehearsed. Rehearsal does offer the participants better control of the content of the broadcast, but it generally has the disadvantage of making the interview sound stilted and planned.

An expert interviewer follows several rules:

1. Prepare for the interview carefully. If it is based on a book, read it ahead of time or at least review notes prepared by an assistant who has read the book.

2. Try to develop the information in an organized way while maintaining a conversational flavor.

3. Keep the spotlight on the guest, recognizing that your role as an interviewer is to do the best possible job of drawing out the guest.

4. Try to avoid replying to the guest's comments with such meaningless remarks as "I see." Instead, use the guest's answer to make a conversational bridge to the next question.

5. Ask one question at a time to avoid confusing the guest and irritating the TV director, who usually likes to put the face of the person who is doing the talking on the line monitor.

6. Attend carefully to what the guest says. One of the most important qualifications of a good interviewer is to be a good listener.

Personality Interviews

In personality interviews the persons interviewed are important primarily because of what has happened to them, what they have done, or the position they hold in the public eye. A personality interview may occur as a feature-story interview presented when the occasion arises, or built as a regular series; it may be a celebrity interview.

Feature-story interviews range from novelties and stunts to eyewitness accounts of disasters. Great flexibility and sensitivity must be possessed by the interviewers. Language, visual image, and delivery must match the mood of the occasion. This seems obvious, and yet reporters have been guilty of bad taste in pursuit of a feature interview after a disaster, capitalizing upon personal grief or using a type of delivery more suited to a sports account. When novelty or stunt interviews are conducted, an interviewer must be careful not to seem superior or to be making fun of the "interviewee." An objective attitude may be hard to maintain when one encounters eccentrics who come to public attention through their activities. The audience may decide to ridicule the person on the basis of the interview, but the interviewer should not slant it in that direction. Avoid correcting grammatical errors made by the interviewees or commenting on gaps in their knowledge. The audience does not like a smart-aleck interviewer; it prefers an interviewer who is genuinely interested in the subject of the interview.

The following rules apply particularly to the interviewing of celebrities:

1. Know as much as possible about your subject.

2. Avoid obvious or trite questions.

3. Keep a file of background material.

4. Do not put celebrities "on the spot" by asking questions that will embarrass them.

5. If you want information on a touchy subject, take an oblique or indirect approach before you get on the air.

6. Don't wait to talk with the celebrity until you are both on the air.

7. Give every personality the plush treatment.

PERSONALITY SHOWS

An important element in network and syndicated programming is the personality show headed by an individual who often acts as a performer and an interviewer. Programs of this nature are often called "desk and sofa" shows because the personalities usually sit behind a desk, their guests on a sofa beside them. These programs usually contain simple performances by the personality and guests—songs, comedy, routines, sketches—and they also invariably contain interviews of some type. Some shows tend to emphasize the performance aspects, others the interviews. One of the leading personality shows is NBC's *Tonight,* which features Johnny Carson. He is essentially a comedy performer who presents monologues and comedy routines and conducts interviews of the personality type. The *Merv Griffin Show,* a syndicated series, is similar in its emphasis. Other syndicated personality shows that emphasize entertainment plus interviews are *The Mike Douglas Show* and *Dinah! The Phil Donahue Show* emphasizes interviews and often concentrates on one guest for the entire program.

The personalities on the "desk and sofa" shows receive assistance from a staff of writers in preparing for their programs. Johnny Carson, for example, employs joke writers who work on his monologues and his comedy skits. He also receives information about his guests, most of whom he does not see until they walk through the curtain to greet him on the air. The notes he receives indicate the events in his guests' lives on which he can base questions. He may also be warned in these notes to stay away from subjects that could be touchy. Personalities on all of these shows are similarly assisted by a staff of writers and production assistants.

EXAMPLE OF A PERSONALITY INTERVIEW

Johnny Carson and Marian Mercer on the *Tonight* show[1]

The interview that follows is typical of the personality interviews featured on the *Tonight* show. Marian Mercer, a Tony award winner for her Broadway performance in *Promises, Promises,* tells Johnny Carson what it is like to appear in a Broadway flop that runs for only one night. The sketch referred to in the interview was a satire on "soap operas" in which Johnny Carson and Marian Mercer appeared just before the interview.

CARSON   . . . On April 18 of this year she opened on Broadway in a play called **A Place for Polly.** And on April 18, she closed in **A Place for Polly.** That happens sometimes. She's a delightful gal. Will you welcome Marian Mercer? (APPLAUSE) I wasn't, you know, doing a put-down introduction.

MERCER: I know. The pain was bad for a while, but I've gotten over it.

[1] Courtesy of NBC.

CARSON: What happened? I didn't get a chance to see **A Place for Polly.** Many people didn't get a chance to see **A Place for Polly.**

MERCER: You know, you're joined by millions. The bad thing was that I really loved doing it, I mean I just loved the character. I guess I have no critical sense any more because I really thought it was going to work.

CARSON: It opened and ran—

MERCER: and closed the next night. In fact, it really opened and closed the same night. I've got to level with you.

CARSON: It didn't have a two-day run. You were trying to stretch the run, right?

MERCER: I didn't even know it had closed because I never read reviews. I just can't bear it. It's just too hurtful. So I went to Asbury Park the night it opened and I didn't know whether it was going to run or what. I came back and I thought I'll go to the theatre at eight o'clock and if it's playing, I'll play, and if it's not playing, I'll just gather up my gear and leave. So that's why I was on Eighth Avenue signalling for a cab at eight-thirty. And I saw everybody I knew in the world. You know, and you just want to creep silently away when that happens and everyone says, "Hi, Marian, how are you?" And I went "oooh."

CARSON: Did you know at any time at all before that it's not going to be a big smash?

MERCER: Yeah, you know when those friends start coming backstage and saying those non-committal things like "You looked beautiful. Where did you get those clothes? Gee, that set—that's the best set I've seen."

CARSON: That is awfully trying on other performers who go back.

MERCER: It's so hard on friends because they don't know what to say. There are several classics. I have a friend, who when he's really put to it and he's just hated what he's seen, he goes back and says, "Well, you've done it. You really have done it."
(LAUGHTER) And that can mean anything.

CARSON: Anything at all.

MERCER: And you always know who's out there—some well-meaning person says, "Hey, your best friend's here tonight." That happened to me during **Polly,** and my best friend didn't come back to see me. She said, "Well, you know, I thought you'd just be besieged by people." I certainly was.

CARSON: I heard once, somebody said once—it was one of those dismal things. It just happened. It wasn't the actor's fault. And he came back and he said. "What do you think?" And he said, "Well, you know, I've never seen you better"—which can mean, again, nothing or anything, you know, and you just have to take it. So you had no after-theatre party at all; you just left town?

MERCER: No, I just left town, got away from it all.

CARSON: Is that terribly depressing? Does it make you not want to get right into another play?

MERCER: Yeah, you feel terrible. But that's part of the game, you know.

CARSON: How long did you spend getting ready for that show?

MERCER: Well, that was the problem. There just wasn't enough time. I think we could have made it work. The preview audiences—some of them just adored it, you know. So you never can tell.

CARSON: Are you going into another play soon?

MERCER: Yeah, hopefully. I can't talk about it, of course . . .

CARSON: This could have been a stepping stone, this sketch here.

MERCER: Oh, that's my comeback.

CARSON: I don't think Clive Barnes reviews our sketches, which is probably just as well. But didn't he say something about you? That you were the only girl in captivity with introverted dimples.

MERCER: What was that? Would those be moles?

CARSON: No, something like that.

MERCER: I don't know what that means. Somebody told me—I had a review once that said I was a combination of Miriam Hopkins and Zazu Pitts. And that did not help me. It simply didn't help me at all. And I got a review once in **Little Mary Sunshine** picking out a gesture that I had done and that's when I stopped reading reviews because I was never able to do that gesture again. You know, because I kept waiting for it. Like here's that wonderful gesture—and it was just so wooden.

CARSON: If I remember before when you were on the show, there's none of your family in the entertainment business, right?

MERCER: No, they're all very conservative, wonderful, solid folk.

GAME SHOWS

Game shows form an important category of programming with a long tradition in radio and in television. There are three principal types: quiz shows, audience participation shows, and panel shows. All three have certain elements in common: spontaneity, structure, and uncertainty of outcome. Good game shows are carefully constructed on the basis of certain premises and then follow a sequence of rules and procedures much like sporting events. Programs of this type occupy much of the three networks' daytime schedules and early evening programming on many stations.

Most successful game shows go considerably beyond the elementary notion of asking questions of an informational nature of contestants. *The Price Is Right* chooses its contestants from the studio audience and confronts them in a competitive situation with the task of estimating the retail price of various items of merchandise. This seemingly simple notion is perfected into a sequence of internal games of great ingenuity that build to a showcase climax where two of the contestants compete to win an entire assemblage of prizes depending upon their acumen in estimating value.

The panel show *To Tell The Truth* exploits the premise that people believe they can tell whether someone is lying. The program has a panel of celebrities who cross-examine three contestants, one of whom is telling the truth about him or herself, while the other two, having been briefed in advance, try to convince the panelists with lies that they are the truthtellers. This format, with contestants obtained from stories in magazines and newspapers around the country, has continued to intrigue home viewers for more than 20 years.

Then there are panel shows in which the game is primarily oriented toward the production of laughs. *Match Game* and *Hollywood Squares* are examples, where contestants are pitted against each other in predicting responses from a panel of celebrities.

Password, a game of word associations, introduced the form of using celebrities teamed with regular contestants as partners. In recent years many other game shows of the quiz type have used this form of competition.

Concentration, another game show with a long record of continuous broadcast, presents contestants in a battle of observation and memory based on a children's game, with the further development of having a rebus revealed in stages until one contestant successfully makes a correct identification.

Game shows use merchandise and cash prizes to add excitement to the program by providing stakes for the contestants. Because they are offered as genuine contests, and because it is a felony under the law to "rig" a broadcast game show through secret help to a contestant, these shows are produced with the utmost care and supervision.

The role of the host or MC of a game show varies, depending upon the nature of the particular game. While all MCs must have attractive personalities, in some game shows they serve primarily as "traffic cops" to keep the show moving. This function is not as easily performed as it may seem, because even in this capacity the MC has to be aware at all times of the sequence of events and must provide the pacing for the show. In a program like *The Price Is Right,* however, which deals mainly with the spontaneous reactions of inexperienced contestants, the MC acts as an on-stage producer in responding to events as they occur during the program. MCs must know how to deal with the recalcitrant as well as the exuberant contestant; they must know when a reply of a contestant is satisfactory; they must keep in mind the perspective of the home audience. They must be able to take anything in stride, from an off-color remark to a participant's panic when the camera goes on, and must deal with it tastefully. They must not ridicule contestants by reference to their nationality, race, or personal characteristics, but they must be able to perceive and exploit humorous situations of a legitimate nature. They must also appear fair to all contestants as well as sympathetic and courteous to those who lose.

An example of a game show is *Match Game,* which is broadcast five days a week by CBS and is syndicated in an evening version as *Match Game, P.M.* The script format for this program is followed by a figure that illustrates the way in which the program is staged and a table showing how the five cameras used in the program pick up the action.

EXAMPLE OF A TELEVISION GAME SHOW SCRIPT

Match Game P.M.[2]

RAYBURN: Welcome to MATCH GAME P.M.
(Ad libs with celebrities)
(Introduces contestants)
Let's meet tonight's contestants,
(_____) and (_____).
(Applause)
(Brief Interview)
              Okay, let's start the game,
              On Match Game "'PM" we'll give each of you three chances to
              match as many of our celebrities as you can. The one who has
              scored the most matches at the end of the third round will be
              the winner . . . and will go on to play the big money super
              match . . . which can pay off over ten thousand dollars.
(Applause)
(To contestant)
              You make the selection. Do you want A or B?
(Contestant selects)
(Read question)
(Music)
(Read question to contestant—get answer)
(Get answers from panel)
(Read 2nd question—get answers)
COMMERCIAL 1
ROUND 2
(To contestant with higher score)
              YOU ARE IN THE LEAD _____ TO _____, SO YOU MAKE
              THE SELECTION. DO YOU WANT A OR B?
(Play game)
ROUND 3
(To contestant with higher score)
              YOU ARE IN THE LEAD _____ TO _____, SO YOU MAKE
              THE SELECTON. DO YOU WANT A OR B?
(Play game) Declare a winner
If the score is tied at the end of round 1 or round 2, the alternate contestant
will choose A or B first.
COMMERCIAL 2
TIE BREAKER
RAYBURN: THIS GAME ENDED IN A TIE—AND WE'LL BE RIGHT BACK TO
              BREAK THAT TIE AFTER THIS.
(COMMERCIAL)
(If enough time remains . . .)
Do a regular Tie-Breaker. Start with the down-stage contestant. (If insufficient
time . . .)
RAYBURN: (TO CONTESTANTS)
              WE DON'T HAVE TIME FOR OUR REGULAR TIE-BREAKER SO
              WE'LL PLAY SUDDEN DEATH. FOR THIS, YOU WILL WRITE

     [2] Courtesy of Celebrity Productions, Inc., Ira Skutch, Producer and Marc
Breslow, Director.

YOUR ANSWERS AND YOU WILL BE PLAYING WITH OUR THREE REGULARS—BRETT, CHARLES AND RICHARD.

(READ QUESTION . . . WRITE ANSWERS)

OK, YOU'RE READY. NOW WE'LL CALL ON OUR REGULARS ONE AT A TIME. THE FIRST ONE OF YOU TO SCORE A MATCH WILL BE THE WINNER.

(PLAY . . . DECLARE WINNER)

RAYBURN: CONGRATULATIONS, YOU'RE OUR CHAMPION. COME ON OVER WITH ME.

(BRING WINNER OVER)

SORRY TO SAY "GOODBYE" TO YOU (LOSER) BUT WE DO HAVE SOME GIFTS FOR YOU BACKSTAGE—AND OUR THANKS FOR PLAYING "MATCH GAME P.M."

(MUSIC)

(APPLAUSE)

(TURNTABLE TAKES OFF LOSER AND BRINGS AROUND "SUPER MATCH.")

SUPER MATCH

RAYBURN: TIME NOW FOR THE BIG MONEY SUPER MATCH—WHERE YOU CAN WIN OVER <u>TEN THOUSAND DOLLARS</u>. TO DO THAT WE HAVE 2 AUDIENCE MATCHES FOR YOU.
WHATEVER YOU WIN IN THESE AUDIENCE MATCHES, YOU WILL HAVE A CHANCE TO MULTIPLY BY TEN.
HERE COMES THE FIRST ONE.
WE POLLED A RECENT STUDIO AUDIENCE AND GOT THEIR BEST RESPONSE TO THIS:

(Help of Panel)

OKAY, YOU'VE WON $_____. WHICH MEANS THAT THE LEAST YOU WILL BE PLAYING FOR IS TEN TIMES THAT— $_____.

(Amount goes on to Neon Sign)

NOW LET'S SEE HOW MUCH MORE YOU CAN WIN WITH THE SECOND AUDIENCE MATCH. HERE IT IS:

(Play with 3 panelists:)

THIS TIME YOU'VE WON $_____. WE MULTIPLY THAT BY 10 WHICH MAKES $_____. WE ADD THAT TO YOUR $_____ WHICH GIVES YOU A POT OF $_____ TO SHOOT FOR.

(Total amount comes on the screen)

TO COLLECT THE $_____, YOU MUST SELECT <u>ONE OF OUR</u> CELEBRITIES—AND MATCH THAT STAR <u>HEAD TO HEAD</u>. WHICH CELEBRITY DO YOU PICK?

(CONTESTANT PICKS ONE)

OKAY.

(TO CELEBRITY)

_____ WRITE DOWN YOUR ANSWER TO "_____"

(WHEN CONTESTANT READY)

OKAY (**contestant**) – (**panelist**) IS READY.
WHAT'S YOUR RESPONSE TO "_____"?

(GETS RESPONSE)

(TO CELEBRITY)

FOR $_____, WHAT'S YOUR ANSWER?

(ANNOUNCE WINNING AND DISMISS CONTESTANT)

COMMERCIAL 3

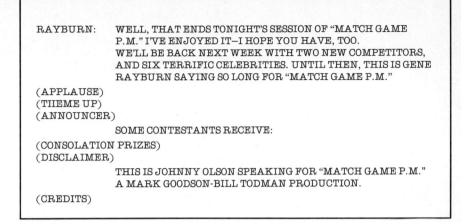

RAYBURN: WELL, THAT ENDS TONIGHT'S SESSION OF "MATCH GAME
P.M." I'VE ENJOYED IT—I HOPE YOU HAVE, TOO.
WE'LL BE BACK NEXT WEEK WITH TWO NEW COMPETITORS,
AND SIX TERRIFIC CELEBRITIES. UNTIL THEN, THIS IS GENE
RAYBURN SAYING SO LONG FOR "MATCH GAME P.M."

(APPLAUSE)
(THEME UP)
(ANNOUNCER)

        SOME CONTESTANTS RECEIVE:

(CONSOLATION PRIZES)
(DISCLAIMER)

        THIS IS JOHNNY OLSON SPEAKING FOR "MATCH GAME P.M."
A MARK GOODSON-BILL TODMAN PRODUCTION.

(CREDITS)

Projects And Exercises

1. Tune in locally produced television and radio interviews in your area and classify them as to type. Do the same for any locally produced game programs. Time with a stopwatch and note format breakdown.

2. Record several class ad-lib interviews and prepare a written transcript. Assign another pair to read these transcripts and compare the results.

3. Study the above transcripts and draw conclusions about characteristics of informal speech style. Then write an interview on a similar subject. Keep the flavor of the ad-lib style, but do not attempt to incorporate all the repetitions, interruptions, and hesitations, nor write in the exact same loose style. Rehearse delivery and present for class as an ad-lib interview. See if the class can detect that it is from script.

4. Prepare and present television interviews with only a few visuals. Select the visuals carefully in order to assure that the interview could not be presented as effectively on radio.

5. Use sound effects (street background—industrial sounds—railroad station or airport—harbor noises—baseball game crowd—theatre lobby—etc.) to simulate a background for a series of "Traveling Mike" or "TV Close-ups" interviews. Adhere to the type of questions appropriate to such a program series.

6. Present a series of informational television or radio interviews entitled "The Hobby Clinic." Keep to an exact three-minute timing accepting a few seconds leeway *under* but not over the time. The interviewer may prepare opening and closing material (reading from script for radio and from cue cards for television), but the remainder of the interview should be ad lib. Conferences with the persons to be interviewed may be held. Brief outline material may be used.

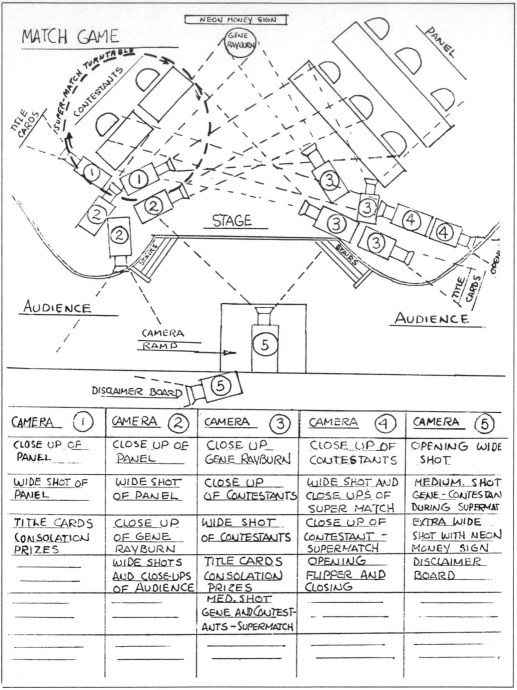

MATCH GAME

CAMERA ①	CAMERA ②	CAMERA ③	CAMERA ④	CAMERA ⑤
CLOSE UP OF PANEL	CLOSE UP OF PANEL	CLOSE UP GENE RAYBURN	CLOSE UP OF CONTESTANTS	OPENING WIDE SHOT
WIDE SHOT OF PANEL	WIDE SHOT OF PANEL	CLOSE UP OF CONTESTANTS	WIDE SHOT AND CLOSE UPS OF SUPER MATCH	MEDIUM SHOT GENE - CONTESTAN DURING SUPERMAT
TITLE CARDS CONSOLATION PRIZES	CLOSE UP OF GENE RAYBURN	WIDE SHOT OF CONTESTANTS	CLOSE UP OF CONTESTANT - SUPERMATCH	EXTRA WIDE SHOT WITH NEON MONEY SIGN
	WIDE SHOTS AND CLOSE-UPS OF AUDIENCE	TITLE CARDS CONSOLATION PRIZES	OPENING FLIPPER AND CLOSING	DISCLAIMER BOARD
		MED. SHOT GENE AND CONTEST-ANTS - SUPERMATCH		

Courtesy of Celebrity Productions, Inc., Ira Skutch, Producer and Marc Breslow, Director.

Figure 25–1   Marc Breslow's Director's Staging Sheet For *Match Game P.M.*

7. Prepare and present a series of 4½ or 9½ minute game or personality programs. A suggested method of procedure: Divide the class into groups by counting off one through four. Assign duties. Number ones are directors; number twos are announcers; number threes are writers; and fours are MCs. Four rounds of this project permit alternation of duties. Each group is permitted to present its choice of program type and format, including specific title, sponsor, radio or television, and station or network. A group other than the performance group assists in technical areas, another group is used for the participants, other groups serve as the audience. Class criticism follows each presentation.

programs

26

"At no period in our history has the function of news and public affairs broadcasting been so critical and important to our national life," said William S. Paley, Chairman of the Board of CBS, in a speech addressed to professional broadcasters.

The movement of world events on both the national and international scenes takes on increasing significance each day in terms of the welfare and security of each citizen. These conditions and circumstances provide the broadcaster with an unprecedented opportunity to move ahead in this field of news and public affairs. We have today within our grasp the opportunity to provide an extraordinary public service in a troubled world and, at the same time, to increase our stature and strength as broadcasters.

The broadcasting of news and, to a more limited extent, commentary and "news-in-depth" is an activity in which practically every television and radio station engages. News operations range from large-scale undertakings involving staffs of news editors, film crews, and special reporters to small-scale operations run by staff announcers. Because of the great audience for news broadcasts and the public faith in the reliability of broadcast news, it is essential that news broadcasters have a high sense of responsibility and the intellectual equipment required for professional journalism. A staff announcer who is required to prepare and present news summaries should at least have a clear knowledge of what constitutes news and of the processes by which news is gathered and edited, a keen sense of news values, and skill in the construction and delivery of newscasts.

WHAT IS NEWS?

"News exists in the minds of men," writes Wilbur Schramm. "It is not an event; it is something perceived *after* the event. It is not identical with the event; it is an attempt to reconstruct the essential framework of the event—*essential* being defined against a frame of reference which is calculated to make the event meaningful to the reader [or listener]."

Millions of events occur daily: your awakening in the morning is an event, just as your failure to awaken on schedule or your death is an event. Which of these events is worthy of a news report? Your rising according to schedule may be a matter of such regularity that even you do not consider it of any significance; should you oversleep some morning, however, you would consider the event of some significance if it made you late for school or forced you to miss an appointment, and you might make a firsthand report of the event to the person you kept waiting. Should you fail to get up in the morning because you had died in your sleep, the event would unquestionably be reported as news to a circle of your social and business acquaintances and might even be reported to the community at large by local newspapers or television and radio stations. Should you fail to rise because you are a victim of a rare sleeping sickness that keeps you in a coma for days, weeks, or months on end, this unusual event might be reported by the press throughout the country. If you happened to be a high government official, the news of your illness or death might be transmitted around the world.

News is related to events that in some way *interest* people. People are interested in reports of events that directly or indirectly affect their own lives, and in reports of any irregularities in the course of human affairs that arouse intellectual or emotional curiosity. News of natural disasters, such as floods, hurricanes, and fires interest many people. Departures from moral and legal codes of behavior interest more people than strict observance of these codes. The commission of a crime, the apprehension of the suspected criminal, and the trial, conviction, or acquittal are events usually reported as news. Important governmental actions, such as the enactment of a law, the issuance of an executive order, or a court decision, are reported as news when they affect our lives in some way. Speeches and interviews by important public officials are newsworthy because they provide clues to future governmental action.

We may see, then, that the occurrence of an event of common interest is the basis for any news story, and that speeches, interviews, and public statements become newsworthy as they are related to past and future events. It is true, of course, that there are several figures in the world whose every public statement serves as material for news reports. The President of the United States is one of those figures because the President's remarks may indicate what our government will do next. There are other public figures who make news almost every time they speak. Television and radio newscasters must maintain at all times a clear understanding of the nature of news so that they will be able to distinguish between news accounts that are worthy of broadcast and stories that are nothing more than promotion or inconsequential statements of opinion.

GATHERING AND DISSEMINATING NEWS

A knowledge of the process by which news is gathered, compiled, and disseminated enables television and radio newscasters to evaluate the reliability of various news items. News may be gathered by on-the-scene reporters who describe an event as they see it. If reporters arrive after an event has occurred, they may interview people who were present at the time and then write secondhand accounts. Reporters seldom witness airplane crashes, but they are often able to interview surviving passengers, people who saw the crash, or people who arrived on the scene shortly after the crash occurred. From this information they reconstruct the event as best they can. In this news-gathering process, possibilities for error exist in the original observation, in the narration of it, and in the semantic difficulties involved in the use of language for descriptive purposes. Readers and listeners do not always interpret words in the sense intended by the reporter.

Some events, however, cannot be *seen*, in the sense that they take place behind closed doors and all that a reporter sees is a sheet of paper stating that something has occurred. A doctor releases a note stating that a patient has passed away, the presidential press secretary releases an announcement of a presidential appointment, or a clerk of the Supreme Court hands out a paper saying that the court will honor an appeal in a very important case. In such instances, reporters have to summarize the history leading up to the event to indicate its current news value.

Some events are purposely staged to provide material for news stories. Public rallies and confrontations are staged to create newsworthy events in order to publicize certain ideas. Specialists in publicity know how to dramatize occurrences in order to attract public attention. An American soldier in Germany who wanted to protest our occupation policy found that he could get no newspaper space for his views until he dramatically created an event by resigning his American citizenship; then his story was carried by all the news-gathering agencies.

When reporters have prepared a written report of an event, they submit it to the newspaper or broadcast station for which they work. There the report may be edited to make it fit space and style requirements. If the story has more than local interest, it will be further edited and then transmitted to the regional or national headquarters of the wire service agency to which the newspaper or station may subscribe. There are two main wire service agencies that gather and disseminate news—the Associated Press and the United Press International. In addition, several organizations provide news and features specifically for broadcasting.

The Associated Press is a membership corporation that provides vast news coverage through a unique arrangement with its affiliated newspapers and broadcasting stations. Those who join AP agree to send to AP headquarters news of any local events that have regional or national interest. This means that AP can depend upon the reporters of all its member newspapers or stations to provide it with news coverage. AP supplements these sources with its own reporters located in many news centers, and large staffs of newsmen in key cities like Washington, New York, and foreign capitals. Into AP's New York headquarters flow the news reports from regional offices, which channel the reports received from individual papers. From overseas come the cable reports of foreign correspondents. AP editors in New York process and rewrite these reports for transmission to all member newspapers, which then use the material to make up their papers. In this way, a story that breaks in some remote community where an AP correspondent or a reporter of an AP newspaper is present can be communicated to the entire AP membership within a matter of minutes.

For television and radio, the Associated Press rewrites the newspaper material and transmits its copy over its own teletype system of communication to subscribing stations. To provide for regional and state coverage, AP stops its national transmissions several times a day for "splits," which are transmitted from regional headquarters to stations within a limited geographical area. Teletype machines are electrically operated typewriters that automatically reproduce copy received over wires at the rate of 66 words a minute. These machines are operated 24 hours a day, because AP transmits material round-the-clock. As many as two hundred or more numbered items may be sent out in a single day—far more than any one station can possibly use in its newscasts. These items include individual news and feature stories, headline summaries, 16 five-and six 10-minute summaries, and feature material, including such items as business and market news, farm programs, weather information, material for women, sports features, commentary and analysis, and even a disc jockey special. Very important news stories come over the teletype labeled "bulletins." Stations may subscribe to AP radio and receive regional, national, and international voiced news programs. For television, AP Photofax and Wire photo services provide spot picture coverage.

The United Press International is a wire service agency owned by the E. W. Scripps Company, which also owns Scripps-Howard Broadcasting, the Scripps-Howard newspaper chain, and NEA, all of which are operated independently. Unlike AP, UPI is not a membership corporation but depends for its news material on its own correspondents and stringers here and abroad. UPI rewrites some news stories for broadcasting transmission and covers others direct with members of its broadcast staff. It transmits its copy over its own teletype system. For radio, UPI provides news scripts via teletype and a broadcast news network service via the UPI Audio Network. The Broadcast Wire (teletype) service provides world, national, and state news, sports, markets, and weather in a variety of forms: headlines, five-minute wrapups, fifteen-minute wrapups, special reports, and backgrounders. During the night UPI transmits special commentary and analysis programs, plus features on such subjects as farming, religion, science, and the women's world. The UPI's system for covering regional and state news through the use of splits is similar to that of AP. It also has a system for identifying breaking stories of great importance.

THE RADIO NEWSROOM

A radio station that schedules news program must subscribe to one or more of the wire service agencies to get its basic news material. Most small stations manage with only one service, and the announcers read the material taken from the news ticker, making practically no changes in it. This type of newscast suffers from the lack of editorial adaptation to local needs and interests, and from inaccuracies or inadvertent bias in the wire service material. Editors in New York headquarters work with care to avoid departures from high-quality news reporting, but all local news editors should double-check material for accuracy and fairness. Another drawback in reading the wire service material without modification is that, when more than one station in the same area engages in this practice, listeners hear identically worded programs over different stations, and competition suffers.

Some radio stations that are network affiliates are now leaving to the networks the primary task of presenting the news of international and national events and are making a specialty of reporting state and local news. A station may employ a reporter to cover local beats or use the telephone to check for news at such key places as the mayor's office, the police department, and the hospitals. Some stations owned by newspapers may have the news-gathering facilities of the newspaper at their disposal, or a station may work out a reciprocal arrangement with a newspaper under which the station receives local news from the newspaper in exchange for advertising the newspaper on the air.

As one might expect, the larger the station the more specialized is the personnel that works on news programming. On a 5000-watt station from five to ten people may work in the news department, whereas on a 250-watt station this number may drop to two or three. Some small radio stations employ no one whose specialty is news broadcasting; the news programs are handled as they come along by the announcer who happens to be on duty at the time. Most newscasts are prepared, at least in part, by the person who presents the news on the air, although some larger stations employ specialized newswriters for this purpose. Instead of merely using the teletyped news as it comes over the wire, the newscasters or editors often rewrite some stories completely to give a local angle or to improve the manner of presentation, retouch other stories to make new and more effective arrangements, include news from local sources, and then put the stories together in the most effective possible order. A large station may also employ a full-time news director who does little or no broadcasting, but whose function is to supervise the news operation, which may also include the presentation of special events, farm programs, and sport shows. When one company operates both a radio and a television station, the news director and staff may be responsible for news broadcasts for both media.

CONSTRUCTING THE RADIO NEWSCAST

The main problems in constructing a radio newscast are deciding what items to include, in what order, and how to present each. The first two problems involve exercises in news judgment and the third involves skill in radio writing. It is well to remember that radio does not have headline type to highlight important stories, nor can a story be buried in the back pages to be caught by only a few. Indications of a story's importance must be made by placing it at the beginning of the newscast, by allowing more time for its presentation, or by directly stating its importance in the report itself. But stories of lesser importance, though they are broadcast later in the program, will still be the center of attention for the 30 or so seconds it may take to read them.

A 15-minute sponsored newscast, which actually runs about 12 minutes, allowing time for commercial announcements, can comfortably handle as many as 20 or 30 different items. Seldom should one story run over two minutes in length, unless it has very unusual interest for the local audience. The items should be arranged within geographical or topical compartments as far as possible, and transitional phrases, such as "On the labor front today," or "Turning now to news from Washington," should be used to hold the units together. It is usually wise to take up national news, foreign news, state news, and local news as separate units. Failure to maintain some organization in the news presentation tends to confuse many listeners.

The choice of stories to be included should be influenced by the audience to be reached at the time the program is broadcast. The time of day also influences the kind of news material available for broadcast. While certain news events, such as disasters, may be reported at any hour, news of public events is generally reported on a fairly well-established schedule. Early morning newscasts usually review the previous evening's news, and mention events scheduled to take place that day. Noon news programs may report on presidential press conferences, congressional committee hearings, and European developments. Dinnerhour newscasts usually have an abundance of news material covering the entire day's events, while late evening newscasts can do little more than restate earlier newscasts or discuss events scheduled for the next day unless an unscheduled event, such as a natural disaster, breaks during the evening. Sundays are generally very dull news days because there is little official activity to make news. If you listen carefully to Sunday newscasts, you will probably discover much greater use of feature stories and summaries of earlier events than you commonly hear on weekday newscasts.

In addition to presenting copy obtained from news services or local sources, many stations include in their newscasts tape recordings made on the scene (called "actualities" or "acks") recorded from local telephone calls, provided by national organizations that syndicate the tapes, or obtained by monitoring foreign broadcasts. The gathering of local news requires the use of special procedures. The most important aid to the newscaster is the telephone, especially one equipped with a device that can be used to record interviews with people in the news or who have witnessed news events. These recordings can then be inserted into the newscast. The telephone can also be employed to keep in touch with the police and fire departments, hospitals and other agencies, and government units where news originates. Larger stations may employ "legmen" who cover these agencies in person.

Some stations may employ people known as stringers who provide information about news events that come to their attention or who can be called when a news event takes place in their area. They are paid a small fee for each story. High school and college students often serve in this capacity. Stations may also wish to encourage members of the audience to report stories they have witnessed, and sometimes prizes are given for the best reports. One problem with this system, however, is that the people who report, known as "tipsters," are often not able to distinguish what is news from what is not. A source of news that should not be ignored is the police radio system and the radio systems of other governmental units. Permission to monitor these frequencies must, however, be obtained from the local originating agencies.

In writing radio news, an editor must avoid carrying over the "inverted pyramid" style of writing used on many newspapers. Newspapers usually try to cram all the essential facts about a story into the opening sentence or paragraph. A radio newscast, on the other hand, uses a narrative technique to relate the facts in a more colloquial fashion that will be instantly intelligible to the listener who, unlike the newspaper reader, cannot dwell on any one sentence or go back to check a confusing word.

Consider the following news story, which appeared in a New York newspaper some years ago:

> Assistant District Attorney Milton Altschuler, of the Bronx, said yesterday that a seventy-five-year-old woman was fatally injured at 4:20 p.m. Wednesday afternoon when she was knocked down by a seventeen-year-old Bronx youth who was playing street football, and that the youth and another boy will be subpoenaed today for appearance in his office on Dec. 1.
>
> The woman, Mrs. Esther Beck, of 27 West 181st Street, the Bronx, was knocked down as she crossed 181st Street at Grand Avenue, and died at 8:40 p.m. at Morrisania Hospital. Mr. Altschuler said that Irwin Chazin, of 44 Buchanan Place, admitted he had run into the woman while catching a football thrown by Charles Gregg, sixteen, of 2181 Davidson Avenue, the Bronx. Other participants in the game are being sought, Mr. Altschuler said.

The story contains the names of four different people, three ages, four hours and days, five addresses, and nine related events—all in 133 words divided into four sentences. Read the story aloud. Note that while it may be satisfactory as newspaper copy, it is awkward for the reader and confusing to the listener. Compare it with the following account, which is a rewrite of the story for radio:

> A game of street football played by Bronx teen-age youths resulted in tragedy yesterday afternoon. Seventeen-year-old Irwin Chazin, of Buchanan Place, was trying to catch a football when he knocked down a seventy-five-year-old woman who was crossing the street at the time. The woman, Mrs. Esther Beck, of West 181st Street in the Bronx, was taken to Morrisania Hospital where she died several hours later. The district attorney's office is investigating the accident and will issue subpoenas for both Chazin and sixteen-year-old Charles Gregg who threw the football. Other participants in the game are also being sought for questioning.

The rewritten story relates the essential facts in 26 fewer words than the newspaper story in a way that is easier both for the announcer to read and for the listener to understand.

In writing a newscast, avoid complex sentence structures and difficult words. Use verbs in active rather than passive voice whenever possible. Whereas newspapers usually employ the simple past tense to describe events that have occurred the previous day, newscasts are often able to use the present or past perfect tense to describe events that have occurred a few hours or minutes before broadcast time.

> The Governor **has signed** a modified version of the new tax bill . . . but he **says he doesn't** like it,

is an example of radio's way of narrating recent events. Tongue twisters and phrasings that might be misinterpreted by listeners should be eliminated from all news copy. When a fairly long story tells about one individual, some variety can be obtained by referring to the person in different ways.

Editorializing on the news through the use of emotionally loaded adjectives or by quoting only one side in a controversy should be scrupulously avoided. Although the practice of describing some individuals involved in political controversy as "handsome and slim" and others as "short, gruff, or pudgy" is quite common in many news magazines and papers, it does not contribute to a fair evaluation of the controversy by listeners. Such descriptive adjectives "personalize" the news to arouse more listener interest, but they often serve to load a news story emotionally in favor of one side or another. This is not to say that descriptive adjectives should be avoided altogether; they should, however, be used with great care in reporting political news. In covering controversial news, efforts should be made to balance the news report by quoting comment from both sides and indicating the sources of all opinions. One national wire service agency at one time reported a Supreme Court decision by devoting one paragraph to the minority opinion and another to the opinion of the lower court that had been overruled. In failing to explain the majority opinion, which had become the law of the land, the wire service was, in effect, guilty of poor and biased reporting. In this instance, a station news editor registered a complaint with the service, and New York headquarters forthwith repaired the error by adding a paragraph from the majority opinion.

Crime news should be handled with extreme care. "Morbid, sensational or alarming details not essential to the factual report, especially in connection with stories of crime or sex, should be avoided," according to the code of the National Association of Broadcasters.

DELIVERING RADIO NEWSCASTS

The most efficient rate for delivering newscasts appears to be somewhere between 175 and 200 words per minute. This rate is somewhat faster than normal radio speaking. Actually, the rate of speech in newscasts should vary according to the content and style of each story. If a newscast is constructed out of stories of widely different topics and events, a responsive reader will derive vocal variety from the changes in meaning and moods of the stories.

The reading should be clear, direct, and confident. A hesitant delivery indicates a lack of assurance, and the radio audience seems to prefer speakers who give the impression that they know what they are talking about. Newscasts should be rehearsed aloud, if time permits, to check the smoothness of sentences and to ferret out any tongue twisters. Pronunciations of place and personal names should be checked in dictionaries or in the pronunciation guides that the wire services provide daily. Many newscasters find it helpful to underline or overscore key words or names in the script and to indicate major pauses or transitions with pencilled notations so that they will have additional cues to aid their interpretation on the air.

To time the newscast, determine the average number of lines of tele-type copy you read in a minute and compute from that the total number of lines you can handle in the broadcast period. Time the final story and clos-ing announcement ahead of time. This technique, called back-timing, lets you know when you must begin your final item in order to finish the pro-gram on time. Several brief additional items should be taken into the studio as a precautionary measure to cover unexpected situations such as a mis-calculation in timing. Few things can be more embarrassing to an announcer than to run short on a newscast and have to fill with announcements or music.

In reading news, an announcer should remember to avoid saying any-thing in any way that might conceivably alarm listeners, for panic is epide-mic, and great damage can be caused by the broadcast of frightening re-ports. The decision to interrupt a program on the air to broadcast important news bulletins or flashes should be made by the news director. Such inter-ruptions should be reserved for bulletins of transcendent importance. With less important news bulletins, the news director must decide whether it is wiser to wait until a station break when the bulletin may be substituted for the scheduled announcement. Decisions like these are exercises in judgment that require a keen sense of news values and cannot be based on rules laid down in advance.

COMMENTARY PROGRAMS

The main difference between programs of news and programs of com-mentary is found in their purpose. A newscast aims to provide news without editorial comment, while a news commentary has as its main purpose the presentation of background information and opinion to enable the listener to interpret the significance of the news. News commentaries have become a highly personal affair in American broadcasting, and there is little con-sistency in the manner of presentation of leading network commentators.

Six different elements can be detected in many news commentaries, however:

1. Narration of straight news report. The available facts are stated, but inferences are not drawn. Editorial judgment determines the selection of reports for the narration of news events, which provides a springboard for interpretative comment.

2. Analyses of personalities and historical forces that indicate the meaning of events. Here the commentator tries to throw light on news developments by providing a frame of reference in which the known facts that preceded or immediately followed an event are assembled to supply interpretative perspective. The commentator points out all the relevant and significant evidence, but he makes no effort to intrude personal conclusions upon the listener.

3. Statements of personal opinion. Here the commentator expresses personal beliefs and judgments on the significance of events. These personal opinions may be expressed outright, but some commentators use the questionable technique of disguising their purely personal belief as expert or majority opinion.

4. Prophecies of future events. The desire to know what is going to happen in advance of its occurrence is a wholly normal desire. Attempts to peer into the future in social and political affairs, however, are extremely hazardous in view of all the uncontrolled variables in human and social behavior and the many limitations on available information. Prophecy, nevertheless, has become a staple of much commentary and, depending on whether it is based on verifiable evidence, "inside information," or simple hunches, it takes forms ranging from outright forecasts to meaningless ambiguities.

5. Editorializing. A large number of television and radio stations present regular editorials. In most cases the station takes a stand with respect to local issues. This practice is encouraged by the FCC, provided those with opposing views are given appropriate opportunities to reply. KGO Radio in San Francisco regularly presents editorials on matters of public concern presented by its General Manager, Michael Luckoff. The station also provides times for rebuttals by people who disagree with the views expressed by the station. The editorial that follows took a position on a proposition to be voted on by the people of California that would place curbs on the development of nuclear power plants. It was broadcast six times on June 4, 1976.

KGO Radio Editorial[1]

THE PLAIN, BASIC ISSUE

Proposition Fifteen is not really complicated.

The operation of nuclear power plants—even with backup systems—still depends ultimately upon human beings, who are subject to error. The failure of a nuclear plant could cause such monumental damage that public safety requires them to be infallible.

Their safety record is not perfect now. The government and nuclear industry both admit to grave past errors. There has been mismanagement, disagreement and coverup of hazards.

What is an acceptable degree of risk? KGO says the public, which incurs that risk, should decide.

[1] Courtesy of KGO Radio.

Proposition Fifteen, though itself imperfect, provides the public that right, through its elected representatives. The guarantees of Proposition Fifteen outweigh its flaws.

KGO endorses a "Yes" vote.

If it carries we believe the economy will not collapse, the state will achieve both effective conservation and alternative energy sources, creating even more jobs.

"Fifteen" is not a nuclear ban! It's the key for a public definition of the crucial question: "How safe is safe enough?"

6. Drama. Here commentators use narrative and dramatic techniques to create an atmosphere of excitement and the aura of importance and prestige. Commentators often build up their own prestige by referring to their associations with men in power or to their broad travels; they may refer to themselves in the third person, or they may set up a conflict between themselves and individuals or groups with whom they differ. Great amounts of dramatic excitement have been created by some much-criticized commentators who make seemingly libelous attacks on the character or motives of persons in public life. This was particularly true in the early years of radio when commentators like Walter Winchell and Fulton Lewis Jr. attracted large audiences.

Occasionally commentators create a news event themselves by revealing previously undisclosed information in the form of an interview with a public figure or the summation of their personal research. For this purpose, some commentators maintain a staff of research assistants and part-time reporters who do the leg work in developing a story.

Following are 10 rules that have been suggested as guides of conduct for commentators:

1. Separate facts from opinions, and clearly identify the source of each.
2. If you are advancing an argument, state the premises on which you base your reasoning.
3. In your choice of topics, don't ride a hobby horse by harping on the same subject day in and day out.
4. Check and recheck all statements of fact to verify their accuracy.
5. Avoid exaggerations.
6. Do not attempt to make yourself appear infallible. Not an overweening self-assurance, but a humility derived from knowing the limitations of your evidence and the pitfalls of prediction should characterize your work.
7. Do not induce panic or extreme insecurity in listeners through excessive emotionalism.
8. Do not prejudice listeners through innuendo, distortions of fact, or suppression of vital information.
9. Do not employ your ability to dramatize an opinion on one side of an issue only.
10. Be prepared to make a sincere and equal retraction if necessary and to provide reply time to those you may attack unfairly in a broadcast.

Shooting a TV Newscast.

TELEVISION NEWSCASTS

Television news programs differ from their radio counterparts in a number of ways, the most obvious difference being that radio emphasizes the word, whereas television emphasizes the picture. One result of this difference is that although TV newscasts can provide an adequate coverage of the day's news, they cannot include as many items as the comparable radio newscast because of the time taken in presenting pictorial material. The cost of producing television news programs is also many times greater than that of producing radio newscasts because of the expense of taping or filming news events.

Competition among networks and among stations in major markets to achieve the highest ratings with their news programs is most intense because in many instances these programs compete head-to-head. Not only does the winning network and station gain prestige, which has a subtle but nevertheless significant impact on the station's success, but the higher ratings usually translate into increased profits.

The production of a half-hour network television newscast requires participation by hundreds of people scattered around the world. Work on a network nightly news program begins about 9:00 A.M. in the New York newsroom. At that time regional bureaus around the United States are contacted to find out what stories they expect to file. These bureaus are located in the major news centers of the nation such as New York, Washington, Chicago, and San Francisco. Coverage from other points in the nation is also provided and from centers throughout the world where news developments are taking place.

The anchor persons arrive about 10:00 A.M., and at that point the process of deciding what is to be included in the nightly newscast begins in earnest. Though the number of stories available can be considered to be almost infinite, the number of possible stories is about 80, and the editors are soon concentrating on about 25. From this group the 14 to 20 stories that will actually be used in the telecast are selected. Through the day, bureaus and correspondents are contacted at regular intervals to keep track of developments, and meetings of the production staff follow these contacts to make decisions about which stories are to be included. By the middle of the afternoon, the basic framework of the newscast has been decided and the writing of the material that will introduce the various segments begins, a process in which the news anchor persons participate. In the field, correspondents are also busy writing their stories. From then until airtime constant changes are made to adjust to the latest news developments.

The pictorial elements of the program arrive in a number of ways. Some are recorded by film cameras and are either brought physically to the originating studio or transmitted on network lines and recorded on tape for use on the broadcast. The main disadvantage of film is that time must be allowed for processing. For this reason the all-electronic video camera is replacing film, a development made possible by the invention of the minicam,

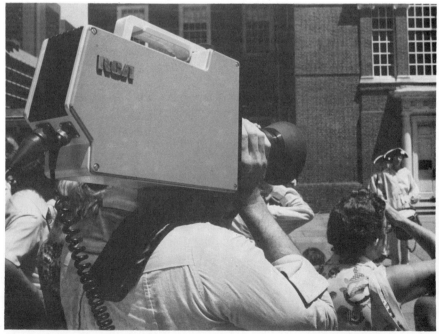

Courtesy of RCA Broadcast Systems

RCA TK-76 Portable Camera (minicam) Covering a News Event.

a small television camera which, with its accompanying video recording equipment, can easily be carried into the field. Its great advantage is that the tape requires no processing but is ready for instant transmission. This process is referred to as electronic news gathering or ENG. The minicam is expected to be used much more extensively than the film camera in network and local news television broadcasting by the 1980s. In addition to filmed and taped inserts, some elements in the network newscast may be picked up live. The minicam has also contributed to this possibility because it has immensely facilitated the process of transmitting events live from remote locations. The transmissions can be sent through phone lines or by microwave facilities.

The production of TV newscasts for stations in major markets follows the pattern just described except that the coverage is limited primarily to the viewing area of the station. Early evening newscasts concentrate on local news events, weather, and local sports, leaving to the networks the primary responsibility for covering national and international news. The scope of the late evening newscasts becomes somewhat broader through the use of excerpts from network broadcasts, which affiliates are permitted to use after they have been broadcast by the networks. The networks also feed additional news and feature materials "down the line," which are video-taped by their affiliates for use on local newscasts.

News directors of local stations begin preparing for the evening newscasts in the morning just as their network counterparts do. One of their important responsibilities is to make assignments to the crews that will be making filmed or taped reports of what is happening in the locations where news events originate. Making these assignments in a meaningful way requires a keen sense of what will be newsworthy by the time the period for the newscast actually arrives. The remote crews are usually comprised of three people: an interviewer who asks questions of those involved in news events, a person who operates the film or tape equipment, and a person who handles the lights and attends to other technical chores. Throughout the day reports, film, and tape roll into the newsroom. Film must be processed and edited, tape edited, the schedule of stories determined and timed, and the material written. In some stations newscasters participate in this process; in others they merely read on the air what others have prepared.

Because the competition for viewers among stations in major markets is so intense, a number of them have engaged outside consultants to provide advice they hope will lead to increasing their audience ratings. In the trade these consultants are known as "show doctors." Two companies of this type dominate the market: Frank N. Magid Associates, which has clients in about 40 cities, and McHugh and Hoffman, Inc., which has clients in about 30 cities. These companies provide advice on such matters as the choice of newscasters, the length of stories, the type of stories to select, and the general flavor of the newscast. One reason an individual who sees newscasts on two stations in widely separated cities may feel that they have the individual touch of the same producer is that both stations have been advised by the same consultant. Thus most large cities have a TV station that features "Eyewitness News" and another that features "Action News."

Stations in small markets cannot afford to hire consultants nor can they support the extensive news-gathering structure made possible by large-station revenues. They can, however, produce local newscasts on a more modest scale if some use is made of the material supplied by one of the wire service agencies. Even so, the costs are considerably higher than most stations are accustomed to spend on radio newscasts. It has been demonstrated, however, that a station can produce a successful news show with a staff of only three full-time people—an operator for a film or TV camera, a director-writer-editor, and a newscaster-supervisor. The camera operator shoots the local news film or tape in the locality, using an automobile to get around; the second person edits the film or tape, writes the narration, backstops as a second camera operator when two stories are breaking at the same time, and directs the news program; the third person is the general supervisor and does the on-camera newscasting as well as reading the narration that accompanies the film or tape. Out of this operation the station obtains each day about five minutes of edited film or tape. With the use of still photographs of people and situations in the news, mounted on art cards and set on an easel, it is possible to give visual variety to even the simplest television newscast. Just as photographs serve to add interest to newspaper reading, so even a still photo of a person or a scene renders a news report more interesting and meaningful to the viewer. Some stations have budgets so small that they cannot even afford a film crew, and some in the smallest markets must rely for pictorial material on stills and on films and tapes from outside sources.

What has been said regarding the skills and approach necessary for success as a radio newscaster may also be said about television newscasters, except that they require one additional skill—the ability to maintain visual communication with an audience. This is not an easy task when one is reading material from a script or from a prompting device located at the camera. Newscasters must develop the facility to pick up script material while at the same time maintaining the illusion of virtually continuous eye contact with those who are watching the broadcast.

The quality and value of television news programs has been the subject of much critical comment. Sometimes questions are raised regarding the value of news film and pictures. Because cameras are often not present when the most interesting and significant news events take place, the picture content of a TV newscast tends to concentrate on ceremonial events, such as the arrival of a foreign ambassador or the dinner that celebrates the successful completion of a fund-raising drive, or on combat action in an armed conflict, or on public confrontations.

The visual elements, moreover, do not explain the significance of events. George Will wrote in the January 10, 1977, issue of *Newsweek:* "As a news gathering instrument a camera is at once powerful and limited. It can never produce a picture of an idea. It can always produce vivid pictures of action." Television cameras, for example, may picture the signing of a treaty, but they cannot summarize what the treaty says except in a very crude way, and they certainly cannot weigh its significance. Where a newscast or commentary aims to stimulate the thought processes of the viewers, it finds no significant advantage in TV over radio, except through the use of visual demonstration materials. In scheduled news events such as a presidential inauguration or a parade, where thought stimulation is not the primary object, television has no peer, but these constitute only a small percentage of the daily fare of news.

In recent years great improvements in television picture coverage have been accomplished, particularly in the process of speeding the picture to the television station. The picture itself is not only likely to be more interesting than it used to be, but it is certainly more up-to-date. Satellite transmission allows network news programs to include coverage of the same day's events from across the world. Local news films can now be prepared for presentation within minutes after they are shot. Films from other areas are brought to the station as quickly as possible by interlocking production schedules with airplane flight times. The development of electronic newsgathering through the use of the minicam has made it possible to present a tape as soon as it is produced or, if the minicam is tied into a coaxial telephone line or microwave facilities, to bring events into a newscast "live" as they are actually happening.

Another frequent criticism of network newscasts is that they are too superficial in their coverage. How can a major story be covered in a minute? is an often-heard question. To meet this problem, some networks planned to increase their news programs from a half-hour to an hour. This proposal, however, met almost unanimous opposition from the network affiliates, which would have to give up an additional half-hour of their local news or other nonnetwork programming, from which they derive substantial revenues.

A third criticism of news programs is that in their attempt to gain listeners they have become too sensational in their approach and content. David Halberstam, a media historian and critic, has condemned networks for trying to make "show-biz" personalities out of their newscasters and proposes to curb what he considers to be the outright sensationalism of local newscasts by reducing them from a half-hour to 15 minutes. Unfortunately, however, sensationalism attracts viewers, and as long as television stations are ruled primarily by market place factors, the practice is likely to continue unabated.

NEWS-IN-DEPTH PROGRAMS

The news departments in radio and television networks and in major radio and television stations produce programs that go beyond the mere reporting of events as they happen from day to day to an examination of these events in depth, including an explanation of their background and a consideration of their impact on society. These programs are of various types. One is the documentary, usually an hour-long television program, which presents information, analysis, and opinion about an important social, political, or ethical problem. Cameras are taken into the field to film or tape events that relate to the problem and to interview people who are associated with it. The producer may film or tape twenty times as much material as will eventually be used. Narrative segments, to provide continuity are then produced in a studio, and this material and that recorded in the field are edited into the final program.

A variation of the documentary is the magazine program, which examines three different topics or problems during an hour period. The CBS program *60 Minutes* is an example.

A recent trend in major television stations is the coverage in depth of an important issue or problem through a number of days. Documentary material is produced and is then divided into segments, which are shown on the station's local news program. The NBC Network on its nightly news show generally apportions somewhat more time to the explanation of a special issue than it does to the usual news event. This segment might be called a mini-documentary.

Another type of news-in-depth program is the press conference or news interview program, which focuses on a news personality as he or she is confronted by a panel of interviewers. The questions may cover a number of different topics, the integrating factor being the subject personality, whose career is connected with the topics or who is considered an expert on them. The broadcast press conference with the President is an example of this type of program, as are the regular network news interview programs that focus on a variety of public figures, among them NBC's *Meet the Press,* CBS's *Face the Nation,* and ABC's *Issues and Answers.*

On a smaller scale, the press-conference program can be used on local or educational stations. A local community leader, public official, or educator who has been involved in the news can serve as the basis for an interesting program produced in simple fashion.

FEATURES

There are now five-minute newscasts and five-minute feature talks and interviews on radio networks that provide affiliated stations with a national service. They deal with a wide variety of subjects and often employ personalities who are known primarily for their work on television. CBS's Walter Cronkite, for example, does a daily commentary on some subject in the news. In addition to his work on television, Edwin Newman serves NBC radio as a *Critic at Large.* The feature program on television is not usually presented as a separate program, but is incorporated into half-hour or hour news presentations. Charles Kuralt has appeared in a TV series called "On the Road," which appeared at intervals on CBS News and magazine programs. *The CBS Evening News* often features editorials by Eric Sevaried, and David Brinkley, before he rejoined the *NBC Nightly News* as a co-anchorman, appeared regularly in a feature called "David Brinkley's Notebook."

In preparing feature programs several considerations should be observed:

Purpose and attitude. The writer of a feature must first decide on the objective of the presentation. Most are designed to inform, some simply to entertain. As long as they manage to amuse, features are generally considered successful.

Some features aim to move their audiences to action or to convince them to accept an idea. Features of this nature must appeal to the deeper feelings of the audience.

Use of time-tested methods. Effective communication by the spoken word is not a development unique to broadcasting. The fundamental principles of oral communication were set forth by Aristotle in his *Rhetoric* and have been amplified by numerous writers. Public speaking, whether from a platform or a studio, should adhere to the essential elements of clear organization of evidence and argument, the need for variety to gain and hold attention, and the use of vigorous and vivid language.

Gain attention immediately. One feature on adventure started with the provocative: "Have you ever met a dinosaur? Probably not. Most *certainly* not, as a matter of fact, because there haven't been any dinosaurs perambulating about the earth for millions of years." The opening of a broadcast feature is crucial. The decision to stay with you or to tune in another station is often made in a few seconds. You may have only the time taken by a person to get up from a chair and walk over to the set to capture his interest. Among the devices that help to capture attention are a startling statement, conflict, suspense, the arousal of curiosity, novelty, and the familiar.

Use simple language. Avoid ornate and literary words and overworked clichés. Use and explain only necessary scientific and technical terms and stay away from professional or trade "jargon." Remember that the audience cannot refer to a dictionary. Strange words and phrases however, may add spice if capitalized on and skillfully incorporated into the speech. *Caution:* Any chef realizes the value of spices, but a good chef realizes, too, the dangers of "too much pepper." The audience is usually unable to follow a long and involved sentence. Short concise sentences that come to the point without qualifying clauses are desirable. Twenty-five words may be a good writing limit on sentences; longer sentences are effective when they are in a loose speech style. Simplicity is essential. Variation in sentence length gives change of pace. The use of contractions, active verbs, and questions is also advisable. The ease of understanding in a "blind" reception situation is the important factor. "Think like a wise man," wrote Aristotle, "but communicate in the language of the people."

Use repetition. The speaker on television or radio has no opportunity to clarify the points of a speech as does the platform speaker, who can see the changes in attention in the audience. Consider for a moment a speaker who is delivering a speech in an auditorium: over at the left a man and woman come down to the fourth row, sit down and chat for five minutes with the people there, then depart, permitting the occupants of the fourth row to listen to the speech again; at the rear, a baby starts to cry; during the last five minutes of the speech twenty people slip into the rear left section, arriving early to hear a violin recital scheduled to be held in the same auditorium at the conclusion of the speech. Speakers would be wholly inadequate if they did not recognize the disturbing effect of such activities on their audience and go over points that might otherwise be missed in the confusion.

Comparable distractions occur in the home, and speakers must subordinate the unimportant to the important by reducing the number of main ideas they want to get across. Frequent restatements and summaries for clarification assist in overcoming these home distractions. All of these considerations must enter into the prepared script.

EXAMPLES OF FEATURE TALKS

1. Walter Cronkite Reporting[2]

In addition to serving five nights a week as the anchor man on the half-hour television news program for CBS, Walter Cronkite also presents a five-minute daily commentary on a news story for the CBS Radio Network. These talks usually deal with a major story in the news such as a war, the Israeli-Arab conflict, or an important action by the President, but they occasionally draw attention to a story that may be hidden on the inside pages of a newspaper, as is the case in the example that follows. Mr. Cronkite's purpose is to enhance public understanding of front-page events or to draw attention to the significance of stories that may be overlooked. His talks are marked by clarity of expression and crispness of style, and in both his writing and his delivery he projects the authority of a man who knows and understands what is happening around the world.

PENNZOIL OPENER

From time to time, it seems we've all become students in a giant Current Events class, with war, protest and politics the only subjects of interest. It's about this same time we get the suspicion that maybe there's something else going on that we're missing. A look, in a moment.

PENNZOIL :60

Most of us recognize the name when it's Richard Nixon or Lyndon Johnson, or Abbie Hoffman, or Julius Hoffman. But what about Charles Huggins or George Wald, or Robert Mulliken or Alfred Kastler? Their work is of a different nature, not in the news, not controversial. They're Nobel Prize winners, in medicine, chemistry and physics.
Or what about Dr. Gobind Khorana of the University of Wisconsin? Yesterday, after five years of work, he announced the first synthesis of a gene.
It's the sort of item many of us glance at, before turning to the sports page. It also is an achievement of major proportions, speeding the day when man will be able to control life itself, maybe even to the point of reproducing himself in the laboratory.
Needless to say, Dr. Khorana, who already has won a Nobel Prize for earlier work, runs no risk of becoming a household name, no matter how

[2] Courtesy CBS News and Walter Cronkite.

important his achievement. And in that respect, he joins a long list of unknowns whose contributions to our everyday life may far excell those of all the politicians and newsmakers put together.

Who—for example—knows of J. Presper Eckert or John Mauchly or Harold Silver, credited with inventing the electronic computer some 25 years ago? And yet, whose life has not been dramatically changed by the computer takeover our society is experiencing?

The computer alone—it can be argued—has done more to revolutionize American society than all the cadres of the Youth Rebellion combined, even though it hasn't received the same attention at cocktail parties.

But it's more than giving the computer its due, or memorizing the names of Nobel Prize winners. We have grown fascinated with Politics and the Conflict Syndrome. And the rest—science and technology and medicine and education—we tend to ignore.

And yet, those are the forces that most affect our lives. The latest Senate speech may be a hot one. But its impact in terms of real change may be far less than the latest classroom lecture on transistors or lasers, fiber optics or electron welding. Campus dissent may get our attention. But we must ask whether we dwell on it. Dozens of other issues—from improving the schools to harvesting the seas to taking care of the mentally ill to curing cancer—are just waiting to be explored.

This is Walter Cronkite. Good Day.

PENNZOIL CLOSE

2. Reasoner Report[3]

In his radio features Harry Reasoner talked about what was on his mind at the moment. A feature may have been inspired by a news item, a personal experience, a current problem, or an amusing aspect of our culture, as in the example that follows. The subjects he chose were light ones, but he discussed even serious problems in a lighthearted way. The tone of his writing and his delivery were familiar and conversational, and he often demonstrated a nostalgic appreciation for some facet of America's past. His usual purpose was to entertain, and he succeeded in doing just that night after night.

Harry Reasoner reporting. The transformation of Christmas cards into joyful newsletters becomes more apparent every year. The story in a moment.

COMMERCIAL

This is the season for Christmas cards and I intend to get mine out any day now. I enjoy getting them, but I was aware, last night, as we looked over a batch of them, of a growing trend: the trend to send out mimeographed or printed newsletters. The theory, I guess, is to bring you up to date on the activities of friends you don't see regularly, and the idea has some merit. But what puzzled the lady who was looking at cards with me was how everyone sounds alike when they sit down to put together one of these missives. Not only do they all sound alike but they all apparently have fantastic, Norman Rockwell type families who could go right from the activities described in the

[3] Courtesy Harry Reasoner.

letter to a jolly television series. The thing is if you've got an ordinary, disorganized family these Christmas newsletters give you an inferiority complex. "Jeremiah disappointed us this year with his fall quarter grades," the newsletters seem to say. "He spent so much time winning the surfing championship and planning ahead for the ski circuit that he only got 4 A's and one sad B. But maybe it's partly my fault. I did take a lot of his time in remodeling the old garage into a combination art gallery and motel. It was a lot of fun and we did it for only 7 dollars and 35 cents." Then, too, newsletters usually contain rather detailed logs of family vacation trips, complete with statistics about various national parks and how to live in a Volkswagen camper.

As I say, it's enough to give your less rugged families feelings of inferiority. This lady I know said that she thought next year **she** would send out a Christmas letter that would be different. I can imagine how it would go, she said—something like this: "Hello, everyone. It's certainly been a fun year for us. Everything got off to a great start in January when jolly old Dad said we couldn't afford a winter vacation. But that didn't matter, because we were all home together, since Flopsie had been expelled from college for smoking pot and Junior flunked out after some trouble with Remedial Swahili. In February one of Sister's little friends gave her a darling little kitten and the scar that Sister got when jolly old Dad found out hardly shows at all. We all looked forward to the happy summer season but abandoned plans for a motor trip when the children flatly refused to travel with each other. But we did enjoy afternoons at Rufus B. Hopwell Memorial Swimming Pool, a splendid structure holding, I'm told, some 65-thousand gallons of constantly circulating water and visited by several hundred citizens every year. In the fall it was back to school for everyone except Junior, who is staying with friends at the Northern Connecticut Correctional Institution and writing frequently about his exciting times. And now its happy holiday time again and your correspondent wonders just where another busy, fun-with-the-family year has gone. Merry Christmas from our house to your house!"

COMMERCIAL

3. Critic at Large—Edwin Newman[4]

One problem faced by feature writers is that they are often required to write about topics that many other people are also treating. In such cases it is often difficult to discover an approach or angle that is different from what other writers have used. Edwin Newman faced this problem when he prepared a feature talk on America's bicentennial year, one of the most discussed topics in the nation's history. The following talk demonstrates how he met that challenge.

This is Edwin Newman, critic at large.

It has probably not escaped your attention that this is not only the first day of the year but the first day of the Bicentennial year, as well. It is no small matter to be alive in the two hundredth year of your country's existence. Not that one should be mystical about it—200 happens to be a round number, and no more significant than 199 or 201. Perhaps it could be argued that while it is

[4] Courtesy of Edwin Newman, NBC News.

more significant than 100, it is less significant than 201. If nations are to be measured by longevity, 201 counts for more than 200 does. But we like round numbers, most of us, and most of us like to take part in celebrations.

One prospect in this year of celebration is disquieting. It is the prospect of an enormous amount of self-examination, unbridled self-examination, self-examination run riot. Self-examination is a fine thing; probably everybody should do it; but it can turn into too much of a good thing very quickly, especially if it leads to a search for so-called national goals. Where are we going? You will hear that question, or in more consciously literary form, whither are we bound?

The correct answer is nowhere or nowhither, at any rate nowhere or nowhither new. It is convenient to believe that we come to a stop every now and then and reverse direction, or shift this way or that, as a result of conscious thought. It isn't so. There is too much accident in the world for that, too many forces beyond our control, too many others who can affect our lives and fortunes for better or for worse.

Obviously, we ought to know what we are about, and so far as we can, we ought to understand the consequences of what we do. But we should not expect a sudden accession of wisdom because the country is 200 years old, or that unexampled good fortune will come upon us; we should not expect our influence to increase, or that the attitudes of others toward us will change.

It's fine to be 200 years old nationally speaking, but the reality is that it doesn't change a thing.

Edwin Newman, NBC News, New York.

Short features or documentaries may be prepared on film or tape for use on all types of programs. The following feature was presented as part of the evening news programs broadcast at 6:00 and 11:00 p.m. by Station WWJ-TV in Detroit. It was one in a series of features on the energy problem presented three times each week by reporter Janis Settle.

EXAMPLE OF A FILM FEATURE

NEWS FOUR, WWJ-TV, DETROIT
"ENERGY HOUSE," BY JANIS SETTLE[5]

LS HOUSE	SETTLE (VO): This is the dream house of Susan and Tom Steele. A brand new energy saving barn on twenty acres in rural Richmond, Michigan. They designed it themselves, with a crock well . . . so no water bills. A propane gas tank to supply a generator . . . for most of their electricity . . . thus lower electric bills. For heat, a fireplace and a stove . . . wood and coal . . . so lower heating bills.
MS CROCK WELL	
MS GAS TANK	
CU GENERATOR	
MS FIREPLACE	
MS STOVE	
LS LIVING ROOM	
SHOT OF CHILD GOING UPSTAIRS THAT SHOWS WOOD WALLS	
SHOT OF KIDS PLAYING UPSTAIRS	

[5] *Courtesy of Janis Settle, Reporter WWJ-TV News.*

THREE-SHOT STEELES AND SETTLE AT KITCHEN TABLE	It is rustic, one large partitioned room downstairs, a simple loft upstairs, all bare wood walls.
TOTAL VO :42	It saves energy, but the home and land cost the Steele's their whole savings, seventy-five thousand dollars. They've been trying to get a forty thousand dollar mortgage for a year now, and have been turned down ten times.
SOF MRS. STEEL :20	INTERVIEW WITH MRS. STEELE (CUE TO BRIDGE) "What to do . . ."
SETTLE ON CAMERA :27	BRIDGE TO SECOND PART OF INTERVIEW (CUE TO INTERVIEW) "As he put it . . ." (CUE TO VO) "No other way . . ."
SOF MRS. STEELE :17	SETTLE (VO): The demand for energy saving homes could easily grow in the next ten years. But the banks can't bet on that now, according to Joseph Olivieri, professor of architecture at the Lawrence Institute of Technology.
MS HOUSE	
OVER SHOULDER SHOT OF SETTLE WITH OLIVIERI IN HIS OFFICE	
TOTAL VO :15	
SOF OLIVIERI :17	INTERVIEW WITH OLIVIERI (CU TO VO) "Sell them on it . . ."
SHOT OF MR. & MRS. STEELE WASHING DISHES IN KITCHEN	SETTLE (VO): The president's plan to encourage energy conservation loans through the federal home loan mortgage corporation could help Mr. and Mrs. Steele. But Congress hasn't addressed that part of the energy proposals yet, and until it does, this family can only write their representatives, and wait. Janis Settle, News Four.
LS HOUSE W/LAKE IN FOREGROUND	
ELS HOUSE LOOKING LONELY WITH LONG THIN DRIVEWAY.	
TOTAL VO :18	
(TOTAL LENGTH 2:36)	

Projects and Exercises

1. Select your favorite network newscaster and explain your selection.
2. Rewrite a leading news story from a local newspaper for radio broadcast.
3. Rewrite a short news account from the inside pages of a newspaper for radio broadcast.
4. Prepare a five-minute world news summary for radio broadcast, drawing on a newspaper for your material.
5. Visit your local radio station and discuss news problems with the news director. Observe the operations of the teletype machine.

6. Prepare a two-minute local news report that might be included in a national news round-up.

7. Prepare a five-minute news summary of local news for broadcast over your local station. Draw upon local and college newspapers and interviews for your material.

8. Using news photographs taken from a newspaper, prepare a short television newscast.

9. Prepare and present features for class listening and criticism.

   a. Prepare a two-minute feature for use by you on an early morning disc-jockey program. Subject: Communitywide used clothing drive to be conducted by the schools.

   b. Same subject—same length—for use by you on consumer's program over the local television station.

   c. Same subject—same length—for use by the local radio sportcaster during the half-time break in a play-by-play account of a game.

sports and special events

27

The largest audiences in television and radio are reached usually when sports and special events are presented. Local stations find these programs useful in competing successfully with large stations. The larger stations and networks compete in obtaining exclusive rights to sporting events and dreaming up new twists for coverage of the spectacular. When the astronauts first walked on the moon, hundreds of millions of people all over the world watched their exciting adventure as it took place. Significant utterances by public officials also draw millions of viewers. President Nixon's resignation speech in 1974 was witnessed by from 70 to 100 million Americans. Audiences of the same size watched the presidential debates between candidates Gerald Ford and Jimmy Carter in 1976. Major sports spectacles, such as the Kentucky Derby, the World Series, and the Superbowl football championship, also attract millions to the television screen. It is estimated that as many as half a billion people in 50 countries have watched the telecast through satellites of World Cup football (soccer) matches.

SPORTS

Sports announcers are daily visitors in millions of homes. Their voices are recognized at once and their pet personal expressions find their way into the vocabulary of sports enthusiasts. Many of the points on general announcing hold true for announcing sports and conducting sports programs. However, the techniques and problems of presenting a running account of a game are highly specialized.

General Considerations

Many early sportscasters entered this field because they had a flair for talking easily and well without script. Even though their descriptions were colorful and exciting, those who knew sports thoroughly found in the broadcasts numerous factual errors, unwarranted excitement, and too much "color" at the expense of describing what was actually taking place. These criticisms are still made of some sportscasters. Most present top-ranking sportscasters know

ABC Covering 1976 Summer Olympics

sports extremely well and make their announcing vital and exciting, but they do not artificially inject excitement into their broadcasts. It has been said, for example, that the game should be exciting but not the broadcaster, whose sole responsibility, at least in radio, is to mirror the action for listeners. As a result of what the broadcaster says, listeners should be able to "see" the game almost as well as if they were actually present in the stands.

Another principle followed by many broadcasters is to show no partisanship in describing games. This quality is especially important for those reporting on regional and national networks to which fans of both teams are listening. Broadcasters reporting games to a strictly local audience, where it can be assumed that almost all the listeners are adherents of the home team, do sometimes "pull" for that team's victory. Such partisanship, if kept under control, is acceptable and is often enjoyed by the listeners. Under no circumstances, however, should the broadcaster's personal feelings be permitted to distort the description of the game. Honesty in reporting is the first requirement.

Another problem facing sports broadcasters is to maintain a proper balance between the straight describing of a game and the transmitting of asides that make the report more colorful. Comments on such matters as a baseball runner's actions, the movements of the coaches, and the idiosyncratic actions of some pitchers help to add interest, but if too much emphasis is placed on them, the listener can lose track of what is happening on the field. The comedy team *Bob and Ray* satirized this tendency once in a sketch in which the color man took over so completely that the listeners ended up not even knowing who had won the game.

Courtesy of National Broadcasting Company, Inc.

Control Room During Coverage of 1977 Presidential Inauguration.

How much should sportscasters become personalities in their own right rather than remaining faceless announcers who are content just to give the facts? There seems to be no absolute answer. The personality of Howard Cosell, for example, seems to dominate the sports programs in which he participates. On the other hand, his partner in broadcasting football, Frank Gifford, usually restricts himself to describing what is happening on the field. Both are highly successful sportscasters.

Effect of Television

With the advent of television, many persons believed that completely new techniques would be required for sportscasting. It was reasoned that since the audience was able to view the action there was little need for the announcer to talk. However, when this was tried, unexpected results ensued. Many viewers simply tuned in the picture on the TV set, but kept the audio off, and used a radio set for the play-by-play description. If one now listens for a brief period to sportscasters' voices only, while they are broadcasting some sports, it is difficult to determine whether they are presenting a radio or a television account. Sometimes they are actually doing both. Stations and sponsors have found it economical in manpower to rely upon "simulcasts,"

Transporting a Camera
During 1976 Winter
Olympics.

*Copyright, American Broadcasting
Companies, Inc.*

although the trend now is to use separate announcers for radio and television. Some sports such as boxing require very little comment when they are being presented on television.

Most sportscasters attempt to keep an eye on a monitor to be informed about what the viewer at home is seeing. They then weave into their commentary references the specific scene shown on the screen. In sports with fast action, such as hockey and basketball, this may not be possible during sustained periods of continuous play.

Television places a premium upon accuracy and knowledge of the game. In radio presentations some sportscasters of national reputation were guilty of calling plays wrong, losing track of a down, or giving incorrect counts of balls and strikes. In order to pull themselves out of a hole they resorted to description of mythical action on the field. Such errors by announcers are detected easily by ardent fans on TV. An announcer who attempts to brazen out an error or oversight by inventing a play that is "off camera" is in for serious trouble. It is imperative that accurate records be kept during the game.

Preparation for a Play-By-Play Report

Each sport has its own vocabulary, pace, traditions, rules, and customs. The sportscaster must learn these traits over a period of years as a player or fan, or in a shorter period of time by concentrating on the literature of the sport and by talking shop with writers and players. In preparing for an individual contest, it is necessary to become familiar with the plays and players. This problem is simplified somewhat if you handle all the home games of a college or professional club. Only the visiting squad and its particular plays must be learned.

Some sports require more memory work than others. Baseball, with its more leisurely pace and relatively static positions of the teams on the field, allows more time to identify the players. In football, however, entirely new teams may come onto the field at one time. The huddle or calling of signals gives a little time for identifying players, but a good memory is most helpful in such situations. The speed of hockey, according to Geoff Davis, who has been a sportscaster in the United States and has covered hockey for the Canadian Broadcasting Corporation, requires one to memorize identifications of players before the game, either by number or physical characteristics. He notes that, added to the speed of the game, the complications created by substitutions of whole lines "on the run" make accurate identification very difficult. A description of a horse race, with numerous entries and rapid changes of position during the race, demands instant recognition of horses and jockeys.

Other aids in preparing for a particular contest may be found in the press releases given out by the teams before the contest. These include information sheets, statistics, form charts, and human interest stories on players. This is termed "filler" or "background" material. Many sportscasters pin these sheets up in the announcing booth or put them together on clip boards for use during lulls in the game and time-out breaks. Sportscasters, particularly those broadcasting on networks, may have the assistance of a researcher, whose function is to assemble statistics and notes about the players, which can be used as the game progresses.

Mechanical Devices and Identification Charts

Mechanical or spotting devices make possible more accurate coverage of events. These devices vary from one sportscaster to another. In broadcasting football, a large pasteboard prepared with individual squares for each player may be used (Figure 27–1). In the center of the board are seven blocks, one for each lineman. Beneath these are four blocks, one for each back. The 11 blocks constitute the starting, first string, or offensive team. On top of the seven blocks are two rows of seven blocks for the substitutes. Below the backs, the same arrangement applies. In order to tell who is playing at any particular moment, the sportscaster need only look at the board, which will have 11 tacks stuck in the appropriate squares. A spotter for each team takes care of this.

Baseball reporters may also use a cardboard with separate name cards

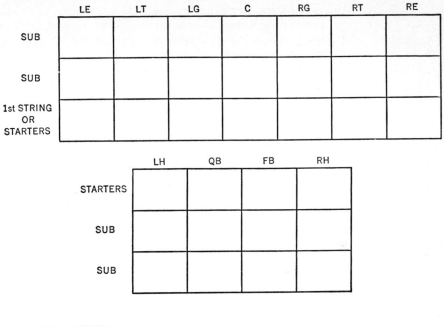

TYPICAL SQUARE

Courtesy of Mel Allen

Figure 27–1   Football Chart for Broadcasting

tacked on it according to position. Some use the tack-up method in basketball and hockey. Others rely on memory because they have to keep their eyes on the ball or puck.

"Recaps" and Audience Orientation

The sportscaster has to look at the playing area most of the time in order to keep the audience informed on the progress of the game. Fans also like to know the facts about what happened earlier in the game because much of their listening is intermittent. Few people tune in at the beginning of a game and stay in front of the set all the way through. And even those people do not keep a score card. Many sports announcers have assistants to compile statistics. Sometimes this task will be combined with the work of a spotter. When there are interruptions in the game, recaps will please those who tune in late. Someone tuning in during the sixth inning is pleased to hear a quick summary, such as: "The Yankees got their three runs in the third" and a rapid and clear review of the details of a big inning. Hockey broadcasters often give the score after every goal and face-off and they frequently review the nature of the scoring. The score may be mentioned as many as 40 times during a single period. In basketball reporting, the score and the time remaining are often given each time a basket is made.

The TV camera can transmit part of the atmosphere of the scene by shots of the time clocks and scoreboard devices used for the audience attending the event in person. Special visual aids may also be prepared for the TV summaries. Plays may be explained and interpreted.

Football, unlike baseball, does not have a standard set of scoring symbols, a fact which requires sportscasters to devise their own systems. One announcer took an ordinary tablet and ruled off several sheets in three vertical columns. To the left of each of these columns he noted the series of "downs" and recorded every play. For example, in a Columbia-Army game he might note 1–10–30–C. That would be Columbia's ball, first down, 10 to go, on the 30-yard line. If the play gained two yards, the next entry would read 2–8–32–C, and so forth. In this manner all plays leading up to the scoring plays were available at all times. The numbers on the jerseys of the players involved on key plays were also set down. In the recap, the sportscaster can take as few or as many of the lead-up plays to the touchdown as are needed. This procedure also adds to the accuracy of the account. The announcer knows at all times what the down is and where the ball is.

A recommended procedure in baseball is to "set" the teams offensively and defensively during the game in order to give those who tuned in late a better understanding of what is happening. One may name the players at their various posts and, if it is a TV broadcast, show them by a cover shot or by a succession of area shots, right half of the infield, then left half, etc. Batting averages as of that moment, not the night before, may be given, comments on where the infield or outfield is playing for a particular hitter, whether a bunt is expected in this situation, and any number of such interpretative analyses may be offered. The name of each batter may be superimposed on the bottom of the screen to reinforce the identification.

Keeping the listener oriented toward the location of the ball in radio is simplified in sports that have a definite geography: "Silver River is ahead by a length coming into the stretch," "It's Notre Dame's ball first down and 10 to go on the 15-yard line," or "There are runners on first and third with one out."

In basketball there were no names for specific locations, so that broadcasters had to invent their own. Thus they follow the ball "to the right corner," "to the baseline," or "to the top of the key." Listeners through the years have become educated to the meaning of these terms and can now follow the game as well as they can follow a football broadcast.

Hockey broadcasters need to work out a series of expressions pleasing to the audience and descriptive enough to cover the very rapid action peculiar to hockey. Examples of this would include the terms to cover the breakaway play, full-length rushes down the ice, player jam-ups near the goal crease, etc.

The viewer's orientation must always be kept in mind in placing cameras and selecting camera shots. Events that are relatively static (in terms of location) such as wrestling or boxing are not as difficult to televise as events where the action takes place over a wider area—baseball, football, horse racing, basketball, and hockey. With these sports, eye-straining pans or a multiplicity of fast cuts in an attempt to keep up with rapid action on the field may be very disturbing to the viewer. Sudden shifts of the basic angle of sight occasioned by cameras located on opposite sides of the playing field may create confusion. The excessive use of the split screen or the upper-corner insert of different players also may be irritating.

Spotters or assistants may work with the sportscaster in keeping track of the play and of incoming substitutions and in compiling statistics for use in recaps or during breaks in the game. Some relieve the regular sportscaster on microphone to handle the color and statistics. The featured play-by-play reporter will be held responsible by the audience, however, for the accuracy of the descriptions of the game in progress.

Daily Sportscast

The peak audiences come with the presentation of the actual sporting event. But large and loyal audiences also follow the many daily sportscasts scheduled at the dinner hour and late evening. Some of these broadcasts are merely summaries of results and the press services provide material for them. Other sportscasts combine press material rewritten for the individual sportscaster, still pictures, both silent- and sound-film clips and interviews. Geoff Davis gives his view of how to proceed:

> The preparation of a daily sportscast differs slightly depending upon the point of view of its origination. For example, in New York, a man beaming to a local audience would have so much action going on in any single day that results alone would take a considerable amount of time. The most efficient means of setting up this type of show is to start with the top sport in season and gradually progress through the less important items. In summer, baseball scores of the major leagues come first followed by "off the diamond news" of this sport, injuries, sales and trades and other executive business of importance. Next come boxing, horseracing and seasonal events of a purely local nature. For a network show out of New York, also lead off with baseball but you must necessarily look across the country and mention national events, big-time fights, Davis cup tennis, international swimming, college sports of importance, etc. The main thing to remember in network presentation is that the program must not be too confined to the local scene.
>
> Interviews have become an important part of every sports reporter's presentation to his public. The thing to remember about interviews is not to overdo them, either in number or in length, because prepare them as you will, like fashions, they come back eventually over the same cycle.
>
> Daily sports broadcasts derive their interest from clear, concise presentation in good taste. Actual delivery is usually somewhat faster than normal, but again it is wise to remember not to overdo the speed because increased rate sometimes gets in the way of clarity.

Directing Procedures

In radio, a local station rarely assigns a director to sports pickups. When present, a director assists in timing, lining up guests for interviews, and listening carefully to the description in order to detect any errors. However, a director is required in television coverage. The director usually is stationed in the "remote" truck or mobile unit that contains the field equipment—camera controls, amplifiers, power supply units, sync generators, switching panels, off-the-air and off-the-line monitors, audio console, and telephone connections with camera operator, sportscaster, and studio master control.

The production of a sports event may be relatively simple or very complex, depending on the nature of the event. A local telecast of a baseball game requires about four cameras to pick up various aspects of the game, about nine microphones, and a mobile unit. The announcing group for each team originates a separate audio report but uses the same telecast of the action, which is directed by a single person. Football, hockey, and basketball broadcasts utilize similar set-ups.

An example of an extremely complicated production operation was the broadcast of the 1976 summer Olympic games from Montreal, Canada, by the ABC network. The broadcast originated from 24 different sites and required coverage by 25 color cameras tied into five mobile units. Some 30 commentators described the action, and 54 tape editors participated in the operation. All together 470 people were in the ABC contingent. The executive producer in the master control location watched 32 monitors in making his selections of the action to be televised at any given moment. The ABC operation was reinforced by 104 cameras from the CBC network, which originated 12 separate signals simultaneously for use by broadcasting teams from 70 different nations. CBC employed 1850 people in its Olympics broadcasting group.

In directing sports events, television directors follow the same general procedure used in studio work. They or the TD instruct the camera operators about upcoming shots and call for appropriate switching from camera to camera as the action of the game and the announcer's comments prescribe. The director decides whether to use an instant replay of the action to clarify and reinforce the highlights of the game. The director is also responsible for timing and inserting live or filmed commercials at the proper moments.

Usually three cameras as a minimum are used for most sports other than boxing and wrestling. Electronic inserts of simultaneous action call for additional cameras. The fast action required of all program and technical personnel demands close teamwork. Ideally, the director, camera operator, and TD should be thoroughly acquainted with the fine points of the sport they are covering. There is little time for deliberation before camera movement or switching to other cameras to follow the play and to obtain proper close-ups. Preestablished patterns and areas of coverage are often assigned to camera operators ahead of the action. The switching must be done fast; often a quick hand signal to the TD is used instead of a vocal command.

Camera placements in a few of the major sports with which the director works are described briefly below.

Baseball. The physical design of the individual ball park and the direction of sunlight may require special locations. The main camera is generally placed behind home plate. It is equipped to follow the ball to any part of the field for close-ups. The location of the other cameras varies considerably—some directors prefer them grouped together on either side of the main camera, others separate them with one along the first-base line and the other between home and third. A camera would be placed along first-base line for coverage of infield plays, close-ups of right-handed batters, and tight coverage of plays at any base including home plate, from a different perspective. A fourth camera placed in the center-field stands provides a view of the action over the pitcher's shoulder. World Series coverage employs additional cameras in the two locker rooms or on the field for pre- and postgame interviews and color.

Football and basketball. It is easy to make mistakes in trying to follow the ball in play in these sports. Football players deliberately try to deceive their opponents about the whereabouts of the ball and may also succeed in deceiving the sportscaster. In basketball the frequent and swift passing of the ball from one player to another makes following it difficult. Observation of practice sessions and briefing by coaches helps in identifying the play patterns a team is likely to follow. In football two cameras are usually placed close together at the 50-yard line in the press box or on top of the grandstand. The third may be stationed alongside the announcer for commercials and summaries and supplemental color coverage. Additional cameras may be located to good advantage on the field itself or at an exit ramp just slightly above field level. Networks utilize a field-level camera placed on a movable dolly along the sidelines. Minicams are also used together with the other cameras to shoot fans, cheerleaders, coaches, band maneuvers, and players on the bench for additional color. In basketball two cameras are placed to pick up good shots of each basket and its surrounding area. Another camera can follow the action through the center of the court.

Boxing and wrestling. Usually two cameras are sufficient for boxing and wrestling because of the limited area of action. One camera can supply a cover shot of the ring and the other camera tight two-shots or close-ups. A special platform is often erected above the spectators but not too far back from the ring. When shots are taken from the rear of the arena, the characteristics of the long lenses makes the fighters appear short and squat. If the announcer is at ringside, he should be stationed on the same side of the ring as the cameras in order not to confuse the viewers in references to "right" or "left." Close-ups of the sportscasters during commercials or interviews are also facilitated. If an additional camera is available, a location that permits "low-angle" shots close to the ringside is desirable and will add considerable dramatic impact to the visual presentation.

SCHEDULED EVENTS

Scheduled special events provide an opportunity for advance preparation. Examples are election night returns, political conventions, dedication ceremonies, banquets, parades, arrival of dignitaries, opening ceremonies of fairs and conventions, fashion shows, and publicity stunts. The station may have an opportunity to adjust the time schedule of some of these events in order to secure a better audience. The atmospheric color achieved by the transmission of "on-location" sights and sounds are important factors in the high degree of interest audiences have in such programs.

The advance preparations for technical pickup facilities affect the polish and smoothness of special events programs. In arranging radio coverage, special audio "loops" and "cueing circuits" are ordered from the local telephone company. If origination points are outside the immediate community, the Long Lines Division of A.T.&T. is called upon to obtain such facilities. Facilities for television remotes are handled either through orders to the telephone company or by the station's own microwave equipment. When the station has sole responsibility, it utilizes a small portable transmitter placed adjacent to the mobile unit on a high point that has a direct line-of-sight approach to the receiving "dish" located on the tower at the station's transmitter. When buildings or hilly terrain interfere with such a line-of-sight connection, another microwave relay link must be used to send the signal to the transmitter in two "hops." It is also capable of transmitting the audio portions.

An outstanding example of complex microwave relays arranged for a one-time broadcast by an individual station was the first live television pickup of an atomic bomb test from Yucca Flats, Nevada. Klaus Landsberg of KTLA, Los Angeles, supervised a dramatic race against time and the elements of nature to install facilities that sent the signal picked up by the cameras at News Nob, seven miles from the scene of the blast, to the station transmitter about 300 miles away. A series of four hops was required from mountain peak to mountain peak including one 140-mile relay over the California desert. Things looked dark indeed at one crucial point. An 8000-foot mountain peak was needed as a relay station, but there was no way to travel up the steep trail except by foot or burro. The U.S. Marines came to the rescue: twenty-four flights of Marine helicopters transported 12,000 pounds of electronic gear, food, gasoline supplies, and four engineers to the peak. The eight-foot receiving dish was tied on by rope. Both a heavy sandstorm and a blizzard knocked out the relay system during test periods. Undaunted, the men worked on; and Landsberg and his staff succeeded in sending to the station, and thence to the nation, the first live television broadcast of an atomic blast. The entire project, including transportation of equipment, location, and installation of the relay links, and arduous checking and testing, took 16 days.

Even when the most careful preparations appear to have been made, mistakes can occur that can create great embarrassment for the originating unit. A good example was the breakdown in the audio line during the televising of the first presidential debate in 1976 between candidates Gerald

Ford and Jimmy Carter. The President of the United States and his opponent in the election stood and fidgeted for 27 minutes before the engineering crew found the malfunction and corrected it. The main problem in this instance was that no backup audio system had been provided. The producers of the succeeding debates made sure that they were not guilty of this oversight.

Script material can be prepared ahead of the scheduled event for the opening and closing announcements, for continuity during emergencies or delays, and for background comments on the occasion, speakers, or other participants. A thorough announcer or writer collects newspaper clippings, maps, press releases, and articles, and writes copy for almost every contingency. Interviews with various personalities can be arranged. The skill with which prepared material and interviews are woven into the ad-lib description of the actual event as it takes place marks the difference between a professional job and an amateurish one. It should be noted that present-day broadcasting does not place a premium on the ability to talk on and on when there is no need to stay at the scene. A switchback to the control point for films, music, or narrative comments by others in the studio is the customary practice. Monitors should be available for use by announcers in remote televised pickups. Otherwise the announcer may be describing a completely different scene from the picture selected for transmission by the director. The commentator must also avoid describing what the viewer can plainly see on the television screen, but at the same time must provide the information needed to make the viewer understand what is being seen.

UNSCHEDULED EVENTS

The other broad area of special events deals with the unexpected. These events may occur during a regular program pickup, such as the explosion of the Hindenberg at Lakehurst, New Jersey, which took place before the eyes of Herbert Morrison, of WLS, who was there to record a routine description of the landing of the giant dirigible. Another such event occurred in 1963 when Lee Harvey Oswald, the alleged assassin of President John Kennedy, was being taken under guard from one location in Dallas to another. As the cameras provided live coverage of the event, the people of the nation saw Oswald shot down by an unexpected assailant. During the presidential election campaign of 1972, a TV crew covering a speech by candidate George Wallace in a Maryland shopping center filmed the shooting that left Wallace a cripple for life. The need to cover unexpected special events may arise at any moment when disaster strikes. Broadcasters, through film and mobile units, have begun to establish a similar reputation for public service—to inform people what to do, where to go, and what is coming next in such crises as hurricanes, tornadoes, floods, and tidal waves. Such broadcasts demand great sincerity and naturalness in presentation. No showmanship tricks, no pretentiousness, no capitalizing on the sufferings of those involved should be tolerated.

AD-LIBBING

Whether the event is scheduled or unexpected, live, filmed, or taped, the announcer must be proficient in extemporaneous speaking. Vivid expressive language, keen observation and accurate description are essential. A brief summary of the scene to orient the audience is a good way to begin the broadcast. A conversational progression from that point should follow. Brief summaries of past activities may also be used if they are necessary for understanding. Avoid long and elaborate summaries. Many announcers work their summaries in along the way rather than at the opening. The rate of speech and the emotional overtones should, of course, be appropriate to the event and its significance. Emotional reactions need not be suppressed; if the event is truly exciting or solemn, it should be reflected in the voice and delivery. Excesses in emotion, however, should be avoided. Stock phrases and repetitive transitional phrases should be avoided. A straightforward progression of ideas and human interest material should be the pattern.

Projects and Exercises

1. Each class member could read aloud and define 25 words or phrases for a particular sport that have special significance and meaning. Select the words and phrases that are distinctive and descriptive of the sport—a vocabulary that would be used by a sports announcer in a broadcast of that sport. "Single wing back" in football and "Texas Leaguer" in baseball are examples.

2. Make an off-the-air recording of a sports event description, radio or television, and have it transcribed in written script form for class analysis and evaluation. Compare it with newspaper accounts. If any sports event is covered by two stations, attempt to have the two announcers recorded as they describe the same thing. Discuss and evaluate the two styles.

3. Monitor television coverage of different sports. Have one class member watch the screen (with the sound off) and describe the game on a tape recorder. Have another class member record the professional description on another tape recorder over a different set. Play back the two recordings for comparison and criticism.

4. Obtain film footage that shows a game in progress. Class members should take turns in describing the game, first as for radio and then as for television during the projection of the film. Class evaluation of different styles should follow.

5. Prepare background material and work out scoring and identification systems. Then take a tape recorder to different practice sessions or actual games for use by class members alternating as sportscasters and spotters. Play back these tapes for class criticism.

6. Cover special events on campus and community via tape recording or film. Prepare advance copy and arrange for interviews to fill in as needed.

28

Programs for children are an important element in network and station programming. The aim of most commercial stations is to entertain the children who are watching. In pursuing this objective, broadcasters face the problem of producing entertainment exciting and interesting enough to hold their young audiences that will not at the same time be damaging to them. Networks wrestled most visibly with this problem in terms of Saturday-morning cartoons for children. For a number of years these programs grew steadily more violent and sensational in their content until the public outcry against violence reached a climax at the end of the 1960s and forced a modification. The cartoons of the seventies depended much more on comedy and fantasy, and the violence still in them took place offscreen and was presented in a "we're not really serious about this" fashion. Another period devoted by some commercial stations to children is just before supper. Syndicated programs such as *Bozo the Clown* and reruns of network series originally produced for general audiences are often shown. Surveys have indicated that children at an early age become interested in adult situation comedies, quizzes, mysteries, detective stories, variety shows, half-hour dramas, and feature movies. To say that all programs broadcast for children by commercial stations are aimed exclusively at entertainment would be inaccurate, however. The *Captain Kangaroo* series broadcast for many years by CBS for preschool children contains significant educational elements, as does the syndicated series *Romper Room.* Occasionally the networks produce programs for children designed primarily to educate.

As one might expect, however, the major effort at producing programs that will be educationally valuable and yet will still be attractive to children has come from public TV stations and production centers. There have been a number of notable successes in this area. One of the first was *The Friendly Giant,* which originated at WHA-TV, Madison, Wisconsin. In a gentle way it provided lessons in life for small children. *Misteroger's Neighborhood* began on the Pittsburgh ETV station and is now distributed nationwide. The producer and personality on the program, Fred Rogers, says that his aim "is to establish an atmosphere in which children can grow in a healthy way . . . through original songs, clearly defined fantasy, and very straightforward age-appropriate dialogue." Roger's main appeal is that he neither plays up to children nor talks down to them. He takes completely seriously the problems of children, which are very important to them. One program, for example, was devoted to telling children how to wait and to be patient.

Public television's biggest success in children's programming and, indeed, one of the biggest successes in television, is *Sesame Street*. Funded jointly by government sources and private foundations, it managed in some cities to outdraw all competing programs in its time period. This success prompted commercial as well as educational stations to telecast the series, with the result that half of the country's twelve million preschool children watched it regularly.

Sesame Street, although full of fun and frolic, is designed to help children aged three to five, particularly those from disadvantaged areas, to prepare for school. Having noted that children are often more fascinated by commercials than by programs, Mrs. Joan Ganz Cooney, the originator of the series, decided to use TV commerical techniques to teach numbers and letters. The program abounds in one-minute spots about various letters and numbers, cartoons, jingles, and dancing symbols. There are also some Muppets (puppets) to hold attention, and attractive people who live on the imaginary "Sesame Street."

Because of the production they require, programs such as *Sesame Street* are beyond the range of most producing groups. It is quite possible, however, to broadcast good children's narrative programs with a small production budget. For many years phonograph companies have been alert to this fact and have produced for children many albums that are simple stories. It is a field in which the smallest television or radio station can be active. Even the station that has no budget for live or taped studio origination can still produce such series by using voice-over narration during visual transmission of drawings on its opaque projectors.

The many volumes of children's literature are excellent program sources if the station does not have a writer for original scripts and an artist to illustrate them. Publishers may authorize use of their stories, and even illustrations, providing a small fee is paid. It may be feasible to work out cooperative arrangements with local book stores to reduce or eliminate the fee. When such a series is produced as a sustainer without a commercial sponsor, either by the station directly, or in cooperation with a local public service organization, the library or public school system, etc., the publisher may permit the use of his story without charge. Many classical and folk stories are in the public domain and may be used at will. These stories generally require some editing and simplifying for children's broadcasts.

In building a series of children's programs, it is important to consider the general interests of children according to age groups. A story well suited for a six-year-old will be too simple for a ten-year-old. Children are less discriminating toward dramatic programs, however. Ten-year-olds will listen to dramatic versions of stories that they themselves will neither listen to in narrative form nor read themselves. Generalizations about the interests of children are difficult to make because of individual differences, but a rough classification may be helpful for those planning series of children's programs. Regional differences, of course, influence these classifications.

Age 4–5

The Mother Goose stories, repetitive jingles and stories dealing with very familiar things around the home or farm. Sample titles: *The Three Bears, Red Hen, Chicken Little, The Pig with a Straight Tail, Noisy Books, Big Dog Little Dog.*

Age 6–7

Stories with a little plot. Familiar transportation methods and animals and some simple fairy stories. Sample titles: *Jack and the Beanstalk, The Tinder-box, Cry Fairy, How the Camel Got its Hump, Golden Touch, The Little Engine That Could, Hop O My Thumb, Honk the Moose, Choo Choo the Little Switch Engine.*

Age 8–9

The fairy story is well liked. Beginning of folk tales and stories from other lands. Continued interest in animal stories. Sample titles: Grimm and Hans Christian Andersen stories, Oz stories, *Winnie the Pooh, The Wind in the Willows, Mother West Wind* series, *Li Lun Lad of Courage.*

Age 10–12

More attention to the outside world and reality instead of fairy stories. Biography and animal stories have great appeal. Adventure, invention, and sports have great interest. Some classic titles: *Treasure Island, Heidi, Swiss Family Robinson, Robin Hood, Hans Brinker, Black Beauty, Tom Sawyer.*

The writer of children's narratives should approach the subject from the child's point of view, not the adult's. Children experience the thrill of a new world unfolding before them and they are highly imaginative. They accept the fantasy of toads and trees talking. The concentrated attention children give to the program makes it possible to have several characters and a simple plot. They will follow and remember correctly many specific details and characters, if they are properly identified. This does not mean that the writer can introduce long descriptive passages; interest must be maintained through action. Direct conversational style is imperative. Classic fairy stories should not be presented as they appear in print, but edited to make the speech smooth and fluent. Horror passages usually can be changed to retain the excitement of the story without inducing fright. A narrative that casually tells about a witch cutting off 67 heads may be accepted, whereas a dramatization of the same event would be too gruesome for broadcast.

EXAMPLE OF ADAPTATION TECHNIQUES (RADIO)

"The Snow Queen," a classic story, rewritten by Ethel Joyce Atchinson.[1] Parallel columns indicate the changes in style between the original version and adaptation.

[1] Courtesy of the author and University of Michigan Department of Speech.

1. The Friendly Beginning

"Now we are about to begin and you must attend; and when we get to the end of the story, you will know more than you do now about a very wicked hobgoblin."

Hello there! This is the story about a wicked old hobgoblin, who was so very, very wicked that—well, just listen to this story about all the terrible things that he did.

2. Description

"The most beautiful landscapes reflected in it looked like boiled spinach and the best people became hideous or else they were upside down and had no bodies. Their faces were distorted beyond recognition and if they even had one freckle it appeared to spread all over the nose and mouth. The demon thought this immensely amusing."

In the mirror the trees looked all brown and wilted, the grass and flowers lost all their color. And the people! In the mirror, people were all upside down. Their noses looked a foot long and the corners of their mouths always turned down. How the demon laughed when he saw how ugly the mirror made people look.

3. Modernizing and Universality

"The roses were in splendid bloom that summer: the little girl had learnt a hymn and there was something in it about roses and that made her think of her own. She sang it to the little boy and then he sang it with her—'where the roses deck the flowery vale, there, Infant Jesus, we thee hail.' The children took each other by the hands, kissed the roses and rejoiced in God's bright sunshine and spoke to it as if the Child Jesus were there."

The roses in the tiny garden were so beautiful that summer. The little girl and boy would make up songs about the roses and dance and sing in the bright sun. The sun, the roses and happiness . . . what a wonderful summer!

4. Creating Suspense

"Kay and Gerda were looking at a picture book of birds and animals one day—it had just struck five by the church clock—when Kay said, 'Oh, something struck my heart, and I have got something in my eye.' The little girl put her arms around his neck, he blinked his eye, there was nothing to be seen."

One day when Gerda and Kay were playing in the garden a terrible thing happened. Just as the clock in the village struck five, Kay screamed! Gerda ran to him! What was the matter, what could it be! Why had Kay screamed so? "Ohhh!" was all that Kay could say. "Oh, Kay," said Gerda, "what has happened?" "I don't know," said Kay, "All of a sudden I had a funny feeling in my heart." "In your heart?" "Yes, and then it got in my eye," said Kay. Gerda didn't know what to think. Was something wrong with her friend?

5. Drawing Imaginative Pictures

"The snow-flakes grew bigger and bigger till at last they looked like big white chickens. All at once they sprang on one side, the big sledge stopped and the person who drove got up, coat and

The snow flakes grew bigger and bigger and bigger until they looked almost like soft white feathery clouds. Suddenly the big sleigh stopped and the driver of the sleigh turned to look at Kay. And do you

cap smothered in snow. It was a tall
and upright lady all shining white, the
Snow Queen herself."

know who the driver was? Standing
right there before Kay was a beautiful
lady all dressed in the purest of white
fur. Tiny sparkling diamonds were
scattered all over her huge muff and hat.
The lady was the most beautiful that
Kay had ever seen as she stood there
before him all white and sparkling, just
like ice and snow when the sun shines on
it. Why it was the Snow Queen herself!

Men or women may be featured in presentations of children's stories.
In television, when men are used, frequently a character role is developed,
such as a Western cowboy, "old timer," clown, "uncle or cousin." Gushiness,
mock enthusiasm, and artificial manners are taboo in the narration of these
tales; the delivery must reveal genuine interest in the story. Exaggerated
characterizations, playing with nonsense words and rhythms, and reacting to
the action in the story with an illusion that the performer is also hearing or
seeing it for the "first time" help in achieving a professional presentation. Direct visual contact is gained in television by talking directly to the lens.
Spontaneous and facile facial expressions and gestures are effective when
they are motivated by the material. Children are suspicious of "over-
playing." The rate of delivery should be somewhat slower in children's narratives than in other types of narratives. Children have to imagine the scene
in radio or to absorb the visual in television. Too rapid a pace, which begin-
ners are likely to set, may confuse them.

Radio

Sound and live or recorded music should be used when appropriate. Several
music bridges are recommended. These permit breaks in attention. Many
children have not learned to take advantage of relatively static passages to
shift attention as adults do. The music bridges almost force them to relax
their attention for a while. Sound effects are also effective production devices. Here you have an interesting contrast. Sound effects in scenes that are
close to the experience of the children—cars, telephone, running, planes,
trains, horses—should be authentic and realistic. Children are quick to spot
the difference between the real sound and the sound effect. It would be better
to let them use their imagination about sounds, or use vocalizations in exaggerated manner, if realistic sound is not possible in these instances. In fantasies and fairy stories, however, children will accept sound of a highly imaginative nature. A slide whistle can be a magic carpet to transport Aladdin's
palace to the Far East, it can be the rapid growth of Jack's magic beanstalk
into the sky, it can be the shrinking of a child into a tiny elf.

Television

We know that a child is able to see the story teller in television. The writer
and director in television also have sound and music, visuals of various
kinds, puppets and marionettes, actors, action, and camera and electronic

tricks to interest and tell the story. Still, programs with relatively simple formats can hold the attention of children. These programs may be produced by a station staff or by organizations or institutions such as schools, universities, libraries, and Junior Leagues, which build programs for broadcast.

SIMPLE FORMATS FOR CHILDREN'S TV PROGRAMS

1. Narrator with stills. Stills may include drawings in the studio or on an opaque projector, RP or regular slides, and photographs. Camera shots vary from full- to shoulder-shots of the story teller as he or she talks directly to the audience. Cut to stills in harmony with story progression. Proportion of camera time allotted to stills and talent depends upon the personality of the performer and the number of available visuals. Variety and heightened interest may result from camera movement during the showing of a visual. A single drawing may be designed to serve for several shots. For example, a neutral still of the lead character may be shot with head shot, extreme close-up of eyes, waist-shot, or as a one-shot at different times in the story while the lead is supposed to be talking or thinking. Zooms in and back may give additional variety. Another example might be a street scene shot in a sequence of different framed shots as the camera tilts up following the character in the story walk along the street. Then the camera pulls back for a cover shot and fades to black as a magic carpet wafts the narrator away from the city. And a final example is a pan back and forth, or dissolves between two cameras, from the face of a mother bird to a fledgling as they discuss problems of learning to fly. Writer, director, and artist should each bear in mind the many uses of visuals as they approach the story. The set for this type as well as those to follow may be only a draped background, a standard set simulating a "circus tent," "magic story room," "garden nook," "old timer's ranch," "giant's castle," etc., or varied from program to program with display-paper sketched background, realistic or stylized set, or rear-screen projection background.

2. Narrator with children in the studio. One, two, or a group of children may gather to listen to the story and engage in dialogue with the narrator. Camera shots that transmit their reactions, usually intriguing and natural, may be employed during the presentation. The children may be requested to reenact segments, participate in rhymes or physical action, or answer questions about the story.

3. Storyteller who draws the illustrations while the narrative is told. This action may be very effective in keeping interest. Pausing while the sketching is in progress may be desirable at times. Finishing a cartoon with a flourish may reinforce a "punch" line. This approach may be varied by having some of the sketches predrawn or partially drawn ahead of air time, or by having another person, an artist partner (either on or off camera), draw while the story is in progress.

4. Narration with stills and off-camera voices for dialogue sections. The voice-over segments may be best used when the camera is on the visuals. Properly used, this technique may approximate a dramatic presentation, but without the need for rehearsing action and memorizing lines. The actors read their speeches "off camera."

5. Narration with pantomime. Child actors or staff members may act out the story in pantomime while it is being told. The characters may or may not be in costume, with or without props and set, in full view or in silhouette.

6. Narration with film. Standard film from library sources or special film may be used. One director secured footage of a German circus that had been photographed by a visitor overseas. He brought into the studio a group of children who watched the film with the narrator and then drew, on camera, their impressions of the individual scenes or characters that interested them most. Film of a local zoo, fire or police station, farm, dairy, bakery, quarry, etc., may be incorporated into the stories or used as "teasers."

7. Performer with other types of visuals. Visuals may be of the cardboard cutout type, standing free or pinned up on boards, felt figures placed on felt board, pipe-cleaner figures, or toy houses, dolls, animals, cars, railroads, farm yards, trees, etc. Movement may be accomplished through animation, pulls, camera "superimps," magnet boards, operating and manipulating toys by wires, or by moving cameras. *The Friendly Giant* series opened with a camera pan along a miniature outdoor set, using toy objects and figures, which the viewing audience accepted as life-size. Then suddenly huge boots were seen as the camera continued to pan, dwarfing the landscape. A slow tilt up and up to the giant's face reinforced the impression of hugeness.

8. Performer, dialogue, singing, with hand puppets or marionettes. This technique has been adopted widely and dates back to the phenomenal success of the *Kukla, Fran, and Ollie* program, which began in 1947. Many variations may be found across the country. Complete stories or sequences may be performed or acted out with pantomime and dialogue. Actors off-camera read the lines. Bill Baird and his puppets also illustrate this type of presentation. A human being may appear on camera working with and talking to the puppets or marionettes. Sometimes humans are dressed in fantastic animal costumes, as are Big Bird on *Sesame Street* and the characters in *The Muppets*.

9. Preschool or kindergarten home-participation. The performer talks directly to the young fry, telling stories, singing songs, demonstrating how-to-do-it projects suitable for their age. Emphasis is upon stimulation of activity by the child. The performer teaches them games and songs, shows them how to construct a cutout puzzle from a magazine advertisement, a tambourine from paper plates, or a tom-tom from a cereal container, interspersed with "exercise sessions." Performers must have an intimate and thorough knowledge of the interests and capabilities of the preschool child, speaking and moving in harmony with the rhythm and frame of reference of the child's world. Excitable, fast chatter and a rapid style are ineffective. The director must remember also that too much camera movement and too many camera cuts may confuse and distract the child viewer.

10. Variety show format. Performers work in regular street clothes or in costume and makeup for a character role. Examples of the latter may be a circus clown, a magician, a Western ranch hand, a magic story lady. Children's talent shows are frequently broadcast. An MC may introduce film shorts and cartoons, specialty vaudeville or circus acts, phonograph-record pantomime units, or broad slapstick comedy sequences. A story line may run through one program or a series. A ventriloquist and dummy partner may also be used.

Many years ago Burr Tillstrom, creator of the *Kukla, Fran, and Ollie* program, described the essential qualities of a TV children's program. His ideas still apply today.

> First among the qualities to be sought after is simple sincerity. The wise showman won't try to do any faking before a young audience: neither will he attempt subtleties. The first they are likely to see through, the second they are not likely to understand.
>
> This is particularly true in television, where characters and situations are much more real and infinitely closer than they ever could be in any other medium. The camera takes you right into the living room, and there is no place to hide; everything you do is seen, and the television camera is almost unbearably honest.
>
> Therefore, the fewer complications involved in a children's program, the better. The simplest props and the least complicated plots have the most appeal. Even adults tire of the too-elaborate.
>
> Secondly, a children's program should be certain of its facts. When anyone on a children's show trips up on pronunciation or on the historical, geographical or arithmetical details, you can be sure the program hears from children and from all ages. As long as the program-planners make sure that the children never see or hear anything unkind, however, the correspondents are correspondingly gentle. Then the corrections are as lovable as a compliment.
>
> A third quality to be aimed at is that of imagination. For while children are intensely practical, they're also highly imaginative. Much of their play is make-believe, and, universally, they love fairy tales, the Oz books and similar fantasies. They find a show that makes that sort of stories real to them a delight.
>
> Informality or intimacy is the fourth point to be stressed for young audiences (although I think it can apply to older audiences as well). Children love to feel that they are a part of the show; and if your audiences are part of you, you are pretty certain of their loyalty.[2]

EXAMPLE OF A CHILDREN'S TELEVISION PROGRAM

Sesame Street.[3]

The scenes on Sesame Street, the basic locale of the series, are recorded on video tape. Inserts are then introduced, either from video tape or from film, as each episode progresses.

[2] Courtesy of *The New York Times* and Burr Tillstrom.
[3] Courtesy of Children's Television Workshop.

An Episode of *Sesame Street* being video-taped.

SHOW NO. 122
CHILDREN'S TELEVISION WORKSHOP
SESAME STREET

1. FILM: SHOW IDENTIFICATION

2. FILM: OPENING SESAME STREET THEME

3. GREETING—TRAFFIC ON SESAME STREET
   Gordon greets—while in the background are sounds of busy street noises—
   horns, vehicles passing, etc. He says that you probably guessed there's a lot
   of traffic on Sesame Street. So it's important to be very careful when you're
   near the street and especially if you have to cross it. Batman knows that.
   SCENIC: Street
   TALENT: Gordon
   S.E.:   Street noises

4. VTR: BATMAN CROSSING STREET
   Show 90, Item 4; Time: :43

5. SUSAN AND GORDON—LISTEN TO TRAFFIC
   Susan arrives holding two kids by the hands. She and Gordon greet. She asks
   Gordon if he's seen how busy the street is today.

   Gordon: Batman and I were just talking about that.

   Susan: And while   and   and I waited at the corner for the traffic light
   to turn green we played a game. We called it Listening to Traffic.

   Gordon: Listening to Traffic?

Susan: All you do is shut your eyes and listen to what's passing in the street. Then try to guess what makes the sound. We'll show you.   ,
and I will close our eyes and you tell us if we guess right.

Gordon: Okay . . . (he looks off) . . . Here comes something now. Sound of a fire siren and clanging bell fades up, is loud for a few moments, then fades off again. Gordon mimes watching it approach, pass, and go off down the street. Meanwhile, Susan and the kids stand with their eyes shut, listening.

All right—can you tell me what that was?

Susan: That's easy.
She asks the kids and they answer that it was a fire engine.

Gordon: Right. Now here comes something else.
The routine is repeated—Gordon looks off, Susan and the kids shut their eyes. S.E. bells of an ice cream truck. The sound of the bells fade up, pass, and fade off, as Gordon turns his head.

Susan: (opens her eyes) I bet we can guess that one too. She asks the children, and if they can't guess, she answers it herself.

Gordon: Good. But shut your eyes again. Here comes another sound.

Gordon looks off. S.E.—the clopping of hoofs and mooing of a herd of cows approaches, passes and fades off. C.U. of Gordon as he watches with surprise. Susan opens her eyes.

Susan: A sound like that on Sesame Street? I don't believe it . . . (to the kids) What did that sound like to you?

The kids or Susan guess a herd of cows.

Gordon: You're right. He laughs. I told you there was a lot of traffic on the street today. Hold it—here comes something.

S.E.—the engine of a racing car approaches, passes, and goes on. Susan opens her eyes.

Susan: I know what that was. A racing car!

SCENIC: Street
TALENT: Gordon, Susan, kids
S.E.:   (a) Fire siren & clanging bell
              (b) ice cream truck bell
              (c) clopping of hoofs and mooing
              (d) Engine of a racing car

6. FILM: RACING CAR BRIDGE

7. BIG BIRD BUILDS A RACE CAR

Big Bird has joined Gordon, Susan.

Big Bird: Wow! That was wonderful! I wish I had a racing car so I could drive around like that! I know. I'll get some boxes and I'll build one. I've built lots of things with boxes—I can build a racing car too.

Susan: Well, you have to be a good driver if you want to drive a racing car, you know.

Big Bird: Oh, I am. I'll show you. When I finish the car I'll drive it up and down the street.

Gordon: Well, you built a truck with boxes, and a space ship and a television set. So there's no reason why you can't build a racing car.

Susan: And if you're looking for boxes, a box salesman went by here just a little while ago. In fact, I think he's seeing Ernie now . . .

SCENIC: Street
TALENT: Gordon, Susan, Big Bird

8. ERNIE AND THE BOX SALESMAN
Show 81, Item 14; Time: 3:54

Projects and Exercises

1. Tune in stations in your area and prepare reports on different types of children's programs currently being broadcast. Compare and evaluate relative effectiveness.
2. Prepare and present five-minute children's programs. These may be original or adaptations. Alternate radio and television presentations. Test for effectiveness by inviting a group of children to the studio. Note carefully the actions of the children during the presentation. Check the places where attention drifted or special interest was shown. Discuss story details with the group following the presentation to check on comprehension.

as a career

"Should I go into radio?" "What about television?" These are questions often asked of station or network staff and of instructors in broadcasting. This chapter deals with those questions.

Television and radio have glamour. They are connected with "show business," hailed so much in song and described at such length in fiction. Show business is not all tinsel and spotlight. In spite of the publicity appearing in magazines and Sunday supplements, few unknowns are catapulted into stardom. It is usually a long, arduous, and grueling struggle before one attains any degree of financial success and security. For every leading actor, starring soloist, and recognized comic, there are hundreds in the shadows who have not "arrived." A performer's union, such as the American Federation of Television and Radio Artists, has many members who do not actually make their living in broadcasting. One survey indicated, for example, that 80 percent of that union's membership made less than $2,000 a year from work in broadcasting. This figure should be borne in mind by those thinking only of the performing positions and the "big time."

However, the fulfillment of a creative desire, the opportunity for self-expression, the excitement of working in a dynamic medium of mass communication, the changing pattern of work in some positions, and the prestige of working in a spotlighted environment are the intangible factors that make television and radio so attractive to aspirants and often outweigh the more material factors.

Each individual should evaluate his or her abilities honestly, using any expert vocational guidance available. A glib "You have a nice voice on the telephone, you ought to be in radio!" or a casual "You photograph so nicely, why don't you go into television!" or an introspective "My, it would be thrilling, working in radio and television, I'd like that!" are not dependable evaluations. Examine and evaluate your experience, your talents, and your capabilities as you review the chapters concerned with the various areas and read the analysis that follows.

THE TELEVISION AND RADIO INDUSTRIES

Although the number of television and radio stations is still increasing, the broadcasting industry seems to be reaching its peak and can no longer be considered a rapidly expanding industry. The number of employees in all capacities working in television and radio industry in the United States rose from approximately 70,000 in 1970 to approximately 80,000 in 1975. Work is so specialized that on-the-job training and experience are necessary. This means that the apprentice system is usually followed.

Two Procedures

Those who seek to enter commercial television and radio as a career may elect one of two general procedures. One method is to seek employment in the profession as soon as possible, going in on a very low level after high school and advancing through the years. Many have followed this method and succeeded. The second method is to take college liberal arts education, including work in the fields of speech, art, drama, music, social sciences, home economics, agriculture, advertising, creative writing, and business, plus specialized work in broadcasting, photography and design. The broadcasting specialization, in many instances, should continue for an additional year beyond the bachelor's degree. The second method delays the beginning of actual work on the job, but most broadcasting executives prefer candidates with college educations. As one station executive phrased it: "Competition in the broadcasting business is too keen! You have to have people who can think, make decisions, judge wisely, and know a lot about a lot of things. College degrees don't guarantee that the people are like that but they are important indications."

The increasing number of colleges and universities with facilities for closed-circuit television as well as equipment for radio enables more students to acquire on-the-job experience at educational institutions as well as at stations. Students who attend an institution where a public television or radio station exists often have opportunities to combine preliminary apprenticeship in broadcasting with college work. Further valuable experience can be gained in closed-circuit operations.

Announcing and Specialties

Announcing is a common method of entering the broadcasting field. The first step is to find a beginning position in a station in a small market. The pay is usually low, but the opportunities to gain experience, not only in announcing but also in other functions, is great, for announcers in small stations must often play a number of roles. If the individual has the required talent and application, he or she can then move up the ladder to higher-paying jobs in larger stations and perhaps even into the networks. It is also possible for announcers to move into management, news, production, or sales positions.

Acting

Careers in acting are limited almost entirely to work in New York City and Hollywood. Only a few stations originate dramas on a regular basis. Even with the increase of television and film work, the field is overcrowded. There are practically no staff positions, and very few long-term contracts. Radio plays have virtually vanished. There is great competition for the acting roles in television. Relatively few opportunities exist for the newcomer to break into acting. Producers and casting directors do not have the time or need to consider inexperienced people. They usually demand previous "credits," indicating considerable theatrical or film experience. Successful models may occasionally move from appearances as models to acting roles in commercials. For those who feel that they are qualified and determined to go ahead and try to become professional actors, it is recommended that they seek experience in college drama of all types, followed by stock, community theater, local TV and radio station jobs, films, and whatever on- or off-Broadway theatrical roles are available. Vocal instruction and training in dance are also desirable. In addition to the casting directors at stations and networks, a great number of different program production firms, advertising agencies, and film producers must be approached for auditions and interviews. There is no central casting agency. Individual contacts must be made and renewed at several hundred locations in New York. The television actor in Hollywood also must compete with the aspiring motion picture hopefuls. Some actors are represented by agents who earn a 10-percent commission when stipends above union scale are received for television and radio work. Few agents, however, will take a chance on representing unknowns. Minimum fee scales are established by the respective trade unions, AFTRA (American Federation of Television and Radio Artists) for television and radio, and SAG (Screen Actors Guild) for film. It is wise for would-be actors who plan a career in New York or Hollywood to have enough funds for an entire year's subsistence. If this is not possible, one should seek part-time employment of a type that permits free daytime periods for "making the rounds."

Specialized Performance Areas

Solo and choral vocalists, solo or orchestral musicians, vaudeville artists, magicians, puppeteers, dancers, and comedians are needed and used in broadcasting. Talent, personality, and experience are the elements required to carve out a career as a performer. It is generally not the training in television techniques that is more important, but the background in the particular branch of show business. Working before a live audience is essential before attempting studio work. Supplemental training in acting or broadcast speech is desirable. Many performers are called upon to speak or act before the camera or on microphone.

Sound-Effects Technicians

There is very limited turnover among sound-effects technicians. There are few positions other than those in network centers. If a position exists in a station or film production unit, it may lead into direction or production.

Script Writers

Station staff writers prepare all types of scripts from continuity, voice-over-film narration, and interviews to commercial copy. This type of position is often the means of obtaining a foothold in broadcasting. Frequently this job is combined with that of traffic clerk or music librarian. Wide general knowledge, "a little about a lot," and more intensive information about music and advertising are useful, in addition to knowing how to write for the ear or eye. Ability to turn out an acceptable script while working under pressure of time is essential. Advancement calls for imagination and creativity. Fresh and interesting ways to present familiar material without resorting to "gimmicks" or tricks are needed. Advertising agency or network staff writers are specialists in commercial and continuity respectively.

Contract and Free-Lance Writers

These writers are employed for program series by stations, networks, independent package companies, and production firms. Experience and specialized skills in the type of program being produced are needed by such writers. Some may develop particular aptitudes for writing children's programs, for thinking up stunts for quizzes, or for finding clever visual approaches to explain medical, scientific, or agricultural subjects. Some discover that they are good at interviewing program guests ahead of broadcast time and preparing questions for an MC or commentator to use. Some show amazing facility in scripting dialogue banter for a "name" personality and guests stars. Comedy "gag"- or "situation"-writers are the highest paid, and suffer the greatest job mortality.

As the television industry grew, there was an increase in dramatic programs, both live and on film. More opportunities developed for writers of plays. However, production of such programs is restricted in the main to New York and Hollywood. It is not easy for the novice to first write, then sell a dramatic script—especially when the person is away from the production centers and unavailable for personal consultations about rewrites. Rod Serling, one of the most successful of television writers, said that those who choose television dramatic writing as a career must realize it is "tough, time-consuming, frustrating and insecure," but on the other hand, "can be satisfying, lucrative and the kind of challenge that comes only with a creative job . . . the singular difference between the successful TV writer and the unsuccessful is just one word—*talent.*"

Producers may elect to seek out writers from fields other than broadcasting for special assignments. A "name" playwright may be signed for a special dramatic series. A journalist or feature magazine writer who is an "expert" in foreign affairs may be recruited for a documentary series in that area. Often a writer or editor experienced in broadcasting techniques may be hired to perform any rewriting needed to prepare such material for the air.

News People

Networks usually hire their editors from the ranks of those who have had experience in news operations. Newscasters on the networks may be former announcers who have shown special skills in delivering the news, or have been trained in journalism and have turned to broadcasting. Some stations prefer that both news editors and newscasters have newspaper experience; others allow these positions to be filled by announcers. Students who have college courses in journalism and broadcasting may be able to secure positions on the news staffs of broadcasting stations directly upon graduation. Some stations favor former athletes for sportscasters. Weather forecasts may be presented by persons with specialized training in meteorology. Supplemental experience in operation of video-tape and audio-tape recorders and film and press cameras is desirable for all news people.

Stage Manager, Facilities Assistant, Stagehand

Another common method to enter the broadcasting field at many stations is by obtaining a position at the "bottom" of the production ladder as a stage manager, facilities assistant, or stagehand. In large cities, union contracts may govern the hiring conditions for these positions. Many stations will select from applicants for these jobs those who appear to be potential candidates for assistant or associate directorships and then directorial positions. Background in technical areas of the theater or experience in television at institutions that provide such training is helpful.

Directors

Few radio stations employ full-time directors. Some television stations promote their directors from within the ranks, others prefer to bring them in from other stations or from the theater or film. Agency and free-lance directors at the national level are generally selected from the network staffs. A knowledge of television techniques is essential. A background in radio, theater, and film is desirable, but many directors have been successful in television without much experience in film. It is recommended, however, that prospective directors seek opportunities to work with film because of the importance of filmed programs in station and network schedules.

Producers

Some stations use this term interchangeably with director. Some describe their employees as producer-directors. Generally the producer exercises administrative and budgetary supervision and has responsibility for the concept, format, and quality of the series. Producers are often selected from the ranks of directors. Persons who have established a reputation in other branches of show business as producers may be employed at the local or network level. Program stars may decide to invest their earnings and become producers. People who exercise overall supervision of a number of series produced by one company are usually known as executive producers. They then assign producers for a specific series or for an individual program within a series who carry out the supervisory functions just described for that series or program.

Unit Managers

In network television, the position of unit manager has been established on an important managerial level. The unit manager, working closely with the producer and the director, is responsible for obtaining all the physical elements required for production and for maintaining budgetary control.

Film and Tape People

A sizable number of positions are available in film and tape departments. Among the functions that must be carried out are checking film and tape in and out, reviewing, editing, processing, and projecting it. Networks and larger stations, as we have noted earlier, also maintain production units that shoot film and tape in the field. These units require interviewers, camera operators, and lighting and sound technicians.

Instruction in cinematography is expanding at a rapid rate at many colleges and universities. The student who is seriously considering a career in film production should learn editing principles and how to use a camera. It may be possible to begin by selling footage to TV stations in the local area. Some news departments purchase free-lance film coverage of spot and feature news. An accumulation of such credits may lead to specific assignment. Experience gained in producing programs on tape and in tape editing is also valuable to a person seeking employment in the television industry.

Camera Operators

There is no consistency within the industry as to whether staff camera operators are affiliated with the engineering department or whether they are a part of programming. The determining factor is usually the union contract in force. Some local stations hire inexperienced persons and give them on-the-job training. Frequently this position is combined with other responsibilities in the programming area.

Artists

Practically every TV station has at least a small art staff. The art director usually has specialized experience in commercial art. Previous training should include design and theatrical staging. Because the smaller stations are interested in employees who are competent in several areas, even limited experience in art may be helpful in obtaining a position at such stations. Lettering skills, cartooning or sketching abilities, and facility in construction of scale models may be put to use.

Production Assistants

Usually such positions are found only at networks and at television stations in metropolitan centers that are very active in programming. The production assistant works with the director and handles details and paper work. The production assistant may be responsible for the following items: marking scripts and distributing copies to various production units, checking facilities lists, obtaining signed tax-withholding forms from talent, keeping rehearsal time sheets for subsequent payment, typing script revisions, obtaining clearance of music, notifying guests of rehearsal times, taking notes for the director during rehearsal, compiling master as-broadcast scripts for filing, and "going out for coffee." General experience in broadcasting, theater, or film and training in shorthand and typing are helpful.

Engineers

Technical qualifications and FCC regulations require special training and skills in broadcasting engineers. Employment is relatively steady and provides gradual advancement over long periods of time. Local radio stations may hire "combination" people—those who can announce and also possess a first class radiotelephone operator's license. Television stations use many more engineers than radio stations. Employers emphasize a thorough knowledge of electrical engineering and physics for those entrusted with supervisory responsibilities at the transmitter and studio. Many engineers are closely allied to the programming areas in TV when assigned as camera operators, lighting directors, microphone boom operators, switchers, and technical directors. In some stations engineers handle video engineering, but when union contracts permit, switching may be handled by the director.

Office Personnel

The general requirements for office work are essentially the same for broadcasting as for any other business. This is an entering wedge for many who later move over into performance or administration. Any special aptitudes shown such as preparation of commercial copy, demonstration, narration, interviewing, art, film, etc., may accelerate a move into programming or production. Positions such as facilities assistant, music librarian, film librarian, and traffic may be considered office positions, but they are closely integrated with programming. No specific experience in broadcasting may be required. They can lead through promotion directly into programming.

Promotion, Public Relations, Publicity

These positions may be combined in smaller organizations with office, program, or commercial positions. The ability to establish excellent relationships with local educational, governmental, civic, and club groups; to write effective publicity releases; to plan showmanlike promotion campaigns; and to carry out merchandising programs is not easily come by. It is an extremely marketable skill. Many of those working in this area come into broadcasting from magazines and newspapers and public relations. Knowledge of audience research techniques is helpful. Those who occupy these positions may report to management of a station and are included in the commercial department

Sales Department

Training in business administration, advertising, bookkeeping, accounting, psychology, and speech are desirable for positions in the sales department. Knowledge of the program side is very useful. Not only time but programs are to be sold. Salespersons in many stations plan programs for clients, assist in selection of talent, and even write commercial copy. As in many businesses the effective salespeople are among the highest paid staff employees. Advancement into general administrative positions from the sales department is a normal progression. Most station managers were previously in charge of sales.

Agencies and Program Production Companies

Not all careers involving television and radio specialization are with stations and networks. Mention has been made of the advertising agency. The student who is interested in the program side alone often does not think of the advertising agency, yet most commercials are conceived, written, produced, and often directed by agency personnel. Those seeking employment as talent, writers, and program production people for this work must apply to the agency. Agencies do not hire staff announcers, but they do employ copy writers, script editors, program supervisors, and producer-directors on a staff basis in their television and radio production departments. Students who plan to enter the business side of broadcasting may find more opportunities with advertising agencies than with stations. The American Association of Advertising Agencies gives annual aptitude examinations in the field of advertising. Results are made available for comparison with national scores and an estimate is given about the phases of advertising activity that seem best suited for the individual person. The test results may be used by applicants seeking positions in advertising agencies.

Independent production companies establish reputations as experts in various kinds of programming; some may work exclusively on musical or cartoon-type commercials; some may purchase the broadcasting rights to an author's works and develop an entire series; or one or several stars may form a production company. There are literally hundreds of such program production companies. Generally these companies employ key people who have "credits" in the particular job classification. Employment may be remunerative but at the same time quite precarious. Short-term contracts with options for continued employment are the practice.

An entry into broadcasting by free-lance packaging of programming

ideas for stations or program production companies should not be overlooked. A program idea, script, and available talent may enable one person
or a small group to enter into business.

Educational and Public Television and Radio

The increased recognition of educational programming by school systems,
community groups, and institutions of higher learning enables young people
to combine specialization in broadcasting with courses and certification in
the teaching profession. A substantial number of positions are available in
the areas of program development, promotion, evaluation, and research. Private businesses, social agencies, civic, labor, and political organizations often
employ persons who build informational broadcasts and films. Non-commercial stations and educational program production centers may have
openings for those interested in a career in broadcasting. Some believe that
the opportunities for creative expression that exist, and the personal satisfaction that comes about because of the content and purposes of public programming, are strong motivating factors to lead one to select educational
broadcasting instead of commercial work as a career. Some approach noncommercial and public broadcasting as an excellent means of learning fun-
damentals and developing skills that may be useful in commercial stations,
networks, agencies, and program production centers.

Women and Minorities in Broadcasting

For many years broadcasting was almost exclusively a male preserve. With
few exceptions men held the positions of power and carried out most of the
functions that did not obviously belong to women because of their sex (such
as, for example, the portrayal of female roles in dramas). Executives, producers, directors, newscasters, and most other people in broadcasting were males.
Women did serve as production assistants in the networks, but they generally
understood that they should not aspire to positions of higher responsibility.
Though women in a number of instances were permitted to tell audiences
about the weather, it was not considered appropriate for them to serve as
newscasters.

    During the last few years there has been a change in this pattern.
Whether the change is a significant one is hotly debated. The FCC requires
stations to report their efforts to broaden employment for women and minorities, and the Equal Employment Opportunity Commission issues regular
studies on this subject. Some representatives of the women's movement argue
that what is taking place constitutes mere tokenism and that the employment of women in broadcasting is still far below what it should be; others
say a significant, slow transition is taking place from a situation in which discrimination existed to one in which a woman with talent and ability will be
able to compete on equal terms with a man.

    Without trying to settle that argument, it does seem that some change
in the employment of women in broadcasting has taken place. This change is
most obvious in the TV newsroom. In many stations women are no longer
relegated to a place before the weathermap, but have moved over to take a

seat at the anchor desk. On networks women regularly serve as reporters, and in 1976 Barbara Walters became a co-anchorperson on a network nightly news broadcast. In 1972 Catherine Mackin became the first floor reporter at a political convention. In 1976 NBC gave her a seat at the anchor desk to report the election returns along with three men. CBS regularly uses a woman—Phyllis George—in presenting its network summaries of sports events.

In addition to winning positions before the camera in performing functions formerly reserved to men, women have also succeeded in other areas. In 1976 Enid Roth became a director for the NBC broadcast of the political conventions after gaining experience directing newscasts for the NBC television station in New York. About the same time ABC appointed a woman, Marlene Sanders, as its vice-president in charge of producing documentary programs. She joined five other women who serve as network vice-presidents. In Chicago, Winifred Chambers is the communications coordinator for the Channel 2 newscasts and serves as the producer of the Sunday morning show *Newsmakers.* Women have even participated in what has always been thought of as a male occupation—the operation of cameras. All three networks employ female camera operators as do a number of stations. Women are also serving as technical directors. The vice-presidents in charge of daytime programming at both the NBC and ABC TV networks have been women, and key network nighttime programming positions with vice-presidential rank have been held by women. There are now also women station managers. Admitting that it is too early to say whether these changes are significant, we can say that there is now no position in broadcasting to which a woman cannot aspire—whereas just a few years ago the doors to a number of occupations were definitely closed to women.

Increasing the employment of minority people in broadcasting constitutes another pressing need. Members of minority groups are now more visible as broadcasters than they were a few years ago and more are employed in nonperforming positions. The Equal Employment Opportunity Commission reported that the percentage of minorities in the broadcasting industry rose from 9.4 percent in 1970 to 15 percent in 1975. There was an improvement in the percentage of all the groups that the Commission classifies as minorities: the percentage of blacks went from .9 percent to 7.1 percent; of Asian Americans from .4 percent to .9 percent; of American-Indians from .1 percent to .3 percent; and of Spanish-speaking Americans or those with Hispanic surnames from 1.7 percent to 2.9 percent. During this same period the percentage of women in the broadcasting industry rose from 25 to 28 percent.

Despite these improvements, in the eyes of many observers the employment of minority people and women is still far below what it should be. Their representation in the managers and sales workers categories is particularly poor. The networks and many stations are carrying out affirmative action programs designed to correct the overall problem, but progress is slow. There is no question that providing both women and minorities with their proper representation among all ranks of radio and televison employees confronts broadcasting with one of its severest challenges.

glossary of studio terms

above-the-line.   Talent elements in a television or radio show, including performers, writers, producers, directors, etc.

abstract set.   A nonrepresentational setting using elements such as drapes, columns, steps, platforms, free-standing flats with various textures and geometrical forms, etc. Such a setting has no definite locale.

actualities.   Words and sounds of actual "on-location" news events recorded on tape or presented "live." Referred to as "acks."

AD (Assistant Director).   At television network headquarters, *Associate Director.*

ad-lib.   To depart from the prepared script with extemporaneous remarks or to proceed without any script or music. Pronouced ăd lib, not äd lib.

aspect ratio.   The ratio of width to height of the television picture transmitted—4 to 3.

audio.   Sound transmission as contrasted to video; radio-frequency circuits, or power circuits.

back-timing.   Timing the closing section prior to broadcast in order to establish the exact "clock" time when such section should begin on the actual broadcast in order to finish smoothly.

back-to-back.   Consecutive programs originating from the same studio.

balance.   Relative placement around microphones and level of volume projection of vocalists, musicians, actors, and sound effects according to desired artistic effects.

Balop.   An opaque projector (reflected light instead of transparent light as in slide projectors). Derived from "Balopticon" manufactured by Bausch and Lomb.

barn door.   Hinged metal flap for television lights. Used to prevent unwanted "spill" light.

BCU.   Big close-up.

beam.   Area of effective microphone pickup—varies according to type of microphone.

below-the-line.   Production elements in a television show, including such items as technical facilities, staging services, studio usage, etc.

bend the needle.   Sudden burst of volume making the needle on the VU meter shoot far past normal maximum peak.

BG.   Background.

509

bible.   Reference book containing statements of station's or network's policies and regulations.

blast.   Too much level, causing distortion.

blowup.   Enlargement of a particular portion of photograph or printed material for legible TV reception.

blue gag.   Off-color material.

board.   The control room audio console. Also referred to as "panel" or "mixer."

board fade.   Fading in or out of the program or any element by manipulation of the volume controls on the control room console.

boom.   1. In radio, a microphone stand with horizontal arm permitting flexible adjustment of microphone position. 2. In television, more elaborate versions for suspension of microphones out of camera range and elevation of cameras for overhead shots. These TV booms may be mounted on movable dollies and operated electrically.

bring it up.   Order for increase in volume.

broad.   A general source of light such as a scoop, fluorescent, or incandescent banks.

burn in.   Image retention on camera tube following completion of shot.

busy.   Anything too complicated or elaborate in design such as a "busy" background. Diverts attention away from desired focus of interest.

canned.   Recorded or transcribed material.

cans.   Headphones.

cartridge.   Receptacle for radio, film, or video-tape elements that can be cued automatically: may contain a complete TV program for institutional, broadcasting, CATV, or home use.

cassette.   Used synonymously with cartridge.

chroma-key.   A specialized form of keying. See *key*.

clean it up.   Order for additional rehearsal to smooth out rough spots.

clearance.   Permission to use copyright material.

closed circuit.   Point-to-point program feed. Contrasted to a "broadcast" presentation.

cold.   1. Starting a broadcast with announcer or dialogue before program theme. 2. Presenting material without rehearsal.

coming up.   Program or portion of program about to begin.

contrast.   The brightness relationships between different elements in picture being transmitted.

copy.   Material to be read. Generally used to refer to announcer's material, either commercial credits or continuity.

corn, corny.   Overly obvious or old and familiar material.

crawl.   Device used to reveal program titles and credits. Motor or hand operation. Speed may be varied.

credits.   Program personnel names—performers, writers, directors, producers, etc., who are given visual (and/or) aural recognition at opening and closing of program.

cross-fade.   See *segue*.

CU.   Close-up.

cue.   1. Hand signal to performer. 2. Word signal in the script to start or stop an effect, speech, movement, or music. 3. Preestablished word signal for switching from one pickup to another. 4. Station or network identification at the close of a program. 5. Music used for background mood music or bridges in dramatic programs. 6. "Cueing" records or transcriptions is to have them ready to play without delay when required.

cue sheet or *cue card.* Large cardboard sheets that contain lyrics, subject outline, or exact words of script. Held next to the camera for reference use by talent or speaker. Referred to also as "idiot sheets."

cushion. Material near the end that may be used wholly, in part, or eliminated in order to complete the program on time.

cut. 1. To eliminate. 2. An individual selection or portion on a transcription.

cyc. (cyclorama). Neutral background, usually a light-colored, cloth backdrop stretched tight to eliminate wrinkles and folds. Frequently used for sky background.

dead. 1. Insensitive side of a microphone. 2. A closed microphone or one that is not connected. 3. Possessing a high degree of sound absorbency. 4. Element in a program that is not to be used.

definition. Distinctness, clarity of detail.

degaussing. To erase previously recorded material from video or audio tape.

depth of field. Distance to or from camera talent or object can move or be moved without becoming out of focus.

detail set. See *insert set.*

diffusor. Material (silk gauze or spun glass) used to soften a beam of light. Attached to the light by a metal-frame holder.

dissolve. Fade-in of picture from black or from the picture to black. Used for a transition from one camera to another with a slight overlapping of the two pictures.

dolly. Movable platform on which a camera or microphone is mounted.

dolly in, dolly out. Movement of camera in towards scene, movement away.

dress. Final rehearsal before performance. A run-through exactly as the program is to be presented.

dry run. Program rehearsal without all of program personnel present such as a run-through without engineer, sound-effects technicians, or camera operators.

echo. Reverberation supplementing voice or music according to effect desired, such as a cave or empty auditorium for speech and extra "brightness" or "life" for music. True echo, repetition of sound with a brief time lag, may be achieved electronically. Acoustical sound reflection, used more frequently, is accomplished by adding extra reverberation in an echo chamber. The echo chamber may be a separate room, tunnel, or labyrinth with a microphone at one end picking up the program coming out of a speaker at the other end. Additional open microphones in other parts of the studio may add reverberation without the use of an echo chamber.

ECU or *ETCU.* Extreme close-up.

EFP Electronic field production. Use of minicams for on-location video-taping of programs or program segments.

ENG. Electronic news gathering. Use of minicams to cover news events for transmission live to studio for simultaneous broadcast or to video-tape events at the scene for later broadcast.

fade. Increase or decrease of audio or video volume. "Take a fade" is a direction to the actor to use a "physical" fade—moving away from or toward the microphone.

fader. Knob on audio or video amplifying equipment. In radio, generally means the volume controls on the control room console. Referred to also as "pot." Technically a potentiometer or attenuator.

feedback. Disturbing hum or whistle caused by a return of portion of an amplifier's output to its input, as when a public address microphone is too close to its loudspeaker.

FG. Foreground.

fill, filler. Material prepared in advance of broadcast for stretch purposes or to fill in dead spots during special events and sportscasts or emergencies.

film clip. Short length of film used within the program.

film loop. A length of film with ends spliced together. It may be projected continuously.

filter. Any device that changes the quality of transmitted sound by elimination of certain frequencies for telephone or "inner-voices" effects and the like. Usually accomplished electrically in the control room.

flexitron. Electronic device that can make the camera picture wave from side to side to create a special effect.

flip cards. Pieces of cardboard in the correct aspect ratio, containing credits, program titles, or commercial slogans. The cards may be pulled away one at a time, flipped up, or flipped down to show material for camera pickup.

fluff. An error or mistake in presentation by the performer or technician.

format. The arrangement of program elements in an established pattern.

45s. Records or transcriptions to be played at 45 revolutions per minute.

frame-up. Camera direction to indicate need for correction of obvious error in composition.

free-lance. Nonstaff.

from the top. Order to start rehearsal from the very beginning of the musical number or script. May also refer to the start of a scene currently being rehearsed.

gain. Degree of amplification of an audio circuit.

gimmick. A new element or change in approach, arrangement, or emphasis in existing program format.

gizmo. A "catchall" word to describe something for which no technical designation is known or when the speaker does not wish to use the correct term.

I.D. Identify or identification.

in the mud. Low level of volume unsuitable for effective transmission.

inky. Small 150-watt spotlight often put on front of camera. Used for lighting eyes or face in a close-up. May be called an "inkie-dinky." Also used to refer to any incandescent light.

IO. Image orthicon tube. Also referred to as "orth."

insert set. Segment of a normal-sized set, such as two stools, a short section of a lunch counter, and a cash register representing a restaurant for a brief scene. Sometimes referred to as a "detail set."

key. An electronic system for inserting a person, a title, or an object into a picture.
kill. Eliminate or cut.

lap. Camera direction calling for a superimposure. "Lap three" would mean that the switcher should super camera three over whatever picture is being transmitted.
leader. Blank film attached to beginning or end of film clip or reel. It is used to aid threading up the film in the projector. May be numbered to show the number of seconds remaining before the picture starts.
level. Amount of volume of transmitted sound.
limbo. A background that is "nothingness." No light reaches any part of the background.
lip sync. 1. Mouthing lyrics during taping or filming in synchronization with previously recorded vocal. 2. Recording separate audio track to match actors' lip movements on screen.
live. 1. An open microphone. Also referred to as "hot." 2. Possessing a high degree of sound reflection. 3. Simultaneous performance and transmission for home reception.
live-on-tape. Program recorded on video tape approximating "live" presentation, i.e., with limited number of interruptions and limited postproduction editing.
log. A detailed chronological listing of a station's complete schedule.
logo. Symbol or trademark.
lose the light. Refers to the tally light. A camera direction indicating that the camera is no longer "hot," *i.e.,* "Move in for a close-up when you lose the light."
LS Long shot.

master. 1. A complete and official script. 2. Authoritative schedule. 3. Transcription or record die kept on file and used to make duplications. 4. The fader on the control console with overall regulation of volume.
MC. 1. Master of ceremonies. 2. Master control room.
MCU. Medium close-up.
MI. Move in (to camera operator).
mix. To manipulate the faders on the control-room console—blending two or more program elements according to desired balance.
mixer. 1. Speech amplifier having two or more inputs. 2. A studio engineer.
monitor. 1. To listen to or to view the program. 2. A screen for checking pictures before or during transmission. A "jeep monitor" used in the studio is movable.
MS. Medium shot.

nemo. A remote, a program originating away from the studio.
NI. Network identification.
noodle. Improvise on piano or other musical instrument.

OC On camera.
off-mike. Location of performer or sound effect back from the microphone.
on-mike. Directly on the beam and near the microphone.
on-the-cuff. A performance without pay.
on-the-nose. Program starting, proceeding, or ending on time.

one-shot. 1. A single appearance on a program series. 2. Close-up of one person in television.

open end. A recorded program with spaces left at the beginning, middle (possibly), and at the end for the insertion of commercials or other messages by the station or network presenting the program.

orth. 1. Image orthicon camera. 2. Image orthicon tube.

PA. 1. Public address system. 2. Press agent.

pan. Move camera horizontally to right or left to follow action or direct attention to another area or subject.

patch. To connect separate pieces of equipment by patch cords so as to route the circuit as desired.

PAX. Private telephone system.

PB. Pull back (to camera operator).

PD. Material in the public domain—not protected by copyright and available for use without payment or permission.

peak. A meter reading indicating the relative volume of transmitted sound. In studio practice, "zero peaks" on the VU meter represent normal upper limits of volume without distortion.

pedestal up (down). Direction to camera operator meaning to raise (or lower) the camera height.

pick it up. Direction to increase the tempo—to speed up performance.

pickup. 1. The produced sound transmission due to relative placement of performers and microphones in a studio or from a remote. 2. A program origination location. 3. Turntable.

pix. Picture.

PL. Private telephone line.

platter. Transcription or record.

play back. To monitor a tape or disc recording immediately after it is made.

plug. Commercial announcement.

plumbicon. TV camera tube.

practical. Prop that is real or that actually works, such as a practical door or window.

prerecorded. Method of recording speech or songs prior to telecast. Performer may then be free to dance or move freely about during playback on the air. Lyrics or speech may be pantomimed in lip sync during the playback.

presence. An "on-mike" pickup that has effective intimacy.

promo. A station or network announcement promoting an upcoming program or event.

prop. Physical materials of a set other than scenery and costumes. Hand props are those handled by actors. Set dressing props are furniture and set decorations.

Q. Cue.

ready. Warning by director or technical director given in control room immediately prior to the command, i.e., "Ready fade in one," "Ready roll film," "Ready music."

read-y. Mechanical or overly precise "word-by-word" reading style.

release.	Direction to camera indicating that it is free to move to the next position.
ribbon.	A velocity microphone.
ride gain.	To regulate the volume level of transmitted sound. Extended to refer to the action of a studio engineer, regulation of levels, and mixing at the control room console.
roll it.	A cue for the start of film.
RP.	Rear-screen projection. Stills or motion pictures projected on a large translucent screen provide a background for the scene.
RPM.	Revolutions per minute.
rough cut.	A tentative preliminary arrangement of program scenes or segments in approximate sequence of presentation. Primarily used in film editing but may refer to video-tape editing.
schmalz.	An overly sweet manner of musical arrangements or presentation; a mawkish style of writing or delivery.
scoop.	1. Distortion (wow) due to the fader's being turned up before the record or transcription attains regular speed. 2. General source of light, usually 500-to 2000-watt lamps. Parabolic shape. Used for base or fill light.
scratch.	Groove noise on record or transcription that makes it unsuitable for broadcast if too intense. Referred to also as "fry."
scrim.	Transparent gauzelike material used for special staging effects.
script.	Complete written collection of all audio and video material and directions for the program as it is to be presented.
segue.	1. An overlapping of two elements as one fades in over another fading out. Sound effects, dialogue, or recorded music may be segued. Referred to as "cross fade." 2. In music, a transition from one number or theme to another.
set up.	1. The relative physical location of performers, microphones, instruments, and sound effects equipment in the studio. 2. To set up is to get ready technically for the program. 3. In filming, a shot within a scene.
78s.	Records to be played at 78 revolutions per minute.
SFX.	Sound effects.
signature.	Theme.
small format VTR.	½-, ¾, or 1-inch video-tape system as contrasted to 2-inch system.
sneak.	A very gradual fade in or out of music or sound so as to be unobtrusive.
soap opera.	A daytime five-a-week serial
SOF.	Sound on film. Film that contains narration or dialogue.
sound truck.	Movable cabinet with multiple turntables and attachments for playing recorded sound effects.
split screen.	Electronic effect whereby portions of pictures from two cameras divide the screen. Frequently used for telephone scene. One part is at left—other at right.
spot	Spotlights. Source of specific and directional light. Used for key or modeling lighting, back lighting, accent lighting etc. Spots range from 250 to 2000 watts.
spread.	1. Time available for stretching a program or any portion of it. 2. In comedy or variety programs the time allotted for audience reactions such as applause and laughter as well as for ad-libbing by performers.

stab. Short musical punctuation played with sharp attack. Also referred to as "sting."

stagger-through. First rehearsal in studio with cameras.

stand by. 1. Order to get ready to begin. 2. A standby is a substitute program ready as a fill in in case of an emergency.

stock footage. Scenes or sequences on film that are not limited to a specialized or one-time use but may be used in different programs. Examples of scenes found on stock footage: Broadway, ocean liner, train passing in the night, storm, airplane view of New York, fields of waving grain, etc.

stretch. To slow down a performance.

strike. To pull down, dismantle, remove sets.

super imp. A superimposition in television—the use of two cameras at the same time, each with its own picture but transmitted as a single picture. More than two cameras may be used for special effects.

sync. Synchronization.

take. 1. A switching direction—"Ready One . . . Take One." 2. Picture or scene held by TV camera. 3. Such a scene so televised or filmed.

take five. Direction for a brief break or recess in rehearsal.

take a level. A prebroadcast test on microphone to determine balance and fader positions on the control-room console.

take it away. An engineering cue to start a program given over a telephone circuit, usually with the identification of pickup added to the cue, such as "Take it away Central Park."

talk-back. Communication system permitting control-room personnel to talk to those in the studio.

tally light. Indicator light on a camera to show when it is "hot," on the air.

TC. Title card. May be extended to refer to any card or graphic.

TD. Technical director.

TelePrompter. A device mounted above the top lens on each camera, or on special stands, permitting the performer to follow the script. Words are typed in extra large type on a continuous roll of paper. Speed of script exposure may be governed by performer's pace of delivery.

telop. 1. An opaque projector. 2. A 3¼" x 4" opaque card used for titles, credits, and art work. Projected from film studio.

33s. 1. Transcriptions prepared for broadcasting and played at 33⅓ revolutions per minute. 2. Long-playing microgroove records.

tight. A program that is so close to its allotted time that any spread might cause it to run over time.

tilt. Move camera vertically up or down.

time check. Synchronization of all clocks and watches involved in timing of a program.

track up. Command to fade up audio on film or VTR.

truck. To move camera parallel to a piece of furniture or set background, or to move with a person crossing the set.

two-shot. Close-up of two persons in television.

under. Music or sound as background for voice. "Under and out" means to fade music or sound down and then out.

VCU.   Very extreme close-up. Also referred to as XCU.

video.   Visual portion of television transmission.

viz.   "Vizmo," an optical system to provide a background behind newscaster or performer.

VO.   Voice-over. Live narration or dialogue presented during projection of silent film or action in the studio.

VTR.   Video-tape recorder.

VU meter.   A meter that indicates electrically the instantaneous volume of sound being transmitted. Readings by volume units (VU) in decibels from minus 20 to plus 3. (Has been called volume indicator, V.I., in the past.)

whodunit.   Mystery melodrama.

winging a show.   Directing a telecast without rehearsal.

wow.   Speed variation resulting in distortion of a record or transcription at the start or during its playing. Referred to as "scoop" when coming at the start.

X/S.   Over or across the shoulder shot. Also referred to as OS.

zoom.   Rapid change of camera pickup effected electronically from long shot to close-up without losing focus.

bibliography

GENERAL

ADLER, RICHARD, ed., *Television as a Social Force: New Approaches to TV Criticism.* New York: Praeger/Aspen Institute, 1975.

ARCHER, GLEASON L., *Big Business and Radio.* New York: American Historical Society, 1939.

———, *History of Radio to 1926.* New York: Amercian Historical Society, 1938.

ARLEN, MICHAEL J., *Living Room War.* New York: Viking, 1969.

———, *The View from Highway One.* New York: Farrar, Straus and Giroux, 1976.

BAER, WALTER S., *Cable Television: A Handbook for Decision Making.* Santa Monica, Calif.: Rand Corporation, 1973.

BANNING, W. P., *Commercial Broadcasting Pioneer.* Cambridge, Mass.: Harvard University Press, 1947.

BARNOUW, ERIC, *The Golden Web: A History of Broadcasting in the United States, 1933–53.* New York: Oxford University Press, 1968.

———, *The Image Empire.* New York: Oxford University Press, 1970.

———, *A Tower in Babel: A History of Broadcasting in the United States to 1933.* New York: Oxford University Press, 1966.

———, *Tube of Plenty.* New York: Oxford University Press, 1975.

BLUM, D. S., *Pictorial History of TV.* Philadelphia: Chilton, 1958.

BLUMLER, J. G., AND D. MACQUAIL, *Television in Politics.* Chicago: University of Chicago, 1969.

BOGART, LEO, *The Age of Television,* 2d ed. New York: Frederick Ungar, 1972.

———, *Premises for Propaganda. The United States Information Agency's Operating Assumptions in the Cold War.* New York: Free Press, 1976.

BOWER, ROBERT T., *Television and the Public.* New York: Holt, Rinehart and Winston, 1973.

BRIGGS, ASA, *The Birth of Broadcasting: The History of Broadcasting in the United Kingdom,* Vol. 1. London, Oxford University Press, 1961.

———, *The Golden Age of Wireless: The History of Broadcasting in the United Kingdom,* Vol. 2. London, 1965.

———, *The War of Words: The History of Broadcasting in the United Kingdom,* Vol. 3. London, Oxford University Press, 1970.

Broadcasting Yearbook, published annually. Washington: Broadcasting Publications.

BROWN, LES, *Television: The Business Behind the Box.* New York: Harcourt Brace & Jovanovich, 1971.

BUXTON, F., & B. OWEN, *Radio's Golden Age* New York: Easton Valley Press, 1966.

CANTRIL, HADLEY, *The Invasion from Mars.* Princeton, N.J.: Princeton University Press, 1940.

———, & G. W. ALLPORT, *The Psychology of Radio.* New York: Harper & Row, 1935.

CATER, DOUGLASS, AND MICHAEL J. NYHAN, *Public Television: Towards Higher Ground.* Palo Alto, Calif.: Aspen, 1975.

———, AND STEPHEN STRICKLAND, *TV Violence and the Child.* New York: Russell Sage Foundation and Basic Books, Inc., 1975.

CHASE, FRANCIS, *Sound and Fury.* New York: Harper & Row, 1942.

CHESTER, E. W., *Radio, Television and American Politics.* New York: Sheed, 1969.

CHILDS, H. L., AND J. B. WHITTON, *Propaganda by Short Wave.* Princeton, N.J.: Princeton University Press, 1942.

CLIFT, CHARLES III, AND ARCHIE GREER, eds., *Broadcast Programming: The Current Perspective.* Washington, D.C.: University Press of America, 1976.

COASE, R. H. *British Broadcasting: A Study in Monopoly.* Cambridge, Mass.: Harvard University Press, 1950.

COLE, BARRY G., ed., *Television: A Selection of Readings from TV Guide Magazine.* New York: Free Press, 1970.

COSTELLO, L. F., AND G. N. GORDON, *Teach with Television: A Guide to Instructional TV.* New York: Hastings House, 1965.

DeFOREST, LEE, *Father of Radio.* New York: Wilcox and Follett, 1950.

DIAMOND, EDWIN, *The Tin Kazoo: Television, Politics, and the News.* Cambridge, MIT Press, 1975.

DIZARD, W. P., *Television: A World View.* Syracuse, N.Y.: Syracuse University Press, 1966.

DOUGLAS, PETER, *Television Today.* London: Osprey Publishing, 1975.

DRYER, S., *Radio in Wartime.* New York: Greenberg, 1942.

DUNNING, JOHN, *Tune in Yesterday.* Englewood Cliffs, N.J.: Prentice-Hall, 1976.

EMERY, WALTER, *Broadcasting and Government: Responsibilities and Regulations,* 2d ed. East Lansing, Mich.: Michigan State University Press, 1971.

———, *National and International Systems of Broadcasting.* East Lansing, Mich.: Michigan State University Press, 1969.

EPSTEIN, EDWARD J., *News from Nowhere: Television and the News.* New York: Random House, 1973.

Evaluation of Statistical Methods Used in Obtaining Broadcast Ratings, Report of the Committee on Interstate and Foreign Commerce, House of Representatives, 87th Congress, 1st Session, House Report No. 193. Washington: Government Printing Office, 1961.

Federal Communications Commission, *Annual Reports.* Washington: Government Printing Office.

Federal Communications Commission, *Public Service Responsibility of Broadcast Licensees.* Washington: Government Printing Office, 1946.

Federal Communications Commission, *Report on Chain Broadcasting.* Commission Order No. 37, Docket No. 5060. Washington: Government Printing Office, 1941.

FRIENDLY, FRED, *Due to Circumstances Beyond Our Control.* New York: Random House, 1967.

————, *The Good Guys, the Bad Guys and the First Amendment: Free Speech vs. Fairness in Broadcasting.* New York: Random House, 1976.

GELLER, HENRY, *The Fairness Doctrine in Broadcasting: Problems and Suggested Courses of Action.* Santa Monica, Calif.: Rand Corporation, 1973.

GILLMOR, DONALD M., AND JEROME A. BARRON, *Mass Communications Law: Cases and Comment.* St. Paul, Minn.: West Publishing Co., 1974.

GOLDSMITH, A. N., AND A. C. LESCARBOURA, *This Thing Called Broadcasting.* New York: Henry Holt, 1930.

GREEN, TIMOTHY, *The Universal Eye,* New York: Stein and Day, 1972.

GROSS, BEN, *I Looked and I Listened.* New York: Random House, 1954.

GUIMARY, DONALD L., *Citizen's Groups and Broadcasting.* New York: Praegar Publishing, 1975.

HARMON, J., *The Great Radio Comedians.* New York: Doubleday, 1970.

————, *The Great Radio Heroes.* New York: Ace, 1967.

HEAD, SYDNEY, ed., *Broadcasting in Africa: A Continental Survey of Radio and Television.* Philadelphia: Temple University Press, 1974.

————, *Broadcasting in America,* 3d ed. Boston: Houghton-Mifflin, 1976.

HEIGHTON, ELIZABETH J. AND DON R. CUNNINGHAM, *Advertising in the Broadcast Media.* Belmont, Calif.: Wadsworth, 1976.

HIMMELWEIT, H. T., et al., *Television and the Child.* London: Oxford University Press, 1958.

The History of Broadcasting in Japan. Tokyo: Nippon Hoso Kyokai, 1967.

HOLE, JULIAN, *Radio Power: Propaganda and International Broadcasting.* Philadelphia; Temple University Press, 1975.

HOLT, ROBERT, *Radio Free Europe.* Minneapolis, Minn.: University of Minnesota Press, 1958.

HUBBELL, R. W., *4,000 Years of Television.* New York: Putnam, 1942.

JOHNSON, NICHOLAS, *How to Talk Back to Your Television Set.* Boston: Little, Brown, 1970.

KAHN, FRANK, ed., *Documents of American Broadcasting,* 2d ed. Englewood Cliffs, N.J.: Prentice-Hall, 1973.

KENDRICK, ALEXANDER, *Prime Time.* Boston: Little, Brown, 1969.

KITROSS, JOHN M., AND KENNETH HARWOOD, eds., *Free and Fair, Courtroom Access and the Fairness Doctrine.* Philadelphia: Broadcast Education Association, 1970.

KLAPPER, J. T., *The Effects of Mass Communication.* New York: Free Press, 1960.

KRASNOW, ERWIN G., AND LAWRENCE D. LONGLEY, *The Politics of Broadcast Regulation.* New York: St. Martins Press, 1972.

KRIS, E., & H. SPEIER, *German Radio Propaganda.* New York: Oxford University Press, 1944.

LANDRY, R. J., *This Fascinating Radio Business.* Indianapolis, Ind.: Bobbs-Merrill, 1946.

LANG, K., AND G. E. LANG, *Politics and Television.* Chicago: Quadrangle, 1968.

LEDUC, DON R., *Cable Television and the FCC.* Philadelphia: Temple University Press, 1974.

LERNER, D., *Sykewar: Psychological Warfare against Germany, D-Day to VE-Day.* New York: Stewart, 1947.

LICHTY, LAWRENCE W., AND MALACHI TOPPING, EDS., *American Broadcasting.* New York: Hastings House, 1975.

Lyle, Jack, *The People Look at Public Television.* Washington, D.C.: Corporation for Public Broadcasting, 1974.

MacNeil, Robert, *The People Machine.* New York: Harper & Row, 1969.

Marconi, Degna, *My Father, Marconi.* New York: McGraw-Hill, 1962.

Mayer, Martin, *About Television.* New York: Harper & Row, 1972.

McGinniss, Joe, *The Selling of the President 1968.* New York: Trident Press, 1969.

McLuhan, H. M., *Understanding Media.* New York: McGraw-Hill, 1964.

Metz, Robert, *CBS—Reflections in a Bloodshot Eye.* Chicago: Playboy Press, 1975.

Mickelson, Sig, *The Electric Mirror: Politics in an Age of Television.* New York: Dodd, Mead, 1972.

Minow, Newton, John Bartlow Martin, and Lee M. Mitchell, *Presidential Television.* New York: Basic Books, 1973.

Murrow, E. R., *See It Now.* New York: Simon and Schuster, 1955.

Nelson, H., and D. Teetler, *Law of Mass Communications.* Mineola, N.Y.: Foundation Press, 1969.

Newcomb, Horace, TV: *The Most Popular Art.* New York: Anchor Books, 1974.

————, *Television: The Critical View.* New York: Oxford University Press, 1976.

Nyhan, Michael J., ed., *The Future of Public Broadcasting.* New York: Praeger Special Studies, 1976.

O'Hara, R. C., *Media for the Millions: The Process of Mass Communication.* New York: Random House, 1961.

Paulu, Burton, *British Broadcasting.* Minneapolis: University of Minnesota Press, 1956.

————, *British Broadcasting in Transition.* Minneapolis: University of Minnesota Press, 1961.

————, *Radio and Television Broadcasting in Eastern Europe.* Minneapolis: University of Minnesota Press, 1974.

————, *Radio and Television Broadcasting on the European Continent.* Minneapolis: University of Minnesota Press, 1967.

Pennybacker, J. H., and W. W. Braden, eds., *Broadcasting and the Public Interest.* New York: Random House, 1969.

Price, Monroe, and John Wicklein, *Cable Television.* Philadelphia: Pilgrim Press, 1972.

Public Television: A Program for Action. New York: Harper & Row, 1967.

Reith, J. C. W., *Into the Wind.* London: Hodder, 1949.

Rivers, William L., and Michael J. Nyhan, eds., *Aspen Notebook on Government and the Media.* New York: Praegar Publishers, 1973.

Rolo, C. J., *Radio Goes to War.* New York: Putnam, 1942.

Schramm, Wilbur, *The Impact of Educational Television.* Urbana, Ill.: University of Illinois Press, 1960.

————, *Television in the Lives of Our Children.* Stanford, Calif.: Stanford University Press, 1961.

————, and Donald F. Roberts, eds., *The Process and Effects of Mass Communication,* 2d ed., Urbana, Ill.: University of Illinois Press, 1971.

Seldes, Gilbert, *The Great Audience.* New York: Viking, 1950.

————, *The Public Arts.* New York: Simon and Schuster, 1956.

Settel, I., and W. Laas, *A Pictorial History of Television.* New York: Grosset & Dunlap, 1969.

_____, *Radio's Second Chance.* Boston: Little, Brown, 1946.

SHANKS, BOB. *The Cool Fire, How to Make it in Television.* New York: W W. Norton and Co., Inc., 1976.

SHAPIRO, ANDREW O., *Media Access: Your Right to Express Your Views on Radio and Television.* Boston: Little, Brown, 1976.

SHERMAN, CHARLES, AND DONALD BROWNE, *Broadcast Monographs No. 21: Issues in International Broadcasting.* Washington, D.C., Broadcast Education Assocation, 1976.

SIEPMANN, C.A., *Radio, Television, and Society.* New York: Oxford University Press, 1950.

SKORNIA, H. J., *Television and Society.* New York: McGraw-Hill, 1965.

SMALL, W., *To Kill a Messenger: Television News and the Real World.* New York: Hastings House, 1970.

SMYTHE, TED C., AND GEORGE A. MASTROIANNI, *Issues in Broadcasting: Radio, TV, Cable.* Palo Alto, Calif.: Mayfield Publishing Co., 1976.

SNOW, MARCELLUS S., *International Commercial Satellite Communications: Economic and Political Issues of the First Decade of Intelsat.* New York: Praegar Publishing, 1976.

STEINBERG, CHARLES, ed., *Broadcasting, The Critical Challenges.* New York: Hastings House, 1974.

STEINER, G.A., *The People Look at Television.* New York: Knopf, 1963.

STERLING, CHRISTOPHER, advisory ed., *Historical Studies in Telecommunications,* 5 books in 6 volumes. New York: Arno Press, 1976. (Reprints of books and pamphlets from various years.)

_____, advisory ed., *History of Broadcasting: Radio to Television.* 34 books. New York: Arno Press, 1974. (Reprints of books and pamphlets of various years.)

Television and Growing Up: The Impact of Televised Violence. Report to the Surgeon General from the Surgeon General's Scientific Advisory Committee on Television and Social Behavior. Washington, D.C.: Government Printing Office, 1972.

Television Factbook, Published annually. Washington, D.C.: Television Digest.

THURBER, JAMES, "Soapland," in *The Beast in Me and Other Animals.* New York: Harcourt Brace Jovanovich, 1948.

TOOHEY, DANIEL, RICHARD MARKS, AND ARNOLD LUTZKER, *Legal Problems in Broadcasting.* Lincoln, Neb.: Great Plains National Instructional Television Library, 1974.

TUCHMAN, GAYE, ed., *The TV Establishment: Programming for Power and Profit.* Englewood Cliffs, N.J.: Prentice-Hall, 1974.

WHALE, J., *The Half-Shut Eye: Television and Politics in Britain and America.* London: Macmillan, 1969.

WHITE, D. M., AND R. AVERSON, eds., *Sight, Sound, and Society.* Boston: Beacon Press, 1968.

WHITE, LLEWELLYN, *The American Radio.* Chicago: University of Chicago Press, 1947.

WILLIS, EDGAR E., *Foundations in Broadcasting: Radio and Television.* New York: Oxford University Press, 1951.

World Communications: A 200 Country Survey of Press, Radio, Television, Film. Paris: Unesco, 1975.

WYCKOFF, GENE, *The Image Candidates.* New York: Macmillan, 1968.

WYLIE, MAX, *Clear Channels: Television and the American People.* New York: Funk & Wagnalls, 1954.

YELLIN, DAVID, *Special: Fred Freed and the Television Documentary.* New York: Macmillan, 1973.

TECHNIQUES

BENSINGER, CHARLES, *Peterson's Guide to Video Tape Recording.* Los Angeles: Peterson Publishing Co., 1973.

BLUEM, A. W., *Documentary in American Television.* New York: Hastings House, 1964.

BRETZ, RUDY, *Techniques of Television Production.* New York: McGraw-Hill, 1962.

COLEMAN, KEN, *So You Want to Be a Sportscaster.* New York: Hawthorn, 1973.

CREAMER, J., AND W. B. HOFFMAN, *Radio Sound Effects.* New York: Ziff-Davis, 1945.

CREWS, ALBERT, *Professional Radio Writing.* Boston: Houghton Mifflin, 1946.

————, *Radio Production Directing.* Boston: Houghton Mifflin, 1944.

DUERR, E., *Radio and Television Acting.* New York: Holt, Rinehart and Winston, 1950.

FANG, IRVING, *Television News,* 2d ed. New York: Hastings House, 1972.

FIELD, STANLEY, *Professional Broadcast Writers Handbook.* Blue Ridge Summit, Pa.: TAB Books, 1974.

GARRY, R., F. B. RAINSBERRY, AND C. WINICK, EDS., *For the Young Viewer.* New York: McGraw-Hill, 1962.

GREEN, M., *Television News: Anatomy and Process.* Belmont, Calif.: Wadsworth, 1969.

HALL, MARK W., *Broadcast Journalism: An Introduction to News Writing.* New York: Hastings House, 1971.

HENNECKE, B. G., AND E. S. DUMIT, *The Announcer's Handbook.* New York: Holt, Rinehart and Winston, 1959.

HERMAN. L., *A Practical Manual of Screen Playwriting for Theatre and Television Films,* Cleveland, Ohio: World Publishing, 1952.

————, AND M. S. HERMAN, *Foreign Dialects: A Manual for Actors, Writers and Directors.* New York: Theatre Arts Books, 1943.

————, *Manual of American Dialects for Radio, Stage, Screen and Television.* New York: Ziff-Davis, 1947.

HILLIARD, ROBERT L., *Writing for Television and Radio,* 3d ed. New York: Hastings House, 1976.

————, AND HYMAN H. FIELD, *Television and the Teacher: A Handbook for Classroom Use.* New York: Hastings House, 1976.

HOFFER, JAY, *Radio Production Techniques.* Blue Ridge Summit, Pa.: TAB Books, 1974.

HYDE, STUART, *Television and Radio Announcing,* 2d ed. Boston: Houghton Mifflin, 1971.

JONES, P., *The Technique of the Television Cameraman.* New York: Hastings House, 1965.

KEHOE, V. J-R., *The Techniques of Film and Television Make-Up.* New York: Hastings House, 1969.

JOHNSON, JOSEPH S., AND KENNETH K. JONES, *Modern Radio Station Practices.* Belmont, Calif.: Wadsworth, 1972.

LEWIS, B., *The Techniques of Television Announcing.* New York: Hastings House, 1966.

LEWIS, C., *The TV Director/Interpreter.* New York: Hastings House, 1968.

Library of Communication Techniques. New York: Hastings House. (Books on the techniques used in television, radio, and motion picture production. Various publication dates and authors.)

Media Manuals. New York: Hastings House. (Manuals on the various techniques used in audio-visual production. Various publication dates and authors.)

MILLERSON, G., *The Technique of Television Producing*. New York: Hastings House, 1968.

NISBETT, A., *The Technique of the Sound Studio*. New York: Hastings House, 1962.

————, *The Use of Microphones*. New York: Hastings House, 1974.

QUAAL, WARD L., AND JAMES A. BROWN, *Broadcast Management: Radio-Television*, 2d ed. New York: Hastings House, 1976.

REISZ, K., *The Technique of Film Editing: Basic Principles for TV*. New York: Farrar, Straus & Giroux, 1953.

ROBINSON, RICHARD, *The Video Primer: Equipment, Production and Concepts*. Westport, Conn.: Hyperion Press, 1974.

SEIDLES, RONALD J., *Airtime*. Boston: Halbrook Press, 1977.

SILLER, B., H. TERKEL, AND T. WHITE, *Television and Radio News*. New York: Macmillan, 1960.

SPOTTISWOODE, R., *The Focal Encyclopedia of Film and Television: Techniques*. New York: Hastings House, 1969.

STASHEFF, EDWARD, RUDY BRETZ, JOHN GARTLEY, AND LYNN GARTLEY, *The Television Program*, 5th ed. New York: Hill & Wang, 1976.

STONE, VERNON, AND BRUCE HINSON, *Television Newsfilm Techniques*. New York: Hastings House, 1974.

TRAPNELL, C., *Teleplay: An Introduction to Television Writing*. San Francisco: Chandler, 1966.

TURNBULL, R. B., *Radio and Television Sound Effects*. New York: Holt, Rinehart and Winston, 1951.

WAINWRIGHT, C. A., *The Television Copywriter*. New York: Hastings House, 1967.

WHITE, P. W., *News on the Air*. New York: Harcourt Brace Jovanovich, 1957.

WILLIS, EDGAR E., *A Radio Director's Manual*. Ann Arbor, Mich.: Ann Arbor Publishers, 1961.

————, *Writing Television and Radio Programs*. New York: Holt, Rinehart and Winston, 1967.

WOOD, W., *Electronic Journalism*. New York: Columbia University Press, 1967.

WYLIE, MAX, *Writing for Television*. New York: Cowles Book Company, 1970.

ZETTL, H., *Television Production Handbook*, 3d ed. Belmont, Calif.: Wadsworth, 1976.

index

The titles of scripts, continuities, and commercial examples are not indexed below but are listed at the front of the book beginning on pp. ix–x.